BASEMENT.

HARMONIZATION
of EUROPEAN
COMPANY LAWS

HARMONIZATION
of EUROPEAN
COMPANY LAWS

NATIONAL
REFORM
and
TRANSNATIONAL
COORDINATION

by ERIC STEIN

Professor of Law

Co-Director of International

and Comparative Legal Studies

University of Michigan

THE BOBBS-MERRILL COMPANY, INC.
A SUBSIDIARY OF HOWARD W. SAMS & CO., INC.
PUBLISHERS • INDIANAPOLIS • KANSAS CITY • NEW YORK

To my wife

UXOR FIDELIS RES PRECIOSA
(Inscription on a tombstone, A.D.
1563, Kristinakyrkan, Jönköping,
Sweden.)

Acknowledgments

In preparing this volume I have sought and received expert advice from many quarters on both sides of the Atlantic. The book could not have been written in its present form without the enthusiastic and competent assistance of Dr. Georg Sandberger from the University of Tübingen Law Faculty who spent most of the academic year of 1968-1969 in Ann Arbor and whose knowledge of the European company law systems was indispensable to me, particularly in the preparation of Chapters IV, VII and VIII.

On the Continent, the following experts read the manuscript and provided me with extensive and authoritative comments: Prof. Dr. Konrad Duden of the University of Mannheim; Hon. Prof. Dr. Ernst Gessler of the University of Bonn Law Faculty, and Dr. R. Franta, both of the Federal Ministry of Justice; Prof. Dr. Bernhard Grossfeld of the University of Göttingen Law Faculty; Prof. Mr. W. L. Haardt of the Law Faculty at Leyden; Prof. Jacques Heenen of the Law Faculty, Free University of Brussels; Prof. Roger Houin of the Faculty of Law and Economic Sciences in Paris; Mr. Paul Leleux of the Legal Service of the European Commission; Dott. Dino Marchetti, Consigliere di Cassazione at the Ministry of Industry, Commerce and Crafts in Rome; Mr. Theodor Vogelaar, Director General, and Dr. Hans Claudius Ficker, both of the European Commission.

On this side of the Atlantic the manuscript was read and helpful comments were offered by Prof. Alfred F. Conard of the Michigan Law School, Prof. Friedrich K. Juenger of the Wayne State University Law School, and Prof. Detlev F. Vagts of the Harvard Law School.

I have also received specific suggestions from Prof. Dott. Giorgio Bernini of the Faculty of Law at Padua, Avv. Dott. Giuseppe Bisconti of Rome and his associates, Mr. Arved

Deringer, Member of the Bundestag and attorney in Bonn and Stuttgart, Dr. Winfried Hauschild of the European Commission, Prof. Richard O. Lempert of the Michigan Law School, and Mr. Guy Vanhaeverbeke of the Secretariat of the Economic and Social Committee of the EEC in Brussels.

Mr. Jean Rey, President of the European Commission, and Dr. Hans von der Groeben, Member of the Commission, received me graciously and repeatedly. Messrs. Michel Gaudet and Theodor Vogelaar, Directors General at the Commission, gave generously of their time and wisdom as did their many collaborators and other members of the staff of the Commission and the Secretariat of the Council of Ministers. Mr. Paul Leleux, whom I mentioned above, was immensely helpful both during his stay in Ann Arbor and again in Brussels.

A portion of the volume was written "on neutral ground" during my term as visiting professor at the three law faculties in Sweden, and I take this opportunity to express my gratitude for the kind invitation and warm hospitality.

I have had countless interviews and correspondence with European scholars, officials, attorneys, and businessmen whose observations are reflected in the book. By this sweeping statement I want to express to them my sincere thanks.

A number of students and young scholars at the Michigan Law School, both American and foreign, provided research assistance. I should mention Mrs. Heika Pfennigstorf of Hamburg who did most of the checking of citations, Miss Catherine Sieklucka, and Messrs. von Bodungen, Puttfarken, and Slot. Mrs. Eleanor Herp typed the text with devotion, speed and accuracy.

My colleague and friend, Prof. Alfred F. Conard, instructed me in the mysteries of corporation law of which he is a master, and gave me the encouragement I sorely needed from time to time.

A grant from the Committee on International Organization of the Social Science Research Council assisted me during the initial stage of research. Subsequently, I received sustained support from the Ford Foundation grant for international and comparative legal studies administered by the University of Michigan. If the concept of the volume strikes the reader as somewhat romantic in scope it is no doubt due to the fact that the idea originated in the heady, eighteenth century atmosphere of the Villa Serbelloni on Lake Como, where I spent an enchanting summer as scholar-in-residence and guest of the Rockefeller Foundation.

E.S.

Ann Arbor, Michigan

January 1970

Selected Basic National Legislative Materials on Commercial Companies

Belgium

Lois coordonnées sur les sociétés commerciales (Law on Commercial Companies), Arrêté royal du 30 novembre 1935, Moniteur, Dec. 5, 1935 (as amended), *cited as Code de commerce.*

Federal Republic of Germany

Handelsgesetzbuch (Commercial Code) of May 10, 1897, RGBl 219, *cited as Commercial Code.*

Aktiengesetz (Law on Stock Companies) of Sept. 6, 1965, BGBl I 1089, *cited as the Law of 1965.* Introductory Law (Einführungsgesetz) of the same date, *id.* at 1185.

Gesetz betreffend die Gesellschaften mit beschränkter Haftung (Law on Limited Liability Companies) of April 20, 1892, RGBl 846 (as amended).

Gesetz über die Rechnungslegung von bestimmten Unternehmen und Konzernen (Law on Financial Accounting by Certain Enterprises and Related Enterprises) of Aug. 15, 1969, BGBl I 1189, *cited as Grossunternehmensgesetz.*

Gesetz zur Durchführung der Ersten Richtlinie des Rates der Europäischen Gemeinschaften zur Koordinierung des Gesellschaftsrechts of Aug. 15, 1969, BGBl I 1146 (Law on the Implementation of the First Directive of the Council of the European Communities for Coordination of Company Law), *cited as Law Implementing First Directive.*

Referentenentwurf eines Gesetzes über Gesellschaften mit beschränkter Haftung, Herausgegeben vom Bundesministerium der Justiz (official draft of a new law on limited liability companies) (Köln-Marienburg 1969).

France

Lois n. 66-537 sur les sociétés commerciales (Law on Commercial Companies) of July 24, 1966, J.O. (France) July 26, 1966 (as amended), *cited as Law of July 24, 1966.*

Décret n. 67-236 sur les sociétés commerciales of March 23, 1967 (Decree on Commercial Companies), J.O. Mar. 24, 1967 (as amended).

Décret n. 67-237 relatif au registre du commerce of March 23, 1967 (Decree on Commercial Register), J.O. Mar. 24, 1967 (as amended).

Ordonnance n. 69-1176 du 20 décembre 1969 modifiant la loi n. 66-537 du 24 juillet 1966 sur les sociétés commerciales, J.O. Dec. 28, 1969; Décret n. 69-1177 du 24 décembre 1969 modifiant le décret n. 67-236 du 23 mars 1967 sur les sociétés commerciales et le décret n. 67-237 du 23 mars 1967 relatif au registre du commerce (both designed to implement the First Directive on coordination of company law).

Italy

Codice civile (Civil Code) of March 16, 1942, Book V, Titles V, VI, VII, XI, *cited as Codice civile.*

Decreto del Presidente della Repubblica, Dec. 29, 1969, n. 1127, Modificazioni alle norme del codice civile sulle società per azioni, in accomandita per azioni e a responsabilità limitata, in attuazione della direttiva 9 marzo 1968, n. 151, del Consiglio dei Ministri delle Communità europee, Gazz. Uff. No. 35, Feb. 2, 1970, at 782 (Decree of the President of the Republic designed to implement the First Directive), *cited as Decree Implementing First Directive.*

La riforma delle società di capitali in Italia, Progetti e Documenti (Milano 1966), *cited as La Riforma.* This collection contains the texts of, and reports on, the Italian draft reform of capital companies. The text of the latest draft is reproduced in 1967 Rivista delle società 370-437.

Luxembourg

Loi du 10 août 1915 concernant les sociétés commerciales (Law Concerning Commercial Companies), 1915 Mémorial 925, *cited as Law of 1915.*

Netherlands

Wetboek van Koophandel (Commercial Code), July 4, 1937, Staatsblad No. 51, Book I, Title III.

Wet tot instelling van een handelsregister (Law on the Establishment of a Commercial Register) of July 26, 1918, Staatsblad No. 493.

Nieuw Burgerlijk Wetboek (New Civil Code), 1960 Staatsblad 205, Book 2, Title 13 (not in force).

Herziening van het ondernemingsrecht, Rapport van de Commissie ingesteld bij beschikking van de Minister van Justitie van 8 april 1960 (Revision of the law of enterprise, Report of the Commission established by order of the Minister of Justice of April 8, 1960), ('s-Gravenhage 1965), *cited as Verdam Report.*

Basic European Community Documents

Treaty Establishing the European Coal and Steel Community, signed on April 15, 1951, 261 U.N.T.S. 140 (1957), *cited as ECSC Treaty.*

Treaty Establishing the European Economic Community, signed on March 25, 1957, 298 U.N.T.S. 3 (1958), *cited as EEC Treaty.*

Treaty Establishing the European Atomic Energy Community, signed on March 25, 1957, 298 U.N.T.S. 167 (1958), *cited as EURATOM Treaty.*

Avis du Comité Économique et Social sur la proposition d'une directive du Conseil tendant à coordonner, pour les rendre équivalentes, les garanties qui sont exigées, dans les États membres, des sociétés au sens de l'article 58, alinéa 2 du traité, pour protéger les intérêts tant des associés que des tiers, 1964 J.O. No. 194 of Nov. 27, 1964, at 3249 (opinion of the Economic and Social Committee on the proposal for the First Directive), *cited as Avis.*

Rapport fait au nom de la commission du marché intérieur sur la proposition de la Commission de la Communauté économique européenne au Conseil (doc. 10/1964-65) relative à une directive tendant à coordonner, pour les rendre équivalentes, les garanties qui sont exigées, dans les États membres, des sociétés au sens de l'article 58, alinéa 2, du traité pour protéger les intérêts tant des associés que des tiers, Rapporteur: M. C. Berkhouwer, Parlement Européen, Documents de Séance, 1966-1967, Doc. 53, May 9, 1966 (report of the Internal Market Committee of the European Parliament on the proposal for the First Directive), *cited as Berkhouwer Report.*

Convention sur la reconnaissance mutuelle des sociétés et personnes morales (Convention on Mutual Recognition of Companies and Legal Persons) signed on Feb. 29, 1968, 1969 Bull. E.C. Supp. No. 2; Rapport concernant la Convention sur la reconnaissance mutuelle des sociétés et personnes morales, présenté par M. Berthold Goldman, Professeur à la Faculté de droit et des sciences économiques de Paris, reproduced with the Convention in 1968 Rev. trim. droit eur. 400, *cited as Rapport Goldman.*

Première Directive du Conseil du 9 mars 1968, tendant à coordonner, pour les rendre équivalentes, les garanties qui sont exigées, dans les États membres, des sociétés au sens de l'article 58, deuxième alinéa, du traité pour protéger les intérêts tant des associés que des tiers, 1968 J.O. No. L65 of Mar. 14, 1968, at 8 (First Directive of the Council on coordination of company laws), *cited as First Directive.*

Sanders, Projet d'un statut des sociétés anonymes européennes, Collection Études, Série Concurrence No. 6, Brussels 1967, *cited as Sanders Report.*

List of Some Abbreviations

A.B.A.	American Bar Association
ABl	Amtsblatt
AcP	Archiv für die civilistische Praxis
AG	Die Aktiengesellschaft
Am. J. Comp. L.	American Journal of Comparative Law
Am. J. Int'l L.	American Journal of International Law
AktG	Aktiengesetz
A.N.S.A.	Association Nationale des Sociétés par Actions
AWD	Aussenwirtschaftsdienst des Betriebs-Beraters
Belgian Code de commerce	Lois coordonées sur les sociétés commerciales of Nov. 30, 1935 (part 1 of the Belgian Code de commerce)
BB	Betriebs-Berater
BGBl	Bundesgesetzblatt
BGHZ	Entscheidungen des Bundesgerichtshofes in Zivilsachen
B.L.D.	Bulletin Législatif Dalloz
Bull. E.E.C.	Bulletin of the European Economic Community
Bull. E.C.	Bulletin of the European Communities
Calif. L. Rev.	California Law Review
CCH	Commerce Clearing House
C.E.E. or CEE	Communauté économique européenne

Clunet	Journal du droit international
C.M.L. Rev.	Common Market Law Review
CCH Comm. Mkt. Rep.	Common Market Reports, Commerce Clearing House, Inc., Chicago, Ill.
Colum. L. Rev.	Columbia Law Review
D.G.	Directorate General
DJT	Deutscher Juristentag
Doc.	Document
Doctr.	Doctrine
E.C.S.C.	European Coal and Steel Community
E.E.C. or EEC	European Economic Community
EURATOM	European Atomic Energy Community
Europe	Europe, Bulletin Quotidien, European Communities, published by Europe, Agence internationale d'information pour la presse, Luxembourg-Bruxelles
F.I.D.E.	Fédération Internationale de Droit Européen
Gaz. Pal.	Gazette du Palais
GG	Grundgesetz für die Bundesrepublik Deutschland
GmbH	Gesellschaft mit beschränkter Haftung
Groeben-Boeckh	Kommentar zum EWG-Vertrag (Baden-Baden 1958)
Harv. Bus. Rev.	Harvard Business Review
Harv. L. Rev.	Harvard Law Review
IAJC	Inter American Juridical Committee

Int'l & Comp. L.Q.	International and Comparative Law Quarterly
Int'l Law Ass'n	International Law Association
J.C.M. Studies	Journal of Common Market Studies
J. Legal Ed.	Journal of Legal Education
J.O.	Journal Officiel des Communautés européennes
J.O. (France)	Journal Officiel de la République Française
Jur.-Cl. Pér.	Juris-Classeur Périodique
JW	Juristische Wochenschrift
JZ	Juristenzeitung
Law & Contemp. Prob.	Law and Contemporary Problems
L.J.	Law Journal
L.Q.	Law Quarterly
Mich. L. Rev.	Michigan Law Review
Model Bus. Corp. Act	Model Business Corporation Act, Revised 1969, by the Committee on Corporate Laws of the American Bar Association (Philadelphia 1969)
N.C.L. Rev.	North Carolina Law Review
NJW	Neue Juristische Wochenschrift
NV	Naamlooze Vennootschap
Nw. U. L. Rev.	Northwestern University Law Review
Parl. Eur.	Parlement Européen
Pas. belge	Pasicrisie belge
Rabels Zeitschrift	Rabels Zeitschrift für ausländisches und internationales Privatrecht

Recueil de la Jurisprudence	Recueil de la Jurisprudence de la Cour, Cour de Justice des Communautés Européennes
Rev.	Revue or Review
Rev. int. droit comp.	Revue internationale de droit comparé
Rev. Marché Commun	Revue du Marché Commun
Rev. trim. droit eur.	Revue trimestrielle de droit européen
RGBl	Reichsgesetzblatt
RGZ	Entscheidungen des Reichsgerichts in Zivilsachen
S.A.	Société anonyme
S.A.R.L.	Société anonyme à responsabilité limitée
U.C.L.A.L. Rev.	University of California in Los Angeles Law Review
U.N.I.C.E.	Union des industries de la Communauté européenne
U.N.T.S.	United Nations Treaty Series
U.S.C.A.	United States Code Annotated
ZHR	Zeitschrift für das gesamte Handelsrecht und Wirtschaftsrecht

Selected Bibliography

(If an item is cited in this volume in an abbreviated form, such form is given in the list below after the full title of the item.)

Books

BAKER and CARY, CORPORATIONS, CASES AND MATERIALS (3rd ed. Brooklyn 1959),
cited as BAKER-CARY, CORPORATIONS.

BÄRMANN, DIE WILLENSBILDUNG IN DEN EUROPÄISCHEN AKTIENRECHTEN (Karlsruhe 1964).

Bastian, *Gesellschaftsrecht,* in 1 JURA EUROPAE No. 30 (France) (München, Berlin, Paris 1966),
cited as Bastian, in JURA EUROPAE.

BATIFFOL, TRAITÉ ÉLÉMENTAIRE DE DROIT INTERNATIONAL PRIVÉ (3rd ed. Paris 1959),
cited as BATIFFOL, TRAITÉ.

BAUMBACH-DUDEN, HANDELSGESETZBUCH (16th ed. München, Berlin 1964).

BAUMBACH-HUECK, AKTIENGESETZ (13th ed. München 1966).

BEBR, JUDICIAL CONTROL OF THE EUROPEAN COMMUNITIES (London, New York 1962).

BEEVER, EUROPEAN UNITY AND THE TRADE UNION MOVEMENTS (Leyden, New York 1960).

BERLE, ECONOMIC POWER AND THE FREE SOCIETY (New York 1957).

BERLE, THE 20TH CENTURY CAPITALIST REVOLUTION (New York 1954).

BLOCH-LAINÉ, POUR UNE RÉFORME DE L'ENTREPRISE (Paris 1963).

VAN BOXOM, RECHTSVERGELIJKENDE STUDIE OVER DE NATIO-
NALITEIT DER VENNOOTSCHAPPEN (Brussels 1964).

BRICE, A TREATISE ON THE DOCTRINE OF ULTRA VIRES (2d
American ed. New York 1880).

BURGARD, DIRECTION GÉNÉRALE ET DIRECTION TECHNIQUE DES
SOCIÉTÉS ANONYMES (Paris 1968).

CAMPBELL & THOMPSON, COMMON MARKET LAW (London,
Leyden, South Hackensack, N.J. 1962).

CHAVEAU, LES SOCIÉTÉS COMMERCIALES (Paris 1967).

CHESNÉ, L'ÉTABLISSEMENT DES ÉTRANGERS EN FRANCE ET LA
COMMUNAUTÉ ÉCONOMIQUE EUROPÉENNE (Paris 1962).

Colombo and Rotondi, *Gesellschaftsrecht,* in 1 JURA EURO-
PAE No. 40 (Italy) (München, Berlin, Paris 1966),
cited as Colombo-Rotondi, in JURA EUROPAE.

COTTINO, LE CONVENZIONI DI VOTO NELLE SOCIETÀ COMMER-
CIALI (Milano 1958).

COULOMBEL, LE PARTICULARISME DE LA CONDITION JURIDIQUE
DES PERSONNES MORALES DE DROIT PRIVÉ (Langre 1950),
cited as COULOMBEL, LE PARTICULARISME.

CRAMTON & CURRIE, CONFLICT OF LAWS, CASES-COMMENTS-
QUESTIONS (St. Paul 1968),
cited as CRAMTON & CURRIE, CONFLICT OF LAWS.

CURRIE, SELECTED ESSAYS ON THE CONFLICT OF LAWS (Durham 1963).

DALSACE, MANUEL DES SOCIÉTÉS ANONYMES (4th ed. Paris
1967),
cited as DALSACE, MANUEL.

Delvaux, *Gesellschaftsrecht,* in 1 JURA EUROPAE NO. 50
(Luxembourg) (München, Berlin, Paris 1966),
cited as Delvaux, in JURA EUROPAE.

DICEY and MORRIS, ON THE CONFLICT OF LAWS (8th ed. London 1967).

DJIAN, LE CONTRÔLE DE LA DIRECTION DES SOCIÉTÉS ANONYMES DANS LES PAYS DU MARCHÉ COMMUN (Paris 1965).

DOHR-PHILLIPS-THOMPSON-WARREN, ACCOUNTING AND THE LAW, CASES AND MATERIALS (3rd ed. Brooklyn 1964).

DRUCKER, CONCEPT OF THE CORPORATION (New York 1946).

EHRENZWEIG, A TREATISE ON THE CONFLICT OF LAWS (St. Paul 1962),
cited as EHRENZWEIG, A TREATISE ON THE CONFLICT OF LAWS.

Esmein, in PLANIOL and RIPERT, 6 TRAITÉ PRATIQUE DE DROIT CIVIL FRANÇAIS (OBLIGATIONS) (2d ed. Paris 1952),
cited as Esmein, in PLANIOL.

EVERLING, DAS NIEDERLASSUNGSRECHT IM GEMEINSAMEN MARKT (Berlin, Frankfurt a.M. 1963),
cited as EVERLING, DAS NIEDERLASSUNGSRECHT.

EVERLING, THE RIGHT OF ESTABLISHMENT IN THE COMMON MARKET (CCH Chicago 1964),
cited as EVERLING.

FERNHOLZ, DIE FUSION VON AKTIENGESELLSCHAFTEN UND DER SCHUTZ VON AKTIONÄREN UND DRITTEN BEI DER FUSION IN DEN RECHTEN DER MITGLIEDSTAATEN DER EUROPÄISCHEN WIRTSCHAFTSGEMEINSCHAFT (Mainz 1965),
cited as FERNHOLZ, DIE FUSION.

FONGHI and SANTA MARIA (eds.), LA RIFORMA DELLE SOCIETÀ DI CAPITALI IN ITALIA—STUDI E DIBATTITI, ATTI DEL CONVEGNO INTERNAZIONALE DI STUDI SULLA RIFORMA DELLA SOCIETÀ PER AZIONI, 3 vols., Venezia 6-7-8 ottobre 1966 (Milano 1968).

FRÉDÉRICQ, L. & S., 1 HANDBOEK VAN BELGISCH HANDELSRECHT (Bruxelles 1962),
cited as FRÉDÉRICQ, HANDBOEK.

FRÉDÉRICQ, L., TRAITÉ DE DROIT COMMERCIAL BELGE, vols. 4-6 (Gand 1950).

GALBRAITH, THE NEW INDUSTRIAL STATE (Boston 1967).

GANSHOF VAN DER MEERSCH (ed.), DROIT DES COMMUNAUTÉS EUROPÉENNES (Bruxelles 1969).

GANSHOF VAN DER MEERSCH, 1 ORGANISATIONS EUROPÉENNES (Bruxelles, Paris 1966).

GARCIN, COGESTION ET PARTICIPATION DANS LES ENTREPRISES DES PAYS DU MARCHÉ COMMUN (Paris 1968),
cited as GARCIN, COGESTION ET PARTICIPATION.

GERBET and PEPY (eds.), LA DÉCISION DANS LES COMMUNAUTÉS EUROPÉENNES (Bruxelles 1969).

VAN GERVEN, PRINCIPES DU DROIT DES ENTENTES DE LA COMMUNAUTÉ ÉCONOMIQUE EUROPÉENNE (Bruxelles 1966).

GODIN-WILHELMI, 1 AKTIENGESETZ (3rd ed. Berlin 1967).

GOLDMAN, COURS DE DROIT DU COMMERCE ET DE LA CONCURRENCE DANS LES COMMUNAUTÉS EUROPÉENNES (Paris 1964-65),
cited as GOLDMAN, COURS.

GORÉ, LA SOCIÉTÉ ANONYME (Paris 1959).

GRAUBARD (ed.), A NEW EUROPE? (Boston 1964).

Van der Grinten, *Gesellschaftsrecht,* in 1 JURA EUROPAE No. 60 (Netherlands) (München, Berlin, Paris 1966).

VON DER GROEBEN and VON BOECKH, KOMMENTAR ZUM EWG-VERTRAG (2 vols., Baden-Baden 1958-60),
cited as GROEBEN-BOECKH.

GROSSFELD, AKTIENGESELLSCHAFT, UNTERNEHMENSKONZENTRATION UND KLEINAKTIONÄR (Tübingen 1968),
cited as GROSSFELD, AKTIENGESELLSCHAFT.

GROSSKOMMENTAR AKTIENGESETZ (2d ed. Berlin 1961),
cited with author of section.

HAMIAUT, LA RÉFORME DES SOCIÉTÉS COMMERCIALES (3 vols. Paris 1966).

VAN HECKE (ed.), DE BALANS EN DE WINST- EN VERLIESREKE-NING IN DE NAAMLOZE VENNOOTSCHAP (Brussels 1965).

Hefermehl, *Gesellschaftsrecht,* in 1 JURA EUROPAE No. 10 (Germany) (München, Berlin, Paris 1966), cited as Hefermehl, in JURA EUROPAE.

VAN DER HEIJDEN and VAN DER GRINTEN, HANDBOEK VOOR DE NAAMLOZE VENNOOTSCHAP NAAR NEDERLANDS RECHT (8th ed. Zwolle 1968), cited as VAN DER HEIJDEN-VAN DER GRINTEN, HANDBOEK.

HÉMARD, TERRÉ & MABILAT, LA RÉFORME DES SOCIÉTÉS COM-MERCIALES (Paris 1967).

HUECK, GESELLSCHAFTSRECHT (13th ed. München, Berlin 1965).

JUENGER and SCHMIDT, GERMAN STOCK CORPORATION ACT (CCH Chicago 1967), cited as JUENGER & SCHMIDT.

JURA EUROPAE. LE DROIT DES PAYS DE LA COMMUNAUTÉ ÉCO-NOMIQUE EUROPÉENNE (München, Berlin, Paris 1966), cited as JURA EUROPAE with author of section, listed under Books.

KEETON and SCHWARZENBERGER (eds.), ENGLISH LAW AND THE COMMON MARKET (London 1963).

KEGEL, INTERNATIONALES PRIVATRECHT (2d ed. München, Berlin 1964), cited as KEGEL, INTERNATIONALES PRIVATRECHT.

KINDLEBERGER, AMERICAN BUSINESS ABROAD (New Haven, London 1969).

KRONSTEIN and CLAUSSEN, PUBLIZITÄT UND GEWINNVER-TEILUNG IM NEUEN AKTIENRECHT (Frankfurt 1960), cited as KRONSTEIN & CLAUSSEN, PUBLIZITÄT UND GEWINN-VERTEILUNG.

LATTIN, JENNINGS & BUXBAUM, CORPORATIONS, CASES AND MATERIALS (Chicago 1968), cited as LATTIN, JENNINGS & BUXBAUM, CORPORATIONS.

LAYTON, TRANS-ATLANTIC INVESTMENTS (Paris 1966).

VAN LEEUWE, FISCALE PROBLEMEN BIJ FUSIES VAN NAAMLOZE VENNOOTSCHAPPEN IN NEDERLAND EN IN ENKELE ANDERE LANDEN, DEELNEMENDE AAN DE EUROPAMARKT (Deventer 1960), cited as VAN LEEUWE, FISCALE PROBLEMEN.

LEFÈBVRE, R. & J., LA RÉFORME DES SOCIÉTÉS COMMERCIALES EN TABLEAUX PRATIQUES (Paris 1966), cited as LEFÈBVRE, LA RÉFORME DES SOCIÉTÉS.

LEFLAR, AMERICAN CONFLICTS LAW (Indianapolis, Kansas City, New York 1968).

LEMEUNIER, LA RÉFORME DES SOCIÉTÉS COMMERCIALES (2 vols. Paris 1966-68).

LOUSSOUARN, LES CONFLITS DE LOIS EN MATIÈRE DE SOCIÉTÉS (Paris 1949), cited as LOUSSOUARN, LES CONFLITS.

LUTTER, DIE GMBH IN BELGIEN, GESELLSCHAFTSRECHT UND STEUERRECHT (Köln 1966), cited as LUTTER, DIE GMBH IN BELGIEN.

LUTTER, KAPITAL, SICHERUNG DER KAPITALAUFBRINGUNG UND KAPITALERHALTUNG IN DEN AKTIEN- UND GMBH-RECHTEN DER EWG (Karlsruhe 1964), cited as LUTTER, KAPITAL.

Del Marmol and Dabin, *Gesellschaftsrecht,* in 1 JURA EUROPAE No. 20 (Belgium) (München, Berlin, Paris 1966), cited as Del Marmol & Dabin, in JURA EUROPAE.

MARTINO, CODICE CIVILE, COMMENTO CON LA GIURISPRUDENZA (4th ed. Roma 1964), cited as MARTINO, CODICE CIVILE.

Mason (ed.), The Corporation in Modern Society (New York 1966).

Mestmäcker, Verwaltung, Konzerngewalt und Rechte der Aktionäre (Karlsruhe 1958),
cited as Mestmäcker, Verwaltung.

Meyssan, Les droits des actionnaires et des autres porteurs de titre dans les sociétés anonymes (Paris 1962).

Minervini, Gli amministratori di società per azioni (Milano 1956).

Molengraaff, Leidraad bij de beoefening van het Nederlandse Handelsrecht (9th ed. Haarlem 1953).

Morand, La législation dans les Communautés européennes (Paris 1968).

Morawetz, 2 A Treatise on the Law of Private Corporations (2d ed. Boston 1886).

Moreau, 1 La société anonyme (Paris 1955).

Mossa, 4 Trattato del nuovo diritto commerciale; società per azioni (Padua 1957).

Van Ommeslaghe, Le régime des sociétés par actions et leur administration en droit comparé (Bruxelles 1960),
cited as van Ommeslaghe, Le régime.

De Page, 1 Traité élémentaire de droit civil belge; principes, doctrine, jurisprudence (3rd ed. Bruxelles 1962),
cited as de Page, Traité élémentaire.

Paillusseau, La société anonyme, technique d'organisation de l'entreprise (Paris 1967),
cited as Paillusseau, La société anonyme.

Pasetti-Trabucchi-Miele, Code des Communautés européennes (2 vols. Milano 1967).

Pennington, Companies in the Common Market (London 1962).

PLAISANT, FRANCESCHELLI, LASSIER, DROIT EUROPÉEN DE LA CONCURRENCE, ARTICLES 85 À 89 DU TRAITÉ C.E.E. (Paris 1966).

PLANIOL and RIPERT, 6 TRAITÉ PRATIQUE DE DROIT CIVIL FRANÇAIS (2d ed. Paris 1952),
cited as PLANIOL, TRAITÉ.

POPESCO-RAMNICEANO, DE LA REPRÉSENTATION DANS LES ACTES JURIDIQUES EN DROIT COMPARÉ (Paris 1927).

QUADRI, MONACO, TRABUCCHI, TRATTATO ISTITUTIVO DELLA COMMUNITÀ ECONOMICA EUROPEA (4 vols. Milano 1965).

RABEL, THE CONFLICT OF LAWS: A COMPARATIVE STUDY (4 vols., vol. 1-3, 2d ed. Ann Arbor 1958-60),
cited as RABEL, CONFLICT OF LAWS.

RENAULD, DROIT EUROPÉEN DES SOCIÉTÉS (Bruxelles, Louvain 1969),
cited as RENAULD, DROIT EUROPÉEN DES SOCIÉTÉS.

RETAIL, FUSIONS ET SCISSIONS DE SOCIÉTÉS (4th ed. Paris 1968).

REYNAUD and BARDOUL, STATUTS DES SOCIÉTÉS COMMERCIALES (Paris 1967).

RIPERT, ASPECTS JURIDIQUES DU CAPITALISME MODERNE (2d ed. Paris 1951).

RIPERT and ROBLOT, TRAITÉ ÉLÉMENTAIRE DE DROIT COMMERCIAL (6th ed. Paris 1968),
cited as RIPERT, TRAITÉ.

RIVERS, VAN DE VEN, WESTBROEK, THE NETHERLANDS BUSINESS CORPORATION CODE (CCH COMM. MKT. REP. No. 16, Oct. 26, 1965).

RODIÈRE, LE DROIT DES SOCIÉTÉS DANS SES RAPPORTS AVEC LA CONCENTRATION (Commission, Études, série concurrence No. 5, Brussels 1967).

RODIÈRE and HOUIN, 1 DROIT COMMERCIAL (4th ed. Paris 1965).

VAN RYN and HEENEN, PRINCIPES DE DROIT COMMERCIAL (4 vols. Bruxelles 1954-66),
cited as VAN RYN, 1 PRINCIPES DE DROIT COMMERCIAL; VAN RYN, 2 PRINCIPES DE DROIT COMMERCIAL.

SANTAGATA, LA FUSIONE TRA SOCIETÀ (Napoli 1964).

SANTINI, SOCIETÀ A RESPONSIBILITÀ LIMITATA (Bologna 1966).

SANTORO-PASSARELLI, DOTTRINE GENERALI DEL DIRITTO CIVILE (8th ed. Napoli 1964).

SERVAN-SCHREIBER, THE AMERICAN CHALLENGE (New York 1968).

SIEBER-HAGENMÜLLER-KOLBECK-SCHERPF, 2 HANDBUCH DER AKTIENGESELLSCHAFT (Köln 1967).

SIMONETTO, DELLE SOCIETÀ (Bologna, Roma 1965).

DE SOLÀ CAÑIZARES, LA CONSTITUTION DES SOCIÉTÉS PAR ACTIONS EN DROIT COMPARÉ (Paris 1959).

SPIRO, THE POLITICS OF GERMAN CODETERMINATION (Cambridge/Mass. 1958).

STEIN and HAY (eds.), LAW AND INSTITUTIONS IN THE ATLANTIC AREA—READINGS, CASES AND PROBLEMS (Indianapolis, Kansas City, New York 1967),
cited as STEIN & HAY, LAW AND INSTITUTIONS.

STEIN and NICHOLSON (eds.), AMERICAN ENTERPRISE IN THE EUROPEAN COMMON MARKET (2 vols. Ann Arbor 1960),
cited as STEIN & NICHOLSON, AMERICAN ENTERPRISE.

STEINER and CANNON, MULTINATIONAL CORPORATE PLANNING (New York 1966).

STEVENS and HENN, STATUTES, CASES AND MATERIALS ON THE LAW OF CORPORATIONS AND OTHER BUSINESS ENTERPRISES (St. Paul 1965),
cited as STEVENS & HENN.

STRAUSS, FRAGEN DER RECHTSANGLEICHUNG IM RAHMEN DER EUROPÄISCHEN GEMEINSCHAFTEN (Frankfurt a.M. 1959), cited as STRAUSS, FRAGEN DER RECHTSANGLEICHUNG.

STRAUSS, GRUNDLAGEN UND AUFGABEN DER AKTIENRECHTSREFORM (Tübingen 1960).

STREET, A TREATISE ON THE DOCTRINE OF ULTRA VIRES (London, Toronto 1930).

TEMPLE LANG, THE COMMON MARKET AND COMMON LAW (Chicago, London 1966).

TRIMARCHI, INVALIDITÀ DELLE DELIBERAZIONI DI ASSEMBLEA DI SOCIETÀ PER AZIONI (Milano 1958).

VERRUCOLI, IL SUPERAMENTO DELLA PERSONALITÀ GIURIDICA DELLE SOCIETÀ DI CAPITALI NELLA COMMON LAW E NELLA CIVIL LAW (Milano 1964).

WANG, DIE EUROPÄISCHE AKTIENGESELLSCHAFT IN DER EWG (Freiburg/Switzerland 1964).

WAUTERS-DE NÉEFF, CODE DES LOIS SUR LES SOCIÉTÉS PAR ACTIONS EN VIGUEUR DANS LES PAYS DU MARCHÉ COMMUN (Bruxelles 1964).

WEDDERBURN, COMPANY LAW REFORM (London 1965).

WIEDEMANN, MINDERHEITENSCHUTZ UND AKTIENHANDEL (Stuttgart 1968).

WIETHÖLTER, INTERESSEN UND ORGANISATION DER AKTIENGESELLSCHAFT IM AMERIKANISCHEN UND DEUTSCHEN RECHT (Karlsruhe 1961).

WILLEBRANDT, DIE VERFASSUNG DER NAAMLOZE VENNOOTSCHAP IM NIEDERLÄNDISCHEN RECHT (Münster 1965).

WOHLFARTH, EVERLING, GLAESSNER, SPRUNG, KOMMENTAR ZUM EWG-VERTRAG (Berlin, Frankfurt a.M. 1960), cited as WOHLFARTH-EVERLING.

DE WOOT, POUR UNE DOCTRINE DE L'ENTREPRISE (Paris 1968).

WÜRDINGER, AKTIEN- UND KONZERNRECHT (2d ed. Karlsruhe 1966).

VAN WYNENDAELE AND WAUTERS-DE NÉEFF, LE DROIT DES SOCIÉTÉS ANONYMES DANS LES PAYS DE LA COMMUNAUTÉ ÉCONOMIQUE EUROPÉENNE (Bruxelles 1961).

Articles

Action accomplie en 1967-1968 par le Conseil de l'Europe dans le domaine du droit, 1969 REVUE DE DROIT INTERNATIONAL ET DE DROIT COMPARÉ 101,
cited as *Action accomplie en 1967-1968 par le Conseil de l'Europe.*

Ankele, *Die Anpassung des deutschen Rechts an die erste gesellschaftsrechtliche Richtlinie des Rates der Europäischen Gemeinschaften und ihre Auswirkungen auf die GmbH,* 1969 GMBH-RUNDSCHAU 52.

Von Arnim, *Das Niederlassungsrecht für Gesellschaften im Gemeinsamen Markt und die Pläne zur Schaffung einer "europäischen" Handelsgesellschaft,* 1965 AWD 346,
cited as von Arnim, *Das Niederlassungsrecht.*

Arnold, *Die Angleichung des Gesellschaftsrechts in der Europäischen Wirtschaftsgemeinschaft,* 1963 AWD 221,
cited as Arnold, *Die Angleichung des Gesellschaftsrechts.*

Ault, *Harmonization of Company Law in the European Community,* 20 HASTINGS L.J. 77 (1968).

Bärmann, *Les Communautés européennes et le rapprochement des droits,* 1960 REV. INT. DROIT COMP. 8,
cited as Bärmann, *Les Communautés européennes.*

Bärmann, *Einheitliche Gesellschaftsform für die Europäische Wirtschaftsgemeinschaft,* 1961 AcP 97,
cited as Bärmann, *Einheitliche Gesellschaftsform.*

Bärmann, *Die europäischen Gemeinschaften und die Rechtsangleichung,* 1959 JZ 553,
cited as Bärmann, *Die europäischen Gemeinschaften.*

Bärmann, *Ist eine Aktienrechtsreform überhaupt noch zulässig?,* 1959 JZ 434.

Bärmann, *Supranationale Aktiengesellschaften,* 1961 AcP 156.

Bastian, *La réforme du droit des sociétés commerciales: Sociétés par actions,* 1968 JUR.-CL. PÉR. DOCTR. 2183,
cited as Bastian, *La réforme des sociétés.*

Bastian, *La réforme du droit des sociétés commerciales,* 1967 JUR.-CL. PÉR. DOCTR. 2121.

Beitzke, *Anerkennung und Sitzverlegung von Gesellschaften und juristischen Personen im EWG-Bereich,* 1964-65 ZHR 1,
cited as Beitzke, *Anerkennung.*

Beitzke, *Internationalrechtliches zur Gesellschaftsfusion,* in VON CAEMMERER, SCHLOCHAUER, STEINDORFF (eds.), FESTSCHRIFT FÜR HALLSTEIN 14 (Frankfurt a.M. 1966),
cited as Beitzke, *Internationalrechtliches zur Gesellschaftsfusion.*

Beitzke, *Zur Anerkennung von Handelsgesellschaften im EWG-Bereich,* 1968 AWD 91,
cited as Beitzke, *Zur Anerkennung.*

Brulliard, *Buts et méthodes de l'harmonisation du droit des S.A.R.L.,* in HARMONISIERUNG DES GESELLSCHAFTSRECHTS UND DES STEUERRECHTS IN EUROPA 27, BERICHT ÜBER DEN VII. INTERNATIONALEN GmbH-KONGRESS in Köln, April 24-26, 1962,
cited as Brulliard, in HARMONISIERUNG.

Bruns, in ENTWICKLUNGSTENDENZEN DES HANDELS- UND STEUERRECHTS, BERICHT ÜBER DIE FACHTAGUNG DES INSTITUTS DER WIRTSCHAFTSPRÜFER IN DEUTSCHLAND e.V., München, Jan. 30-31, 1964 (Düsseldorf 1964),
cited as Bruns, in ENTWICKLUNGSTENDENZEN.

Bülow, *Das Verhältnis des Rechts der europäischen Gemeinschaft zum nationalen Recht,* in AKTUELLE FRAGEN DES EUROPÄISCHEN GEMEINSCHAFTSRECHTS; GEMEINSCHAFTSRECHT UND NATIONALES RECHT, NIEDERLASSUNGSFREIHEIT UND RECHTSANGLEICHUNG, EUROPARECHTLICHES KOLLOQUIUM 1964, 28 (Stuttgart 1965),
cited as Bülow, in AKTUELLE FRAGEN.

Von Caemmerer, *Entwurf einer europäischen Gesellschafts-form*, in VON CAEMMERER (ed.), EUROPÄISCHE HANDELSGE-SELLSCHAFT UND ANGLEICHUNG DES NATIONALEN GESELL-SCHAFTSRECHTS, WISSENSCHAFTLICHES KOLLOQUIUM DER FACHGRUPPE EUROPARECHT 54, Bad Ems, May 5-6, 1967 (Frankfurt a.M., Berlin 1968),
cited as von Caemmerer, in EUROPÄISCHE HANDELSGESELL-SCHAFT.

Von Caemmerer, *Europäische Aktiengesellschaft*, in BIEDEN-KOPF, COING, MESTMÄCKER (eds.), FESTGABE FÜR HEINRICH KRONSTEIN 171 (Karlsruhe 1967),
cited as von Caemmerer, *Europäische Aktiengesellschaft*.

Von Caemmerer, *La riforma tedesca delle società per azioni del 1965*, 1967 RIVISTA DELLE SOCIETÀ 165,
cited as von Caemmerer, *La riforma tedesca*.

Von Caemmerer, *Rechtsvereinheitlichung und internatio-nales Privatrecht*, in VON CAEMMERER, SCHLOCHAUER, STEINDORFF (eds.), FESTSCHRIFT FÜR HALLSTEIN 63 (Frank-furt a.M. 1966).

Cerexhe, *La reconnaissance mutuelle des sociétés et per-sonnes morales dans la Communauté économique euro-péenne*, 1968 REV. MARCHÉ COMMUN 578,
cited as Cerexhe, *La reconnaissance*.

Chayes, *The Modern Corporation and the Rule of Law*, in MASON (ed.), THE CORPORATION IN MODERN SOCIETY 25 (New York 1966),
cited as Chayes, in MASON.

Conard, *Corporate Fusion in the Common Market*, 14 AM. J. COMP. L. 573 (1965-66),
cited as Conard, *Corporate Fusion*.

Conard, *Harmonisation des législations commerciales des Etats-Unis*, 1967 TRAVAUX ET CONFÉRENCES, UNIVERSITÉ LIBRE DE BRUXELLES, FACULTÉ DE DROIT 33 (Brussels 1967),
cited as Conard, *Harmonisation des législations*.

Conard, *La mosaïque des droits de sociétés des Etats-Unis,* 1967 TRAVAUX ET CONFÉRENCES, UNIVERSITÉ LIBRE DE BRUXELLES, FACULTÉ DE DROIT 47 (Brussels 1967),
cited as Conard, *La mosaïque.*

Conard, *Organizing for Business,* in 2 STEIN & NICHOLSON (eds.), AMERICAN ENTERPRISE IN THE EUROPEAN COMMON MARKET 1 (Ann Arbor 1960),
cited as Conard, *Organizing for Business.*

Corporations Formed Pursuant to Treaty, (Note) 76 HARV. L. REV. 1431 (1963),
cited as *Corporations Formed Pursuant to Treaty.*

Cox, *The Study of European Institutions,* 3 J.C.M. STUDIES 114 (1965).

Dalsace, *Aperçu critique sur le projet de loi sur les sociétés commerciales,* 1965 REVUE DES SOCIÉTÉS 1,
cited as Dalsace, *Aperçu critique.*

Deringer, *Organschaft, Umwandlung und Publizität,* 1968 AG 211.

Desmyttere, *L'imposition des sociétés dans le cadre du Marché commun,* in INSTITUT D'ÉTUDES EUROPÉENNES, UNIVERSITÉ LIBRE BRUXELLES (ed.), L'HARMONISATION DANS LES COMMUNAUTÉS 39 (Brussels 1968).

Dieu, *La reconnaissance mutuelle des sociétés et personnes morales dans les Communautés européennes,* 1968 CAHIERS DE DROIT EUROPÉEN 532,
cited as Dieu, *La reconnaissance mutuelle.*

Dippel, *Die Reform des Aktienrechts (zugleich ein Beitrag zur Geschichte des Aktienwesens),* 1965 DEUTSCHE RICHTERZEITUNG 315, 353.

Dittner, *Die handelsrechtliche Publizität ausserhalb der Aktiengesellschaft,* GUTACHTEN FÜR DEN 45. DEUTSCHEN JURISTENTAG (München, Berlin 1964).

Döllerer, *Rechnungslegung nach dem neuen deutschen Aktiengesetz und ihre Auswirkungen auf das Steuerrecht,* 1965 BB 1405,
cited as Döllerer, *Rechnungslegung.*

Dorat des Monts, *Vers un droit européen des sociétés commerciales,* 1965 JUR.-CL. PÉR. DOCTR. 1896,
cited as Dorat des Monts, *Vers un droit européen.*

Drobnig, *Conflict of Laws and the European Economic Community,* 15 AM. J. COMP. L. 204 (1966-67).

Drobnig, *Kritische Bemerkungen zum Vorentwurf eines EWG-Übereinkommens über die Anerkennung von Gesellschaften,* 1966 ZHR 93,
cited as Drobnig, *Kritische Bemerkungen.*

Droz, *Technique de rapprochement des législations en matière de sociétés,* in KATHOLIEKE UNIVERSITEIT LEUVEN (ed.), EUROPEES VENNOOTSCHAPSRECHT 21 (Antwerpen, Leuven, Gent, Brussel, Kortrijk 1968),
cited as Droz, in EUROPEES VENNOOTSCHAPSRECHT.

Drucker, *Companies in Private International Law,* 17 INT'L & COMP. L.Q. 28 (1968).

Ducouloux-Favard, *Avec le nouveau régime des sociétés commerciales, le droit français s'est-il rapproché du droit italien?,* 1967 RIVISTA DELLE SOCIETÀ 1357.

Duden, *Aktienrechtsreform in Deutschland, Frankreich und England,* 1967 RABELS ZEITSCHRIFT 51.

Duden, *Das Für und Wider einer europäischen GmbH,* 1962 GMBH-RUNDSCHAU 76.

Duden, *Internationale Aktiengesellschaften,* 1962 RABELS ZEITSCHRIFT 90,
cited as Duden, *Internationale Aktiengesellschaften.*

Duden, *Umwandlung und Take-over,* in VON CAEMMERER, NIKISCH, ZWEIGERT (eds.), 1 FESTSCHRIFT FÜR DÖLLE (Tübingen 1963),
cited as Duden, *Umwandlung und Take-over.*

Durand and Latscha, *Obstacles tenant au droit fiscal,* in COOPÉRATIONS, CONCENTRATIONS, FUSIONS D'ENTREPRISES DANS LA C.E.E., Colloque Paris, Oct. 26-28, 1967, 1968 REV. MARCHÉ COMMUN 6,
cited as Durand & Latscha, in COOPÉRATIONS.

Duvieusart, *Le rôle des parlements nationaux et du Parlement européen dans le développement des Communautés,* in INSTITUT D'ÉTUDES EUROPÉENNES, UNIVERSITÉ LIBRE BRUXELLES (ed.), INSTITUTIONS COMMUNAUTAIRES ET INSTITUTIONS NATIONALES DANS LE DÉVELOPPEMENT DES COMMUNAUTÉS 75 (Bruxelles 1968),
cited as Duvieusart, in INSTITUTIONS COMMUNAUTAIRES.

Eisenberg, *The Legal Roles of Shareholders and Management in Modern Corporate Decisionmaking,* 57 CALIF. L. REV. 1 (1969),
cited as Eisenberg, *The Legal Roles of Shareholders.*

Ernst, *Harmonisation des politiques commerciales et politique commerciale commune de la C.E.E.,* in INSTITUT D'ÉTUDES EUROPÉENNES, UNIVERSITÉ LIBRE BRUXELLES (ed.), L'HARMONISATION DANS LES COMMUNAUTÉS 207 (Brussels 1968),
cited as Ernst, in L'HARMONISATION.

Esser, *Die Aufgaben der Publizität im Aktienrecht,* 1963 AG 31.

Everling, *Europäisches Gemeinschaftsrecht und nationales Recht in der praktischen Rechtsanwendung,* 1967 NJW 465,
cited as Everling, *Europäisches Gemeinschaftsrecht.*

Everling, *Niederlassungsfreiheit und freier Dienstleistungs-verkehr in der EWG*, 1961 BB 1257,
cited as Everling, *Niederlassungsfreiheit.*

Everling, *Die Rechtsangleichung in der Europäischen Wirt-schaftsgemeinschaft auf dem Gebiet des Niederlassungs-rechts*, in AKTUELLE FRAGEN DES EUROPÄISCHEN GEMEIN-SCHAFTSRECHTS 60, EUROPARECHTLICHES KOLLOQUIUM 1964 (Stuttgart 1965),
cited as Everling, in AKTUELLE FRAGEN.

Ficker, *Die Arbeiten der Kommission der Europäischen Wirtschaftsgemeinschaft auf dem Gebiet des Gesellschafts-rechts*, 1967 NJW 1160.

Ficker, *Die Entwicklung eines "Federal Corporation Law" durch die Rechtsprechung in den Vereinigten Staaten von Amerika*, in VON CAEMMERER, MENTSCHIKOFF, ZWEIGERT (eds.), 2 FESTSCHRIFT FÜR RHEINSTEIN 1059 (Tübingen 1969).

Ficker, *Federal Corporations als Vorbild für die Europäische Aktiengesellschaft*, 1969 AWD 182.

Fikentscher & Grossfeld, *The Proposed Directive on Com-pany Law*, 2 C.M.L. REV. 259 (1964-65),
cited as Fikentscher & Grossfeld, *The Proposed Directive.*

Foyer, *L'harmonisation des législations européennes sur les sociétés*, 1967 L'INTÉRÊT EUROPÉEN 1.

Foyer, *La proposition française de création d'une société de type européen*, 1965 REV. MARCHÉ COMMUN 268.

Franceschelli, *Harmonisation du droit des sociétés en ce qui concerne les pouvoirs des organs sociaux*, in HARMONISA-TION DU DROIT DES SOCIÉTÉS 52, 3ème COLLOQUE DE DROIT EUROPÉEN ORGANISÉ PAR L'ASSOCIATION DES JURISTES EURO-PÉENS, Paris, Nov. 25-27, 1965,
cited as Franceschelli, in 3ème COLLOQUE.

Garnier, *Théorie des bénéfices et des pertes,* 1967 Jur.-Cl. Sociétés, vol. 2, fasc. 18-3.

Geiler, *Die sog. Internationalen Juristischen Personen-Grenzrechtliche Probleme,* 1933 Mitteilungen der Deutschen Gesellschaft für Völkerrecht 177,
cited as Geiler, *Die sog. Internationalen Juristischen Personen.*

Genton, *La représentation et l'influence des "opérateurs économiques" dans la Communauté européenne,* in Institut d'études européennes, Université Libre Bruxelles (ed.), Institutions communautaires et institutions nationales dans le développement des Communautés 75 (Bruxelles 1968),
cited as Genton, in Institutions communautaires.

Van Gerven, *Le droit d'établissement dans la Communauté économique européenne et la législation sur les sociétés dans les Etat-membres,* 1965 Revue pratique des sociétés civiles et commerciales 53,
cited as van Gerven, *Le droit d'établissement.*

Gessler, in Entwicklungstendenzen des Handels- und Steuerrechts, Bericht über die Fachtagung des Instituts der Wirtschaftsprüfer in Deutschland e.V., München, Jan. 30-31, 1964 (Düsseldorf 1964),
cited as Gessler, in Entwicklungstendenzen.

Gessler, *Europäisches Gesellschaftsrecht am Scheideweg,* 1969 Der Betrieb 1001,
cited as Gessler, *Europäisches Gesellschaftsrecht am Scheideweg.*

Gessler, *Gegenseitige Anerkennung von Gesellschaften und Juristischen Personen im EWG-Bereich,* 1967 Der Betrieb 324.

Gessler, *Grundfragen der europäischen Handelsgesellschaft,* 1967 BB 381,
cited as Gessler, *Grundfragen.*

Gessler, *Das neue Aktienrecht,* 1965 BB 677.

Gessler, *Les pouvoirs des dirigeants des sociétés anonymes et des sociétés à responsabilité limitée,* in HARMONISATION DU DROIT DES SOCIÉTÉS, 3ème COLLOQUE DE DROIT EUROPÉEN ORGANISÉ PAR L'ASSOCIATION DES JURISTES EUROPÉENS 1, Paris, Nov. 25-27, 1965,
cited as Gessler, in 3ème COLLOQUE.

Gessler, *Probleme und Wege von Aktienrechtsreformen,* 1966 JURISTISCHE BLÄTTER 169.

Gessler, *Ziele und Methoden der Harmonisierung des Gesellschaftsrechts der GmbH,* in HARMONISIERUNG DES GESELLSCHAFTSRECHTS UND DES STEUERRECHTS IN EUROPA 9, BERICHT ÜBER DEN VII. INTERNATIONALEN GMBH-KONGRESS IN KÖLN, April 24-26, 1962,
cited as Gessler, in HARMONISIERUNG.

Goldman, *Le droit des sociétés internationales,* 1963 CLUNET 320.

Goldman, *Obstacles tenant au droit interne des sociétés,* in COOPÉRATIONS, CONCENTRATIONS, FUSIONS D'ENTREPRISES DANS LA C.E.E., Colloque Paris, Oct. 26-28, 1967, 1968 REV. MARCHÉ COMMUN 297,
cited as Goldman, in COOPÉRATIONS.

Goldman, *Le projet de convention entre les États membres de la Communauté économique européenne sur la reconnaissance mutuelle des sociétés et personnes morales,* 1967 RABELS ZEITSCHRIFT 201,
cited as Goldman, *Le projet.*

Goldman, *La reconnaissance mutuelle des sociétés dans la Communauté économique européenne,* in ETUDES JURIDIQUES OFFERTES À LÉON JULLIOT DE LA MORANDIÈRE 175 (Paris 1964),
cited as Goldman, *La reconnaissance.*

Goldman, *The Convention Between the Member States of the E.E.C. on the Mutual Recognition of Companies and Legal Persons,* 6 C.M.L. Rev. 104 (1968-69), cited as Goldman, *The Convention.*

Van der Grinten, *Contre une société de type européen,* 1964 De naamlooze vennootschap 8.

Van der Grinten, *Erkenning van vennootschappen en rechtspersonen in de Europese economische gemeenschap,* 1966 Sociaal-economische wetgeving 201, cited as van der Grinten, *Erkenning van vennootschappen.*

Van der Grinten, *Het europees vennootschapstype,* in Katholieke Universiteit Leuven (ed.), Europees vennootschapsrecht 37 (Antwerpen, Leuven, Gent, Brussel, Kortrijk 1968), cited as van der Grinten, in Europees vennootschapsrecht.

Von der Groeben, "Approximation of Legislation: The Policy of the Commission of the European Communities," Address before the European Parliament, Strasbourg, Nov. 27, 1969, *Publications Services of the European Communities* 8289/5/1/1970.

Von der Groeben, *Auf dem Wege zu europäischen Aktiengesellschaften,* 1967 AG 95, cited as von der Groeben, *Auf dem Wege.*

Von der Groeben, "Competition Policy as Part of the Economic Policy in the Common Market," Address before the European Parliament, Strasbourg, June 16, 1965, *Publications Services of the European Communities* 8/58/5/VI/1965/5, cited as von der Groeben, "Competition Policy."

Von der Groeben, *Vers des sociétés anonymes européennes, nécessité et possibilité de créer une société européen,* 1967 Rev. trim. droit eur. 224, cited as von der Groeben, *Vers des sociétés anonymes européennes.*

Von der Groeben, *Zur Politik der Rechtsangleichung in der Europäischen Wirtschaftsgemeinschaft*, 1967 ZEITSCHRIFT FÜR RECHTSVERGLEICHUNG (Vienna) 129,
cited as von der Groeben, *Zur Politik der Rechtsangleichung.*

Grosser, *The Evolution of European Parliaments*, in GRAUBARD (ed.), A NEW EUROPE? 219 (Boston 1964).

Grossfeld, *Die Anerkennung der Rechtsfähigkeit juristischer Personen*, 1967 RABELS ZEITSCHRIFT 1,
cited as Grossfeld, *Die Anerkennung.*

Guglielmetti, *Le direttive della CEE in materia di società e l'interpretazione dell' articolo 54.3.g del Trattato*, 1966 RIVISTA DELLE SOCIETÀ 1012.

Gutzwiller, *Die sog. Internationalen Juristischen Personen-Grenzrechtliche Probleme*, 1933 MITTEILUNGEN DER DEUTSCHEN GESELLSCHAFT FÜR VÖLKERRECHT 116,
cited as Gutzwiller, *Die sog. Internationalen Juristischen Personen.*

Hallstein, *Angleichung des Privat- und Prozessrechts in der Europäischen Wirtschaftsgemeinschaft*, 1964 RABELS ZEITSCHRIFT 211,
cited as Hallstein, *Angleichung des Privat- und Prozessrechts.*

Hauschild, *Obstacles tenant au droit interne des sociétés*, in COOPÉRATIONS, CONCENTRATIONS, FUSIONS D'ENTREPRISES DANS LA C.E.E., Colloque Paris, Oct. 26-28, 1967, 1968 REV. MARCHÉ COMMUN 317,
cited as Hauschild, in COOPÉRATIONS.

Hauschild, *Die europäische Aktiengesellschaft*, in VON CAEMMERER (ed.), EUROPÄISCHE HANDELSGESELLSCHAFT UND ANGLEICHUNG DES NATIONALEN GESELLSCHAFTSRECHTS, WISSENSCHAFTLICHES KOLLOQUIUM DER FACHGRUPPE EUROPARECHT 81, Bad Ems, May 5-6, 1967 (Frankfurt a.M., Berlin 1967),
cited as Hauschild, in EUROPÄISCHE HANDELSGESELLSCHAFT.

Hay, *Four Lectures on the Common Market: Trade Provisions—German and French Company Law—Establishment*, 24 U. Pitt. L. Rev. 685 (1963).

Van Hecke, *Erkenning, zetelverplaatsing en fusie*, in Katholieke Universiteit Leuven (ed.), Europees vennootschapsrecht 149 (Antwerpen, Leuven, Gent, Brussel, Kortrijk 1968),
cited as van Hecke, in Europees vennootschapsrecht.

Van Hecke, *Nationality of Companies Analysed*, 1961 Nederlands tijdschrift voor internationaal recht 223.

Heenen, *Le projet de première directive en matière de société, validité des engagements de la société*, in Katholieke Universiteit Leuven (ed.), Europees vennootschapsrecht 109 (Antwerpen, Leuven, Gent, Brussel, Kortrijk 1968),
cited as Heenen, in Europees vennootschapsrecht.

Heenen, *La représentation des sociétés anonymes et des sociétés de personnes à responsabilité limitée*, in Harmonisation du droit des sociétés 20, 3ème colloque de droit européen organisé par l'Association des Juristes Européens, Paris Nov. 25-27, 1965,
cited as Heenen, in 3ème Colloque.

Hellner, *Unification of Law in Scandinavia*, 16 Am. J. Comp. L. 88 (1968).

Hémard, *La réforme des sociétés par actions en France et la loi du 24 juillet 1966*, 1967 Rivista delle società 132,
cited as Hémard, *La réforme des sociétés*.

Houin, *Où en est le droit des sociétés dans le Marché commun*, 1968 Rev. trim. droit eur. 131,
cited as Houin, *Où en est le droit des sociétés*.

Houin, *Les pouvoirs des dirigeants des sociétés anonymes et des sociétés à responsabilité limitée et la coordination des*

législations nationales dans la C.E.E., 1966 REV. TRIM. DROIT EUR. 307,
cited as Houin, *Les pouvoirs des dirigeants.*

Houin, *Le projet italien de réforme du droit des sociétés par actions,* 1967 RIVISTA DELLE SOCIETÀ 148,
cited as Houin, *Le projet italien.*

Houin, *Le régime juridique des sociétés dans la Communauté économique européenne,* 1965 REV. TRIM. DROIT EUR. 11,
cited as Houin, *Le régime.*

Houin, *Les sociétés de type européen,* 1962-64 TRAVAUX DU COMITÉ FRANÇAIS DE DROIT INTERNATIONAL PRIVÉ 19 (séance du 7 déc. 1963),
cited as Houin, *Les sociétés de type européen.*

Houin, *La société européenne,* in INSTITUT D'ÉTUDES EUROPÉENNES, UNIVERSITÉ LIBRE BRUXELLES (ed.), L'HARMONISATION DANS LES COMMUNAUTÉS 79 (Brussels 1968),
cited as Houin, in L'HARMONISATION.

Houin, *Le Traité de Rome et les fusions en droit commercial français,* 1960 ANNUARIO DI DIRITTO COMPARATO E DI STUDI LEGISLATIVI 84.

Houin and Goré, *La réforme des sociétés commerciales,* 1967 RECUEIL DALLOZ SIREY CHR. 121,
cited as Houin & Goré, *La réforme des sociétés.*

Huiskamp, *The Harmonisation of Legislation of E.E.C. Member States Concerning Turnover Taxes,* 5 C.M.L. REV. 177 (1967).

Hutchings, *Obstacles tenant au droit fiscal,* in COOPÉRATIONS, CONCENTRATIONS, FUSIONS D'ENTREPRISES DANS LA C.E.E., Colloque Paris, Oct. 26-28, 1967, 1968 REV. MARCHÉ COMMUN 6,
cited as Hutchings, in COOPÉRATIONS.

Ipsen, *Das Verhältnis des Rechts der europäischen Gemeinschaft zum nationalen Recht,* in AKTUELLE FRAGEN DES EUROPÄISCHEN GEMEINSCHAFTSRECHTS 1, EUROPARECHTLICHES KOLLOQUIUM 1964 (Stuttgart 1965).

Jeantet, *La sécurité des tiers dans leurs rapports contractuels avec les représentants d'une S.A.R.L. ou d'une S.A. française,* in HARMONISATION DU DROIT DES SOCIÉTÉS 30, 3ème COLLOQUE DE DROIT EUROPÉEN ORGANISÉ PAR L'ASSOCIATION DES JURISTES EUROPÉENS, Paris, Nov. 25-27, 1965,
cited as Jeantet, in 3ème COLLOQUE.

Jennings, *The Role of the States in Corporate Regulation and Investor Protection,* 23 LAW & CONTEMP. PROB. 193 (1958),
cited as Jennings, *The Role of the States.*

Jepsen, *Die Genehmigung des Gewerbebetriebs ausländischer juristischer Personen in der Bundesrepublik Deutschland,* 1966 AWD 21,
cited as Jepsen, *Die Genehmigung des Gewerbebetriebs.*

Kaysen, *The Corporation: How Much Power? What Scope?,* in MASON (ed.), THE CORPORATION IN MODERN SOCIETY 85 (New York 1966),
cited as Kaysen, in MASON.

Lamberth, *Der Richtlinienentwurf der EWG-Kommission zur Koordinierung der Publizitätspflicht juristischer Personen,* 1964 AWD 69,
cited as Lamberth, *Der Richtlinienentwurf.*

Latham, *The Body Politic of the Corporation,* in MASON (ed.), THE CORPORATION IN MODERN SOCIETY 21 (New York 1966),
cited as Latham, in MASON.

Leboeuf, *Obstacles tenant au droit fiscal,* in COOPÉRATIONS, CONCENTRATIONS, FUSIONS D'ENTREPRISES DANS LA C.E.E., Colloque Paris, Oct. 26-28, 1967, 1968 REV. MARCHÉ COMMUN 487,
cited as Leboeuf, in COOPÉRATIONS.

Lecourt, *Concentrations et fusions, facteurs d'intégration,* in COOPÉRATIONS, CONCENTRATIONS, FUSIONS D'ENTREPRISES DANS LA C.E.E., Colloque Paris, Oct. 26-28, 1967, 1968 REV. MARCHÉ COMMUN 6,
cited as Lecourt, in COOPÉRATIONS.

Leleux, *Corporation Law in the United States and in the E.E.C.,* 5 C.M.L. REV. 133 (1967-68),
cited as Leleux, *Corporation Law.*

Leleux, *Le droit des sociétés aux États-Unis et dans la C.E.E.—Perspectives de leur évolution,* 1968 REV. TRIM. DROIT EUR. 50.

Leleux, *Faut-il créer la société commerciale européenne pour faciliter l'intégration économique dans la C.E.E.,* 1968 JOURNAL DES TRIBUNAUX 109,
cited as Leleux, *Faut-il créer.*

Leleux, *Harmonisation des droits des sociétés,* in VON CAEMMERER (ed.), EUROPÄISCHE HANDELSGESELLSCHAFT UND ANGLEICHUNG DES NATIONALEN GESELLSCHAFTSRECHTS, WISSENSCHAFTLICHES KOLLOQUIUM DER FACHGRUPPE EUROPARECHT 7, Bad Ems, May 5-6, 1967 (Frankfurt a.M., Berlin 1968),
cited as Leleux, in EUROPÄISCHE HANDELSGESELLSCHAFT.

Leleux, *Le rapprochement des législations dans la Communauté économique européenne,* 1968 CAHIERS DE DROIT EUROPÉEN 129,
cited as Leleux, *Le rapprochement.*

Leleux, *La société commerciale européenne instrument juridique de l'intégration économique?,* 1967 SOCIÉTÉ ROYALE D'ÉCONOMIE POLITIQUE DE BELGIQUE 1 (séance du 15 novembre 1967).

Lindberg, *The European Community as a Political System: Notes Toward the Construction of a Model,* 5 J.C.M. STUDIES 344 (1966-67).

Loussouarn, *Droit international de commerce,* 1959 REV. TRIM. DROIT EUR. 246.

Loussouarn, *Le rapprochement du droit des sociétés dans le cadre de la Communauté économique européenne,* in INSTITUT D'ÉTUDES EUROPÉENNES, UNIVERSITÉ LIBRE BRUXELLES (ed.), L'HARMONISATION DANS LES COMMUNAUTÉS 9 (Brussels 1968),
cited as Loussouarn, in L'HARMONISATION.

Loussouarn, *Les sociétés étrangères en France,* 1958 JUR.-CL., DROIT INTERNATIONAL, fasc. 564, No. 13.

Lutter, *Die Angleichung des Gesellschaftsrechts nach dem EWG-Vertrag,* 1966 NJW 273.

Lutter, *Die Erste Angleichungs-Richtlinie zu Art. 54 Abs. 3 Lit.g) EWGV und ihre Bedeutung für das geltende deutsche Unternehmensrecht,* 1969 EUROPARECHT 1.

Lutter, *Das neue französische Gesellschaftsrecht,* 1967 NJW 1153.

Lutter, *Die Rechtsangleichung im Gesellschaftsrecht,* in VON CAEMMERER (ed.), EUROPÄISCHE HANDELSGESELLSCHAFT UND ANGLEICHUNG DES NATIONALEN GESELLSCHAFTSRECHTS, WISSENSCHAFTLICHES KOLLOQUIUM DER FACHGRUPPE EUROPARECHT 5, Bad Ems, May 5-7, 1967 (Frankfurt a.M., Berlin 1968),
cited as Lutter, in EUROPÄISCHE HANDELSGESELLSCHAFT.

Lutter and Schlosser, *Die Publizität der GmbH in den Rechten der EWG,* 1967 GMBH-RUNDSCHAU 109,
cited as Lutter & Schlosser, *Die Publizität der GmbH.*

Maeijer, *Aanpassing van de Nederlandse wetgeving aan de eerste E.E.G. richtlijn en de rechtsgeldigheid van de verbintenissen van de vennootschap,* 1969 NAAMLOOZE VENNOOTSCHAP 151,
cited as Maeijer, *Aanpassing.*

Marchal, *Nécessité économique des concentrations et fusions,* in COOPÉRATIONS, CONCENTRATIONS, FUSIONS D'ENTREPRISES DANS LA C.E.E., Colloque Paris, Oct. 26-28, 1967, 1968 REV. MARCHÉ COMMUN 25, cited as Marchal, in COOPÉRATIONS.

Marty, *Les sociétés internationales,* 1962 RABELS ZEITSCHRIFT 73.

Mathijsen, *Les entreprises communes,* in GANSHOF VAN DER MEERSCH (ed.), DROIT DES COMMUNAUTÉS EUROPÉENNES 1119 (Bruxelles 1969).

Mayens, *Het eerste ontwerp van richtlijn ter coördinatie van het vennootschapsrecht, publiciteitsvereisten-nietigheid,* in KATHOLIEKE UNIVERSITEIT LEUVEN (ed.), EUROPEES VENNOOTSCHAPSRECHT 87 (Antwerpen, Leuven, Gent, Brussel, Kortrijk 1968), cited as Mayens, in EUROPEES VENNOOTSCHAPSRECHT.

Miller, *Toward the "Technocorporate" State—An Essay in American Constitutionalism,* Reprint No. 3, PROGRAM OF POLICY STUDIES IN SCIENCE AND TECHNOLOGY (George Washington University, Washington, D.C. undated).

Minervini, *Alcuni problemi connessi alla creazione di una società di tipo europeo,* 1966 RIVISTA DELLE SOCIETÀ 984.

Minervini, *Società per azioni: riforma anno zero,* 1967 RIVISTA DELLE SOCIETÀ 1280.

Möhring, *Aktuelle Wirkungen des EWG-Vertrages auf das Kartellrecht, das Niederlassungsrecht, den Dienstleistungsverkehr und das Agrarrecht,* 1965 NJW 1633, cited as Möhring, *Aktuelle Wirkungen.*

Möhring, *Das neue Aktiengesetz,* 1966 NJW 1, 87.

Möhring, *Rechtsvereinheitlichung und Rechtsgarantien im EWG-Bereich,* 1965 NJW 2225.

Motte, *Obstacles tenant au droit interne des sociétés*, in COOPÉRATIONS, CONCENTRATIONS, FUSIONS D'ENTREPRISES DANS LA C.E.E., Colloque Paris, Oct. 26-28, 1967, 1968 REV. MARCHÉ COMMUN 392,
cited as Motte, in COOPÉRATIONS.

Müller-Freienfels, *Legal Relations in the Law of Agency: Power of Agency and Commercial Certainty*, 13 AM. J. COMP. L. 193 (1964).

Nicholson, *Assimilation in the European Common Market of Laws Affecting Companies*, 9 AM. J. COMP. L. 358 (1960).

Nicholson, *The Significance of Treaties to the Establishment of Companies*, in STEIN & NICHOLSON (eds.), 2 AMERICAN ENTERPRISE IN THE EUROPEAN COMMON MARKET 153 (Ann Arbor 1960),
cited as Nicholson, *The Significance of Treaties.*

Nye, *Comparative Regional Integration: Concept and Measurement*, 22 INTERNATIONAL ORGANIZATION 855 (1968).

Van Ommeslaghe, *L'application des articles 85 et 86 du Traité de Rome aux fusions, aux groupes de sociétés et aux entreprises communes*, 1967 REV. TRIM. DROIT EUR. 457.

Van Ommeslaghe, *La création d'une société commerciale de type européen*, 1960 JOURNAL DES TRIBUNAUX 457.

Van Ommeslaghe, *Les groupes de sociétés*, 1965 REVUE PRATIQUE DES SOCIÉTÉS CIVILES ET COMMERCIALES 153.

Van Ommeslaghe, *La première directive du Conseil du 9 Mars 1968 en matière de sociétés*, 1969 CAHIERS DE DROIT EUROPÉEN 495, 619,
cited as van Ommeslaghe, *La première directive.*

Van Oven & van Leeuwe, *La fusion des sociétés anonymes en droit néerlandais*, in FUSIONS DES SOCIÉTÉS, RAPPORTS

AU COLLOQUE INTERNATIONAL DE DROIT EUROPÉEN, Bruxelles, Oct. 12-14, 1961 (Bruxelles 1962),
cited as van Oven and van Leeuwe, *La fusion.*

Patry, *La société anonyme de type européen,* Mémoirs publiés par la Faculté de Droit de Genève No. 18, 29 (Genève 1964).

Reese and Kaufmann, *The Law Governing Corporate Affairs; Choice of Law and the Impact of Full Faith and Credit,* 58 COLUM. L. REV. 1118 (1958),
cited as Reese & Kaufmann, *The Law Governing Corporate Affairs.*

Renauld, *Aspects de la coordination et du rapprochement des dispositions relatives aux sociétés,* in KATHOLIEKE UNIVERSITEIT LEUVEN (ed.), EUROPEES VENNOOTSCHAPSRECHT 47 (Antwerpen, Leuven, Gent, Brussel, Kortrijk 1968),
cited as Renauld, in EUROPEES VENNOOTSCHAPSRECHT.

Renauld, *Aspects de la coordination et du rapprochement des dispositions relative aux sociétés,* 1967 CAHIERS DE DROIT EUROPÉEN 611.

Renauld, *Etude comparative de la réglementation des fusions de sociétés en droit belge et dans certaines législations étrangères,* 1955 REVUE PRATIQUE DES SOCIÉTÉS CIVILES ET COMMERCIALES 1.

Renauld, *Les fusions des sociétés en droit belge,* 1962 REVUE DE DROIT INTERNATIONAL ET DROIT COMPARÉ 217,
cited as Renauld, *Les fusions.*

Renauld, *Réflexions sur l'évolution du droit des sociétés anonymes dans le Marché commun,* 1967 REVUE DES SOCIÉTÉS CIVILES ET COMMERCIALES 117.

Renauld, *Les travaux de réforme du droit des sociétés par actions en Belgique et le projet italien,* 1967 RIVISTA DELLE SOCIETÀ 218.

Renault, *Le droit d'établissement et la libre prestation de services dans la Communauté économique européenne,* 1966 JUR.-CL. PÉR. DOCTR. 1977.

Rengade, *Les mesures spéciales d'information requises des sociétés dont les actions sont cotées en Bourse,* 1965 JUR.-CL. PÉR. DOCTR. 1966.

Rigaux, *Le critère de nationalité et la notion de personne morale dans l'article 58 du Traité CEE et dans les dispositions d'application,* in KATHOLIEKE UNIVERSITEIT LEUVEN (ed.), EUROPEES VENNOOTSCHAPSRECHT 10 (Antwerpen, Leuven, Gent, Brussel, Kortrijk 1968), cited as Rigaux, in EUROPEES VENNOOTSCHAPSRECHT.

Rigaux, *Les personnes morales en droit international privé,* 1964 (XXIV) ANNALES DE DROIT ET DE SCIENCES POLITIQUES 241.

Rittner, *Die handelsrechtliche Publizität ausserhalb der Aktiengesellschaft,* Gutachten, Verhandlungen des fünfundvierzigsten Deutschen Juristentages, Vol. 1, Part 4 (1964), cited as Rittner, *Die handelsrechtliche Publizität.*

Rodhe, *Svensk aktiebolagsrätt och harmoniseringen av EEC-Ländernas aktiebolagslagar,* in FESTSKRIFT TILL HÅKAN NIAL, STUDIER I CIVILRÄTT OCH INTERNATIONELL RÄTT 460 (Stockholm 1966).

Rodière, *L'harmonisation des législations européennes dans le cadre de la C.E.E.,* 1965 REV. TRIM. DROIT EUR. 336, cited as Rodière, *L'harmonisation des législations.*

Rostow, *To Whom and for What Ends Is Corporate Management Responsible,* in MASON (ed.), THE CORPORATION IN MODERN SOCIETY 46 (New York 1966), cited as Rostow, in MASON.

Van Ryn, *Faut-il instituer la "société européenne"?,* 1967 JOURNAL DES TRIBUNAUX 377.

Van Ryn, *La société européenne,* in INSTITUT D'ÉTUDES EURO-
PÉENNES, UNIVERSITÉ LIBRE BRUXELLES (ed.), L'HARMONI-
SATION DANS LES COMMUNAUTÉS 65 (Brussels 1968),
cited as van Ryn, in L'HARMONISATION.

Sacco, *Industrial Concentration in Europe,* 2 LO SPETTA-
TORE INTERNAZIONALE 53 (Eng. ed. No. 1 1967),
cited as Sacco, *Industrial Concentration.*

Sanders, *La fusion des sociétés,* in CONTRIBUTIONS NÉER-
LANDAISES AU SIXIÈME CONGRÈS INTERNATIONAL DE DROIT
COMPARÉ, Hambourg 1962, at 72 (Amsterdam 1963),
cited as Sanders, *La fusion.*

Sanders, *Reform des Aktienrechts in den Niederlanden,*
1965 AG 284,
cited as Sanders, *Reform des Aktienrechts in den Niederlanden.*

Sanders, *La société commerciale européenne,* 1968 RIVISTA
DELLE SOCIETÀ 233.

Sanders, *Vers une société anonyme européenne?,* 1959
RIVISTA DELLE SOCIETÀ 1163.

Scholten, *Company Law in Europe,* 4 C.M.L. REV. 377
(1967-68),
cited as Scholten, *Company Law in Europe.*

Scholten, *The European Company,* 4 C.M.L. REV. 9 (1967-
68).

Scholten, *Riesame delle disposizioni della legge olandese
sulle società di capitali con particolare riguardo alla tutela
degli azionisti,* 1967 RIVISTA DELLE SOCIETÀ 242.

Scholten, *La société européenne,* in INSTITUT D'ÉTUDES EURO-
PÉENNES, UNIVERSITÉ LIBRE BRUXELLES (ed.), INSTITUTIONS
COMMUNAUTAIRES ET INSTITUTIONS NATIONALES DANS LE
DÉVELOPPEMENT DES COMMUNAUTÉS 47 (Bruxelles 1968),
cited as Scholten, in INSTITUTIONS COMMUNAUTAIRES.

Schultsz, *Harmonisation du droit des sociétés en ce qui concerne les pouvoirs des organes sociaux,* in HARMONISATION DU DROIT DES SOCIÉTÉS 78, 3ème COLLOQUE DE DROIT EUROPÉEN ORGANISÉ PAR L'ASSOCIATION DES JURISTES EUROPÉENS, Paris, Nov. 25-27, 1965,
cited as Schultsz, in 3ème COLLOQUE.

Schwartz, *De la conception du rapprochement des législations dans la Communauté économique européenne,* 1967 REV. TRIM. DROIT EUR. 238.

Schwartz, *Zur Konzeption der Rechtsangleichung in der Europäischen Wirtschaftsgemeinschaft,* in VON CAEMMERER, SCHLOCHAUER, STEINDORFF (eds.), FESTSCHRIFT FÜR HALLSTEIN 474 (Frankfurt a.M. 1966),
cited as Schwartz, *Zur Konzeption der Rechtsangleichung.*

Seidl-Hohenveldern, *European Companies,* 1959 J. BUS. L. 120 (London).

Simonetto, *Ritocchi alla normativa delle società contenuti nel decreto pres. 29 dic. 1969 n. 1127,* 1970 (II) RIVISTA DI DIRITTO CIVILE 148.

Sinay, *Le droit nouveau de la constitution des sociétés commerciales et de leurs modifications statutaires,* 1966 REVUE DES SOCIÉTÉS 246.

Sinay, *La proposition de directive européenne en matière de sociétés commerciales et le projet de loi française,* 1965 GAZETTE DU PALAIS DOCTR. 38,
cited as Sinay, *La proposition de directive européenne.*

Sinay, *La société anonyme de type nouveau du projet de loi français sur les sociétés commerciales,* 1966 GAZETTE DU PALAIS DOCTR. 50.

Sinay, *Vers un droit des groupes de sociétés, l'initiative allemande et le Marché commun,* 1967 GAZETTE DU PALAIS DOCTR. 70.

Skaupy, *Europäisches Gesellschaftsrecht,* 1966 AG 13.

Stein, *Assimilation of National Laws as a Function of European Integration*, 58 AM. J. INT'L L. 1 (1964), cited as Stein, *Assimilation*.

Stein, "Decision-Making in International Institutions," University of Chicago Graduate School of Business, Conference, April 1968 (unpublished).

Steinmann, *Über den Publizitätszweck in Europäischen Aktiengesellschaften*, 1966 AG 187.

Storm, *Statute of a Societas Europaea*, 5 C.M.L. REV. 265 (1967-68), cited as Storm, *Statute of a Societas Europaea*.

Le Tallec, *Koordinierung des Gesellschaftsrechtes in der Europäischen Wirtschaftsgemeinschaft*, 1963 AWD 114, cited as Le Tallec, *Koordinierung des Gesellschaftsrechtes*.

Teitjen, *Rapport de synthèse*, in COOPÉRATIONS, CONCENTRATIONS, FUSIONS D'ENTREPRISES DANS LA C.E.E., Colloque Paris, Oct. 26-28, 1967, 1968 REV. MARCHÉ COMMUN 539, cited as Teitjen, in COOPÉRATIONS.

Temple Lang, *The Right of Establishment of Companies and Free Movement of Capital in the European Economic Community*, 1965 U. ILL. L.F. 684.

Thibièrge, *Le statut des sociétés étrangères*, in 1 LE STATUT DE L'ÉTRANGER ET LE MARCHÉ COMMUN 240, 57ᵉ CONGRÈS DES NOTAIRES DE FRANCE, Tours 1959 (Paris 1959).

Trebuth, *Obstacles tenant au droit fiscal*, in COOPÉRATIONS, CONCENTRATIONS, FUSIONS D'ENTREPRISES DANS LA C.E.E., Colloque Paris, Oct. 26-28, 1967, 1968 REV. MARCHÉ COMMUN 508, cited as Trebuth, in COOPÉRATIONS.

Turq, *Obstacles tenant au droit fiscal*, in COOPÉRATIONS, CONCENTRATIONS, FUSIONS D'ENTREPRISES DANS LA C.E.E., Colloque Paris, Oct. 26-28, 1967, 1968 REV. MARCHÉ COMMUN 524, cited as Turq, in COOPÉRATIONS.

Uniken-Venema, *Coordination du droit des sociétés dans la Cee*, 1966 RIVISTA DELLE SOCIETÀ 994.

Vagts, *The Multinational Enterprise: A New Challenge for Transnational Law*, 83 HARV. L. REV. 739 (1970), cited as Vagts, *The Multinational Enterprise.*

Vagts, *Reforming the "Modern" Corporation: Perspectives from the German*, 80 HARV. L. REV. 23 (1966), cited as Vagts, *Reforming the "Modern" Corporation.*

Vanhaeverbeke and Genton, *The Economic and Social Committee*, EUROPEAN COMMUNITY 14 (London, May 1968).

Vasseur, *Argumente für eine europäische Handelsgesellschaft*, 1965 ZHR 177.

Vasseur, *Pour une société de type européen*, Mélanges offerts à René Savatier 903 (Paris 1965).

Vasseur, *Quelques arguments pour une société de type européen*, 1965 REVUE DES SOCIÉTÉS 18.

VerLoren van Themaat, *Probleme der Rechtsangleichung im Gemeinsamen Markt*, 1962 BB 1131.

VerLoren van Themaat, *Die Rechtsangleichung als Integrationsinstrument*, in HALLSTEIN AND SCHLOCHAUER (eds.), FESTSCHRIFT FÜR OPHÜLS 243 (Karlsruhe 1965).

Vernon, *Multinational Enterprise and National Sovereignty*, 1967 HARV. BUS. REV. 156.

Vignes, *Le droit d'établissement et les services dans la Communauté économique européenne*, 1961 ANNUAIRE FRANÇAIS DE DROIT INTERNATIONAL 668.

Vignes, *La société (commerciale) européenne, état des travaux*, 1967 REV. MARCHÉ COMMUN 344.

Visentini, *Opinioni e discussioni sulla riforma delle società per azioni*, 1967 RIVISTA DELLE SOCIETÀ 469.

Walker, *Foreign Corporation Laws: A Current Account*, 47 N.C.L. REV. 733 (1969).

Walker, *Foreign Corporation Laws: The Loss of Reason*, 47 N.C.L. REV. 1 (1968).

Weiner, *Legislative Recognition of the Close Corporation*, 27 MICH. L. REV. 273 (1929).

Wiethölter, *Die Gründungskontrolle bei Aktiengesellschaften*, DEUTSCHE LANDESREFERATE ZUM VI. INTERNATIONALEN KONGRESS FÜR RECHTSVERGLEICHUNG 225, Hamburg 1962 (Special Publication of RABELS ZEITSCHRIFT, Hamburg 1962).

Wilhelmi, *Das neue Aktiengesetz*, 1965 AG 153, 187, 217, 247, 307, 349.

Willemetz, *Faut-il envisager la création d'une société de type européen?*, 1960 REVUE DES SOCIÉTÉS 364.

Willemetz, *Une société du type européen*, 1960 REV. MARCHÉ COMMUN 38.

Würdinger, *Zur Publizität der GmbH im nationalen und europäischen Bereich*, 1964 GMBH-RUNDSCHAU 151.

Yntema, *"Autonomy" in Choice of Law*, 1 AM. J. COMP. L. 341 (1952).

Yntema, *The Objectives of Private International Law*, 35 CAN. B. REV. 721 (1957).

Zweigert, *Der Einfluss des europäischen Gemeinschaftsrechts auf die Rechtsordnungen der Mitgliedstaaten*, 1964 RABELS ZEITSCHRIFT 601.

Zweigert, *Grundsatzfragen der europäischen Rechtsangleichung, ihrer Schöpfung und Sicherung*, in VON CAEMMERER, NIKISCH and ZWEIGERT (eds.), 2 FESTSCHRIFT FÜR DÖLLE 401 (Tübingen 1963), cited as Zweigert, *Grundsatzfragen der europäischen Rechtsangleichung*.

Summary Table of Contents

Table of Contents

INTRODUCTION

In this study we are concerned with "assimilation of laws" of nation-states which are in the process of integration into a wider community of a still uncertain pattern or dimension. The concept of "assimilation of laws" connotes making national laws more similar, not necessarily in the words they use but rather in their economic and social impact.[1]

Social scientists very tentatively offer a series of factors that exert integrative influence upon people, including transactions or interactions among persons or groups, knowledge of each other, shared functional interests, previous integrative experience ("spill-over"), governmental effectiveness, system of decision-making, and—last but not least—homogeneity in the sense of similar social, economic and other characteristics.[2] If homogeneity proves to be such a factor, and if law is viewed as a set of "normative criteria of action representing feelings of obligation, legitimacy and the like," then a process of making national laws more similar may upgrade homogeneity and thus advance integration.

---

[1] In the title of this volume I employed the term "harmonization" because it has a commonly understood meaning which I thought would convey the general idea of the book more effectively than the somewhat novel term "assimilation." I did so, however, at some risk of compounding the already rampant terminological confusion since—as I shall explain in the first chapter—the term "harmonization" is used in the Treaty establishing the European Economic Community in a sense which is different from the commonly understood one.

[2] See for instance Jacob and Teune, *The Integrative Process: Guidelines for Analysis of the Bases of Political Community*, in JACOB & TOSCANO (eds.), THE INTEGRATION OF POLITICAL COMMUNITIES at 11-12 (Philadelphia 1964). Other factors suggested are: geographical proximity, the "character" or "motive" pattern of a group, the sovereignty-dependency status of the community, external threat. RUSSETT, INTERNATIONAL REGIONS AND THE INTERNATIONAL SYSTEM: A STUDY IN POLITICAL ECOLOGY at 3, 10 and *passim* (Chicago 1967).

Perhaps a certain degree of homogeneity is necessary for any mutual assimilation, but once the assimilation begins a feedback effect may occur which increases homogeneity which in turn escalates assimilation. Again, if, as has been suggested, "cohesiveness among individuals and among communities of individuals can be measured by—and is probably promoted by—the extent of mutual relationship or interaction among them,"[3] then assimilation of laws which facilitates transactions and interaction would contribute to integration. Finally, since the process of legal assimilation requires extensive comparative studies, it unquestionably increases "the knowledge of each other" on the part of the national élites concerned; and it may also advance, perhaps in a marginal measure only, the shared functional interests and governmental effectiveness with ultimate impact upon integration dynamics.

Even while proposing these intriguing hypotheses, I wish to dispel any expectation that this volume was designed to supply conclusive data in their support or rebuttal. In the first place, the very nature of the subject matter makes this impossible since one cannot possibly offer empirical evidence that assimilation of national laws, coordinated in a regional context, has increased homogeneity and advanced integration when the process has hardly begun. Quite apart from this inherent obstacle, my objective is much more modest. I have been interested in the role of the law in European integration from its very inception as an aspect of the more general problem of the role of the law in international organization. By definition, this approach puts at least as much emphasis on the dynamics and methodology of the process as on the resulting new norms of positive law. For reasons which need no elaboration, the initial lawmaking in the European Community centered on branches of administrative law removed from, and superimposed upon, the central body of the law as it is traditionally con-

---

[3] JACOB & TEUNE, *id.* at 23.

ceived. When Community lawmaking first began to "spill-over" into the area of corporation law, a "core" discipline of private law, I decided to record in some detail—in the form of a "case study"—the "birth" of the first "Community law" designed to coordinate national legislation in this vital field. As I became engrossed in the panorama of the initial organizational difficulties, the interaction of the various Community institutions, the interplay of the emerging special interests, I realized that the developments in the Community arena have been profoundly conditioned by, and could not be seen in isolation from, the processes of national reform that have been in more or less advanced stages of progress in the nation-states concerned. This meant that at least some attention had to be given to the national instrumentalities of company law reform. An elementary sense of loyalty to the discipline of the law required that the examination of the processes on the national and Community levels be complemented with a responsible analysis of the resulting positive Community norm—but this in turn appeared of limited value unless accompanied by an elucidation of the impact of the regional norm on the underlying rules of the national laws. As I completed the study of the first Community law my attention was naturally attracted to further undertakings in this field, including a new treaty and a host of preparatory drafts extending across the entire field of company law. Through this logical progression that a wiser man would have anticipated at the outset, I was drawn inexorably from the reasonably familiar grounds of transnational institutions into the treacherous highways and byways of company law of the six national systems. As a result, although the core of the volume deals with the "political dynamics" of the assimilation process (to borrow Lindberg's term) it is heavily encrusted by an analysis of existing and projected company law norms. While I fully realize the danger of falling between the proverbial two chairs, I nevertheless dare to hope that the book will be of some interest not only to lawyers concerned with corporation, compara-

tive and international law, but to political and other social scientists as well. I would also hope that as the assimilation process unfolds, others will pursue the theoretical perspectives projected by the hypotheses mentioned earlier.[4]

---

[4] A word about terminology is in order. The term "transnational" is used in this volume to indicate a state of integration extending beyond intergovernmental cooperation and marked by a direct interaction of groups and individuals of varied nationalities. Again, since this volume is mainly concerned with differences and similarities among six national laws, the English terms employed to connote the various boards and institutional arrangements provided for in these laws were selected with a view to preserving, as much as possible, the nuances of the national terms. Consequently the terminology applied here is not designed primarily to evoke the institutional equivalents in American corporation laws as would presumably be the case if this were a handbook on European company laws for American lawyers.

Chapter 1

THE FUNCTION OF ASSIMILATION OF LAWS IN THE EUROPEAN COMMUNITY SYSTEM[1]

1. The Community as an economic system

Assimilation of national laws is one of a number of processes in an intricate design for a progressive coalescence of the national economies of the six "sovereign" Member States (Belgium, Federal Republic of Germany, France, Italy,

---

[1] On this generally see Stein, *Assimilation of National Laws as a Function of European Integration,* 58 Am. J. Int'l L. 1 (1964). Extensive literature has now become available on this topic: Schwartz, *Zur Konzeption der Rechtsangleichung in der Europäischen Wirtschaftsgemeinschaft* in von Caemmerer, Schlochauer, Steindorff (eds.), Probleme des Europäischen Rechts, Festschrift für Walter Hallstein 474, with comprehensive citations to earlier literature at 478-79 n.7 (Frankfurt a.M. 1966); VerLoren van Themaat, *Die Rechtsangleichung als Integrationsinstrument,* in Hallstein & Schlochauer (eds.), Zur Integration Europas, Festschrift für Carl Friedrich Ophüls 243 with citations at 243-44 n.2 (Karlsruhe 1965); Hallstein, *Angleichung des Privat-und Prozessrechts in der Europäischen Wirtschaftsgemeinschaft,* 1964 Rabels Zeitschrift 211; Anne Limpens, *Harmonisation des législations dans le cadre du Marché commun,* 1967 Rev. int. droit comp. 621; Leleux, *Le rapprochement des législations dans la Communauté économique européenne,* 1968 Cahiers de droit européen 129; von der Groeben, *Zur Politik der Rechtsangleichung in der Europäischen Wirtschaftsgemeinschaft,* 1967 Zeitschrift für Rechtsvergleichung 129. *See also* EEC Commission, *Eighth General Report on the Activities of the Community 1965,* Table 7, at 89 ff.; *Ninth General Report on the Activities of the Community 1966,* Table 8, at 91 ff.; *Tenth General Report on the Activities of the Community 1967,* Table 6, at 118 ff.; Approximation of Legislation, Work undertaken between 1 Jan. 1958 and 31 Mar. 1966, 1966 Bull. E.E.C. Supp. No. 8, at 3 ff. and Approximation of Legislation, Work undertaken between 1 Jan. 1958 and 31 December 1967, 1968 Bull. E.C. Supp. No. 5 at 7 ff. For 1968 see *Second General Report on the Activities of the Communities 1968,* Table 4, at 75; for 1969 see *Troisième Rapport Général sur l'activité des Communautés 1969,* Table 13, at 97.

Luxembourg, Netherlands) into a "Common Market" and eventually into an economic union.[2] The Common Market embraces in the first place the "four freedoms": Freedom of movement of goods, freedom of movement for workers, freedom for individuals and companies to enter business and to supply services across frontiers, and freedom of movement of capital throughout the territory of the Community. A system of rules is to assure a legal order for a fair, qualified competition, and governmental measures as well as private restrictive arrangements distorting such competition are proscribed. A common Community-wide policy must govern agriculture, transportation and commercial relations with the outside world; national economic and monetary policies are to be "co-ordinated" so as to advance growth with stability and social policies are to be "harmonized." Thus the Treaty contemplates a coherent economic system which is to assure conditions essentially akin to a national integrated market. The system is in the nature of a market economy tempered by social welfare considerations, strong public control of agriculture and transportation, and moderate public guidance of the economy. The guidance aims at the "magic triangle" objectives: balanced growth, stability, and higher living standards.

2. Patterns of lawmaking: three categories

To make this system work, the Treaty provides a basis for a coherent legal order which in specified limited segments penetrates the national legal orders and breaches their integrity more deeply than does the legal order of traditional international organizations. This is one reason why law and lawyers have played such a significant part in the life of the Community.

Lawmaking, which aims at the assimilation of national laws of the Member States, cannot be discussed in isolation

---

[2] Art. 3 of the Treaty Establishing the European Economic Community (298 U.N.T.S. 3 (1958)) describes the "activities" designed to achieve the Treaty purposes specified in Art. 2.

from other lawmaking activities in the Community, particularly since in a number of instances assimilation is conceived as a supplementary device to these other lawmaking processes. We may think of three basic categories of lawmaking in terms of the objectives of the Community scheme:[3]

a. The first category is aimed at assuring a "national treatment" throughout the Community territory for the nationals and companies of the Member States, their goods and services and capital. Or, expressing it in a negative way, the objective is to remove all restrictions which discriminate on the basis of nationality.

b. The second category of lawmaking serves to put into effect "common" Treaty rules (as in the field of competition) and "common" Community policies. The Treaty requires, as I suggested earlier, the Community institutions to evolve common policies on agriculture and transport, and a common commercial policy toward third states.

It is useful to keep in mind when examining this category that integration has been conceived from the very beginning as a progression, an evolutionary process. Even within a nation-state, a legal norm is the ultimate expression of the will and values of the society; only after the conflicting economic and social forces have been composed may the resulting consensus crystallize into a general norm. In the Community we note a multitude of activities directed toward what the EEC Treaty calls "co-ordination"—co-ordination of economic and monetary policies, social, regional and energy policies of the Member States. With certain exceptions these confrontations of national policies have not progressed far enough to affect national laws directly. Thus for example, when the Council of Ministers decides to under-

---

[3] Gaudet, *Incidences des Communautés européennes sur le droit interne des États membres,* 1963 ANNALES DE LA FACULTÉ DE DROIT DE LIÈGE 5.

take a Community-wide inquiry into the wage rates within certain sectors of industry, or when the Council recommends a co-ordinated use by the Member Governments of national budgetary policies to cope with the vagaries of the business cycle, the effect on national laws is, if anything, incidental. But if we assume that the process blocked out by the Treaty will continue to take its course at a pace determined by the prevailing political and economic conditions, we must expect that the lawmaking activities in this category will expand as agreement is reached on common policies in the various fields.

In both these categories the desired legal objective is achieved either directly by a "self-executing" provision of the Treaty,[4] or by an "act" of the Community institution. This act may take the form of a federal-type "regulation" which changes national laws directly; or it may constitute a "decision" or "directive" which compels the national lawmaker to adjust national law through the national lawmaking processes; or it may be a "decision" addressed to, and directly binding, an individual.[5]

---

[4] *E.g.*, Art. 85 as interpreted by the Court of Justice in Case 13-61, de Geus en Uitdenbogerd v. Bosch & Van Rijn, 8 Recueil de la Jurisprudence 89 (1962); 57 AM. J. INT'L L. 129 (1963); and Art. 12 as interpreted in Case 26-62, van Gend en Loos v. Tarief-commissie, 9 Recueil de la Jurisprudence 1 (1963).

[5] The principal forms of the acts of the Council of Ministers and the Commission are defined in Art. 189 of the Rome Treaty which reads as follows:

"The Council and the Commission shall, in the discharge of their duties and in accordance with the provisions of this Treaty, issue regulations and directives, take decisions and formulate recommendations or opinions.

"Regulations shall have general application. They shall be binding in every respect and directly applicable in each Member State.

"Directives shall be binding upon every Member State to which they are addressed as to the result to be achieved, but the form and means of enforcing them shall be left to the national authorities.

"Decisions shall be binding in every respect upon those to whom they are directed.

"Recommendations and opinions shall have no binding force."

c. The third category of lawmaking is aimed at what the Treaty calls "approximation" of national laws of the Member States "to the extent necessary for the functioning of the Common Market" (Article 3(h)). It is this category that is of particular relevance to our study.

3. The "approximation" of law

(a) The concept

The particular function of approximation is to reduce or eliminate disparities in national laws, regulations or administrative practices where they constitute obstacles to economic intercourse which cannot be removed through other legal devices specifically authorized in the Treaty. In other words, approximation tackles obstructive legal disparities which cannot be eliminated by measures designed to strike down governmental barriers to the free flow of goods and factors of production, prohibited subsidies, dumping, protectionist indirect taxes, and private restrictive practices. Where disparities in national laws contribute to disparities in the cost of production and in competitive conditions generally, approximation of these laws in selected spheres (such as social benefits and working conditions) is to act as a catalyst in the automatic leveling-off process inherent in the Common Market, and thereby make it easier for the governments to accept common Community-wide policies.

It is inherent in the Community system of "delegated powers" that the common institutions may not act except on the basis of a more or less specific grant of power in the Treaty. This principle holds true also for the approximation-of-laws activities. The clause in Article 3(h) mentioned earlier, is only a general principle and we must therefore look to the more specific provisions of the Treaty which define the fields where approximation is authorized and the procedure through which it is to be achieved. The conditions under which the institutions may act and the procedures differ from one provision to the other.[6]

In most, but by no means all, instances where the Treaty contemplates approximation, the independent, "executive" Commission has the legal authority to propose, and the Council of Ministers to enact, directives which are legally binding on the Member States. The Commission must see to it that the Governments adopt the necessary national measures implementing the directives and, if they should fail to do so, the Commission must institute a proceeding which culminates in a declaratory judgment by the Court of Justice of the Communities against the delinquent member. If the Commission fails to act, any Member State may bring the matter before the Court. The Court of Justice has the final authority to interpret the directive and to say whether a national measure constitutes a proper implementation of the directive. Although the Treaty is silent on the subject, it may be reasonable to assume that a national court will interpret the national implementing measure in the light of the directive. There is even some authority that in certain circumstances a directive will be held directly applicable in national courts.[7] Thus, if a question should arise in a pro-

---

[6] These provisions authorizing approximation in specific areas are:
Art. 27: customs legislation,
Art. 54, par. 3 (g): company law (see p. 36 *infra*),
Art. 56, par. 2: legislation on aliens based on public order, health and security,
Art. 57, pars. 2 and 3: legislation concerning access to and exercise of, certain self-employed activities,
Art. 70: exchange controls on movement of capital,
Art. 99: indirect taxes,
Arts. 111 and 113: unification of commercial policy,
Art. 112: subsidies for export to third countries,
Arts. 117 and 118: social legislation,
Arts. 100 and 101-102 contain more general authorization clauses and are discussed p. 49 *infra*.
For a detailed discussion see Stein, *Assimilation* at 6-29; Leleux, *Le rapprochement* at 137 and *passim*.

[7] Conseil d'État (Belg.) 3ᵉ chambre, Oct. 7, 1968, in 1969 CAHIERS DE DROIT EUROPÉEN 343; Kellermann, *Les directives de la CEE dans*

ceeding before a national court as to the scope or meaning of such directive, the national court of last resort will be bound to refer this preliminary question to the Court of Justice of the Communities for a binding determination in accordance with Article 177 of the Treaty. To this extent, uniform interpretation of the approximation directives and of the national implementing measures could be assured.

(b) Terminology—Special characteristics

A word about the terminology of the Treaty may be useful. The Treaty employs a number of different terms, such as "approximation," "harmonization," and "co-ordination," all of which may connote the reduction of differences among the laws of the Member States. But the treaty does not employ them consistently to indicate different concepts. A comparison of the four official texts of the Treaty leads to the perhaps surprising conclusion that there is no meaningful difference between the terms;[8] they imply a process which

---

l'ordre juridique néerlandais, id. at 247; *see also* BEBR, JUDICIAL CONTROL OF THE EUROPEAN COMMUNITIES at 187 (London 1962); Desmedt, *Les deux directives du Conseil de la C.E.E. concernant la police des étrangers,* 1966 CAHIERS DE DROIT EUROPÉEN 55, 69-71; Pepy, *Les questions préjudicielles dans les Traité's de Paris et de Rome et la jurisprudence de la Cour de Justice des Communautés Européennes,* 1965 CAHIERS DE DROIT EUROPÉEN 194, 211.

[8] Only the French text of the Treaty Establishing the European Coal and Steel Community (E.C.S.C.) is authoritative. 261 U.N.T.S. 140 (1957). An English translation was published by the E.C.S.C. High Authority and in 1962 by Her Majesty's Stationery Office in London. The Dutch, French, German and Italian texts of the EEC Treaty and of the Treaty Establishing the European Atomic Energy Community are equally authoritative. 298 U.N.T.S. 3 (1958) and 298 U.N.T.S. 167 (1958). Two different English translations were published: one in 1958 by the Interim Committee for the Common Market and Euratom, Brussels (subsequently reprinted by the Publishing Services of the European Communities), and the other in 1962 by Her Majesty's Stationery Office. There is no authoritative English text of any of the three treaties. Lochner examined the texts of the three treaties and concluded that there was no fundamental difference between the following terms used in the German text: Angleichung, Annäherung, Anpassung, Harmonisierung, Abstimmung, Koordinierung, gemeinsames Vorgehen, enge Zusammenarbeit. He attempted, however, to find

may conceivably lead as far as the creation of a uniform rule, but may stop short of such result. However, the concept of "co-ordination" is used also in a non-normative context, such as "co-ordination of economic policies," which need not involve any change in the law.

We conclude that approximation of laws in the first place has a very special function in the Treaty scheme, that is to bring about adjustment in national laws where they impede the coalescence process. This function not only controls the direction of the effort but also supplies it with a motive force. Second, the new institutions provide an "organized impulse" as well as a measure of enforcement and uniform interpretation. In both respects approximation, and for that matter "assimilation" of law in the broader sense defined above,[9] differ, at least quantitatively, from the "uniform law" movement in the United States and in Scandinavia, from the "unification-of-law" efforts that have flourished on the Continent in this century, and from the restatement and development-of-law activities in the United Nations and its specialized agencies such as the International Labor Organization. Of course the true significance of the differences can be measured only by the results accomplished.

4. A decade of transition, how much progress?

I have dealt elsewhere with the early achievements of the Community system in the field of assimilation.[10] This book is an attempt to analyze the assimilation process in the area

---

some difference in the "gradation of intensity." Lochner, *Was bedeuten die Begriffe Harmonisierung, Koordinierung und gemeinsame Politik in den Europäischen Verträgen?*, 1962 ZEITSCHRIFT FÜR DIE GESAMTE STAATSWISSENSCHAFT 35. In the same vein *Leleux, Le rapprochement* at 147; *but see contra* Renauld, *Aspects de la coordination et du rapprochement des dispositions relative aux sociétés,* 1967 CAHIERS DE DROIT EUROPÉEN 611. *See also* Polach, *Harmonization of Laws in Western Europe,* 8 AM. J. COMP. L. 148 (1959); *cf.* STRAUSS, FRAGEN DER RECHTS-ANGLEICHUNG IM RAHMEN DER EUROPÄISCHEN GEMEINSCHAFTEN 18 (Frankfurt a.M. 1959).

9 *See* p. 1 *supra.*

10 Stein, *Assimilation,* 58 AM. J. INT'L L. 1 (1964).

of company law. It would therefore exceed the bounds of this study if I were to undertake a detailed evaluation of the manifold activities extending over more than a decade of the Community existence. A few general observations, however, may be necessary to complete the framework for our inquiry.

It is not surprising that assimilation of law has progressed furthest in those areas where greatest progress was made in the implementation of the Treaty. By July 1, 1968, eighteen months in advance of the Treaty schedule, the movement toward a customs union among the Six was virtually completed.[11] Except for a few agricultural products, tariffs, quotas and equivalent restrictions on the free flow of goods have been dismantled for intra-Community trade and the common external tariff toward the outside world erected. As for the bulk of agricultural products, the common marketing organizations with a unified price-support system and joint financing of agricultural export subsidies, based on a formidable superstructure of new Community law, also reached the final stage of completion.[12] Since the uniform prices had been set at high levels the production increased dramatically and the resulting surpluses in some agricultural products have placed a heavy financial burden on the member Governments. Although trade with third countries has risen considerably, trade among Member States has expanded more rapidly so that it now accounts for 45% of the Members' total exports, compared with 30% in 1958.[13]

---

[11] Van der Mensbrugghe, *Vers l'achèvement de l'union douanière dans la CEE*, 1969 CAHIERS DE DROIT EUROPÉEN 181; *Second General Report on the Activities of the Communities 1968*, at 21-25.

[12] *See in general,* Olmi, in GANSHOF VAN DER MEERSCH (ed.), DROIT DES COMMUNAUTÉS EUROPÉENNES at 1766-1822 (Brussels 1969); *Second General Report on the Activities of the Communities 1968* at 135-80. *See further, Dix ans de politique agricole commune,* 1967 REV. MARCHÉ COMMUN 160; *L'Europe agricole va-t-elle changer de cap?,* 1969 *id.* at 112; Olmi, *Common organisation of agricultural markets at the stage of the single market,* 5 C.M.L. REV. 359 (1967-68).

[13] *The European Common Market—Progress Report,* 1969 WORLD BUSINESS 5 (No. 17).

With the internal tariff barriers removed, the "non-tariff" obstacles to trade became starkly visible, and this is where "approximation" came into play. Thus, although the national Governments lost their authority to modify the external tariff, national customs officials have continued to administer it; differences in national customs regulations, such as customs clearance and valuation procedures or definition of the "origin" of goods, threatened to defeat the uniformity of the common external tariff. For this reason a series of directives and regulations has been adopted to meet this difficulty.[14] Similarly, it became apparent that the flow of goods and fair competition have been obstructed by disparities—if not by the very existence—of national regulations on safety standards and inspection procedures for appliances, tools, and motor vehicles, on product labeling and packaging, and on controls of pharmaceuticals. An extensive approximation plan, envisaging a host of directives, was elaborated but only a fraction has been put into effect thus far.[15] In the Commission's own words, after seven years of efforts, the pharmaceutical sector is "a striking example of the almost complete sealing-off of markets by national laws."[16] More progress has been made in the field of food controls and veterinary and phytosanitary regulations where

---

[14] *Second General Report on the Activities of the Communities 1968*, at 25-29; van der Mensbrugghe, in Droit des Communautés européennes at 1740-65; Dubois, *Ce qui a été accompli et ce qui reste à faire pour le fonctionnement harmonieux de l'union douanière*, 1968 Rev. Marché Commun 1017.

[15] On May 28, 1969, the Council of Ministers adopted a resolution establishing an extensive program for the elimination of non-tariff obstacles envisaging a series of decisions to be made by the Council before Jan. 1, 1971. [1969] J.O. C76 of June 17, at 1. *See also* Bonn, *Les entraves techniques aux échanges intracommunautaires*, 1969 Rev. Marché Commun 369; Goldman, in Droit des Communautés européennes at 2206-54.

[16] Commission, Spokesman's Group, P (69) 49, Sept. 1969. *See generally* Seidel, *The Harmonization of Laws Relating to Pharmaceuticals in the EEC*, 6 C.M.L. Rev. 309 (1968-69).

a number of approximation directives has come into effect
in conjunction with the agricultural policy.[17]

It also became clear that the disparity of indirect taxes on
transactions in goods and services, particularly the widely
applied turnover tax, seriously impaired the customs union
because they directly affected prices, could be manipulated
for protectionist purposes and necessitated continued frontier controls inside the Community. The directives designed
to harmonize the turnover tax represent perhaps the most
far-reaching assimilation thus far, although their full implementation has been delayed.[18] Efforts to adjust important
state monopolies so as to remove discriminatory purchasing
and marketing practices have hardly begun to be felt, although in this field the Commission has only the power to
recommend remedial action to the Governments.[19]

The legal framework for free movement of workers has
been established by a set of regulations so that workers of

---

[17] *First General Report on the Activities of the Communities 1967,*
at 162-63; *Second General Report on the Activities of the Communities
1968,* at 175-78.

[18] *See* p. 168 *infra.*

[19] In November and December 1969, the Commission issued recommendations to the Federal Republic, France and Italy concerning state
monopolies in a variety of products including alcohol, potassium,
matches, explosives, salt, and the French arrangements governing imports of petroleum products. COMMISSION, GROUP DU PORTE PAROLE,
P-2, Jan. 1970. Earlier action centered mainly on tobacco products. See
also on a related topic the Commission directive based on Art. 33 (7)
designed to eliminate procurement practices by national, regional and
local authorities which discriminate against suppliers in other Member States. *Id.* at 1P (69) 189, Nov. 10, 1969. *See generally* van der
Mensbrugghe, in DROIT DES COMMUNAUTÉS EUROPÉENNES at 1761-65;
Franceschelli, *Les monopoles nationaux de caractère commercial visés
dans l'article 37 du Traité C.E.E. et leur aménagement,* 1968 REV.
MARCHÉ COMMUN 855; *Second General Report on the Activities of the
Communities 1968,* at 54; and *First General Report on the Activities
of the Communities 1967,* at 68. In the context of elaborating a common policy in the tobacco sector, France and Italy undertook an
important commitment to terminate by 1976 their respective state
monopolies for importing and wholesale marketing of manufactured
tobacco. EUROPE No. 506 (new series) Feb. 10, 1970, at 4-5.

any Member State are now free to seek employment any-where in the Community on an equal basis with local workers. The realization of this important "freedom" has been favored by persistent labor shortages in the Commu-nity.[20] To make sure that labor mobility is not impaired by the application of differing national public-order and security regulations on entry and sojourn of aliens, these regulations have been partly "co-ordinated" by directives.[21] Again, an effort was made in the form of a series of direc-tives to harmonize at least provisionally those national laws and practices governing standards of admission to various occupations and professions;[22] here diversity may have cur-tailed freedom of access to entrepreneurial activities and supply of services across national frontiers—a subject which I shall discuss in some detail later in this book. Suffice it to say here that a substantial number of directives has been adopted by the Council to improve freedom of establish-ment and supply of services.

Two early directives had gone some distance toward re-moving restrictions on the movement of capital, more spe-cifically on direct investment, short and medium term loans, issues of foreign securities and transactions therein;[23] but many such restrictions remain and the national capital mar-kets are still both relatively undeveloped and substantially isolated. Although the dramatically expanding Eurodollar

---

[20] See generally Troclet, in Droit des Communautés européennes at 1823-54; ter Heide, The Free Movement of Workers in the Final Phase, 6 C.M.L. Rev. 466 (1968-69).

[21] See Desmedt, supra note 7.

[22] See p. 24 infra.

[23] [1960] J.O. 921 and [1963] J.O. 62; see Second General Report on the Activities of the Communities 1968, at 65-66; see also Segré, Capital movements in the European Economic Community, Banca Nazionale del Lavoro, 1962 Quarterly Rev. (Mar.) 78; Truquet, Le développement d'un marché européen des capitaux, pt. 1, and Lieber-herr, pt. 2, 1967 Rev. Marché Commun 565, and 614. See generally EEC Commission, The Development of a European Capital Market, Report of Group of experts appointed by the EEC Commission (Brus-sels Nov. 1966).

market has provided the beginnings of a "European" capital market, it has caused concern because it has been almost unregulated and could pose a threat to national currencies in time of financial crisis.[24]

In the context of a common commercial policy toward third states, common rules have been adopted on antidumping measures and administration of quotas and procedures on imports from third states, members of GATT.[25] The Six assumed a common posture in GATT negotiations for tariff concessions and concluded, through the Community institutions, a few trade agreements of limited importance and a series of "association agreements" with Greece, Turkey, the French-African states and certain other countries. Only most recently has the Council laid down certain ground rules for commercial relations with "state-trading" countries.[26]

In the field of competition, the basic Community legislation on restrictive agreements and practices has been laid down in the form of "quasi-federal" regulations. In Italy and Luxembourg, and for all practical purposes in Belgium, the

---

[24] *The Eurodollar Market*, 1969 WORLD BUSINESS 9 (No. 17); Duhamel, *Les courants de devises hors du circuit des banques centrales (Les euro-marchés) II*, 1969 BANQUE 947.

[25] Regulation No. 459/68, [1968] J.O. L93, at 1 (April 17), concerns antidumping (English translation in CCH COMM. MKT. REP. ¶ 3883); see on this subject also, Beseler, *EEC Protection Against Dumping and Subsidies from Third Countries*, 6 C.M.L. REV. 327 (1968-69). On the three regulations adopted in 1968 on drawing up a common liberalization list for imports, procedure for management of quotas and a special import procedure for specified products see *Second General Report on the Activities of the Communities 1968*, at 381-83. These regulations constitute only a framework for a policy to be filled by the Council.

[26] *First General Report on the Activities of the Communities 1967*, at 381-91; and *Second General Report on the Activities of the Communities 1968*, at 371-75. Regarding alignment of trade agreements with third countries, the Council took a decision on October 9, 1961, [1961] J.O. 1273, providing a procedure for consultations on negotiations of trade agreements with third countries. ANANIADÈS, L'ASSOCIATION AUX COMMUNAUTÉS EUROPÉENNES (Paris 1967).

EEC Treaty was the first "antitrust" law ever enacted.[27] The requirement of "notification" of restrictive agreements caused the Commission to be swamped by some 40,000 notifications concerning in large measure agreements of a marginal competitive impact. A great deal of the Commission's energy was absorbed by its effort to obtain recognition of its jurisdiction in this field. After a slow start a number of individual cases has come up for decision by the Commission and the Court of Justice, particularly in the vertical restrictive agreements area. Thus the rule was established by the Court outlawing clauses in exclusive dealership agreements that would prohibit parallel imports or exports and thereby in effect restore the isolation of national markets.[28] More recently, substantial fines were imposed by the Commission in two cases involving "unnotified" horizontal restrictive arrangements of considerable importance,[29] and the Court offered some clarification of the respective enforcement roles of national authorities and the Community institutions.[30] In the field of monopolies, the Treaty limits itself to prohibiting *abuse* of "a dominant position." The Commission's policy has been to encourage concentration and to a certain extent cooperation within the Community in order to facilitate adjustment to the new dimensions of the Common Market.[31] The Commission has also been

---

[27] BLAKE (ed.), BUSINESS REGULATION IN THE COMMON MARKET NATIONS (3 vols., New York 1969).

[28] Établissements Consten and Grundig-Verkaufs-GmbH v. Commission, Case 56 & 58/64, 12 Recueil de la Jurisprudence 429 (1966), CCH COMM. MKT. REP. ¶ 8046.

[29] Commission Decision (quinine cartel) IV/26, 623 of July 16, 1969, [1969] J.O. L192, at 5 (Aug. 5), CCH COMM. MKT. REP. ¶ 9313; Commission Decision (dyestuff manufacturers) IV/26, 267 of July 24, 1969, [1969] J.O. L195, at 11 (Aug. 7), CCH COMM. MKT. REP. ¶ 9314.

[30] Wilhelm v. Bundeskartellamt, Case 14/68, 15 Recueil de la Jurisprudence 1 (1969).

[31] *See generally* Lassier, *Dix ans de politique européenne de la concurrence,* 1967 REV. MARCHÉ COMMUN 167; Mok, *The Cartel Policy of the EEC Commission 1962-1967,* 6 C.M.L. REV. 67 (1968-69); MESTMÄCKER, DIE VERMITTLUNG VON EUROPÄISCHEM UND NATIONALEM RECHT

engaged in a scrutiny of financial subsidies made available by Member Governments to certain industrial sectors (film, shipbuilding, iron and steel, computers, etc.) and it has made findings regarding the competitive impact of some fifteen national general subsidy schemes submitted to it in accordance with the Treaty.[32] Similarly, in the context of "approximation of legislation" the Commission has been examining in detail a number of national statutes and regulations which may constitute distortions of competition, with a view to ordering their modification, but the impact in this field and in the area of subsidies has been quite limited.

In the field of general economic policy, voluntary cooperation through a network of committees rather than institutionalization has been the trend. The Council has made a series of recommendations on short-term cyclic policies. A group of experts, and another group of government officials, have worked out medium-term policy "programs" which, although initially quite general, will no doubt provide an increasing impulse toward national "programming" and Community centered coordination of national "programs." In this field, and in the monetary area, serious differences persist among national policies which have prevented effective coordination.[33] The unhappy experience in connection with the French devaluation and German revaluation in 1969 led to the approval of a plan for mutual assistance in monetary crisis-situations which, however, represents only a limited step toward a solution.[33a]

IM SYSTEM UNVERFÄLSCHTEN WETTBEWERBS (Bad Homburg, Berlin, Zürich 1969).

[32] On subsidies in general see Colliard, in DROIT DES COMMUNAUTÉS EUROPÉENNES at 2172-83; *Second General Report on the Activities of the Communities 1968,* at 55-60.

[33] *Second General Report on the Activities of the Communities 1968,* at 108-33. *See also* Commission Memorandum on Medium-Term Guidelines for the Economic Policy of the European Community, CCH COMM. MKT. REP. No. 127, Feb. 3, 1970.

[33a] *EEC Monetary Reserve Pool,* 22 INT'L FINANCIAL NEWS SURVEY 57 (Feb. 20, 1970).

Owing in no small measure to the limited powers given to the Commission in the Treaty, the progress in the development of a common social policy has been minimal. Apart from some ventures such as vocational training, national social welfare and labor laws remain basically unchanged, and the limited assimilation that has taken place was confined principally to the agricultural sector. However, worker mobility has been encouraged by detailed Community regulations protecting migrant workers against any loss of their social security benefits as they move from one Member State to another, and by provisions for retraining and relocation assistance from Community funds which, however, benefited Italy, more than any other Member.[34]

Although the Treaty gives the Community comprehensive powers in the field of transportation policy, the work in this area has produced limited results, partly due to an excessive emphasis on the technical aspects in disregard of the important underlying political-economic considerations on which an agreement is difficult to obtain. Only in mid-1968, in the face of a threat of unilateral action by the Federal Republic, did the Council adopt a series of measures concerning mainly road transport (one involving harmonization) which could be viewed as the beginning of a common policy.[35] Similarly, the attempts to work out a common "energy policy" that would comprise all sources of energy (coal, oil, water, nuclear materials) have thus far remained largely unsuccessful.[36]

---

[34] On social policy see in general, Troclet, in DROIT DES COMMUNAUTÉS EUROPÉENNES at 2349-2424; Second General Report on the Activities of the Communities 1968, at 292-332.

[35] See generally Rodière, in DROIT DES COMMUNAUTÉS EUROPÉENNES at 1921-70; Second General Report on the Activities of the Communities 1968, at 263-78; Robert, Doubts on a Common Transport Policy, 5 C.M.L. REV. 193 (1967-68); Dousset, Bilan et perspectives de la politique commune des transports, 1967 REV. MARCHÉ COMMUN at 174.

[36] On Dec. 18, 1968, the Commission submitted to the Council a document entitled "First Guidelines for a Community Energy Policy." 1968 Bull. E.C. Supp. No. 12. The document outlines the general

Although it has been generally recognized that research and innovation are vital to economic growth, the studies of the Working Group on Scientific and Technical Research Policy were interrupted as a result of the political controversy over the participation of non-member states, particularly the United Kingdom. The decision to resume work was made only in December 1968 and the Group reported on a variety of subjects.[37] In the field of regional policy, efforts have been made to harmonize national regional policies and to stimulate new regional activities and means of development through such measures as coordinated subsidies, railroad tariff rates, European Investment Bank credits and special studies.[38]

Although many Treaty deadlines remained unfulfilled, the "transitional period" came to an end on December 31, 1969 as envisaged by the Treaty. After half a decade of stagnation, the "summit" meeting at The Hague and the follow-up sessions of the Council of Ministers in December 1969, evidenced a revival of the determination to proceed toward an economic union. Within the framework of a definitive arrangement for financing the common agricultural policy, it was agreed in principle that, by the mid-nineteen-seventies, the proceeds from levies on agricultural imports and from customs duties on industrial imports, and a portion of the revenues from the value-added tax will flow into Community treasury, so as to provide the Community with its own resources. The European Parliament will be given limited budgetary powers over these substantial funds in order to assure a measure of "political control" on

objectives and proposes means of action. A similar outline of action already exists in the form of the General Objectives prescribed by the ECSC Treaty and in the Target Programs for nuclear energy under the EURATOM Treaty. *Second General Report on the Activities of the Communities 1968,* at 251-55.

[37] *Second General Report on the Activities of the Communities 1968,* at 206 and generally at 203-45.

[38] *Id.* at 278-92.

the Community level. A plan for a monetary union was to be worked out during 1970. Finally, an adjustment in the French position following General de Gaulle's retirement appeared to clear the way for negotiations with the United Kingdom and other states, with a view to their admission to Community membership.[39]

---

[39] Communiqué of the Meeting of Heads of State or Government at The Hague on December 1 and 2, 1969, Translation, News from European Community, December 5, 1969, Eur. Community Information Service, Washington, D.C. For the Council of Ministers resolutions on the Community resources and budgetary powers of the European Parliament of Dec. 19-22, 1969, and Feb. 5-7, 1970, see CCH COMM. MKT. REP. ¶¶ 9337 and 9344. On March 4, 1970, the Commission submitted a plan for the establishment of an economic and monetary union before 1980. CCH COMM. MKT. REP. No. 133, Apr. 29, 1970.

Chapter 2

COMMERCIAL COMPANIES AND ASSIMILATION OF LAWS IN THE EEC TREATY: THE "CONSTITUTIONAL" FRAMEWORK

In modern economy, capital companies came to be the dominant mode for the conduct of business; they became not only the principal buyers and sellers of goods, but the major borrowers and lenders of capital flowing between countries, and the principal conveyors of new technology. Groups of companies, joined by a common parent but including diverse nationalities play a major part in national economic life and in international economic intercourse.[1] It is therefore not surprising that the Community scheme is particularly concerned with companies and earmarks segments of national company laws for assimilation.

In the first place, if a company is to help integrate national markets into a "Common Market," as the American corporation has contributed to the creation of a single continental market in the United States, the legal order must enable it—the authors of the Treaty realized—to progress from the classic import-export pattern to a stage where it creates more or less permanent "establishments" beyond its own state's frontiers. In American constitutional parlance, the company which has been engaged in "interstate" business only, must be free to "enter" another State with a view to doing "intrastate" business there. The establishment in the other state in due course becomes an organic part of the

---

[1] GALBRAITH, THE NEW INDUSTRIAL STATE at 83-96 (New York 1968); Vernon, *Multinational Enterprise and National Sovereignty*, 1967 HARV. BUS. REV. 156.

local economic life, but it still remains subject to the parent company's overall planning and direction. In fact, the EEC Treaty includes specific and detailed provisions to achieve this first objective, and it is not surprising that the first and most intensive assimilation effort centered on the "freedom of establishment."

Second, if a company is to take advantage of a greatly enlarged market, and if it is to meet the increased capital demands not only for expansion but also for research and development, it should be able—within the limits of effective competition—to combine and merge with other companies and transfer its operations across national frontiers and generally to select the most economical patterns. As far as this second objective is concerned, the Treaty provides little more than a conditional commitment on the part of the members for further governmental negotiations toward an adjustment of national laws.

1. Freedom of establishment for companies

The legal basis for accomplishing the first of the two objectives described in the preceding section—the "free entry" into business across frontiers—is found in that part of the Treaty which deals with the "freedom of establishment and supply of services," one of the Treaty quartet of freedoms essential for opening up the national markets.[2] Each Member State is required to adjust its laws progressively so that, by the end of the "transitional period" (that is by the end of 1969) at the latest, nationals and companies of the other Member States will be treated the same way as

---

[2] EEC Arts. 52-66. Ehring in GROEBEN-BOECKH, 1 KOMMENTAR ZUM EWG-VERTRAG 163 (Baden-Baden 1958); EVERLING, THE RIGHT OF ESTABLISHMENT IN THE COMMON MARKET *passim* (CCH Chicago 1964); Wohlfahrt-Everling at 165-76; RENAULD, DROIT EUROPÉEN DES SOCIÉTÉS at 2.01-2.73 (Bruxelles 1969); *Les aspects économiques de la liberté d'établissement et de prestation de services dans la Communauté économique européenne,* Conférence internationale Pont-à-Mousson, France, 9 et 10 juin 1967, Commission des Communautés européennes (undated).

local nationals and companies when they wish to establish themselves locally in non-salaried activities, or when they wish to "supply services" from their home base to customers or clients across national frontiers.[3] The immediate purpose of this "freedom" is, first, to remove the barriers that national frontiers set to entrepreneurial and organizational skills of Member States' nationals and companies, and—in a broader context—to advance the objective of a more effective utilization of available resources in the enlarged market, particularly through industrial specialization.[4]

As is the case in other nation-states, the national systems of the Six are ridden with laws and practices discriminating against aliens in matters of access to business and other economic activities. The task of identifying and loosening these barriers has proved an undertaking of mammoth proportions. In order to provide a workable framework for a progressive implementation of this part of the Treaty, the Council of Ministers of the Community adopted, in December 1961, two "General Programs" which defined in broad terms the categories of discriminatory restrictions on access to the many specified occupations and professions, and fixed deadlines within which these restrictions must be removed.[5] On the basis of these Programs—although after considerable delay and in disregard of the deadlines—the Commission proposed, and the Council has adopted, some thirty direc-

---

[3] Campbell and Thompson give the following illustrative examples of "services" falling under the Treaty: " (i) the supplier moving to the recipient, as for example, for the purpose of having consultations, giving expert advice, giving entertainment, or maintaining machinery; (ii) the recipient moving to the supplier, as in the case of the tourist trade, or for medical treatment abroad; (iii) the service itself being moved, as in the transmission of a film for showing, or the dispatch of an expert opinion." CAMPBELL & THOMPSON, COMMON MARKET LAW 48-49 (London 1962).

[4] EEC Commission, *Action Program of the Community for the second stage* at 17, par. 19 (Brussels, Oct. 24, 1962); *First General Report on the Activities of the Community* at 58 (Sept. 1958).

[5] General Program for the Removal of Restrictions on the Right of Establishment, and General Program for the Removal of Restrictions on the Free Supply of Services, [1962] J.O. 32-46.

tives—and many others are in the process of elaboration—
identifying the specific provisions of national laws and regulations and the practices which the members must abolish
or modify.[6]

(a) The two components of the freedom of establishment

The Treaty "freedom of establishment" has two components:[7] (1) freedom of non-discriminatory access to, and
exercise of non-salaried activities; and (2) freedom to organize and manage—without discrimination—enterprises, in
particular companies as this term is defined in the Treaty.[8]

Included in this freedom is not only the right to establish
agencies, branches and subsidiaries, but also, among others,
the right of access to courts, to sources of supply, to the
various sources of financing (subject to the Treaty provisions
on removal of restrictions on the flow of capital),[9] as well as
the right to benefit from government concessions and licenses, to enter into contracts and acquire property of any
kind, to participate in government contracts and social welfare schemes, to join "professional" organizations, and to
benefit from whatever subsidies are accorded by the government[10] on equal footing with local nationals and companies.

---

[6] For a list of the directives see Approximation of Legislation, Work
undertaken between 1 Jan. 1958 and 31 December 1967, 1968 Bull.
E.C. Supp. No. 5, at 4-6. Forty-five directives are listed as being in
various stages of preparation. For 1968 see *Second General Report on
the Activities of the Communities 1968,* at 67 ff. Thirty-two directives
were reported as having been adopted in the Third General Report.
Troisième Rapport Général sur l'activité des Communautés 1969, at
88.

[7] Art. 52.

[8] Arts. 52 (1), 58.

[9] Arts. 67-69.

[10] Title III, General Programs, [1962] J.O. 32-46. Statement by Mr.
Colonna di Paliano, Member of the E.E.C. Commission, before the
XVth *Round Table on European Problems* concerning company law,
at 6 (Brussels, mimeogr., June 8, 1965). Synthèse des discussions, I-II,
2251/III/C/65 F, Rev. 2., March 29, 1965.

The freedom is not an absolute freedom; the obligation which the Member States had assumed is in fact—to use the language common to commercial treaties—an obligation to assure "national treatment," that is the treatment no worse but also no better than that enjoyed by nationals and companies of the receiving state. The design is, we must remember, to equalize the competitive conditions in the Community arena.[11] Moreover—and this is a further limitation—a national of a Member State who wishes to exercise his "freedom of establishment" by organizing an "agency, branch or a subsidiary" in another Member State, must first himself be "established" in the Common Market,[12] that is he must have a place from which he operates his business or practices his profession, an economic base or link in one of the Common Market countries, not necessarily that of his nationality. This limitation is a consequence of the Community's character as a regional arrangement.[13]

(b) The benefiting companies: a divergence in a conflict-of-laws rule

Companies are to benefit from this freedom in the same way as individual nationals.[14] This is a logical enough proposition but its implementation has posed problems, owing to the distinction that is made in the law between natural and "legal" (juridical) persons, such as companies. The beneficiary companies are not defined in terms of their "nationality"[15] or nationality of their management or shareholders:

---

[11] Art. 52 is a specific instance of Art. 7 which prohibits "any discrimination on the grounds of nationality." Ehring, in 1 GROEBEN-BOECKH at 164. See generally STEINDORFF, DER GLEICHHEITSSATZ IM WIRTSCHAFTSRECHT DES GEMEINSAMEN MARKTES (Berlin 1965).

[12] Art. 52(1); EVERLING at 64.

[13] Further as to the concept of "establishment" see Conard, Organizing for Business, in STEIN & NICHOLSON (eds.), 2 AMERICAN ENTERPRISE IN THE EUROPEAN COMMON MARKET—A LEGAL PROFILE at 13-17 (Ann Arbor 1960); Renault, Le droit d'établissement et la libre prestation de services dans la Communauté économique européenne, 1966 JUR.-CL.PÉR. DOCTR. 1977.

[14] Arts. 52(2), and 58.

[15] EVERLING at 74 n.48.

according to Article 58 the benefit goes to all companies[16] "organized in accordance with the law of a Member State *and having their registered office, central administration or principal place of business* within the Community."[17]

There is today practically no disagreement that the prerequisites with respect to the company's link with a Member State listed in Article 58 are alternative rather than cum-

---

[16] The term *"sociétés"* or *"Gesellschaften"* must be interpreted in broadest terms to comprise all legal persons (including cooperatives) and "unincorporated" associations without a legal personality which exist according to the laws of any Member State and which engage in economic activities in furtherance of the economic interests of the shareholders or partners. Art. 58 (2) as interpreted by EVERLING at 67-70.

[17] Emphasis added. For an analysis of Art. 58 and the relevant national law see Nicholson, *The Significance of Treaties,* in 2 STEIN AND NICHOLSON at 166 ff.; Conard, *Organizing for Business,* at 61-66; EVERLING at 74-77. RENAULD, DROIT EUROPÉEN DES SOCIÉTÉS 1.01 ff.; Grossfeld, *Die Anerkennung der Rechtsfähigkeit juristischer Personen,* 1967 RABELS ZEITSCHRIFT 1, at 16-17; Beitzke, *Anerkennung und Sitzverlegung von juristischen Personen im EWG-Bereich,* 1965 ZHR 1.

"Registered" or "statutory" seat (siège statutaire, satzungsmässiger Sitz), is the "seat" indicated in the articles of incorporation. It would correspond to the "principal office . . . within the state" or "initial registered office in this state" called for by the Delaware and Illinois Acts respectively. Conard, *id.* at 62. Conard likens the concept of "central administration" to the "home office" of an insurance company in the U.S. (at 61). "Principal place of business" (principal établissement) in Belgian law means the same as the "real seat," that is the seat of the central administration. Art. 197 of the Lois coordonnées sur les sociétés commerciales of Nov. 30, 1935, (Belgian Commercial Code, coordinated laws of 1935) hereinafter referred to as Code de commerce. *See also, e.g.,* Art. 1 of the French decree of Dec. 22, 1967 on bankruptcy of an individual merchant giving jurisdiction to the court of the "principal establishment," and Art. 2505 of the Italian Codice civile referring to "principal object of the enterprise." Since Art. 58 refers also to "central administration" the term principal établissement, Hauptniederlassung, must have a different meaning here than in Belgian law. Renauld correctly remarks that it is not easy to understand what is meant by this term and he suggests that, pursuant to the Italian doctrine, it could be taken to mean the place where the company maintains "the most important portion of material means whereby it pursues its purpose." RENAULD, DROIT EUROPÉEN DES SOCIÉTÉS at 2.31.

ulative.[18] However, one may ask whether a company which maintains only a registered office within the Community could still claim freedom of establishment in the other Member States, not unlike a Delaware corporation wishing to "enter" another State of the Union with a view to "doing business" there. Two considerations must be kept in mind:

First, national law and dominant conflict-of-laws doctrine in all but one Member State view a company as a "national" of the state in which it has its "real seat" (*siège social, siège réel*), that is its central administration, its "brain or nerve center"[19] where the main operational decisions are made. It is the law of the state of the company's "real seat" that determines its legal existence and governs its internal affairs. The scope and application of the "real seat" rule vary from one Member State to another, but only in the Netherlands, under the influence of English law, the rule is not followed. Instead, in the Netherlands, as in the United Kingdom and the United States,[20] the courts look to the law of the state of incorporation in which the formalities for the company's formation were complied with and where the company has its registered office.[21] Thus a company, in-

---

[18] Goldman, *Le projet de convention entre les États membres de la Communauté économique européenne sur la reconnaissance mutuelle des sociétés et personnes morales,* 1967 RABELS ZEITSCHRIFT 201-32. *But see contra,* Audinet, *Le droit d'établissement dans la Communauté économique européenne,* 1959 CLUNET 982, at 1016. *See generally* Loussouarn, in *L'harmonisation* at 17-20.

[19] Latty, *Pseudo-Foreign Corporations,* 65 YALE L.J. 137, at 167 (1955-56).

[20] EHRENZWEIG, A TREATISE ON THE CONFLICT OF LAWS at 412, 417 (St. Paul 1962).

[21] Conard, *Organizing for Business* at 61-65; RENAULD, DROIT EUROPÉEN DES SOCIÉTÉS at 2.28-2.35, 2.65-2.66, 6.04-6.07.
Netherlands: Law of July 25, 1959, [1959] STAATSBLAD No. 256; VAN DER HEIJDEN-VAN DER GRINTEN, HANDBOEK VOOR DE NAAMLOZE VENNOOTSCHAP at 76, 83-85 (8th ed. Zwolle 1968); RABEL, 2 THE CONFLICT OF LAWS: A COMPARATIVE STUDY at 34 (2d ed. Ann Arbor 1960).
France: Art. 3 of the Law of July 24, 1966 provides: "Companies whose [real] seat (*siège social*) is situated on French territory are sub-

ject to French law. Third persons may rely on the registered seat but the company may not invoke it as against third parties if its [real] seat is situated in another place" [*i.e.* in a place other than the registered seat]. See comment in LEMEUNIER, 1 LA RÉFORME DES SOCIÉTÉS COMMERCIALES at 14. However, Art. 154 of the same law (which follows the earlier rule contained in the Ordinance of January 7, 1959) sanctions a transfer of the seat to another country, upon approval in an extraordinary shareholders' meeting, without the loss of legal personality of the company but only if the receiving country has concluded with France a "special convention" permitting the acquisition of its "nationality" and preserving the legal personality upon transfer to its territory. *See* Franco-Belgian Treaty of Oct. 6, 1927 (J.O. (France) of Nov. 5, 1927). *See also* BATIFFOL, DROIT INTERNATIONAL PRIVÉ No. 193 ff. (3rd ed. Paris 1959).

Federal Republic: A company incorporated in a State of the United States for the exploitation of Mexican mines, with its main office in Hamburg, fraudulently sold shares there to German residents; in a suit by defrauded shareholders, the courts refused to consider it as an American corporation and apply the law of the state of its incorporation; since it failed to comply with the German stock company law requirements in Germany it was not considered a German stock company and the court applied the German law on noncorporate associations. RG Mar. 31, 1904, 1904 Deutsche Juristenzeitung 555, 1904 JW 231. *See also* 92 RGZ 73, 76 (1918), 7 RG 68 (1882). Where, however, the company does not have its real seat in Germany and the state of the company's real seat follows the rule of the law of incorporation (*e.g.,* a Delaware corporation with its real seat in Kentucky), German courts will apply the law of incorporation with respect to that company and not the law of the real seat. The case of the Eskimo Pie Corporation, 117 RGZ 215, at 217 (1927). There is some question whether German law has ever really settled on the "real seat" rule and some German writers advocate the "law of incorporation" rule. Beitzke, *Anerkennung und Sitzverlegung* at 13 and references there.

Belgium: Art. 197 of the Code de commerce provides that all companies whose "principal establishment" is in Belgium are subject to Belgian law, and Art. 196 states that companies organized and having their seat (siège) abroad may conduct their operations and appear in courts in Belgium. The Cour de cassation (dec. of Nov. 12, 1965, Lamot v. Société Lamot Ltd., 1966 REVUE PRATIQUE DES SOCIÉTÉS 136) held that these provisions allowed an English company to transfer its "real seat" to Belgium without a loss of legal personality but subjected the company to mandatory rules of Belgian company law. *See* p. 41 *infra* on seat transfer.

Luxembourg: Art. 159 of the Law of Aug. 10, 1915 on commercial companies follows the Belgian Art. 197, and Art. 158 follows the Belgian Art. 196.

Italy: Art. 2505 of the Codice civile states: "Companies organized abroad which have on the territory of the [Italian] State the seat of their administration or the principal object of the enterprise (sede

corporated in the Netherlands, but maintaining only a registered office there, would be considered as validly organized by Dutch courts[22] but might run into difficulties in the other Member States. More specifically, until the newly negotiated Convention[23] comes into effect, such a company could be denied recognition as a legal person or, in any case, it could at least be held subject to parts of the company law of the State where its "real seat" (central administration) is located.

Second, if a company has nothing but a registered office in the Community it would hardly be considered as meeting the requirement of being "established" in the Common Market which an individual must show as a prerequisite for his exercise of the freedom to set up "agencies, branches, or subsidiaries" in another Member State.[24] Accordingly, the General Program has prescribed that for a company to be

---

dell' amministrazione ovvero l'oggetto principale dell' impresa) are subject to all provisions of the Italian law, including those on the validity of their constitutive act." *See also* Arts. 2506-2510, and Art. 2437 of the Codice civile.

On United States see EHRENZWEIG, A TREATISE ON THE CONFLICT OF LAWS 408 ff.; LEFLAR, AMERICAN CONFLICTS LAW 55-68 (Indianapolis, Kansas City, New York 1968); on the United Kingdom see DICEY & MORRIS, ON THE CONFLICT OF LAWS 481 ff. (8th ed. London 1967).

For further discussion see p. 42 *infra* in connection with seat transfer, and p. 397 in connection with the new Convention on Mutual Recognition of Companies, etc.

[22] The stock company laws of the Member States provide that the articles of incorporation must designate a "seat" which must be, at least inferentially, in the State in which the formalities of incorporation are carried out; except in the Netherlands, the "seat" is interpreted to mean the "real seat" in the sense of central administration. Conard, *Organizing for Business* at 61-62; KOLLEWIJN, AMERICAN-DUTCH PRIVATE INTERNATIONAL LAW, 3 BILATERAL STUDIES IN PRIVATE INTERNATIONAL LAW at 16 (New York 1955); VAN DER HEIJDEN VAN DER GRINTEN, HANDBOEK at 75-76.

[23] *See* p. 394 *infra.*

[24] To claim this right a national of a Member State must be "established in the territory of any Member State." Art. 52 (1) second sentence. *See* p. 27 *supra.*

able to profit from the freedom of establishment in the Community it must show that its business activity constitutes "a continuous and effective link with the economy of a Member State,"[25] a new concept the content of which remains to be defined. In 1965, the French Minister of Justice pointed to the substantial differences in the "severity" among the laws of the Member States and was not at all satisfied that this provision in the General Program would prevent the working of a new Gresham law according to which the most "liberal" law will "chase out" (*chaser*) the stricter law.[26]

The "real seat" rule was predicated on the assumption that a company would operate in a single state. The purpose of the rule was to assure that the bulk of the legal relationships within the company system will be governed by the law of the state where most of its transactions take place, so that the company could not "escape" the policy and law of that state. In the establishment context this rule has been restricted, if not excluded by the clear language of Article 58; similarly, it has been sharply curtailed in the field of recognition by the new Convention concluded on this subject by the Member States. Beyond this, its general suitability in an increasingly transnational regional market has been questioned. Yet there exists some concern, as illustrated by the view of the former French Minister, lest the entrepreneurs make their organizational decisions not on the basis of normal business considerations but rather with a view to obtaining advantages in terms of greater legal freedom such as is afforded by the Netherlands law, as compared for instance with the strict German law. If this concern has any basis in reality, making national company laws more similar would appear the obvious answer.[27]

---

[25] Title I of the General Program at 36.

[26] Foyer, *L'harmonisation des législations européennes sur les sociétés*, 1965 L'INTÉRÊT EUROPÉEN 1, at 4.

[27] See for detailed considerations, p. 36 *infra*. Brulliard, *Buts et méthodes de l'harmonisation du droit des S.A.R.L.*, in HARMONISIERUNG

(c) Efforts to limit Article 58 to "true" Community companies

It is not uncommon for states by legislative fiat to exclude foreign controlled enterprises from specified benefits available to local companies even if the foreign enterprises are organized as local companies under local law. Such benefits may relate to taxation, subsidies, exchange controls, investment incentives, government contracts and licenses, etc.[28]

Scholten reveals that in the course of the negotiations for the EEC Treaty, the French delegation proposed to add a new section to Article 58, according to which a Member State could ask the Commission "to exclude from the benefits" of the freedom-of-establishment chapter "companies which, although established within the Common Market under the laws of a Member State, were subject to a preponderant influence exercised by residents of third countries or were dominated by capital foreign to the Community." Still according to Scholten, this proposal was rejected[28a] and in fact there is no provision to this effect

DES GESELLSCHAFTSRECHTS UND DES STEUERRECHTS IN EUROPA 27-28 (Köln 1962); Fikentscher & Grossfeld, *The Proposed Directive on Company Law*, 2 C.M.L. REV. 259, at 262 (1964); Ehring, in 1 GROEBEN-BOECKH at 36; 74 Harv. L. Rev. 1447 (1960-61). *See generally* Ficker, *Die Arbeiten der Kommission der Europäischen Wirtschaftsgemeinschaft auf dem Gebiet des Gesellschaftsrechts*, 1967 NJW 1160; Renauld, *Réflexions sur l'évolution du droit des sociétés anonymes dans le Marché commun*, 1967 REVUE PRATIQUE DES SOCIÉTÉS CIVILES ET COMMERCIALES 117-54.

[28] Van Hecke, *Nationality of Companies Analysed*, 1961 NEDERLANDS TIJDSCHRIFT VOOR INTERNATIONAAL RECHT 223, at 232. However, such legislation must be distinguished from cases where the "control theory" is employed for general conflict-of-laws purposes, that is where a company is held governed by foreign law because it is owned or controlled by foreigners, even though it is organized under local law and maintains its central administration within the state. BATIFFOL, DROIT INTERNATIONAL PRIVÉ at No. 196.

[28a] Scholten, *Company Law in Europe*, 4 C.M.L. REV. 377, at 386 (1967). Scholten reports that the French proposal did not form part of a new text dated Feb. 4, 1957. "At the beginning of February, the French delegation reserved the right to propose the inclusion elsewhere in the Treaty of provisions covering the type of [foreign controlled]

in Article 58 or anywhere else in the Treaty. Yet when it came to practical application of the establishment and supply-of-services provisions, in several contexts certain member Governments were reluctant to accept the broad definition of beneficiary companies in Article 58 or, at any rate, sought to limit the scope of the benefits derived from the freedom of establishment. For example, early in 1967, a French decree imposed the requirement of prior notification upon a broad spectrum of direct-investment transactions by "foreign" nationals even if no movement of capital across French frontiers was involved, and the French Minister of Economic Affairs was given the authority to order a delay or "adjournment" of such transactions. No distinction was made in the decree between nationals and companies of the other Member States and "third" states. The Commission considered this in violation—among others—of the freedom-of-establishment provisions but France pointed to the dramatic increase in foreign ("third country") investments in the Community and implied that foreign controlled subsidiaries organized in other Member States and even in France could not be considered Community companies at least for the purpose of the French decree. In its "reasoned opinion" initiating an enforcement proceeding against France, the Commission demurred and took the view that no distinction could be made for purposes of the freedom of establishment or movement of capital on the basis of "control criteria" derived from the origin of the capital or the nationality of the directors or shareholders.[29]

---

corporation just mentioned. Nothing was done about this, however, ..." *Id.*

[29] Written Question No. 333/69 by M. Glinne, [1970] J.O. C 3 (Jan. 10) at 14. EUROPE, April 22, 1969, No. 319 (new series) at 7-8. The Commission also relied on Art. 221, see p. 47 *infra,* and Art. 67 (with the first directive on free movement of capital of May 11, 1960). The Commission did not accept the contention that Art. 70, allowing safeguard measures in connection with movements of capital within the Community would supply a defense. As for freedom of movement of capital, it should be noted that Art. 67 requires removal of restric-

(d) Some compliance problems in the field of establishment and services

Noncompliance with the directives in the field of freedom of establishment has posed problems in several Member States. Thus, France has been slow in lifting its traditional requirement of the foreign merchant's identity card (*carte de commerçant*) for the benefit of the nationals of the other Member States, including sales representatives, and this has led to questions in the European Parliament and to enforcement proceedings under Article 169.[30] Again, the French regulations of 1967 enacting controls over the purchase by French companies of "foreign" patents was held by the Commission to be a new restriction, contrary to the "standstill" provision in Article 62 which prohibited new curtailments of freedom to supply services.[31] Finally, enforcement proceedings aimed at inducing the French Government to remove French nationality as a prerequisite to admission to certain positions were discontinued only after the necessary adjustment in French law had been made.[32]

tions, "to the extent necessary for the proper functioning of the Common Market," "on the movement of capital *belonging to persons resident* in the Member States and any discrimination based on the nationality or place of residence of the parties or on the place in which such capital is invested."

[30] EUROPE, April 15, 1969, No. 314 (new series) at 6; *id.,* April 30, 1969, No. 325 (new series) at 7; Written Questions No. 217 and 324 by Mr. Apel, [1969] J.O. C 6 (Jan. 22) at 5 and C 58 (May 10) at 4; Written Question No. 299 by Mr. Vredeling, [1969] J.O. C 46 (Apr. 9) at 7. The same type of restrictions ordered removed for the benefit of Community nationals included the German requirement of a "professional card" for traveling salesmen, the Belgian requirement of a professional card, and the limited duration of the authorization for aliens in Luxembourg law. *See, e.g.,* Directive on the realization of the freedom of establishment and free supply of services for activities derived from wholesale trade, dated Feb. 25, 1964, [1964] J.O. 863.

[31] EUROPE, April 16, 1969, No. 315 (new series) at 6; Written Question No. 323 by Mr. Deringer, [1969] J.O. C 50 (Apr. 21) at 8.

[32] EUROPE, April 29, 1969, No. 324 (new series) at 9. See a proceeding against France for the removal of French nationality requirement for the management positions in mining companies, EUROPE,

Similarly, the Commission took steps against Italy for requiring reciprocity as a condition for admission to mining and oil exploration, and against Luxembourg for failure to implement the directives in a variety of fields. In an interim report prepared for the Council, the Commission noted that the deadlines set in the directives have been respected only in rare instances but "[o]n the whole the Member States have carried out these commitments, even if they have been slow in doing so."[32a]

(e) Freedom of establishment and the protection of shareholders and "third parties": Article 54, par. 3(g)

The draftsmen of the Treaty evidently assumed that existing differences among national company laws would also stand in the way of the freedom of establishment and increased transnational activities. They provided in Article 54, which lays down the procedure for the realization of the freedom of establishment, that the Council of Ministers, with the Commission, was to see to

> co-ordinating, to the extent that is necessary, and with a view to making them equivalent, the guarantees required in Member States from companies . . ., for the purpose of protecting the interests both of the associates [shareholders] of such companies and of third parties. . . .[33]

May 28, 1969, No. 340 (new series) at 8. France did remove the nationality requirement in this field by Decrees No. 69-687 and 69-688 of June 19, 1969, [1969] J.O. (France) 6337. See also problem in Belgium raised by the Commission with the Belgian Government, Europe, May 5, 1969, No. 326 (new series) at 6.

[32a] Commission Spokesman's Group, 1P(70) 19, Feb. 7, 1970; Europe, Feb. 13, 1970, No. 509 (new series) at 6-8. The Commission's report has not been published.

[33] Nicholson, *The Significance of Treaties* at 177; Everling, in 1 Groeben-Boeckh at 171-75; Arnold, *Die Angleichung des Gesellschaftsrechts in der Europäischen Wirtschaftsgemeinschaft*, 1963 AWD 221, at 222.

Perhaps the most immediate consideration behind that provision was that Member States would find it difficult to remove the traditional restrictions or special formalities imposed upon foreign companies and to admit and treat them as national companies, unless they met certain standards with respect to the protection of their creditors and shareholders.[34] Although in principle the "coordination" was not made a condition precedent to the removal of such restrictions, it nevertheless was to be completed before the end of the transitional period which was to be also the ultimate deadline for the full realization of the freedom of establishment.[35] Whether or not this was the intention of the authors of the Treaty, the "coordination" provision—as we shall see—has become a principal Treaty basis for the activities aimed at assimilation of company laws.

(f)   The "chicken-egg" controversy about Article 54, par. 3(g)

A serious difficulty arose between the Federal Government of Germany and the EEC Commission, which in this affair was supported with a varying degree of vigor by all the other five members, in a matter involving the relationship between the "coordination of guarantees" under Article 54, par. 3(g) and the removal of restrictions on the freedom of establish-

---

[34] Jepsen, *Die Genehmigung des Gewerbebetriebs ausländischer juristischer Personen in der Bundesrepublik Deutschland,* 1966 AWD 21. *See also* p. 38 *infra* for a specific illustration.

[35] The Commission noted in its report for 1968 that it would be difficult for the Council to complete the freedom-of-establishment program and that it had under consideration a draft of a "global directive" which would provide for removal of restrictions on access to a great number of activities. *Second General Report on the Activities of the Communities 1968,* at 65. There was some controversy as to whether the end of the transitional period would automatically bring about freedom of establishment for those activities which had not been dealt with in the Council directives. *See* p. 48 *infra.* In the case of the medical, para-medical and pharmaceutical professions, the gradual removal of restrictions upon the freedom of establishment and supply of services is made "subject to the coordination for their exercise in the various Member States," EEC Art. 57 (3).

ment. In the process of elaborating the first series of directives on establishment and services, the Commission listed among the national provisions to be repealed certain sections of the German stock company law and of the German Code regulating trade, crafts and industry (*Gewerbeordnung*) which required any "foreign" legal person desiring to exercise an activity on the territory of the Federal Republic to obtain a special authorization from the Minister of Economic Affairs of the Land (State) concerned.[36] The Commission took the position that these German provisions were discriminatory restrictions against foreign companies and could not be applied to the companies of the Member States.[37]

---

[36] Section 292 of the Stock Company Law of 1937 (see also § 105 of the Versicherungsaufsichtsgesetz). Landmann-Rohmer, KOMMENTAR ZUR GEWERBEORDNUNG, § 12 n.2 (11th ed., München 1956). On the modification and repeal respectively of these provisions see note 41 *infra*. For an example of a directive ordering the repeal see Directive on the realization of the freedom of establishment and free supply of services for activities derived from wholesale trade, dated Feb. 25, 1964, [1964] J.O. 863.

[37] The Legal Service of the Executives of the Communities advanced the following arguments (JUR/CEE/1509/62 of June 21, 1962):

1. The Treaty assimilates companies to physical persons and no additional or other conditions than those set forth in Art. 58 as interpreted by the General Program (see *supra* note 5, at 25) can be required from companies.

2. The benefit of the right to create establishments of secondary nature cannot be made subject to prior coordination. The authors of the Treaty were fully aware that the company laws in Member States were far from uniform but they accepted the inherent difficulties because they thought that the scope of the right of establishment would be substantially reduced if it were to be limited to physical persons only. Clearly, inconveniences might arise from the differences in the company laws as they might arise from differences in rules concerning access to non-salaried activities generally. This is why the Treaty, in addition to suppressing discrimination, provided for coordination both of national provisions for access to non-wage earning activities (Article 57) and of certain limited aspects of the company laws (Article 54, par. 3(g)). But just as the coordination of the rules on access was not required as a condition precedent to the freedom of establishment *except* with respect to medical and pharmaceutical

The German Government objected on the ground that a repeal of these provisions could be demanded only after the coordination envisaged in Article 54 had been completed. The Ministerial authorization—the Federal Government claimed—far from constituting a *discrimination* against aliens, served to assure *equality* between national and foreign companies; the authorization procedure enabled the Minister to inquire whether in certain respects the guarantees for the protection of creditors in the foreign company's law were comparable with those accorded in German law. The authority of the Minister was discretionary[38] and he could refuse authorization for instance to a foreign company whose minimum capital was inferior to the minimum required of corresponding German companies. This meant of course that a number of foreign companies could be excluded because the minimum capital requirements differed

---

professions, so the coordination of company laws could not be required as a condition precedent to extending the right of establishment to legal persons. If the authors of the Treaty had wanted to have it otherwise they would have said so as they did say it expressly in connection with medical and pharmaceutical professions.

3. The General Program in Title I did not add anything to the conditions of Articles 58 and 52(1), and in Title III it specifically listed among restrictions which had to be eliminated a requirement of authorization as a condition to access to, or exercise of, an activity. Moreover, the General Program included a special title (Title VI) headed "Coordination of guarantees required from companies" but did not establish any link between this coordination and freedom of access, except, of course, that in the same title this coordination was "contemplated" before the expiration of the second year of the second stage, that is at the latest at the end of 1963. But the term "contemplated" clearly showed that this was not an imperative obligation as that laid down in the "Timetable" in Title IV of the General Program. It was understood therefore that at least some of the activities would be freed necessarily before the end of 1963. The Council also made a special declaration of interest in the coordination with respect to crafts and retail business but did not make any such statement on coordination under 54 par. 3 (g).

[38] Sieg-Leifermann, GEWERBEORDNUNG, § 12 No. 5 (München and Berlin 1966).

from country to country.[39] These and other requirements in national company laws, the Federal Government argued, must first be coordinated before German authorities could be deprived of their power to protect their citizens against foreign fly-by-night companies. Moreover, in all these years no authorization has been refused in Germany; but this, it was argued on the other side, could have been due to the fact that hitherto only large international companies of unquestionable reliability had sought to create branches or agencies in Germany.

The deadlock continued for two long years and only after the Commission's proposal had reached the Council of Ministers, the highest and final forum in the lawmaking hierarchy, did the Germans abandon their opposition since it then became clear beyond doubt that they would be outvoted.[40] Some eighteen months later, the Federal Parliament enacted the appropriate changes in the German law.[41] This

---

[39] Loussouarn, *Étude sur l'harmonisation des droits des sociétés dans les états membres de la CEE*, EEC Doc. 2117/IV/64-F at 25 ff.; LUTTER, KAPITAL, SICHERUNG DER KAPITALAUFBRINGUNG UND KAPITALERHALTUNG IN DEN AKTIEN- UND GMBH-RECHTEN DER EWG at 57 (Karlsruhe 1964). *See* p. 200 *infra*. I am advised by Prof. Gessler that the minimum capital requirement is the only "guarantee" considered by the Minister.

[40] The issue was actually settled by the Council's approval of the Directive on access to wholesale trade (see *supra* note 36, p. 38), which provided a precedent for other directives.

[41] Art. I of the Gesetz zur Durchführung von Richtlinien der EWG über die Niederlassungsfreiheit und des freien Dienstleistungsverkehrs of Aug. 13, 1965, Bundesgesetzblatt (BGBl) I, 849, amended § 12 of the Gewerbeordnung so that an authorization can be refused only if the activities of the foreign company are contrary to the public interest, especially if reciprocity ("mutuality") is not assured and if the law under which the foreign company was organized does not prescribe the same standards with respect to the amount of required capital as the German law. The same article added a new § 12a which exempted from the requirement of an authorization companies organized according to the law of an EEC Member State which have connection with the Community either through their seat or through a close economic link with a Member State. Bilateral treaties with non-member states were to prevail over § 12. Art. II of the same law repealed § 292 of the Stock

incident illustrates the depth of the feeling on the part of the Federal Government, cheered on by the German commentators,[42] when faced with the prospect of having to change federal legislation of this type even though the legal position of the Federal Government was difficult to sustain.

2. Improving "mobility" of companies: recognition, seat transfer and merger ("fusion") of companies (Article 220)—"European" conventions

It is inherent in the nature of companies as legal persons that—in reality and in law—they cannot exercise the freedom of establishment in the same manner as natural persons. In the first place, an individual can physically move from one state across the frontier to exercise his freedom of establishment by entering a business or profession in another state; a company, on the other hand, according to the laws of most Member States, could not move its "real seat" to another state without risking more or less disagreeable legal consequences.[43] It has been said that in Germany at any rate such a move would entail "automatically . . . the dissolution and liquidation" of the company,[44] but no judicial decision appears to support such drastic result, al-

Company Law of 1937. Jepsen, *Die Genehmigung des Gewerbebetriebes* at 21.

According to German Law, a German limited liability company would not be allowed to carry on certain types of banking (mortgages on real estate and vessels). Could a foreign limited liability company of another Member State be excluded from that type of banking in the Federal Republic? Apparently the Commission would answer this question in the affirmative because the restriction related to an activity rather than company capacity and struck German and foreign companies equally. This was considered a case for coordination, however. The same type of limitation upon limited liability companies applies in France (Art. 6, Law of June 13, 1941 on the banking profession).

[42] EVERLING at 78.

[43] EVERLING at 73 n.45. Ehring, in 1 GROEBEN-BOECKH at 182. Beitzke, *Anerkennung* at 33.

[44] RABEL, 2 CONFLICT OF LAWS at 52.

though the resolution deciding upon the transfer may be annulled.[45] In any case, and this is the situation for instance in Belgium, the courts in the receiving state, even though recognizing the company's continuing existence as a legal person, will apply mandatory rules of that state's company law to its internal affairs and the company will thus be held subject to two laws.[46] Moreover, a company which has its

[45] 7 RG 68 (1882). Conard in an address before the American Foreign Law Association, New York, Sept. 25, 1969 (verifaxed).

[46] A company incorporated in the United Kingdom in 1927 transferred its "real seat" to Belgium in 1932. In 1959, a suit was filed in a Belgian court to have the company dissolved. The plaintiff apparently first argued that the company had ceased to exist when it moved its central administration to Belgium. He contended further that if the company had not dissolved in 1932 it dissolved in 1957, which was more than 30 years after its incorporation in the United Kingdom. Belgian law limits corporate existence to 30 years. The Belgian Cour de cassation found no basis in Belgian law for the proposition that the company had ceased to exist when it moved its seat to Belgium in 1932; on the contrary its legal personality under English law continued to be recognized in Belgium. However, upon moving its seat to Belgium the company became subject to the mandatory rules of Belgian law including the 30-years rule. Yet the court held that the company did not expire in 1957, 30 years from the incorporation in the United Kingdom, but would continue until 1962. Since the suit was instituted in 1959 the plaintiff's complaint was denied. The judgment was based on Art. 197 of the Belgian Code de commerce (see *supra* note 21). Dec. of Nov. 12, 1965, Lamot v. Société Lamot Ltd., published in 1966 REVUE PRATIQUE DES SOCIÉTÉS 136, with opinion of Avocat général Dumon, and in 1966 REVUE CRITIQUE DE JURISPRUDENCE BELGE 392, with a note by van Ryn; see also note by Leleux in 1967 CLUNET at 140. Since Luxembourg and Italy have similar provisions (Art. 159 of the Luxembourg Law of Aug. 10, 1915 and Art. 2505 of the Codice civile) the decision is of interest for these countries as well. Italian law takes into account a possible transfer abroad in that it accords a dissenting stockholder the right of withdrawal. Art. 2437 of the Codice civile. Art. 154 of the new French company law of 1966 follows the earlier rule contained in the Ordinance of January 7, 1959 and sanctions the transfer of the seat to another country, upon approval in an extraordinary shareholders' meeting, without the loss of legal personality of the company, but only if the receiving country has concluded with France a "special convention" permitting the acquisition of its "nationality" and preserving the legal personality upon transfer to its territory. *See also* Art. 3 of the French Law of July 24, 1966. *See generally* p. 29 *supra* and p. 410 *infra*.

registered and real seat in one Member State cannot in principle "move" to another State by transferring so to speak *both* seats there, without losing its legal personality. In other words, as the law stands today, and in the absence of a new treaty arrangement, it is generally impossible for a company by such a "move"—and a simple charter amendment—to relinquish its original governing law and "nationality" and to acquire a new governing law and nationality, and at the same time to retain continuity of its legal personality.[47] In anticipation of the need for an adjustment of the law which will result from greater mobility in a single transnational market, the Member States undertook in Article 220 of the Treaty to negotiate with each other, "in so far as necessary," with a view to ensuring the preservation of the legal personality of their companies in case of a seat transfer. In the same vein, foreseeing the need for larger companies in a widened market, they agreed to negotiate with a view to making legally possible "fusion" between companies that are organized under different national laws; the existing national laws generally do not provide for international fusion.[48] Although negotiations on transnational fusion have made substantial progress[49] the work on seat transfer has not gone beyond initial studies.

Again, companies are capable of setting up branches, agencies and subsidiaries in another Member State provided, however, their legal personality is "recognized" in that state. An unrecognized company would not be able to obtain the necessary commercial license, conclude contracts, hold property or sue or be sued;[50] yet nothing is said in the "estab-

---

[47] *See* Rigaux, *Les personnes morales en droit international privé,* 1964 ANNALES DE DROIT ET DE SCIENCE POLITIQUE 241, at 259-64 (Vol. 24, No. 4).

[48] *See* p. 387 *infra.* EVERLING at 73; Ehring, in 1 GROEBEN-BOECKH at 182; Beitzke, *Internationalrechtliches zur Gesellschaftsfusion,* in FEST-SCHRIFT FÜR HALLSTEIN 14-35.

[49] *See* p. 387 *infra.*

[50] Beitzke, *Anerkennung,* 1964-65 ZHR 1; Grossfeld, *Die Anerkennung der Rechtsfähigkeit juristischer Personen,* 1967 RABELS ZEIT-

lishment" chapter about recognition. But since a denial of recognition would defeat the freedom of establishment it would seem that the Treaty intended recognition to go hand in hand with the progressive realization of the freedom of establishment.[51] For most practical purposes mutual recognition of companies has already been assured among the Member States by a network of treaties, by legislation (in Italy, Belgium and Luxembourg) or by case law (in the Federal Republic of Germany).[52] However, because of the differences and gaps in the protection, and because the question of recognition could arise outside the context of freedom of establishment or supply of services, the members undertook, also in Article 220, to negotiate with each other for a uniform and more perfect recognition. The negotiations have led to the signature of the first treaty designed to supplement the EEC Treaty, the Convention on Mutual Recognition of Companies and Legal Persons.[53] I shall deal with this Convention in some detail later in this book.[54] Suffice it to say here that, even in this Convention which was to assure "automatic recognition" of companies, the Member

SCHRIFT 1; van Gerven, *Le droit d'établissement dans la Communauté économique européenne et la législation sur les sociétés dans les États-membres,* 1965 REVUE PRATIQUE DES SOCIÉTÉS CIVILES ET COMMERCIALES 53-64.

[51] See particularly Title IIIA of the General Program, which lists among the restrictions that must be removed restrictions on rights whose exercise is traditionally viewed as conditioned upon the recognition of the company's legal personality, such as the right to contract, hold property, appear in court, etc. Nicholson, *The Significance of Treaties* at 170.

[52] On the actual state of recognition in the Member States see p. 397 *infra.*

[53] This Convention was signed on Feb. 29, 1968. Commission of the European Communities, Brussels, P-14/68. For the text see 1968 REV. TRIM. DROIT EUR. 400-23. For the English unofficial translation see CCH COMM. MKT. REP. ¶ 6083 and 1969 Bull. E.C. Supp. No. 2, at 7. To the extent that it is required for purposes of the freedom of establishment, recognition could have been decreed by "directives" issued under the law-of-establishment chapter. Beyond that, another source of authority would have to be relied on. EVERLING at 271 n.40.

[54] *Infra* p. 394.

States have retained the power to refuse recognition to a company which, although organized under the law of a Member State, has its "real seat" outside the Community territory *and* has no real link with the economy of the Community. But recognition may in no circumstances be refused a company whose registered office and real seat are in the Community, even though the two are located in different Member States. Yet this new rule that dilutes the "real seat" doctrine is made subject to a qualification: the Member State on whose territory a company organized under the law of another Member State has its real seat will be free to require such a company to comply with those rules of its own company law for which it deems there is an absolute necessity. The Member States may feel less constrained to insist on this qualification as the national company laws become more similar. One can thus discern a link between the treaty-making under Article 220 and the coordination under Article 54, par. 3(g).

It will be noted that the Convention on mutual recognition of companies and to a certain extent the projected treaty on transnational fusion are oriented toward conflict-of-laws problems, and are designed essentially to modify the national choice-of-law rules concerning companies by introducing—as treaty law—uniform conflict rules more suitable to a single market.[55]

3. Removing territorial restrictions: industrial property rights-bankruptcy

Neither the method of unifying conflict-of-laws rules nor the coordination of "internal" laws under Article 54, par. 3(g) appeared adequate in those fields where the very exist-

---

[55] However, some "internal" rules are at times included as well, as for instance in the draft of the fusion treaty. Art. 220 served as a legal basis for the negotiation of the Convention on Jurisdiction and the Enforcement of Civil and Commercial Judgments which was signed on Sept. 27, 1968. English text in 1969 Bull. E.C. Supp. No. 2, at 1.

ence of diverse legal systems had posed obstacles to the creation of a single market. Thus in the area of industrial property, the limited territorial scope of the national patent impairs the unity of the Common Market and makes possible market division through patent licenses. What was needed therefore was a federal-type "European" patent which would be valid throughout the territory of the Member States. The drafts of the several Conventions on industrial property intended to provide the necessary "European" law repose also on a broad interpretation of Article 220,[56] as does the proposed Convention on bankruptcy. In the latter field also, coordination or even unification of national laws would not fill the need and for that reason the draft would provide for a single bankruptcy proceeding with the effect upon all the debtor's property, wherever located within the territory of the Member States, akin to the federal bankruptcy law.[57] The same rationale and the same legal

---

[56] Two draft conventions dealing with a European system of patent law have been prepared but are not in force as yet. The Draft Convention for a European System for the Grant of Patents was drafted at the seventeen nation International Patent Conference (including the Six) held at Luxembourg on Jan. 13-16, 1970. Taking this Convention into account, the EEC Commission prepared the second convention, the Draft Convention Relating to a European Patent for the Common Market to be concluded only between the Six. The second Convention to a large extent supplements the first and it replaces an earlier draft which was published in 1962. Neither of the two current drafts is complete. For the two texts see CCH COMM. MKT. REP. ¶ 5503 ff. and ¶ 5751 ff. The 1962 text was published as Avant-Projet de Convention relatif à un droit européen des brevets élaboré par le group de travail "brevets" (1962); Froschmaier, *The Draft Convention on Patents in the Common Market*, 11 INT. & COMP. L.Q. Supp. 4, at 50 (1962); Froschmaier, *Some Aspects of the Draft Convention Relating to a European Patent Law*, 12 INT. & COMP. L.Q. 886 (1963). The Conventions on trademark law, on models and designs, and on proposed new industrial property institutions have been in preparation.

[57] Avant-projet de Convention relative à la faillite et aux procédures assimilées, C.E.E. Comm. Doc. 4368/1/IV/67-F, Apr. 28, 1967; for an analysis see Noël, *Aperçus sur le projet de convention européenne relative à la faillite, aux concordats et aux procédés analogues*, 1968 REV. TRIM. DROIT EUR. 703-19.

basis have been invoked in the negotiations for a "European company" which—some hope—would also be grounded in Community law.[58]

A special procedure has been evolved for the negotiation of these "European" Conventions. They are to be linked more or less closely to the communal institutions, particularly the Court of Justice of the Community.[59] Of course the Member States may always resort to ordinary treaties when they feel that the basis of Article 220 is not appropriate.

4. Article 221: free access to portfolio investment

The Member States were required, by the end of 1960, to permit nationals of the other Members to participate financially in the capital of companies on an equal footing with their own nationals, "without prejudice to other provisions of the Treaty."[60] This rule contained in Article 221, which probably has now become "self-executing" in the national laws of the Member States, has raised compliance problems in Belgium, France, Italy and the Netherlands. The Commission has invoked this article, along with the provisions on the freedom of establishment and movement of capital, in its effort to induce Member States to remove discriminatory restrictions.[61]

---

[58] See p. 443 infra.

[59] See p. 404 infra.

[60] According to Thiesing in 2 GROEBEN-BOECKH at 392, "other provisions" relate principally to Art. 52 (2) and Art. 67 ff. Art. 221 benefits all nationals of other member countries who desire to participate financially in a local company while Art. 52 (2) limits the benefit only to those nationals who "establish" themselves locally through participation in organizing and managing a company. Arts. 67 to 73 deal with freedom of movement of capital. Unlike Art. 221 which came into effect "at the end of the third year of the transitional period" the provisions concerning capital movement contemplate a *progressive* removal of the restrictions on such movement to be completed by the end of the transitional period, but—unlike Art. 221 which benefits only nationals—the latter provisions benefit all residents in the Member States. *Id.* at 382.

[61] This was the case in the Commission's "reasoned opinion" concerning French restrictions on direct-investment transactions, note 29, p.

Obviously the delimitation between Articles 52(2) and 221 is not clear. For instance, the freedom to acquire an absolute majority of shares (or even a controlling interest) could perhaps fall within the scope of Article 52(2) as an aspect of the freedom of establishment, and if this were the case its realization would be subject to the progressive implementation of the freedom of establishment in the various branches of the economy over the transitional period. On the other hand, acquisition of shares below the level of control would fall under the "self-executing" provision of Article 221 with full effect since 1960.[62] This difference would cease to be relevant at the end of 1969 upon the expiration of the transitional period, if one were to assume, in the light of the opinion of the Court of Justice of the Communities rendered in the *Lütticke* case, that the establishment provisions also became fully self-executing with the lapse of the transitional period.[63]

34 *supra*. Again, pursuant to the Commission's demand, based on Art. 221 as well as on the establishment provisions, Belgium was to modify its law in order to remove the requirement for an authorization by the Ministry of Justice as a prerequisite for a take-over of a Belgian company by a company of a Member State, Heenen, *Le projet de première directive en matière de société. Validité des engagements de la société*, in EUROPEES VENNOOTSCHAPSRECHT 109, at 112, 113 (Antwerpen 1968). It is reported that the Belgian Government has not modified its law and instead it will probably extend the requirement of such authorization so as to apply also to a take-over by a Belgian company. *See also* 1967 REV. TRIM. DROIT EUR. 73 to the effect that the French Ordonnance of Aug. 26, 1944 which provides that only French citizens can own shares in a stock company engaged in newspaper publishing business is contrary to Art. 221.

62 What if a national law provided that only those vessels are allowed to fly the national flag which are owned by companies whose majority of the shareholders are local nationals? It is reported that in such a case the Commission would apply Art. 52 (2) rather than the self-executing Art. 221.

63 *See* Case 57/65, Firma Alfons Lütticke GmbH v. Hauptzollamt Saarlouis, 12 Recueil de la jurisprudence 293 (1966), CCH COMM. MKT. REP. ¶ 8045 (1966). Although it is quite plausible, I doubt that this interpretation would be accepted since it would place too great a burden upon the Court of Justice, and, according to the European

5. The general "approximation of laws" clause: Article 100

Article 100 of the Treaty—one of the "common rules" governing competition—calls for "the approximation of such legislative and administrative provisions of the Member States as *directly affect the establishment or functioning of the Common Market.*"

This general or "catch-all" clause equips the common institutions with a potentially broad power base for approximation by directives, above and beyond the specific authorizations described earlier in this chapter. The words "directly affect" suggest substantial discretion. Any type of residual obstacle to the economic intercourse and competitive conditions postulated in the Common Market, including presumably legal uncertainty and insecurity which is due to disparities among national laws, would constitute a proper basis for prescriptive approximation of these laws. In fact, the article has been invoked as affording legal authority for approximation directives in the field of taxation, procedures for awarding government contracts, safety, health and control of pharmaceuticals.[64]

In the initial stages of Community life a lively, even though somewhat academic, controversy centered on the question to what extent this general clause could be invoked as an additional legal basis for the approximation of national company laws in the more general interest of an "undistorted" competition, above and beyond the coordination under Article 54 which presumably was to serve the specific—albeit also competition-related—objective of the freedom of establishment.[65] The major difference between the two articles from the operational viewpoint is in the voting formula. While Article 100 prescribes unanimity in

---

concepts of the role of the judiciary, it would give the Court too much power. That Court would ultimately have to determine which national restrictions are in violation of the Treaty even when no appropriate directive had been enacted.

[64] *See supra* note 15, p. 14.

[65] Schwartz, *Zur Konzeption der Rechtsangleichung* at 480.

the Council of Ministers, Article 54 allows decisions by qualified majority. Before it adopts a directive pursuant to either of the two articles, the Council must consult the European Parliament to obtain a political judgment on the proposal, and the Economic and Social Committee, in which are represented the various groups likely to be affected by the directive; but Article 100 limits this requirement only to instances where national legislation (as distinguished from mere administrative regulations) in a Member State is to be modified. Yet the impact of Article 100 in the company law field proper has been limited, if not nil, thus far.

Of some relevance to our study is Article 101, included in the same "approximation" chapter, which gives the Council of Ministers the power, on the Commission's proposal, to issue directives designed to remove a "distortion" of competitive conditions caused by differences in national laws, and the following Article 102 which establishes a procedure before the Commission aimed at preventing the occurrence of new distortions from autonomous changes in national legal systems.[66]

6. The scheme for a "European company"

There is no provision in the EEC Treaty for a "federal-type," Community-wide commercial company, just as there is no clause for a federally incorporated commercial enterprise in the United States Constitution. In the United States, ideas to this effect have been advanced in the Congress as one possible means, based on the Congressional power over interstate commerce, to control excessive corporate power and curb possible abuses. Proposals for a "European"

---

[66] On these articles, and on the undefined concept of "distortion," see Stein, *Assimilation* at 6-8 with references to literature; Leleux, *Le rapprochement* at 144-46. For instances in which these articles were invoked see 1968 Bull. E.C. Supp. No. 5, at 16-19; *Second General Report on the Activities of the Communities 1968*, Table 4, at 75; *Troisième Rapport Général sur l'activité des Communautés 1969*, Table 13, at 97.

commercial company, which I shall explore in some detail,[67] have been under consideration in the EEC, but for a different, if not the opposite, purpose: to facilitate growth, particularly through concentration among enterprises across national frontiers.[68]

7. The Treaty framework: summary and comparison with a federal framework[69]

(a) Freedom of establishment or "entry"

Aware of the crucial role that companies must play in the market-coalescence process, the authors of the Treaty concentrated in the first place upon opening the national markets to the entry of companies of other Member States by employing the familiar principle of "national treatment," a device derived from international commercial treaties, but supplemented in a significant way by the grant of an authority to the Community institutions empowering them to enforce this principle through normative prescriptive acts. As these acts come into effect, a Member State is no longer able to require a company of another Member State to seek prior authorization for setting up a branch or supplying services in its territory, and generally it must make sure that the company is treated in the same way as a local company. Nor can a company be denied the right of establishment on the ground that it has only a registered seat in the Member

---

[67] *Infra* p. 424.

[68] *See* p. 428 *infra*.

[69] For an enlightening comparison see generally Leleux, *Le droit des sociétés aux États-Unis et dans la C.E.E.—Perspectives de leur évolution*, 1968 Rev. trim. droit eur. 50; English version in Leleux, *Corporation Law in the United States and in the E.E.C.*, 5 C.M.L. Rev. 133 (1967-68). On commercial laws specifically see Conard, *Harmonisation des législations commerciales des États-Unis* and *La Mosaïque des droits de sociétés des États-Unis*, in 1967 Travaux et Conférences, Université Libre de Bruxelles, Faculté de droit, 33-46 and 47-58 (Brussels 1967). On the "federal-type" features of the EEC system generally see Hay, Federalism and Supranational Organizations (Urbana and London 1966).

State under whose law it is organized as long as it can show a genuine link with the Community's economy.

In the United States, a difference is drawn in theory between a natural person and a corporation in this context. According to the old and discredited doctrine, a corporation does not legally exist outside the state of its incorporation. A State of the Union may "exclude" a "foreign" company incorporated in a sister State, since for historical reasons a "legal person" such as a corporation is not entitled to the benefits of a citizen under the privileges and immunities clause in Article IV, Section 2 of the Federal Constitution. But in practice, the objective of a free entry and recognition of basic legal personality is achieved by federal control against discriminatory treatment which is grounded in the equal protection clause of the Fourteenth Amendment and which comes into play once a State "admits" *any* "foreign" corporation. Again, "free supply of services" across State lines (as well as free movement of goods and capital) is protected by the interstate commerce clause which generally confines State regulatory powers to "intrastate" commerce and precludes them from "unduly" burdening interstate commerce. Within these limits, however, the States have the authority to prescribe certain conditions before a foreign corporation "qualifies" to engage in intrastate business, and they do so in so-called "qualifying statutes,"[70] a survival of the franchise theory of corporate existence. Historically, the statutes were deemed necessary to enable local courts to assert jurisdiction over the foreign corporation in the interest of the local parties by providing for a service of process within the State but, in view of the progressively expanding scope of

---

[70] The qualifying statutes as a rule include provisions designed to facilitate service of legal process within the State on the foreign corporation, to preclude tax evasion, to provide information concerning corporate affairs, and at times even to regulate certain aspects of the foreign corporation's internal affairs (see p. 54 *infra*). *See Sanctions for Failure to Comply with Corporate Qualification Statutes: An Evaluation*, 63 COLUM. L. REV. 117 (1963); LEFLAR, AMERICAN CONFLICTS LAW at 56.

judicial jurisdiction over out-of-State parties and events, this particular rationale of the qualifying statutes seems to have lost its vitality.[71]

At what point the transactions of the foreign corporations cease to be privileged interstate business and begin to amount to "doing business within the State" has been the subject of a continuing flow of litigation, particularly since different standards apply for the exercise of the State regulatory power, its power to tax and its judicial jurisdiction, and the standards change in the light of the changing business realities. In addition to the limitations imposed upon State powers by the interstate commerce clause, these powers are also subject to federal control in accordance with the due process clause of the Fourteenth Amendment.

(b)   Conflict of laws: recognition and law governing company's internal affairs

Pursuant to the choice-of-law rule followed in all the Member States except the Netherlands, the law of the state of the company's "real seat" (central administration) governs its legal personality and internal affairs. This rule curtails the possibility of transnational transfer of the company's head office, and "mobility" is further curtailed by the impossibility of moving the seat to another state without jeopardizing legal personality, and by the failure of national company laws to provide for transnational fusion. However, to remedy these impediments the Member States have been negotiating "European Conventions" intended to contain essentially (but not exclusively) uniform conflict-of-laws rules which would encourage mobility of companies.

In the United States, in principle, a court will look to the law of the State of incorporation not only to decide on the recognition of the corporation's legal personality, but also—in the absence of a statutory provision of the forum,

---

[71] Walker, *Foreign Corporation Laws: The Loss of Reason,* 47 N.C.L. Rev. 1 (1968); Walker, *Foreign Corporation Laws: A Current Account,* 47 N.C.L. Rev. 733 (1969).

at any rate—for the rules to govern the corporation's internal affairs. Thus, a multistate company and its branches in different States are permanently governed by identical law, the law of the State of incorporation; and this legal situation prevails even if the company initially had established its head office outside the State of incorporation or transferred it subsequently to another State. There are, however, instances in which, according to Ehrenzweig, "courts in this country have, particularly for certain regulatory purposes, come to pay increasing attention to the law of the corporation's 'commercial domicile,' often identified as 'the center of authority . . . the actual seat of its corporate government,'" a definition reminiscent of the "central administration" in civil law.[72] Moreover, in the more recent legislation, certain States have attempted to modify the general conflict-of-laws rule by inserting in the "qualifying statute" rules designed to govern certain aspects of the internal affairs of foreign corporations that would displace the relevant rule in the law of the State of incorporation.[73] Such an attempt may lead to a possible conflict between a policy of the receiving (forum) State and the federal interest in the uniform treatment of corporations and its shareholders throughout the Union. There is yet not enough case law to suggest at which point the Federal Supreme Court may strike down such a State law imposing its own rule on the foreign corporation's internal affairs. The Supreme Court could possibly rely upon the due process clause (in the absence of sufficient contacts of the foreign corporation with the forum State),[74] or upon the full-faith-and-credit clause

---

[72] EHRENZWEIG, A TREATISE ON THE CONFLICT OF LAWS at 412 and cases cited there.

[73] See, e.g., a California statute in Western Airlines v. Sobieski, 191 Cal. App. 2d 399, 12 Cal. Rptr. 719 (1961); Western Airlines v. Schutzbank, 258 Cal. App. 2d 218, 66 Cal. Rptr. 293 (1968). Kaplan, Foreign Corporations and Local Corporate Policy, 21 VAND. L. REV. 433 (1968).

[74] See, e.g., New York Life Ins. Co. v. Dodge, 246 U.S. 357 (1918); Home Ins. Co. v. Dick, 281 U.S. 397 (1930).

in Article IV, Section 1 which requires each State to recognize the public acts, records and judicial proceedings of every other State. Thus far, the federal judiciary has invoked this latter clause with vengeance to enforce nationwide recognition of sister State judicial judgments, but has been most reluctant to rely on it as a ground for intervening in the choice-of-law processes in the courts.[75] Nor has the Congress chosen to legislate in the choice-of-law field although it would have ample power to do so under this clause and perhaps under the interstate commerce clause as well. In isolated instances, courts have refused to apply the law of incorporation when they were faced with a "tramp" or "pseudo-foreign corporation," the bulk of whose activities centered in the State of the forum, although it had been incorporated in another State.[76]

In a sense, we may note an interesting convergence of the trends in the EEC and in the United States: while within the EEC the movement is toward the rule of incorporation (or registered seat) in the field of establishment and recognition, if not in the general area of choice of law, in the United States selected aspects of the law of the place of the corporation's effective operations seem to be getting more attention than has been generally assumed, even though, of course, there is never any question of subjecting a foreign corporation to the whole body of the law of the receiving State.[77] The Conventions among the EEC members, grounded in Article 220, could be compared with some poetic license to "interstate compacts" which the States of the Union may

---

[75] Reese & Kaufman, *The Law Governing Corporate Affairs: Choice of Law and the Impact of Full Faith and Credit*, 58 COLUM. L. REV. 1118 (1958). The case in which this clause was actually relied upon, United Commercial Travelers v. Wolfe, 331 U.S. 586 (1947), applied to a narrow situation and has been rendered highly dubious as a precedent by more recent developments, Clay v. Sun Ins. Office, 377 U.S. 179 (1964). Kaplan, *Foreign Corporations and Local Corporate Policy*, 21 VAND. L. REV. 433, 436 (1968).

[76] Latty, *Pseudo-Foreign Corporations*, 65 YALE L.J. 137 (1955).

[77] Leleux, *Corporation Law in the United States and in the E.E.C.*, 5 C.M.L. REV. 133, at 145 (1967-68).

conclude among themselves, if the Congress consents,[78] but no such compact exists in the field with which we are here concerned.

(c)   Coexistence of local company laws and their assimilation

The EEC Treaty assumes that the national company laws will continue to exist but requires a degree of "coordination" among them, and for that purpose it gives the Community institutions the power to issue binding "directives" designed to equalize the protection of shareholders and "third parties" afforded by these laws.

In the United States, federal institutions do not possess a comparable general power to compel the States of the Union to bring about adjustments in their own corporation laws, and, to the extent that Congress could legislate in the field, particularly on the basis of the interstate commerce clause, it has refrained from doing so. It is thus accurate to say that corporation law—in the narrow sense—remains within the province of the States. Moreover, the attempts at a unification of State corporation laws through voluntary cooperation have met with little success. Those who question the need for an extensive assimilation of national laws in the EEC often point out that in the United States the coexistence of fifty-one different corporation laws[79] has not prevented the emergence of a vast, integrated market of continental proportions, in which multistate companies appear to function with the greatest of ease and efficiency. The EEC Commission dispatched one of its senior attorneys to the United States to explore this argument, and his able report demonstrates the pitfalls of easy analogies. It shows above all,

---

[78] U.S. Constitution, Art. I, Sec. 10. But the U.S. Supreme Court indicated that such consent was not required to agreements having no tendency to increase the political powers of the States or to encroach on the just supremacy of the Federal Government. Virginia v. Tennessee, 148 U.S. 503, at 518 (1893).

[79] The laws of the fifty States and the federal law of the District of Columbia.

that any meaningful inquiry must extend beyond the company laws of the States of the Union to other State laws and certain federal legislation as well.[80]

---

[80] Leleux, *Corporation Law* at 175-76.

Chapter 3

THREE INTERLUDES

---

1. Company law in the American "Common Market": a paradigm for the Community? An impressionistic interlude

It is important in the first place to keep in mind that the numerous corporation statutes in the States of the Union show a degree of similarity, due to the influence of common-law principles which are drawn upon by courts and parties in the absence of specific written rules and which also guide the legislators.[1] Moreover, the general organizational pattern of the corporation and the distribution of powers between the management and the shareholders' meeting are broadly similar. However, and this is of great significance, the extent to which internal affairs of corporations are regulated varies greatly from one State to another, from the "strict" California statute to the "permissive" Delaware law. In Jennings' words, the incorporation statutes of the more "liberal" States are "essentially enabling acts, which contain many loopholes for an irresponsible management and a minimum of protective provisions in the interest of shareholders."[2] Apart from the underlying laissez-faire philosophy, this development has a historical explanation. In the late nine-

---

[1] Leleux lists the concept of fiduciary duty of directors and officers toward the corporation, the derivative suit, the right of shareholders to inspect the corporation's books and the power of the board of directors to declare dividends. Leleux, *Corporation Law in the United States and in the E.E.C.*, 5 C.M.L. REV. 133, at 152 (1967-1968).

[2] Jennings, *The Role of the States in Corporate Regulation and Investor Protection*, 23 LAW & CONTEMP. PROB. 193, at 194 (1958).

teenth century, with New Jersey leading the parade, followed by Delaware, some States began to amend their statutes so as to give the widest freedom to corporate promoters and managers, in order to lure out-of-state businesses to incorporate in the State and thereby avoid more restrictive legislation at their real business home. Increased revenue from fees and taxes was the principal objective. The federal framework and the "rule of incorporation" described above, as well as the absence of any feeling of loyalty to the "home" State on the part of business made this possible. The State of Delaware which added tax incentives to its liberal corporation law was decidedly the winner in "the race of laxity." Even today, more than one-third of the corporations listed on the New York Stock Exchange are still incorporated in Delaware's "corporate haven."[3] In 1964, Delaware was in the twelfth place only in new incorporations, with the important industrial States, New York and California, in the lead, but the average initial capital of newly incorporated businesses has remained markedly higher in Delaware. The significance of Delaware as a "corporate domicile" of large multistate corporations appears to have increased after the enactment of the New Delaware corporation law of 1967.[4]

In a sense, the Delaware law, drafted professionally by selected corporation lawyers with the corporation's interest in mind, has functioned as a uniform national law and produced a significant body of case law; but the "charter mon-

---

[3] 1965 DIGEST OF THE DELAWARE CORPORATION LAW at 1 (41st ed. 1965) *reprinted in* STEVENS & HENN, STATUTES, CASES AND MATERIALS ON THE LAW OF CORPORATIONS AND OTHER BUSINESS ENTERPRISES at 27 (St. Paul 1965). *See generally* Conard, *La mosaïque* at 51-55.

[4] STEVENS & HENN at 26, giving figures for 1964. Leleux, *Corporation Law* at 150. *See also* Eisenberg, *The Legal Roles of Shareholders and Management in Modern Corporate Decision-making,* 57 CALIF. L. REV. 1, at 61 (1969). DEL. CODE ANN., tit. 8 (Spec. Gen. Corp. Law Pamphlet 1967). For a discussion of six major areas covered by this law see Comment, *Vestiges of Shareholder Rights Under the New Delaware Corporation Law,* 57 GEO. L.J. 599 (1969). For an intriguing account of the legislative history see Comment, *Law for Sale: A Study of the Delaware Corporation Law of 1967,* 117 U. PA. L. REV. 899 (1969).

gering" trend was certainly not conducive to a formal unification of State laws.[5]

The National Conference of Commissioners on Uniform
State Laws recommended a Uniform Business Corporation
Act in 1928 after many years of study. The Act was conceived as a means to correct abuses and coincided with the
beginning of a substantial movement to modernize corporation laws. However, only four states adopted it with modifications. In 1943 it was "demoted" to a Model Act[6] and in
1957 it was withdrawn by the Conference altogether.[7] An-

---

[5] Kaplan writes: "The general corporation laws of many states
have been watered down in order to deter local enterprises from the
temptation of Delaware incorporation. For example, the Governor of
Michigan, in his 1921 message to the Michigan Legislature, stated that
it was useless to pass a stringent corporation act because 'all of our
corporations will come back to us as foreign corporations.' Despite
such competition as Michigan's, the ingenuity of the Delaware legislature has outpaced the efforts of other states to provide equal attrac-
tions to the organizers of corporations. Corporations still stream out of
states such as Illinois to avoid the requirement of cumulative voting.
Despite the opinion of the Secretary of State of Michigan, expressed
in 1934, that 'Michigan's new Corporation Code, Act 327, Public Acts
of 1931 has given to Michigan corporations practically all the advantages which might be received under incorporation in any outside
state,' Michigan corporations still move to Delaware. In addition to
lower capital stock or franchise taxes in Delaware, other advantages
which induce corporate managements to seek incorporation in Delaware include greater freedom to pay dividends and make distributions;
greater ease of charter amendment and less restrictions upon selling
assets, mortgaging, leasing, and merging, due to the lower percentage
of shareholder approval required and also by virtue of lesser rights of
appraisal for dissenting minority shareholders; freedom from mandatory cumulative voting; permission to have staggered boards of directors; lesser pre-emptive rights for shareholders; clearer rights of in-
demnification for directors and officers; greater freedom of action in
many crucial respects for management; and a climate of opinion,
thought to be prevalent in the legislature and courts, generally favorable to management and generally unreceptive to the dissident minority shareholder." Kaplan, *Foreign Corporations and Local Corporate
Policy*, 21 VAND. L. REV. 433, at 436-37 (1968), footnotes omitted.

[6] HANDBOOK OF THE NATIONAL CONFERENCE OF COMMISSIONERS ON
UNIFORM STATE LAWS AND PROCEEDINGS at 72 (Chicago 1943).

[7] Model Acts are employed "where in the judgment of the
National Conference [an act] is not a subject upon which uniformity

other, less ambitious and somewhat more successful effort was made by the American Bar Association which published its initial draft of a Model Business Corporation Act in 1946.[8] This Act which underwent a series of revisions has had a definite influence on some more recent legislative reforms; it has served as a general model for some twenty medium or small States but was, for instance, not followed by the recent important new corporation law of New York and the innovating North Carolina Act. Although criticized by some as an "invitation to irresponsibility,"[9] the Act was intended primarily as an enabling act: "[t]he policing must be left to the blue-sky laws and other statutes of that character, and to case law defining fraud and delineating the obligations of majorities to minorities."[10]

In fact, the laxity of State corporation laws and the resulting abuses and speculative excesses led to the enactment in every State, except Delaware, of "blue-sky laws" purporting to regulate the issue and trade in corporate securities; but

---

between the states is necessary or desirable, but where it would be helpful to have legislation which would tend toward uniformity where enacted. . . ." 9 UNIFORM LAWS ANNOTATED (U.L.A.) 115 (1957). *See also id.,* Supp. at 61 (1967). Garrett, *Model Business Corporation Act,* 4 BAYLOR L. REV. 412 (1951-52). However, the Uniform Partnership Act, published in 1914, has been a great success; it was adopted by some 40 states. Conard, *La mosaïque* at 48-49.

[8] Model Business Corporation Act, Revised 1969, by the Committee on Corporate Laws of the American Bar Association (Philadelphia 1969).

[9] Harris, *The Model Business Corporation Act—Invitation to Irresponsibility?,* 50 Nw. U.L. REV. 1, 2 (1955-56) quoted in Jennings, *The Role of the States* at 198; Eisenberg, *The Legal Roles of Shareholders* at 60. For an appraisal of the criticism of state statutes generally see Vagts, *Reforming the "Modern" Corporation: Perspectives from the German,* 80 HARV. L. REV. 23-24 (1966).

[10] A member of the A.B.A. Committee quoted in Campbell, *The Model Business Corporation Act,* 11 Bus. LAW. 98, at 99-100 (1956). For the experience in other federal systems (Canada and Australia) see *Symposium on the Revised Draft Uniform Companies Act (Memorandum and Articles)—1960,* 3 ALBERTA L. REV. 89 (1963); Sawer, *Federal-State Co-operation in Law Reform: Lessons of the Australian Uniform Companies Act,* 4 MELBOURNE U.L. REV. 238 (1963).

these statutes also failed to afford adequate protection because they were confined to intrastate commerce and the
enforcement was difficult.

It was only after the Wall Street crash, and in the context
of the New Deal reforms, that the Federal Government
stepped in. Drawing upon its power to regulate interstate
commerce, the Congress adopted the Securities Act of 1933
and the Securities Exchange Act of 1934. This legislation,
and the rulemaking of the new, powerful federal agency,
the Securities and Exchange Commission (SEC), laid the
groundwork for an elaborate, and certainly after the 1964
amendment, a most pervasive regulatory system, with far-
reaching integrating impact upon the entire legal framework
within which corporations function. Continuing disclosure
and reporting requirements are imposed not only on corporations listed on stock exchanges but also on those with at
least 500 shareholders and $1,000,000 worth of assets. In-
formation supplied to investors in compliance with an
extensive disclosure obligation is checked both at the time
of the first issue of securities and in subsequent trading at
the stock exchange, and also in over-the-counter transactions.
Anti-fraud provisions offer protection against misleading
information and manipulation of the market, and "insider
trading" is prohibited. Stock exchanges and stock brokers
were made subject to registration and supervision by the
SEC whose orders are enforceable in federal courts. On the
basis of the anti-fraud provisions, these courts have developed rules for the conduct of the management, and the
stockholders may invoke these rules through derivative
suits; thus, in this sense it is possible to speak today of a
federal corporation law, enforceable by the SEC and the
federal courts.[11] To this should be added the supervisory

---

[11] Fleischer, *Federal Corporation Law—An Assessment*, 78 HARV.
L. REV. 1146 (1965); Ficker, *Die Entwicklung eines Federal Corpora-
tion Law durch die Rechtsprechung in den Vereinigten Staaten von
Amerika*, in VON CAEMMERER, MENTSCHIKOFF & ZWEIGERT (eds.), FEST-
SCHRIFT FÜR RHEINSTEIN at 1059 (Tübingen 1969).

function by the stock exchanges which require the acceptance by the corporations of a code of behavior as a condition
to listing,[12] and also the "self-discipline" of the accounting
profession which is nationally organized and has been seeking to develop nationwide uniform methods and practices.

The growth of the American corporation would have been
unthinkable without the continent-wide, centralized capital
market (both national stock exchanges are in New York),
effectively organized to channel savings toward the most
profitable enterprises throughout the territory of the Union.
The Federal securities regulations have contributed to the
growth of confidence in the stock market on the part of the
financial community including the large institutional investors, and the extensive "publicity" through disclosure has
made it possible for the success of an enterprise to be reflected in the stock exchange quotations, and this benefits
the shareholder as well.

The integrating factor of the federal power extends, however, beyond the sphere of securities regulations. Federal
power is incomparably broader than the "Community power"
in the EEC. The currency, monetary policy, foreign commercial policy (and for that matter of course general foreign
and defense policies), bankruptcy law, patents and copy-
right are all within the exclusive jurisdiction of the Federation which also regulates interstate transport and communication media. These media, and an extensive network of
highways bind the Continent together—along with other
factors such as common language and the mobility of the
restless people. Again, Congress has legislated extensively
in the antitrust, labor and social welfare fields, mainly on
the ever-expanding basis of the interstate commerce clause;

---

12 The "listing agreements" cover rules on such matters as prohibition of non-voting shares, requirement of shareholders' meeting consent to capital increase, duty of the board to provide information on
significant occurrences within the corporation which may affect the
stock value, etc. 1968 New York Stock Exchange, Company Manual
A2, at 27.

and the Federal Government has exerted immense influence through its procurement and research-and-development support policies. Last, but certainly not least, one must mention the federal power to tax, since by far the most important corporate tax is the federal income tax on corporations.

Despite the high degree of integration, the system suffers from serious flaws as seen by a multistate corporation. Although its internal affairs are governed by a single law, the law of the State of incorporation, such corporation must comply with the qualifying statutes of every State in which it does business, with federal as well as State regulatory legislation on such matters as corporate securities and labor relations. However, the most significant problem arises from the "enormous disparity" of State tax laws, particularly income tax laws, but also legislation on capital stock, gross receipts, sales and use taxes. The principal inconvenience is administrative: the duty to comply with a variety of complex, differing and possibly conflicting rules. Instances where an enterprise has been subjected to double or even multiple State taxation of the same income probably occur, but are said to be quite rare and, on the contrary, at times multistate income escapes State taxation completely. A multistate corporation needs sophisticated legal advice, at the headquarters and often also in other States where it has major operations, to guide it through the complexities of the system. This necessity explains in part the highly valued position of a lawyer as advisor, incomparably more important in America than in Europe where, moreover, some of the consulting functions are performed by non-lawyers.[13]

As one means to remedy the situation the National Conference of Commissioners on Uniform State Laws prepared a Uniform Division of Income for Tax Purposes Act with two objectives in mind: to promote uniformity in the allocation of corporate income for tax purposes among the

---

[13] Keesling & Warren, *California's Uniform Division of Income for Tax Purposes Act,* 15 U.C.L.A.L. Rev. 156, at 157 (1967-68).

States, and to relieve pressure for Congressional legislation. By mid-1969, nineteen States and the District of Columbia had enacted most or all of its provisions. But the Act fails to face the problem of the multistate corporate business conducted by affiliated corporations, be they divisions of a single corporation or subsidiaries of the parent.[14]

In 1959, the Federal Supreme Court held that a State could impose tax on the income of a corporation derived from its activities within the State, although those activities were exclusively in interstate commerce.[15] Within months, in response to the pressure from the multistate business community, Congress enacted a law limiting the jurisdiction of the States to tax income from such activities[16] and— what has proved more important—it instituted a broad study of the problem. Moreover, in a rare demonstration of "cooperative federalism," eighteen States have entered into an "interstate compact" which embraces, but goes beyond, the Uniform Act, and sets up a Multistate Tax Commission with powers of compulsory arbitration of apportionment disputes and with facilities for research and recommendations of uniform standards.[17] This undertaking was spon-

---

[14] California, one of the States that has adopted the Uniform Act has met this problem by requiring that the allocation of income be made on the basis of a "combined report" whereby the combined income of all of the affiliated corporations is first allocated to sources within and without the State on the basis of a fixed formula based on property, payroll and sales within each State, and the California income is then apportioned among the corporations which are doing business in California. *Id.* at 174. On the problem generally see ALTMAN & WARREN, ALLOCATION OF INCOME IN STATE TAXATION (1st ed. 1946).

[15] Northwestern States Portland Cement Co. v. Minnesota, 358 U.S. 450 (1959).

[16] Public Law 86-272 (1959). The law precludes such tax if the only activity within the State is soliciting orders or using an independent "contractor" to make sales within the State.

[17] Among the parties to the compact are important States: Illinois and Texas. There are 10 associate members, including California, Michigan, Massachusetts, and Pennsylvania. *See* MULTISTATE TAXATION —INCLUDING TEXT AND EDITORIAL EXPLANATION OF MULTISTATE TAX COMPACT AND PROPOSED REGULATIONS UNDER COMPACT (Prentice

sored by the Council of State Governments at the initiative of State officials and legislators.

Today, considerations relating to State taxes (mainly income and property taxes) and environmental factors such as access to market and the labor situation, influence executive decisions on the location of business to a much greater extent than the degree of stringency of the corporation law.

Even this impressionistic sketch makes clear the striking differences between the United States continental system and the emerging European system. Any detailed discussion would exceed the purpose of this diversion from our main theme. Suffice it to point out a few obvious factors that are directly relevant to our study. Apart from the ethnic divergence among the European states, the historic antagonisms and traditionally limited mobility of the people, the powers granted to the Community institutions are still quite limited. Above all, the taxation power for all practical purposes remains in the hands of the national governments, although the "approximation" provisions in the Treaty would provide a legal basis for a far-reaching assimilation. The national governments conduct independent foreign policies, and their national economic and monetary policies diverge to a point that the conflicts interfere with the working of the Common Market. The absence of a "political will" to coordinate national policies stymied the progress toward a true economic union although the year's end developments of 1969, mentioned earlier, have given rise to bright hopes of forward movement. National capital markets are underdeveloped and despite some progress in the suppression of obstacles to capital movements, exchange restrictions still exist in certain member countries on both considerable long-term transactions, such as the issuing of shares and granting of loans of a purely financial nature, and on an entire series of

Hall, Inc., Englewood Cliffs, New Jersey, undated); MULTISTATE TAX COMMISSION, THE MULTISTATE TAX COMPACT (pamphlet, 1969).

short-term capital movements.[18] In the corporation law field
specifically, it is important to keep in mind that the "guarantees" and safeguards designed to protect shareholders and
"third parties," which in Europe are generally grounded in
company law, are found in the United States principally
in federal and state legislation on corporate securities and
other regulations imposed upon the financial community.

2. Company law as a subject for international unification

If it can be said that a glance at a federal system offers
some helpful insights into the problem of assimilation of
company laws, the next obvious step is to consider the
efforts undertaken in this field at the international level.

International conflict-of-laws rules and problems of entry
and establishment concerning companies have been traditionally the subject of international agreements. Treaties,
bilateral and multilateral, abound in this field[19] and I shall

---

[18] Report of a Group of Experts Appointed by the EEC Commission, EEC COMMISSION, THE DEVELOPMENT OF A EUROPEAN CAPITAL
MARKET 85-95 and *passim* (Brussels Nov. 1966).

[19] *On conflict-of-laws* (private international law) see for instance:
Hague Convention of June 1, 1956, concerning recognition of legal
personality of foreign companies, associations and foundations,
RECUEIL DES CONVENTIONS DE LA HAYE 28 (The Hague 1966). CÓDIGO
BUSTAMANTE (or Code of Private International Law) adopted by
the Sixth Pan American Conference held in Havana in 1928, and
Treaties of Montevideo of 1889 and 1940; *see* ALFARO DE LA CERDA,
EL CÓDIGO BUSTAMANTE Y SUS RATIFICACIONES (Santiago 1938); RABEL,
1 THE CONFLICT OF LAWS 32, 33, 36, 37 (2d ed. Ann Arbor 1958); OAS,
Inter-American Juridical Committee (IAJC), Opinion on the Possi-
bility of Revision of the Bustamante Code (Washington, D.C. 1951)
considers a revision of the Code in relation to the two treaties of
Montevideo and the American *Restatement of the Law of Conflict of
Laws;* in 1966 the IAJC issued a draft code, see *Work accomplished
by the IAJC* during its regular meeting 16-56 (Washington, D.C. 1967).
See also International Law Association, *Report of the 49th Conference,* Hamburg, 1960, at 62-92 (1961). *On entry:* Council of Europe,
European Convention on Establishment of Companies of 1966, European Treaty Series No. 57, not in force; it was ratified by Luxembourg
only (Sept. 18, 1968) and signed by Belgium, the Federal Republic and
Italy. *Action accomplie en 1967-1968 par le Conseil de l'Europe* at
151. See also the numerous bilateral treaties of friendship, commerce

take some into account in the chapter on recognition of companies.[20] There is, however, a very limited record of successful unification on the international level of "internal" or "municipal" rules governing capital companies.

It is probably useful to view the integration process as a continuum reaching from a loose cooperation among nation-states to a federation. From that perspective one should at least mention the monumental unification of German private law, including commercial law with basic rules on companies. In the 1850s, the Diet of the *Zollverein* (Customs Association) approved the Prussian draft commercial code as a basis for discussion; and it was adopted first by Prussia in 1861 and in the next few years by most of the German States. In 1870, it was adopted by the North German Federation, and thereafter by the German Empire. Thus, the commercial code, and subsequently also the special company laws, came within the exclusive jurisdiction of the central government.[21]

The generally negative record on the international level may be due as much to the difficulty of the task as to the absence of a feeling on the part of the élites concerned that unification in this field was needed. Indeed, the law governing business associations is one of the "core" disciplines; in some of its aspects it is linked intimately to the doctrinal foundations and historically determined concepts of the entire legal system. In addition, it often reflects a delicate balance between conflicting economic, social and even polit-

---

and navigation, and bilateral treaties of establishment. On bilateral treaties see WILSON, UNITED STATES COMMERCIAL TREATIES AND INTERNATIONAL LAW (New Orleans 1960); Walker, *Provisions on Companies in United States Commercial Treaties*, 50 AM. J. INT'L L. 373 (1956).

On the methods and forums generally see UNIFICATION OF INTERNATIONAL PRIVATE LAW, REPORT OF THE AMERICAN BAR ASSOCIATION SPECIAL COMMITTEE ON INTERNATIONAL UNIFICATION OF PRIVATE LAW (Am. Bar Foundation, Chicago 1961).

20 *See* p. 397 *infra*.

21 Keeton, *The Zollverein and the Common Market,* in KEETON & SCHWARZENBERGER (eds.), ENGLISH LAW AND THE COMMON MARKET 1, at 3 (1963).

ical interests in the national arena and, as we have already noted, it is also organically tied to other vital fields of law, such as taxation.

The sense of a need for undertaking unification or assimilation in this field, in the face of the glaring difficulties, seems to have arisen thus far only on the regional level—in the Nordic Council, in the European Community, in the Council of Europe, in the Central American Common Market—where homogeneity is higher, and the on-going or prospective intensification of business relations offers an economic reward and supplies the incentive.

The greatest progress has been made in Scandinavia where the regional institutional framework is minimal but the ethnic affinity is highest and the unification-of-law tradition goes back to the second half of the nineteenth century. There, the idea was first advanced more or less casually in the Nordic Council meeting of parliamentarians by a Swedish deputy, a judge turned politician, in more modest terms of a unification of selected *aspects* of company law. In 1961, referring to the changes resulting from the European Common Market the Council recommended exploration of this subject. After the national authorities in Finland, Denmark, Norway and Sweden had considered the matter, the project was broadened to comprise drafting a complete uniform Scandinavian stock company law. The work on the uniform law became effectively linked with, and received an impetus from, the on-going or projected national reforms. Even the relatively modern Swedish stock company law of 1944, enacted in the aftermath of the Kreuger affair, required updating, particularly a simplification of the extraordinarily cumbersome company formation procedure.[22] The Norwegians also felt a need for modernizing their law of 1957, especially in the direction of strengthening the

---

[22] The only way of avoiding intolerable delay in the formation of stock companies is for Swedish attorneys to organize, and keep a supply of, "paper companies" which are made available to clients as needed. This has been a common practice in Sweden.

protection of shareholders and sanctioning new types of
securities. Finland definitely needed a new company act to
replace its 1895 statute. However, a major difficulty arose
from the fact that the Danish experts who had been working
on a reform of their permissive and obsolescent 1930 law
since 1957, had already made considerable progress at the
time and actually published a draft text in 1964. Although
the Danish Government decided to delay its draft and refrain from presenting it to the Parliament the margin of
flexibility of the Danish contingent in the negotiations for
a uniform Scandinavian law was reduced.[23] A concomitant
difficulty has been the attitude of the Danish industrial
circles, reportedly still adverse to a meaningful financial
disclosure, as compared with the posture of the Swedish
industry which is marked by a somewhat greater "openness."
The fear of the dominant Swedish economic power and
generally the structural differences in the dimension and
organization of the industry in the countries concerned have
also been complicating factors. On the other hand, the fact
that only one major corporate form exists in all the states
concerned—the limited liability company is not known there
—has simplified the work. In 1969, a working level agreement was reached on a tentative text of a uniform stock
company law, but the necessary national legislation is still
some distance off. Moreover, for reasons suggested above, the
draft is conceived as a first, more or less basic, uniform
legislation in the field and it contains intentional ambiguities in several important provisions. The provisions that
are susceptible to several interpretations will allow the member states to continue their divergent national rules on such
matters as the structure of company organs and the use of
bearer shares, at least until further uniform legislation is
agreed upon.[24]

---

[23] Hellner, *Unification of Law in Scandinavia*, 16 AM. J. COMP.
L. 88, at 97 (1968).

[24] Preparatory studies on limited liability companies have been
in progress in the *Council of Europe* but there is no indication of

any action at this time. Jean and Anne Limpens, *Problème de la coordination des mouvements d'unification,* in RAPPORTS BELGES AU VIIᵉ CONGRÈS INTERNATIONAL DE DROIT COMPARÉ, UPPSALA, 6-13 Aug. 1966, 41, at 56 (Brussels 1966). Baade, *The Council of Europe: Its Activities Relating to Law,* 15 AM. J. COMP. L. 639, at 644 (1966-67). On request from the Council of Europe made in 1957, the International Institute for Unification of Private Law considered the possibility of introducing the principles of the "trust" into civil law countries; the "investment trusts" received special consideration and in 1966 the Institute advised drafting of a model law on "mutual funds" (contractual or trust deeds: *fonds de placement*) and "investment companies" *(sociétés d'investissement).* UNIFICATION OF LAW, 1966 YEARBOOK 58-64 (Unidroit, Rome 1967). In 1968 the Committee of Ministers of the Council of Europe decided to discontinue work on limited liability companies. *Action accomplie en 1967-1968 par le Conseil de l'Europe* at 191.

Studies on stock company law were instituted in the *Nordic Council* as early as 1925. VAN DER GUCHT, 1 MATIÈRES SUSCEPTIBLES DE FAIRE L'OBJET D'UN MOUVEMENT D'UNIFICATION DU DROIT at 22 (Centre interuniversitaire de droit comparé, Bruxelles, undated); Rainer, *La coopération nordique sur le plan législatif en 1963 et 1964,* UNIFICATION OF LAW, 1964 YEARBOOK 197, 201 (Unidroit, Rome 1965); WENDT, THE NORDIC COUNCIL AND CO-OPERATION IN SCANDINAVIA 55, at 57 (Copenhagen 1959); von Eyben, *Inter-Nordic Legislative Co-Operation,* in 1962 SCANDINAVIAN STUDIES IN LAW 63, reports on the appointment in 1960 of a commission on company law. In a recommendation adopted in 1961 the Nordic Council suggested to the member governments, with special consideration of the changed economic, commercial and political relations resulting from the European Common Market, that they explore the possibility for a more uniform Nordic legislation on stock companies in order to assure legal equality among their citizens with regard to access to activities as founders, members of management, directors, etc., in stock companies. 1961 Nordisk Råd, 9th Sess., Copenhagen, at 1368. *See also* 1966 Nordisk Råd, 14th Sess., Copenhagen, at 1255. Agreement was reached in early 1969 among governmental commissions from Denmark, Finland, Norway and Sweden on a text of a uniform stock company law which was to be made public in late 1969 and in due course submitted by each of the governments to the respective national parliaments. For uniform Scandinavian legislation on partnership see WENDT, *supra* this note at 56. *National* reforms in this field have been under consideration in Scandinavia and a new draft company law was published in Denmark in 1964. Rainer, *supra* this note at 197, 201; Hellner, *Unification of Law in Scandinavia* at 97, relying mainly on the Finnish expert, Prof. Curt Olsson, *Lakimiespäivien Pöytäkirja,* in XVIII SUOMEN LAKIMIESLIITON 93 (1967). *See also* Expanded Nordic Economic Co-operation, *Report by the Nordic Committee of Governmental Officials* at 39 (unofficial translation sponsored by the Nordic Council, Stockholm 1969).

Unification of company law is contemplated also in the new Nordic Economic Union Treaty which was to be signed in the spring of 1970.[24a] Since two Scandinavian states (Denmark and Norway) are likely to become full members of the EEC along with the United Kingdom, they will be required to accept and implement the EEC directives and Conventions, in the framing of which they played no part,[24b] and to participate in further assimilation work, along with the present members. Thus we may witness an intriguing convergence, if not a confrontation, of two regional assimilation processes. The convergence will be all the more inter-

On developments in the Central American Common Market, see FRANKLIN, KOZOLCHYK et al., PROYECTO DE BASES Y COMENTARIOS SOBRE LA SOCIEDAD ANÓNIMA MULTINACIONAL, PROYECTO REFORMA JURÍDICA, Universidad de Costa Rica-AID, Facultad de Derecho; Kozolchyk & Torrealba, *Proyecto Revisado de Bases y Comentarios sobre la Sociedad Anónima Multinacional en Centroamerica*, 1968 REVISTA DE CIENCIAS JURÍDICAS 23 (Costa Rica). The Institute for Latin American Integration in Buenos Aires has sponsored a comparative study of legislation on corporations in Latin American Free Trade Area (LAFTA) countries. The purpose of the study is "to establish priorities in the process for standardizing commercial legislations, to make possible multinational action by Latin American companies." Prof. Héctor Alegría of Argentina was asked to prepare a report on the basis of individual country studies. Boletín de la Integración (Engl. version), Aug. 1968-Aug. 1969, at 62.

Some unification efforts have, however, been successful in the field of partnership and other unincorporated associations. WENDT, *supra* this note at 56. In December 1964 the EEC Commission requested the International Institute for Unification of Private Law in Rome to undertake studies in this field which were completed in 1966. UNIFICATION OF LAW, 1966 YEARBOOK 66-68 (Unidroit, Rome 1967).

[24a] CCH COMM. MKT. REP. ¶ 9353. The signature did not take place because Finland was unable to sign.

[24b] In Commission's Opinion on Application for Membership of United Kingdom, Ireland, Denmark, and Norway, submitted to the Council Oct. 1, 1969, the Commission stated: "In any event, the accession of new members to the Communities entails their acceptance not only of the Treaties, but also of the decisions [in the general sense of the term] that have been issued since the Treaties were adopted." CCH COMM. MKT. REP. No. 24, Dec. 22, 1966, at 6.

esting because of the inclusion of the United Kingdom, whose legal system has its roots in common law rather than in civil law which forms the underpinning of the legal order in the Member States. The EEC Commission observed in this connection that "[a]lthough the English system of company law differs in many respects from the continental systems (guaranteed minimum capital, structure of management, role of the shareholders' meeting), the protection of the rights of third parties and of the entrepreneurs (Article 54(3)(g) of the EEC Treaty) is not so different that substantial difficulties could result for the accession of the United Kingdom. . . ."[24c] Moreover, the British Government has already agreed to modify its law to the extent necessary for the creation of a "European company,"[24d] and it has recognized that "[c]onsiderable amendment of our national law might eventually be involved" as a result of the Conventions negotiated in accordance with Article 220.[24e]

As we proceed, in the following pages, to observe and evaluate the progress of the assimilation of company laws in the Community, including the modest first directive, we must keep in mind the achievement or, to be more accurate, the lack of achievement elsewhere, and the difficulties encountered on the international level and even in the federal context.[25]

[24c] *Id.* at 50.

[24d] *Id.* at 50.

[24e] LEGAL AND CONSTITUTIONAL IMPLICATIONS OF UNITED KINGDOM MEMBERSHIP OF THE EUROPEAN COMMUNITIES, Cmnd. 3301, No. 36, at 13 (May 1967).

[25] On the particular difficulty of assimilating company laws see Lutter, *Die Rechtsangleichung im Gesellschaftsrecht,* in EUROPÄISCHE HANDELSGESELLSCHAFT UND ANGLEICHUNG DES NATIONALEN GESELLSCHAFTSRECHTS, WISSENSCHAFTLICHES KOLLOQUIUM DER FACHGRUPPE EUROPARECHT, WISSENSCHAFTLICHE GESELLSCHAFT FÜR EUROPARECHT— am 5/6 Mai 1967 in Bad Ems, 5, at 30 (Frankfurt/M.—Berlin, 1968); Kalbe, *Änderungen des ersten Richtlinienvorschlags zur Koordinierung des Gesellschaftsrechts in der EWG,* 1966 AWD 466-68.

3. Modern corporation and law reform[26]

(a) Corporation as a new subsystem

Earlier in this book, I sought to identify those features of the EEC Treaty which bear evidence of the recognition on the part of its authors of the role which a "modern corporation" plays in the economy. Given the technologically determined need for large capital and for the management of many men, the corporation is an inevitable product of an industrialized society on both sides of the Atlantic. As the central "institutional device for large-scale organization of energies and resources," its role is no longer purely economic or commercial; it has changed both practice and theory of private property; it has become the chief agency for private organized research and innovation replacing the small inventor. In the United States, at any rate, corporations are "the hope for fund raisers for institutions of higher learning and principal consumers of the products of those institutions," the principal advertisers in the newspapers and television, and "the leading purveyor of influence and pressure on public officials" at all levels of government. In fact, corporate enterprise undercut the conditions which made it possible for the market to regulate the exercise of economic power, and "in the process, the modern corporation emerged as the first successful institutional claimant of significant unregulated power since the nation-state established its title." Although the "monopolistic corporation" has been the traditional devil in the miracle plays of anti-capitalist propaganda it has now become the principal target of the new crusade for the salvation of the environment. The great corporations are "political systems in which their

---

26 See generally MASON (ed.), THE CORPORATION IN MODERN SOCIETY (reprinted by Atheneum, New York 1966); BERLE, ECONOMIC POWER AND THE FREE SOCIETY (New York 1957); BERLE, THE TWENTIETH CENTURY CAPITALIST REVOLUTION (New York 1954); DRUCKER, CONCEPT OF THE CORPORATION (New York 1946); Eisenberg, The Legal Roles of Shareholders at 1; Vagts, Reforming the "Modern" Corporation at 23.

market, social and political influence goes far beyond the functional efficiency in the economy."[27] In any case, it is accurate to say that we live today in a corporate society, marked by distinct collectivist features which have contributed to the current "crisis of identity" and "alienation" of young people in particular.

(b) Is a reform necessary?

It would be a mistake to overestimate the role of corporation law and its reform—and for that matter of law reform in general—in any analysis of current social ills and needed remedies. Yet, as Mason pointed out, although many people in the United States have ideas on what to do about the corporation, there is little more than a "cacophony of voices" which has produced no firm view either in the general public or in the minds of legislators.[28] While there have been recently some significant revisions of state and federal laws, particularly the 1964 amendment to the securities legislation, many American lawyers would agree with Vagts' position that the corporation is in less urgent need of repair than other institutions.[29] This is in contrast with the trends on the Continent which I have attempted to outline in a synoptic form in the next chapter of this book. In all the Common Market countries comprehensive reforms have either just been completed or hold a relatively high spot on the current agenda. Yet even in France, where the need for a revision of the age-old basic company law was felt perhaps most strongly long before the seminal events of May 1968, it has been recognized that the new law, fashioned essentially by business-oriented lawyers, will have little more than

---

[27] Berle, *Foreword* to MASON, THE CORPORATION IN MODERN SOCIETY at IX (New York 1966); Chayes, *The Modern Corporation and the Rule of Law,* in MASON at 26-27, 37; Latham, *The Body Politic of the Corporation,* in MASON at 218; Mason, *Introduction,* in MASON at 1-2.

[28] *Id.* at 2.

[29] Vagts, *Reforming the "Modern" Corporation* at 25.

a marginal impact on the role of "the 'enterprise' in its three-fold reality, economic, human and public,"[30] and that the more penetrating reforms would have to be formulated in a different context. As for the EEC, the work on company law coordination and the supplementary Conventions has been given increasing emphasis, but we must keep in mind that coordination or "approximation" in the sense defined above is the avowed objective, *not* reform. In fact, with one possible exception—harmonization designed to promote equalization of working and living conditions *in an upward direction*—the Treaty does not speak of what one would call a "reform." This has been stressed on the Commission staff level as a doctrinal reason why coordination need not, and often cannot, lead to the adoption of the most modern or progressive rule.[31] Yet at the policy level, some of the Commission members who have sought to evolve a broader, programmatic framework for Commission action—for instance the energetic Colonna di Paliano or the thoughtful Dr. von der Groeben—speak of a common "industrial policy" which would help the Community industry to adjust to the changing competitive conditions. The content of this concept is not exactly crystal clear[32] but it includes a broad, across-the-board adjustment and modernization of what is becoming known in Europe as the "economic law," the entire normative framework of private and public law within which a commercial enterprise functions.[33]

---

[30] De Woot, Pour une doctrine de l'entreprise at 49 (Paris 1968).

[31] Leleux, *Le rapprochement* at 140.

[32] *See, e.g.,* a statement by Mr. Colonna di Paliano in *Le Figaro,* June 27, 1969; The Communities' Work Programme (20th March 1969), 1969 Bull. E.C. Supp. No. 4, at 11-12. The extensive Commission paper entitled "La politique industrielle de la Communauté, Memorandum de la Commission au Conseil," COM (70) final, Mar. 18, 1970, Bruxelles, was published after the completion of this book.

[33] For a recent survey of the content of the concept "economic law" see Limpens, *Contribution à l'étude de la notion de droit économique,* 1966 Il diritto del'economia 5.

(c) Topics of the reform

Despite the differences in the developmental stages of the industrial society on the two sides of the Atlantic (and for that matter within Western Europe as well), the principal topics pursued in the reform debate have been quite similar.

(i) Functional differentiation

In the first place, the modern corporate structure must serve an increasing variety of enterprises, ranging still from a small family undertaking to the conglomerate monster of the 1960s. In contrast with the United States, the problem is simplified in five of the six Common Market states by the availability of *two* principal corporate forms, the stock company corresponding to our corporation and the limited liability company which could best be described as an institutionalization of our close corporation. Only the first type, the stock company, is empowered to offer shares to the public and list them on stock exchanges, and it is "obliged to endure the glare of publicity on its financial affairs." The other type, the limited liability company, is confined to offering its "shares" to a select few, its "shares" are non-negotiable, its management structure simple and, until recently at any rate, it has enjoyed relative privacy.[34] However, the very availability of the two forms has raised a host of problems, including the questions to what extent the promoters should be left free to choose between them and just how much more privacy should the limited liability company enjoy. The EEC Commission also grappled with the "privacy" problem in drafting the disclosure provisions in its first coordination directive. Even where the "dichotomy" of corporate form did not exist, as in the Netherlands and in the United States, a differentiation appeared necessary when it came to intro-

---

[34] Conard, *Organizing for Business* at 46-61; on the advantages of this "dichotomy" see Weiner, *Legislative Recognition of the Close Corporation*, 27 MICH. L. REV. 273 (1929); *see also* DeVries & Juenger, *Limited Liability Contract: The GmbH*, 64 COLUM. L. REV. 866 (1964).

ducing new requirements (as in the field of financial disclosure) which, while appropriate for economically significant and publicly held enterprises, would prove disfunctional for "a midget."

Again, new needs of the business and financial community required new and special forms, for instance for investment funds and real estate development enterprises, which on the Continent have been reflected in the company law reforms. In the same vein, new and more varied forms of securities have been introduced there.

(ii)　Schism between ownership and control

By far the most significant issue in the reform debate has been the proverbial "disassociation" between corporate ownership and control. In smaller, closely held corporations, the owner exercises control by means of the voting powers of the common stock, but these cases, it is said, have been growing rarer every year. The widely held assumption has been that "[i]n comparatively few large publicly-held corporations, managerial control is in fact exercised by or for substantial stockholding interests. . . . The current prototype, increasingly, is that of a corporation with stock widely scattered among individuals, investment trusts, or institutional investors who faithfully vote for the incumbent management and resolutely refuse to participate in its concern."[35] More recently, Professor Eisenberg concluded on the basis of available statistics that the AT&T prototype is quite atypical and that the pattern of stock distribution in the overwhelming majority of corporations, even those publicly held, is such that many shareholders must be assumed to be legitimately interested, and expect to participate, in structural decisions at any rate.[36] Nevertheless, the

---

[35] Rostow, *To Whom and for What Ends is Corporate Management Responsible,* in MASON at 53.

[36] Eisenberg reports that there are almost no data on the distribution of shares by a number of shareholders of the approximately 1,200,000 active corporations in the U.S. (other than financial institu-

image of the "new feudalism" based on an indifferent shareholder and an all powerful, self-perpetuating management,
has not only raised the question of the legitimacy of the
management power, but it added a new dimension to the
more general issue of corporate purpose and control of
corporate power. There has been, on the other hand, a clear
recognition of the need for strong and flexible management,
capable of rapid decisions. A variety of solutions has been
envisaged to meet the situation.

The *first* and most obvious approach, which is mirrored
in all the national reforms, is to attempt to restore "stockholder democracy" through such measures as giving the
stockholder more information by improved disclosure, better
protection through tightened proxy rules, cumulative voting
and remedies based on anti-fraud rules, and more power
through reviving the shareholders' meeting as a meaningful
source of authority for the administration and review of
the corporation's performance.[37]

A *second* school of thought envisages a change in the
organizational structure of the corporation by establishing
a special corporate organ with a duty to supervise the
management on behalf of the shareholders. But in a discussion of such a special supervisory organ the question in-
evitably arises whether the shareholders are the only "constituency" whose interests must be taken into account. What,
if any, other corporate constituencies or "subpublics" should
be recognized: workers, suppliers, customers, consumers, the
local community, the "public" generally, and what institutional form should the recognition of their interests assume?
Should these constituencies participate in the company's

---

tions and wholly-owned subsidiaries), but he estimates that only 7,500
have 300 or more shareholders and about 35,000 corporations are in
the 10-300 shareholder range. Eisenberg, *The Legal Roles of Shareholders* at 40-44; *see also* Vagts, *Reforming the "Modern" Corporation*
at 32; *cf.* Folk, *Recent Developments in Corporation Statutes*, 20 J.
LEGAL ED. 511, 519 (1968).

[37] Rostow, *To Whom and for What Ends is Corporate Management Responsible,* in MASON at 53.

decision-making and, beyond this, should they share in its benefits? Is "maximization of business profits" no longer the exclusive corporate purpose and, if so, what other purposes should be taken into account? In large measure, as we shall see, those in charge of company law reforms have succeeded in avoiding a confrontation on these issues or at least channeling it into a debate on special legislation, outside the scope of the traditional company law. In the EEC, the issue of the scope of corporate constituencies was linked to the technical interpretation of Article 54, par. 3(g) which speaks of the protection of shareholders and "third parties"; some labor groups asserted that "third parties" included not only creditors but employees as well.[38]

The *third* and most radical variant is public ownership, or some form of direct governmental control of management. Public ownership has played a substantially larger role in Western Europe, particularly in Italy and France, than in the United States. Yet the experience in the United Kingdom and in France (where in 1968 workers' discontent erupted in a publicly owned enterprise) has not made this solution any more attractive than it had been before. Only in Italy, where substantial new nationalizations took place quite recently, have other forms of direct public control of companies been seriously advanced in the context of a general company law reform.

At the opposite end of the spectrum is the *fourth* school, sometimes known as the "managerialists" who would seek to achieve ends of social, or more generally public, policy simply by increasing management power. They proceed on the theory that while shareholders are interested only in profits, and client-groups only in their own welfare, management is in a position to balance the claims of all groups dependent on the corporation, including not only client-

---

[38] Memorandum by the Secrétariat Syndical Européen (C.I.S.L.) and Organisation Européen de la C.I.S.C.-C.M.T., *summarized in* LE DROIT ET LES AFFAIRES, LE BI-MENSUEL DU MARCHÉ COMMUN, No. 152, May 12, 1969, C. 975 (Paris).

groups and shareholders, but the general public—in a position, that is, to run the corporation in the public interest.[39] Although there have been some changes in the selection process, training and attitudes of management in the direction of evolving professional standards, Kaysen and others are skeptical of the inclination and ability of the "professionalized" management to serve as instruments of public policy.[40] Vagts' findings suggest that the trend toward "managerialism" is much less distinct among European executives than among their American counterparts. The German executives, he believes, tend to be "more independent, self-willed, and bent upon success in strictly business terms, and less dependent on their colleagues' approval of their public-spiritedness."[41]

(d) "The American challenge": a new reform impulse?

In his recent study Gilpin poignantly refers to the "momentous transformation" which has been taking place in the international economy of the West, "with profound consequences" for the position of Western Europe. "At the same time an immense common market of over a hundred million people is forming in Western Europe, a true Atlantic economy composed of North America and Western Europe is evolving because of recent technical advances in transportation and communication. The jet airplane, the communications satellite, and the declining costs of oceanic transportation have moved the United States and Western Europe ever closer together and made one united Western economy a technical possibility."[42] The relative success in 1967 of

---

[39] See Eisenberg, The Legal Roles of Shareholders at 21, and references to literature there; Andrews, Toward Professionalism in Business Management, 1969 HARV. BUS. REV. 49.

[40] Kaysen, The Corporation: How much Power? What Scope?, in MASON at 43; Eisenberg, The Legal Roles of Shareholders at 22.

[41] Vagts, Reforming the "Modern" Corporation at 43.

[42] GILPIN, FRANCE IN THE AGE OF THE SCIENTIFIC STATE at 39 (Princeton 1968). See generally SERVAN-SCHREIBER, THE AMERICAN CHALLENGE (New York 1968); JOHNSON, THE WORLD ECONOMY AT THE CROSSROADS (Oxford 1965).

the Kennedy round of negotiations for reduction of tariffs has contributed to this trend, and the growing realization in the United States of the dependence of the dollar upon European support has improved the prospect for some policy coordination.

It is of course a long step from a "technical possibility" of an Atlantic-wide market to an economic and political reality. In fact, the intermittent friction between the United States and the Community[42a] and the renewed pressures for

---

[42a] Some of the controversial issues are dealt with in the following excerpt from an address delivered by M. Maurice Schumann, French Minister of Foreign Affairs, before the French National Assembly on Apr. 28, 1970:

"Economically, the development of an independent Europe cannot fail to bring the United States to agree to, or rather to confirm, an important choice which is also—let us admit it—a difficult choice. It will soon be 20 years since the declaration of May 9, 1950, on France's initiative, committed Europe to the path of reconciliation and union. Since then, encouragement from the United States has never been lacking. Even today the most authorized officials voice the same line.

"However, Mr. Schaetzel, United States Ambassador to the European Communities, and Mr. Davis, Assistant Secretary for Domestic and International Business, who are not just private citizens, recently, without mincing their words, made a case against the Common Market based on three main grievances: The common external tariff is too high; the common agricultural policy is an obstacle to the development of American exports to the European market and to the markets of nonmember countries, and the preferential system from which the Six allow the African states to benefit upsets the rules of international trade.

"Our answer: First of all, the common external tariff is lower than the American tariff, even when one excludes the nontariff obstacles which hamper the development of European sales to the United States. Next, the surplus in the United States' agricultural trade with Europe has doubled in 10 years, even if the volume of sales did once drop 12% in relation to the previous year. Lastly, if the total sum of American aid to Africa does not exceed $130 million, or 9% of the funds granted by the United States to foreign countries, the duty of Europe, like the duty of France, is to give the African states the privileged aid demanded at one and the same time by the consolidation of their independence, by the respect of traditional ties and currents and by resistance to subversion, that is, to more or less underhanded neocolonialist undertakings.

protectionist legislation in the United States Congress could be viewed as harbingers of a new trend in the opposite direction. However, even the present situation, as it has actually developed, is marked by a distinct change of competitive conditions. With the removal of most of the internal barriers within the Common Market, competition has increased across national borders within the Community, and, with the common external tariff lowered in response to the Kennedy round agreements, across the frontiers of the Community as well. Initially, at any rate, major American companies, experienced in multinational operations, rather than European companies, have taken full advantage of the emerging single market by acquisitions, joint ventures and new subsidiaries. They have done so not without losses and miscalculations, but on the whole most successfully. The influx of foreign capital and know-how has brought unquestionable benefits to the Community and until the 1960s the American "penetration" has not been viewed as a serious threat to Western Europe's competitive position. The French Government, itself oscillating in its attitude toward American investment, unsuccessfully urged the Commission to help establish a common Community policy on foreign investments, but other Member States were opposed.[43] By the early 1960s, however, the growth rate of the American economy leaped ahead and at the same time science had become a major factor in the innovation of technologies of great economic importance; it was in these advanced tech-

---

"But, however justified and necessary these replies may be, we must be careful lest they feed a polemic that without fail would end up either impeding the growth of the Community, or making it the subject of a permanent dispute between Western Europe and the New World. Did not Mr. Schaetzel go so far as to establish a relation between the effects of the trade policy of the Six and the stationing of American forces in Europe?" Ambassade de France, Service de Presse et d'Information, No. 1370, at 3-4.

[43] Newburg, *Legal and Financial Planning for the International Corporations Doing Business in the European Common Market*, in PRIVATE INVESTORS ABROAD, PROBLEMS AND SOLUTIONS 1, at 25 (Albany, New York 1967).

nologies that the United States was forging ahead. As the high stakes of the competitive struggle became apparent to corporate planners, European business and governmental observers began to stress what they considered a number of competitive advantages American corporations had over their European rivals which were apt to destroy the Atlantic economic balance. "First, American corporations have access to a huge and fluid capital market, in contrast to the small, slow moving, and nationally oriented capital markets of western Europe. Second, American firms enjoy immense 'economies of scale' and have decades of experience dealing with a large, mass market. Finally, American management and labor are equipped by attitude and experience to accept and promote rapid technological change."[44] Both the size of the American corporation and the huge governmental subsidies of research and development have been in the focus of this argument.[45]

These considerations are reflected, albeit marginally, in the national company law reforms, but even more clearly in the changing attitudes within the EEC Commission. The "industrial policy," in which assimilation of company laws was to play a part, has been pressed as one means for helping European industry to rationalize its production and to concentrate so as to overcome the "handicap of size," and to stimulate Community-wide progress and cooperation in research and development, in order to bridge the "scientific" or "technological gap." In this sense one could view the "American challenge" as an impulse for reform, a thought that we shall pursue further in the chapters that follow.

---

[44] GILPIN *supra* note 42, at 46.

[45] *See also* LAYTON, TRANS-ATLANTIC INVESTMENTS (The Atlantic Institute, Paris 1966); KINDLEBERGER, AMERICAN BUSINESS ABROAD at 75 ff. (New Haven and London 1969). *See generally* BEHRMAN, SOME PATTERNS IN THE RISE OF THE MULTINATIONAL ENTERPRISE (Chapel Hill 1969); ROLFE and DAMM (eds.), DIRECT INVESTMENT IN PERSPECTIVE (New York 1970); Vagts, *The Multinational Enterprise: A New Challenge for Transnational Law*, 83 HARV. L. REV. 739 (1970).

Chapter 4

EUROPEAN COMPANY LAWS: DIVERGENT BUT CONVERGING?

1. The not-so-similar national laws in the EEC: some highlights

The six company law systems share basic concepts which were enunciated in the Napoleonic Civil and Commercial Codes. The French law on stock companies of 1867, in part reflecting English legislation, had served as a common model for the corresponding laws in Belgium, Italy and Luxembourg, and in certain respects it influenced also the first legislations in Germany. However, the process of divergence began at an early date. The requirement of governmental approval for the establishment of a stock company—a residue of the "concession" (franchise) system—was abolished and replaced by an increasingly detailed scheme of rules governing not only the formation but also the functioning of companies and designed to protect both the shareholders and "third parties" (principally creditors); and a less complex set of rules has evolved for the limited liability companies.[1] In the Netherlands, however, these rules were and

---

[1] For an effective introduction to the various forms of business organization in the national laws of the Six see Conard, *Organizing for Business* at 46-60 with an explanation of the limited liability company at 51-60. *See also* PENNINGTON, COMPANIES IN THE COMMON MARKET (London 1962); Loussouarn, *Le rapprochement* at 11; VAN OMMESLAGHE, LE RÉGIME DES SOCIÉTÉS PAR ACTIONS ET LEUR ADMINISTRATION EN DROIT COMPARÉ at 80 ff., 112 ff.; Houin, *Le régime juridique des sociétés dans la Communauté économique européenne*, 1965 REV. TRIM. DROIT EUR. 11, at 12; Lacan, *Pour une société anonyme de type européen, Caractéristiques essentielles des sociétés anonymes dans les six pays de la C.E.E.*, 1967 REV. TRIM. DROIT EUR. 319; Scholten, *Company Law in Europe*, 4 C.M.L. REV. 377 (1967-68).

still are substantially more liberal since the prerequisite of administrative authorization has been retained. Moreover, only in the Netherlands the limited liability company does not exist so that the stock company form, like the American corporation, must accommodate both small and large enterprises. In general, as a result of the important British interests in the Dutch multinational enterprises, Dutch law has come under strong British influence of which the "rule of incorporation" mentioned earlier is one manifestation. The rule suited well the large Dutch enterprises which have become accustomed to operations on a worldwide level. The "liberal" law designed to attract foreign capital for instance allows directors to issue shares of the authorized capital, permits a stock company to purchase up to fifty percent of its own shares[2] and makes possible arrangements similar to voting trusts, with certificates equivalent to non-voting shares. Only the Netherlands law fails to provide any statutory guarantee against exaggerated valuation of contributions in kind to the capital and has no provisions on legal reserves.[3] For a time, the Belgian *Commission bancaire*,[4] a body reminiscent of the United States Securities and Exchange Commission, refused to admit the shares of the giant Dutch companies (Philips, Unilever) to the Belgian stock exchange because of what it considered inadequate legal protection. I have already mentioned that the

---

[2] Art. 41a of the WETBOEK VAN KOOPHANDEL (Netherlands Business Corporation Code) (An American Translation by Rivers, van de Ven and Westbroek, CCH Chicago, 1965, at 20) provides that the corporation may acquire its own fully paid shares but only up to the amount of par value authorized in the articles of incorporation. The Minister of Justice, however, authorizes only provision for acquisition not to exceed 50%. This limitation was included in the new Netherlands law, which, however, has not come into effect as yet. VAN DER HEIJDEN-VAN DER GRINTEN, HANDBOEK at 499. *See* p. 322 *infra*.

[3] BALEKJIAN, LEGAL ASPECTS OF FOREIGN INVESTMENT IN THE EUROPEAN ECONOMIC COMMUNITY at 99 (New York 1967); VAN OMMESLAGHE, LE RÉGIME at 245. Only the Netherlands law fails to *require* the appointment of an auditor; in fact, however, apparently all "open" stock companies employ the services of "an accountant."

[4] *See* p. 265 *infra*.

liberal rules in the Netherlands law, combined with the "rule of incorporation," have caused concern of an excessive concentration of foreign and Community capital in the Netherlands, although others have argued strongly that considerations other than differences in company laws— tax and labor legislation, market factors, national loyalty— determine the basic business decisions.[5]

Again, important differences appeared from the very outset in the internal organizational pattern of the stock company. In contrast with the classic French-type single board, the so-called administrative council (*conseil d'administration*) , the German legislator, as early as 1870, made compulsory the two-tier pattern of the executive board (*Vorstand*) and supervisory council (*Aufsichtsrat*), and the pattern was further elaborated in successive reforms, particularly those of 1937 and 1965.[6] Other marked features which became part of German law more recently, distinguished it from the other systems: the elaborate rules on "related companies" (*Konzernrecht*) and, above all, the controversial workers' right of "codetermination" (*Mitbestimmungsrecht*) enabling workers' representatives to participate in the company's decision-making.[7]

In 1940, the French Vichy Government modified the stock company organizational scheme. Since that time, the administrative council (*conseil d'administration*) is required to elect a president who assumes responsibility for the management as president-general manager (*Président-Directeur-Général*).[8] Some were of the opinion that by adopting this law France "has caught up with good business practice,"

---

[5] The differences in the Dutch law have posed a problem in the efforts to harmonize conflict-of-laws rules relating to companies at the level of Benelux and at The Hague Conferences. Van Hecke, *Nationality of Companies Analysed,* 1961 NEDERLANDS TIJDSCHRIFT VOOR INTERNATIONAAL RECHT 223, at 228.

[6] Vagts, *Reforming the "Modern" Corporation* at 50.

[7] *See* p. 95 *infra.*

[8] In the alternative, another person may be appointed to the job of general manager (*Directeur-Général*) but the President remains responsible for the management.

although others criticized it as a totalitarian innovation reflecting the *Führerprinzip.* At any rate, the Vichy law remained on the books after World War II and its scheme
was incorporated in the new 1966 Law which, however,
as we shall see, added an alternative optional form, quite
similar to the German system.[9] The original French-type
system of a single board (administrative council) has continued in effect in Belgium, Luxembourg, and substantially
also in the Netherlands and Italy.[10]

---

[9] On the 1940 law see Conard, *Organizing for Business* at 98-99.

[10] On some of the important differences between the American
board of directors and the European boards see Conard, *Organizing
for Business* at 88-89, 91-102. Conard states:

"Successful European companies, like their American
counterparts, generally have a chief executive in whom all
reins of authority are concentrated. . . .

"However, we must avoid assuming that the executive
power is held by the presiding officer of the governing board,
as it usually is in the United States. Although a European governing board usually elects a president, the presidency of that
board signifies something more like being an American
'chairman of the board' than being an American 'president'.
. . . Even in France, where the president is required by law
to assume responsibility for the company's management, he
has the choice of delegating the authority to a subordinate
general manager, or exercising it himself under the compound title of 'president and general manager' (président-
directeur-général).

"In Germany, the president of the [supervisory council]
(that is, the board elected by the shareholders) is forbidden to
be an executive; the executive power must be wielded by
a subordinate board (the Vorstand), or its president (German stock companies having two boards and possibly two
presidents).

"A striking peculiarity of European management structures is the power of the shareholders in the statutory plan.
The legislator has not designed them to be a mere electoral
college, to choose the leadership to which the company
shall be entrusted. The shareholders are generally the supreme
governing body, and the governing board is merely their
agent, responsive to their will. Even in Germany, where the
reforms of 1937 were intended to give increased independence
to the executive board, the shareholders have distinctly
greater powers than are usual in the United States. This

To the normative differences must be added substantial structural dissimilarities: thus, for example, in France about one-half of all companies, large and small, are organized as stock companies whereas in Germany the most common corporate form is the limited liability company.[11]

2. National reforms and Community coordination: a "symbiosis"?

(a)   No more "unilateral" reform?

The EEC Treaty came into effect in 1958. In 1965, Professor Houin of the Paris law faculty, a leading French expert in the EEC Commission's activities at Brussels and an important actor in the French law reform, suggested that the alluring prospect of a true European company law should have discouraged the Member States from

---

conception expresses itself in many ways, such as the rule that dividends must be declared or at least confirmed by the shareholders rather than by the governing board alone, as in America.

"The most important aspect of shareholder supremacy is the power to remove top management, which may be stated as a general principle of European company law, subject to some qualifications. . . . A qualification must be noted in Germany, where the shareholders' removal power affects the highest board (Aufsichtsrat) but not the subordinate executive board (Vorstand). . . .

". . . A third peculiarity of European boards is that, with a few exceptions, the board members may act as a joint executive. They do not need to act through officers; they may, by virtue of their positions, act to negotiate and sign contracts. In short, most of the European laws make no provisions for the separation of policy-making and executive functions which are basic to American thinking about management structure.

"In small enterprises this may be all to the good. Many American writers have been suggesting that we should in America provide for boardless management in 'close corporations,' and have cited European experience to support their contention. But it is obvious that larger concerns need a plural board, with a systematic delegation of executive functions. . . ."

[11] See p. 245 infra.

reforming their national legislation "unilaterally." Yet the opposite appears to be the case and "one has the impression that each Member State hastens to complete the reform of its own national law as if that reform should strengthen his position in the European framework."[12] In fact, the most recent reform in the Federal Republic was enacted in 1965, to be followed by a new law in France in 1966.

The question then is, what has been the interaction between the Community effort and the work on national reforms? With this question in mind, I shall consider in the following sections the principal characteristics of the national reform work in a sharply foreshortened historical perspective and with an emphasis on the reform process.

(b) The German stock company law of 1965: modernizing a modern law[13]

(i) A glimpse at the history

In Germany "the history of the stock company law is a history of its reform."[14] In contrast with France, the succes-

---

[12] Houin, *Le régime* at 27. For a more detailed discussion and references, particularly to the position of Prof. Bärmann see p. 162 *infra*. *See also* von der Groeben, *Vers des sociétés anonymes européennes — nécessité et possibilité de créer une société de type européen*, 1967 REV. TRIM. DROIT EUR. 224.

[13] *See generally* Vagts, *Reforming the "Modern" Corporation* at 23 ff.; Steefel & Falkenhausen, *The New German Stock Corporation Law*, 52 CORNELL L.Q. 518 (1967); Juenger, in JUENGER & SCHMIDT, GERMAN STOCK CORPORATION ACT, TRANSLATION, INTRODUCTION (CCH Chicago 1967); HUECK, GESELLSCHAFTSRECHT 107 (13th ed. München, Berlin 1965); WÜRDINGER, AKTIEN-UND KONZERNRECHT 10 (Karlsruhe 1966); Gessler, *Das neue Aktienrecht*, 1965 BB 677; Kohler, *New Corporation Laws in Germany (1966) and France (1967) and the Trend Towards a Uniform Corporation Law for the Common Market*, 43 TUL. L. REV. 58 (1968); Wilhelmi, *Das neue Aktiengesetz*, 1965 DIE AKTIENGESELL-SCHAFT 153, 187, 217, 247, 307, 349; Möhring, *Das neue Aktiengesetz*, 1966 NJW 1, 87; Dippel, *Die Reform des Aktienrechts (zugleich ein Beitrag zur Geschichte des Aktienwesens)*, 1965 DEUTSCHE RICHTER-ZEITUNG 315, 353; von Caemmerer, *La riforma tedesca delle società per azioni del 1965*, 1967 RIVISTA DELLE SOCIETÀ 165; Duden, *Aktienrechts-reform in Deutschland, Frankreich und England*, 1967 RABELS ZEIT-SCHRIFT 51, at 76.

[14] WIETHÖLTER, INTERESSEN UND ORGANISATION DER AKTIENGESELL-

sive reforms in Germany have offered a relatively timely response to the changing role of the stock company in a changing economy. The winds of liberalism swept away the last vestiges of the franchise system so that since 1870, an entry into the commercial register has been the prerequisite for a stock company to come into existence as a legal person. Since that year also the German stock company law has been federal in nature.

The law of 1884 was intended to do away with the then prevalent abuses of the corporate form and consequently it increased sharply the regulatory features, particularly the civil and criminal responsibility of the incorporators and of the administration. The large and interlocking enterprises which had emerged after the First World War caused an ever widening gap between the shareholders and the management, the "disassociation" between ownership and control, and this led to a critical review of the stock company's organization (particularly of the central role of the shareholders' meeting). The proposed structural changes stimulated in turn a debate on the need for ordering the respective roles of capital, labor, and management in a separate body of "law of the enterprise" (*Unternehmensrecht*).[15]

The 1930-1931 proposals of the Ministry of Justice were dominated by the new ideas and also aimed at eliminating the deficiencies that had appeared during the great depression. Only a part of these proposals became the law in 1931, that is, provisions relating to the preparation of the balance sheet, extension of credit to members of the executive board, acquisition of a company's own shares, and—most importantly—the introduction of "independent" auditors as a new means of supervision.[16]

SCHAFT IM AMERIKANISCHEN UND DEUTSCHEN RECHT at 35 (Karlsruhe 1961). *See also* Duden, *Aktienrechtsreform in Deutschland, Frankreich und England,* 1967 RABELS ZEITSCHRIFT 51.

[15] RATHENAU, VOM AKTIENWESEN (Berlin 1918); Geiler, *Die wirtschaftlichen Strukturwandlungen und die Reform des Aktienrechts,* in ENQUÊTE-BERICHT 1927, at 52 ff.

[16] Von Caemmerer, *La riforma tedesca* at 169.

Finally, in 1937, drawing upon Anglo-American corporate experience with a powerful board of directors and skillfully capitalizing upon the *Führerprinzip* which the National Socialist Government had sought to impose upon the entire economy,[17] the Ministry of Justice succeeded, with the support from Hjalmar Schacht as Minister of Economic Affairs, to put through a general reform which substantially realized the proposals of the early thirties. The greatly strengthened executive board (*Vorstand*), removable for "good cause" only, became the organ in charge not only of the day-to-day operations but also of policy-making and dealing with outsiders, with the supervisory council (*Aufsichtsrat*) selecting the executive board and overseeing it on behalf of the shareholders. The powers of the shareholders' meetings were reduced to include the election (or removal) of the supervisory council, charter amendments and the distribution of dividends.[18]

After the Second World War, important changes occurred in the composition of the supervisory council. In 1951, the workers were granted by special legislation the right of "codetermination" first in the coal, iron and steel producing industry. In that sector, the supervisory council of enterprises with over 1000 employees is composed of equal numbers of representatives of shareholders and employees; in addition a "labor director," who is responsible for labor relations and must be approved by the workers, is a member of the executive board. The law setting forth a "constitution for enterprises," adopted the following year, accorded the employees one-third representation on the supervisory council of all stock companies, excepting family owned companies

---

[17] HUECK, GESELLSCHAFTSRECHT 112 (13th ed. München, Berlin 1965).

[18] Von Caemmerer, *La riforma tedesca* at 167; WÜRDINGER, AKTIEN- UND KONZERNRECHT at 12; HUECK, GESELLSCHAFTSRECHT at 110. For a comparison between the American board of directors and the organs of a German stock company see Conard, *Organizing for Business* at 100-01.

with less than 500 employees, and in all limited liability companies employing more than 500 workers.[19] Moreover, "plant" or "workers councils" organized in all enterprises with more than five employees have a voice in questions of personnel and working conditions. Finally, in the so-called "economic committees" (*Wirtschaftsausschüsse*) management discusses questions of business policy with labor representatives.[20]

The "codetermination" was enacted "over the protests and dire predictions of the industry" and over the opposition of a substantial sector of the Bar as well.[21] The labor unions having eschewed demands for nationalization some time ago, have been pressing for an extension of codetermination.[22] This issue—whether "codetermination" should be

---

[19] Law on Codetermination (Mitbestimmung) of Employees in Supervisory Councils and Executive Boards of Enterprises in the Coal, Iron and Steel Producing Industry of May 21, 1951, [1951] BGBl I 347, and the supplementing Law of Aug. 7, 1956, [1956] BGBl I 707; The Law on the Constitution for Enterprises (Betriebsverfassungsgesetz) of Oct. 11, 1952, [1952] BGBl I 681. Vagts, *Reforming the "Modern" Corporation* at 64-75; von Berenberg-Gossler, *Die Einführung der paritätischen Mitbestimmung der Arbeitnehmer in Grossunternehmen als Sozialisierungsmassnahme gegen Art. 15 GG* (GG—Grundgesetz, Constitution of the Federal Republic of Germany), 1968 DIE AKTIEN-GESELLSCHAFT 67 and 108; DE SCHWEINITZ, LABOR-MANAGEMENT CONSULTATION IN THE FACTORY, THE EXPERIENCES OF SWEDEN, ENGLAND, AND THE FEDERAL REPUBLIC OF GERMANY (Honolulu 1966). For a most recent study see *Workers' Participation in Management in the Federal Republic of Germany,* Country Studies Series, No. 4, in INT'L INSTI-TUTE FOR LABOUR STUDIES, 1969 BULLETIN 94-148. *See generally* GAR-CIN, COGESTION ET PARTICIPATION DANS LES ENTREPRISES DES PAYS DU MARCHÉ COMMUN (Paris 1968).

[20] The plant councils have existed since 1920, but the economic committees were created by the 1952 law. Law of Feb. 4, 1920, [1920] RGBl I 147; Law of Feb. 15, 1922, [1922] RGBl I 209. On plant councils in the Member States see Boldt et al., *La représentation des travailleurs sur le plan de l'entreprise dans le droit des pays membres de la C.E.C.A.,* COMMUNAUTÉ EUROPÉENNE DU CHARBON ET DE L'ACIER, HAUTE AUTORITÉ (Luxembourg 1959).

[21] Vagts, *Reforming the "Modern" Corporation* at 66.

[22] See proposal by the Social-Democratic group in the Bundestag, Bundestagsdrucksache V/3657, Entwurf eines Gesetzes über die Unter-

broadened—has caused a rift in the Christian Democratic party and more recently it has created a controversy within the Free Democratic Party as well.[23] The Social Democrats, on the other hand, give "codetermination" a large share of credit for the labor peace that has prevailed in post-war Germany and, in response to pressures from the unions, they have been ready to demand its extension. A report submitted to Chancellor Brandt by a Commission of nine professors and six "permanent" consultants, chaired by Professor Kurt Biedenkopf of the Bochum Law Faculty, may well provide a further impetus for this demand.[23a] On the basis of a broad, fact-finding inquiry extending over a period of two years, the Commission concluded that in principle "codetermination" has been a success. Although the Commission did not go so far as to endorse a general extension of the principle of equality or "parity" of workers' representation on the supervisory council as demanded by the unions, it did recommend an increase both of the number of workers' representatives (beyond the present one-third) and of their legal authority in all enterprises with one to two thousand employees. In a rare display of harmony, the report was

---

nehmensverfassung in Grossunternehmen und Konzernen, Dec. 16, 1968, and Bundestagsdrucksache V/3660, Entwurf eines Gesetzes zur Erhaltung der Mitbestimmung der Arbeitnehmer in den Aufsichtsräten und Vorständen der Unternehmen des Bergbaus und der Eisen und Stahl erzeugenden Industrie, Dec. 18, 1968; Deutscher Gewerkschaftsbund, *Entwurf eines Gesetzes über die Mitbestimmung der Arbeitnehmer in Grossunternehmen und Grosskonzernen,* 1968 RECHT DER ARBEIT 185.

23 *Differenzen wegen der Mitbestimmung,* Frankfurter Allgemeine Zeitung, June 22, 1968, No. 142, p. 4, col. 2-3; *Disharmonie in der CDU über die Mitbestimmung, id.,* June 19, 1968, No. 139, p. 1, col. 1; *CDU-Arbeitnehmer engagieren sich für mehr Mitbestimmung, id.,* June 18, 1968, No. 138, p. 3, col. 3-5; *More Codetermination in Industry? Union Says Yes, Employers No,* THE BULLETIN, issued by the Press and Information Office of the German Federal Government, Vol. 16, No. 26, at 195, 197, July 23, 1968.

23a Mitbestimmung in Unternehmen, Deutscher Bundestag, 6. Wahlperiode, BUNDESTAGSDRUCKSACHE VI/334. The report contains more than 400 pages. The Commission was appointed in 1968 by the then Chancellor Kiesinger, a Christian Democrat.

received favorably by both the Social Democrats and the Christian Democrat opposition, although the unions felt it did not go far enough. The business community, however, voiced its opposition in strongest terms,[23b] on the ground that the proposed extension would give labor unions excessive influence on company policy, not necessarily in the interest of the rank and file of union membership. As part of a counter-offensive, spokesmen for industry have suggested legislation aimed at strengthening the legal position of the individual worker in the enterprise, a direction currently pursued by Italian labor unions and the Italian Parliament.

(ii)   The neo-liberalists and the virtuoso drafter

The same post-World-War II period which produced "co-determination" saw the beginning of a grand debate in professional, scholarly and business circles on a new stock company reform, which in the first place centered on improving the company's capability for gathering large-scale capital. The means explored included broader disclosure, more information in annual statements, restriction upon "hidden reserves" and more active involvement of shareholders. The prevailing "neo-liberalist" doctrine advocated the widest possible ownership of shares as a means for reducing further the class conflict and improving the working of the "social market economy" (*soziale Marktwirtschaft*).[24] Again, since about seventy percent of all German stock companies have become interrelated by stock ownership or by other ties,[25] the discussion turned toward improving the legal safeguards on economic power by assuring greater transparency.

[23b] *See, e.g.,* Apel, *Mehr Mitbestimmung-keine Parität-Zum Bericht der Mitbestimmungskommission,* 1970 BB 89; Delcour, *Le patronat reste hostile à l'extension de la cogestion proposée par la commission Biedenkopf,* Le Monde, Sélection hebdomadaire, from Feb. 12 to Feb. 18, 1970, p. 3, col. 1-3.

[24] On neo-liberalism see NAWROTH, DIE SOZIAL-UND WIRTSCHAFTS-PHILOSOPHIE DES NEOLIBERALISMUS (Köln 1962).

[25] Gessler, *Das neue Aktienrecht,* 1965 BB 677, at 681.

The ideas for specific modifications emerged from the lively confrontations in professional journals and gatherings. The actual drafting of the new law was done for all practical purposes by Ernst Gessler, a high official in the Federal Ministry of Justice, with the support of a staff of three. In contrast with the practice in the other Member States of the EEC, there was no officially appointed commission to advise him. Gessler has had a lifetime experience in the Ministry and was already concerned with the 1937 reform. He has been "honorary" (part-time) professor at the University of Bonn where he has lectured on company law and he has written extensively in that field. He was also the forceful leader of the German delegation in Brussels until his retirement in 1970.

A first official "pre-draft" of the reform law (*Referentenentwurf*) which did not engage the responsibility of the Minister of Justice was published in 1958[26] and was the subject of extensive comment by interested parties.[27] The next phase of the reform process was the publication of the official government proposal (*Regierungsentwurf*), accompanied by an extensive explanatory statement. Authored again by Gessler, after a study of the great mass of criticism and observations on the earlier draft, the new text was submitted to the Parliament in 1960[28] where it was considered

---

[26] Referentenentwurf eines Aktiengesetzes, published by the Federal Ministry of Justice, Köln 1958. The "small" stock company law reform of 1959 introduced certain changes. Law of Dec. 23, 1959, [1959] BGBl I 789.

[27] *See* Begründung zum Entwurf eines Aktiengesetzes (Reasons for the Draft of a Stock Company Law), BUNDESTAGSDRUCKSACHE III/1915, at 92. A great number of the comments and articles appeared in the periodical *Die Aktiengesellschaft*. Among the extensive literature *see, e.g.,* STRAUSS, GRUNDLAGEN UND AUFGABEN DER AKTIENRECHTS-REFORM (Tübingen 1960); HENGELER, KREIFELDS, BEITRÄGE ZUR AKTIEN-RECHTSREFORM (Heidelberg 1959); MARBURGER AUSSPRACHE ZUR AKTIEN-RECHTSREFORM (Marburg 1959).

[28] Regierungsentwurf eines Aktiengesetzes und eines Einführungs-gesetzes zum Aktiengesetz, BUNDESTAGSDRUCKSACHEN III/1915, and IV/171.

during the third and fourth Parliamentary periods. To this law the Economic Committee of the Bundestag devoted 40 sessions, the Legal Committee 19 sessions, the Labor Committee 6 sessions, and a special Subcommittee of the Legal Committee 23 additional sessions.[29] In accordance with the rules of procedure allowing Parliamentary Committees to hold hearings,[30] no less than 39 expert witnesses were heard in the Economic Committee. The law was finally approved shortly before the lapse of the fourth Parliamentary period on May 25, 1965,[31] only a few months after the publication in Brussels of the first draft of the first coordination directive of the EEC.

A number of comparative studies appeared in the late fifties and early sixties which examined solutions in foreign laws and unquestionably exerted influence on the German lawmakers. Thus aspects of American law, including particularly rules on company accounts, financial documents and disclosure requirements, were introduced into the debate by Prof. Kronstein, a refugee from the Nazis, who after the war held university teaching appointments in both the United States and in Germany, and by the younger generation of German legal scholars who had received part of their advanced training in the United States.[32]

---

[29] Schriftlicher Bericht des Rechtsausschusses (12. Ausschuss) Bericht des Abgeordneten Dr. Wilhelmi, zu BUNDESTAGSDRUCKSACHE IV/3296, at 1 (Report of the Legal Committee). The proceeding was based not only on the government bill but also on two bills proposed by the Social Democratic group.

[30] § 73 Rules of Procedure (Geschäftsordnung) of the Bundestag.

[31] The Law of Sept. 6, 1965, [1965] BGBl I 1089, effective Jan. 1, 1966. This law will be cited here as the Law of 1965. For the Introductory Law (Einführungsgesetz) of the same date and effective date see id. at 1185. For an English translation see JUENGER & SCHMIDT, GERMAN STOCK CORPORATION ACT (CCH Chicago 1967).

[32] See, e.g., KRONSTEIN & CLAUSSEN, PUBLIZITÄT UND GEWINNVERTEILUNG IM NEUEN AKTIENRECHT (Frankfurt 1960); MESTMÄCKER, VERWALTUNG, KONZERNGEWALT UND RECHTE DER AKTIONÄRE (Karlsruhe 1958); WIETHÖLTER, INTERESSEN UND ORGANISATION DER AKTIENGESELLSCHAFT IM DEUTSCHEN UND AMERIKANISCHEN RECHT (Karlsruhe

(iii)   What of the EEC coordination?   Some national attitudes

Since Gessler, who drafted the German reform law, was also the principal German expert in Brussels, we can safely assume that full information on the work in the EEC was available in Bonn. In fact, the Legal Committee of the Bundestag considered the draft of the First Directive, particularly from the viewpoint of its compatibility with the EEC Treaty.[33] But the effort in Brussels apparently did not have any visible repercussion on the framing of the German law. Neither the material published by the government in support of the new law nor—subject to a few exceptions—the extensive reform literature[34] refers to the coordination on the Community level, and even the then Secretary of State in the Ministry of Justice, Walter Strauss, a strong partisan of a united Europe and subsequently a judge on the Court of Justice of the Communities, did not mention the EEC aspect in his study on the German reform published in 1960.[35] The absence of any discernible concern may be explained at least in part by the time sequence, since the German bill was already more or less crystallized when the preparatory labors began in Brussels. Again, in contrast with the French official stance, the initial governmental view in Germany attributed limited significance to the coordination function of the EEC in this field. Finally, it may have

---

1961). Kronstein's work exerted influence on the new rules for financial documents and Mestmäcker's ideas influenced the new law on "related companies" *(Konzernrecht);* Esser, *Die Aufgaben der Publizität im Aktienrecht,* 1963 DIE AKTIENGESELLSCHAFT 31. The German reformers considered Anglo-American law as early as 1926 at the 34th Deutscher Juristentag in Köln. Verhandlungen des 34. DJT zu Köln I, 258-331, II, 611-798, 874-79.

[33] Deringer, Débats, Compte rendu in extenso des séances, [1966-1967] EUR. PARL. DÉB. No. 85, at 56.

[34] Among the exceptions see Bärmann, *Ist eine Aktienrechtsreform überhaupt noch zulässig?,* 1959 JZ 434; Möhring, *Das geltende Aktienrecht und die "Notwendigkeit" einer Reform,* 1964 DEUTSCHE RICHTERZEITUNG 235, 236.

[35] LUTTER, KAPITAL at 26-27, referring (at 27) to STRAUSS, GRUNDLAGEN UND AUFGABEN DER AKTIENRECHTSREFORM at 5.

been felt that the German reform law, designed as it was to modernize further the "strictest" system in the Community, would certainly meet—and most likely exceed—whatever standards will be evolved in the coordination work.

In many respects German law has been considered as the principal model in Brussels. Yet, initially at any rate, the German reform process may be said to have had a negative impact on the Community effort. The German experts in the Ministry of Justice, realizing that—apart from the divergence of the Netherlands system—it was primarily the advanced nature of the German law that had caused the legal asymmetry within the Community, feared that their law and their national reform might be impaired or diluted by the coordination process.[36]

The Social Democratic party, although recognizing the need for some modifications of the prevailing law, such as a further extension of the disclosure obligation, was not in favor of overhauling the entire stock company law at the time.[37] Addressing the Bundestag in the name of the Social Democratic group as late as in the final stage of the debate, Dr. Reischl spoke of a "premature reform"; it would have been better, he felt, to await the results of the EEC coordination effort which will require further changes in the law, and in this view he was supported by a Christian Democrat. A more rational way to proceed, Dr. Reischl argued, would have been first to review the law governing enterprises in general, and the determining factor in this review would be the size and economic impact of the enterprise; a unitary concept of "enterprise law" would then provide a framework for an overall company law reform. However, it was obvious

---

[36] Gessler, *Die Bestrebungen zur Harmonisierung des Handelsrechts in EWG-Raum,* in ENTWICKLUNGSTENDENZEN at 23.

[37] The Social Democratic group in the Parliament actually submitted two bills of its own, one on improving the disclosure for stock companies, limited liability and "related companies" (*Konzerne*), Bundestagsdrucksache IV/203, and the other on the protection of minorities in capital companies, Bundestagsdrucksache IV/204.

to a spokesman for the Free Democrats that at the bottom of
the socialist argument for a prior "enterprise law" reform
lay the objective of extending the workers' "codetermination" in the company's affairs which, he thought, should be
discussed separately in the next session of the Bundestag;
the purpose of the new stock company law, on the other
hand, was quite different, that is, to improve the protection
of small shareholders through greater disclosure and clearer
definition of the responsibility of the management. As for the
coordination in the EEC, German interests in the EEC called
for the application of the old principle that "those who have
an idea and put it on paper are ahead of the race"; this was
confirmed by the experience with the harmonization of the
turnover tax, since the existing French law was essentially
accepted by the other Member States as the EEC law.[38]

The principal German industrial circles, which were opposed to the national reform for reasons of their own, used
the still somewhat nebulous prospect of a coordination on
the Community level as an argument in support of their
opposition to the proposed national reform. The basic attitude of the industry, in Germany and for that matter in
other Member States as well, has been that company law
should be "neutral" and should not be used to advance the
objectives of any particular economic policy. Moreover,
under the circumstances a reform would mean only more
restrictions on the management and further tightening of
the protection of shareholders and creditors. In particular,
German industry viewed with disfavor a further restriction,
if not elimination, of the "hidden reserves" which was a
major purpose of the reform.[39]

---

[38] Deutscher Bundestag, 4. Wahlperiode, 187. Sitzung, May 25,
1965, Bundestagsdrucksache IV/3296, Third Reading, Dr. Reischl
(SPD) at 9406-9407; Mr. Seidl (CDU/CSU) at 9412; Dr. Aschoff (FDP)
at 9411-12. On turn-over tax harmonization see p. 168 *infra*.

[39] Bärmann, *Einheitliche Gesellschaftsform* at 125; DEUSS, DAS
AUSKUNFTSRECHT DES AKTIONÄRS IN DER HAUPTVERSAMMLUNG DER AKTIEN-
GESELLSCHAFT NACH § 112 AKTG UND ALS PROBLEM DER AKTIENRECHTS-
REFORM (München 1962).

In a general way it may be said that the innovations in the law were decided upon by the majority of the Christian Democrats and the Social Democrats, with the Free Democratic Party as a rule supporting conservative solutions.

(iv) The new law: some salient features

The explanatory statement accompanying the Government draft bill suggests that the lawmaker had in mind a definite socio-political concept of the stock company.[40] The final text, however, is a blend of two contradictory models. The first sees the stock company as an essential component of the legal-economic order, designed to help "the little fellow" increase his capital (the people's share, *Volksaktie*) and thus to counterbalance the concentration of large fortunes in the hands of the few. According to the second paradigm, however, the function of the stock company law is merely to provide an efficient organizational framework in which the stockholder's role is to supply the required capital; his right to information and the rules on accounts and disclosure serve to ensure the security of the investment and no other purpose.[41] Neither of the two models has been applied in full in the new law which has the following significant features:

1. In the first place, a further effort is made to reconcile shareholder-owner control with management autonomy. Although the 1965 Law retains the two-tier system, it stresses the collegial character of the executive board[42] and introduces several significant new restrictions on the administration's discretion. The final authority of the shareholders' meeting with respect to the distribution of profits is defined

---

40 BEGRÜNDUNG ZUM ENTWURF EINES AKTIENGESETZES, BUNDESTAGS-DRUCKSACHE III/1915, at 92 ff.

41 WÜRDINGER, AKTIEN-UND KONZERNRECHT at 13; Duden, *Aktien-rechtsreform* at 58-59.

42 § 77 of the Law of 1965. This applies of course only if the executive board consists of more than one person.

more clearly[43] and the unrestrained discretion of the executive board and the supervisory council as regards building hidden reserves by arbitrarily understating assets and overstating liabilities is eliminated in the new valuation rules inspired by American practice.[44] On the other hand, the administration is free to build open reserves but the shareholders are given remedies to compel appropriate dividend distribution.[45]

2. The new formulation of the rules on accounting and financial statements, already enacted in large measure in the 1959 reform law, serves to improve disclosure.

3. The management's reporting duty towards the supervisory council is broadened,[46] the number of positions a member is allowed to hold in such councils is limited and, more significantly, interlocking arrangements through appointments of executive board members to supervisory councils of other companies are prohibited.[47]

4. The legal position of the individual shareholder is strengthened. The grounds on which the management may refuse to supply information are now formulated in more precise terms and such refusal is subject to full judicial review.[48] The new "proxy rules" governing the right of the banks to vote the shares deposited with them are designed to intensify the participation of the shareholder in the company's decision-making by according him the right to issue instructions to the bank and assuring him of more adequate information. However, the practical effect of the new rules may well be limited, since the law still permits blanket

---

[43] §§ 58, 148 ff., 174 of the Law of 1965. In principle, the executive board and the supervisory council establish the annual financial statements and they may allocate up to one-half of the year's net profits to free reserves.

[44] § 153 ff. of the Law of 1965. *See also* p. 246 *infra.*

[45] §§ 58, 174 of the Law of 1965.

[46] § 90 of the Law of 1965.

[47] §§ 90, 100 of the Law of 1965.

[48] §§ 131, 132 of the Law of 1965.

proxies which, contrary to the Government's original text modified in the Bundestag, need not relate to a specific meeting and can be issued in advance for a period of up to fifteen months, and in practice will be automatically renewed.[49]

5. The protection of minority shareholders is improved by loosening the prerequisites for the access to judicial remedies, such as the action for damages against the administration, or appointment of special auditors.[50]

(v)   The law on "related companies"

6. The most far-reaching innovation, however,—"without precedent in corporate legislation"—is the comprehensive set of rules governing "related enterprises," the famous *Konzernrecht,* replacing the fragmentary provisions of the 1937 Law. The new law attempts to face the reality of the dialectic contradiction between the legal separateness and factual interdependence of affiliated or "related companies"; it does not undertake to "untangle this webwork" or even to put a brake on the trend toward further concentration of economic power. This latter task is left to the Law Against Restraints of Competition which contains limited provisions on concentration.[51]

In the first place, since one objective of the new rules is to provide a clearer picture of the corporate interrelationships, any "enterprise" whose holding in a German stock company amounts to at least twenty-five percent, is required

---

[49] §§ 128, 135 of the Law of 1965. Juenger, in JUENGER & SCHMIDT at 19-20; Gessler, *Das neue Aktienrecht,* 1965 BB 677, at 679; Möhring, *Das neue Aktiengesetz,* 1966 NJW 1, at 8. The Legal Committee and the Economic Committee of the Bundestag suggested that the rule allowing a proxy to be issued for a specific meeting only and after the call for the meeting would be too burdensome for small shareholders and would infringe their rights to appoint an agent. This opinion prevailed over the original Government text. Juenger, *id.* at 20.

[50] §§ 147, 142 par. 2, 120, 258 par. 2, 247 of the Law of 1965.

[51] §§ 22, 23 of the GESETZ GEGEN WETTBEWERBSBESCHRÄNKUNGEN (Law Against Restraints of Competition) (1966 BGBl I 37).

to notify the latter which must publish the notification. Failure to comply with the reporting requirement causes suspension of the shareholder's rights of the delinquent enterprise. This and other reporting requirements are to provide the creditors and investors with information about the holdings and acquisitions and to assure the enforceability of other rules in this field.[52] It is interesting to note that the move by the Social-Democratic group in the Bundestag to reduce the threshold figure from twenty-five percent to ten percent so as to conform to the law of France ("our immediate neighbour and besides us the greatest EEC partner") met with the opposition of both the Government and the majority in the Bundestag.[53]

Second, a company may assume the direction of another company in pursuit of its own interest *only* on the basis of a formal agreement ("control agreement," agreement to transfer or pool profits or to lease or surrender a business). Such agreement is subject to requirements resembling those prescribed for charter amendments (approval by qualified majority of shareholders, entry into the commercial register, etc.). Moreover, the controlled company and the creditors are protected by provisions prohibiting impairment of that company's capital, and the "outside shareholders" (those not connected with the controlling group) are given either a right to a reasonable dividend or an option to withdraw upon appropriate compensation.[54]

Finally, a company that has acquired a controlling interest in (and thus *de facto* control over) another company, must not use its power to the prejudice of the controlled party without affording it specific compensation within the same fiscal year, and subject to stringent provisions on liability for damages. The controlled company must report annually

---

[52] §§ 20, 21 of the Law of 1965.

[53] It was also noted that the 10% figure applied in the United States and was recommended in the Jenkins Report for the United Kingdom. BUNDESTAGSDRUCKSACHE IV/3296, at 9214. *See* § 16a of the Securities Exchange Act of 1934.

[54] §§ 291, 292, 308-310 of the Law of 1965.

all transactions induced by, or serving the interest of, the controlling enterprise.[55]

Thus the agreements and practices that evolved "as a result of corporate inbreeding and of peculiarities of German turnover and corporate income taxation" are made the subject of statutory recognition and regulation, and the adjustment of the conflicting interests is sought in a more systematic and "scientific" way than in the American case law which is based on fiduciary duties and liabilities of majority shareholders.[56]

The new law does not incorporate or modify the existing rules on "codetermination" (*Mitbestimmung*) of workers; this—the Government explained in its report—would be "premature."[57]

(c) The new French Law on Commercial Companies of 1966: a moderate modernization

In contrast with the latest German reform, the French reform process was not limited to the stock company but

---

[55] §§ 311, 312-315, 317, 318 of the Law of 1965.

[56] Juenger, in JUENGER & SCHMIDT at 15-16; Karplus, *The German Integration Agreement as Corporate Guaranty*, 19 BUS. LAW. 295 (1963); *see generally* Haskell, *The New West German Law of "Related Business Units,"* 24 BUS. LAW. 421 (1969).

[57] BEGRÜNDUNG ZUM ENTWURF DES AKTIENGESETZES, BUNDESTAGS-DRUCKSACHE III/1915, at 96. However, the Law refers to the special laws on codetermination (*supra* note 19, p. 95), as they affect the composition of the executive board and the supervisory council, and establishes procedures for settling disputes concerning the applicability of their provisions. See particularly §§ 76 par. 2, 95 par. 2 to 99.

Two important laws, enacted after the 1965 reform, should be mentioned here: Umwandlungsgesetz (Law on Transformation of Legal Form of Enterprises) in the version of Nov. 6, 1969, [1969] BGBl I 2081, and Gesetz über steuerliche Massnahmen bei Änderung der Unternehmensform (Law on Tax Measures in Connection with Changing the Form of an Enterprise) of Aug. 14, 1969, [1969] BGBl I 1163. This legislation provides far-reaching possibilities for a tax-free transfer of assets of partnerships and other unincorporated enterprises to stock companies and limited liability companies, and vice versa. The "transformation" is accomplished by universal succession, as in the case of a fusion. The tax privilege is denied in specified circumstances in order to prevent evasion of codetermination.

was aimed from the outset at bringing together and updating the entire archaic body of the company law, scattered in a bewildering multiplicity of texts. In its final and decisive stages, the reform process interacted effectively with the early efforts in Brussels.

(i)   Why the reform?   "Obscurantisme impénétrable"

Company law provisions were dispersed in the Civil, Commercial and Penal Codes, in the basic law on stock companies of 1867 which, however, was itself modified not less than thirty times during its century-old existence, in the 1925 law on limited liability companies and in a great variety of other, often contradictory, texts. In addition, as time passed, statutory law became increasingly divorced from the reality and practice, with courts filling in the "gaps." If it was hard for a French lawyer to find his way through this labyrinth, a foreigner was baffled by its "impenetrable obscurantism." As the French Government pointed out in the introduction to the reform bill, the need for consolidation and clarification became particularly pressing when France and the other members of the EEC undertook to expand their commercial relations, to extend freedom of establishment and to coordinate their legislation.[58]

(ii)   The reform process: a succession of Commissions

The first effort to consolidate the many texts was undertaken in 1941 by a group of practitioners under the leadership of M. Maurice Polti, then President of the National Association of Stock Companies (A.N.S.A.). The Association,

---

[58] Projet de loi sur les sociétés commerciales, No. 1003, Assemblée Nationale, Annexe au procès-verbal de la séance du 23 juin 1964, Exposé des motifs at 2-3; M. Le Douarec, Rapport fait au nom de la Commission des lois constitutionnelles, de la législation et de l'administration générale de la République sur le projet de loi (No. 1003) sur les sociétés commerciales, Assemblée Nationale, No. 1368, Annexe au procès-verbal de la séance du 14 Mai 1965, Tome 1, at 3-5.

which comprises the most important stock companies in the country, supplies its members with legal and tax documentation and defends their interests before legislative and administrative bodies. The result of its undertaking was examined by a committee within the Ministry of Commerce and Industry and by other commissions.

After the liberation, in 1947, the Minister of Justice appointed a commission to prepare a reform of the Commercial Code and of the company law. The Commission consisted of four law professors, four judges, and six practitioners in commercial and company law, and it was presided over first by Professor Escarra and, after his death, by Professor Amiaud. In 1961, before this group was able to put the finishing touches on its "code of company law," the new Minister of Justice, M. Michelet, took the project out of its hands in order to speed up the work with a view to an early submission of a proposal to the Parliament. The Government of the young Fifth Republic considered it desirable at the time to "occupy" the Parliament with relatively noncontroversial legislation, and the pending commercial law reform was thought eminently suitable for this purpose. As a result, a group of officials in M. Michelet's own Ministry took over and came up with a new draft, introducing such radical innovations as a German-type "codetermination" that would allocate one-half of the seats on stock company administrative councils to employees. However, M. Baumgartner, the Minister of Finance, opposed the draft because of the strong hostility on the part of business and industry.

In the face of the opposition, the Minister of Justice felt compelled to withdraw the proposal. He appointed a new "consultative organism" whose task it was to submit a draft that presumably would be more in the "classic" mold. The new body, generally referred to as the "Pleven Committee," was composed of M. Pleven as chairman, Senator Molle, M. Polti, then also a member of the French Economic and Social Council, M. de Balasy, and representatives of the

several Ministries concerned. M. Molle, a notary, has been a
member of the "center-left" group in the Senate. The late
M. Polti was professionally connected, as I mentioned earlier,
with the association of the major stock companies, and
although not politically active, was a "conservative" in the
sense that he viewed the reform principally as a means for
encouraging private investment and avoiding any dampening
of entrepreneurial dynamism. M. de Balasy, originally a presiding judge of a chamber at the *Tribunal de commerce de
la Seine,* apparently also without any definite political
affiliation, has held prominent positions in the administration of chemical and banking concerns. Finally, M. Pleven,
an elder statesman and respected deputy of the moderate
center-left in the National Assembly, has had considerable
practical experience, including contacts with American
companies. The selection of these men was obviously designed to reassure the business sector. Since they were
intimately acquainted with the working of companies and
corporate problems of the day, they would be able to
identify the areas where limited reform was desirable and
feasible without serious interference with the functioning of
companies. The Committee was directed, as a first step, to
obtain the views of interested groups and persons on problems raised by the proposed modifications of the law, and to
suggest which of these views should be taken into account—
a rather unusual procedure in the French system. Accordingly, between May 1961 and January 1962, the Committee held no less than 63 meetings and it heard 48
groups and individuals from all walks of life, including
attorneys, law professors, representatives of banks, chambers
of commerce, employers, labor unions, and even "two
foreigners," members of the British and American organizations of accountants. A draft "Code of company law" containing some 600 articles was then completed, but it was
reportedly kept secret until 1964 so that even leading attorneys in Paris were kept in the dark.

On instructions from the new Minister of Justice, M. Foyer, this text was again modified by a group of magistrates and professors, and in the process it was stripped of a great number of provisions (some 200 articles) which were to be included in implementing decrees. This assertion of executive power, although strongly criticized by M. Pleven and others in the Parliament,[59] was considered necessary in order to maintain the new constitutional division of power between the executive and legislative branches, prescribed by the 1958 Constitution.[60] Paradoxically, this modification defeated at least in part a paramount objective of the reform, that is the maximum possible consolidation of all the relevant provisions in a single text;[61] moreover, a new element of uncertainty was injected since the implementing decrees are subject to judicial review by the Conseil d'État.[62]

(iii) EEC radiation

Prior to submitting the "Foyer draft" to the National Assembly in June 1964, the Minister undertook "to make it conform to the latest directives of the European Community."[63] The original draft of the first coordinating directive was published by the EEC Commission also in 1964. As we shall see, not only did the French delegation in Brussels have a decisive impact on the selection of the topics for the first coordinating directive but it influenced its content as well.

---

59 DÉB. PARL., Assemblée Nationale, June 1, 1965, [1965] J.O. (France, June 2) at 1663-64.

60 Art. 34 of the 1958 Constitution. *See also* Art. 41. M. Le Douarec counted no less than 61 references to future implementing decrees in the new draft. RAPPORT LE DOUAREC at 11.

61 RIPERT & ROBLOT, TRAITÉ ÉLÉMENTAIRE DE DROIT COMMERCIAL 531-34 (6th ed. Paris 1968). Hémard, *La réforme des sociétés par actions en France et la loi du 24 juillet 1966,* 1967 RIVISTA DELLE SOCIETÀ 132, at 136; Tomasi, *Das neue französische Gesellschaftsrecht,* 1966 AWD 661.

62 RAPPORT LE DOUAREC at 11.

63 M. Molle, Rapporteur de la Commission des lois, DÉB. PARL., Sénat, Apr. 14, 1966, [1966] J.O. (France, Apr. 15) at 117.

In the European Parliament, the French contingent, led by
M. Pleven, played an active part in the discussion of that
directive and offered a series of amendments. The draft
directive was reproduced in full in the 1965 report of the
French National Assembly's Committee on the proposed
reform law, and in the Parliamentary debates the Government invoked some of the provisions of the draft—long
before it was adopted—to justify certain aspects of the proposed law.[64] But of course the work in Brussels at that time
had not progressed far enough to have a more pervasive
impact.

In the parliamentary proceedings one finds several references to the company laws of the other Member States and
to the EEC Treaty; and in at least one instance the assertion
was made that in pursuing the harmonization within the
Common Market the new French law will "tend to favor
concentration on the European level" and penetration of
foreign, German and American, capital with the result that
"a true policy of national independence" will be compro-
mised.[65]

Outside the government circles, a part of the French
literature dealing with the reform also manifested considerable interest in comparing the proposed law with other
legal systems and in exploring its relationship to the EEC
coordination effort.[66] The idea of coordinating national
legislation on the EEC level, moreover, was favored by the
traditional French propensity toward governmental central-

---

[64] M. Foyer, Minister of Justice, DÉB. PARL., Assemblée Nationale,
June 1, 1965, [1965] J.O. (France, June 2) at 1661. *But see* M. Pleven,
id. at 1667-68. *See* p. 301 *infra. See also* Houin & Goré, *La réforme des
sociétés commerciales,* 1967 RECUEIL DALLOZ-SIREY, CHR. 121, at 126.

[65] M. Guy Ducoloné (Communist party) in the National Assembly,
[1965] J.O. (France, June 2) at 1668.

[66] *E.g.,* Houin & Goré, *La réforme des sociétés commerciales* at
121; Sinay, *La proposition de directive européenne en matière de
sociétés commerciales et le projet de loi français,* 1965 GAZETTE DU
PALAIS, DOCTR. 38; Dorat des Monts, *Vers un droit européen des sociétés commerciales,* 1965 JUR.-CL. PÉR., DOCTR. 1896.

ization and a penchant for symmetry. In the earlier stages
of the French reform, the failure to publish the draft was
criticized not only in France but also in the Federal Republic, presumably because it made timely transnational
discussion difficult.[67] There is some evidence that a portion
of the French Bar that was unhappy with the Escarra-Amiaud
draft because it had been influenced too strongly by academic
lawyers, turned to the Community arena, and this—it is said
—explains in part the energetic initiative of the Paris Bar
in favor of the so-called European company which was later
officially put forward at Brussels by the French Government.[68]

(iv) In the Parliament

After a detailed and meticulous examination in the National Assembly's Law Committee, the Government draft
was discussed in the Assembly on the basis of the report by
M. Le Douarec and voted in first "reading" in June 1965;
more than 400 amendments were tabled and more than
one-half of the articles modified. The Senate had before it
the reports by Senators Molle, Dailly and Le Bellegou, as
well as 548 amendments. When it took up the draft in April-
May 1966 it approved the text with 487 amendments. A
mixed Assembly-Senate Committee worked out an agreed
text now counting 509 articles which was finally adopted in
July 1966.[69]

---

[67] LUTTER, KAPITAL at 27; Dalsace-Bernard, *Der Vorentwurf des
französischen Aktiengesetzes*, 1963 ZHR 185; Carteron, *Quelques re-
marques sur le projet de réforme des sociétés commerciales*, 1965 REVUE
DES SOCIÉTÉS 245; Dalsace, *Aperçu critique sur le projet de loi sur les
sociétés commerciales*, 1965 REVUE DES SOCIÉTÉS 1.

[68] *Infra* p. 432.

[69] Law No. 66-537 of July 24, 1966, [1966] J.O. (France, July 26),
cited as Law of July 24, 1966. See also the explanation by M. Le
Douarec, Assemblée Nationale, June 1, 1965, [1965] J.O. (France,
June 2) at 1663. On the reform law generally see Bastian, *La réforme
du droit des sociétés commerciales: Sociétés par actions*, 1968 JUR.-CL.
PÉR., DOCTR. 2183; R. & J. LEFÈBVRE, LA RÉFORME DES SOCIÉTÉS COM-

I shall return to the parliamentary proceeding in the context of the general discussion of the role of parliaments in national company law reforms. Suffice it to point out here that the Senate, perhaps more than the Assembly, played a significant role, chiefly due to a handful of its members who were both good legal technicians and experienced practitioners. These men undertook to align the "Foyer draft," which was prepared by bureaucrats and academics without much experience in business affairs, with the "realities" of company life. In fact, many of the adopted amendments restored the provisions of the original "Pleven draft." Generally, the debate was technical and not more than some twenty lawyer-members took part in it. This was due to the fact that the entire reform effort was essentially a product of technicians in which political parties showed little interest. The parties of the left, especially the Socialists and Communists, were indifferent, since in their eyes the reform would not serve the social and economic goals which they pursued. Only on one point, the introduction of the German-type two-tier system of company structure, did the debate take a somewhat political turn; I shall return to it in the next section. Even the proposed judicial control over company formation that was urged by the Government as a step toward greater legal security and harmonization with other Member-State laws was debated in terms of its practical implications rather than as a political issue; and it was defeated in the Senate due to the traditional mistrust on the part of businessmen toward public authorities, including the courts.

MERCIALES EN TABLEAUX PRATIQUES (Paris 1966, Supp. 1968); LE-MEUNIER, LA RÉFORME DES SOCIÉTÉS COMMERCIALES, Loi no. 66-537 du 24 juillet 1966, Décret no. 67-236 du 23 mars 1967 (2 vols. Paris 1966-68); HÉMARD, TERRÉ & MABILAT, LA RÉFORME DES SOCIÉTÉS COMMERCIALES, Décret no. 67-236 du 23 mars 1967, Commentaire analytique (Paris 1967); Houin & Goré, *La réforme des sociétés commerciales,* 1967 RECUEIL DALLOZ-SIREY, CHR. 121-176; RIPERT, 1 TRAITÉ; Lutter, *Das neue französische Gesellschaftsrecht,* 1967 NJW 1153.

(v)   The new law—toward a new labyrinth?

The new law "does not bring about any revolutionary modifications . . . and tackles basic questions in rather rare instances;"[70] it remains within the traditional mold of company law and, above all, it avoids the controversial problem of restructuring the law of the enterprise. Nevertheless, politically the reform fitted nicely the French Government's declaratory policy of massive institutional "renovation."

In the words of the Minister of Justice, the reform sought to assure

> a greater security for those who deal with a company, better guarantees for the associates and shareholders, a modernization of the structure of our commercial companies, and finally, adaptation of the legal framework to present necessities, especially to concentration. . . . The proposal offers the possibilities . . . both with a view to an international unification of company law which certainly is desirable but probably still a long way off, and, if modern legislation is to turn in that direction, with a view to a reform of the enterprise. . . .[71]

Despite its youth the new law has already been amended a dozen times[72] and the basic implementing decree of March

---

[70] M. Molle, Rapporteur de la Commission des lois, Déb. parl., Sénat, Apr. 14, 1966, [1966] J.O. (France, Apr. 15) at 117.

[71] Minister of Justice M. Foyer, *id.* at 116.

[72] Law No. 67-16 of Jan. 4, 1967, J.O. (France) Jan. 6, 1967, modifying Law No. 66-537 of July 24, 1966, J.O. July 26, 1966; Law No. 67-559 of July 12, 1967, J.O. July 13, 1967, modifying and completing Law No. 66-537 of July 24, 1966, J.O. July 26, 1966; Law No. 67-563 of July 13, 1967, J.O. July 14, 1967, reforming legislation on bankruptcy and judicial procedure; Ordinance No. 67-695 of Aug. 17, 1967, J.O. Aug. 18, 1967, modifying and completing Law No. 66-537 of July 24, 1966, J.O. July 26, 1966; Ordinance No. 67-833 of Sept. 28, 1967, J.O. Sept. 29, 1967, creating a Commission on Stock Exchange Transactions; Ordinance No. 67-834 of Sept. 28, 1967, J.O. Sept. 29 and Oct. 3, 1967, providing for various measures with a view to facilitating the adaptation of structures of enterprises; Ordinance No. 67-836 of Sept. 28, 1967, J.O. Sept. 29, 1967, designed to encourage savings and

23, 1967, has also been followed by a series of modifying and supplementing texts.[73]

(vi) Some features of the new law

Some of the principal features of the new law are as follows:

1. Distinction is drawn between companies[74] "making a public offering of their securities" (whether or not listed

---

the development of the financial market; Law No. 68-696 of July 31, 1968, J.O. Aug. 2, 1968, concerning transitory provisions of the Law of 1966 (rectification Aug. 14, 1968); Law No. 69-12 of Jan. 6, 1969, J.O. Jan. 8, 1969, modifying 3 articles of the Law of 1966; Law No. 69-717 of July 8, 1969, J.O. July 1969, extending the deadline for the modification of company charters to conform to the Law of 1966; Ordinance No. 69-1176 of Dec. 20, 1969, modifying Law No. 66-537 of July 24, 1966, on commercial companies, J.O. Dec. 28, 1969; the last mentioned ordinance and a decree cited in the following note were designed to implement the First Directive on coordination of company law.

[73] The Decree No. 67-236 of Mar. 23, 1967, on commercial companies, J.O. (France) Mar. 24, 1967, was modified by the following measures: Decree No. 67-1112 of Dec. 19, 1967, J.O. Dec. 21, 1967 (added a paragraph to Art. 206); Decree No. 68-25 of Jan. 2, 1968, J.O. Jan. 13, 1968; Decree No. 68-857 of Oct. 3, 1968, J.O. Oct. 4, 1968; Decree No. 69-1177 of Dec. 24, 1969, J.O. Dec. 28, 1969, implementing the First Directive; Decree No. 29-1226 of Dec. 24, 1969, J.O. Dec. 21, 1969.

The important Decree No. 67-237 of Mar. 23, 1967, J.O. Mar. 24, 1967, concerning the commercial register, has been modified by the following: Decree No. 68-26 of Jan. 2, 1968, J.O. Jan. 13, 1968; Decree No. 68-109 of Feb. 2, 1968, J.O. Feb. 4, 1968; Decree No. 69-1108 of Dec. 5, 1969, J.O. Dec. 13, 1969; Decree No. 69-1177 of Dec. 24, 1969, J.O. Dec. 28, 1969, implementing the First Directive. See also arrêté ministériel of Dec. 5, 1969, J.O. Dec. 13, 1969, replacing an earlier arrêté, which specifies the data and documentation that must be submitted in support of an application for entry into the commercial register.

Another significant implementing measure is Decree No. 69-810 of Aug. 12, 1969, J.O. Aug. 29, 1969 (rectification in J.O. Sept. 12, 1969), concerning professional organization and status of auditors (commissaires aux comptes) of companies.

[74] Both stock companies (sociétés anonymes) and limited partnerships with shares (commendatory share companies, sociétés en

on a stock exchange) which must have a minimum capital of 500,000 francs (about $100,000) and small companies whose minimum capital must be 100,000 francs ($20,000)[75] and whose formation is subject to less stringent formalities. In a limited liability company, the number of associates is limited to a maximum of 50 in order to avoid "multiplicity of membership" which leads to an undesirable "predominance" by a group of associates.[76] However, since no other Member State of the European Community sets a maximum limit for the capital of this company (only Spain and Switzerland do so in Europe) the new law also eschews such requirement.[77] The major limited liability companies must appoint at least one auditor (*commissaire aux comptes*) but the supervisory council required under the 1925 law was abolished. Again, in order to increase legal certainty and "taking into account the legislation of the states of the Community [that is, the Federal Republic and Italy] and the views of certain French authors," the new law provides that any commercial company acquires legal personality only when it is registered in the commercial register. Under the old law the company's legal personality came into ex-

---

commandite par actions). The Senate voted to abolish the latter but the Assembly did not agree. Limited partnerships with shares resemble limited partnerships in that some members are liable for firm's debts, while others are not, but they differ from limited partnerships in their power to issue transferable shares. They have had a historical role as precursors of the modern stock company and limited liability company. *See* Conard, *Organizing for Business* at 50, n.69, giving the various national names in the Member-State laws.

[75] Art. 71. Art. 72 provides: "Companies are deemed to make a public offering if their securities are entered on the official list of a stock exchange (and are so deemed from the date of entry), or if they have recourse either to banks, financial institutions, or stockbrokers [*agents de change*], or use any publicity device whatever for the placement of any kind of securities." (Translation by Abelman, revised by Sieklucka, edited by Conard, University of Michigan Law School, Student edition, 1967.)

[76] PROJET DE LOI, EXPOSÉ DES MOTIFS, *supra* note 58, at 6.

[77] *Id.* at 7. The minimum capital is fixed at 20,000 francs. Art. 35 of the Law of July 24, 1966.

istence immediately upon its constitution and without any further formality such as entry into a register.[78]

2. The shareholders' protection is extended, among others, by granting a minority recourse to the court with a view to obtaining recall or replacement of an auditor[79] or appointment by the court of an *ad hoc* expert[80]—an innovation inspired in part by German law. Generally, the new law increases the professional prerequisites for auditors and seeks to broaden substantially their role and responsibility. Whereas before 1966 their function was merely to "verify" the financial statements, they are now required to "certify" that the statements offer a "true and fair view" of the company's affairs (*certifient la régularité et la sincérité*) which presumably requires a more thorough examination.[81] Again, the company administration is required to forward certain documents and information to the shareholders[82] in order to give them a better insight into the company's affairs.

3. The protection of third parties who deal with the company is also enhanced. Although, as I mentioned earlier, the proposal for judicial supervision over the formation of companies was defeated, the final text requires the found-

---

[78] Art. 5 of the Law of July 24, 1966. *Id.* at 4. *Cf.* Ducouloux-Favard, *Avec le nouveau régime des sociétés commerciales, le droit français s'est-il rapproché du droit italien?*, 1967 RIVISTA DELLE SOCIETÀ 1357, at 1367. The author suggests that this innovation is a step away from the "old Napoleonic notion of a company as a contract" but this has been questioned. For other measures designed to increase certainty and security see Arts. 6, 480, 7.

[79] Art. 225. *Cf.* § 137 German Stock Company Law of 1937, § 163 par. 2 German Law of 1965.

[80] Art. 226. This solution was included in the proposal of M. Pleven; HEURTEUX, L'INFORMATION DES ACTIONNAIRES ET DES ÉPARGNANTS; ÉTUDE COMPARATIVE (Paris 1961); Rengade, *Les mesures spéciales d'information requises des sociétés dont les actions sont cotées en Bourse (Décret No. 65-999 du 29 nov. 1965)*, 1965 JUR.-CL. PÉR. DOCTR. 1966.

[81] Arts. 218, 228.

[82] Art. 162, supplemented by Arts. 138, 139 of the Decree No. 67-236. *See also* Arts. 356-357 on subsidiaries and holdings.

ers of a company formally to affirm that they have complied with all the legal prerequisites; and the former system under which a company could be considered invalid ("null and void," the so-called system of "nullities") was replaced in substantial measure by arrangements which enable the company to cure the defects.[83] Third party protection was further improved by a somewhat clearer definition of the powers of the company's organ entitled to act on its behalf and by the provision precluding the company from relying, in relation to outsiders, on restrictions upon the power of representation written into the company charter. In these areas, as we shall see, the radiation of the first Community directive is clearly visible.

4. Criminal penalties for disregarding the specified rules concerning formation and functioning of companies are consolidated and extended.[84]

5. New or modified provisions concern the preparation and disclosure of financial statements[85] and certain types of securities. Finally, in a substantial measure the reform fills the gap in the French law on statutory merger ("fusion") but it includes only a few rules on subsidiaries, holdings and reciprocal holdings.

(vii) The new, two-tier system: how much employee "participation"?

As a major innovation, the new law introduces a German-type, two-tiered administration, consisting of an executive board (*directoire*) and a supervisory council (*conseil de surveillance*), not as the exclusive stock company form but as an added optional alternative to the existing system, a single-tier administrative council with the president-general manager.[86] This change may prove a significant aspect of the

---

83 On the modifications in response to the First Directive on co-ordination see p. 304 *infra*.

84 Arts. 423-489.

85 *See* p. 255 *infra*.

86 Arts. 118-150. It must be kept in mind that there are significant differences between the German and the new French two-tier

French reform from the viewpoint of assimilation of law in the Community. The new form, which allows for a sharp distinction between the functions of management and representation on the one hand and supervision on the other, was inserted in the bill at the stage of the parliamentary proceeding only. The initiative came from the left wing of the ruling Gaullist party led by M. René Capitant, the chairman of the lower chamber's Law Committee, whose amendment (offered jointly with M. Le Douarec) was adopted by the National Assembly and substantially modified in the Senate.[87] Some support for the new form was based on the argument that it would encourage German companies familiar with it to organize subsidiaries in France. But the principal motivation of its protagonists was the hope that they would be able to press the assimilation toward the German model a step further and include in the new supervisory council not only the representatives of the shareholders but of the workers as well. This expectation, however, has not materialized. In fact, the Assembly rejected even a last minute amendment, offered by M. Capitant and accepted by the Government, to the effect that the new supervisory council and the "plant committee" ("*comité d'entreprise*,") an employees' committee organized on the enterprise level to advise on the problems of the enterprise,[88] "may constitute mixed commissions of equal representation [from

---

systems. In French law, shareholders retain most of their prerogatives and the auditors (*commissaires aux comptes*) also preserve all their powers and duties.

[87] Hémard, *La réforme des sociétés* at 141. For a discussion of the advantages and disadvantages of the two-tier system, based on German experience see p. 335 *infra*.

[88] Ordinance of Feb. 22, 1945, amended by Law No. 46-1065 of May 16, 1946, and Law No. 66-247 of June 18, 1966. Under the current law two members of the comité d'entreprise may attend the sessions of the administrative council of stock companies in an advisory capacity. The comité d'entreprise is entitled to receive the balance sheet, the statement of profit and loss, and the reports of the auditors and of the administrative council, and it may convene the auditors to obtain their explanation of the documents.

the two bodies] to examine all questions relating to the conduct of the enterprise" and eventually to hold joint meetings.[89] In support of his amendment M. Capitant argued that under the already prevailing law two representatives of the plant committee may attend the meetings of the administrative council in an advisory capacity, and that a bill was pending before the Parliament which would extend this arrangement to the new supervisory council.[90] However, even a Socialist deputy spoke against the amendment on the ground that the matter should be considered in the context of the "reform of the enterprise" rather than as a part of the company law reform.[91]

In August 1967, the Government enacted three ordinances designed to create a worker's *legal right* to "participation" in a portion of an enterprise's profits that is reinvested for expansion purposes, with a corollary substantial tax benefit for the enterprise. Any enterprise with more than 100 employees, regardless of the nature of its activity or of its organizational form, is subject to the new arrangement.[92]

---

[89] Assemblée Nationale, Séance June 10, 1966, Débats parlementaires, [1966] J.O. (June 11) at 1940. On the problem generally see *Workers Participation in Management in France: The Basic Problems*, COUNTRY STUDIES SERIES NO. 3, in INTERNATIONAL INSTITUTE FOR LABOUR STUDIES, 1969 Bull. 54-99 (No. 6, June 1969).

[90] A bill was introduced in the Parliament that would authorize two representatives of the plant committee to attend the sessions of the new supervisory council. M. Capitant, Assemblée Nationale, Séance June 10, 1966, Débats parlementaires, [1966] J.O. (June 11) at 1940.

[91] M. Germain, *id.* at 1941.

[92] Ordinances No. 67-693, 67-694, and 67-695 of Aug. 17, 1967. The last-mentioned ordinance modified the new 1966 law on commercial companies which prohibited a company to acquire its own shares except for the purpose of reducing its capital for reasons other than losses (Art. 217). The new ordinance which was followed by implementing decrees allows purchase by the company of its own shares also for the purpose of "workers' participation." J.O. Aug. 18, 1967. The evolution in this direction began as early as 1955. See also Art. 33 of Law No. 65-566 of July 12, 1965, J.O. July 13, 1965. For explanation see a pamphlet by the Ministry of Economy and Finance, Information Service, La participation des salariés aux fruits de l'expansion des entreprises—S.1. Mesures nouvelles, *Trésor-Impôts*, Diffusion 12-67-3. *See also* Rapport de la Commission d'Étude du problème des droits des salariés

These legal texts came into effect on January 8, 1968, and subsequently were extended to employees of some 30 state-owned enterprises. However, some felt that thus far a relatively small number of firms concluded the required agreements with the workers concerning the terms of the "participation," and organized labor's attitude is reported to range "from indifference to hostility."[93] In defending the program against those who "affect to discredit or minimize its importance," President Pompidou indicated in September 1969, that during the first year of its active application, agreements involving some 4,000 firms and two million workers had been negotiated, with many more to be signed before the end of 1969.[94]

---

sur l'accroissement des actifs dû à l'autofinancement, July 1966, Rapport synthèse des travaux, Annexes. The Commission was chaired by M. Raymond Mathey, conseiller maître à la Cour des comptes. Savatier, *Die neue französische Gesetzgebung über die Beteiligung der Arbeiter am Unternehmensgewinn,* 1968 RECHT DER ARBEIT 215.

Cf. § 71 par. 1 (2) of the German Stock Company Law of 1965 which allows a stock company to acquire its own shares for the purpose of offering to sell them to employees. The provision is to make acquisition by employees possible at a price favorable to them. A more far-reaching provision which would have authorized issue of shares to employees gratis upon capital increase out of "company means" was not adopted.

[93] Gerwitz, *French Widen 1967 Plan to Share Profits,* Int'l Herald Tribune, March 25, 1969, p. 7, col. 1; Farnsworth, *Renault Workers Indifferent to Stock-Sharing Plan,* New York Times, Jan. 16, 1970, p. 2 C, col. 3-6.

[94] Le Monde, Sélection hebdomadaire—From Thursday, Sept. 18 to Wednesday, Sept. 24, 1969, La conférence de presse du Chef de l'État, p. 3, col. 3. In December 1969, the French Government approved a bill to extend the program to the 80,000 employees of the state-owned Renault automobile manufacturing company. Early newspaper reports indicated a reserved attitude on the part of Renault workers, "little different" from that of the Volkswagen employees who received preferential rights in a distribution in 1960. "German studies have found that the workers were mainly interested in selling out at the highest price. Few of the workers own Volkswagen shares today." Farnsworth, preceding note. See Gesetz über die Überführung der Anteilsrechte an der Volkswagenwerk Gesellschaft mit beschränkter Haftung in private Hand (Law on the Transfer of Rights of Participation in the Volkswagenwerk Limited Liability Company to Private Ownership) of July 21, 1960, [1960] BGBl I 585.

The policy of "participation" in all walks of life (schools, factories, government) emphasized after the traumatic disorders of May 1968 reopened the public debate of the workers' representation in company organs. The most articulate advocate of this policy, M. Capitant, was made Minister of Justice and he was represented as wanting "to contract into a single body the two main 'groups,' thus creating a cooperative society of salaried workers and the owners of capital." One observer commented that

> "[i]t really is astonishing to see the belief persisting in high places, where dreams circulate of nothing other than partnership between capital and workers, that legal texts can put an end to class strife."[95]

The problem in his view was to improve the flow of information in a company "from the top to the bottom" and to decentralize the authority, thus ending the "imperial system of management" reflecting the excessive centralization inherited from Napoleonic institutions. While rejecting changes that could impair the competitiveness of the industry, he suggests "a gradual imposition of converging solutions, throughout Europe," with the Economic and Social Committee of the EEC perhaps invited first to prepare a synthesis of the many ideas "in the wind."

In a widely discussed book published in 1963, Bloch-Lainé suggested that in a company a "college of directors" should have full powers to direct the management while a triangular "supervisory commission," consisting of representatives of shareholders, personnel and the government would exercise supervision.[96]

There is, however, no indication that the opposition on the part of the employers' groups to any radical structural

---

[95] Drouin, *Death Knell for Imperial System of Company Management in France,* Le Monde, English ed. July 11-July 17, 1968, p. 4.

[96] BLOCH-LAINÉ, POUR UNE RÉFORME DE L'ENTREPRISE at 73-74 (Paris 1963). The book is based on a project initiated by Club Jean Moulin. *Id.* at 7.

modification has subsided and the French labor unions have shown little interest in, if not actual hostility toward, the German-type of "codetermination." It was above all General de Gaulle himself, with some of his Ministers, notably M. Capitant, who had favored workers' codetermination. M. Capitant left the Government and was replaced by the more conservative M. Pleven. The idea of "concertation" seems to have replaced "participation" in the jargon of the day. Since President Pompidou wants to broaden his majority by gaining support from the Center parties where codetermination is most unpopular, there seems to be little likelihood for the time being that the present, modest, advisory workers' participation will become in France a genuine codetermination.

(viii)   Changing French practice?

Of the 2187 *new* stock companies formed in 1968, 29 chose the new two-tier form, as did 13 of the 1256 companies newly established during the first six months of 1969; no corresponding figures are available for transformations of "old" companies into the new type.[97] However, according to one estimate, a total of some 300 companies, *old and new,* has adopted the new optional form thus far.[98] Many apparently are small family companies in which a shareholder, who owns a majority of the stock, often the head of the family, wants more independent power to run the enterprise without the constraints of the old line administrative council, and thus prefers a vague surveillance by the supervisory council.[99]

---

[97] I am indebted to the Association Nationale des Sociétés par Actions (A.N.S.A.) of Paris for making this information available to me. According to its letter of Aug. 29, 1969, the above figures were derived from a count of new stock companies mentioned in the *Bulletin Officiel des Annonces commerciales.*

[98] This estimate was suggested by Professor Houin.

[99] I am told that another feature that is proving attractive is the greater job security of the executive board members who, in contrast with the members of the old line administrative council or president, are entitled to indemnity if removed without just cause.

I was able to identify only two important companies, both in the banking sector, that have changed over to the new form. Of the two, of particular interest is the *Compagnie bancaire,* a powerful commercial banking concern which controls a number of other stock companies, each of which is engaged in a specialized field of banking.[100] The immediate impulse for the transformation of this company was the resignation of its founder from the all-powerful position of president-general manager. In the new scheme the former administrative council in effect became the supervisory council. In view of the relatively limited functions of this body, the departing founder was able to retain the chairmanship and thereby a measure of influence over the company. The new executive board, which in effect has replaced the president-general manager, is composed chiefly of the former principal executive officers of the company who held simultaneously important positions in the administration of the banking firms controlled by the *Compagnie bancaire.* The new arrangement was in part designed to avoid what would otherwise have been a delicate personnel problem of choosing the successor to the outgoing founder, and it was also to assure a greater "cohesion" within the group.[101]

On the basis of the present evidence, it certainly cannot be said that French practice has embraced the new system with enthusiasm, and it is much too early for offering any estimate of the future development. For one thing, it would take some time to overcome a built-in reluctance on the part of businessmen to take the risks of a new and untried institution. The second obstacle is due to the fact that until 1969, members of the new executive board (*directoire*) were treated as independent entrepreneurs rather than employees for tax and social security purposes and thus suffered serious dis-

---

[100] La Banque de Neuflize, Schlumberger, Mallet & Cie, is the other company.

[101] Le Monde, June 6, 1969 p. 18, col. 1-2; Allocution du Président, Assemblée Générale Ordinaire de la Compagnie bancaire en date du 8 Mai 1969.

advantages, as compared with the president-general manager and other executives in the old system. The change in the treatment, announced in early 1969, should encourage recourse to the new form. Finally, the concern persists among businessmen that a widespread adoption of the new system might stimulate new legislation on workers' representation in the supervisory council.

(d) The projected new commercial code in Belgium: toward a more "efficient" company structure

The present Belgian company law is contained in Title IX of the first book of the Commercial Code that was derived from the 1807 French Commercial Code. The original text was reshaped by the law of 1873 (again strongly influenced by the French law of 1867) which in turn has been repeatedly amended over the years.[102] Perhaps the most important innovation was the introduction in 1935 of the limited liability company following the example of France (1925) and Germany (1892). Despite its age, the present text, based on a 1935 consolidation, has been considered generally quite functional in the sense that it has provided a broad framework for the company associates to order their legal relationships in the company charter. The courts, the *Commission bancaire* and the legislature have helped provide some of the more urgent adjustments required by the changing business reality.[103] However, evolving ideas on the corporate role in modern economy and the declining confi-

---

[102] Particularly in 1913, 1919, 1934, 1935, 1953, 1958, 1961, 1962, 1967. The last over-all "consolidation" dates from 1935. Lois coordonnées sur les sociétés commerciales of Nov. 30, 1935, hereinafter referred to as Code de commerce. For an English translation see OSTERWEIL, BELGIAN COMPANY LAWS, CCH COMM. MKT. REP. No. 42, Oct. 25, 1966, Part I (Chicago 1966).

[103] On the Commission bancaire see *supra* p. 88, *infra* p. 265, and VAN RYN, 2 PRINCIPES DE DROIT COMMERCIAL at 345 (Brussels 1957). *See generally* Renauld, *Les travaux de réforme du droit des sociétés par actions en Belgique et le projet italien*, 1967 RIVISTA DELLE SOCIETÀ 218, 219; *see also* L. & S. FRÉDÉRICQ, 1 HANDBOEK VAN BELGISCH HANDELSRECHT (Brussels 1962).

dence in the often abused limited liability company form brought forth voices calling for a more fundamental revision of such features as the all-powerful shareholders' meeting, the cumbersome French-type administrative council and the inadequate supervision by the auditors.[104]

(i)   The "technicians'" Commission of 44

The current reform undertaking contemplates a comprehensive revision of the entire commercial code, including a new codification of the provisions governing all types of companies. Although a new form, a "company with a variable capital" (*société à capital variable*), is introduced on the French pattern, the principal thrust of the proposed reform is directed at the stock and limited liability companies. As for the other types of companies, the new text would essentially incorporate the present provisions as they have been interpreted by the courts.

A Commission for the Revision of the Law on Commercial Companies was established in 1951.[105] In January 1952, the Minister of Justice, Mr. Moyersoen, appointed no less than 44 members to it.[106] Again, lawyers are in an overwhelming majority but, in contrast with the Dutch Verdam Commission, the only political figure of a national repute is the Chairman, Mr. Paul Struye, a prominent member of the Christian Social Party and President of the Senate.[107] The political affiliation of most of the other members is not known and few of them are actually members of a political party. Law professors, drawn carefully in almost

---

[104] On the 1953 amendment dealing with the financial documents and special auditors see VAN RYN, 1 PRINCIPES DE DROIT COMMERCIAL at 425 ff. (Brussels 1954); VAN OMMESLAGHE, LE RÉGIME at 129 ff.; *see also* VAN RYN, 2 PRINCIPES DE DROIT COMMERCIAL at 4.

[105] Arreté Royal of Oct. 19, 1951.

[106] One member died and apparently was not replaced.

[107] Mr. Struye belongs also to the select group of attorneys admitted to practice before the Supreme Court (avocat à la Cour de cassation).

equal proportion from the Free (non-Catholic) University at
Brussels and the Catholic University at Louvain,[108] and
practicing attorneys[109] provide the largest two groups; they
are followed by judges,[110] representatives of banking,[111]
industry,[112] and the Ministry of Justice.[113] The Commission
did its work in six sections, each dealing with one or more
company forms, and only certain basic questions were considered in the plenary Commission. As is usually the case,
only some (fewer than twenty) members did their full share
of the work, a dozen participated in some measure, with the
remaining more than a dozen a total loss.[114] The drafting
task was completed for all practical purposes in 1969, and
in 1970, the text was in the process of final review before
the Conseil d'État.[115]

(ii) Accent on the comparative method

Perhaps more than any other national legislation, the
Belgian Commission's proposals are based on, and "inspired"
by, a systematic comparison with other legal systems, including, in the first place, the laws of the other Member
States of the Community. This is due in no small measure to

[108] Four professors from the Free University at Brussels, five from
the University of Louvain, one from the University of Liège. Most of
these also practice law or hold other positions in banking or industry.

[109] Nine members.

[110] Six members including one prosecutor.

[111] Five members including two technical advisors, apparently not
lawyers.

[112] Two members connected with the Federation of Belgian Industries and a counsel of the Société Générale de Belgique.

[113] Three officials. Other members include one official each from
the Ministry of Economic Affairs and the Ministry of Agriculture, a
notary, a reviseur d'entreprise (accountant), an official of the Commission bancaire, the Secretary General of the Center for Studies of
Companies, an Inspecteur général des Finances, and a legal advisor of
the EEC Commission.

[114] The last group included more than one-half of all the judges,
three of the professors, and the official of the Ministry of Economics.

[115] The original series of some twenty documents prepared by the
sections of the Commission was consolidated into a single text.

the personal influence of a tiny group of able comparative-oriented legal scholars who, in addition to teaching law, engage in successful transnational law practice on behalf of major Belgian and foreign industrial and financial interests. It obviously was no accident that the best known scholars in *comparative* commercial and civil law (such men as Professors van Ryn, Heenen, Limpens, van Ommeslaghe) have been appointed to the Commission and have been perhaps the most active members of that body. The crucial section on "stock companies" was chaired by Professor van Ryn; his associate in law practice and colleague at the Brussels Law Faculty, Professor van Ommeslaghe, known for his comparative study of patterns of company administration,[116] and Professor Heenen of the same faculty who also serves as a house counsel for a large bank, played prominent parts.[117] The Belgian government has evidently encouraged the outward look—a logical position for a country whose foreign trade represents some 40% of the national product.

Mr. Paul Leleux, the senior legal advisor in the EEC Commission in charge of company law matters, a Belgian national and former member of the Brussels Bar, has been also a member of the Belgian Commission, and that Commission's work became geared quite closely to the Community effort at an early date. The Belgian experts have been instrumental in offering compromise solutions in the various Community fora[118] and, conversely, several provisions in the new Belgian text were actually inspired by the Community drafts, for instance, the article denying the company the possibility of invoking, as against a third party, a restriction on its organs contained in its charter.[119]

----

116 Van Ommeslaghe, Le régime.

117 The representative of the Commission bancaire also played an important role.

118 *But see* Lutter, Die GmbH in Belgien, Gesellschaftsrecht und Steuerrecht at 27 (Köln 1966).

119 *See* p. 292 *infra*. Prof. Jacques Heenen, in addition to teaching commercial law and commercial comparative law at the Free Univer-

Generally speaking, the Belgian draft is largely a compromise between the newly reformed French law and the German system; but it introduces the German two-tiered administration not as an optional alternative but as the exclusive organizational structure for a stock company. The leading members of the reform Commission were so convinced of the virtues of the German system that they did not want to give company founders any choice.

In the spring of 1968, following the adoption of the first coordination directive by the EEC Council of Ministers, a special three-man Commission of professors was formed in Belgium for the specific purpose of assisting the officials of the Ministry of Justice in the drafting of a law that would implement the directive in Belgian law. This task was made more difficult by the fact that, whereas the directive applies only to certain specified company forms, the general provisions of the Belgian code deal with all the company forms.

---

sity of Brussels, has been in charge of the legal department of the Société Générale de Banque in Brussels since 1953, presently with the title of Director. He has been president of the Legal Committee of the Fédération Bancaire de la C.E.E. since 1963, has served as an expert appointed by the Belgian Government on the EEC working group "54(3)g," has been president of one section and member of two other sections of the Belgian national Commission for revision of company law. He also has been a member of the Benelux Commission for the study of unification of the law.

Prof. Pierre van Ommeslaghe teaches civil law, also at the Free University, and practices law in Brussels. He served as a government-appointed expert on the working group "54(3)g" and on the Belgian delegation in the negotiation of Conventions under EEC Art. 220. Since 1966 he has been special consultant of the EEC Commission on company law. He was a member of the Belgian national Commission for revision of company law, and since 1968 has served as an expert assisting the Government of Luxembourg in the reform of Luxembourg company law.

Prof. Jean van Ryn has taught at the Free University of Brussels in the field of commercial law since 1938. He has been in law practice as avocat à la Cour d'Appel and avocat à la Cour de Cassation and has served as a government expert on EEC working groups on company laws. He was president of the important section on stock companies of the Belgian national Commission on revision of company law. He is the author, with Prof. Heenen, of the basic multi-volume treatise on Belgian commercial law.

(iii)   The stock company: basic approach—no "codetermination"!

Effective management combined with effective supervision were the Commission's basic, twin objectives. General custom, new practices, business needs, protection of the various interests and the necessity to correct existing abuses were taken into account.[120] The Commission did not feel called upon to study in depth the relationship between capital and labor, and having received various opinions on the subject and weighed foreign experience, it rejected the idea of workers' representation in company organs. Would not the workers' representatives be looked upon as intruders with the result that important deliberations would take place outside the particular organ? Moreover, the Commission opined, the character of the stock company as an institution of private law would be entirely undermined. Instead, the present "plant council" (*conseil d'entreprise*) at the plant level, a body separate and independent from company organs, was viewed as the first step in the right direction toward capital-labor cooperation; and the competence of this institution could be extended, the Commission believed, without tampering with the structure of the company.[121]

The stock company form should be available only to undertakings of certain importance. To this end, a minimum capital requirement is imposed (one million Belgian francs, $20,000), the two-tiered system of administration introduced, the liability of the organs broadened, the qualifications of auditors made more demanding, and the disclosure obligation made more stringent by detailed rules on financial statements and by extending the powers of the *Commission bancaire*. The lawmaker would thus compel about one-half of all the existing stock companies to assume another form of organization. There is to be no special regime for family-owned or close stock company since they can choose the

---

[120] *See generally* LOEB-MAYER, LE PATRONAT INDUSTRIAL BELGE ET LA CEE (Bruxelles 1965).

[121] On the plant council see GARCIN, COGESTION ET PARTICIPATION at 281 ff.

limited liability company form which is designed to suit
their purpose.

(iv) Stock company: some specific modifications

1. The Commission decided not to follow the German
and Italian pattern of judicial control over the formation of
the company and, instead, to retain the present requirement
of a notarial instrument (*acte authentique*) for this purpose,
a position also strongly defended by the Belgian delegation
in the EEC. However, the minimum prescribed number
of incorporators was reduced to two, and a stock company
acting alone would be able to incorporate a subsidiary; this
would be the first and only instance within the EEC orbit
where a "one man" company could be organized initially by
a single shareholder. Acquisition of all shares by a single
shareholder would no longer cause automatic dissolution
but would render him liable jointly with the company.[122]

2. The Anglo-American concept of "authorized capital"
is accepted so that new shares may be issued (albeit within a
specified time limitation) without recourse to the cumbersome charter-amendment process.

3. German law has served as the model for the modification of the company's organizational structure—perhaps the
most important feature of the proposal.[123] The present law
authorizes delegation by the administrative council (*conseil
d'administration*) of day-to-day business only;[124] in practice
a *comité de direction* is entrusted with the direction of the
business in disregard of this provision; the council convenes
only from time to time to check on, rather than direct the
management.[125] The reform in effect embraces this practice
in that it requires the constitution of an executive organ

---

[122] On the "one man" company in the EEC generally see p. 327
infra.

[123] For a comparative survey see Renauld, *Les travaux de réforme,*
1967 RIVISTA DELLE SOCIETÀ 218, at 225.

[124] CODE DE COMMERCE Art. 63.

[125] VAN OMMESLAGHE, LE RÉGIME at 428, 450.

(*administrateurs gérants*) and of a supervisory council (*conseil du surveillance*). The executive is no longer removable at will but it is more effectively supervised, in view of the organic division between managerial and supervisory functions and personnel. The proposal deviates somewhat from the German model in that it would require the executive to obtain the consent of the supervisory council on questions of general policy.[126] Still in line with the German law, the principle of the general competence of the shareholders' meeting,[127] the "sick organ" of the stock company, is abandoned as unworkable in view of the indifference of the shareholders,[128] and the shareholders' meeting is left with only such powers as are expressly conferred upon it by the charter or by the law, including (contrary to German law) the power to remove the executive; the power to appoint the executive is with the supervisory council.[129] This hybrid solution suggests perhaps that the reformers were not yet ready to jetison entirely the ancient "mandate" theory of a legal person.[130]

4. As a further improvement, the *ultra vires* doctrine is curtailed; in conformity with the first EEC directive,[131] the company is bound by transactions exceeding its charter purpose vis-à-vis a third party acting in good faith.

5. The protection of minority shareholders is strengthened by giving the minority the right to sue the management

---

126 § 111, par. 4, of the German Stock Company Law of 1965 states that managerial functions cannot be delegated to the supervisory council but makes it possible only to provide in the charter that *specified types of transactions* (*e.g.*, acquisition of interest in another company, real estate transactions) may require approval by the supervisory council.

127 CODE DE COMMERCE Art. 70.

128 VAN RYN, 1 PRINCIPES DE DROIT COMMERCIAL at 381.

129 "By law" the shareholders' meeting has also the power to decide on the balance sheet, to appoint and remove the supervisory council, to approve the management's accounts, and to make "constitutional" decisions regarding the company.

130 *See* p. 286 *infra*. *See also* VAN RYN, 1 PRINCIPES DE DROIT COMMERCIAL at 380-81.

131 *See* p. 289 *infra*.

on behalf of the company, and by voiding contractual obligations to vote in accordance with instructions and acts
constituting an abuse of majority power (*détournement de
pouvoir*) in the shareholders' meeting.

6. The existing rudimentary provisions concerning the
financial statements[132] are supplemented by more detailed
rules, including certain valuation principles developed by
courts. Following the French example, bondholders' rights
vis-à-vis the company are also strengthened. Convertible
bonds have been authorized since 1962, and now the Anglo-
American warrants (*bons de subscription*) and the German-
type non-voting preferred stock are also added as available
types of securities.

7. The proposal contains the first statutory treatment of
mergers in Belgian law, but in the field of "related companies" (in the sense of the German *Konzernrecht*) it is spotty:
the rules on holdings deal only with the more striking instances of abuse to the prejudice of the shareholders or
creditors of the controlled company,[133] and there is no
provision for consolidated financial statements. However,
holding of 10% or more of the shares in another company
must be reported—a percentage advocated unsuccessfully,
as we have seen, by the Social Democrats in Germany but
applicable in France and in the United States.

(v) Other companies

Statistics suggest that the Belgian law governing the limited liability company form has served its purpose of offering
an organizational shell for close or family undertakings,[134]
although the incidence of bankruptcies has been high. An
earlier law had already sought to improve their credit-

---

132 CODE DE COMMERCE Arts. 77-80.

133 *E.g.*, prohibition of acquiring the parent company's shares and
of reciprocal holdings above 10%.

134 In 1965, there were in Belgium about 31,000 limited liability
companies, as compared with 18,000 stock companies. LUTTER, DIE
GMBH IN BELGIEN at 4.

worthiness by raising the minimum capital figure to 250,000 Belgian francs ($5,000)[135] and requiring valuation by a court appointed *"reviseur d'entreprise,"* as is prescribed for stock companies.[136] The reform proposal carries this objective further by adding new instances of personal liability of the founder and the managing associate in the event of bankruptcy. The second objective of the reform is to facilitate the process of transformation of stock companies into limited liability companies that will become necessary, as was explained earlier, when the new stock company provisions are adopted, and for this purpose the existing limitation on the number of associates in a limited liability company is dropped (in contrast with the new French law) and the transfer of quotas ("parts") in that company is made easier.[137] Finally, numerous rules heretofore applicable to stock companies only are extended to these companies (financial statements, obligatory auditors, merger provisions).

Newly introduced into Belgian law is the company with a variable capital—a combination between the stock company, limited liability company, and a cooperative—whose capital in excess of the prescribed minimum figure may be varied without a charter change.[138] It may be suited, provided

---

[135] *See* Art. 1 of the Law of June 26, 1967.

[136] Art. 2 of the Law of June 26, 1967, and Art. 29 bis of the Code de commerce (Art. 1, Law of June 30, 1961).

[137] At present, transfer to outsiders requires consent of the other associates; the proposed text gives them an acquisition option only in conformity with German law.

[138] The capital in a "cooperative company" is also "variable" but the new law restricts the use of that company to an undertaking which pursues a profit objective of its members rather than its own. This restriction appears to be the reason for introducing the new type of "mixed" company. It must set a minimum capital which can be reduced by charter amendment to the obligatory minimum amount of 250,000 Belgian francs ($5,000). The capital in excess of this minimum amount is "variable." It may be increased by subscription or reduced by withdrawal of an associate. The "parts" are all registered in the name of the associates and cannot be transferred, even by succession, unless the charter allows it. The charter may require the associates to contribute new capital. The company may choose either the stock company or the limited liability company organizational structure.

it becomes acceptable credit risk, for enterprises involving a personal element but could also serve as a substitute for small stock companies that will be required to reorganize into another form.

(e) The projected reform of stock company and limited liability company law in Italy: an "opening to the left"?

The Italian Commercial Code of 1882, which contained the company law, was based on French law. The new text in the Civil Code of 1942 took German law into account but in some respects it adopted new solutions.[139]

(i) The controversial innovating ideas

The problem of reforming commercial company law in Italy was posed on the governmental level in connection with certain new ideas on safeguarding competition. For this reason, it was the Minister of Industry and Commerce, Sig. Colombo, who took the initiative in December 1959, and appointed a Commission of experts, with Professor Francesco Santoro-Passarelli as chairman. Because of the special focus of its task and the brief deadline, the Commission decided to limit its study to a reform of stock companies listed on stock exchanges.[140] This Commission's report,[141] completed

---

[139] CODICE CIVILE of March 16, 1942, Book V, Titles V, VI, VII, XI (Arts. 2247-2554, 2621-2642 supplemented by Arts. 99-107, 109, 204-219). A number of special laws has been adopted after the effective date of the Code.

For a translation into English see THE ITALIAN CIVIL CODE, Translated by Beltramo, Longo, Merryman (Dobbs Ferry, N.Y. 1969). The Codice civile was modified by the Decree of the President No. 1127 of Dec. 29, 1969, implementing the First Directive, GAZZ. UFF. No. 35, Feb. 2, 1970, at 782.

[140] Officially, Sig. Colombo was the chairman and Prof. Santoro-Passarelli presided in his stead. Other members of the Commission were the Chief of the Legislative Office in the Ministry of Industry, the Chief of the Minister's Cabinet, a member of the Consiglio di Stato, the Directors General for Industrial Production and for Internal Commerce and seven professors. LA RIFORMA DELLE SOCIETÀ DI CAPITALI IN ITALIA, PROGETTI E DOCUMENTI at 31 (Milano 1966). Circolare N. 183, Associazione fra le Società Italiane per Azioni, Rome, July 27, 1965.

[141] LA RIFORMA 1966, at 31-49. For a brief reference to American

in 1961 but kept secret until 1964, disclosed a basic difference of opinion on the two principal innovating ideas, that
is, *first,* whether the college of auditors (*collegio sindacale*) of
the large companies, which is now elected by the shareholders' meeting, should instead be appointed by a public body,
in order to assure better protection for small stockholders;
and *second,* whether a new type of non-voting share (later
dubbed the investor share, *azione di risparmio*)[142] should be
created. The report does not mention the EEC or the coordination effort in Brussels.

A second attempt at drafting a reform proposal was made
outside the government, within the Association of Italian
Stock Companies. Finally, when it became generally accepted that the scope of the reform should be broadened,
the responsibility was transferred to the Ministry of Justice,
and it was that Ministry, acting in concert with the Ministry
of Industry and Commerce, that appointed a new commission of officials and professors early in 1964, under the
chairmanship of Professor Alfredo de Gregorio.[143] This
Commission was directed to prepare a draft that would align
and "integrate" the stock company and limited liability company law and make it conform to the governmental "programmatic agreement," presented to the Parliament in 1963

---

law in the report of the Santoro-Passarelli Commission see *id.* at 48;
see generally Sassi, *La riforma della società per azioni sotto il profilo
tecnico-aziendale,* 1967 RIVISTA DELLE SOCIETÀ 501.

142 Henrich, *Reformbestrebungen im italienischen Aktienrecht,*
1964 DIE AKTIENGESELLSCHAFT 275. On the possible impact of the 1959
German "small reform" on the Italian stock company law see Mengoni, *La rappresentanza dei soci nell'assemblea secondo il progetto
tedesco di riforma della legge sulla società per azioni,* 1961 RIVISTA
DELLE SOCIETÀ 303. Prof. Mengoni was a member of the Commission.

143 The new Commission was composed of professors and officials
designated by the Ministers of Justice, Industry, Budget, Finance,
Treasury (Tesoro), and the Bank of Italy. A number of these members,
including Prof. Santoro-Passarelli, were previously members of the first
Commission. LA RIFORMA 1966, at 50. In Italy, the Ministry of the
Treasury is in charge of government expenditures, the Ministry of
Finance deals with government revenues through taxation, and the
Ministry of the Budget is to perform a coordinating function.

by the first Moro government of the Center-Left coalition. The agreement which was approved by the Parliament in December 1963, embraced the innovating ideas supported by the majority of the Santoro-Passarelli Commission. In this manner the company law reform became a component of a new policy platform which, under the strong influence of the Socialist Party, envisaged among others the institution of economic planning ("programmation") machinery in the national government.[144]

In the course of 1964, the new Commission prepared a draft law of 130 articles which was modified somewhat by an Interministerial Committee chaired by Minister Piccioni, and published[145] together with the critical observations of the four dissenting members of the Commission[146] and an extensive explanatory report.[147] It is perhaps indicative that although this proposal also centered on strengthening the "guarantees" of the shareholders through such means as improved disclosure and flow of information which at the time was a primary subject of the work in Brussels, the lengthy government report contains not a single comment on the coordination work in the Community, not a single reference to the EEC Treaty or for that matter to the law of another state; nor is there any evidence that the Italian delegation in Brussels participated actively in the work on the national reform as was the case in France, the Federal Republic, the Netherlands, and Belgium.

(ii) The first reference to the EEC

The Minister of Justice submitted the modified draft to the National Council of Economy and Labor on July 15,

---

[144] For the text of the extract from the governmental "programmatic agreement" see LA RIFORMA 1966, at 3-4.

[145] 1966 RIVISTA DELLE SOCIETÀ 93 ff; LA RIFORMA 1966, at 51-104.

[146] 1966 RIVISTA DELLE SOCIETÀ at 397 ff; LA RIFORMA 1966, at 168-84.

[147] 1966 RIVISTA DELLE SOCIETÀ at 125 ff; LA RIFORMA 1966, at 105-67.

1965, and the Council rendered its opinion in January, 1966.[148] The opinion takes note of the trend, within and outside the Common Market, toward up-dating "the valuable instrument that is the stock company" and recognizes the need not only "to harmonize the company laws of the six countries," but also to provide a special "European" structure for companies, so as to facilitate their "autonomy in all the countries" as well as concentration and greater dimension.[149] It is perhaps not without significance that, in the extensive official documentation, the first references to the EEC appear in a document elaborated not by government officials or a ministerial commission, but by a consultative body of representatives of the various economic and social interest groups.[150] The opinion of the Council reflects in large measure the attitude of the industry, and it was influenced by the able staff member of the Association of Italian Stock Companies, dott. Gino De Gennaro, who was also a member of the De Gregorio Commission and who lectures at the Rome University law faculty.

Subsequently, the draft law was expanded to 150 articles and substantially reworked by a high-level Interministerial Committee composed of the Minister of Justice (Republican Party), Minister of Finance (Socialist Party), the Minister of Budget (Socialist Party), the Minister of Industry and Commerce (Christian Democratic Party), the Governor of the Bank of Italy, the Accountant General, an official of the Ministry of Finance, a representative of the Association of Italian Stock Companies, the chairman of the board of Olivetti and two law professors. In redrafting the text, the Interministerial Committee took into account a plethora of comments and suggestions offered by individuals, special interest groups and conferences, including particularly the

---

148 *Parere del Consiglio Nazionale dell 'Economia e del Lavoro,* in LA RIFORMA 1966, at 185-248.

149 LA RIFORMA 1966, at 196, 198-99. *See also* 226, 230.

150 For the composition of the Council see Art. 2 of the Law No. 33 of Jan. 5, 1957.

International Conference on Studies Concerning the Reform of Stock Companies, held in Venice in October of
1966.[151] It was this Conference that provided a unique forum
for a confrontation of the Italian reform with comparable
undertakings not only in the other members of the EEC but
also in Switzerland, the United Kingdom, and Spain.

The Interministerial Committee accepted only some and
rejected other suggestions made by the National Council of
Economy and Labor; most of these suggestions were directed toward mitigating government control and preserving
greater management discretion.[152]

(iii) Accent on policy

Because of the link to the governmental program, the
company law reform has been viewed, more consciously
than in the other EEC countries, as a problem of national
economic and political policy. But as in the other countries,
the central consideration reflected in the reports appears to
be the emergence of the large enterprise, organized for
mass production and drawing on public savings, in which
the management is divorced from the mass of absentee shareholders. Existing means of protection for the individual
shareholder are to be strengthened and new forms of such
protection become necessary in large enterprises and in the
new investment and financing organizations.[153] With this
stated purpose in view, the current draft would introduce a
variety of more or less radical modifications:

---

151 *Il movimento di riforma della società per azioni in Europa*,
1967 RIVISTA DELLE SOCIETÀ 1-307. FONGHI & SANTA MARIA (eds.),
LA RIFORMA DELLE SOCIETÀ DI CAPITALI IN ITALIA-STUDI E DIBATTITI, ATTI
DEL CONVEGNO INTERNAZIONALE DI STUDI SULLA RIFORMA DELLA SOCIETÀ
PER AZIONI, Venezia, 6-7-8 ottobre 1966 (3 vols. Milan 1968).

152 For the text of the Interministerial Committee's report and
modified draft law see 1967 RIVISTA DELLE SOCIETÀ 353-69 and 370-437
respectively. This is the latest text of the reform thus far.

153 *See, e.g.*, the report (relazione) of the De Gregorio Commission,
in LA RIFORMA 1966, at 105-06; Opinion of the National Council of
Economy and Labor in 1966 RIVISTA DELLE SOCIETÀ at 190.

1. In order to avoid the abuse of the limited liability privilege by non-productive undertakings, the freedom of choosing the forms in which an enterprise may be organized is substantially reduced. A clear distinction is drawn between operating and holding companies,[154] and companies listed on the stock exchange are made subject to a special legal regime. Since the number of shareholders in the limited liability company is limited to 25,[155] major enterprises would in effect be compelled to assume the form of a stock company. New minimum capital levels, reflecting the current value of the lira, are set at 100 and 10 million lire (approximately $161,000 and $16,100) for the stock company and limited liability company respectively.[156] In the same vein, in order to reduce the discretionary powers of the management, the articles of incorporation must define the charter purpose with "specificity," and, in the case of the stock company, the purpose must involve production or trade or supply of services.[157] A court may order dissolution of a company if it exceeds its charter purpose but the company cannot invoke the *ultra vires* character of a transaction as against third parties.[158]

2. With the exceptions made for holding and investment companies, the freedom of one company to acquire stock in another is strictly limited, even though the National Council of Economy and Labor dissented sharply and its dissent was shared by the Governor of the Bank of Italy and the

---

[154] Tax penalties are imposed, contrary to the advice from the National Council of Economy and Labor, in case an operating company fails to engage in an entrepreneurial activity.

[155] Art. 58 of the draft modified by the Interministerial Committee, 1967 RIVISTA DELLE SOCIETÀ at 397.

[156] Arts. 2 and 57, *id.* at 370 and 397. The 1942 minima were 1 million and 50,000 respectively. The new levels are considerably higher than those existing or proposed in the other EEC states.

[157] This excludes for instance a group venture for building apartment houses for rental to members of the group. Houin, *Le projet italien,* 1967 RIVISTA DELLE SOCIETÀ 148, at 151.

[158] Art. 1, 1967 RIVISTA DELLE SOCIETÀ at 370.

Christian-Democratic Minister of Industry and Commerce.[159]
Similarly, the 1942 rule limiting reciprocal participations[160]
and designed to avoid the watering-down of the company
capital is made substantially stricter by devices considered
more effective than those employed in the new French law
for the same purpose.[161]

3. Except in the case of banks and insurance companies,
it is no longer possible to include in a company charter a
provision requiring the consent of the company's administrative council or shareholders' meeting for any transfer
of stock by its shareholders.[162]

4. A series of proposed modifications aims at enabling
the shareholders to exercise their rights more effectively:

(a) The content of the financial statements is made more
specific, complete reports on the administration are required,
the disclosure requirement is increased (*e.g.*, holdings of ten
percent or more have to be reported), and the minimum
number of shareholders entitled to call a shareholders' meeting is reduced.

(b) In Italy, as in Germany, shares are as a rule deposited
with banks which play a controlling role in shareholders'
meetings. These banks obtain proxies from their depositors
and apparently vote the shares often in the interest of the
management which for them is an important clientele.[163]
The draft, again contrary to the opinion of the National
Council of Economy and Labor, severely confines the use of
proxies in major companies and prescribes penalties for the
violation of these rules. Some fear that these rules would
not compel the stockholders' attendance but rather would

---

[159] Relazione in LA RIFORMA 1966, at 355.

[160] Art. 2361 CODICE CIVILE.

[161] Houin, *Le projet italien* at 154.

[162] Art. 7, 1967 RIVISTA DELLE SOCIETÀ 372-73. *Compare* with Art.
275 of the French Law of July 24, 1966, offering a more flexible solution.

[163] Visentini, *Opinioni e discussioni sulla riforma delle società
per azioni,* 1967 RIVISTA DELLE SOCIETÀ 469, at 471, 477-78.

make it impossible to comply with the quorum requirement for the shareholders' meeting.[164]

(c) The action for annulment of a shareholders' meeting decision is no longer available to an individual shareholder and can be filed by a minimum quorum of shareholders only;[165] but the action is made more effective and an independent action for damages is also available to each shareholder.[166]

5. In a certain sense, one could speak of a two-tier system in the present Italian stock company. In addition to the "administrators" (*amministratori, directors*), a college of auditors (*collegio sindacale*) is given substantial powers of supervision over the administration, and we are reminded of the German supervisory council.[167] On paper, this power goes beyond mere verification of accounts, but in reality this organ has not been more effective than the auditors (*commissaires aux comptes*) in France, due to lack of independence from the administration and often also lack of competence.[168] The original reform proposal was twofold: *first,* only professionally qualified persons would be eligible for appointment as auditors (*sindaci*) and the auditing function could be entrusted to the newly introduced special companies of certified public accountants (*società di revisione*) that would offer speedy and expert team service; and *second,* the auditors would no longer be elected exclusively by the shareholders' meeting but at least in part would be appointed by

---

164 Relazione, 1967 RIVISTA DELLE SOCIETÀ 353, at 358. Houin, *Le projet italien,* at 156. *Cf.* French Law of July 24, 1966, Art. 161, which does not purport to limit proxies.

165 Art. 9, 1967 RIVISTA DELLE SOCIETÀ at 374. This was characterized as a "step backwards" from Art. 2377 of the Codice civile which allows individual action.

166 Art. 18, *id.* at 377.

167 However, the shareholders' meeting elects under the existing law not only the college of auditors but—in contrast with the German law—the *"amministratori"* as well. Arts. 2364(2), 2383 of the CODICE CIVILE.

168 Relazione of the De Gregorio Commission, in LA RIFORMA 1966, at 124.

a judge (President of the *Tribunale*), or—in companies admitted to the stock exchange—by a new public "supervisory organ" instituted within the Bank of Italy under the Governor of the Bank.[169] The first aspect has been retained, along with provisions strengthening the prerequisites and authority of the auditors. However, the second aspect, although it conformed to the governmental program, met with a storm of opposition which saw in it excessive governmental intervention in the company's affairs and unnecessary cumulation of controls. As a result, this perhaps most radical feature of the reform which deviated from all the other EEC company laws was greatly diluted in the majority version of the Interministerial Committee[170] but, at the insistence of the Socialist Minister of the Budget, the question was left open for decision by the Council of Ministers.[171]

6. Another far-reaching phase of the original proposal, however, has been retained. While the establishment of a stock company with a capital exceeding one billion lire would require the authorization by the Minister of the Treasury, the admission to the stock exchange would be subject to a further special approval by the same Minister, following extensive public disclosure of the financial data. Moreover, either the Bank of Italy, or an *ad hoc* governmental body is to exercise continuing supervision not only as regards the availability to the public of the necessary

---

[169] Relazione of the Santoro-Passarelli Commission, in LA RIFORMA 1966, at 43-45. Relazione of the De Gregorio Commission, *id.* at 124-26, 142-43.

[170] Arts. 26-29, 48, 90 and 145, in 1967 RIVISTA DELLE SOCIETÀ at 380, 381, 392, 407, 408, 434, 435. Pursuant to Art. 48, if a company listed on a stock exchange fails to entrust the auditing function to a company of certified public accountants inscribed in a special government-approved list, the "supervisory organ" will appoint the president of the company auditors' group (collegio sindacale) and one substitute auditor. According to Art. 29, minority shareholders may ask the President of the local Tribunale to appoint one auditor and one substitute auditor to join the auditors elected in the regular way by the stockholders' meeting.

[171] Relazione, in 1967 RIVISTA DELLE SOCIETÀ at 364.

information, but also in order to assure the "regularity" of the company management. Although the scope of the supervision, as originally conceived, has been pared down[172] it would still exceed the powers of the comparable Commissions in France and Belgium, as well as those of the Board of Trade in the United Kingdom or the Securities and Exchange Commission in the United States, whose function pertains only to assuring the integrity of the information relating to the company.[173] As a counterpart to the tight governmental control, these companies would be given the authority to issue a new type of "investor shares" (*azioni di risparmio*), entitling the holder to preferential treatment in the distribution of profits and capital, as well as to most of the usual stockholders' rights, excepting, however, the right to vote.[174] The assumption is that governmental supervision would take care of the interest of the mass absentee shareholders who at any rate are not concerned with the management. The Interministerial Committee, again relying on the governmental program, rejected the suggestions by the National Council of Economy and Labor to allow the issue of these shares as bearer shares, and to reduce the scope of the preferences.

The Interministerial Committee failed to reach unanimity on the entire text and several important questions were left open, as I indicated above, for a "political" decision by the Council of Ministers. The first National Economic Program for 1966-1970, elaborated through the new planning mechanism and approved in 1967, reaffirmed in emphatic terms the early goals of the reform, including the establishment of the public "supervisory organ," which was to function both "in public interest" and in the interest of minority share-

---

[172] Relazione of the Interministerial Committee, in 1967 RIVISTA DELLE SOCIETÀ 351, at 361-62.

[173] Houin, *Le projet italien* at 162.

[174] Art. 2351 of the CODICE CIVILE served as a precedent.

holders.[175] However, like so many other carefully elaborated reform proposals, the draft has not reached the Parliament,[176] and it has been gathering dust in the files of the
Ministry of Justice.

The question has been raised whether the governmental
agreement underlying the draft was still binding, in view
of the lapse of the legislative period for which it was
adopted. The reform draft—it has been suggested—should
now be reviewed in the broader European context, particularly with a view to adopting the German-type two-tier
structure for a stock company, since this would also open
the possibility for workers' participation in accordance with
Article 46 of the Italian Constitution, which heretofore has
remained a dead letter.[177] The Italian labor unions, however,
remain opposed to such participation and the Italian delegation in Brussels appears to be hostile to the two-tier
system itself.

From the viewpoint of the legislative technique, the Italian draft is conceived, in contrast with the Belgian, French
and German reforms, not as a self-contained, complete new
law, but as a partial reform, a "novella" modifying certain
provisions of the Codice civile but leaving others in effect.
This formal characteristic, it has been pointed out, might
cause some difficulties in practical application although "the
way remains open for further elaboration in the direction
of a unification."[178]

---

[175] Par. 39 of the Testo integrale del programma economico nazionale 1966-1970, reproduced in Pola, Il programma economico italiano 1966-1970, at 157 (Milano 1967). The program was approved by
Law No. 685 of July 27, 1967. For a comment see Minervini, *Società
per azioni: riforma anno zero,* 1967 RIVISTA DELLE SOCIETÀ 1280.

[176] On the fate of proposals for reforming Italian government
machinery see Barzini, *The Anatomy of Expertise,* 30 ENCOUNTER 32,
at 37 (Jan. 1968).

[177] Minervini, *Società per azioni: riforma anno zero,* 1967 RIVISTA
DELLE SOCIETÀ 1280, at 1281, 1285-86. GARCIN, COGESTION ET PARTICI-
PATION at 513 ff.

[178] Asquini, in LA RIFORMA 1966, at 5.

*(f)   The beginning of a partial reform in the Netherlands: response
to social-economic pressures*

(i)   General recodification: no great change

In the Netherlands, the Government has been in the
process of recodifying the civil law and the commercial law,
"consolidating" it into a single New Civil Code (*Nieuw
Burgerlijk Wetboek*). The second "book" of the code, entitled "Legal Persons" and dealing also with stock companies, was approved in Parliament by the law of May 12,
1960,[179] but it is not expected to come into force within the
next few years. Consideration is being given, however, to
bringing the second book into effect without waiting until
work on the entire Code has been completed.[180] Except for
the inclusion of new provisions on mergers, only few changes
were made in the existing stock company law—mostly of an
editorial nature, or to remove ambiguities that had arisen
in the interpretation of the existing law—because "that law
is of a still rather recent date and in general has fulfilled its
purpose well."[181] However, the new system is said to have
some interesting doctrinal consequences. Since the stock
company is included in the book on "Legal Persons" and
governed also by its general provisions, it can no longer be
viewed primarily as a contract (on the basis of the contractual theory of companies) but rather as an "institution."[182]

---

[179] 1960 STAATSBLAD at 205.

[180] VAN DER HEIJDEN-VAN DER GRINTEN, HANDBOEK at 30-31. For
an "American" translation of the presently applicable law see RIVERS,
VAN DE VEN, WESTBROEK, THE NETHERLANDS BUSINESS CORPORATION
CODE, CCH COMM. MKT. REP. No. 16, Oct. 26, 1965. Another translation, by the INTERNATIONAAL JURIDISCH INSTITUUT at The Hague, was
published in Leyden in 1957.

[181] ONTWERP VOOR EEN NIEUW BURGERLIJK WETBOEK, opgesteld
door Prof. E.M. Meijers, Toelichting, eerste gedeelte, Book 1-4, at 148
('s-Gravenhage 1954).

[182] VAN DER HEIJDEN-VAN DER GRINTEN, HANDBOEK at 30-31.

(ii) The Verdam Commission: focus on "neuralgic" areas

Of more direct interest to us, however, is a partial reform that has been in progress in the Netherlands. A commission was appointed by the Minister of Justice in 1960 with the task of identifying those areas where economic and social considerations, rather than legal-technical factors, called for adjustment or new solutions. In view of these terms of reference, the commission's membership was selected so as to secure not only professional expertise but also the representation of the major political parties. Although lawyers of every variety were in substantial majority, there were also party leaders, economists, bankers, and a psychologist-educator. Professor P. J. Verdam, a member of Parliament for the Anti-revolutionary Party and a member of the Social and Economic Council, former Minister of Justice and professor of law (not of company law but of ancient legal history) was appointed chairman.[183]

The "Verdam" Commission had at its disposal reports from the employers' association as well as from the Liberal Party. In his original instructions the Minister of Justice suggested several areas for exploration: financial disclosure ("publicity"), division of the tasks between company organs and their proper functioning, and the right of workers to "codetermination" in the sense of their membership in a

---

[183] The membership list is given in the Commission's report entitled Herziening van het ondernemingsrecht, *Rapport van de Commissie ingesteld bij beschikking van de Minister van Justitie van 8 April 1960*, at 1 ('s-Gravenhage 1965) (cited as VERDAM REPORT). The political constellation was as follows: Anti-revolutionary Party 2, Catholic Party 4, Liberal Party 3, Christian Historical Party 2, Socialist Party 5. *See generally* Scholten, *Riesame delle disposizioni della legge olandese sulle società di capitali con particolare riguardo alla tutela degli azionisti,* 1967 RIVISTA DELLE SOCIETÀ 242. In terms of a broad generalization, at the present time the Catholic Party is essentially a center party (with a left and a right wing); the Liberal Party is the most conservative party on the "right wing," the Socialists form the "left wing," the Anti-revolutionary Party is somewhat "left of center" and the Christian Historical Party is somewhat "right of center." The Catholic and Socialist Parties are the largest ones.

supervisory council along the German pattern. After four years of work, the Commission produced concrete proposals on all these questions, intended mainly to improve the protection of the shareholders, the public, as well as the workers, and it added also a text on increasing the powers of the existing plant councils.[184]

(iii) The Verdam Report and the EEC

A significant phase of the Verdam Commission's work— particularly in the field of financial statements and disclosure where the present Dutch law is practically meaningless and where the Commission suggested a separate new law—fell squarely within the scope of Article 54 of the EEC Treaty. Yet the Report which the Commission submitted in 1964 fails to mention the Treaty.[185] This could not be due to any lack of information about the happenings in Brussels, since a member of the Verdam Commission and its Secretary, Mr. L. de Vries, an official in the Ministry of Justice, has been a member of the expert group on coordination of company law in Brussels and thus was fully informed. Several factors may explain the Report's silence. First, as in the case of the German reform, the Commission's work had been greatly advanced, if not largely completed, before the Brussels working group became fully active. Second, in the final stage of its deliberations, the Commission did take note of the draft of the first directive, published, it will be recalled, in 1964 only, but decided to put it aside,[186] reportedly on the assumption that the crucial part of the draft directive dealing with disclosure would be modified (as was actually the case); thus a "wait and see" attitude toward the eventual "European" rule was felt to be in order. Finally, the Brussels

---

[184] GARCIN, COGESTION ET PARTICIPATION at 624, 733 (text of the law on plant councils of May 4, 1950).

[185] *See generally* VAN HECKE (ed.), DE BALANS EN DE WINST- EN VERLIESREKENING IN DE NAAMLOZE VENNOOTSCHAP (Brussels 1965).

[186] Sanders, *Reform des Aktienrechts in den Niederlanden,* 1965 AG 284 n.2. The author was a member of the Verdam Commission.

effort, at its inception at any rate, met with a hostile attitude
on the part of the small élite group in the Netherlands (in
and outside the government) that was privy to it. This
group saw in the coordination proceeding nothing less than
a direct threat to the Dutch liberal company law which the
industry in particular wished to preserve and which the
other Member States would no doubt want modified in the
direction of stricter regulation. Again, the Dutch official
and unofficial circles reflected the conviction—due in part
to the continuing British influence in the Netherlands—
that no major projects in the Community beyond the customs union stage, such as the proposed "European company," should be undertaken pending the enlargement of
the membership. In fact, the veto of the United Kingdom's
application for membership in 1963 alienated the Netherlands officials, parliamentarians and the informed public
profoundly, and the resulting change in the official Dutch
posture became apparent across the spectrum of the Community activities. Netherlands legal literature dealing with
national reform was almost without exception critical of the
Brussels work.[187]

The Verdam Commission Report, although ignoring the
coordination effort in Brussels, drew upon United States
legislation concerning the Securities and Exchange Commission;[188] its innovating proposal for a new judicial remedy to compel company compliance with disclosure obligations is fashioned, as the Commission expressly pointed out,
after the Anglo-American injunction.[189]

(iv) The two-tier system and workers' "codetermination"

It was the German law, of course, that was used by the
Commission as a starting point for an examination of both

---

[187] VAN DER HEIJDEN-VAN DER GRINTEN, HANDBOEK at 33-34 and
references cited in n.3, at 34-35; *see also* p. 192 and note 45 *infra*. One
exception was the article by Sanders, cited in the preceding note.

[188] Commission's report, *id., e.g.* at 35, 39.

[189] *Id.* at 6, 34, 41, 128.

the two-tier system and the connected problem of workers'
representation, the latter having proved, not surprisingly,
the most controversial and time-consuming item in all the
Commission's work. Even the "minimal" proposal which
would introduce this institution of codetermination for the
first time into the Netherlands law in a limited form, was
adopted by a narrow margin of nine to seven, with the
Catholic Party split but the Socialists united in favor.[190]
The new arrangement would apply only to a very small
fraction of the 30,000 Dutch stock companies, namely only
to those whose stock was listed on the stock exchange
or which were controlled by such companies. For these
companies the council of auditors ("supervisors," *commissarissen*) which under the present law is optional,[191] would
become obligatory, and what is more important, its powers
would be greatly expanded and defined in the law itself in
the image of the German supervisory council.[192] In practice
most Dutch companies of any magnitude already have a
council of auditors.[193]

(v)　The three draft reform laws

The Social and Economic Council rendered its opinions
first on those portions of the Commission's proposed reform
that concerned the contents and disclosure of financial state-

---

190 The vote reflects the political alignment: the affirmative votes
came from the two members of the Anti-revolutionary Party, all five
Socialists and two of the four members of the Catholic Party. The
other two joined the Christian Historical Party members and the three
Liberals in casting the negative votes. According to the proposal, the
workers would be entitled to elect one of the "commissarissen." VER-
DAM REPORT at 9.

191 Sec. 50 of Book I, Title 3 of the Commercial Code speaks of
"one or more auditors."

192 At present, if the council of auditors is established, the charter
must define its duties.

193 It may be of interest to note here that in voting on whether
the new definition of the tasks of the council should include the words
"within the framework of public welfare" the two Liberals dissented.
VERDAM REPORT at 78.

ments and the shareholders' and workers' right of inquiry into the conduct of the management, and the Government submitted two draft statutes on these subjects to the Parliament on May 13, 1968.[194] By that time, the Social and Economic Council had also formulated its opinion on the third subject, the increase of powers of the existing plant councils, but it was not until October 6, 1969, that the Government submitted a draft statute dealing with this matter.[195] This draft, which is in the form of an entirely new constitutive law for plant councils, would increase their powers even beyond the suggestions made by the Verdam Commission and the Social and Economic Council. The disputed chapter of the Verdam Report dealing with workers' codetermination at the time remained before the Social and Economic Council and the Netherlands Government showed no signs of wanting to hurry the matter.

On September 19, 1968, acting principally in response to the Community's first directive and the coordination stimulus generally, but also with a view to advancing the overall reform of the Netherlands company law, the Netherlands Minister of Justice appointed a new nine-member Commission with Professor van der Grinten as chairman.[196] Eight members were company law experts and the ninth, Professor VerLoren van Themaat, former Director General of Competition in Brussels, was an authority on European Community law. This Commission was given the specific mandate to advise whether it would be desirable (a) to introduce the limited liability company form into the Netherlands law, (b) to modify the rules concerning the safeguarding of company capital (a subject of the "second directive" in preparation at Brussels), (c) to introduce new rules for the protection of shareholders in connection with the

---

[194] Draft Laws No. 9595 and 9596. *See* p. 261 *infra* for a more detailed discussion. The two drafts were approved with a number of amendments by the Second Chamber in April 1970.

[195] Draft Law No. 10,335.

[196] Decree No. 299/668 of July 9, 1968.

issuance of certificates and the so-called "oligarchic clauses,"[197] and (d) to enact rules on holding and related companies in the image of the German *Konzernrecht*. Finally, the Commission was to study other questions that might arise in connection with harmonization of company law in the Community.

A year later to the day, on September 19, 1969, the Social and Economic Council produced an opinion on the remaining portion of the Verdam Report dealing with workers' codetermination. The very fact that the Council was able to arrive at a compromise was quite unexpected and the content of the opinion caused general surprise. Spurred by the unanimous endorsement of the compromise by the representatives of employers and workers, as well as by government-appointed "crown" members in the Council, the Netherlands Government now seems to be eager to translate the opinion into law.

The solution proposed by the Council is quite novel and it differs radically from the patterns prevailing in other Member States and under discussion in Brussels. The new organizational regime would not be limited to companies listed on the stock exchange and affiliates controlled by them as was suggested by the Verdam Report; it would apply to all companies with assets in excess of 10 million guilders which employ one hundred or more workers and thus have a plant council. All these companies would be required to establish a supervisory council, endowed with substantial powers, including the power to appoint the administrative council or "managing committee" (*bestuur* or *directie*) and to dismiss it (after consultation with the shareholders' meeting), to draw up annual financial statements (which would have to be approved, but could not be modi-

---

[197] Clauses inserted in the company charter in order to make sure that a shareholder or a group of shareholders will be able to maintain control of the company, *e.g.*, a clause restricting the competence of the stockholders' meeting. VAN DER HEIJDEN-VAN DER GRINTEN, HANDBOEK at 304-06.

fied by the shareholders' meeting), and to veto certain management decisions. In contrast with the German model, members of this supervisory council would not be appointed by the shareholders' meeting but would be selected by a procedure of controlled cooptation. In case of a vacancy, the shareholders, management (*bestuur*), members of the council itself, as well as members of the plant council, would be free to bring forward names of candidates. The supervisory council would then designate a candidate who would be deemed elected unless he is vetoed by the shareholders' meeting or the plant council.[198] The new system represents an attempt to bring the influence of "capital" and labor into balance. The Van der Grinten Commission was asked to study the matter and prepare an appropriate statutory text.

(g) The prospect in Luxembourg: in the Belgian pattern

The Luxembourg law on commercial companies of Aug. 10, 1915, is "strongly inspired" by Belgian law.[198a] The smallest of the Six, Luxembourg has been least active in the field of company law reform. However, the government has obtained the services of Prof. van Ommeslaghe, one of the leading Belgian experts on company law, active both in the Belgian national commission and in the Community, and it is generally assumed that Luxembourg will adopt the new Belgian Commercial code as a model for its new law.

---

[198] Exceptions and dispensations are envisaged for wholly-owned subsidiaries whose parent companies adopted the new system and for companies linked to foreign companies. On the opinions of the Social and Economic Council see Verdam, *Het S.E.R.-advies over de onderemingsstructuur*, 1969 NV 137; Löwensteyn, *Het advies van de Sociaal-Economische Raad over de wijziging van de structuur van de Naamloze Vennootschap*, 1969 NV 140.

[198a] Arendt, *Notice introductive au droit des sociétés dans le Grand-Duché de Luxembourg*, in COLLECTION JUPITER, 1 RECUEILS PRATIQUES DU DROIT DES AFFAIRES DANS LES PAYS DU MARCHÉ COMMUN, RÉGIME DES SOCIÉTÉS, 1e PARTIE (Paris 1959). For the text of the law (as amended) see *id.* 3e Partie. See also the text of the Law of July 31, 1929, on holding companies, *id.*, which, with its tax implications, is credited with establishing Luxembourg as a favorite financial center.

3. Some institutional aspects of national reforms

(a) Lawyers' monopoly: The "Commission" device

Perhaps the most striking feature, common to the national reform processes in all the Member States, is the control exercised by lawyers. This is a logical consequence of the traditional institutional arrangement that attributes the competence for company law reform to the Ministry of Justice. Even where the initiative comes from another executive department, as was the case in Italy, the Ministry of Justice takes over in due course. Moreover, when other Ministries come into the picture—and this usually occurs when the proposed text has already substantially crystallized —it is the legal personnel in these Ministries that carries the working-level responsibility. The Ministries of Justice have also the responsibility for assuring national representation in the coordination work of the EEC. Nevertheless, the German Ministry of Economic Affairs has sent its own man to the meetings in Brussels, but this official—some felt— being himself a member of his Ministry's legal department, has not pressed for a broadening of the context to include economic considerations but by an atavistic reflex has joined in the "lawyers' approach." Again, the Verdam Commission in its reform proposal went beyond the competence of the Ministry of Justice in outlining changes to be made in the plant councils law which falls within the scope of the Ministry of Social Affairs; yet the Ministry had no expert representative on the Commission.

Except in the Federal Republic, the pattern has been for the Minister of Justice to initiate the process by appointing a commission of experts within which—in some instances at any rate—company-law expertise was tempered by representation of political trends and special interests which, again more often than not, were articulated by trained lawyers or lawyer-politicians. It is on the basis of a report and text elaborated by such a commission that the Ministry of Justice proceeds to draft the text for approval by the Government and submission to the Parliament. In France and in Italy, early "private" models were prepared by lawyers in professional organizations of stock companies with the idea that they would exert appropriate influence on the reform, and some of the same lawyers would later reappear as members of a government appointed commission.

In the Federal Republic, the commission device was dispensed with and the drafting was done from the outset within the Ministry of Justice itself. The most frequently advanced explanation has been that, in view of the strong influence exerted upon the Federal Government by organized special interests, only the "impartial civil servant," insulated within the four walls of his "technical" ministry, is able to resist the pressures where these interests are as directly concerned as in the company law field. There has been some criticism of this procedure in the *Bundestag,* and one also hears complaints that the deputies have been receiving copies of legislative drafts from the Executive Departments at much too late a stage. As a result, the *Bundestag* has under consideration a modification of its rules of procedure to the effect that the Ministries would be expected to present a draft bill to the appropriate Committee of Parliament as soon as such draft was made available to nongovernmental organizations for consultation purposes.

(b) Consultations with interest groups

These consultations are an integral part of lawmaking in all Member States although the modalities vary, and in some Member States the process is in part institutionalized. We have noted the consultations in the Economic and Social Council in France, the Social and Economic Council in the Netherlands, and the National Economic and Labor Council in Italy, all of which were established to provide a more formal, orderly and open arena for the expression of special interests. The Belgian Government might also decide to consult the *Conseil Central de l'Economie* (Central Council for Economy). These bodies, whose influence in reality has been rather limited, except in the Netherlands, had served as a model for the Economic and Social Committee of the Community established by the EEC Treaty.

In the Federal Republic where no comparable body exists, the Ministry of Justice began consultation on the last reform with professional and interest groups simultaneously with inter-ministerial consultations as soon as the officials completed and published a pre-draft (*Referentenentwurf*) that did not officially commit the Minister. The process continued following the publication of the official government text (*Regierungsentwurf*) which already reflected the results of the first round of consultation. After this text had been submitted to the Parliament, the groups were given an opportunity to press their views in extensive hearings held by the Economic Committee.[199]

Foremost among the groups that participated actively in the public discussion were the *Bundesverband der deutschen Industrie* (Federal Association of German Industry), the *Bundesvereinigung der deutschen Arbeitgeberverbände* (Federal Association of German Associations of Employers, grouping together banks, insurance companies and others), the *Deutsche Gewerkschaftsbund* (Association of Labor Unions), and—among the legal-professional associations— the *Deutscher Juristentag*.

The governing body of the last mentioned association— itself representative of lawyers in government, practice and industry—organized a similarly representative special committee for the specific purpose of studying the draft reform law. In the course of this study, extensive opinions and reports were prepared on various aspects of the law which served as a basis for detailed debates at widely attended meetings, open to any member of the profession.[200] These meetings represented perhaps the most meaningful and informed confrontation of expert views and special interests in the entire process.

---

[199] *See* p. 99 *supra.*

[200] *See, e.g.,* the proceedings of the 39th, 41st and 46th meetings.

(c)   The role of Parliaments

Some Continental scholars speak of a "crisis of parliamen-
tarism" in modern industrial democracy.[201] It is said that
a major cause for the reduced role of the parliaments and
the trend toward a "technocracy" has been the increasingly
complex and technical nature of governmental problems
which the legislative branch has not been equipped to handle. In order to cope with this difficulty and to assure a
degree of technical expertise in the Parliament, the Government of the French Fifth Republic has encouraged civil
servants in all branches, including the judiciary, to take leave
of absence from their jobs and run in Parliamentary elec-
tions; a group of such deputies has functioned as "affiliates"
of the Gaullist party, but some civil servants have been
elected even on opposition tickets. In the Federal Republic,
almost one-fifth of all the deputies in the Bundestag are
civil servants on temporary inactive status.[202]

Be that as it may, the experience with national company
law reforms in Germany and even in France, where the Constitution of 1958 had drastically curtailed the authority of
the Parliament, points the other way and reveals a very lively
role of the legislative branches. For one thing, the subject
matter has been traditionally within the competence of the
legislature, and, considering the high proportion of lawyers
among the lawmakers, it was certainly not beyond at least
a general comprehension by a substantial group among
them. In France, as we have noted, close to 500 amendments

---

201 For a criticism of this view see WHEARE, LEGISLATURES at 227-
34 (London, New York 1963). *See generally* Grosser, *The Evolution of
European Parliaments,* in GRAUBARD (ed.), A NEW EUROPE? at 219
(Boston 1964); Cox, *The Study of European Institutions, etc.,* 3 J.C.M.
STUDIES 114 (1965). On the French Parliament generally see Williams,
THE FRENCH PARLIAMENT-POLITICS IN THE FIFTH REPUBLIC (New
York, Washington 1968).

202 Of the 518 members of the 5th Bundestag (1965-1969) 100 may
be considered to fall in this category: 55 Christian Democrats, 39
Social Democrats and 6 Free Democrats. STEINMANN, 4 HANDBUCH DER
BUNDESREPUBLIK DEUTSCHLAND at 15 (Bonn 1967).

to the Government bill were offered in the Parliament, a
major part of which was accepted by the Government.[203]
The significant additions to the bill made during the
Parliamentary proceeding, included not only the new "two-
tier" system for the stock company administration, but also
the provisions on mergers and convertible bonds. On the
other hand, the Parliament forced the exclusion of a number of provisions such as cumulative voting and judicial
control over company formation and refused to eliminate
limited partnership with shares as was proposed in the
bill. Moreover, the Government was prompted into promising further significant reforms at an early date, including
legislation on "related companies" and nonvoting stock.[204]
However, a company law expert complained that while
certain of the amendments submitted in the Parliament
were useful, others were not, and they often conflicted with
the letter and spirit of the bill. Portions of the bill that
were formulated after extensive study and with great care
before submission to the Parliament, were dropped in the
course of the parliamentary proceeding. The debate was
at times improvised and quite sparsely attended, "a proof
that absenteeism was not the privilege of shareholders at
shareholders' meetings." It was the Law Committee of the
Senate that in his view brought some order into the confusion.[205] The scene depicted by the French expert is of course
not uncommon in any parliament. Yet the additions and
modifications effected in that course of the parliamentary
proceeding were quite far-reaching and thus the part played
by the legislative branch went beyond the formal function of legitimation which, in any case, is important in a

---

[203] *See* p. 113 *supra*. M. Drouot L'Hermine, in PARLEMENT EURO-
PÉEN, Débats, Compte rendu in extenso des Séances, VII/66, [1966-1967]
EUR. PARL. DÉB., No. 85, at 68.

[204] LEFÊBVRE, LA RÉFORME DES SOCIÉTÉS COMMERCIALES EN TABLEAUX
PRATIQUES 9-10 (Paris 1966).

[205] Hémard, *La réforme des sociétés par actions en France et la
loi du 24 juillet 1966*, 1967 RIVISTA DELLE SOCIETÀ 132, at 136, 137.

democratic system. The legitimation by elective representatives was perhaps particularly important during the Gaullist
phase of the Fifth Republic when emphasis was on the
mythical approval of the people and referendums, rather
than on parliamentary democracy.

In the Federal Republic, the *Bundestag* dealt with the
stock company reform bill over a period of not less than
two and a half years in a succession of Committees.[206] It is
said that the dialogue between the chairman of the Legal
Committee, Dr. Wilhelmi, co-author of a commentary on
company law and leading expert on that subject in the
lower House, and Dr. Gessler, of the Ministry of Justice,
also author of an authoritative commentary on partnership
law who defended the government bill before the Committee, turned into a stimulating seminar on company law to
the delight and enlightenment of the lawyer-deputies.[207]

Dr. Aschoff of the Free Democratic Party, Chairman of
the Economic Committee and often a spokesman for industry, made it clear in the debate that the parliamentary
facilities were inadequate; the Committees, he said, should
be given additional staff to help them cope with such major
pieces of legislation as the company law reform:

> [N]ot only Mr. Wilhelmi and myself but almost all
> of us had to spend weeks—day and night—not only in
> Committee sessions but in conversations with economic
> groups and with experts, to such an extent that the
> matter is not practicable. I believe one should have the
> courage to say, in connection with such a law as this,
> that the repeated conversations—back and forth—with
> the interested persons and experts must have a certain
> limit for a member of the Parliament who wants to

---

206 *Supra* p. 99.

207 The indefatigable Dr. Wilhelmi is given credit for assuring
that the Legal Committee's version did not differ appreciably from the
text which later emerged from the Economic Committee. Dr. Aschoff,
in DEUTSCHER BUNDESTAG, 4. WAHLPERIODE, 187. Sitzung, May 25, 1965,
BUNDESTAGSDRUCKSACHE IV/3296, Third reading at 9411.

maintain his self-respect. I should be the last one to quarrel with the proposition that on occasion I must procure the missing data through discussions with experts, and that I am obligated to learn the interest and position of the various groups. But this must not go so far as to allow that the line between expert consultation and very concrete demands be transgressed until the very last hours, so as to impair the standing of a deputy.[208]

The record shows that the statement—as much a complaint as a sigh of relief at the completion of the job—was greeted with applause from the Free Democrats and the Christian Democrats. It illustrates not only the serious predicament of the Parliaments throughout Europe due to the shortage of independent staff and advice, but also the intensity of pressures exerted by special interests upon parliamentarians, probably not less pervasive in Europe than in the United States. The example of the amply staffed and funded committees of the United States Congress has provided a stimulus for the current effort to improve the procedures in the German Parliament. In Belgium, where according to the Constitution the two chambers of the legislature have "a right of inquiry," a system of legislative hearings would, it has been suggested, give some reality to this right and would make the participation of interest groups both more direct and more overt.[209] We have seen earlier,[210] that the Rules of Procedure of the Bundestag allow its Committees to hear outside experts. The Economic Committee took full advantage of this provision in considering the new stock company law. In France, the Committees of the Parlia-

---

208 *Id.*

209 Le Soir, June 15-16, 1969, p. 1, col. 5.

210 *Supra* p. 99. § 73 of the GESCHÄFTSORDNUNG DES BUNDESTAGES, 1952 BGBl. II 339. *See generally* ODEWALD, DER PARLAMENTARISCHE HILFSDIENST IN DEN VEREINIGTEN STAATEN VON AMERIKA UND IN DER BUNDESREPUBLIK DEUTSCHLAND (Berlin 1967).

ment did not follow this pattern and generally the appearance of outsiders in these Committees is quite rare. Yet the Pleven Committee, although appointed by the executive, was headed by a leading deputy and its improvised "hearings" in some measure were a substitute for legislative hearings.

The German *Bundestag* has also sought to influence the coordination process in Brussels and the deputies played an active part in the debate on the first directive in the European Parliament, as did certain members of the French Parliament.

4. Are national reforms contrary to the Treaty? Some political realities

(a) The Treaty law

Since there is no specific Treaty provision on the subject, it is not surprising that learned writers are divided on the question whether, after the adoption of the Treaty, the Member States have remained free to embark upon national reforms of company law. At one pole of the spectrum, Bärmann and, to some extent, Lutter believe that independent national reform may no longer be admissible as a matter of positive law;[211] at the other pole Minervini perceives no legal restraints whatsoever—and on the contrary advocates urgent action on the Italian reform in order to enable the Italian delegation "to represent the Italian thesis" in Brus-

---

[211] Bärmann, *Ist eine Aktienrechtsreform überhaupt noch zulässig?*, 1959 JURISTENZEITUNG 434; Bärmann, *Einheitliche Gesellschaftsform für die Europäische Wirtschaftsgemeinschaft*, 1961 ARCHIV FÜR DIE CIVILISTISCHE PRAXIS at 104; Bärmann, *Die Europäischen Gemeinschaften und die Rechtsangleichung*, 1959 JURISTENZEITUNG 553, and *Les communautés européennes et le rapprochement des droits*, 1960 REV. INT. DROIT COMP. 8, at 44; Lutter, *Die Rechtsangleichung* at 27-28. *But see contra*, Zweigert, *Der Einfluss des europäischen Gemeinschaftsrechts auf die Rechtsordnungen der Mitgliedstaaten*, 1964 RABELS ZEITSCHRIFT 601; Duden, *Internationale Aktiengesellschaften*, 1962 RABELS ZEITSCHRIFT 89, at 106.

sels.[212] Finally, Houin takes an in-between position when he questions the wisdom of uncoordinated national reform as a matter of sound legal policy.[213]

Three arguments have been advanced in support of the illegality of independent national reform. First, since so many aspects of the individual national reform laws concern protection of third parties and shareholders within the meaning of Article 54,[214] and since this protection is still quite uneven within the Community, a coordination will require modifications in the laws of every Member State. Consequently, any uncoordinated change in national law— the argument goes—would necessarily hamper, if not entirely frustrate, Community action and thus be contrary to Article 5 of the Treaty in which the Member States undertook to cooperate in the execution of the Treaty and to facilitate the work of the Community.[215] Second, to the extent that there is "reason to fear" that a national reform provision could cause "a distortion" by increasing the divergence among existing national laws and thereby interfering with conditions of competition, the Member State concerned would violate its obligation under Article 102, if it proceeded with the enactment without prior consultation with the Commission. The Court of Justice of the Communities interpreted this Article as specifically designed to avoid aggravation of legal divergence, but thus far the Article has been invoked by the Commission in a handful

---

212 Minervini, *Società per azioni: riforma anno zero*, 1967 RIVISTA DELLE SOCIETÀ 1280, at 1281. The author seems to labor under the impression that *both* the coordination and the decisions on the establishment of a "European type" company require a unanimous consent.

213 Houin, *Le projet italien de réforme du droit des sociétés par actions*, 1967 RIVISTA DELLE SOCIETÀ 148, at 149.

214 It could be argued that the entire company law directly or indirectly deals with such a protection. *See* p. 174 *infra*.

215 Lutter, *Die Rechtsangleichung* at 28. Art. 5(1) provides: "Member States shall take all measures, whether general or particular, appropriate to ensure the carrying out of the obligations arising out of the Treaty and resulting from the acts of the institutions of the Community. They shall assist the latter in the achievement of its tasks."

of cases only.[216] Finally, if it could be said that a given
national reform affected national economic policy, Article 6
would come into play in which the Members undertook
the legal obligation, "in close collaboration with the institutions of the Community," to coordinate their economic
policies to the extent necessary for achieving the objectives
of the Treaty.[217]

It would be for the Court of Justice ultimately to determine whether in principle any independent national reform
in this field was incompatible with the general obligations
of Article 5, or whether any particular provision in a given
reform law was contrary to the other articles of the Treaty
mentioned above. I see no indication today that either the
Commission or any other interested party would wish to
press such an issue.

Actually, the Commission's valiant attempt to assert its
coordinating authority in a much more modest context was
not an unqualified success. In proposing the first coordinating directive under Article 54, par. 3(g), the Commission
insisted that, after the directive comes into effect, the Members will have to inform it of all the proposed legislation
and regulations in the field governed by the directive, and
that they must do so sufficiently in advance so as to allow
the Commission to present its observations on the proposals
to the governments.[218] These observations would presumably be directed toward coordination and avoidance of further divergence. The Economic and Social Committee

---

[216] Judgment of July 15, 1964 in Case 6/64, Costa v. ENEL, 10
Recueil de la Jurisprudence 1141, at 1160-61 (1964). For a complete
list of instances in which the Commission invoked Art. 102 see *First
General Report on the Activities of the Communities 1967,* par. 3, at
89 (Feb. 1968); *Second General Report on the Activities of the Communities 1968,* at 88-89 and table 4, at 75, and *Troisème Rapport Général sur l'activité des Communautés 1969,* table 13, at 97.

[217] See Commission's answer to Written Question No. 37/68 by
Mr. Vredeling concerning the proposed French law on creating a
company of "European interest." [1968] J.O. C68 (July 9) at 3.

[218] Art. 16, First Draft of 1964 and Art. 16, Second Draft of 1966,
COM (66) 366 final, Oct. 3, 1966, at 22.

agreed with the Commission and it went even further in suggesting that all proposed modifications of national company laws be submitted to the Commission in advance of the enactment; the Commission in turn would be required to submit appropriate observations thereon not only to the national parliaments and other national authorities concerned but to the European Parliament and the Economic and Social Committee as well.[219] The Committee of the European Parliament which dealt with the first directive raised the question whether, in the interest of coordinating the national reforms, the Commission should not organize an *ad hoc* group of national experts who would "determine the essential points of a general harmonization of the company law in the Member States"; but the Commission rejected this thought on the ground that such body would duplicate the work of its existing working group on company law.[220] However, the Commission asserted that it must examine national reform proposals not only to see that they did not violate the Treaty (notably Article 221[221]) but also with a view to "taking into account the predominant criteria of these reforms in elaborating its proposals for [Community] directives."[222]

The Commission clung to its original position tenaciously until the eleventh hour, and it received some encourage-

---

219 Avis du Comité Economique et Social sur la proposition d'une directive du Conseil tendant à coordonner, pour les rendre équivalentes, les garanties qui sont exigées, dans les États membres, des sociétés au sens de l'article 58, alinéa 2, du traité pour protéger les intérêts tant des associés que des tiers, [1964] J.O. No. 194, Nov. 27, 1964, 3249/64, at 3256/64.

220 BERKHOUWER, RAPPORT SUR LA PROPOSITION DE LA COMMISSION DE LA COMMUNAUTÉ ÉCONOMIQUE EUROPÉENNE AU CONSEIL (doc. 10/1964-65) relative à une directive tendant à coordonner, pour les rendre équivalentes, les garanties qui sont exigées, dans les États membres, des sociétés au sens de l'article 58, alinéa 2, du traité pour protéger les intérêts tant des associés que des tiers, [1966] EUR. PARL., DOCS. No. 53, at 3 par. 8 and 10 par. 8 (May 9, 1966).

221 *See* p. 47 *supra*.

222 BERKHOUWER REPORT at 10 par. 12-14.

ment from the national experts and two or three governmental delegations. It encountered, however, a strong opposition, particularly on the part of the German and French
delegations, and as a result, the group of officials within the
framework of the Council of Ministers discarded the Commission's version and substituted for it the much less specific "standard" clause, previously approved in other directives:
"Member States shall see to it (*veillent*) that the text of the
essential [most important] provisions of national law which
they will adopt in the field governed by the present directive shall be communicated to the Commission." The Commission argued that this provision was devoid of any practical meaning since the national law, once adopted, could be
readily found in national official journals; what mattered
was to make sure that the texts were made available to the
Commission for its comments (and also to the other Member
States) *before* they became law. The argument, however, fell
on deaf ears and at the very last moment, after the rest of
the directive had received unanimous agreement, the Commission spokesman decided not to press for a showdown on
this issue in the Council of Ministers. In its meeting on
March 9, 1968, the Council included the disputed provision
in the final text of the directive but it did note for the record
that the Commission maintained its insistence on *advance*
communication of the proposed national legislation and that
it intended to raise this issue again. Moreover, the Ministers
approved a statement to the effect that the question was
covered by an earlier agreement, reached in connection with
another directive, whereby "the representatives of the Member Governments, meeting within the forum of the Council,"
had assumed the obligation to communicate to the Commission, *if at all possible, and at a stage which is of the greatest
interest for the Commission,* proposals falling within the
scope of directives in the field of the right of establishment,
supply of services and approximation of national laws.[223]

---

[223] The above agreement was made at the time of the adoption
of the directive No. 64/221/CEE ("Coordination entry and sojourn")

Evidently, the Governments were not prepared to concede that the Commission had the authority, as a matter of Treaty law, to review national legislative proposals, or that it could or should be granted such authority by formal Council act; they were willing to accept an ambiguous clause in the directive and a somewhat more specific, yet still quite loose obligation in the form of a separate inter-governmental agreement, rather than in a formal Council act. The agreement constitutes an authoritative interpretation of the directive by the individual Member Governments. This attitude illustrates in a telling manner the reluctance of the Governments to accept any limitations on their lawmaking authority beyond those specified in the Treaty.

(b) A "coordinated" or "spontaneous" assimilation?

In contemplating the problems of the legality and wisdom of the conduct of the Member States, several factors should be kept in mind.

First, during the earlier years of the Community, a sharp disagreement existed on how much freedom of lawmaking the Member States had relinquished in accepting Article 54, par. 3(g). More generally, even the informed élites laboring on national reforms were not familiar as yet with the complex EEC Treaty and, as in other fields in which the Treaty "intruded" upon national law, a period of "education" was necessary.

Second, the German and French reform laws had their origins before the Treaty came into existence, and all the national reforms, considered above, may be said to have been initiated before the Community coordination activities became reasonably continuous and predictable in 1963-1964. Yet the reform pressures in the national arenas, stemming predominantly from "technicians," mostly lawyers within

---

but it was to apply to other directives in the field of the right of establishment and supply of services as well as approximation of legislation in accordance with Art. 100.

and outside the governments, continued after the adoption of the Treaty.

Finally, if the function of the assimilation of laws was to advance the Common Market the reverse effect was also contemplated in the Treaty.[224] For instance, the Treaty rules on social policy are based on the assumption that the working of the single market will "favor the harmonization of social systems" which in turn will result in an equalization of the working and living conditions of the workers in an upward direction; "the approximation of legislative and administrative provisions" was to play a supplementing role in what was conceived as a more or less automatic process.[225]

Again, perhaps the most far-reaching assimilation accomplishment thus far, which sooner or later will affect every citizen from Kiel to Catania, has been the adoption in April 1967 of two directives requiring all Member States to introduce the same type of a "value-added tax" (TVA) in place of the old "cascade" or multistage, cumulative turnover tax.[226] The Member States rely on indirect taxes as a source

---

[224] VerLoren van Themaat, *Die Rechtsangleichung als Integrationsinstrument* at 246.

[225] Art. 117. Kahn-Freund, *Labor Law and Social Security*, in 1 STEIN & NICHOLSON at 297.

[226] [1967] J.O. 1301. Huiskamp, *The Harmonisation of Legislation of E.E.C. Member States Concerning Turnover Taxes*, 5 C.M.L. REV. 177 (1967). For an English translation of the directives see CCH COM. MKT. REP. ¶¶ 3111 and 3135. As indicated above, France already had a TVA system, the German Federal Republic adopted it in January 1968, and the Netherlands on January 1, 1969. Luxembourg intended to meet the original 1970 deadline but Italy and Belgium were unable to meet it—Belgium because of inflation and budgetary problems, and Italy because its Parliament has been working on a general overhaul of the tax system. Responding to a request by the two last mentioned countries, the Commission proposed to the Council a postponement for one year, that is, to January 1, 1971, and it also proposed that a timetable should be set for harmonizing the rates of the tax. Commission of the European Communities, Press Release IP (69) 162, October 2, 1969. Luxembourg was reported to have decided also to seek postponement of the effective date. On Dec. 9, 1969, the Council adopted the "Third Directive," [1969] J.O. L320 (Dec. 20) at 34. By virtue of

of revenue to a substantially greater extent than, for instance, the United States, and consequently the matter was of vital importance for the national governments. Although the Treaty directed the Commission to explore the possibilities of "harmonizing the turnover taxes,"[227] the radical and relatively rapid Community action became feasible only because France had adopted the new system in 1954 in the process of its own national reform,[228] and it was followed by the Federal Republic of Germany where the new system entered into effect in 1968.[229] Without question, the dominant objective of the French legislation was national, that is to bring some order out of the chaos of the extremely complicated, discriminatory and economically inefficient French sales taxes, and to provide an incentive for a modernization of French industry by making the new tax deductible on expenditures for capital goods. However, the difficulties and frictions which the old system had caused in the dramatically increased flow of goods across national frontiers within the Community, and the potential anticompetitive impact of the old tax upon the structure of the single market had a marked influence upon the decision of the Federal Government and of the other member governments to accept the French system. Since the two most influential members had already made their decision the Commission was able, with their support, to perform a significant function of coordination by proposing concrete solutions to the Ministers of Finance and helping persuade the other members, particularly Italy and the Netherlands, to relinquish their opposi-

this directive the deadline for the introduction of the TVA was moved from Jan. 1, 1970 to Jan. 1, 1972, but the flat rates for calculating compensatory charges on imports and refunds of the cumulative turnover tax on exports could not be increased beyond the Oct. 1, 1969 level.

[227] Art. 99.

[228] For the amended text see Law No. 66-10 of Jan. 6, 1966, and Law No. 67-1114 of Dec. 21, 1967.

[229] Turnover Tax Law (Umsatzsteuergesetz, Mehrwertsteuer) of May 29, 1967, BGBl. I 545, amended by Law of Oct. 18, 1967.

tion. Thus in the end the Council of Ministers was in a position to approve the outlines of the new system unanimously. The assimilation process in the turnover-tax field has "spilled over" the frontiers of the Common Market to Denmark, Norway, Sweden and Austria, and the British Government reportedly has been reconsidering an earlier negative decision on the new system.[230] In fact, TVA has its advocates in the United States as well.[231]

If modernization was the principal incentive for the assimilation in this instance, the ease of calculating the new turnover-tax with precision for the purpose of its refund on exports and imposition of a compensatory charge on imports in intra-Community trade was a significant consideration as well.[232]

Perhaps a somewhat analogous, although much more complex, evolution has begun in the field of company law: if modernization of the corporate form is a principal impulse for the national reforms, the interest in facilitating transnational intercourse and stimulating structural changes made necessary by the enlarged market comes also into play. The pattern that is emerging may differ from that contemplated by the authors of the EEC Treaty; yet the Commission would have a significant role to play in drawing upon, and seeking to coordinate what is essentially "spontaneous assimilation." It is, however, clear that as long as the law-

---

[230] *A Fiscal Innovation: The Value-Added Tax,* First National City Bank, New York, Monthly Economic Letter, July 1968, 81, at 82.

[231] For a critical discussion see Surrey, *Implications of Tax Harmonization in the European Common Market,* 1968 TAXES—THE TAX MAGAZINE 398, at 402-05.

[232] One of the aims of the new tax on value added was the avoidance of the distortion of competition caused by the flat-rate refund on exports and flat-rate compensation charges on imports employed under the old system. These flat rates in practice have invariably favored integrated companies and also could easily conceal a subsidy on exports or, conversely, a protectionist charge on imports. The new system allows exact calculation of the refunds and compensatory charges.

making in Brussels is in the hands of the national and transnational executive branches, with no effective parliamentary participation, and as long as the areas of agreed common
policies remain limited, the important issues of company
law, such as the degree of financial disclosure, the basic
structure of the stock company administration, the workers'
right of codetermination or—to use the French terminology
—"participation," must still be determined in the first place
through, or in close dependence upon, the national political
processes.

Chapter 5

EARLY PROBLEMS OF ASSIMILATION: THE TERRITORIAL IMPERATIVE OF THE EUROCRATS

1. Distribution of competence within the Commission

When the Commission's organizational chart was first drawn the competence for the freedom-of-establishment part of the Treaty (including Article 54, par. 3(g)) was allocated to the Directorate General for the Internal Market (*D.G. III*), supervised by a Commissioner of Italian nationality. The "approximation-of-law" chapter (including the general Article 100)[1] went to the Directorate General of Competition (*D.G. IV*), a small empire with responsibility for anti-trust, government subsidies, tax harmonization and a host of other matters, supervised by Commissioner Dr. Hans von der Groeben, a lawyer-economist with experience in government administration and in German industry. For reasons which are not apparent, D.G. IV was also assigned whatever competence the Commission could derive from Article 220.[2] That provision places the burden of action not upon the Commission but upon the Member States who are to negotiate with each other on a series of matters some of which concern company law. D.G. IV established a separate "directorate" for "harmonization of law" which was to comprise also company law. This division of competence, based in part on undefined and novel concepts, between two major bureaus led by different Commissioners, added to the already serious coordination difficulties which could be ex-

---

[1] See p. 49 *supra.*
[2] See p. 41 *supra.*

pected even under ideal conditions in a collegiate and multinational institution such as the Commission.[3]

(a)   The case for "coordination" by D.G. III: Article 54 as the king-pin "lex specialis"

In the internal debate which from time to time erupted into the open, the D.G. III argued—and in this it was supported by the influential Legal Service—that Article 54, par. 3(g), as a *lex specialis* in the field of coordination of company law, had absolute priority over Article 100; this latter article was a *lex generalis* and thus constituted only a subsidiary or residuary, "last resort" authority that could be drawn upon only if—in a given area of company law—there was no other, more specific, source of authority in the Treaty.[4] Since there was practically no provision in any national company law—and that included rules on internal organization of companies—that would not concern the protection of either third parties or shareholders, "practically the entire company law" was comprised within that article[5] (and thus within the jurisdiction of D.G. III) and only quite secondary aspects may be laid aside in the exploratory comparative studies at any rate.[6] This broad reach was not

---

[3] On the difficulties of coordination of the assimilation-of-law work within the Commission generally see Stein, *Assimilation* at 8-12.

[4] JUR/CEE/3960/64. *See also* Note in support of oral statement by M. Colonna di Paliano, Exéc. III/Sec. (65)544, Feb. 22, 1965, par. C.
     Art. 100 requires a finding of "direct incidence" of the difference in national laws upon the Common Market; Art. 54, par. 3 (g) assumes such incidence and does not require any such finding.

[5] Dr. H. Bruns, Director in D.G. III, in ENTWICKLUNGSTENDENZEN DES HANDELS- UND STEUERRECHTS, BERICHT ÜBER DIE FACHTAGUNG DES INSTITUTS DER WIRTSCHAFTSPRÜFER IN DEUTSCHLAND E. V. AM 30.-31. JANUAR 1964 IN MÜNCHEN 24, at 25 (Düsseldorf, 1964). *See also* JUR/CEE/3960, at 3 par. 3. LOUSSOUARN, ÉTUDE SUR L'HARMONISATION DU DROIT DES SOCIÉTÉS DANS LES ÉTATS MEMBRES DE LA COMMUNAUTÉ ÉCONOMIQUE EUROPÉENNE, 2117/IV/64-C, at 8, takes the same position.

[6] Note in support of an oral statement by M. Colonna di Paliano, Exéc./III/Sec. (65) 544, Feb. 22, 1965, par. G. *See also* Réponse aux questions posées à M. Colonna di Paliano par les membres de la

restricted by the provision that the coordination was to be carried out with a view to render "equivalent" the protective guarantees, since such equivalence might in some instances require a uniform rule (in which case the appropriate directive would have to be quite detailed and precise), while in others a certain degree of differences among national laws may be allowed to persist.[7] Complete unification was not the objective of coordination; this was evident from the fact that the chosen instrument for coordination was a "directive" which was not suitable for unification; moreover, the differences among the laws of the Six were so substantial as not to permit immediate unification without prior coordination; finally, company law fell within the competence of parliaments, and unification could not be undertaken by the Community unless the European Parliament which was an advisory body only, were given new, truly legislative powers.[8] In any case, while it could not be excluded *a priori* that certain laws concerning companies might eventually and conceivably become subject to approximation under Article 100 (by D.G. IV) it was out of the question—for legal and practical reasons—to think in terms of two successive phases of harmonization.[9]

Perhaps the most telling argument in an institution, eager to preserve and upgrade its own powers vis-à-vis the Member States, was based on the voting formula: Article 54, par. 3(g) allowed the Council to act by qualified majority, while Article 100 required unanimity. The principle of majority decision was one of the most crucial manifestations of the particular character of the Community institutions and must be preserved in all instances where it has been authorized; more

---

Commission parlementaire du Marché Intérieur, addressed to M. Carboni, Président de la Commission Marché Intérieur du Parlement Européen 2250/II/C/65-F, Rev. 1, April 1, 1965, at 9, par. B.

[7] JUR/CEE/3960/64, at 3, par. 3.

[8] Exéc. III/Sec. (65) 544, Feb. 22, 1965, par. 2d; 2250/III/C/65-F, at 14.

[9] JUR/CEE/3960/64, at 4, par. 4.

importantly, as a practical matter, if unanimity should be
required in the company law field, it would almost certainly be impossible to reach any meaningful results, considering the fact that on some points one of the six legislations (the reference is obviously to the Netherlands) did not
have as elaborate rules, offering as much protection, as the
other five. Thus there was no hope for any assimilation without a majority vote, and such vote was possible only under
Article 54. To talk about an approximation through Article
100 or unification through new treaties (both requiring unanimity and, incidentally, falling within the jurisdiction
of the competing D.G. IV) was to pursue a vain illusion.

(b) The case for "approximation" by D.G. IV

The counter argument by D.G. IV was—as could be expected—that a coordination under Article 54 must be limited, as was implied in the concept of "equivalence," to a few
basic "guarantees," such as publication of the company
charter and balance sheet and the maintenance of company
capital, with all other aspects left in the competent hands of
D.G. IV to be dealt with under Article 100. Again, the
unanimity requirement in Article 100, far from being a disadvantage, would encourage Member States to cooperate
readily in this delicate field, without fear of being outvoted;
they would be more hesitant if a majority formula were to
apply as would be the case under Article 54. Finally, two
arguments were pressed in opposition to *any* activity by D.G.
III and, of course, they were angrily denied by it: *First,* the
Commission must not take any action in this field until the
entire company law complex has been thoroughly explored
and a "unified concept" was evolved:[10] in national legal
systems a rule represented a compromise between conflicting
interests, a part of a carefully balanced whole, and a lawmaker could not tamper with it without having a clear idea

---

[10] *See, e.g.,* Arnold, *Die Angleichung des Gesellschaftsrechts* at
221-25. The author was formerly an official of D.G. IV.

what the impact of the proposed change would be on the whole and what final shape the entire company law should take.[11] *Second,* before any specific decisions are taken, the Commission must undertake a study of national company laws with a view to making them "neutral," by "approximation" under Article 100, with respect to concentration and competition. In other words, the company law must be adjusted so that it "neither encourages nor discourages any tendency by firms to concentrate, thus making it consonant with the principles of competition."[12] It has been suggested that this course, obviously influenced by German economic doctrine,[13] would revive—on the Community level—the fruitless debate which on the national level punctuated the company law reform in Germany.[14]

The protagonists in the jurisdictional quarrel were of course lawyers and legal arguments were employed with brilliance in defense of the "tribal territory." An added element which played a still greater role in the antitrust field was the fact that D.G. IV was under the influence of the German neo-liberal economic thought while on the other side the D.G. III and the Legal Service tended to reflect the Franco-Italian concepts of the wider role of government in national economy. The controversy was without any

---

[11] Dr. Bruns felt that an attempt to evolve an overall view of the company law based on a "unified conception" was not the proper method for a coordination. Bruns, in ENTWICKLUNGSTENDENZEN at 24-29.

[12] Memorandum of the Commission on the Action Programme of the Community for the second stage, par. 45 (Brussels, Oct. 24, 1962).

[13] For details see GROSSFELD, AKTIENGESELLSCHAFT, UNTERNEHMENS-KONZENTRATION UND KLEINAKTIONÄR at 44-49 (Tübingen 1968).

[14] Gessler, in ENTWICKLUNGSTENDENZEN at 13. Would for instance the modern German law on related enterprises (Konzernrecht) promote concentration by recognizing the existence of and regulating the interlocking relationships among enterprises? Does a provision on self-financing or a limitation on the formation of hidden reserves or the attribution of the authority to directors to propose dividends advance concentration? Dr. Bruns of D.G. III viewed "competition neutrality as a criterion, perhaps as an objective, but hardly as a basis for an extensive approximation in the field of company law." *Id.* at 24-29.

doubt a major cause of the initial delay in the Commission's work; it gradually lost in intensity and was resolved in 1967 in connection with the "merger" of the executive bodies of the three Communities.[15] In the ensuing reorganization, responsibility for *all* assimilation-of-law work relating to commercial and particularly company law and tax law matters was concentrated in a single, new Directorate General[16] which was placed under the supervision of Commissioner von der Groeben, the former master of D.G. IV; the responsibility for antitrust and subsidies was transferred under the jurisdiction of the Dutch Commissioner Sassen. Since all the officials dealing with company law matters were now assembled in a single Directorate General the former foes became allies and peace was restored.

Most of the Commission staff whom I had encountered were able men and women dedicated to the "European idea." As in any major organization, the power position of a bureau in the Community arena has determined the prestige and advancement possibilities of the officials, and the prospect of these rewards has been a major motivation for the fierce tribal loyalty which at times has cut across other allegiances—to the Community itself, to the nation-state and the national civil service from which many of the

---

[15] Treaty establishing a single Council and a single Commission of the European Communities, [1967] J.O. 152, at 2. The Treaty came into effect on July 1, 1967.

[16] The new Directorate General for the Internal Market and the Approximation of Legislation is headed by T. Vogelaar, formerly a Director General in the Legal Service. The new Directorate General is composed of four Directorates: Freedom of establishment, services and general affairs; approximation of commercial and economic legislation; banking and insurance, company law; taxation. See the "organigram" in the Commission's Press Release 1 P (68)79. Mr. Vogelaar received his law degree at the University of Amsterdam in 1942 and after the War acted as liaison officer to the British Military Government in Germany. He was legal adviser to a large international corporate group with its head office in Amsterdam until 1958. Thereafter he became associated with the EURATOM Commission and until his latest appointment he was Director General in the Legal Service in charge of EURATOM problems.

individual actors have come and to which they may want to return.

2. The slow start: enter first national élites

On the scale of priorities, assimilation of company law necessarily ranked behind such crucial matters as the removal of internal tariffs and quotas and common agricultural policy. It took D.G. III until 1961 before it was able to establish the working group "company law 54(3)(g)," while the D.G. IV working group on company law problems was appointed even later, in November 1962, almost five years after the Treaty had come into effect. Each national Ministry of Justice selected one or more expert members—lawyers of course—either from its own ranks or from a national law faculty;[17] the membership of the two groups overlapped to a considerable extent which tended to mitigate somewhat the antagonism of the competing Directorates.[18] In theory, these experts serve in their personal capacities, with the task of providing expert advice to the Commission; they are not supposed to represent their governments and they do not commit their governments. In fact, however, their position has been ambiguous, since they have often been treated as spokesmen for their national authorities. Because of their high official rank or scholarly standing (or both), these experts have had considerable influence

---

[17] The principal members of the D.G. III group since June 27, 1962 were: *Belgium:* Professors van Ryn, Heenen, and van Ommeslaghe of the Free University of Brussels, Mr. Warnant of the Ministry of Justice, and Mr. Gelders of the Commission bancaire; *Federal Republic:* Prof. Gessler and Dr. Franta of the Ministry of Justice, Mr. Gördel and Dr. Kötter of the Ministry of Economic Affairs; *France:* Messrs. Baudouin, Cotte, and Mabilat of the Ministry of Justice, Prof. Houin of the University of Paris; *Italy:* Mr. Coriasco of the Ministry of Grace and Justice, Mr. Cochetti of the Ministry of Interior (the membership of the Italian delegation varied); *Luxembourg:* Messrs. B. Delvaux and J. Delvaux, attorneys, Mr. Elter and Mrs. Schmidt of the Ministry of Justice; *Netherlands:* Mr. de Vries and Mr. de Die of the Ministry of Justice.

[18] For the membership of the D.G. IV group see note 31 *infra*.

within their Ministries which were to instruct them as to the position they were to take in the working group. For this reason—and because of the technical nature of most of the problems—they have often been in the happy position of writing their own instructions in the national capital to guide them when they appeared in Brussels. They have also served—as was described earlier—as an organic link between the national reform work and the Community effort.

The jurisdictional controversy was not the only reason for the slow start. For one thing, during the early phase, only a very limited staff was available in the Commission to do the necessary preparatory work, one or two senior officials with several young "interns" (*stagiaires*) in each of the two Directorates General, and this was at the time when the total personnel already counted some 2500.[19] Again, there was the understandable difficulty in setting priorities in the field of company law, determining the procedure, selecting the proper legal form for the assimilation act, and—above all—assembling the necessary information about the national laws in the face of an appalling dearth of suitable comparative studies.[20]

(a) The working group on "coordination": the unsuccessful questionnaire

The staff of D.G. III, plagued at the outset by serious leadership problems, concentrated on the elaboration of the two General Programs in the field of establishment and

---

[19] At present, after the reorganization following the "merger of the executives," each of the divisions in the Directorates responsible for coordination and approximation of laws (*see* p. 178 *supra*) consists of a division head, 2 or 3 officials and 2 or 3 "interns" (*stagiaires*).

[20] In its Fourth General Report on the activities of the Community the Commission states—with an obvious sigh—that in the field of approximation of legislation "the particular nature and importance of the comparative studies . . . obviously prevent one to expect concrete results within a brief period of time," CEE, *Quatrième Rapport Général sur l'activité de la Communauté 1961*, at 74.

services which set the end of 1963 as the deadline for the completion of the coordination of company laws under Article 54. This deadline, although clarifying in some measure the general priorities, was obviously quite unrealistic already at the time of the adoption of the two Programs in December 1961.[21]

Happily, the text of Article 54 at least eliminated one uncertainty, since it specifies the legal form of the acts through which coordination is to take place, that is "the directives," which are defined by the Treaty as acts

> binding upon every Member State to which they are addressed as to the result to be achieved, but the form and means of enforcing them shall be left to the national authorities.[22]

In the initial preparatory work that led to the first coordination directive, the staff first had hoped to procure the necessary information on the relevant aspects of national company laws by addressing detailed, uniform questionnaires to national governments which, however, to put it mildly, did not respond with enthusiasm. The governments criticized the excessively broad scope of the questions and pointed out that certain questions were framed to fit some, but not other, legal systems, while other questions could lead to misunderstandings due to translation difficulties.[23] The answers were on the whole incomplete and tardy; moreover, an effective analytical comparison which had to be

---

21 *See* p. 25 *supra.* Actually, the first coordination directive was not *proposed* to the Council until early 1964. The coordination process, however, according to the Treaty itself, was to be completed by the end of the transitional period, that is, by the end of 1969.

22 Art. 189. This article defines also the other legal acts through which the Council or Commission may act in other matters. *See* p. 8 *supra.*

23 See for instance III/C. 7987/61-F (Belgium), III/C/4561/60-F, Aug. 9, 1960; one questionnaire which the Commission staff described in the introduction as "simple," contained no less than 19 pages of questions, 3225/III/C/63-F, March 29, 1963.

undertaken after the answers had been received, was beyond the knowledge and the manpower potential of the Commission staff. It was for this reason that the officials turned to outside private sources, and a consistent practice has developed of commissioning scholars and learned institutions with the preparation of analytical comparative studies on selected aspects of national company laws. In 1965, in view of its increased need for advice, the Commission appointed five scholars, all until then members of the "54(3)g" working group, as its own permanent special consultants on company law.[24]

One difficulty encountered in the working group particularly during the early years was the fact that the successive chairmen, members of the Commission staff, however hard working and erudite, could not match the national experts' knowledge of their respective national company laws based on lifelong experience, and thus found it difficult to provide the necessary leadership.

(b) The working group of D.G. IV: mergers or recognition of companies?

Unlike the built-in deadline for "coordination," neither the approximation provisions of Article 100 nor the undertakings in Article 220 set any time limits. In theory at any rate, the central question with respect to Article 100 was: what aspects of company laws could be said to "directly affect the establishment or functioning of the Common Market" at a time when the Common Market itself was little more than an alluring mirage? When the suggestions for an exploration of the "unified concept" of the company law and its "neutralization" for competition purposes ended

---

[24] The special consultants were: Professors Houin (France), van Ommeslaghe (Belgium), Würdinger (Federal Republic), Miccio (Italy), and Mr. Scholten (Netherlands).

in a blind alley,[25] D.G. IV turned to Article 220 which, however, presented a particular problem.

This article, inserted in the Treaty as an afterthought only a few weeks before it was signed,[26] did not assign any role to the Commission or for that matter to any other institution of the Community; it simply enunciated that Member States "shall, in so far as necessary, engage in negotiations with each other" on specified topics. Nor did the article say what legal form the result of the negotiations was to take.[27] Nevertheless, the Commission assumed the initiative and saw to it that a series of working groups was established to prepare new conventions on the "European" patent and trademark,[28] on judicial jurisdiction and recognition and execution of judgments in civil and commercial matters,[29] on bankruptcy[30] and—last but not least—on selected problems of company law. The legal form of a "convention"— a traditional international treaty—was chosen primarily because it was politically the most palatable instrumentality: it preserved the prerogatives of national parliaments and,

---

[25] See p. 177, note 12 supra. Art. 100 has of course been relied on as a basis for assimilation in fields other than company law. Schwartz, Zur Konzeption der Rechtsangleichung at 480 ff. See also tables referred to in note 1, p. 5 supra. "The wishes of governments and requests of economic groups" were taken into account in selecting priorities. EEC, Third General Report on the Activities of the Community 1960, at 120.

[26] Scholten, Company Law in Europe at 386.

[27] Theoretically, there would be a choice between a simple declaration, an informal understanding, possibly a Council directive or regulation under Art. 235 which allows the Council with the Commission to adopt measures necessary to fill a gap in the Treaty, an agreement by representatives of the six Governments meeting in the forum of the Council, or finally a treaty imposing specified obligations or containing a uniform law which the members would undertake to adopt; see p. 445 infra.

[28] See p. 46 supra.

[29] Text in 14124/IV/67/Fin and Report by the Chairman M.P. Jenard, director in the Belgian Ministry of Foreign Affairs and External Commerce, and in 1969 Bull. E.C. Supp. No. 2, at 17. English text also in CCH COMM. MKT. REP. ¶ 6003.

[30] Draft in 5267/XIV/68-F (1968).

at the same time, it offered the possibility of adopting "self-executing" rules of common European law in those areas where the EEC Treaty did not authorize the adoption of such rules by the Community institutions or where the authority was unclear.

In contrast with the Article 54 group, a creature of the Commission with the task to prepare drafts for the Commission, the groups under Article 220 were appointed by the Member Governments and, in theory, they function as intergovernmental conferences, with the Commission providing supporting staff and services. The chairmanship is held by one of the government experts and not by a Commission official as in the Article 54 group, and the product—thus far in all cases a draft convention—is not forwarded "for approval" to the Commission but (at the insistence of the French Government) directly to the President of the Council of Ministers and to the Member Governments; the Commission renders its opinion on the draft.

Under the able chairmanship of the French member, Professor Berthold Goldman of the Paris Law Faculty, the Article 220 group on company law[31] had to determine its

---

[31] The following were the principal participants in this working group: *Belgium:* Messrs. de Granges de Surgères, Director at the Ministry of Justice, Jenard, Director at the Ministry of Foreign Affairs, Prof. van Ryn and one other official from each of the above Ministries; *Federal Republic:* Messrs. Bülow, Franta, and Prof. Gessler, all of the Federal Ministry of Justice, Dr. Kötter and Mr. Rambow of the Federal Ministry of Economic Affairs; *France:* Mr. Baudouin of the Ministry of Justice, Prof. Goldman and Prof. Houin, both of the Faculty of Law and Economic Sciences of Paris, an official of the Ministry of Economy and Finance and of the Ministry of Industry; *Italy:* Mr. Castelli, Section Director of the Ministry of Interior, Prof. Miccio, Ministry of Grace and Justice, Mr. Terrana, Ministry of Industry and Commerce; *Luxembourg:* Mr. B. Delvaux, Attorney; *Netherlands:* Mr. Scheffer of the Ministry of Justice, Miss van Heukelom of the Ministry of Foreign Affairs, and another official from the Ministry of Justice. *Observers:* Mr. van Hoogstraten, Secretary General of the Hague Conference on Private International Law, and a legal advisor from the Secretariat of the Council of Ministers. A number of *Commission* staff from the Legal Service, D.G. IV and D.G. III also participated regularly.

own priorities among the topics listed in Article 220, that is, the mutual recognition of companies, the maintenance of their legal personality in case of a seat transfer, and merger ("fusion") of companies subject to the law of different Member States. As we saw above, the recognition was tackled first, not because of any pressing practical need, but rather because of the direct systemic relationship to the freedom of establishment, and also because of the relatively noncontroversial and traditionally "international" nature of the subject, and the availability of substantial comparative materials which offered the prospect of a relatively speedy accomplishment. At this early stage of the Common Market, it obviously was not very necessary to enable a company to transfer its "seat" from one Member State to another, but if the group had been guided by practical considerations of the commercial world it would have taken up international mergers first. However, for one thing, a feeling prevailed in the high reaches of the Commission hierarchy that any move toward facilitating international mergers should await the formulation of the Commission's policy on concentrations and monopolies. But the staff which was assigned this latter task was more than fully absorbed by evolving a policy for the application of Article 85 on cartels and other restrictive agreements; only in 1963 were arrangements made for eight university professors to undertake two studies, one on the application of Article 86 regarding dominant enterprises, and the second on the relationship between the "cartel policy" and the "concentration policy," with particular attention to the possibility of applying the anti-cartel rules of Article 85 to mergers, somewhat along the lines of the United States antitrust law. The reports became

---

The Chairman, Prof. Berthold Goldman, has taught at the Law Faculty in Dijon, and since 1960 in Paris. He is editor-in-chief of several periodicals in the field of comparative and international law and is widely known as a consultant on legal matters.

available late in the fall of 1964 only,[32] at a time when the clamor for intra-Community mergers as a means of combating the American "invasion" became more persistent not only in France but in certain circles in Germany and Italy as well. The first statement on the concentration policy, based on the scholarly studies and rejecting in principle the possibility of applying Article 85 to concentrations, was made by Dr. von der Groeben before the European Parliament in June 1965.[33] Some officials, particularly in French circles within the Commission, questioned the need for the delay in the work on facilitating international mergers and discerned in it an "excessive" emphasis on the antitrust aspects reflecting German economic philosophy—and ultimately the American influence.

Another complicating factor was the relationship between company law and tax law since, from the practical viewpoint, the tax obstacles to international mergers appeared much more formidable than those posed by company law.[34] However, the tax division of D.G. IV had become entirely enmeshed in the harmonization of the turnover tax which called for priority treatment, because of its direct impact on prices and the flow of goods across the frontiers. As a result, the tax aspects relating to company law were put aside for all practical purposes until 1964, and that lent an air of artificiality to the initial work on mergers in company law.

---

[32] ÉTUDE RÉLATIVE AUX MOYENS DÉCOULANT DE L'ARTICLE 86 DU TRAITÉ, RAPPORT DE SYNTHÈSE DU GROUPE I (MM. les Professeurs Samkalden, Président, Houssiaux, Rapporteur, Lombardini, Fikentscher, 14.190/IV/64-F); ÉTUDE DES RAPPORTS EXISTANT ENTRE LA POLITIQUE EN MATIÈRE D'ENTENTES (Article 85) ET LA CONCENTRATION D'ENTREPRISES, RAPPORT DE SYNTHÈSE DU GROUPE II de MM. les Professeurs Müller, Président, Philips, Rapporteur, Bernini, Mercillon, 7574-6/IV/64-F.

[33] Von der Groeben, *Competition Policy* at 20; *see also* Concentration of Enterprises in the Common Market, Memorandum of the EEC Commission to the Member Governments, CCH COMM. MKT. REP. No. 26, Mar. 17, 1966.

[34] Conard, *Corporate Fusion in the Common Market,* 14 AM. J. COMP. L. 573, at 583 (1965-66). *See* p. 383 *infra.*

Be that as it may—the D.G. IV working group was not ready to turn to the merger problem until it had completed the draft convention on mutual recognition of companies in mid-1965. By that time the group had before it a scholarly report on company law problems posed by international mergers which was prepared by Professor Rodière of the Paris law faculty and was to serve as a basis for its work.[35]

3. The expanding arena of debate

(a) The early public posture of the Commission

In the internal dialogue within the Commission and among its staff the issue was, as we have seen, how to divide Community power between two competing bureaus, even though the power with respect to the outside world was defined in somewhat unrealistically broad terms. Two sets of values were involved: *first,* a transnational *common* interest in advancing integration through assimilation of law and increasing the power of the Community vis-à-vis the Member States; and *second,* a *particularized* interest in upgrading the power position of one bureau at the expense of another.

It was not surprising that the Commission's public posture was, to say the least, ambiguous and its statements on the company law program few and far between. Commission President Hallstein's speech in 1964 before the Max Planck Institute in Hamburg, important as it was as the first effort to trace a more general policy framework for the fragmented, multipronged, and disconnected harmonization work carried on in the many bureaus of the Commission, threw no light on such concrete problems as the desired scope of the coordination or the specific role of Article 100 in company

---

35 R. RODIÈRE, LE DROIT DES SOCIÉTÉS DANS SES RAPPORTS AVEC LA CONCENTRATION (E.E.C. Commission, Études, série concurrence No. 5, Brussels 1967).

law.[36] In the annual reports on its activities the Commission
was quite reticent and from the outset stressed the work
under Article 220 about which, as we have seen, there was
relatively little controversy.[37] No specific mention was made
of the coordination under Article 54 in the first six reports[38] or in the Commission's 1962 "Action Program" which
seemed to envisage, in oracular terms, a multistage assimilation of undefined but vast proportions.[39]

---

[36] Hallstein, *Angleichung des Privat-und Prozessrechts* at 231.

[37] The first reference was in the EEC, *Third General Report on
the Activities of the Community 1960,* at 119, 123-24. The General
Program for the removal of restrictions on the freedom of establishment purports only to set a deadline for the coordination, without
giving the least indication of its scope *(see supra* p. 37), but the very
brevity of the time period allocated suggests perhaps a limited scope.

[38] The first specific reference to that article was in paras. 52 and
54 of the EEC, *Seventh General Report on the Activities of the Community 1964,* at 56, 57.

[39] It is said under the general rubric "Approximation of Legislation" and the heading "Company law":

> In this field the Community has several long-term tasks
> to cope with. One aim already mentioned is to adjust Member
> States' company law in such a way that it neither encourages
> nor discourages any tendency by firms to concentrate, thus
> making it consonant with the principles of competition.
> Preparatory work has already begun. The Commission will
> intensify and speed it up, so as to reach an interim solution,
> if possible, during the second stage.
> During the same stage, the Commission will press forward
> its work on the approximation of legislation, undertaken
> under Article 100, and also work on the recognition of the
> legal personality of companies, on the transfer of a company's
> registered office from one State to another, and mergers of
> companies under the law of different countries.
> During the third stage further steps will be taken
> towards the harmonization of company law: the Commission
> will then be able to submit proposals for directives or for the
> preparation of European conventions.

Memorandum of the Commission on the Action Programme of the
Community for the second stage, par. 45 (Brussels, Oct. 24, 1962). The
reference in the quoted text to the "[o]ne aim already mentioned"
is apparently to par. 26 under the heading "Concentration of Firms"
in which

(b)   National values injected

The creation of the working groups meant, as we have seen, a first modest broadening of the arena beyond the corridors of the Commission office building and the beginning of a confrontation with the first line (predominantly governmental) *national* élites. It meant an injection into the Community system of national values, such as the attachment to national law, preservation of national power, and the protection of national enterprise. The confrontation concerned again power, a division of power between the Community on the one hand and the national power centers on the other.

The meetings of the working groups are closed; but we find an instructive illustration of the early confrontation that spilled over into the public domain in an exchange between two German nationals, Professor Gessler, the German expert in both working groups dealing with company law, who was also, as we have seen, the principal actor in the German national reform, and Dr. Bruns, an able Director in D.G. III. In this exchange, Professor Gessler vigorously attacked the Commission's Action Program for "approximation of legislation" both because of its ambitious scope and because it would require a series of consecutive, piecemeal changes in national laws.[40] Article 54, par. 3(g)

---

it is felt to be particularly important to see that concentration having no justification from the standpoint of the economy at large should at least not be artificially encouraged. In practical terms, this means that the first step must be to secure greater neutrality in respect of competition in company law, tax law and the law on industrial property. . . .

On this problem see also Hallstein, *Angleichung des Privat-und Prozessrechts* at 231.

[40] "I ask myself with a certain preoccupation, whether one can expect a harmonious company law from so many and so different harmonizations." Gessler, in ENTWICKLUNGSTENDENZEN at 10-11.

Dr. Herbert Bruns left the Federal Ministry of Finance to join the Commission staff in 1958. He was in charge of the work on freedom of establishment and supply of services, and after the "merger" of the "executives" he became director of the Directorate dealing with

was limited, he argued, by its purpose to facilitate freedom
of establishment, so that the diversity of national rules must
be preserved to the greatest possible degree; and Article 100
might not have any, or at the most a very marginal application to company law, since that law was "in the first place
a law of organizational forms" whose "influence on the
market is *a priori* quite limited."[41]

In his response Dr. Bruns readily conceded the narrow
interpretation of Article 100 but not of Article 54. The more
interesting aspect of the reply, however, was his artful
management of the national and Community values involved. First, addressing himself to the preoccupation in the
German quarters, he thought that the German stock company law generally provided quite effective guarantees
which, strengthened still further by the national reform
then in progress, were likely to serve as a model. It will be
the legal systems of those *other* Member States which "historically date from an earlier epoch" that will be made
the subject of a critical examination. Thus the Federal
Republic should be greatly interested in the coordination
and the Federal Government itself must *welcome* coordination since, he recalled, it had sought to block a measure in
the field of the freedom of establishment pending such
coordination.[42] On the Community level, Dr. Bruns argued,
the determining issue was whether the assimilation should
be limited to technical aspects—that is, whether it was to
serve merely as a means of establishing competitive conditions—or whether the objective should be to achieve "uniform legal concepts" with a highly integrative effect, a
"Leitbild" (a "guiding image") of the economic and social

---

harmonization of company law and establishment of banks and insurance companies. He resigned in 1969 to become a member of the
board of an insurance concern, the Nordstern Allgemeine Versicherung
AG, Köln/Berlin.

41 *Id.* at 13.

42 *Id.* at 26. *See* p. 38 *supra.*

order for Europe.[43] But returning quickly to his original *argumentum ad hominem,* he wanted to reassure Professor Gessler that the Commission was following the latter's counsel of wise self-limitation and was seeking practical results— through two directives—not unification or even the highest possible "approximation." It would be relatively simple, Dr. Bruns concluded, to say in abstract terms which legal solution offers the strongest protection and at what kind of guarantee one should aim in any given case. But national company laws were grounded in national traditions and formed a part of the law that had grown in national "separateness" (*Absonderung*). The Commission staff therefore must carefully feel its way in order to find out to what extent it was possible to loosen the concepts that were firmly rooted in national law if in its view they did not guarantee the necessary degree of legal security in the Community.

(c) The Commission as a client and "establishment": from "conflict" to "collusion"

The Commission's growing reliance on outside experts led to an expansion of the ranks of the engaged élites in still another direction. In the early and mid-sixties, these "non-governmental" experts, principally law professors who as a rule were also active in some gainful law work, saw to it that the debate spread into legal periodicals and professional meetings throughout the Community. In the United States, the "client" relationship between members of the academic community and the federal executive departments (principally Defense and State) has been the subject of criticism by the "anti-establishment" forces. Analogous relationships began to emerge on a transnational level between the bureaus of the Commission and their academic consultants, as is illustrated by the sharp but competent polemic between two French scholars of the same Paris law

---

[43] Quoting Prof. Müller-Armack, former Federal Secretary of State for Economic Affairs. *Id.* at 27.

faculty. Professor Houin, a French expert on the "54(3)g" working group, and later a special consultant to the Commission, has been closely associated with D.G. III and advocated a broad interpretation of that article; while on the opposing side Professor Rodière, who advised D.G. IV, supported a restrictive interpretation and limited coordination only.[44] To Rodière, greater freedom for market forces and companies was the controlling principle of interpretation; in Houin's view, the coordination clause in Article 54, par. 3(g) was concerned not with greater freedom, but, on the contrary, with necessary limitations on the freedom of foreign companies to escape guarantees required of local companies.

With one possible exception, the division between the advocates of a broad and narrow interpretation did not appear to be determined by national allegiance.[45] Only in

---

[44] Houin, *Le régime juridique des sociétés dans la Communauté économique européenne,* 1965 Rev. trim. droit eur. 11, at 16 and *passim;* Rodière, *L'harmonisation des législations européennes dans le cadre de la C.E.E., id.* 336, 337, 343-57. Prof. Roger Henri Houin has taught commercial law at Rennes, and since 1958 in Paris. He was avocat à la cour de Paris (1933-1938), secretary-general of the national Commission for the reform of the Civil code (1946-1964), and since 1968 councillor at the Conseil d'État "en service extraordinaire." He served as a government-appointed expert on EEC working group "54(3)g" and more recently has been special consultant on company law to the Commission at Brussels. He is editor-in-chief of the leading French commercial law review and of the French review on European law.

[45] Among those advocating a restrictive interpretation one may list: *Germany:* Everling, Das Niederlassungsrecht im Gemeinsamen Markt at 41; Gessler, *Ziele und Methoden der Harmonisierung des Gesellschaftsrechts der GmbH,* in Harmonisierung des Gesellschaftsrechts und des Steuerrechts in Europa, Bericht über den VII. Internationalen GmbH-Kongress in Köln, April 24-26, 1962, at 9 ff. (Köln 1962); *France:* Rodière, *L'harmonisation des législations* at 16 ff.; *Belgium:* Renauld, *Aspects de la coordination* at 613; *Netherlands:* Uniken-Venema, *Coordination du droit des sociétés dans la Cee,* 1966 Rivista delle società 994, at 1002-03; Scholten, *Company Law in Europe* at 379. These last two authors offer the most restrictive interpretation. Scholten refers to the legislative history of the EEC Treaty at 383-86. For a nuanced analysis see van Ommeslaghe, *La première directive* at 506-08.

the Netherlands, those favoring a restrictive construction appeared to rule supremely. In Germany and France the views were divided, with the practitioners outside the "academia" displaying somewhat greater skepticism toward the assimilation work and some in France inclining to the "European company" as a preferable alternative. What had begun as an abstract and highly conceptual debate, often centering upon a sterile, textual or at the most contextual interpretation of the Treaty, became, as we shall see, gradually more concrete and meaningful, as the Commission's specific proposals became available for specific criticism. The writings by the national experts and the Commission staff have been the principal sources in the legal literature; as these experts became more familiar with the company laws of the Six their contributions have acquired a more "comparative" tinge and have become more focused on specific issues. The interest generated by the Commission's work has led to what one may call a flowering of comparative company law studies in the universities and in the some forty new centers of European studies.[46]

Among those advocating broad interpretation: *Germany:* Arnold, *Die Angleichung des Gesellschaftsrechts* at 223; von Arnim, *Das Niederlassungsrecht für Gesellschaften im Gemeinsamen Markt und die Pläne zur Schaffung der "europäischen" Handelsgesellschaft,* 1965 AWD 346, at 347, considers as "guarantees" all essential provisions which determine the life of the company from its formation to its dissolution. Probably also Möhring, *Aktuelle Wirkungen des EWG-Vertrages auf das Kartellrecht, das Niederlassungsrecht, den Dienstleistungsverkehr und das Agrarrecht,* 1965 NJW 1633, at 1640; Bärmann, *Les Communautés européennes* at 10; Beitzke, *Anerkennung* at 42; Fikentscher & Grossfeld, *The Proposed Directive* at 260; Lutter, *Die Rechtsangleichung im Gesellschaftsrecht* at 34; *France:* Houin, *Le régime* at 16; Sinay, *La proposition de directive européenne* at 45; *Italy:* Guglielmetti, *Le direttive della CEE in materia di società e l'interpretazione dell' articolo 54.3.g del Trattato,* 1966 Rivista delle società 1012; Lansa, *Attività e tendenze della Communità economica europea in tema di società,* 1966 Rivista delle società 1034.

46 Several doctoral theses have been written on this subject and thorough studies have been prepared by young scholars in connection with their first appointment to a professorial position. *E.g.,* Lutter, Kapital, Sicherung der Kapitalaufbringung und Kapitalerhaltung

The initial "conflict"-type relationship between the Community staff and the national élites, such as was illustrated by the Gessler-Bruns debate, has lost some sharpness as the working groups have come down to specific issues, and it has gradually turned into a "collusion" relationship within the Community system. This process of transformation will become apparent in the next chapter.

IN DEN AKTIEN- UND GMBH-RECHTEN DER EWG (Karlsruhe 1964); for theses in progress see EUROPEAN COMMUNITY INSTITUTE FOR UNIVERSITY STUDIES, UNIVERSITY STUDIES ON EUROPEAN INTEGRATION, vol. 4, 1967, vol. 5, 1969 (Brussels).

Chapter 6

THE MAKING OF THE FIRST COORDINATION DIRECTIVE: A CASE STUDY

In the normal course of the Community lawmaking process, a working-group draft of a directive is approved by the Commission after consultation with interested nongovernmental groups. The Commission transmits the approved text to the Council of Ministers which consults formally with the Economic and Social Committee and with the European Parliament. The Council may then adopt the Commission's proposal by a qualified majority vote, but if it wishes to modify the proposal it may do so by a unanimous vote only, unless the Commission is prepared to accept the modification.[1]

1. The Hobson's choice: what topics to coordinate?

If coordination was to embrace practically the entire company law (and this was a part of the Community mythology), the working group of D.G. III would have been faced with a sisyphian task, a monumental study of six legal systems, which would have to be completed within a brief period of time.[2] If, on the other hand, the group decided "to begin

---

[1] EEC Arts. 54, 148, 149.

[2] According to Art. VI of the General Program for the Removal of Restrictions on the Freedom of Establishment, *supra* note 5, p. 25, the national laws of the Member States were to be coordinated before the expiration of the second year of the second stage of the transitional period, that is, according to Art. 8 of the Treaty, before December 31, 1963. Everling, *Niederlassungsfreiheit* at 1259; LeTallec, *Koordinierung des Gesellschaftsrechtes in der EWG*, 1963 AWD 114. The time limit set forth in the General Program has been greatly exceeded. In the first draft of the first directive on the coordination of company law

195

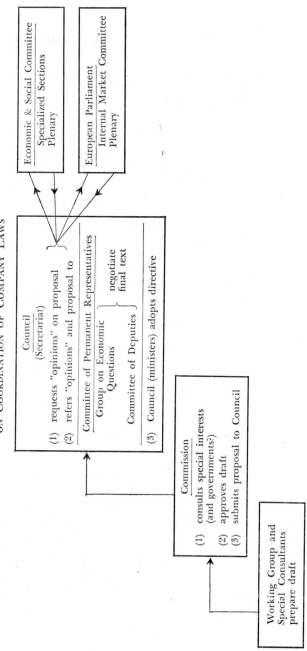

FLOW CHART OF DIRECTIVES
ON COORDINATION OF COMPANY LAWS

Economic & Social Committee
Specialized Sections
Plenary

European Parliament
Internal Market Committee
Plenary

Council
(Secretariat)
(1) requests "opinions" on proposal
(2) refers "opinions" and proposal to

Committee of Permanent Representatives
Group on Economic Questions
Committee of Deputies   } negotiate final text

(3) Council (ministers) adopts directive

Commission
(1) consults special interests (and governments?)
(2) approves draft
(3) submits proposal to Council

Working Group and
Special Consultants
prepare draft

at the beginning" by singling out several more or less specific problems for treatment in a series of directives it
opened itself to the objection of a "piece-meal" approach
which presumably was not acceptable either to the national
parliaments or to the business community, and was viewed
as destructive of the coherence of the legal systems. Nevertheless, the decision was made to seek some practical results
as rapidly as possible[3] and to proceed with a first directive
that would be limited both horizontally to certain company
forms and vertically with respect to subject matter.

(a) Horizontal limitation: only "capital" companies covered

The first directive was to apply not to all companies which
according to Article 58 of the Treaty were to benefit from
the freedom of establishment, but only to those which were
"most prominent in the international sphere" (and thus
most likely to seek the benefit of freedom of establishment
abroad),[4] and in which individual liability was limited so

([1964] J.O. 3245), the Commission set as a deadline for the Member
States to enact the necessary changes in their national laws the 1st of
January, 1965. After that date had passed without the adoption of the
directive by the Council, the Commission considered that it should be
possible to adopt the directive before the end of 1966 (BERKHOUWER
REPORT at 9). The hope to meet this deadline was indicated in the
second draft of the Commission (Proposition revisée d'une Directive du
Conseil, COM (66) 366 final Oct. 3, 1966) which fixed the 1st of July,
1967, as the date by which the changes in national laws were to be
executed. However, the directive was not adopted until March 9,
1968, and the final deadline for modification of national laws was set
eighteen months after the notification of the Member States.

3 Bruns, in ENTWICKLUNGSTENDENZEN at 27.

4 Explanatory Memorandum (at 14) to the first draft of a Proposal
for a Council Directive to Coordinate and Render Equivalent the
Guarantees Required in the Member States of Companies Defined in
Art. 58, Second Paragraph of the Treaty, to Protect the Interests of
the Members of Such Companies and of Third Parties, Submitted to
the Council on Feb. 21, 1964, [1964] J.O. 3245; unofficial English text
in 1964 Bull. E.E.C. Supp. No. 3, at 10. Cited as "First Draft," reproduced with the Opinion of the Economic and Social Committee (AVIS).
Revised proposal of the directive dated Oct. 3, 1966, in Commission
Doc. 1966, COM (66) 366 final of the same date, cited as "Second

that the company assets were the only "guarantee" with respect to creditors,[5] that is, stock companies, limited partnerships with shares and limited liability companies.[6] Other reasons for selecting these companies were that "their purposes are practically the same or that on certain points they are subject to identical or similar national rules," and last, but not least, to include some, but not all, company forms in this group might encourage "getting round the law."[7]

This selection, dictated by a sense of urgency,[8] was applauded by some,[9] and only reluctantly accepted—for practical reasons—by others, including the majority of the Economic and Social Committee.[10] In accepting the limitation,

---

Draft." Final Text, as adopted, on Mar. 8, 1968, in [1968] J.O. L65 (Mar. 14) at 8-12. English text in the Annex p. 515 *infra,* and also in CCH COMM. MKT. REP. ¶ 6083.

According to Uniken-Venema, *Coordination du droit des sociétés* at 1004, the argument of the Commission in the text above did not carry any conviction, for "activity" did not mean "establishment." *But see* M. Molle, Reapporteur de la Commission des lois, DÉB. PARL., SÉNAT, [1966] J.O. (France) at 117.

[5] Eighth preambular para. of the proposed directive, *First Draft,* in AVIS at 3246; *Final Text,* [1968] J.O. L65 (March 14), at 8.

[6] Art. 1 enumerates specifically the company forms in the national laws included. This means exclusion from coordination, for the time being, of partnerships and limited partnerships, e.g., "sociétés en nom collectif" and "sociétés en commandite simple" in France (see Conard, *Organizing for Business* at 50) and of "foundations" and cooperatives.

[7] Working paper 456/III/C/63-F, at 9. 1968 Bull. E.C. No. 3, at 14, II. CCH COMM. MKT. REP. ¶ 1375.02.

[8] Sixth preambular paragraph, [1964] J.O. 3245, [1968] J.O. L65, (March 14), at 8.

[9] Fikentscher & Grossfeld, *The Proposed Directive* at 265-66, welcomed particularly the inclusion of the limited liability company because it is "very widely interchangeable" with the stock company, and "a transformation into a limited liability company is able (sic) to produce only too easily an escape from the provisions laid down in respect of the joint stock company." Similarly, approving at least temporary limitation, GOLDMAN, COURS at 215, and Dorat des Monts, *Vers un droit européen* at par. I, 3.

[10] Avis du Comité économique et social at 3249-3256, approved in the 41st session held at Brussels, Oct. 27-28, 1964, by a vote of 68 to 7. Dorat des Monts, *Vers un droit européen* at par I.

the Committee urged that the coordination be extended as quickly as possible to other types of legal persons, including cooperatives and "foundations" (*fondations, Stiftungen*) some of which play an important role in national economies.[11]

(b) Vertical limitation: only three subjects chosen

When it came to choosing the specific subjects the ideas on priorities differed widely. Theoretically, the discussion was of course in the context of what coordination was "necessary" in the sense of Article 54. In reality, most of the individual national experts wished to focus first either on those aspects which in their own company law were deficient and required reform, or on those areas where less strict provisions in other Member States posed a potential problem. Thus Dr. Gessler, obviously concerned at the loss of power by the German authorities to keep out foreign under-

---

11 Avis at [1964] J.O. 3250. The Specialized Group for Non-Salaried Activities and Services, a subsidiary body of the Committee, actually urged that the Commission's proposal be amended to include foundations organized for profit, but the Committee did not accept this view. ZUSÄTZLICHE STELLUNGNAHME, July 30, 1964, CES 195/64 fin. at 3. The Committee stated that, if foundations were not included, this would be an inducement to abuse this legal form. [1964] J.O. 3250, par. II, 2. Dorat des Monts, *Vers un droit européen* at par. I, 3 urged that the problem of the scope of the application of the proposed directive be viewed more from the economic than the legal viewpoint. He suggested that any obligation (such as disclosure) imposed on an association should not be linked to its legal form but to the actual importance it has in the economy. This criterion, employed in the First Draft with respect to the limited liability company which was to be required to disclose its financial situation only if its balance sheet total exceeded one million units of account ($) (Art. 2, par. 1, sect. 1), should be determinative for all associations. Le Tallec, *Koordinierung des Gesellschaftsrechtes* at 114, thought that the decision to include only the three mentioned companies, was made on the assumption that other types of associations would not be interested in international business activities. But consider the German Zeiss Foundation and its worldwide business. For the structure of this Foundation and its legal and economic aspects see Mayer, *The Carl Zeiss Foundation*, 10 J. PUB. L. 384 (1961).

capitalized "dwarf" companies,[12] urged concentrating first on provisions governing the minimum required company capital, availability and maintenance of the capital, but also the rules concerning the authority of company organs to act on its behalf and publication of information on the legal status of companies, all of which called for a reform in *other* Member States.[13] The Belgian delegation laid particular emphasis on strengthening the protection of minority shareholders. The Netherlands experts continued to assert that no coordination was necessary; they argued that although the

---

[12] *Supra* p. 40.

[13] Gessler, *Ziele und Methoden,* in HARMONISIERUNG at 18; Gessler pointed out that it was possible, before the enactment of the new French Company Law (Loi No. 66-537 of July 24, 1966), to derive from the prescribed minimum number of incorporators and minimum face amount of a share the minimum capital of 700 French francs, Art. 23 of the Law of 1867, and Art. 28 of the Décret of August 4, 1949. Bruns, in ENTWICKLUNGSTENDENZEN at 17; similarly EVERLING at 84 n.63. The 1966 Company Law introduced the concept of a minimum capital by requiring in its Art. 71 that all stock companies which make public offering must have 500,000 francs ($100,000) minimum capital; for all other stock companies a minimum of 100,000 francs ($20,000) is required. This new law brings the French law in line with the German law (not considering recent changes in monetary values), except that the German stock company law does not employ the distinction between companies which do and which do not make public offering, and thus provides only for a 100,000 DM ($27,300) minimum for all stock companies. The similarity also prevails with respect to the limited liability company for which in both countries 20,000 francs or marks is necessary. Art. 35 of the French Law of July 24, 1966; § 5 of the Law on Limited Liability Companies (Gesetz über die Gesellschaften mit beschränkter Haftung). In Luxembourg the required capitalization is still minimal. The minimum number of incorporators taking one share each of the minimum face amount would bring the total capital to 350 Luxembourg francs ($77). Loi sur les sociétés commerciales of Aug. 15, 1915, Arts. 26, 27, 37. In the Netherlands, apparently the Ministry of Justice allows not infrequently incorporation of stock companies with a capital amounting to not more than 1,000 guilders (about $276); an actual minimum amount is not required. Art. 36d of the Netherlands WETBOEK VAN KOOPHANDEL. Belgium has no minimum capital requirement as yet, but one million francs ($20,000) is contemplated to be the requirement in the reform law. In Italy one million lire (about $1,600) is the minimum required to form a stock company. Art. 2327 CODICE CIVILE.

Netherlands company law was much less elaborate there
have not been any more numerous bankruptcies under that
law than under the strict legislation of its neighbor to the
East.[14] However, a French civil service official employed in
D.G. III, brought with him to Brussels a draft of a questionnaire prepared originally, as reported by Professor Houin, by
the so-called Hamel Committee at the Secretariat of State for
Economic Affairs in Paris. This paper was limited to three
topics: publication of information in connection with the
formation of companies, the extent of the authority of company organs in relation to third parties, and circumstances
under which a company was considered invalid ("null and
void"). The same questionnaire, designed to elicit information on national rules governing these topics, was sent by the
EEC Commission to the Member Governments. The re-
sponses were submitted to the working group which in the
end embraced a somewhat broadened version of the original
French selection of topics.[15] The idea apparently was that

---

14 Bruns, in ENTWICKLUNGSTENDENZEN at 26.

15 Houin, *Le régime* at 14. Paul Leleux, a legal advisor at the
Legal Service of the Commission, writes that the selection was based
substantially on "studies made in France where there were complaints
of a certain degree of legal chaos" in two of the three areas selected, to
wit: " 'publicity' which was extremely insufficient, and the causes of
'nullity,' which, until the adoption of recent French law [of 1966],
represented a puzzle for lawyers and business men." Leleux, *Harmonisation des droits des sociétés*, in EUROPÄISCHE HANDELSGESELLSCHAFT
UND ANGLEICHUNG DES NATIONALEN GESELLSCHAFTSRECHTS, WISSENSCHAFT-
LICHES KOLLOQUIUM DER FACHGRUPPE EUROPARECHT, WISSENSCHAFT-
LICHE GESELLSCHAFT FÜR EUROPARECHT, 5/6 Mai 1967, Bad Ems, 37,
at 47 (Frankfurt/M.-Berlin 1968. Houin who prepared the questionnaire in the Hamel Committee disagrees with this analysis. He asserts
that the choice of subjects was not based on considerations of French
law but rather on an effort to identify, *in the laws of the Six*, important
points, affecting interests of third parties, on which a first study could
be usefully focused, as is contemplated in Art. 54, par. 3(g). First, "publicity" appeared important, he reports, not because the French legislation was defective (such legislation was not substantially modified by
the Law of 1966 and to a large measure it served as a basis for the
First Directive) but because purely local publicity, effected in a
variety of different forms, did not appear suitable for an enlarged
Common Market. Second, as regards the power of management with

the three topics lent themselves to a treatment separate from other aspects of company law, since the coordinating rules could be designed so as to apply to the entire group of the companies concerned, while subsequent directives would co-ordinate separately other aspects (such as minimum capital requirements).[16] In effect, the first directive was to serve as a "trial run" for the coordination process and was to be dealt with quickly on a priority basis. This, we shall see, proved to be an illusion.

The selection of the topics was criticized both within and outside the working group because, so went the argument, on one hand, it did not include the truly urgent matters, and on the other hand, it exceeded the authority under Article 54, par. 3(g).[17]

Nevertheless the working group proceeded with the draft-ing of the coordinating rules in these three areas, and the draft was formally approved by the Commission, published and transmitted to the Council on February 19, 1964,[18] and the Council then instituted the next phase in the law-making process, consultation with the Economic and Social Committee and the European Parliament.

---

respect to third parties, the German system which had already been in effect in France for limited liability companies, appeared worthy of general acceptance. Third, the Hamel Committee was aware of the criticism abroad of the French system of "nullities" of companies, and it appeared useful to study how this problem was solved in the other Member States.

[16] Bruns, in ENTWICKLUNGSTENDENZEN at 27. See for additional explanation Leleux, *Harmonisation des droits* at 47-48.

[17] Leleux, *Harmonisation des droits* at 47. Uniken-Venema, *Co-ordination du droit* at 1008-09. The Economic and Social Committee also suggested a number of other rules which it thought ought to be coordinated: payment of capital, audits of accounts, number of share-holders. AVIS at 3250.

[18] [1964] J.O. 3245-48, *First Draft.* Until 1964 the working group met not more than three times a year for sessions of 2-3 days. How-ever, in 1964 it had already met six times. BERKHOUWER REPORT at 8, par. 19.

2. Consultations with transnational economic and political groups

These consultations begin as a rule, when a working group of national experts and Commission staff reaches a more or less general agreement on a draft of a directive— and prior to the submission of the draft to the Commission for formal approval. The multiphased consultation process of mutual enlightenment and persuasion broadens the circle of the élite beyond the national and transnational bureaucracy directly concerned, and beyond the group of scholars linked with it.

(a) "Bilateral" consultations with economic interest groups

Perhaps because this process had not been firmly established as yet at the time when the first draft of the first co-ordination directive became available, the Commission staff omitted the first stage—that is "bilateral" consultation with the interested economic and professional groups organized on the Community level. By contrast, in 1968 the draft of the second coordination directive[19] was submitted, with a request for an opinion, to the three professional "summit" organizations grouping together national associations of industry, banking and the legal professions, that is, the Union of Industries of the European Community (*Union des Industries de la Communauté, UNICE*), the Federation of Banks of the EEC (*Fédération Bancaire de la C.E.E.*), and the Consultative Commission of the Bar of the Six Countries of the EEC (*Commission Consultative du Barreau des Six Pays de la CEE*) established for this purpose by the International Union of Attorneys (*Union Internationale des Avocats*). These three organizations are now regularly consulted on matters of company law.[20] Yet the number of

---

[19] *See* p. 316 *infra.*

[20] Initially, labor unions were not included in the consultation process in this field. But labor unions were consulted on the proposed

persons in the transnational secretariats and committees of these nongovernmental organizations, who actually become familiar with the complex technical texts and directly involved in the preparation of the opinions on behalf of the organizations, is quite limited. Thus, the opinion of the *Fédération Bancaire* on the second coordination directive was drafted by a house counsel of a leading national bank who (in addition to his law faculty position and law practice) has served simultaneously on the national company law reform commission and also was a national expert on the Commission's working group. This may be perhaps an extreme, if not unique, instance illustrating the dearth of expert talent in this field.

The impact of the "summit" organizations on lawmaking in the Community has often been reduced by their inability to arrive at a common position. This probably would have been the case with respect to the first directive's provisions on financial disclosure where divisions were clearly along national lines. However, the effort itself to agree on a common posture has probably had some integrating impact on the professional organizations, particularly since the Commission has consistently made it clear that it will attribute little weight to divided counsel, and also has refused to have relations with *national* interest groups, lest it come into conflict with Member Governments.[21]

---

directive concerning "internal fusion" of companies. *See* p. 382 *infra*. On the role of the unions see generally BEEVER, EUROPEAN UNITY AND THE TRADE UNION MOVEMENT (Leyden 1960).

[21] Pryce, *Interest Groups in the Community*, EUROPEAN COMMUNITY at 13 (London, May 1968). According to this author there are now some three to four hundred Community-wide associations of national groups. On the interest groups in the Community generally see FISCHER, DIE INSTITUTIONALISIERTE VERTRETUNG DER VERBÄNDE IN DER EUROPÄISCHEN WIRTSCHAFTSGEMEINSCHAFT (Hamburg 1965); RITTSTIEG, WIRTSCHAFTSVERBÄNDE UND EUROPÄISCHE GEMEINSCHAFTEN, EINE UNTERSUCHUNG ZUR INSTITUTIONALISIERTEN INTERESSENVERTRETUNG (Hamburg 1967).

(b) Institutionalized consultations: the "opinion" of the Economic and Social Committee

(i) Committee structure

When the Commission's proposal for the first coordination directive was received by the President of the Council of Ministers, his first move was, in letters dated March 25, 1964, to request the Economic and Social Committee and the European Parliament to render their "opinions" on the proposal in accordance with Article 54 of the Treaty. This marked the beginning of the second, highly formal and institutionalized, phase of consultations with both the economic and the political quarters in the Community. The "opinions" (*avis*) of the two bodies are not "binding" in the normative sense either upon the Commission or the Council who together hold the power to "make" Community law. The actual influence of these opinions upon the lawmakers has varied, although in this particular instance it was probably greater than has been usually the case.

The Economic and Social Committee's one hundred and one members are appointed by the Council of Ministers according to a nationality key fixed by the Treaty[22] from lists compiled by the Member Governments, and they are to represent the numerous categories of economic and social life in the Community.[23]

The Committee does most of its work in eight specialized sections dealing with the main fields covered by the Treaty which in effect function as parliamentary committees. In order to reflect the transnational socio-economic reality, the Committee members have formed three groups: employers,

---

[22] 24 members from each of the Federal Republic, France, and Italy, 12 from Belgium and the Netherlands, 5 from Luxembourg. Art. 193.

[23] Art. 193 states that the Committee is to include, in particular, representatives of producers, farmers, transport operators, workers, merchants, artisans, the professions and representatives of the general interest.

workers and the heterogeneous "general interest" group.[24] The "general interest" group has been viewed by the workers with considerable suspicion, as in effect concealing additional representatives of employers. With some exceptions, as in the case of transport policy, the alignment in the Committee has generally followed group loyalty rather than national allegiance. The specialized sections are serviced by the Committee secretariat counting some 100 personnel, while the groups must rely on outside organizations (the first group relies on UNICE, the second group on the "summit" labor union organizations) for staff assistance.

The first coordination directive was assigned to the Specialized Section on Economic Questions whose President, M. de Précigout of the employers' group, was persuaded to assume also the office of section rapporteur, an unusual cumulation of functions which obviously would not remain without effect on the tenor of the final opinion.[25] M. de Précigout, a lawyer connected with the textile industry in France, and Vice-President of the influential national association of French industry (*Conseil National du Patronat Français,* CNPF) also served as a member of the French Economic and Social Council, and in both capacities had an opportunity to speak with authority on the French national reform. To avoid ruffled feathers and a jurisdictional controversy, the Specialized Section on Non-Wage-Earning

[24] Vanhaeverbeke & Genton, *The Economic and Social Committee,* EUROPEAN COMMUNITY at 14 (London, May 1968). *See generally* Genton, *La représentation et l'influence des opérateurs économiques dans la Communauté européenne,* in INSTITUTIONS COMMUNAUTAIRES ET INSTITUTIONS NATIONALES DANS LE DÉVELOPPEMENT DES COMMUNAUTÉS 75 (Bruxelles 1968); LES GROUPES DE PRESSION DANS LA C.E.E. (Europa Instituut, Université d'Amsterdam, 1965); ZELLENTIN, DER WIRTSCHAFTS- UND SOZIALAUSSCHUSS DER EWG UND EURATOM (Leyden 1962). In 1968, there were 27 members in the employers' group, 34 in the workers' group, 40 in the general interest group including farm producers, craftsmen, tradesmen, journalists, and members of liberal professions.

[25] Actually M. de Précigout took over the rapporteurship only after the originally appointed rapporteur resigned his function.

Activities and Services was asked to provide a supplementary report on four specific questions, considered to fall within its particular competence.

(ii) Minority opposition by Dutch-German industry

In the deliberations of the two Sections, and for that matter in the plenary of the Committee as well, two issues proved sharply controversial: first, the legality and wisdom of the directive in general, and second, the provision concerning financial disclosure. Even those members who did not possess any expertise in company law were able to understand some aspects of these questions, and it is not surprising that those who opposed the second expressed also their doubts, in more or less emphatic terms, on the first issue.

In this first exposure to the "private sector," the Commission's draft encountered a determined opposition by a small minority alliance of Dutch and German industrial interests. While the Dutch industry presented a united front and its spokesman went so far as to formally propose recommittal of the draft to the Commission,[26] there were minor defections from the German employers' group and only a mild support for the opposition from a spokesman for the Federation of Belgian Industries.[27] The workers' group was solidly with the majority which favored the directive, and this included all the German and Dutch members of the labor group; the third or "general interest" group, with one exception to be noted below, also formed a part of the majority.

The opposition was led by Mr. van de Woestijne, a professor at the Technical College in Delft who, although a member of the "general interest" group, succeeded another Dutch professor who had maintained close ties with the Dutch oil industry.[28] The dissenters demanded to know

---

[26] Prof. van de Woestijne, Comité Écon. et Soc., CES 316/64, *Compte rendu des délibérations* Nov. 20, 1964, 4lème Session plénière, Oct. 27 and 28, 1964, at 13.

[27] M. de Bièvre, *id* at 19.

[28] The Netherlands Government as a matter of policy discusses the appointments to the *Community* Economic and Social Committee

in what respect the divergence of national company laws had jeopardized the exercise of the freedom of establishment, so as to make coordination "necessary," within the meaning of Article 54. Moreover, "partial" harmonization without a "complete view" of the intended "global harmonization" was improper and risked introducing new discriminations.[29] The majority of the Section on Economic Questions, after hearing the staff member of the legal service of the Commission expound on the problem, chose to assume the legality of the proposal by implication (recognizing that the Court of Justice would have the last word). However, the other Section, perhaps under the "law oriented" influence of its rapporteur, Sig. de Cesare, a former member of the Italian Consiglio di Stato, dealt with the question of legality in some considerable detail without any hesitation and rejected the minority onslaught on the legality in ringing terms.[30] In its final opinion, the majority of the plenary Committee upheld the legality of the directive but suggested that since the divergence of national laws could affect not only the exercise of the freedom of establishment but also the competitive conditions as well, "the legal bases of the directive" might be enlarged, implying no doubt a possible recourse to Article 100.[31]

---

with the *national* Social and Economic Council and sees to it that, in the case of a resignation, the successor reflects the views of the same interests and organizations.

[29] Van de Woestijne, in *Compte rendu des déliberations* at 12; Bölger, *id.* at 16-17; Seibel, *id.* at 20.

[30] Rapport de la Section spécialisée pour les questions économiques sur la Proposition d'une Directive du Conseil tendant à coordonner pour les rendre équivalentes, les guaranties qui sont exigées dans les États membres, des sociétés au sens de l'article 58, alinéa 2 du Traité, pour protéger les intérêts tant des associés que des tiers, Rapporteur: M. de Précigout, Sept. 28, 1964; Rapport complementaire, July 31, 1964, and Avis complementaire, July 30, 1964 de la Section pour les activités non salariés et les services sur quelques points relatifs à la Proposition de directive, etc.

[31] Avis du Comité Economique et Social at 3249; on this point see also Rodière, *L'harmonisation des législations* at 336, 343 ff.

More significant, however, was the policy posture of the Committee majority which urged the Commission to proceed energetically beyond the first directive toward the coordination of other topics, toward clear-cut rather than compromise solutions, even if this meant more far-reaching "harmonization," in the interest of clarity and simplicity. Even a "harmonization" of the general principles of civil, commercial and criminal law was "desirable," but it required "careful study and great prudence." Several provisions of the Commission proposal were criticized as not going far enough and indulging in an "appearance of harmony," only to conceal persisting "different realities." Moreover, the majority desired to strengthen the arrangement for assuring the Commission's coordinating role in the adoption of national reform laws.[32]

(iii)   The showdown on financial disclosure—the outcome

There was unanimous agreement, M. de Précigout explained, on requiring "publicity" for the financial statements of those companies which "draw upon public capital markets"—a criterion first employed in French law—and a "rather large majority" was ready to go further and to support the original stance of the Commission which would have extended this obligation to all capital companies.[33] However, since such extension would result in flooding the public repositories of information with data on economically insignificant companies and thus reduce the efficacy of the "publicity" system, a large majority was ready to accept the exception for companies with assets of not more than one million dollars as proposed by the Commission, but only if the exception was broadened to cover not solely small limited liability companies, but small stock companies as well.[34] This was a concession to the Dutch view pressed by

---

[32] Avis, *passim*.

[33] Van de Woestijne, in *Compte rendu des déliberations* at 10.

[34] *Id.* at 11.

the spokesmen not only for the Dutch industry, but for the Dutch labor unions as well[35] who pointed out that, since the limited liability company form did not exist in Dutch law, the small "close" stock companies which took its place in the Netherlands would be subject to discrimination, unless they were given the same treatment. It was also argued that confining the exception from the disclosure obligation to limited liability companies would encourage an "escape" from the stock company to the limited liability company form.[36] The view was also advanced that it would be possible for a company to manipulate its balance sheet so as to show assets below the minimum level in order to remain within the exception,[37] and there was a general feeling that the exemption criterion based on the amount of the assets ought to be reviewed.

The most noteworthy feature of the relatively brief debate was a confrontation between two German nationals, Mrs. Hesse, a member of the workers' group and official of the German white-collar workers' union,[38] and Mr. Seibel, a member of the employers' group connected with the Chamber of Industry and Commerce in the Federal Republic. The issues were the same as those debated hotly in the Federal Republic in connection with the national disclosure legislation, and concerned both the rationale and the criteria for the disclosure obligation.[39] Reflecting the position of the Social Democrats and labor union spokesmen in Bonn, Mrs. Hesse asserted[40] in the Committee debate that disclosure

---

[35] Prof. van de Woestijne, id. at 12; Mr. ter Heide, id. at 24.

[36] M. de Précigout, id. at 13.

[37] Prof. van de Woestijne, id. at 12.

[38] Union of German Employees (Deutsche Angestellten-gewerkschaft).

[39] Infra p. 247.

[40] Compte rendu des délibérations at 14-17. She was supported by Mr. Brand of the "general interest" group, at 17-19, Mr. ter Heide of the workers' group, at 23-24, and basically also by Mr. Rollinger of Luxembourg, who is close to small business groups in that country, at 17.

must serve not only to protect creditors and shareholders, but must also assure the transparency of the national economy in the public interest. Mr. Seibel, on the other hand, took the view that, at the Community level at any rate, the consideration of any interest beyond that of creditors and shareholder-investors exceeded the powers of the Community institutions. This view, we shall see, was echoed by the German Christian Democratic voices in the European Parliament. Similarly, the divergence among the Dutch employers and workers reflected the corresponding debate in the Netherlands, surrounding the Verdam Commission Report.

On one aspect, however, there was general agreement in the Economic and Social Committee: whatever the scope of the disclosure obligation, the content of the financial statements and the procedure for their preparation and verification which differed greatly from one Member State to another, must be coordinated to assure comparability. This position became the central point in the next phase of the consultation process, the proceeding before the European Parliament, and in addition to presenting a weighty question for which the Commission had no immediate answer, it was employed by the opponents of the coordination as a handy delaying device.

In the final Committee vote—at the end of a single plenary session devoted to the subject—67 members voted in favor of the "opinion" supporting the directive subject to the qualifications indicated earlier, and 7 opposed it. The negative votes were cast by four Dutch and two German members of the employers' group,[41] and by Professor van de Woestijne.

The tenor of the Committee "opinion" reflects substantial French influence, exerted very likely in no small measure through the able French Section President and rapporteur. In contrast with the proceedings in the European Parlia-

---

[41] Messrs. Bölger, Jonker, Kuipers, and Schrijvers of the Netherlands; Messrs. Kley and Seibel of the Federal Republic. *Id.* at 26.

ment, one discerns little impact of the spokesmen for the German industry, perhaps because those circles have attributed little importance to the Committee. This generally skeptical attitude might be explained in part by the fact that although the Committee has its national counterparts in Belgium, France, Italy and the Netherlands, no comparable body exists in Germany, and in fact the Federal Government originally was opposed to its establishment as a Community institution. German industry is thus accustomed to pressing its interests directly with the Government or with the members of the Parliament. The German workers, on the other hand, have consistently selected top union talent for service on the Committee, and seem to pay considerable attention to its work.

(iv) The EEC Commission's response

The Commission staff that labored assiduously to help indoctrinate the Committee members in the mysteries of company law and Treaty interpretation, was evidently pleased by the outcome, particularly since the affirmative opinion of the Committee provided a welcome compensation for the widespread criticism which the draft had encountered in professional literature. The energetic Dr. Bruns expressed this sentiment when he addressed the Committee plenary session immediately after the vote. He announced that in view of the "particularly valuable" opinion of the Committee, the Commission would deviate from the established procedure and return the draft to its working group before the institution of the proceeding within the Council of Ministers; this move would enable the group to review the proposal in the light of the modifications proposed by the Committee. This promise was fulfilled and—as we shall see—the First Draft was modified substantially. However, not all the modifications proposed by the Committee or by the European Parliament were accepted.

(c) Institutionalized consultations continued: the "opinion" of the European Parliament

If the Commission's proposal fared reasonably well in its first confrontation with organized economic interests, it sailed into stormy weather when it came before the "transnational politicians." To start with, it met with the most common and yet the most exasperating maneuver in parliamentary practice, a thinly disguised but effective delaying tactic.

(i) The composition of the European Parliament

Like the Economic and Social Committee, the European Parliament must be heard but need not be obeyed by the lawmakers in the Community. Each national parliament sends a specified number of its own members to the European Parliament, and the national contingents more or less accurately mirror the power positions of the national political parties in the national arenas, except that until very recently Communists were kept out.[42] The Italian contingent now includes Communist Party members. The deputies are organized in three transnational political groups, the Christian-Democrats, the Socialists, and the Liberals (with affiliates), and the French *Union Démocratique Européenne* (U.D.E.), comprising the Gaullist supporters. The positions on more important matters are determined as a rule in group caucuses, and—as in national parliamentary bodies—most of the work is done in standing committees of limited membership.[43]

(ii) The labors of the Internal Market Committee

The request for the Parliament's opinion on the first coordination directive was received by the "Bureau" in

---

[42] The "Big Three" Parliaments send 36 deputies each, Belgian and Dutch Parliaments send 14 each, and 6 come from Luxembourg. EEC Treaty Art. 138.

[43] The number of members in 1966 was as follows: Christian Democrats 61, Socialists 35, Liberals with affiliates 26, UDE 15.

late March 1964, and it was assigned to the Internal Market Committee. As is the case with all the official positions in the Parliament, the crucial jobs of rapporteur are distributed in equal proportion among the four political groups; within each group, the most interested deputy is given the assignment. In this instance, by a decision of the Internal Market Committee of April 23, 1964, the rapporteurship went to the Committee Vice President, Mr. Berkhouwer, a member of the "liberal" group and of a Netherlands conservative party, and a law-trained spokesman for the Dutch industry.[44] Mr. Berkhouwer succeeded, very likely with some assistance from his Christian-Democrat colleague and co-national, the Committee President Mr. Blaisse, whose ties with the industry were, if anything, even closer,[45] to delay the submission of the report for more than two years—a feat which is quite uncommon in the annals of the Parliament. This delay was made subject to a rare public criticism in the plenary debate.[46] Mr. Blaisse did not return to the European Parliament after 1966.

The Internal Market Committee met nine times between December 1964 and April 1966. Initially, the Committee had before it only the proposed text of the directive with a

---

[44] The official biography provides the following data on Mr. Berkhouwer: doctor of law, attorney, member of the board of directors of two stock companies, substitute member of the Consultative Council of Benelux, member of the Chamber of Deputies since 1956 for the Popular Party for Freedom and Democracy (V.V.D.). PARLEMENT EUROPÉEN, ANNUAIRE 1965-66, at 32 (Luxembourg 1966).

[45] The official biography contains the following data on Mr. Blaisse: doctor of law, Institute of Technology, Hanover, secretary of the Philips Gloeilampenfabriek at Eindhoven, Secretary of the Federation of Industry, director at the directorate general of foreign relations at the Ministry for Economic Affairs, economic consultant since 1952, member of the second chamber from 1952 for the Popular Catholic Party (K.V.P.). PARLEMENT EUROPÉEN, ANNUAIRE 1965-66, at 36. Most recently Mr. Blaisse has become part-time professor at the Technical College at Delft where he lectures on legal and economic aspects of international organizations.

[46] Deringer, in [1966-67] PARL. EUR., DÉBATS, Compte rendu in extenso des séances, Doc. No. 85, at 56.

brief "motivation" (statement of reasons) prepared by the Commission staff. In view of this scanty information, the rapporteur first addressed a questionnaire to the Commission—a procedure that is not common but was employed in several instances before—intended to elicit further data on the proposed directive, and on the Commission's current and projected work in the company law field generally. The Commission replied on May 6, 1965, to the twenty-three questions posed to it; these answers and a brief sketch of the pertinent national laws, prepared by the Committee Secretariat,[47] apparently constituted the only written information made available to the Committee as a basis for its deliberations on this complex technical subject. Several members of the Commission staff appeared before the Committee and gave a detailed oral explanation of the proposed text but no "independent" company law experts were heard. On March 21, 1966, and on April 25, 1966, the Committee finally approved the report and a resolution with an "opinion" proposed for adoption in the plenary, by a vote of 20 with two abstentions.[48] The vote evidently did not reflect the sharp controversy within the Committee.

Paradoxically, the report did not support, and in fact was in conflict with, the proposed "opinion," and this was a cause of an understandable bafflement for the Commission.[49] The report was strongly critical of the proposed directive and stated that in several respects the Commission exceeded the legal basis of Article 54 of the Treaty.[50] Some of the

---

[47] The Parliament has its own staff and each Committee is assigned several staff members.

[48] BERKHOUWER REPORT at 2. The vote on Mar. 21, 1966 was subject to further consideration of the statement of reasons to be included in the report. This vote took place on Apr. 25, 1966 but there is no indication of the outcome.

[49] Commissioner Colonna di Paliano, in [1966-67] PARL. EUR., DÉBATS, Doc. No. 85, at 69.

[50] BERKHOUWER REPORT at 35, par. 74. Specifically, the report raised the question whether the problem of invalidity ("nullity") of companies was outside the scope of recognition of companies because

legal arguments advanced to show that the proposed directive was illegal were more convincing than others.

In the first place, the report relied on the traditional rule laid down by the Permanent Court of International Justice to the effect that treaties limiting state sovereignty must be given a restrictive interpretation. This is only one of the principles of interpretation, and one may wonder how relevant it is when it comes to interpreting the EEC Treaty which differs in many respects from the common "variety of treaties.

Second, it was said in the report that some articles in the directive were so detailed and specific as to leave hardly any freedom to the national legislator, and this feature was contrary to the Treaty which defined directives as "binding upon the Member States as to the result to be achieved, but the form and means of enforcing them shall be left to the national authorities";[51] in effect, the proposed text would require Member States to adopt a "uniform law" whereas Article 54 authorizes "coordination" only. There is some support for this criticism in the literature.[52] On the other hand, other writers have pointed out that the directives of the Community, generally speaking, have been becoming progressively more specific;[53] some felt that the "equival-

---

the effect of invalidity was territorially limited. The report apparently confused the two provisions of the EEC Treaty which are often mentioned together, namely, Art. 220 and Art. 54; only the former deals with recognition of companies, but the latter, on which the directive was based, does not. Although one may argue about the urgency of coordinating the rules on invalidity in the first coordination attempt, it is hardly possible to contend that the rules specifying the grounds on which a company may be declared not validly constituted do not concern the protection of—especially—third persons who would want to be certain about the legal status of the company with which they deal.

51 Treaty Art. 189. BERKHOUWER REPORT at 25.

52 Rodière, L'harmonisation des législations at 340.

53 Sohier & Megret, Le rôle de l'executif national et du législateur national dans la mise en oeuvre du droit communautaire, SEMAINE DE BRUGES, 1965, 107, at 114. See generally Waelbroeck, The Application of EEC Law by National Courts, 19 STAN. L. REV. 1248, at 1272-75 (1967); OLDEKOP, DIE RICHTLINIEN DER EWG at 178-90 (Göttingen

ence" of guaranties required in Article 54 may in certain instances be achieved only when "form and substance" are connected so closely as to become merged, and that the Community institutions were given the necessary range of power in the interest of achieving substantial equivalence;[54] thus even a uniform law could be imposed in a directive if the only means to achieve effective harmonization was through "uniformity of time, means and forms";[55] in any event, after a directive is adopted the Member States would still be free to transform it into national law through means of their choice, that is, by a statute, a government decree or administrative order.[56]

Finally, the report attempted to draw certain conclusions from a judgment of the Court of Justice of the Communities in the widely discussed case of *Costa v. E.N.E.L.* In the plenary debate of the Parliament, a deputy characterized these conclusions as "slightly erroneous," a description apparently tempered by parliamentary courtesy.[57]

1968); Ipsen, *Richtlinien-Ergebnisse,* in HALLSTEIN (ed.), FESTSCHRIFT FÜR OPHÜLS 67 (Karlsruhe 1965).

[54] Lutter, *Die Angleichung des Gesellschaftsrechts nach dem EWG-Vertrag,* 1966 NJW 273, at 274.

[55] Zweigert, *Der Einfluss des europäischen Gemeinschaftsrechts auf die Rechtsordnungen der Mitgliedstaaten,* 1964 RABELS ZEITSCHRIFT 601, at 643. *See also* Zweigert, *Grundsatzfragen der europäischen Rechtsangleichung, ihrer Schöpfung und Sicherung,* in VON CAEMMERER, NIKISCH, ZWEIGERT (eds.), 2 FESTSCHRIFT FÜR DÖLLE 401, at 418 (Tübingen 1963). Von Arnim, *Das Niederlassungsrecht* at 347, although preferring clear and definite unification of law over mere approximation with its necessarily uncertain results, doubts whether Zweigert's opinion would be upheld. Houin, *Rapport général sur la fusion des sociétés,* in FÉDÉRATION INTERNATIONALE DE DROIT EUROPÉEN, 3ème Colloque international de droit européen, Paris, Nov. 1965, 9, at 22.

[56] RABE, DAS VERORDNUNGSRECHT DER EUROPÄISCHEN WIRTSCHAFTSGEMEINSCHAFT at 42 (Hamburg 1963); Gaudet, *Rechtliche Aspekte der Niederlassungsfreiheit im Gemeinsamen Markt,* 1961-62 ZHR 66, at 87.

[57] BERKHOUWER REPORT at 26, par. 24, 25. Costa v. E.N.E.L., Case No. 6/64, 10 Recueil de la Jurisprudence 1141, at 1163 (1964). The statement in the plenary was by Deringer, in [1966] PARL. EUR., DÉBATS, No. 85, at 56-57.

In a more weighty observation, based as much on policy as on legal considerations, the report castigated the Commission for having failed to offer any evidence, obtained through inquiries from banking, industrial or commercial quarters, that decisions concerning the location of company facilities and activities were in fact influenced by differences in national company laws rather than by considerations relating to taxes, foreign exchange restrictions and transport cost. Another objection was that the Commission appeared to proceed "in slices" rather than first evolving an overview, a *"conception d'ensemble,"* based on a thorough comparative study of "the legal problems in general, and the administrative, commercial and accounting practices in the Member States."[58]

(iii)   A paradox, a paradox . . .

Along with the negative report, the Internal Market Committee adopted a resolution containing the proposed "opinion" in which the European Parliament was to express its pleasure (*"se félicite"*) at the Commission's initiative and approve the draft directive, subject to certain modifications. The principal modification, again reflecting the Netherlands-German coalition of interests, aimed at broadening still further the exemption from financial disclosure and postponing the disclosure obligation for limited liability companies and Dutch close companies, pending coordination of provisions prescribing the content of the financial statements. The resolution asked that the Parliament

---

In the *E.N.E.L.* case the Court held that Art. 53, prohibiting new restrictions on the freedom of establishment, must be interpreted in the light of Art. 52 requiring no better than national treatment. The argument in the *Report* was that Art. 54 must also be interpreted in the light of Art. 52. Referring to the *Report,* Scholten concluded that the Court's decision points to a restrictive interpretation of Art. 54. Scholten, *European Company Law,* 4 C.M.L. REV. 377, at 391 (1967). One may wonder how relevant this argument is to the problem of the legality of the First Directive.

58 BERKHOUWER REPORT at 35, par. 78.

be advised of the other sectors of company law earmarked for coordination, and it stressed the need for an overview.

The contradiction between the report and the resolution can be explained if one reconstructs the happenings in the Internal Market Committee which began its difficult, and in many respects painful, proceedings in Rome during December 1965. Of the more than twenty Committee members, apart from Mr. Berkhouwer who obviously set the tone, only Mr. Blaisse and Mr. Deringer, a member of the Federal Parliament, and to a lesser degree his socialist colleague, Mr. Seuffert, were actively interested in this aspect of the Committee's work. The first draft of the report was prepared by Mr. Berkhouwer alone, and was said to have been replete with factual errors; the author proposed to say flatly that the disclosure provisions were illegal and that no action should be taken on the directive—a view reminiscent of the position taken by Professor van de Woestijne in the Economic and Social Committee. Moreover, a move developed in the Committee to refer the legal aspects to the Legal Committee of the European Parliament which would have meant another postponement, as well as a danger that a restrictive interpretation of Article 54, par. 3(g) would be "frozen" at this early junction. The members of the Commission staff who arrived in Rome from Brussels, succeeded in persuading the Committee to forego this move. If the Commission officials and the sympathetic members of the Internal Market Committee had attempted to modify the text of the report radically enough to reflect their own views, still another year's delay would no doubt have been inevitable. Consequently, the tactical decision was made to concentrate on the more important of the two documents, the resolution with the "opinion." The Commission staff had the difficult task of instructing the Committee members in the technicalities of company law, and the painful nature of this process is illustrated by the fact that it took four long meetings of the Committee to deal with just the first four articles of the draft.

(iv)   Profile of a Community lawyer

Perhaps the most active participant in the parliamentary proceeding was Mr. Deringer of the Christian Democratic group in the European Parliament, a deputy for the Christian Democratic Party in the Bundestag and member of its Legal Committee, and last but not least, a successful attorney, representing substantial corporate clients and trade organizations particularly in matters of the new European law, including antitrust law and agricultural regulations. He has been engaged in practice before the German authorities and courts, and before the EEC Commission and Court of Justice; at the same time, he has played a role in the framing of national legislation in the Bundestag and in the formation of the Community policy in the European Parliament. He was able—for instance—to address the Commission in the European Parliament on matters of interest to industry in the form of parliamentary questions which, according to the Treaty,[59] the Commission was required to answer. Moreover, as an effective chairman of the newly created Legal Committee of the European Parliament, he sought to explore ways of increasing the power and influence of that body.[59a] Keeping in mind the rather negative attitude of important sectors in his own Parliament and of the German industry toward breaching the privacy of limited liability companies,[60] Mr. Deringer may well have been inclined to join Mr. Berkhouwer in seeking the recommittal of the draft directive to the Commission. But a realistic appraisal of the parliamentary situation convinced him that a majority (including his own German Socialist colleagues) would not be amenable to such an

---

[59] EEC Art. 140.

[59a] Mr. Deringer was defeated in the 1969 election for the Bundestag by a Social Democrat.

[60] The changes in the Federal law imposing disclosure on certain large limited liability companies were still three years off, as was the publication of the new draft law on limited liability companies requiring these companies to make their balance sheet publicly available.

unprecedented rebuff to the Commission. Nor was he prepared to carry the opposition so far as to cause serious prejudice to the Commission's standing. Thus he disassociated himself from Mr. Berkhouwer in a statement made on behalf of the Christian Democratic group in the plenary. In that statement he criticized the delay in the completion of the Committee report on the ground that it had damaged the reputation of the Parliament, and he also took issue with some of the legal arguments in the report.[61] He concentrated on two points which he considered essential for his objectives—the postponement of the effective date of the disclosure obligation for limited liability companies, and the preservation and extension to other Members, to the greatest extent possible, of the German rule excluding the *"ultra vires"* doctrine. He succeeded in carrying with him an "almost unanimous" Committee,[62] and eventually the plenary as well.

(v) Plenary debate: the "groups" speak

The plenary debate extended over three sessions, and it was much more lively and better attended than an average debate in the European Parliament. In the opening summary of his report Mr. Berkhouwer, the rapporteur, sought to explain the delay and dispel any possible impression of partiality; but his position on the substance of the directive was quite negative.

In accordance with the established pattern, he was followed by the spokesmen for each of the four political groups, starting with Mr. Deringer who spoke in the name of the Christian Democratic group within which there was relatively little interest in this subject. He carefully rejected the implication in the rapporteur's speech that either he, Deringer, or the opinion of the Legal Committee of the Bundestag (on which Mr. Berkhouwer also relied) had reached the

---

61 [1966] PARL. EUR., DÉBATS, No. 85, at 56 rejecting the relevancy of the *E.N.E.L.* case.

62 *Id.* at 58.

conclusion that the directive exceeded the legal basis in the Treaty. He made it clear that the Christian Democratic group did not take a position on the issue of legality—very likely because it was divided on the disclosure provision— and proceeded to state his personal opinion to the effect that disclosure by limited liability companies was not required for the protection of either the creditors or the investor-shareholders; whether it was necessary for the protection of workers or the public was a political question unrelated to the freedom of establishment, and the protection of these interests was not a proper basis for a directive. He also adumbrated that one of the reasons why "certain Member States" were so vigorously opposed to some provisions in the directive was that the Commission relied on Article 54, allowing majority vote on such an important matter, rather than on Article 100 requiring unanimity—an argument we have seen advanced earlier by the staff of D.G. IV. He pressed for the modification of the Commission's text on the two issues described above which were close to his heart; he urged the Commission to present promptly and at one time all the provisions which unquestionably required coordination; and he pointedly enumerated what he considered the advantages of a "European company" form as compared with the coordination of company law, particularly if it was to occur "by little slices."

The position of the Socialist group was stated in a brief (five paragraph), perfunctory, and ambiguous statement by Mr. Seuffert, a successful German attorney with a corporate practice in the tax field who has since become a judge and Vice President at the Federal Constitutional Court. While mildly praising the directive as "a first step on a long and difficult journey" and finding Mr. Deringer's proposal to postpone the disclosure for limited liability companies "regrettable" (this would presumably be expected from him as a member of the Socialist group), he found the reasons motivating the proposal for a delay "perfectly well founded."

It was perhaps not a coincidence that many of the deputies actively interested in this subject were members of the Liberal group whose views were presented by M. Jozeau-Marigné, a notary representing the Independent Republican Party in the French Senate. Yet neither he nor M. Pleven, his group and party colleague, and chairman of the important French national committee on company law reform, who also intervened vigorously in the plenary debate, was a member of the Internal Market Committee. Their absence from the Committee was perhaps the reason why the Liberal group submitted a series of amendments as late as at the plenary stage of the proceeding. Mr. Jozeau-Marigné indicated that his group also had considered proposing that the directive be referred back to the EEC Commission because it wished to avoid "multiple consultations of our national parliaments" on piecemeal coordination measures, but decided against such a move for fear of jeopardizing two years of work. Instead, the group decided to propose specific improvements of the text, including one designed to "assure" that it remained within the scope of Article 54.[63] The most important two amendments, however, were, *first*, to eliminate the postponement in the disclosure obligation (and here the speaker pointedly referred to the remarks in the German Federal Parliament that protection of third parties can no longer be delayed); and, *second*, to limit this obligation further, so as to exempt not only the Dutch "close" stock companies with assets of not more than one million dollars but *all* stock companies of that size "that do not draw upon public savings"—which has been the yardstick employed by French law.[64]

In a spirited discussion Mr. Colonna di Paliano, a member of the Commission, supported the first amendment and urged that the postponement provision be dropped; Messrs. Deringer, Berkhouwer and Blaisse argued that it should be

---

[63] *Id.* at 62-84.

[64] *Id.* at 62. *See* Art. 72 of the Law of July 24, 1966.

maintained, and the plenary followed their view and rejected the amendment.[65] But the other Liberal amendment,
which sought to introduce the French law criterion into
the exemption from the disclosure and was strongly pressed
by M. Pleven, was adopted despite the negative posture by
Commissioner Colonna di Paliano and sharp opposition by
the German deputies, both Socialist and Christian Democrat, who argued that this criterion had no legal meaning in
German law. Another Liberal amendment advanced by the
French deputies that would have required every Member
State to assure publication of data on companies in a *local*
newspaper and a reference to such publication in a single
centralized file maintained for the entire country, again in
the French image, was not accepted.[66]

The last of the four groups to present its view was the
Gaullist *Union démocratique européenne*. M. Drouot L'Hermine, carefully avoiding what he called the "technical content" of the directive, criticized the Berkhouwer Report as
not going far enough and called for as rapid a harmonization of legislation as possible, "if we want really to build a
Europe which, sooner or later, will turn into a political
Europe."[67] He asserted that of the six Member States, the
Federal Republic and France were the two countries which
proved by their acts that they took very seriously the importance of evolving a European commercial law. Recalling
that France was often blamed for not being "European"
enough, he referred to the massive effort, led by M. Pleven,
to fit the French company law into a "European plan" and
he stressed, "in the name of my group," the French origin
of the proposal for a European company. Having delivered
his address, which was as eloquent as it was general, M.

---

65 *Id.* at 91.

66 *See id.* at 91-93, 99-100. Commissioner Colonna di Paliano did
not accept the amendment. It was supported by Pleven and Armen-
gaud.

67 *Id.* at 68.

Drouot L'Hermine left the hall, as Mr. Berkhouwer regretfully observed, not to return for the rest of the debate.

The most emphatic individual defense of the legality of the directive came, as in the Economic and Social Committee, from Italian quarters. Sig. Battaglia of the Liberal group, a member of the right-of-center Italian Liberal Party in the Italian Senate, stressed an argument particularly germane to Italian law, that coordination of national legislation was necessary in order to reduce the tendency—prevalent in Italy—to impose local law on foreign companies.[68]

Commissioner Colonna di Paliano restated the position of the Commission on the legal issues, in addition to commenting on the amendments.[69] As a member of a collegiate body, he was in a difficult position when urged to take a position on new amendments, submitted on the floor, that would modify the text approved by the Commission. In general, when pressed he took a negative view of amendments that would substantially deviate from the Commission's text, and supported those amendments that sought to restore the original Commission text, modified in the Parliamentary Committee.

The plenary debate and the attitudes taken on the amendments were, at least in some measure, instructive in revealing the alignment of the groups and individuals. However, the final vote on the resolution and "opinion" was anticlimatic and without much interest. The only negative vote was cast by Sig. Carboni, a professor of maritime law from Cagliari, Sardinia, a Christian Democrat in the Italian Senate. The good law professor dissented because of his passionate attachment to the *ultra vires* doctrine[70] which he was prepared

---

68 *Id.* at 65-66.

69 *Id.* at 69-73; 86; 90; 92; 93; 99; 100.

70 See p. 292 *infra.*

to defend single-handedly to the last drop of his southern blood.[71]

(vi) Aftermath: the "Second Draft"

With the consultation stage completed, the Commission's working group—as anticipated by Dr. Bruns—reopened its discussion on those aspects of the directive raised in the consultation proceedings. However, the Commission staff alone prepared a new draft, which the Commission approved without prior reference to the working group and which it forwarded to the Council of Ministers in October 1966.[72] This Second Draft reflected a number of suggestions made by the Economic and Social Committee and some, but not all, amendments proposed by the European Parliament. Above all, the Commission did not embrace the European Parliament's view on financial disclosure. Although it agreed to extend the exemption from disclosure so as to cover not only *small* limited liability companies but also the Dutch close stock companies, the Commission did not agree to broaden the exemption still further to all small stock companies that did not draw upon public capital markets. In addition to the fact that the latter concept was unfamiliar outside the French system, such broadening of the exemption, the Commission explained, would free from disclosure "too many stock companies whose financial situation is of interest to third parties"; it would constitute "a step backward" from the level of the law in Germany, Belgium, Luxembourg, and Italy, and it was not acceptable to the majority of governmental experts.[73] It soon appeared, however, that the acute disagreement on this major political issue remained unresolved and would cause further delay and controversy.

---

[71] [1966] PARL. EUR., DÉBATS, No. 85, at 95.

[72] COM (60) 366 final (Oct. 3, 1966).

[73] *Second Draft,* EXPOSÉ DES MOTIFS, COM (66) 366 final (Oct. 3, 1966) at 2.

3. The final stage of lawmaking: the Council of Ministers

(a) The Committee of Permanent Representatives: conflict or "collusion" with the Commission?

The preparatory work for the busy Ministers is done within the multi-tiered framework of the so-called Committee of the Permanent Representatives[74] which on its highest level consists of the Ambassadors heading the national Permanent Missions of the Six to the Communities in Brussels. The Ministers in the Council have a dual responsibility, first, as "representatives of the Member States" and, second, as members of a Community institution;[75] and the members of the Committee of Permanent Representatives have the same dual status. However, since in theory at any rate all the decisions must be made by the Council itself, actual decision-making cannot be delegated to the Committee. This principle is to assure that the power of final decision remains in the hands of the politically "responsible" Ministers, and is not usurped by "faceless bureaucrats." With the exception of the Permanent Mission of Luxembourg which is quite small (three persons), each Permanent Mission maintains a staff of twenty to twenty-five officials drawn mostly from the Ministries of Foreign Affairs, but also included are officials on detached service from Ministries for Economic Affairs, Finance and other departments. Only the Federal Republic maintains a careful balance between diplomats and officials of the Ministry of Economic Affairs which reflects the division of responsibility for Common Market matters in the Federal Government, a source of continuing difficulty in the formulation of German policy.

---

[74] EEC Art. 151, EURATOM Art. 121, *Merger Treaty* Art. 4. The latter Treaty speaks expressly of "permanent representatives." Thus their appointment now takes place in execution of the "Merger Treaty" and not in execution of an intergovernmental agreement as was the case before. Noël, *Le Comité des représentants permanents,* in INSTITUTIONS COMMUNAUTAIRES ET INSTITUTIONS NATIONALES DANS LE DÉVELOPPEMENT DES COMMUNAUTÉS 9, at 10, 24 (Brussels 1968).

[75] Noël, *Le comité des représentants permanents* at 41.

In the German Mission, a high ranking member of the Foreign Office acts as the Permanent Representative, but his deputy is a senior official of the Ministry of Economic Affairs.

The Committee meets weekly both at the ambassadorial level of the Permanent Representatives themselves and at the level of the Deputies who, with the one exception noted above, are also career diplomats of superior rank. The Ambassadors deal with matters of substantial political significance, including those concerning foreign relations of the Community. The Deputies handle all the other matters, and these comprise not only "routine business" but also "technical" proposals which, however, may have also certain political implications, as in the case of the first coordination directive. It is noteworthy that the conclusions of the Deputies are not reviewed by the Ambassadors but are submitted directly to the Ministers.[76] Some fifteen permanent working groups, staffed by the Permanent Missions and national officials commuting from the capitals, prepare the work for the Committee sessions, with the assistance of the Secretariat of the Council of Ministers. The Secretariat is composed of some 500 persons who, like the Commission staff, are transnational "civil servants" employed by the Communities.

As one could expect, tension has existed between the Commission complex and the Permanent Representatives' "establishment" which in principle is expected to act as "the eyes and ears of the national governments"[77] and to defend their prerogatives and those of the Council, as against the Commission's assertions of power. The influence of the Committee has clearly grown at the expense of the Commission in certain matters which did not require the Commission's formal initiative. Thus for instance the preparatory work for the "European company" was entrusted by the

---

[76] Noël, *Le comité des représentants permanents* at 25.

[77] Houben, Les conseils de ministres des Communautés européennes at 142 (Leyden 1964), *quoting* Handelingen Tweede Kamer der Staten-Generaal II, Dec. 10, 1958, 454.

Ministers, at the insistence of France, to the Committee rather than to the Commission. However, the Permanent Representatives have gradually become more "Community conscious." What initially may have been described as a "conflict" relationship between the "supranational" Commission and the nationally instructed Committee, has progressively evolved into a cooperation, albeit an uneasy one, at least when the power relationship between the two is not directly involved. The Committee not only influences the Commission but it also interprets and defends the Commission's positions in national capitals.

(b)   The directive before the Committee of Permanent Representatives

(i)   The actors

When the Commission submitted the 1966 text (Second Draft) of the directive to the Council it in effect exercised its Treaty authority to withdraw its proposal at any time before the "final action" by the Ministers[78] and substitute a new one. When the new text reached the Council of Ministers, it was first referred, along with the two "opinions" of the European Parliament and the Economic and Social Committee, to a standing working group of the Committee of Permanent Representatives, the Group on Economic Questions. In this Group, we meet again some of the familiar faces from the national Ministries of Justice that appeared earlier as national experts in the Commission's working group.

In a great number, if not in most instances, an agreement is reached by the Six Governments and the Commission on the substance of the Commission's text before it reaches this final phase in the lawmaking process. At times, however, when agreement cannot be reached—and this was the case with our directive—significant questions are left open for resolution in the Council framework. Moreover, the full impact of pressures, exerted locally on the national gov-

---

[78] Art. 149 (2).

ernments by economic interest groups, often becomes felt
at this stage of the proceeding only and must be taken into
account. Again, the clearance process within the national
governments moves in this phase, as a rule for the first time,
vertically to the highest echelons and horizontally to all the
interested departments other than that with primary competence. Finally, the seasoned "old hands" in the Permanent
Missions review the proposal for its compatibility with more
general national policies toward the Community and with
Community precedents in the same or related fields,
and also weigh its effect as a precedent for the future. No
wonder therefore, that new solutions and significant modifications are often brought about by the national representatives.

The actors in this phase of the proceeding may be grouped
into four categories. First, the national delegations primarily
press the postures determined in their respective capitals
and reflecting "national interest." Second, the Commission
staff, also bound at least in a general way by instructions,
aims at preserving the Commission text and particularly
those aspects of the proposal that in their view best advance
Community interests. Third, the Secretariat of the Council
of Ministers poses as a "neutral" and "administrative" factor;
but at times it is capable of suggesting new avenues, precisely because it enjoys a degree of freedom from any instructions. Last but not least, the Chairman of the Group
and the Chairman of the Committee assume the position of
"Presidential impartiality" by relinquishing their posts on
their respective national delegations to other national officials; they exert pressure on the national delegations and on
the Commission's staff toward advancing the negotiations and
disposing of the matter as promptly as possible. Under this
pressure, the effectiveness of which varies depending upon
the energy and ingenuity of the Chairman, national instructions are loosened, new alliances created, and "Presidential
compromises" are considered. The national delegations of
course are in the best bargaining position because they are

capable of trading concessions. The Commission has little to
bargain with beyond the implied threat of withholding consent to the modification of its text.[79] In theory, if the Commission refused to accept a modification the text could not
become law unless approved by a *unanimous* Council, and
in most cases the Commission would be able to enlist the
support of at least one Member Government for its position.
Moreover, if the modification of the Commission's text,
made without its consent, should be so radical as to constitute in effect a new solution, the Council act might be subject to annulment by the Court of Justice.[80]

(ii) A partial consensus

In the case of our directive, the process was simplified on
the one hand by the fact that the senior officials of the Ministries of Justice who did most of the negotiating at this
stage, had been involved in the enterprise from the very
outset, starting at the Commission working group level, and
no other Ministries claimed substantial concurrent interest.
On the other hand, the thorny "political" problem of financial disclosure remained unsettled because of the German
and Dutch opposition; and—as we shall see—the Italian
delegation introduced a series of new demands in the field of
company invalidity which it was not prepared to abandon
at least as long as the German delegation maintained its
negative stand on the disclosure.

The Group on Economic Questions met throughout the
first part of 1967, with the Commission staff present as active
participants since the proceeding was based on a formal
Commission proposal. The Belgian chairman, a high official
of the Ministry of Justice, working closely with the Com-

---

[79] EEC Arts. 149 par. 1, 173.

[80] In fact, in case of such a radical modification, even if it is approved by the Commission, it is probably necessary for the Council to
refer the new text again to the Economic and Social Committee and
to the European Parliament, if consultation on the matter involved is
prescribed by the Treaty.

mission's legal advisor, also a Belgian national, played a prominent part at this stage in reducing the area of disagreement. However, in June 1967 the Group, unable to make further progress, decided to pass on to the higher echelon the two problems on which the deadlock persisted. Considerable pessimism prevailed in the Group at that time, and it was felt more or less generally that the matter might have to go as high up as the Council of Ministers itself, possibly with the participation of the Ministers of Justice.

When the proceedings began before the Committee of Permanent Representatives at the Deputies' level, the German officials were on one extreme end of the spectrum. They were unalterably opposed to any provision imposing a disclosure obligation upon limited liability companies, pending coordination at the Community level of the content of the financial documents; but at the same time they insisted that the directive must exempt from any obligation whatsoever all such companies which fall below a specified minimum size. It may be relevant to note here that the draft of the new Federal law subjecting German limited liability companies for the first time to a limited disclosure requirement was not to be published until some two years later.[81] At the other extreme were the Belgian and Italian officials who opposed any delay or exemption from the disclosure duty. The Commission representatives made every effort to maintain the Commission's 1966 formula which, they claimed, had the support of five delegations, and they were particularly opposed to fixing the floor for the disclosure obligation—at one time the then German Chairman proposed the figure of $2,500,000 of assets as a "Presidential compromise" that did not prove particularly helpful—and at the same time deferring the effective date of the obligation.[82] A series of compromise proposals was suggested by

---

[81] See p. 248 infra.

[82] The Commission staff argued that when the coordinated content of the balance sheet and the profit-and-loss statement shall have been worked out, it might well be that all Governments would agree

several delegations designed to conciliate the divergences.[83] The chairmanship passed to the German delegation on July 1, 1967, and in the ensuing difficult negotiations a compromise gradually emerged with respect to the Italian and German demands in the field of invalidity of companies.

(iii) Disclosure problem "resolved"

It took another six months before the Deputies reached a unanimous agreement on the disclosure provision in early December 1967. Thereafter they referred the text back to the Group with instructions to adjust the remaining differences and to complete the redrafting. The final text imposed the general disclosure obligation on all the companies covered by the directive, but it postponed the disclosure obligation of limited liability companies and Dutch close stock companies (which were defined in the directive) until the effective date of a further directive. This additional directive was to (a) coordinate the content of the balance sheet and the statement of profit and loss, and (b) relieve some of these companies, whose assets were less than the minimum amount to be fixed in that directive, of the obligation to

---

to remove the floor entirely and impose disclosure on *all* companies or at least reduce the floor to, say, $500,000. Thus this question must not be prejudiced in the first directive.

[83] The first such proposal, while imposing a general disclosure obligation would have allowed Member States to delay compliance for companies presently not subject to disclosure until after about 1969, with an instruction to the Commission to propose a further directive coordinating the content rules and to examine whether a distinction should be made among the various types of companies. The second variant would have provided in effect for a delay in the disclosure by limited liability companies and the Dutch close companies until the effective date of the other directive which would not only coordinate the content of disclosure but also "the conditions and details" thereof for these companies. The Belgian and Italian delegations did not consider this a compromise since no legal obligation would be imposed with respect to the exempted companies. Finally, the Italian delegation proposed a third variant which would have imposed the obligation to publish the balance sheet upon *all* companies but postponed obligatory disclosure of the profit-and-loss statement pending further coordination.

publish "all or a part of" these documents. The Council of Ministers was to adopt the second directive within two years —and in a separate declaration the Council of Ministers directed the Commission to submit an appropriate draft before December 31, 1968. The compromise satisfied the German insistence on the delay and the Commission's opposition to a fixed floor for an exemption.

Just before Christmas 1967, a consensus was confirmed on the entire directive, except that the Commission continued to insist on its own text of the article relating to its coordinating role with respect to prospective changes in national company laws. Finally, this issue also was resolved[84] and the text became Community law upon approval by the Council on March 9, 1968.[85] The Member States became obligated to effect all the necessary modifications in their laws and regulations within eighteen months and to inform the Commission thereof at once.[86]

Along with the directive, the Council approved seven interpretative declarations which were proposed to it by the Committee of Permanent Representatives. I shall take note of these interpretations in the next chapter.

Since a consensus had been reached in the Committee of Permanent Representatives among the national delegations and the Commission, the proposal appeared on the Council's agenda as one of the so-called "items A" which are disposed of by a formal approval and without any debate, unless a Minister or a member of the Commission should demand a discussion, in which case the item is taken up in the next meeting. Since no such demand was made, the approval by the Council became a formality, and one may wonder to what extent the Foreign Ministers were aware of

---

84 *Supra* p. 166.

85 [1968] J.O. L65 (Mar. 14) at 8-12.

86 Art. 13. For a longer period afforded to certain Dutch stock companies see Art. 13, par. 2. The eighteen months' period lapsed on Sept. 14, 1969 and only the Federal Republic completed the national modification process by adopting an appropriate law. *See* p. 311 *infra*.

the content of the directive. For all practical purposes the final decision on the directive, including the solution of the "political" problem of financial disclosure, had been made before the matter reached the "political forum" of the Ministers.

This procedure obviously enhances the status and the power of the Committee of Permanent Representatives.[87] In order to be able to exercise this power effectively, the Permanent Representatives, and particularly the Deputies, must be in position to comprehend the technical aspects of a proposal without becoming lost in the technicalities. They must avoid the impression that they seek to replace the experts on the subject, and at the same time they must be able to identify, and deal with, the political problems involved— obviously no mean task for professional diplomats, if one considers the wide range and technical complexity of the subjects on their agenda.

Two characteristics of this phase in the lawmaking should be noted. First, the process of broadening the circle of actors which begins immediately after a "pre-draft" is prepared by the Commission staff, is dramatically reversed in this final stage, and only the miniscule, intimate group of national and Community officials, mostly diplomats (and in our case senior law officials), remains in the arena. Second, in contrast to the previous proceedings, this phase takes place without any publicity whatsoever, in an atmosphere amounting almost to mystery, where abstract legal argument is eschewed, bargaining is the order of the day, and solutions at times are reached in the privacy of the chairman's office.

---

[87] Noël, *Le comité des représentants permanents* at 41.

Chapter 7

THE FIRST DIRECTIVE AND ITS IMPACT ON NATIONAL COMPANY LAW

The three areas which were selected for coordination in the first directive were *first,* making public certain information concerning companies, a complex of rules subsumed in national laws under the heading of "publicity"; *second,* the rules on *ultra vires* acts of company organs; and *third,* invalidity (or "nullity") of companies.[1]

1. Making public legal and financial information on companies ("publicity")

The problem here was—a Commission official wrote—to inquire whether the various national means of "publicity" offered adequate protection to third parties, whether they were "equal" in their effect and sufficiently centralized, and whether the civil and criminal sanctions were such as to induce compliance.[2]

The directive undertook to coordinate national rules governing "publicity" of two types of information: first, data on the company's legal status and second, data on its financial condition.

(a) Information on the legal situation of companies

The purpose of this aspect of "publicity" was "to enable third parties to know the basic documents relating to the

---

[1] *See generally* Ault, *Harmonization of Company Law in the European Economic Community,* 20 Hastings L.J. 77, at 89-113 (1968).

[2] Le Tallec, *Koordinierung des Gesellschaftsrechtes* at 114. *See generally* Lutter & Schlosser, *Die Publizität der GmbH* at 109.

company and certain information . . . particularly the identity of persons authorized to act on its behalf."[3] The coordination proved relatively noncontroversial, since provisions to this effect existed in all the national laws governing "capital" companies.[4] The coordination rules require making publicly

---

[3] The preamble of the First Directive, [1968] J.O. L 65 (March 14), at 8-9 (Final Text).

[4] In the *Federal Republic of Germany*, the basic organizational documents of any new capital company (stock company, limited partnership with shares, limited liability company) must be filed with the publicly accessible commercial register where an appropriate entry is made. §§ 36-39 of the Law of 1965, §§ 7-10 of the Limited Liability Company Law, and § 9 of the COMMERCIAL CODE. A notice is then published in the *Bundesanzeiger*, the central official bulletin and also in another periodical (usually a local newspaper), as a rule designated by the court to carry official announcements. The notice gives the content of the entry, the essentials of the charter, the founders, their special advantages, and the valuation of contributions in kind. §§ 25 and 40 of the Law of 1965, § 10 of the COMMERCIAL CODE, § 10, par. 3, of the Limited Liability Company Law.

In *France*, newspaper publication is required as a prerequisite to the entry into the commercial register of any newly organized company. The specified basic data (name, seat, purpose, duration, capital, personally obligated associates, authorized persons and organs, etc.) must be published—upon completion of other prescribed formalities—in the officially designated paper in the *"Départment"* (district) of the company's seat (home office). More data must be included in the case of a stock company (Art. 285, Décret No. 67-236 of Mar. 23, 1967). The filing with the commercial register must be accompanied by copies of the charter and documents of appointment of the authorized representatives. A new requirement is the declaration that all statutory prerequisites have been met. Art. 6, Law of July 24, 1966. Art. 55, Décret No. 67-237 of Mar. 23, 1967, which was again modified in response to the First Directive. *See* p. 304 *infra*. After the entry in the register there follows another publication, containing again all the essential data, in the Bulletin officiel des annonces commerciales, Art. 286, Décret No. 67-236. The extensive requirement of newspaper publication is apparently due to the desire to assure financial support of the local press. HÉMARD, LA RÉFORME DES SOCIÉTÉS COMMERCIALES, DÉCRET No. 67-236, comment on Art. 286, at 237 (Paris 1967).

In *Belgium* and *Luxembourg* also, the copies of the basic documents must be filed with the office of the commercial court (Art. 10 of the Belgian CODE DE COMMERCE, Art. 9 of the Luxembourg Law of Aug. 10, 1915) and published subsequently in the *Moniteur* and the *Mémorial* respectively. While publication of the extracts suffices in the case of a limited liability company, a full text must be published in the case of a stock company. Arts. 6, 7, Belgian CODE DE COMMERCE; Art. 8, Luxembourg Law of 1915. An entry must then be made in the register.

In the *Netherlands,* the notarized stock company contract and the ministerial certification of "no objection" must be published in the Dutch journal for official announcements, the *Staatscourant* (Art. 36 f, WETBOEK VAN KOOPHANDEL) and entered in the commercial register (Arts. 1, 8, 31, HANDELSREGISTERWET 1918). This register must also show the names and particulars of each member of the management and of the council of auditors.

In *Italy,* filing of the charter with the register of the enterprises is required by Art. 2330, par. 1, of the CODICE CIVILE (the filing is made with the *cancelleria del Tribunale* since no register has been established; Art. 101, Disposizioni per l'attuazione del codice civile e disposizioni transitorie) and the appropriate authority makes the entry into the register upon examination of the legality of the charter. Notification is made to the Chamber of Commerce and there is a requirement of publication in a journal. For limited liability companies the filing is required by Art. 2475 of the CODICE CIVILE.

Essentially the same principles apply to *charter amendments.* *Germany:* § 181 of the Law of 1965, § 54, par. 2 of the Limited Liability Company Law; *France:* Art. 287, Décret No. 67-236; *Belgium:* Art. 12 of the CODE DE COMMERCE; *Luxembourg:* Art. 11 of the Law of 1915; *Netherlands:* Art. 45e, WETBOEK VAN KOOPHANDEL and Art. 19, HANDELSREGISTERWET; *Italy:* Art. 2436 CODICE CIVILE, for limited liability companies Art. 2494 CODICE CIVILE. The German and French laws which do not provide for publication of the complete text of the charter require filing of the amendment and entry (§ 181 of the Law of 1965, Art. 58 of the Décret No. 67-237). In France, however, Art. 59 of the Décret No. 67-237 requires in addition the filing of the complete amended version. *See* p. 241 infra.

All six legal systems require an entry at the occasion of a declaration of *liquidation* or *invalidity. Germany:* §§ 263, 273, of the Law of 1965, § 65 of the Limited Liability Company Law, § 10 of the COMMERCIAL CODE; *France:* Arts. 368, 391, 392 of the Law of July 24, 1966; Arts. 290, 291, Décret No. 67-236; Art. 38 ff., Décret No. 67-237; *Belgium:* Art. 12, par. 2, CODE DE COMMERCE; *Luxembourg:* Art. 11, par. 2, Law of 1915; *Netherlands:* Art. 55b, WETBOEK VAN KOOPHANDEL, Art. 21, HANDELSREGISTERWET; *Italy:* Arts. 2453, 2456, 2497 (for limited liability companies), CODICE CIVILE. Similarly, publication in papers is required as above.

Appointment and removal of persons entitled to represent the company are also subject to the above requirements. *Germany:* § 81 of the Law of 1965, § 39 of the Limited Liability Company Law, § 10 of the COMMERCIAL CODE; *France:* Art. 8 of the Law of July 24, 1966; Art. 33, Décret No. 67-237; *Belgium:* Art. 12 of the CODE DE COMMERCE; *Luxembourg:* Art. 11, par. 2 of the Law of 1915; *Netherlands:* Art. 19 of the HANDELSREGISTERWET; *Italy:* Arts. 2383, par. 4, 2385, 2487 (for limited liability companies) of the CODICE CIVILE.

available the text of the articles of incorporation[5] with all amendments,[6] the name of persons authorized to bind and to represent the company and to participate in its management or supervision,[7] the names of the auditors where they are required by law, as well as the termination of the functions of these persons, any change in the company's seat (*siège social*),[8] the amount of the capital subscribed (if the articles of incorporation make provision for "authorized" capital), the dissolution, any judicial decision declaring the company "null and void," and information concerning its liquidation.[9]

---

[5] Art. 2, par. 1 (a): "the act constituting the company and the charter, if it is the subject of a separate act"; 1 (c): "after each amendment of the act constituting the company or the charter, the full text of the amended act in the up-to-date version." The term "charter" is used in this book to describe the articles of incorporation and any subsequent amendments.

[6] Art. 2, par. 1 (b): "amendments to the acts referred to in (a), above, including any extension of the duration of the company."

[7] Art. 2, par. 1(d): "the appointment, the termination of office, as well as the names of persons, who, as an organ of the company prescribed by law or as members of such organ (1) have the power to bind the company in relation to third parties or to represent it in court, (2) take part in the administration, supervision or control of the company." The measures of "publicity" must indicate whether persons who have the power to bind the company may do so alone or must act jointly. The last mentioned provision required an amendment of German law. *See* Art. 2, Nos. 2, 3, 8, 16, 22; Art. 3, Nos. 1, 2, 8 of the Federal Law on the Implementation of the First Directive of the Council of the European Communities for Coordination of Company Law (Gesetz zur Durchführung der Ersten Richtlinie des Rates der Europäischen Gemeinschaften zur Koordinierung des Gesellschaftsrechts) of Aug. 15, 1969, BGBl I 1146. Gustavus, *Die registerrechtlichen Bestimmungen des Gesetzes zur Durchführung der ersten EWG-Richtlinie zur Koordinierung des Gesellschaftsrechts*, 1969 BB 1335; Einmahl, *Die erste gesellschaftsrechtliche Richtlinie des Rates der Europäischen Gemeinschaften und ihre Bedeutung für das deutsche Aktienrecht*, 1969 AG 131, 167, 210. On the government proposal of that law see Ankele, *Die Anpassung des deutschen Rechts an die erste gesellschaftsrechtliche Richtlinie des Rates der Europäischen Gemeinschaften und ihre Auswirkungen für die GmbH*, 1969 GMBH-RUND-SCHAU 52.

[8] Even if such a change does not involve a change in the articles, which is often the case where the new seat is located in the same city. GOLDMAN, COURS at 216. Art. 2, par. 1 (g).

[9] Art. 2, par. 1 (e), (h)- (j).

Both French and German writers viewed it as a helpful innovation that a complete, up-to-date text of the articles of incorporation will have to be filed after each amendment. The German law had to be modified to conform to this provision.[10] It will no longer be necessary for an interested party to engage in the often laborious task of plodding through the successive amendments in order to determine the legal position of a company which has existed for some time.[11] The French Government already had implemented this idea in 1967,[12] well in advance of the adoption of the directive. Again, any person—even if he could not show a special right or interest—would be able to obtain copies or extracts from the file, a provision which went further than even the German law, and since it was retained in the final text it required a modification of that law.[13]

---

[10] Skaupy, *Europäisches Gesellschaftsrecht*, 1966 AG 13, at 15. In the Federal Republic, the Law Implementing First Directive, Art. 2, Nos. 9 and 11, modified §§ 181 and 248 of the Stock Company Law of 1965, and Art. 3, No. 5, modified § 54, par. 1 of the Limited Liability Company Law to require filing a complete, up-to-date text of the charter after each amendment. In Italy Art. 10 of the Decree Implementing First Directive modified Art. 2436 of the Codice civile to the same effect.

[11] Gessler, in ENTWICKLUNGSTENDENZEN at 18; GOLDMAN, COURS at 216. See the comment by the Economic and Social Committee on the unclear formulation of Art. 2, paras. 1-3, of the *First Draft*, AVIS, in [1964] J.O. 3251. Because the preparation of a "consolidated" text of articles of incorporation of existing companies might prove a difficult job, the directive would allow ample time for its completion. *See Final Text*, Art. 13 (3).

[12] Art. 59 of the Décret No. 67-237 of Mar. 23, 1967.

[13] Art. 3(3) *Final Text*. Lamberth complained that this provision went too far; it went beyond the German law under which anyone could inspect the commercial register but only a person able to show a special interest was allowed to read the documents in the file and obtain copies. Lamberth, *Der Richtlinienentwurf* at 70. Law Implementing First Directive, Art. 1, No. 1, amending § 9, par. 2 of the COMMERCIAL CODE, dispenses with the requirement that a person requesting a copy prove a legal interest. For Italy see Art. 20 of the Decree Implementing First Directive. See generally the modifications of the Codice civile effected by this Decree: Art. 1, Art. 2 (adding a new Art. 2330 bis), requiring publication of the charter in the *Bol-*

(b)   Disclosure of financial data: the political problem

The initial position of the Commission staff was logical and simple enough: in view of the limitation on the individual liability of the shareholders in all the companies covered, *all* these companies must make a disclosure of their financial condition annually. This in substance has been the rule in two of the Six (Belgium, Italy)[14] and the coordination would thus be made on the level of the strictest rule. No consideration was given at this stage to the question, whether the national rules prescribing the *content* of the financial documents were adequate or of a comparable effectiveness.

It was the Commission staff's view that, since companies without any international reputation will be crossing the frontiers in increasing numbers, it will be imperative for third parties, dealing with such foreign companies, to be in a position to know their financial position. The fact that a great number of these companies will be family enterprises of a limited size was held irrelevant, because the knowledge of the financial standing of precisely these small companies will be essential, as they broaden their scope of activities in the Common Market. Again, many such small companies should have chosen a more suitable organizational form (presumably not allowing for a limitation of liability) and would have to do so in the future, if they insisted on avoiding disclosure.[15] Originally, the staff proposed an identical dis-

---

lettino ufficiale delle società per azioni e a responsibilità limitata; Art. 16 of the Decree, modifying Art. 2475 of the Codice civile, extended this requirement to limited liability companies); Arts. 4, 7, 8, 10-21. For a critical comment on the Decree see Simonetto, *Modifica-lampo delle norme sulle società con decreto del Presidente della Repubblica,* 1970 RIVISTA DI DIRITTO CIVILE 61 (1970).

[14] Belgian CODE DE COMMERCE Art. 137; Italian CODICE CIVILE Art. 2493, Art. 2435 for limited liability companies; Würdinger, *Zur Publizität der GmbH im nationalen und europäischen Bereich,* 1964 GMBH-RUNDSCHAU 151.

[15] Doc. de travail pour la réunion des 19 et 20 février, 1963, 456/III/C/63-F, Jan. 7, 1963, at 12. The above reasoning was linked specifically to stock companies. Similar considerations would govern with respect to the other types of companies affected by the directive. *See generally* Gessler, in ENTWICKLUNGSTENDENZEN at 18.

closure obligation for all the companies covered by the directive, regardless of their size; but, in view of a strong opposition in the working group, the limited liability companies whose balance sheet total did not exceed one million dollars were exempted in the first draft.[16] This compromise solution was offered by the Commission staff, and only grudgingly accepted by the Belgian and Italian experts; it was rationalized on the grounds that a large number of small limited liability companies did not and would not normally carry on business outside their own country,[17] and that the risk of a large scale "flight to the limited liability company" will be negligible. Nevertheless, when the text of the proposal was made public, this provision caused a veritable tempest in France and Germany, not to speak of the Netherlands.

An atmosphere of unreality surrounded the discussion within the Commission. This was due not only to the lack of the necessary detailed knowledge on the part of the national experts of the laws and relevant economic facts in the other Member States, but also to the absence of an agreement on the framework within which the exploration should be conducted. A variety of problems became apparent only gradually in the laborious process of mutual education:

(1)   The basic criteria for the disclosure rule: should the obligation be determined by the organizational form of the company or by the economic importance of the enterprise?

(2)   The beneficiaries in whose interest disclosure was introduced: should the disclosure be primarily for the benefit of the creditors, shareholder-investors, employees, the public at large—and the related questions, whether the disclosure obligation should be employed to advance national economic and social policies, and, if so, whether this task should be left

---

[16] Art. 2, par. 6, *First Draft,* maintained in Art. 2, par. 7 of the *Second Draft.*

[17] Explanatory Memorandum, 1964 Bull. E.E.C. Supp. No. 3, at 14. In support of the exemption, Fikentscher & Grossfeld, *The Proposed Directive* at 266.

to the national lawmaker, at least in the first instance, before coordination is attempted on a transnational level.

(3)   The structural divergences in the organization of industry and commerce in the Member States, and the differences in national laws and practices, including accounting practices.

(4)   The divergent estimates of the disadvantages suffered by the disclosing companies in their competition with other Community enterprises and with foreign enterprises.

(5)   The role of the Community lawmaker in determining the disclosure obligation.

The fact that pressures for an increased flow of information have been "in the air" in the Member States as part of a general syndrome of increased "democratization" or participation, added to the political charge of the issue. The technical advances in the storing and dissemination of information, which were obviously relevant, apparently were not considered. Nor did the Commission stress that more effective disclosure might accelerate the improvement of European capital markets which has been in the forefront of the Community effort, obviously because of the fear of being accused of exceeding the Treaty basis for the directive.

(i) The situation in the Federal Republic: a search for a new criterion

(1)   The two basic factors

If one were to identify the two factors which more than any other variable had determined the attitude of the German delegation in Brussels, it would be unquestionably the organizational pattern of German business and industry, and the state of the German law.

In the *first* place, in 1960 there were in the Federal Republic no less than 37,984 limited liability companies with a total capital of 14.5 billion DM; by 1963 these figures rose dramatically to 46,800 and 21.7 billion respectively, to reach 58,024 and 29.7 billion in 1966. On the other hand, in 1960 there were only 2,573 stock companies,[18] and this number actually dropped by 1963 and 1966 to 2,548 and 2,420 although the total capital rose from 32 to 39 and 48 billion.[19] The impact of the 1959 partial reform and particularly of the 1965 Stock Company Law is clearly reflected in these figures.[20]

Second. Historically, whether a German enterprise was required to make public disclosure of its financial data depended (with few exceptions) until 1969 on the legal form in which it was organized and on no other criterion.[21] According to the law of the Federal Republic, stock companies and limited partnerships with shares are subject to strict disclosure provisions which include extraordinarily detailed rules on the scheme and content of the balance sheet and the profit-and-loss statement, and require verification by certified accountants, filing with the public commercial register and publication in the *Bundesanzeiger,* the official periodical.[22]

---

[18] This figure includes both stock companies and limited partnerships with shares (Kommanditgesellschaften auf Aktien).

[19] Lutter, Kapital at 37-38; 1967 Statistisches Jahrbuch für die Bundesrepublik Deutschland at 200. In 1963 in France, in Belgium, and in Italy the proportion of stock companies (including limited partnerships with shares) to limited liability companies was only about two to one (in France 51,477 to 106,474 but the capital figures were 86 billion francs to only 15 billion). The number of limited liability companies in Italy is estimated only. Lutter, *id.* at 36; in 1968, there were in Italy 40,888 stock companies and limited partnerships with shares, with a total capital of 9,758 billion lire. The figures for 1964 were 40,992 and 8,450 billion. 1969 Annuario Statistico italiano at 290 (Roma 1969).

[20] On the reforms see generally *supra* p. 97. On the two important German laws dealing with transformation of legal form of enterprises see *supra* p. 107 n.57.

[21] Exceptions were listed in Entwurf eines Gesetzes über die Rechnungslegung von Grossunternehmen und Konzernen (Draft Law Concerning the Annual Statements of Large and Related Enterprises), Bundesratsdrucksache 296/68, Begründung at 13. This draft became law in a somewhat modified form on Aug. 15, 1969, BGBl I 1189, under the title Gesetz über die Rechnungslegung von bestimmten Unternehmen und Konzernen (Law on Financial Accounting by Certain Enterprises and Related Enterprises).

[22] The Stock Company Law of 1965 (§ 178). The same law requires that the financial documents of the company (and an annual report)

Smaller stock companies are relieved only from the duty to
specify separately the income and cost items in the profit-
and-loss statement.[23] The Law of 1965, inspired in part by
American practice, has introduced several significant innovations, such as a new obligation for the "controlling company"
(*Konzernobergesellschaft*) to prepare consolidated financial
documents and reports, and this obligation applies even to
a limited liability company, if its "controlled" subsidiary is a
stock company.[24] Again, although the management still retains substantial discretion in the choice of the valuation
and depreciation methods, its freedom in the actual valuation of assets has been reduced further, in the interest not
only of creditors but of the shareholders as well, and the
possibility of creating the notorious "hidden reserves" has
been greatly restricted. Allegedly an element of creditor protection, such reserves resulted from understating assets and
overstating liabilities, and in effect enabled the management
to manipulate profits so as to defeat the shareholders' statutory right to designate the amount of profit for distribution
as dividends. Under the present law, hidden reserves can
result only from the application of valuation and depreciation methods conforming to proper accounting principles,
and these methods must be set forth in the annual report.[25]

be drawn up by the executive board (Vorstand) (§ 148), audited
separately by certified public accountants (§§ 162-169) and the supervisory council (Aufsichtsrat) (§§ 170-171), and finally filed with the
commercial register (§ 177). *See generally* KRONSTEIN & CLAUSSEN,
PUBLIZITÄT UND GEWINNVERTEILUNG. The rules concerning the content
of the balance sheet specify no less than 47 individual items (§ 151),
those on the profit-and-loss statement 32. Gross income and cost items
must be given. The possibilities for deviation from these rules are
limited and specified (§ 161). Banks, transport, loan, and certain hous-
ing construction enterprises may follow different rules. § 17, Introductory Law to the Stock Company Law of 1965 (Einführungsgesetz).

[23] § 157, par. 4. This benefits companies with a balance sheet total
not exceeding 3 million DM (about $819,000) or 10 million DM
($2,730,000) for family enterprises, if not listed on a stock exchange.

[24] § 329 of the Stock Company Law of 1965 and § 28 of the
Introductory Law.

[25] §§ 149, 160 of the Stock Company Law of 1965. The 1937 Law
restricted overstating of assets to preclude repayment of the capital

On the other hand, with the single exception mentioned above, the law requires no disclosure from limited liability companies, even though some of the large German enterprises, such as BOSCH, are organized in this form—and in this respect, paradoxically, German law lagged behind the laws of certain Member States. The fundamental issue of whether the legal form of the enterprise should be the exclusive criterion to govern the disclosure obligation became the subject of a sharp political controversy, which was resolved—at least for the time being—only when the Parliament adopted the new law on financial accounting by large enterprises[26] in 1969, more than a year *after* the enactment of the First Directive in Brussels.

(2) Changing winds and widening concerns on national level: the new law

On the national level, the basic posture of the German authorities began to evolve, partly under the impact of the Social Democratic party, when in 1966 that party became a partner in the Grand Coalition Government, and probably to some extent also in response to the transnational pressures generated in Brussels. The problem, as seen in the Ministry of Justice and in the Parliament, was on the one hand to avoid encroaching upon the *"Intimsphäre"* or "entrepreneurial privacy,"[27] and on the other hand to give the creditors some insight into the financial position of the enterprise. Consequently, the Ministry of Justice appeared inclined to include in the proposal for a reform of the German limited liability company, then in preparation, a compromise provi-

---

and thus was designed to protect creditors. The management remained free to build hidden reserves through understating. This meant a double impairment of the shareholder: his claim to dividends was reduced and the listed price of the share may have been depressed. Gessler, *Bedeutungswandel* at 159; WÜRDINGER, AKTIEN- UND KONZERNRECHT at 159; Juenger, in JUENGER & SCHMIDT at 17. The possibility that the management could dissolve the hidden reserves in order to conceal losses posed a threat to the creditors as well.

26 *See* note 21, p. 245 *supra.*

27 GROSSUNTERNEHMENSGESETZ, ENTWURF at 15.

sion, requiring such companies to make only their balance sheet available for public inspection and *not* the profit-and-loss statement. This, in fact, was the solution adopted in the proposal published in 1969.[28] It was obviously due to the sharp distinction drawn in the Federal Republic between the two major corporate forms that while the creditors' interest remained paramount in the debate on the disclosure obligation of limited liability companies, the investor-shareholder protection became unquestionably the predominant consideration with respect to stock companies.[29]

A more telling sign of the changing winds was the new law on "large enterprises," mentioned above, which was proposed by the Federal Government to the Parliament in May 1968 and adopted in August 1969. This law extended the disclosure obligation to any enterprise of a specified substantial size, *regardless of its legal form,* including individual business proprietorships (*Einzelkaufmann*).[30] The law represents the first substantial deviation in German history from the principle that the legal form of the enterprise is the sole criterion for disclosure purposes.

Actually, the immediate impulse for the new legislation was supplied by the case of Alfried Krupp whose Ruhr em-

---

28 § 152, Referentenentwurf eines Gesetzes über Gesellschaften mit Beschränkter Haftung, Herausgegeben vom Bundesministerium der Justiz (Köln-Marienburg 1969). (Official draft of a Law on Limited Liability Companies, published by the Federal Ministry of Justice.) Only filing with the commercial register would be required, no publication in a bulletin, etc. *See also* Würdinger, *Zur Publizität der GmbH* at 152. Kreplin doubts that the real informational value of balance sheets is commensurate with the necessary administrative costs incurred at the courts of registry. He believes that erroneous management decisions, and the resulting impairment of creditors, will not be prevented by such "publicity," and he also points out that the requirement anticipates (and goes beyond) the present obligation under the First Directive, which limits the disclosure obligation as regards limited liability companies to such companies of certain minimum size. Kreplin, *Der Referentenentwurf eines neuen GmbH-Gesetzes im Urteil der Wirtschaft,* 1970 BB 93, at 97.

29 Gessler, *Bedeutungswandel* at 130, citing von Caemmerer.

30 Grossunternehmensgesetz § 1.

pire faced a serious crisis in March 1967. Not being subject
to any disclosure obligation, Krupp apparently deluded himself and the public into believing that his available capital
was about twice the amount of what corresponded to reality.
In order to avert a national calamity and save the 100,000
jobs of the Krupp employees, the Federal and Länder
Governments had to resort to public funds to guarantee
bank loans in excess of half a billion marks. It was this
experience that prompted Rembert van Delden, the West-
phalian textile industrialist and maverick Christian Democrat member of the Bundestag, to offer the first bill that
would have extended the disclosure duty to some 20,000
enterprises falling within a new statutory criterion.[31] This
criterion of "size" would be determined by the combined
effect of three factors: total assets, the annual turnover, and
the size of the work force. Van Delden's plea that "the cloak
of the Christian affluent society must fall," fell on deaf ears
among his Christian Democratic colleagues, but the bill was
taken up by the then Social Democratic Minister of Justice,
Dr. Gustav Heinemann. As a former member of the board
of the *Rheinische Stahlwerke* (Rhine Steelworks), Dr. Heinemann was aware of the negative attitude on the part of the
industry, and in order to broaden the support for the bill,
he reduced its scope so as to affect only 170 enterprises. In
the critical meetings of the Cabinet, Minister Schmücker, a
Christian Democrat, advocated voluntary disclosure as a substitute, while his colleague, Franz-Josef Strauss, the Minister
of Finance and leader of the Christian Social Union, urged
thorough hearings of the industry as a prerequisite to any
legislation. Among other arguments, Strauss pressed the
proposition that a one-sided extension of disclosure would
not fit into the EEC scheme, and he called a German member of the EEC Commission, Dr. von der Groeben, to Bonn
as a supporting witness. Dr. von der Groeben, it will be
recalled, was in charge of the Commission's Directorate Gen-

---

[31] Der Spiegel, May 27, 1968, No. 22, at 75-76.

eral for Competition (D.G. IV) up to the time of the reorganization in mid-1968. However, in an interministerial meeting called for this purpose, Dr. von der Groeben is said to have expressed the conviction that the new disclosure requirement would not impair the competitive position of the German industry in the EEC. The confrontation between Heinemann and Strauss extended through two Cabinet meetings. Finally, the Social Democratic Minister of Economic Affairs Schiller, working with the Federal Cartel Office, devised a compromise formula, according to which the ceiling figures of the three factors mentioned above were multiplied by 2.5, with the effect that only 70 "large enterprises" would fall within the scope of the bill.[32] This formula was approved by the Cabinet but Strauss left the meeting before the vote.[33]

In the "motivation" accompanying the bill, the Federal Government stressed the economic and social impact of the major enterprises on suppliers, customers, financial institutions, employees and the regional or national labor markets, on the structure and financial position of entire cities and on the government itself, which in the past was forced—as the Krupp experience illustrated—to bail out such enterprises with public funds in order to avoid an unacceptable harm. In fact, the Government pointed out, most of the

---

[32] In 1969, Deputy Rembert van Delden was accused of leading a group of Christian Democratic deputies intent at scuttling the compromise Schiller bill and preventing any law from being passed. Die Zeit, Feb. 4, 1969, at 16.

[33] According to the text submitted to the Parliament and adopted in the new law, an enterprise becomes subject to disclosure if at least two of the following three indices occur (the figures in brackets indicate the original government proposal): total assets exceed 125 million DM (50 mill.); turnover in the preceding year exceed 250 million DM (100 mill.); average employment in the preceding year exceed 5,000 (2,000). § 1, GROSSUNTERNEHMENSGESETZ. For the original Social Democratic party proposal of a Law for the Improvement of the Publicity for Stock Companies, Limited Liability Companies and Related Companies see BUNDESTAGSDRUCKSACHE IV/203. Lamberth, *Der Richtlinienentwurf* at 69, thought that this proposal was generally considered a suitable basis for discussion. *See also* Rittner, *Die handelsrechtliche Publizität* at 45-50.

large post-war bankruptcies involved enterprises that were not subject to disclosure.[34] Finally, the disclosure information was indispensable for an understanding of the economy in general by private and governmental decision-makers. It is interesting that four years earlier, when the question came before the 45th *Deutscher Juristentag,* a committee of this influential professional group of German lawyers voted by a very small majority *against* any extension of the disclosure to even the largest limited liability enterprises, and a press commentator noted the absence in the debate of any reference to the spectacular financial difficulties of the Stinnes and Schlieker empires, or the insolvency of the Borgward Company.[35] One is reminded of the debate in the United States that surrounded the enactment in Congress of the 1964 legislation, deviating for the first time from the "securities offered to the public" criterion for the disclosure obligation, and imposing a continuing reporting duty upon companies with more than one million dollar assets and at least five hundred shareholders.[36]

Although the German industrial interests were reluctant in principle to accept any extension of the disclosure, perhaps the more important consideration underlying their negative attitude was the concern that the labor unions (and the Social Democratic party on their behalf) might seek to apply the new criterion of size, used in the Heinemann-Schiller bill, to the requirement of "codetermination" by workers in the decision-making of the enterprise—and there is evidence that this is precisely what the unions had in mind.[37] Nevertheless, the bill became law although in the process of enactment the disclosure obligation of individual business proprietorships and unincorporated business asso-

---

[34] GROSSUNTERNEHMENSGESETZ, ENTWURF at 14.

[35] HANDELSBLATT, Sept. 19, 1964.

[36] 15 U.S.C.A. § 78*l* as amended Aug. 20, 1964, Pub. L. No. 88-467.

[37] *See* p. 94 *supra.*

ciations (*Personenhandelsgesellschaft, i.e.,* partnership and
limited partnership) was diluted somewhat.[38]

(3) German posture on transnational level

During the Brussels negotiations on the disclosure provision of the First Directive in 1963-1968, German spokesmen
remained adamantly opposed to an extension of the disclosure requirement to limited liability companies. A spectrum
of arguments was advanced, in the first place, against the
broad proposition that *any* company in which associates
enjoy the limited liability privilege must be subject to disclosure. It would be unfair, it was urged from the German
side, to subject companies with limited liability, other than
stock companies, to any disclosure requirement whatsoever,
as long as simple partnerships and individual merchants (including such "large enterprises" as Oetker and Flick) with
whom these companies compete are not subject to an identical requirement.[39] Moreover, if a third party plans to enter
into a transaction with a foreign limited liability company,
that party—it was argued—would be free to demand information on the company's financial situation and, in case
of a refusal, abandon the deal.[40] A potential creditor, rather
than relying on the published information, in any case was

---

[38] *E.g.*, § 5, par. (1), no annual report required, § 5, par. 2 (4),
GROSSUNTERNEHMENSGESETZ. Generally the disclosure obligations of unincorporated enterprises are substantially less exacting.

[39] This may not be considered a convincing argument since
creditors in limited liability companies may rely only on the company's assets while partners in a partnership and individuals are liable
without limitation. However, from the economic viewpoint there is
some truth in the competition argument. The opponents of financial
disclosure do not object so much to the disclosure of assets serving
as a clue for *creditors,* but rather to the publication of information
on sales figures, the drop or increase in inventories and similar data
in the profit-and-loss statement which provide the *competitors* with
valuable material. Against the argument of the disclosure duty as "a
correlate of the limited liability" see Rittner, *Die handelsrechtliche
Publizität* at 156, and the sources cited there.

[40] Gessler, in ENTWICKLUNGSTENDENZEN at 18. This argument could
be invoked by any company, including the stock company, against
disclosure.

more likely to demand security in a tangible form. It was
the potential investor in a company—as was also pointed
out by the EEC Economic and Social Committee—for whom
the published documents may be of primary importance
as the principal source of information;[41] yet the shares or
"quotas" *(Anteile)* in a limited liability company are not
readily negotiable as are the shares of the stock company,
and—as a rule—when available, are not bought by the
general public, but rather only by persons interested in
the management who in any event would want to have
more detailed information beyond that required by the disclosure rule.[42]

It was said further by the opponents of disclosure, that
the limited liability company form is often chosen for a
family business, despite possible tax disadvantages (as compared with a stock company), because it has certain characteristics of a partnership, and yet allows for a greater
variety of solutions, particularly in case of death and succession. The "privacy" of the company would be destroyed
by a disclosure obligation and "publication havens" (analogous to tax havens) would be sought abroad, particularly
for such businesses as management consultants or patent exploitation, where the prospect of disclosure would frighten
away   clients and help competitors.[43] Even if the antidis-
closure argument, based on competitive prejudice, was of
questionable validity as a general proposition,[44] it was never-

---

[41] Avis at 3252.

[42] Deringer, in [1966] PARL. EUR. DÉBATS, No. 85, at 58. *See also*
in the same vein Gessler, in HARMONISIERUNG at 11 ff. But Skaupy
points out that in reality, a potential creditor eager to do business
with a company may be unwilling to demand more information than
he can obtain from the published documents. Skaupy, *Europäisches
Gesellschaftsrecht* at 15-16.

[43] Lamberth, *Der Richtlinienentwurf* at 70. For other arguments
see Centrale für GmbH, *Zur Harmonisierung der Publizitätspflicht der
GmbH in der EWG,* 1964 GMBH-RUNDSCHAU 23; Skaupy, *Europäisches
Gesellschaftsrecht* at 16.

[44] This argument was rejected by the Federal Government with
respect to disclosure by stock companies as being "without any basis."
Statement of reasons for the GROSSUNTERNEHMENSGESETZ, ENTWURF at 15.

theless said that small and middle-sized limited liability companies that produce a single product, should not be required to disclose data from which the competitor would be able to reconstruct the costs and price formation (such as the figures on the turnover tax).

The Federal Government is required by law to inform the Parliament prior to the final adoption of any Community act that could result in a modification of German legislation.[45] Accordingly, both chambers were given an opportunity to comment on the Commission's first draft of the First Directive, and they expressed opposition to the provision that would have required extending disclosure to limited liability companies with more than one million dollar assets, principally on two grounds: first, in the present state of the law, there was no assurance that the financial documents published by companies in the Member States would be comparable in content and reliability,[46] and second, the criterion of one million dollar assets would in any event be improper.[47] The *Deutscher Juristentag* group calculated that the one-million dollar (four million DM) asset criterion would include some 8,000 German limited liability companies and rejected it by an almost unanimous vote, but there was some support among the lawyers for a three-to-ten million DM ceiling subject to certain qualifications.[48]

The position of the Parliament foreshadowed in part the disclosure criteria adopted five years later in the law

[45] Art. 2, Law Concerning the Treaties of March 25, 1957, Establishing the European Economic Community and the European Atomic Energy Community, dated July 27, 1957, 1957 BGBl II, 753. Other provisions of this law were subsequently amended.

[46] STELLUNGNAHME DES BUNDESRATS, BUNDESRATSDRUCKSACHE III/64 and the *Report of the Legal Committee of the Bundestag* of Apr. 23, 1964, BUNDESTAGSDRUCKSACHE IV/2190, cited in Skaupy, *Europäisches Gesellschaftsrecht* at 16.

[47] The Bundesrat thought it would be necessary to take as the sole or additional basis the amount of company capital (Stamm- or Eigenkapital) and/or the turnover figure. *Id.* preceding note.

[48] HANDELSBLATT, Sept. 19, 1964. *See generally* Rittner, *Die handelsrechtliche Publizität* at 159-60.

concerning "large enterprises." The fact that in the national arena the disclosure issue became enmeshed in a controversy with strong political overtones, involving questions of economic policy and apt to affect thousands of small enterprises, obviously reduced, at least for a time, the margin of discretion of the Federal negotiators on the transnational level.

(ii) The situation in France: broad disclosure for listed stock companies

(1) The organizational pattern and national law

In contrast with Germany, France has a multitude of stock companies, many of them quite small; in fact, in France there are only twice as many limited liability companies as there are stock companies, as contrasted with a ratio of about twenty-eight to one prevailing in the Federal Republic, and this structural difference is necessarily reflected in the disclosure rules.

Each French stock company must now file its balance sheet, a statement of profit and loss, and an operating income statement *(compte d'exploitation général)* with the recording office of the court *(Tribunal)* for deposit at the commercial register, which is open to public perusal.[49] In addition, a substantially more extensive disclosure by publication in an official periodical is required only of stock companies whose shares are listed on a stock exchange and whose balance sheet total exceeds 10 million francs, and also of the subsidiaries of certain importance *(whatever their legal form and even if not listed on the stock exchange)* in which these companies hold at least one-half of the capital, and finally of companies engaged in certain specified activities such as banking and insurance.[50] Again, the stock companies whose

---

[49] Art. 293, Decree No. 67-236 of March 23, 1967, J.O. (France) of March 24, 1967, at 2866, as modified by Decree No. 68-25 of Jan. 2, 1968, J.O. (France) of Jan. 13, 1968.

[50] *Id.* Arts. 294-299 as modified. In addition to annual publication of the three basic financial documents mentioned above, with specified annexes plus the inventory of the securities portfolio (Art.

shares are listed on the stock exchange, but whose balance
sheet total does not exceed 10 million francs, must make
available to any shareholder on request specified financial
information.[51] Like the law in the Federal Republic, French
law prescribes precise rules regarding the content and
modalities of presentation of the information required of the
company, including—and this is important—information
concerning its subsidiaries and holdings.[52]

---

294), there is a requirement of periodic publication in the course of
the year (Art. 296). The provision concerning the subsidiaries was
originally included in the Decree No. 65-999 of Nov. 29, 1965,
abrogated by Law No. 67-559 of July 12, 1967, J.O. (France) of July 13,
1967. In view of the identity of the present law with Decree No. 65-
999 the literature dealing with that Decree remains relevant. See
Dalsace, in RECUEIL DALLOZ, Feb. 16, 1966, at 89; also the letter of the
Ministry of Finance to A.N.S.A. dated Jan. 18, 1966, published in
DROIT DES SOCIÉTÉS, March 3, 1966, at 20. See also Arts. 484, 485 of
the new Law No. 66-537 of July 24, 1966, concerning fines in case of
violation of the disclosure provisions.

[51] Art. 297, Decree No. 67-236 as modified. The financial documents included here are the balance sheet, the profit-and-loss statement and, if requested by a shareholder, also the "compte d'exploitation général" as specified, and an inventory of securities in the
portfolio.

[52] Art. 357 of the Law of July 24, 1966, prescribes that "all companies" possessing subsidiaries or holdings must attach to their
balance sheet a "table" describing "the situation of the said subsidiaries and holdings." A model for the table was to be given in a
decree. This requirement is not limited to companies whose securities
are listed on a stock exchange. In pursuance to Art. 357 of the Law
of 1966, Decree No, 67-236 of March 23, 1967, introduced the model
table and the table was modified by virtue of Art. 4 of Decree No. 68-
857 of Oct. 3, 1968, J.O. (France) of Oct. 4, 1968. According to Decree
No. 66-236, in case of a stock company, the "table" (annexed to the
balance sheet) is filed with the registry of the court (Arts. 247, 293 as
modified by Decree No. 68-25 of Jan. 2, 1968); and as for the companies with listed securities and their subsidiaries, the table must be
also made available to shareholders or, as specified, it must be published (Arts. 294-298, as modified, particularly Art. 295, No. 3). When
the value of the holding in the other company exceeds 1% of the
reporting company's capital, each such holding must be described
separately, while all the lesser holdings may be grouped together in
two basic categories: subsidiaries (at least 50% owned by the parent)
and other holdings, but French and foreign companies must be
grouped separately. Annex (Tableau I) to Decree No. 67-236. These

(2) The new French "S.E.C."

In 1967, the French Government ordered the institution
of a Commission on Stock Exchange Transactions *(Commission
des opérations de bourse)* with more extensive powers
than its antecedents.[53] The principal innovations were, first,
any company that proposes to make a public offering
of its securities must obtain prior clearance from the Commission of an appropriate prospectus and, second, all "insiders" are required to change the bearer shares they or their
family hold in the company or its affiliates into registered
shares or to deposit them with a bank;[54] and they must
promptly disclose any acquisition or alienation of these
shares. Penalties are imposed in case of failure to comply.[55]

provisions remain in force for companies which do not attach to their
balance sheet a consolidated balance sheet and accounts, taking into
account the situation of their subsidiaries and holdings; however, by
virtue of Art. 5 of Decree No. 68-857 of Oct. 3, 1968, those companies
that choose the consolidated form need give only "global information"
on all their subsidiaries and holdings, distinguishing only between
French and foreign ones. Actually, according to Art. 5 of the same
Decree, until Dec. 30, 1970, global information with respect to foreign
subsidiaries and holdings was to suffice even for companies which
did not provide consolidated accounts.
  On the French *plan comptable* see RODIÈRE & HOUIN, 1 DROIT
COMMERCIAL at 119 (4th ed., Paris 1965); KOECHLIN, DROIT DE L'ENTRE-
PRISE at 118 (Paris 1964). On the need for harmonization between
the *plan comptable* and the rules determining the application of the
Code général des Impôts with respect to information which companies
are required to supply see Dorat des Monts, *Vers un droit européen*
at par. 11.
  [53] Ordinance No. 67-833 of Sept. 28, 1967, J.O. (France) of Sept.
29, 1967. English translation in 7 INT'L LEGAL MATERIALS 1063 (Sept.
1968). *See also* Decree No. 68-23 portant organisation administrative
et financière de la Commission des opérations de bourse of Jan. 3,
1968, J.O. Jan. 13, 1968; and Decree No. 68-30 supprimant le Comité
de bourse des valeurs et fixant certaines attributions de la Commission
des opérations de bourse institué par l'ordonnance No. 67-833 du 28
sept. 1967, of Jan. 3, 1968, J.O. Jan. 13, 1968.
  [54] Art. 8 of Ordinance No. 67-833 of Sept. 28, 1967, added a new
Art. 162-1 to the Law of July 24, 1966, and this article was again
amended by Art. 4 II of the Law No. 69-12 of Jan. 6, 1969.
  [55] Arts. 153-2 and 153-3 (and generally Arts. 153-1 to 153-6 and
203-2) of the Decree No. 67-236 of March 23, 1967, added by Art. 1
of the Decree No. 68-857 of Oct. 3, 1968, J.O. (France) of Oct. 4, 1968.

In general, the Commission is to exercise continuing supervision over the flow of information to the shareholders and to the public from publicly held companies and over the functioning of the stock exchanges. To this end its personnel has substantial powers of investigation.

In its first Annual Report the Commission stated that 85% of the companies concerned had met their obligations within the prescribed time limits; the Commission had examined 236 "prospectus"-type documents and it recommended improvement in the quality of the information and harmonization of accounting rules.[56]

(3)   Opposition to EEC draft on disclosure

When the EEC Commission's proposal for the First Directive was published, a competent observer noted a strong opposition in France to the inclusion of *any* compulsory disclosure provision, particularly as regards limited liability companies which in that country often are quite insignificant enterprises and which in principle are still not required to disclose financial information.[57] It has been suggested that the intensity of this opposition was due in part to the still lingering effects of the obsolete concept of a company as

---

[56] *Rapport Annuel 1968*, J.O. (France), Documents administratifs No. 5, Apr. 7, 1969 (*First Annual Report* to the President of the Republic), summarized in Le Monde, Apr. 5, 1969, p. 23, col. 1-2. On the Commission generally see Boitard, *La commission des opérations de bourse*, 1968 JUR-CL. PÉR., DOCTR. 2161; Chatenet, *Efficacité des divers systèmes institutionels de contrôle des règles d'information*, 1969 BANQUE 81; Canac, *La commission des opérations de bourses*, 1968 GAZ. DU PALAIS, DOCTR. 59; Will, *Die französische Börsenkommission*, 1970 ZHR 229; Huyck, *The French Capital Market: Institutions and Issues*, 16 AM. J. COMP. L. 219 (1968).

[57] GOLDMAN, COURS at 215. A limited liability company is obligated to make a disclosure only if it is a subsidiary of a parent company which is subject to the disclosure obligation, under the conditions defined in Art. 298 of Decree No. 67-236 of Mar. 23, 1967, as explained *supra* p. 255. Prof. Houin advises that this rule may not be always observed in practice, despite the threat of penalties in Art. 485 of the Law of July 24, 1966, as amended.

a "contrat librement conclu"[58] which underlay the French law of 1867 but was abandoned in Germany at an early date; but the structure of the French industry, particularly the great number of small stock companies, the long protectionist tradition shunning competition, and the accent on "privacy," offer a better explanation. The existence of the multitude of minor stock companies (in contrast with the pattern in the Federal Republic) was perhaps the strongest motivation for the French inspired move in the European Parliament to exempt all small stock companies "that do not draw upon public savings" from the disclosure obligation in the First Directive.[59]

(iii)   The situation in the Netherlands:
more information for stockholders and employees

The Netherlands law, as we have seen, is the only one among the Six that does not provide for the limited liability company form. The role of the limited liability company is assumed in fact by the stock company under circumstances not dissimilar to the American close corporation.

(1)   No meaningful disclosure rules now

The law governing disclosure in the Netherlands concerns only a minute fraction of stock companies, and it is so general as to be meaningless. Yet the great, publicly owned, Dutch concerns have gone a long distance toward conforming voluntarily to modern reporting standards.[60] Pressures for

---

[58] Wang, Die europäische Aktiengesellschaft in der EWG at 97 (Freiburg/Switzerland 1964) quoting Ripert. The law of July 24, 1966 (Art. 505), repealed Art. 15 of the Code de commerce in which the notion of the company as a contract was expressly stated. See Pleven in Déb. Parl., Ass. Nat., June 1, 1965, [1965] J.O. (France, June 2), at 1666, complaining that the notion of company contract has not been defined.

[59] See p. 255 supra.

[60] The law prescribes in general terms that all stock companies must prepare a balance sheet and a profit-and-loss statement for adoption by the stockholders' meeting, but the filing with the office of the commercial register (accessible to the public) is prescribed only

improved disclosure have come in the Netherlands not only from unions and the Socialist Party, but—interestingly enough—to some extent also from the industry which has hoped to fend off demands for the German-type workers' "codetermination" by increased disclosure of financial data.[61]

The Verdam Commission, mentioned earlier, has proposed that a new law be adopted which would prescribe detailed rules (some 33 paragraphs, not as detailed as the German rules, however) on the content of the financial documents. An interesting new remedy, an injunction fashioned after the Anglo-American common law, could be obtained from a special chamber of the Amsterdam Court of Appeal ("the enterprise chamber") by any party able to show material interest in the development of the company, in order to compel the company's compliance with the rules governing financial data.[62] The proceeding before the court, however, would take place behind closed doors (as in family and tax matters) to avoid premature or distorted disclosure.[63] Moreover, the Commission proposed that the

---

if (a) the articles of incorporation authorize bearer shares in excess of 50,000 guilders; or (b) the company has issued bearer debentures or bearer "certificaten" for registered bonds; or (c) its shares or debentures or "certificaten" are listed on the stock exchange; or the company's business consists of accepting money from third parties for deposit or insurance. Moreover, only those companies that fall within these categories must follow a simple list of separate entries in preparing their balance sheet. Scholten, *Company Law in Europe* at 392; Art. 42, WETBOEK VAN KOOPHANDEL; Rivers, van de Ven, Westbroek, *The Netherlands Business Corporation Code* at 22, CCH COMM. MKT. REP. No. 16, Oct. 26, 1965.

Only about 500 of the 30,000 stock companies are listed on the stock exchange and the paid-up capital of 80% of all stock companies does not exceed 100,000 guilders. Sanders, *Reform des Aktienrechts in den Niederlanden* at 284-85; VERDAM REPORT at 37.

[61] On the proposed "codetermination" in the Verdam Commission see VERDAM REPORT at 9, 17, 98. *See* p. 150 *supra*.

[62] Sanders, *Reform des Aktienrechts in den Niederlanden* at 285, describes the proposal for a modified criterion for disclosure obligations. *See also* VERDAM REPORT at 36-42.

[63] It is interesting to note that the Government dropped the "closed-doors" feature in this context in Draft Law No. 9595 on

Commercial Code be amended so as to empower the same court, on request from a national labor union, to order an examination of the management's record and, if that should appear necessary, the dismissal of the management or of the supervisory council.

However, when it came to the question of broadening the disclosure of the financial documents *to the public,* only four of the five socialists were in favor, the fifth, a law professor and former attorney with substantial practice, broke the socialist ranks and joined the majority opposing the idea.[64] In fact, the majority of the Commission proposed to limit the disclosure to the public further[65] but the Social and Economic Council rejected this proposal and followed the Commission's minority, which would have broadened the obligation substantially.[66]

(2) The two proposed new laws: waiting for the EEC

The two draft laws (Nos. 9595 and 9596) which the Netherlands Government submitted to the Parliament on May 13, 1968, follow generally the portions of the Verdam Commission Report[67] which had been approved in substance by the

---

this subject, so that normal procedure would apply; but the Government preserved it in Draft Law No. 9596 for the proceeding of inquiry into the management instituted by shareholders or workers.

[64] VERDAM REPORT at 36 n.2.

[65] The disclosure would apply only to those companies that actually issued bearer shares in the amount exceeding 250,000 guilders. VERDAM REPORT at 37.

[66] The minority would have included unlisted stock companies with capital in excess of 500,000 guilders, even if they issued no bearer shares. *Id.* at 37.

[67] Draft Law No. 9595 on the preparation and content of the balance sheet, statement of profit and loss and report thereon, contains some 46 articles amending several articles of the Commercial Code concerning company law and also other laws; Draft Law No. 9596 concerns the right of inquiry into the management of the company by shareholders and workers. Both Draft Laws were approved, with a number of amendments, by the Second Chamber of the Parliament in April, 1970.

Social and Economic Council,[68] with one important exception. There would be no *immediate* change in the disclosure to the public, even though the flow of information to the shareholders would be significantly broadened. However, as further Community directives become available, additional legislation was to be introduced that would extend the disclosure obligation, albeit in an attenuated form (publication of a less detailed balance sheet), to closely held stock companies with a balance sheet total of at least 8,000,-000 guilders (about $2,220,000) subject to certain exemptions.[69] At any rate, one immediate and significant effect of bill No. 9595, if enacted, would be to submit the larger close stock companies (with minimum capital of 500,000 guilders or about $137,500) to an obligatory verification by auditors.[70]

More stringent rules—though by far not as stringent and comprehensive as in German law—would apply to the structure and content of the balance sheet and the profit-and-loss statement.[71] However, in contrast with German law, no valuation standards would be prescribed; any valuation method commonly employed in practice would be acceptable, but the method adopted and any subsequent change therein would have to be described in the annual report. In the interest of securing a clear financial picture, the formation of hidden reserves would be discouraged by the requirement of a separate entry.[72] Although no fixed scheme would be laid down for the balance sheet, the obligation to include detailed and separate information regarding the individual asset and liabilities items does not differ substantially from the corresponding obligation in German law.[73] Although the

---

[68] Opinions of May 20, 1966, and May 19, 1967.

[69] The company could be exempted if it is a subsidiary and complies with provisions still to be enacted.

[70] Draft Law No. 9595, Art. 39.

[71] The financial documents are to provide an effective insight into the financial condition and rate of profits of the enterprise and also the credit-worthiness and liquidity. Art. 2 of Draft Law No. 9595.

[72] *Id.* Arts. 5 and 6.

[73] But goodwill and "going concern" items may be listed as assets. *Id.* Art. 11.

companies would have to follow a simple scheme in the preparation of their profit-and-loss statement, they would be free to adopt any accounting and reporting method commonly used in the particular type of business.[74] In general, the emphasis is not on a unification of financial reporting, but rather on flexibility that would conform to the needs of individual enterprises and allow adjustments to modern accounting methods. An effort is made to mitigate the risks that this approach entails for the comparability of financial documents, by prescribing minimum requirements and legitimizing the methods customarily employed in a given field of business.

Again, *all* companies would be required to report to their shareholders on their holdings (and changes therein) in other companies, with more detailed information required in cases of majority holdings.[75] Exceptions from this new and important obligation (based on a certain limited amount of capital involved or an administrative act of exemption) are fashioned—the Government explanation asserts—after the American model. There would be no general exemption (but some alleviation) for reporting holdings abroad.

In the Netherlands, where by far the most stock companies are quite small, perhaps the strongest opposition to increased disclosure has come from middle class quarters, particularly the Brabant Catholics who own family businesses in the textile and shoe manufacturing fields. Their principal concern has been the advantage gained by the competitor from the disclosure. One has also heard the argument that disclosure facilitates undesirable "take-over" transactions by revealing the financial situation of the potential "victim." Whatever may have been the view of the large industrial companies on the disclosure issue, they were unalterably

---

[74] *Id.* Arts. 28 and 29.

[75] *Id.* Arts. 12-15. In those cases the company concerned would have a choice either to submit a consolidated balance sheet, or to include in its annual report a separate or consolidated balance sheet of its subsidiaries.

opposed to the entire coordination effort in the Community on the more general grounds which I have mentioned above.[76] In Brussels, the Dutch delegation concentrated its energy on pressing the proposition that, since the limited liability company form did not exist in the Netherlands, and its economic purposes were performed by the close stock company, the latter must be treated the same way as the limited liability company, and thus must be included in the one-million-dollar exemption from disclosure, lest there be an unlawful discrimination. Although the EEC Commission refused at first to agree, the Economic and Social Committee of the Community was sympathetic,[77] the Committee of the European Parliament embraced the Netherlands view, and the Commission eventually followed suit in the second modified draft of 1966.[78] The equality of the Netherlands close companies with the small limited liability companies was maintained for this purpose in the final text of the directive which—and this is noteworthy—sets forth its own definition of what constitutes a close company *under the law of the Netherlands.*[79]

(iv)   The Situation in Belgium, Luxembourg and Italy

(1)   Belgium: few rules but more in prospect

As I indicated earlier in connection with the discussion of the proposed Belgian reform, the present Belgian rules concerning the content of the financial documents are rudi-

---

[76] *Supra* p. 87.

[77] *Supra* p. 209.

[78] *Second Draft,* Art. 2, par. 1 (f).

[79] *Final Text,* Art. 2, par. 2(a) to (c). Scholten, *Company Law in Europe,* at 393-94, raises technical objections to this solution.
In the general area of "publicity," Draft Law No. 10,400 "for the adaptation of the Netherlands legislation to the first directive of the Council of the European Communities of Mar. 9, 1968 relating to company law," submitted by the Government to the Parliament on Nov. 4, 1969, proposes changes in Arts. 37b, 37c, 45e, 55b, 56e of the COMMERCIAL CODE, and in Arts. 8, 19, 30a, 31 and 32 of the HANDELSREGISTERWET. *See* Maeijer, *Aanpassing.*

mentary,[80] with no provisions for the valuation and depreciation standards.[81] Stock companies must file their balance sheet and profit-and-loss statement with the recording office of the commercial court and publish them in the annex to the official journal, the *"Moniteur"*;[82] the limited liability companies, however, must file the balance sheet only and there is no requirement of publication in a journal.[83] The reform proposal would essentially preserve this pattern, leaving the management with broad discretion in the valuation of the assets, although the method employed would have to be specified. A more detailed set of rules concerning the organization and the content of the financial documents would also be added.[84]

(2) The Belgian "Commission bancaire"

The Belgian picture would not be complete, however, without mentioning an administrative agency, the *Commission bancaire,* organized in 1935[85] which, although endowed with limited powers, has evolved into an organ whose impact has greatly exceeded the expectations of its founders. The Commission must be notified fifteen days in advance of any public offering of securities or listing on a stock exchange,

[80] Arts. 77 ff., 127 of the Belgian CODE DE COMMERCE. An annual inventory, balance sheet and profit-and-loss statement are required without any more detailed indications of the content and scheme.

[81] The court-made standard of review of the company's discretion requires "prudence, sincerity and good faith." Cour de cass. Judgment of Apr. 22, 1929, Pas. belge 1929, I, 164.

[82] The same applies to limited partnerships with shares (sociétés en commandite par actions). The above two documents, the inventory and the reports by the administrative council (conseil d'administration) must be forwarded to the shareholders with the invitation to the annual meeting.

[83] Arts. 80 and 137 of the CODE DE COMMERCE.

[84] The company management would have to specify the valuation method in the explanation to the balance sheet. Similar treatment is envisaged for limited liability companies. The possibility of including rules on holdings along the line of a *Konzernrecht* was apparently considered but put aside pending further study.

[85] Arrêté royal No. 185 of July 9, 1935.

and it must be given specified information.[86] In the interest
of capital market protection, the Commission may order a
postponement or reduction of the offering, and if the company's statements to the public appear misleading and are
not corrected, it may prohibit the offering for a time;[87]
at its behest, the Finance Minister may prohibit listing of
a security on a stock exchange.[88] Moreover, companies
drawing on the capital market are required to file their
balance sheet with the Commission annually.[89] Particularly
as a result of its advisory activities, the Commission has
been a significant factor in preventing violations of company law.[90] Its decisions have also introduced, or made
general, certain practices, such as shareholder's pre-emptive
rights, which are not to be found in statutory law.[91] The
Commission has acquired a mass of information through
intimate contacts with industry, conducted with great discretion in an atmosphere of secrecy.

In Luxembourg the law concerning stock companies coincides with the law of the Belgian neighbor[92] but, in contrast
with Belgium, limited liability companies are relieved even
of the obligation to file the balance sheet; the associates,
however, have a right of access to the financial documents.
The *Commissaire au contrôle des banques* performs functions
analogous to those of the Belgian *Commission bancaire*.[92a]

(3) Italy: middle of the spectrum

If we view the statutory standards governing the content
of financial documents as a continuum, the presently applicable Italian law is situated somewhere between the strict

---

[86] *Id.* Art. 27.

[87] *Id.* Arts. 28 and 29.

[88] *Id.* Art. 32.

[89] *Id.* Art. 33.

[90] Van Ryn & Heenen, 2 PRINCIPES DE DROIT COMMERCIAL at 345.

[91] Leleux, *Corporation Law* at 159.

[92] Law of Aug. 10, 1915, Arts. 9, 72, 75.

[92a] Arrêté grand-ducal of June 19, 1965, concerning banking and
credit operations and issues of securities, Mémorial A No. 33 of June
1965, at 610.

German rules and the "liberal" Benelux rules.[93] The valuation rules leave a broader margin of free choice to the management than exists in German law.[94] A stock company is required to file the balance sheet, the management and the auditors' reports, and the minutes showing the approval by the shareholders' meeting, with the office of the court *(cancelleria del Tribunale)*, and to publish a summary of the balance sheet in the "provincial" (district) bulletin *(Foglio annunzi legali)*, and the full text in the central bulletin *(Bollettino ufficiale delle società per azioni e a la responsibilità limitata)*.[95] Article 9 of the Decree implementing the First Directive now requires stock companies to file and publish also a profit-and-loss statement. A limited liability company must file and publish the balance sheet in the same manner, although some writers believe that publication in the bulletins is not obligatory.[96]

---

[93] HENRICH-CEREGHETTI, DAS ITALIENISCHE AKTIENRECHT, *Einleitung (Introduction)* by Henrich at 19 (Frankfurt 1965). Art. 2424 of the CODICE CIVILE.

[94] Art. 2425 of the CODICE CIVILE.

[95] *Id.* Art. 2435. The "register of enterprises" provided for by the Codice has never been established so that the transitional provisions of Art. 100 of R. Decree No. 318 of Mar. 30, 1942, Disposizioni di attuazione del codice civile e disposizioni transitorie, continue to apply. This article has been interpreted to the effect that pending the establishment of the "register of enterprises," the filing and publication requirements prescribed by the superseded Commercial Code and subsequent modifying laws remain in force. Corte di cass. dec. No. 3618 of Nov. 28, 1953; 1953 Foro It. Mass. 695.

[96] CODICE CIVILE Arts. 2491 and 2493. COLOMBO-ROTONDI, in JURA EUROPAE, No. 40.00, 17, 18; 40.20, 4. Santini is of the opinion that publication is not required for limited liability companies. SANTINI, SOCIETÀ A RESPONSIBILITÀ LIMITATA at 217 (Bologna 1966). *But see* Corte di cass. dec. No. 177 of Jan. 24, 1955, upholding generally obligation to publish with respect to limited liability companies. The argument in support of the obligation to publish has been that the lawmaker had intended all forms of publicity applicable during the "transitional" period mentioned in the preceding note to apply also to limited liability companies, although these companies did not exist prior to the integrated Codice civile. On this assumption, the reference to limited liability companies was added in the title of the central official bulletin.

The proposed reform would make the rules concerning the content of financial documents much more specific, and it would broaden the disclosure requirements particularly for listed companies.[97]

According to the present Italian law, admission of an issue to the stock exchange requires authorization by the local chamber of commerce and approval of the Ministry of the Treasury,[98] and the company requesting admission must show a minimum capital of 1,000 million Lire (about $1,540,000).[99] Again, formation of a stock company with a capital in excess of 500 million Lire or a capital increase beyond this level requires special governmental approval.[99a] The reform pro-

---

[97] Each stock company would have to show in its balance sheet its holding in another ("related") company amounting to 10% or more of its own or the related company's capital (Art. 3 of the reform proposal), as well as the majority holding in another ("controlled") company (Art. 4), and an annex would have to specify essential data of the balance sheets of the companies concerned. Balance sheets would have to be accessible to shareholders. Art. 34 of the reform proposal. *Cf.* Art. 2432, par. 3 of the CODICE CIVILE. Detailed rules would govern the items in the profit-and-loss statement, whereas the present text prescribes an outline only for the balance sheet. Art. 35 of the reform proposal. While the present law leaves the content of the annual report to the discretion of the management, the new law would provide detailed guidance, *e.g.*, separate treatment of the diverse sectors of the company's activities with reference to the financial documents and the cost, prices, investments, the valuation and depreciation principles adopted and changes therein, changes in the various asset and liability items with explanations, salaries, pensions, obligations, etc. In addition, listed companies would have to report on holdings of their own shares and they would have to report also *semiannually*. Art. 38. There would be no changes in the rules governing valuation and reserves: for text of reform proposals see 1967 RIVISTA DELLE SOCIETÀ 370. *See* p. 140 *supra.*

[98] The Bank of Italy certifies only that necessary authorizations have been obtained. The requirement for admission of securities to a stock exchange is determined by the chamber of commerce pursuant to Law No. 272 of March 20, 1913; PELLERI, ORDINAMENTO DELLA BORSA IN ENCICLOPEDIA DELLA BANCA E DELLA BORSA at 276 (Roma, Milano 1968).

[99] On June 8, 1960, this minimum amount was fixed by the Comitato interministeriale per il credito e il risparmio.

[99a] The approval is granted by the Ministry of the Treasury, acting in agreement with the Ministry of Industry, Commerce and Crafts,

posal would introduce a *continuing* supervision of listed companies by a supervisory agency within the Bank of Italy which would receive and publish the relevant information.[100]

(4)   Impact of national laws in EEC forum

The fact that in Italian and Belgian law the disclosure obligation extends—albeit in a varying degree—also to limited liability companies, proved to be a determining factor in the position taken by the delegations of these two Member States in the EEC coordination proceedings. Their officials and experts were extremely reluctant to accept any limitation on, or exemption from, the principle of disclosure which would constitute a retrograde step in their national laws. In Italy, moreover, certain groups within the Government appeared particularly interested in disclosure provisions because of the influx of foreign companies into Italy. The Italian delegation fought against the curtailment and postponement of the disclosure obligation to the very last moment of the proceeding within the framework of the Council of Ministers. The German delegation was the most articulate antagonist of an extension of the disclosure requirement to limited liability companies, and in taking this position it also defended the existing Federal law, despite the fact that the official circles at that time had already inclined toward a certain modification of that law on this issue. In its final text, the directive did impose an obligation to publish the balance sheet and the profit-and-loss statement in principle upon all three types of the companies concerned (including limited liability companies)[101] but it exempted temporarily both the limited liability companies and the Dutch close stock companies, pending further coordination.[102]

---

and after consultation with the Comitato interministeriale per il credito e per il risparmio. Law No. 428 of May 3, 1955, Gazz. Uff. No. 121 of May 27, 1955.

[100] Arts. 41, 51, 54 of the reform proposal, *supra* note 152, p. 140.

[101] The other two types were stock companies and limited partnerships with shares.

[102] *Final Text*, Art. 2, par. 1 (b). *See* p. 233 *supra*.

(v)   The content of financial documents, or how to achieve comparability

The Commission's drafts of 1964 and 1966 were confined simply to the requirement of publication of the balance sheet and the statement of profit and loss; they did not purport to define in any way the minimum content of these documents or the modalities of their compilation and verification. Yet this problem became a central factor in the EEC proceeding after 1966. Although France and the Federal Republic, as we have seen, had detailed, albeit different, rules on this subject, the Benelux countries had little, if any, while the state of the law in Italy was somewhere between these two groups. Thus it was argued that, in the absence of detailed and comparable rules governing the content and verification of the financial documents, any informed reading and any meaningful comparison would be impossible, and, on the contrary, the data disclosed were bound to create false impressions and misunderstandings. This argument was advanced particularly in the debate within the Federal Republic, and it was pressed by German spokesmen in Brussels and in the European Parliament. The Commission delayed any work in this vital and technically complex field, in part apparently because it did not recognize the significance of the problem for some considerable time, in part again because of the jurisdictional conflict among the Directorates General, and, finally, because the tax division, which would do the preparatory studies, was occupied by other matters.[103]

Be that as it may, the Commission did nothing in this difficult field until 1966 when the *Institut der Wirtschaftsprüfer in Deutschland e.V.* (Institute of Public Accountants) in Düsseldorf took the initiative, organized a study group composed of accounting experts from five Member States (all except Luxembourg), and offered assistance to the Commission. The Commission gratefully accepted and the result was a preliminary draft of a new directive on the coordination of

---

[103] Some preparatory work was done by private organizations, the Union des experts comptables and the Union des analystes financières.

annual financial documents which was completed in 1968.[104] In the meantime, however, as we have seen, the delay in the preparatory work on this subject became the most effective argument in support of avoiding or delaying *any* coordination of the disclosure rules.

One commentator sought to absolve the Commission of any blame for the delay on the ground that the problems of accounting methods, and particularly valuation and depreciation, were so closely connected with the tax and general economic policies that, without a close coordination of national policies in these areas, no realistic effort was feasible, and "all company law reform must remain superficial and imperfect."[105]

We have noted earlier that national authorities, concerned with company law reform, had given considerable attention to United States securities legislation and to the working of the Federal Securities and Exchange Commission. However, only the Belgian *Commission bancaire* and the *Commissaire au contrôle des banques* in Luxembourg have approached the American pattern. It is perhaps too early to comment on the working of the French Commission on Stock Exchange Transactions, and the prospects for an Italian supervisory agency are uncertain.[106] Although the general trend appears to point toward the establishment of a supervisory body, the dominant opinion in the Federal Republic holds any such body unnecessary, in view of the strict and detailed rules of the Federal law governing stock companies.[107]

The question was raised, what solution would be ultimately desirable on the transnational level of the EEC. Leleux of the EEC legal staff considered two alternatives: "[A] somewhat far-reaching standardization" of the national rules, or "the introduction of Community provisions for

---

[104] Doc. IV-2/2800/68/F. *See* p. 354 *infra.*

[105] Fikentscher & Grossfeld, *The Proposed Directive* at 266.

[106] *Supra* note 100.

[107] §§ 162, 170, 177, par. 1, Stock Company Law of 1965.

which a European agency would be responsible." In his view, the example of the United States favors the second alternative:

> [H]armonization presents very great difficulties when the actions of the authorities in the various countries are based on different ideas, and even if harmonization is achieved, the disadvantages of having parallel but multiple procedures that have to be gone through are obvious. The advantages that there would be in having a set of Community regulations and a federal-type agency to enforce them are undeniable, both because this would encourage unification in related fields, as we can see from the S.E.C.'s example, and because it would prevent the decision as to where issues should be floated being based not on economic considerations but on the issuing corporation's desire to escape rules it considered too strict. Furthermore, will it not be necessary to have an agency of this kind to ensure respect for the legal provisions—which will still be national provisions—relating to groups of corporations and to intercorporate stockholdings when the corporations concerned are in several different countries? Otherwise, how would it be possible to ensure that any given provision of one member country's statute will be respected by a parent corporation, subsidiary or affiliate which comes under the law of another country? Classical private international law does not seem to provide an adequate answer to these questions.[108]

Director General Oleffe of the Belgian *Commission bancaire* suggests another variant: "Europe must find something between the SEC and the Commission Bancaire. Perhaps every member country of E.E.C. could create a system of control with a federation of these control agencies at the top. . . ."[108a]

---

[108] Leleux, *Corporation Law* at 159-60.
[108a] Robert Ball, *The Declining Art of Concealing the Figures*, 76 FORTUNE 136, at 171 (Sept. 15, 1967).

(vi)   An American comment on European reporting

An American observer, viewing the European practice at
the time when the First Draft of the directive was published
(in 1964), was struck by the fact that financial reports (with
the exception of large Dutch or American-controlled concerns operating in Europe) generally were issued three
months later than those issued by their counterparts in the
United States. Reports by large British and Dutch companies
were "reasonably good with balance sheets reflecting the
condition of the company fairly accurately" and income
statements "approximating the earning power." In Germany
and France, the reports were "fairly accurate," but German
balance sheets were generally understated (a defect which, as
we have seen, the 1965 law had sought to correct), and the
French tended to hide sales figures in subsidiaries where sales
did not need to be disclosed. Belgian reports lay somewhere
between the above two groups' standards, "while Italian
income statements are virtually useless for security analysis
purposes."[109] Three years later, in 1967, a French expert
thought that both French and Italian reports were "too
vague and general to be really useful."[110] Reporting practices
have been generally improving in Europe as European companies have been encouraged to seek new capital. If American interest in European investment is allowed to continue,
pressures from potential American investors and the practices of American subsidiaries in Europe will work in the
direction of a generally improved reporting practice.

---

[109] *European Companies Lag Far Behind Those in the U.S. on
Earnings Reports,* New York Times, Feb. 16, 1964, at F1, col. 4, at F5,
col. 1-7, quoting American investment concerns specializing in foreign
issues.

[110] Houin, *Le projet italien* at 155. *See also* KRONSTEIN & CLAUSSEN,
PUBLIZITÄT UND GEWINNVERTEILUNG at 98; WÜRDINGER, AKTIEN- UND
KONZERNRECHT at 158 ff.; Robert Ball, *The Declining Art of Conceal-
ing the Figures,* 76 FORTUNE 136, at 138 (Sept. 15, 1967).

(c)   Methods of "publicizing" information on companies: a "cartesian" solution?

National laws in the Community prescribe one or more of the following means of publicizing information: filing with the clerk of the court or an administrative bureau; entry into a commercial or company register; insertion into a journal for legal notices.[111] Had the Commission followed a "cartesian" approach, it would have tried to design a single "ideal" system consisting of the "best" features of these three basic methods[112] which are applied differently from one State to another, and even within the same State with respect to different documents and different types of companies.

(i)   Too little coordination in First Draft

The Commission's First Draft, however, followed a much less ambitious avenue: it left the Member States free to continue employing any or all of the three methods, subject to certain *minimum* requirements.[113] However, the Member States were to make sure that a file was instituted for each company (either at a central register or at one of the commercial or company registers) which would contain, in an up-to-date form, all the documents and information which was to be made public according to the directive.[114] The

---

[111] Lutter & Schlosser, *Die Publizität der GmbH* at 109; Rittner, *Die handelsrechtliche Publizität* at 76-112.

[112] Comm. Doc. du travail 2829/III/C62-F, March 29, 1962.

[113] Art. 3(1), *First Draft.* Thus if the method of publication through insertion in a journal was adopted, the publication would have to be centralized in the same, single official journal. Art. 3 (2), *First Draft.* If a Member employed several methods cumulatively for the same document or information, an arrangement would have to be made (and the form of this was also left to the State concerned) to avoid discrepancies and to specify which method would control in relation to third parties. Art. 3 (4), *First Draft.* A State was to be free to employ different methods for different types of information or company. However, the same method had to be employed for the same type of company with respect to information that could be invoked against third parties, but this rule did not include the consolidated text of the articles of incorporation. Art. 3 (3), *First Draft.*

[114] *See* p. 241 *supra,* on the modification of the law in the Federal Republic.

Economic and Social Committee welcomed the institution
of a central file for each company in all Member States, but it
wondered why the Commission had failed to take the next
logical step, that is to require that in all states information
in the file be made controlling with respect to third parties,
regardless of any other method of publication prescribed in
the State.[115] The European Parliament pursued this suggestion with enthusiasm,[116] and it proposed an appropriate
amendment[117] which the Commission gladly accepted. The
original hesitation in the working group was due particularly
to unwillingness on the part of the Belgian Government to
relinquish its treasured method of publication in a special
journal as the controlling channel. The main argument in
favor of this method was that filing alone did not meet the

---

[115] Avis at 3253. The Economic and Social Committee made
another practical suggestion: since the specified documents must be
deposited in the company's file, where publication in a journal was
also required it should be limited to a summary containing also a
reference to the file where the full text could be found. This suggestion in substance was followed in the final text. Furthermore, the
Committee urged that uniform deadlines for the publication be fixed in
the directive. *Id.*

[116] The Committee for the Internal Market (BERKHOUWER REPORT
at 31) welcomed the prospect of obtaining all desired information as
quickly as modern commerce required. The *Report* took also the
side of the Economic and Social Committee on the point that the
central file should be controlling with respect to third persons in
case its content should be inconsistent with information made public
through other means. It argued that in intra-Community trade a
third party would rarely seek information in person at the business
seat of his foreign trading partner. This was the reason why Art.
4, par. 5, was introduced which enabled a third party to acquire
the necessary information (by mail) from the officials in charge of
the central file. If, however, a third party could not rely on the
information from the central file, because information made public
through other methods would prevail in case of a divergence, then he
had to consult the information published elsewhere in any event, and
the filing in the central file would be useless and superfluous.

[117] The proposed modification to Art. 4, par. 4 of the *First Draft*,
in Avis at 1522. The Liberal group in the European Parliament
proposed a further "centralization" of the publicity along the French
pattern but the amendment was not adopted. M. Jozeau Marigné,
in [1966] PARL. EUR., DÉBATS, No. 85, at 63.

business needs, since those who were in a continuing business relationship with the company could not keep a constant watch over the file or register for any new information; it was less inconvenient to follow announcements in a bulletin. The final compromise, accepted only at a very late stage, under heavy influence from the German and Belgian delegations, adds publication in a journal as a second *obligatory* method, in addition to the company file.[118]

(ii) Central file and publication in bulletin—effect on third parties

Thus, the final version of the directive provides, in the first place, that the full text of each document and other information which a company is required to make public must be made part of the company's central file at the register, *or* it must be transcribed in its entirety in the register; if the latter alternative is followed an entry must be made in the company's file referring to the text in the register. Second, either the entire text, or a summary, or an appropriate reference to the text in the file or register must be published in the national bulletin.

The effect of this "publicity" with respect to third parties is governed by a curious compromise: the company cannot invoke, as against a third party, a document which was not published or noted in a national bulletin, unless the company is in a position to prove the third party's knowledge thereof;[119] but in case of a discrepancy, it is the text in the

---

[118] *Final Text,* Art. 3. The Commission explained that the modification in the *Second Draft,* adding the obligatory publication in a journal, had served a number of purposes: it was to soothe the opposition of those Governments strongly attached to their traditional publication in official journals; it also was to defeat the reproach that the filing, as the only means of publication, would fail to reach the public effectively and make all interested persons aware of the changes in the company's situation; finally, it was to take the wind out of the sails of those who condemned the rigidity of the directive and claimed that it was illegal, because it left too little freedom to the Member States. Motivation of the EEC Commission to the Second Draft, COM (66) 366 final, at 3.

[119] Pursuant to a qualification inserted in this provision, despite considerable doubt on the part of the Commission staff, transactions

central file or register and not the text in the bulletin that must prevail with respect to a third party. The third party, however, may rely on the text in the bulletin, unless the company is in a position to prove that the third party knew the text in the file or register.[120] Moreover, the third party may always rely on the document and information, even before they are "published," unless by national law they have no legal effect without "publicity,"[121] that is, unless "publicity" has a constitutive rather than declaratory effect. The provisions concerning the burden of proof of knowledge were modified in the successive drafts, and the originally employed concept of "good faith" (*bona fide*) third parties was eliminated, apparently because it was not uniformly understood in the national laws.

In this context we may note that in the German, Italian and the new French law, the company becomes a legal person only when entered into the register; "publicity" in this instance has a constitutive effect,[122] while in the other three Member States its effect is merely declaratory. When the effect of the "publicity" of a legal act concerning a company is not constitutive, failure to "publish" deprives the company in all Member States of the possibility to rely on that act *vis-à-vis* a third party acting in good faith, but the third party

---

occurring before the sixteenth day after publication in the bulletin may still not be relied on by the company against third parties who prove that it was "impossible" for them to learn of the publication. *Final Text,* Art. 3, par. 5, second sentence. How will the "impossibility" be proved? The clause was inserted at the insistence of the German delegation and it reflects in part § 15, par. 2 of the German COMMERCIAL CODE which, however, did not limit the "probatio diabolica" to a fixed period. However, § 15, par. 2 has now been amended by Art. 1, No. 2(a), of the Federal Law Implementing First Directive to conform to the directive.

120 *Final Text,* Art. 3, par. 6 (2).

121 *Final Text,* Art. 3, par. 7.

122 *Germany:* § 41 of the Stock Company Law of 1965, § 11 of the Limited Liability Company Law; *France:* Art. 5, par. 1 of the Law of 1966; *Italy:* Arts. 2330, 2331 CODICE CIVILE; Art. 2475(2) for the limited liability company.

in turn retains the option to rely on the act if it wishes to do so.[123]

In a sense, the two methods of publicizing information which the directive makes obligatory may be viewed as a minimum Community standard; where national law requires other additional methods they will remain applicable unless the law is modified.

Similarly, to the extent that the directive purports to regulate the *legal effect* of the "publicity" it confines itself in principle to the effect on third parties, leaving the rest to the domain of the respective national laws. The rules concerning the impact on third parties[124] came close to the provisions of

---

[123] In *Belgian* and *Luxembourg* law, failure to "publish" the act constituting the company as required by law deprives the company of any access to the courts (Art. 11, par. 3 of the Belgian CODE DE COMMERCE; Art. 10, par. 3 of the Luxembourg Law of 1915); third parties may take advantage of the failure to publish but the company cannot rely on it.

In the *Netherlands* law the failure to publish, in the official journal, the company's charter (Art. 36g of the WETBOEK VAN KOOPHANDEL), a charter amendment (*id.* Art. 45e), or the act of dissolution (*id.* Art. 55b), and the failure to enter into the commercial register (Art. 31 HANDELSREGISTERWET) have similar consequences.

Failure to register has the same result in *Italy:* Art. 2193 of the CODICE CIVILE. The new *French* law contains the same principles (Arts. 43, 44, Decree No. 67-237). In Italy, in the Federal Republic, and now in France, a company becomes a legal person only upon inscription in the register and purported actions on behalf of the company prior to registration entail personal liability (see preceding footnote and also *infra* p. 282 on "civil" effects of failure to comply with required "publicity"). However, in French law, where publication in a journal is required in addition to an entry into the register, failure to do the former does not seem to have the same *civil*-law consequences and this would constitute a difference from the German and other Members' laws. But see Art. 8 of the French Law of 1966 on failure to publish changes in the organs. Art. 283 of Decree No. 67-237 provides only that the legal representatives of companies are responsible for compliance with the requirements of "publicity," and if the company fails to meet the requirements within a specified time, any interested person may ask the president of the commercial court (*tribunal de commerce*) to appoint a "mandatory" who would see to the compliance.

[124] *Final Text,* Art. 3, paras. 5 and 7, Art. 8.

the German Commercial Code and the related principles of
what may be viewed as "customary law" developed by
German courts. Nevertheless, the directive diverged enough
to require in Germany a statutory provision which modified
the principles.[125] In contrast with the Federal Republic
where a statute was required, in France and in Italy the
modifications were made by executive action.[126] Actually all
of the Six must modify their law to some extent to conform

---

[125] The original principles were formulated as follows: "Whoever
(1) causes an incorrect entry to be made, or (2) fails to have removed
an incorrect entry concerning his affairs, which is known to him though
not caused by him, is estopped from invoking the incorrectness of the
entry as against a third person who has in good faith relied on this
apparent legal situation (Rechtsschein)." BAUMBACH-DUDEN, HANDELS-
GESETZBUCH (16th ed. München, Berlin 1964) § 15, note 5 B, C; *see
also* 22 BGHZ 235, 238 (1956), 131 RGZ 12, 14 (1930). A new par.
3 was included in § 15 of the COMMERCIAL CODE by Art. 1, No. 2(b)
of the Federal Law Implementing First Directive. This new paragraph
modifies the above principles so as to make it possible for a third
party, acting in good faith, to rely on an incorrect publication or
entry against a person whose affairs are involved, even if that person
did not cause, or fail to have removed, the incorrect version. The new
text goes beyond the scope of the directive in several respects. It appeared impossible to limit this provision only to companies dealt with
in the directive, or to confine it to information which the directive
requires to be published. Again, the new paragraph covers also cases
"more significant in practice," where *not only* the published text or
fact, but the entry in the register as well, is faulty or altogether missing. If the entry is incorrect but the published text or fact is accurate
the original principles, as stated above, apparently continue to apply.
See explanation in Entwurf eines Gesetzes zur Durchführung der
Ersten Richtlinie des Rates der Europäischen Gemeinschaften zur
Koordinierung des Gesellschaftsrechts, BUNDESTAGSDRUCKSACHE V/3862,
at 10-11 (Feb. 13, 1969). *See also* Art. 8 of the First Directive, *Final
Text;* Gessler, in 3ÈME COLLOQUE at 1 ff.
    On the problems arising from the implementation of this aspect
of the First Directive see Olshausen, *Neuerungen im System der
handelsrechtlichen Rechtsscheingrundsätze zur Publizitätswirkung des
Handelsregisters,* 1970 BB 137; see also on the application of the
implementing law, Gustavus, *Anmeldung und Eintragung der Ver-
tretungsverhältnisse einer GmbH nach dem Koordinierungsgesetz,* 1970
BB 594.

[126] See preceding note on the Federal Law Implementing First
Directive. France: Ordinance No. 69-1176 of Dec. 20, 1969, modifying
Law No. 66-537 of July 24, 1966, on commercial companies, inserting

to the new provisions, the Federal Republic probably less than the others.

On a late initiative from Italian quarters[127] the Council of Ministers approved, along with the directive, a supplementary declaration in which it noted the inconvenience faced by a company with operations abroad, which must comply with the "publicity" requirements both at its home office and in those other Member States where it maintained an agency or a branch. The Council asked the Commission to propose a solution for this difficulty "as soon as possible." Perhaps the Italians had in mind a single central file and a single register to cover the company's operational bases anywhere in the Common Market area. But here again the controlling consideration may have been the idea that concentrating the "publicity" for a foreign company's Italian branches in that company's home state would add another contact with that state for choice-of-law purposes, and thus would render it more difficult for an Italian court to impose Italian law on the foreign company's Italian branch.[128] It is, however, unlikely—after the experience with the first directive—that the Commission would hasten to submit such a proposal to the Ministers.[129]

---

a new Art. 4-1 in the 1966 Law. Italy: Decree Implementing First Directive, Art. 4 (modifying Art. 2383 of the CODICE CIVILE), Art. 15 (adding Art. 2457 ter to the CODICE CIVILE), Art. 18 extending the new article to limited liability companies.

127 The proposal was made in the Group for Economic Questions within the Committee of Permanent Representatives.

128 Art. 2505 of the Italian CODICE CIVILE provides that if a company organized abroad has either its central administration or the center of its economic interests in Italy, it is subject to Italian law.

129 At the initiative of the same group, the Group for Economic Questions, the original text of Art. 3, par. 1, was modified (the words "de chaque registre du commerce" were replaced by "d'un registre du commerce") so as to avoid the necessity for a company with several domestic branches to keep a separate file at each register in which each domestic branch is entered. Thus a single file covering all its *domestic* branches will suffice.

(iii)   Required information on company's stationery

To enable any businessman to determine readily the locale of the publicly available information about a company, the directive requires that the company's stationery and order forms indicate the register where the file is kept, as well as the legal form of the company, its seat and, where applicable, the fact of the liquidation proceeding.[130] If the company's capital is mentioned on its papers, the amount of the subscribed *and* paid-in capital must be given.[131]

(d)   Penalties for failure to disclose

Finally, in order to assure the necessary enforcement, the directive requires the Member States to prescribe "appropriate sanctions" against those responsible[132] for the failure to effect the disclosure of the financial documents or to comply with the rules concerning information on company stationery and other papers.[133] Presumably, criminal or administrative law penalties are contemplated here—a rather rare instance

---

[130] Art. 4, *Final Text.* This provision required new legislation *inter alia* in Germany. Gessler, in ENTWICKLUNGSTENDENZEN at 19. Federal Law Implementing First Directive, Art. 2, Nos. 7 and 17; Art. 3, Nos. 3 and 10. Similarly, in Italy, Art. 2250 of the CODICE CIVILE was modified by Art. 1 of the Decree Implementing First Directive.

[131] Art. 4, last par. The indication of the capital which was required in the *First Draft* is no longer obligatory. This modification was a compromise between those favoring an obligatory indication of the capital and those who did not think that "a" capital figure constituted any "guarantee" to a third party, but on the contrary feared that it would result in misconceptions about the economic potential of the company, if in reality the capital was diminished through losses. Skaupy, *Europäisches Gesellschaftsrecht* at 16. As a reason why the *Second Draft* required indication of the subscribed and paid-in capital in case the capital is mentioned at all, it is stated by the Commission, COM (66) 366 final at 4, that the simple indication of the subscribed capital could lead to a "fictitious" guarantee if the subscribed capital had not been paid in completely; furthermore, it was necessary to prevent a company from including authorized capital.

[132] *Final Text,* Art. 5.

[133] *Final Text,* Art. 6. The *First Draft* and *Second Draft* referred to "mesures repressives."

of Community law reaching into this sensitive area of national law.[134] "Civil" consequences consist, as we have seen, of depriving the company of the possibility to rely on unpublished documents or data in relation to third parties.[135] Actually, as Professor Goldman pointed out, national patterns for the enforcement of the "publicity" rules differ widely, and the directive attempts coordination on a limited basis.[136] Since the text left each Member free to determine the nature of the contraventions and the severity of the punishment, the Economic and Social Committee concluded that the provisions represented "no real harmonization."[137] At the opposite pole, a former Dutch Minister of Justice questioned the legality of this provision on the ground that it exceeded the legitimate scope of a directive which is to leave national authorities free to decide the manner of enforcement: "The purpose of the directive," he wrote, "is publication and not how municipal law penalizes those who fail to do so."[138]

2. Validity of undertakings entered on company's behalf— quo vadis ultra vires?

While the problem of financial disclosure raised significant issues touching upon economic policy, the *ultra vires* rules reflect certain basic concepts of private law, and the effort to coordinate them led to a confrontation not only of technical differences but of divergent doctrines as well.

---

[134] The EEC Treaty itself provides in Art. 87, par. 2(a), for "regulations or directives" to enforce certain rules in the antitrust law field by "fines and penalties," and fines have been in fact imposed by the Commission.

[135] *See* p. 276 *supra.*

[136] GOLDMAN, COURS at 218. The Economic and Social Committee did not appear to have understood the Commission's text and reasoning in the *First Draft* (*see* AVIS at 3253, par. C(2)) and no one can blame the Committee in view of the obscure nature of the text and the Commission's failure to explain it.

[137] AVIS at 3253.

[138] Scholten, *Company Law in Europe* at 396.

The two opening articles in this section of the directive proved relatively noncontroversial: the first, which embodies almost word for word the 1966 French law,[139] provides that persons who act on behalf of a company in the process of organization, before it has acquired its legal personality, shall be liable, "in the absence of contractual arrangements to the contrary," jointly and indefinitely, unless the company itself assumes the undertakings.[140] The second article (relating also to the "civil" effects of "publicity") prescribes that completion of the formalities of "publicity" with respect to the appointment of company officials shall preclude the company from invoking any irregularity in such appointment against a third party, unless the company is in a position to show that the third party was aware of such irregularity.[141] It was, however, the immediately following series of provisions concerning the effect of limitations on the powers of company organs in their dealings with third parties that caused considerable difficulties.

(a)   The doctrinal difference: Germany vs. the Five

Three different types of limitations on the company organs' powers were involved: those derived from the company's charter purpose (*objet social*), those imposed upon the company organ by national law, and those contained in the company charter (or in a decision of one organ restricting the powers of another organ).

---

[139] Art. 5 of the Law of July 24, 1966.

[140] *Final Text*, Art. 7. This article was Art. 8 in the *First Draft* which was included in the section on "Publicity." The clause "in the absence of contractual arrangements to the contrary" was included at the insistence of the German delegation despite doubts on the part of the Commission's lawyers. *Cf.* § 41 of the German Stock Company Law of 1966 and Art. 2331 of the Italian CODICE CIVILE.

[141] *Final Text*, Art. 8. This article constituted the second paragraph of Art. 10 in the *First Draft*. See comment by Dorat des Monts, *Vers un droit européen* at par. 12. The first paragraph of the same article in that draft was dropped as unnecessary in the final editing stage.

The advanced state of German law in this area, as compared with the law of the other Five, became the determining factor in the coordination strategy. Although the other Member States went a long way toward recognizing the value of the modern solutions in German law, they were not prepared to embrace them entirely. It is difficult to say to what extent these Members were influenced by their attachment to different doctrinal concepts, rather than by a policy divergence on how to reconcile the interests of third parties (security of transactions) on the one hand, and the interests of the company (and of the shareholders) on the other—the perennial problem in company law.

In all Member States, *except* in the Federal Republic of Germany, there has flourished the obsolete principle of *spécialité statutaire* which corresponds to the equally obnoxious doctrine of *ultra vires* in Anglo-American law.[142] According to this principle, since a company was created as a legal person to achieve a certain purpose (*objet social*), it was capable of performing only such legal acts as were within its purpose;[143] beyond its purpose, "it did not exist" and thus

---

[142] Brice, A Treatise on the Doctrine of Ultra Vires (2d American ed., New York 1880); Reese, The True Doctrine of Ultra Vires in the Law of Corporations (Chicago 1897); Street, A Treatise on the Doctrine of Ultra Vires (London 1930); Sieklucka, Ultra Vires, American Jurisprudence (unpublished paper) in Univ. of Mich. Law Library, Ann Arbor 1969); Ballantine, *Proposed Revision of the Ultra Vires Doctrine,* 12 Cornell L.Q. 453 (1927); Carpenter, *Should the Doctrine of Ultra Vires be Discarded?,* 33 Yale L.J. 49 (1923-24); Darter, *Ultra Vires in Georgia,* 16 Mercer L. Rev. 320 (1964); Ham, *Ultra Vires Contracts Under Modern Corporate Legislation,* 46 Ky. L.J. 215 (1958); Harno, *Privileges and Powers of a Corporation and the Doctrine of Ultra Vires,* 35 Yale L.J. 13 (1925); Stevens, *A Proposal as to the Codification and Restatement of the Ultra Vires Doctrine,* 36 Yale L.J. 297 (1927). In the United States today corporate charters confer, or can be readily amended to confer, almost unlimited freedom to engage in any kind of business. Thus the problem of a company acting *ultra vires* has almost disappeared as a practical problem in business and law. Rostow, in Mason at 51.

[143] *France:* Rodière & Houin, 1 Droit commercial No. 489, referring to No. 393; Moreau, 1 La société anonyme 204 (Paris 1955). *Netherlands:* Art. 2.1.5.a. Nieuw Burgerlijk Wetboek; Molen-

was "congenitally" incapable of acting. As a consequence, the company itself could refuse to be bound by any transaction falling outside its purpose, even if the transaction had been approved by the shareholders' meeting, and the other party to the transaction could also refuse to be bound.

In Germany, however, in response to pressures for greater legal security, the *ultra vires* concept was formally eradicated from commercial law before the First World War, so that limited liability and stock companies may be bound by a transaction even if it falls outside their charter purpose.[144] The question then in Germany is no longer whether a transaction was within the company's charter purpose, but rather only whether the organ that acted on behalf of the company held the necessary power to bind it.[145] And in this respect also, we encounter what until most recently was a striking divergence between the German law and the laws of the other Members.

On the one hand, in the Federal Republic a company organ's power of "direction" and representation was for all practical purposes defined by law and could not be varied by a charter provision unless the law itself authorized such variation.[146] In the other legal systems, on the other hand, a large discretion was left to the founders and shareholders in ordering the distribution of power among the company organs, with full impact upon third parties dealing with the com-

---

GRAAFF, LEIDRAAD BIJ DE BEOEFENING VAN HET NEDERLANDSE HANDELS-RECHT at 271 (9th ed., Haarlem 1953); VAN DER HEIJDEN-VAN DER GRINTEN, HANDBOEK No. 235, at 386 ff. (less emphasis than in previous editions). *Belgium:* DE PAGE, 1 TRAITÉ ÉLÉMENTAIRE DE DROIT CIVIL BELGE No. 510 (3rd ed., Bruxelles 1962); VAN RYN, 1 PRINCIPES DE DROIT COMMERCIAL No. 364. *Italy:* MOSSA, 4 TRATTATO DEL NUOVO DIRITTO COMMERCIALE, SOCIETÀ PER AZIONI at 412 (Padua 1957). *See generally* VAN OMMESLAGHE, LE RÉGIME No. 228, at 475.

[144] On legal capacity generally see FABRICIUS, RELATIVITÄT DER RECHTSFÄHIGKEIT (München, Berlin 1963).

[145] VAN OMMESLAGHE, LE RÉGIME at 475-81, and references therein; BAUMBACH-HUECK, AKTIENGESETZ § 82 n.2 (13th ed., München 1966); Schmidt, in GROSSKOMMENTAR AKTIENGESETZ § 74 n.7 (2d ed., Berlin 1961); WÜRDINGER, AKTIEN- UND KONZERNRECHT at 118 ff.

[146] WÜRDINGER, *id* at 122.

pany. At the base of this divergence has been the historical difference between the German *"Organtheorie"* and the *"Mandattheorie"* embraced in the other Members which stemmed from Roman law and was embodied in the Napoleonic Codes.[147] According to the "mandate theory," the relationship between the company and the person or body that deals on its behalf with a third party was conceived essentially as that between a principal and agent; traditionally, in that relationship the scope of the agent's authority to bind the principal contractually to third parties is determined by the "mandate" received from the principal. On the other hand, in the German doctrine, ever since the mid-nineteenth century the distinction has been drawn—and it has been reflected in both the Civil and Commercial Codes—between a representative's *"power* to represent" the represented person *(Vertretungsmacht),* and the *"authority* to represent" actually granted by the represented person *(Geschäftsführungsbefugnis).*[148] It might occur—and this would reflect our own concept of "apparent authority"—that, although an agent had no "authority" to bind his principal, he was nevertheless vested with the "power" to do so; the lack of "authority" then would have consequences only between the principal and the agent—the latter might be liable for damages to the former—but it would have no influence on the validity of the contract with the third party. The principal would be obligated to the third party just as much as if the agent had acted with "authority." The "power" can be vested in the representative either by legally relevant conduct of the represented person, or by the law (statute) itself. The first

---

147 Art. 1984 of the French CODE CIVIL. Art. 1737 ff. of the Italian CODICE CIVILE of 1885, replaced by Art. 1387 ff. of the 1942 CODICE CIVILE.

148 IHERING, MITWIRKUNG FÜR FREMDE RECHTSGESCHÄFTE, 1858 IHERINGS JAHRBUCH 67, at 131; Laband, *Die Stellvertretung bei dem Abschluss von Rechtsgeschäften nach dem allgemeinen Deutschen Handelsgesetzbuch,* 1866 ZHR 183. *See* Müller-Freienfels, *Legal Relations in the Law of Agency: Power of Agency and Commercial Certainty,* 13 AM. J. COMP. L. 193, at 197 (1959).

alternative occurs in the normal principal-agent situation where the principal authorizes the agent to act for him; here "power" and "authority" usually coincide. The second alternative, "representative power by operation of the law," exists if the represented person is himself incapable of acting without a representative, as in the case of minors, legally incapacitated persons, or legal persons such as commercial companies. In such situations, the scope of the power to represent is determined by law and cannot be left to the discretion of any person. As applied to legal persons, the "*Organtheorie,*" unlike the "mandate theory," holds that a legal person has the capacity to act through its organs, and the acts of its organs are not considered acts of its agents, but rather acts of the legal person itself, executed through its organs within their respective powers which are defined by law.[149] The company has its own will which is formed through the "acts of will" of its organs,[150] and the recognition of an organ's function carries with it the impossibility of limiting this function by a decision of another organ of the same company, except where authorized by law. This would make it impossible to limit the functions and powers of the executive board *(Vorstand)* of a stock company by a clause in the company charter, since the charter is viewed as a manifestation of the will of the shareholders' meeting, which is another "organ."[151]

(b)   The not-so-different legal reality

To present the legal situation in the Six in terms of such stark doctrinal contrast would be both a mockery of reality

---

[149] ENNECCERUS-NIPPERDEY, 1 LEHRBUCH DES BÜRGERLICHEN RECHTS at 617 (15th ed., Tübingen 1959); BÄRMANN, DIE WILLENSBILDUNG IN DEN EUROPÄISCHEN AKTIENRECHTEN at 21 (Karlsruhe 1964).

[150] This may have important legal consequences for imputing the organs' knowledge of facts, good faith, etc., to the company.

[151] Lietzmann, *Die Vertretungsmacht gegenüber Dritten im Schnittpunkt der geplanten europäischen Aktiengesellschaft,* 1961 AG 125; Lietzmann, *La représentation de la société à l'égard des tiers par la direction,* 1960 DROIT EUROPÉEN 327.

and an argument against any chance for coordination. In
Germany, the courts have blunted the impact of the unrestrained "power to represent" by protecting the company in
case of collusion between the company's representative and
a third party, or in case of a blatant excess of authority of
which the third party was aware.[152] In the other Five, there
is little evidence that legal security has suffered seriously as a
consequence of the continuing obeisance to the *ultra vires*
doctrine.[153] In the first place, the matter seldom arises in
practice, since the charter-purpose clauses are drawn as a
rule in broad terms,[154] and second, the effect of *ultra vires*
has been diluted in all these national legal systems, with the
exception of Belgium, by a variety of devices, some of which
are reminiscent of our "apparent authority" doctrine.[155]
Thus, for instance, annulment of a transaction is allowed
against a third party, acting in good faith, only if the act
"objectively" appears entirely outside the charter purpose.[156]
Only the Belgian Cour de cassation appears to apply the doctrine with great vigor.[157] The trend toward a reduced application of *ultra vires* is illustrated by the proposed Italian
reform law. On the one hand that law would prescribe that
the statement of the charter purpose of a stock company
must contain "a specific indication of the [company's] activi-

---

[152] FLUME, 2 ALLGEMEINER TEIL DES BÜRGERLICHEN GESETZBUCHES
at 788 (Berlin, Heidelberg, New York 1965); 52 RGZ 96, 99 (1902);
145 RGZ 311, 315 (1934). The company, however, has the burden of
proof.

[153] *See* AVIS at 3254, which considers *ultra vires* still a "general
principle of law." RODIÈRE & HOUIN, 1 DROIT COMMERCIAL No. 489
referring to No. 393; MOREAU, 1 LA SOCIÉTÉ ANONYME at 204.

[154] For a comparison of the European and American practice of
writing such clauses see Conard, *Organizing for Business* at 74-75.

[155] Comm. Working paper 465/III/C/63-F at 16. BERKHOUWER
REPORT at 33.

[156] VAN RYN, 1 PRINCIPES DE DROIT COMMERCIAL BELGE No. 430;
COULOMBEL, LE PARTICULARISME at 217; VAN DER HEIJDEN-VAN DER
GRINTEN, HANDBOEK Nos. 234 and 235, at 381 ff.; VAN OMMESLAGHE,
LE RÉGIME at 481.

[157] Cour de cassation, Judgment of May 31, 1957, 1957 REV.
PRATIQUE DES SOCIÉTÉS 289.

ties" so as to reduce the discretion of the management to change the company's activities without changing its charter; it is assumed that such discretion could be used against the shareholders' interest. On the other hand, however, in order to protect the interest of third parties and the security of transactions, the company would no longer be in the position to challenge the validity of its transactions in relation to third parties on the ground that it exceeded the charter purpose.[158]

As for the "mandate theory," it has also been criticized by leading authorities in France,[159] and the national trend has been distinctly toward an increasingly specific statutory definition of the powers of the organs in the sense of the *"Organtheorie."*[160]

(c) Limitation by law and by charter purpose: toward a new formula

In the light of this state of the law, it was no wonder that the German delegation in the Brussels working group pressed

---

[158] LA RIFORMA 1966, at 109. Santoro-Passarelli for instance embraces entirely the "Organtheorie" in his analysis of the legal person. He points out, however, that only through a "laborious" process has an organ of a legal person acquired "autonomous status" as against the concept of agency, and that in fact the two institutions are still confused in certain articles of the present Codice civile, including Art. 2384. SANTORO-PASSARELLI, DOTTRINE GENERALI DEL DIRITTO CIVILE 272-73 (8th ed., Napoli 1964). Art. 2384 extends to stock companies the application of Art. 2298 which provides that the "amministratore" who represents the company may undertake all acts falling within the charter purpose, subject to limitations derived from the charter or from his power of representation (procura). The limitations may not be invoked against a third party if they are not inscribed in the register of enterprises [see p. 267 *supra*] or if it is not proven that the third party was aware of them. Art. 2384 has now been modified by Arts. 5 and 6 of the Decree Implementing First Directive, see immediately following sections (c) and (d).

[159] In France, *see, e.g.,* Esmein, in PLANIOL at 62; POPESCO-RAMNICEANO, DE LA REPRÉSENTATION DANS LES ACTES JURIDIQUES at 262 (Paris 1927).

[160] *See* Arts. 98 and 113 of the French Law of July 24, 1966, amended by Law No. 67-559 of July 12, 1967, defining more specifically the powers of the administrative council and of its president; both articles were amended again. *See* p. 298 *infra.*

as strongly as it could for the abandonment of the *"ultra vires"* doctrine, under the banner of security of transactions and protection of third parties throughout the Community. It is perhaps also not surprising that the other Five were not prepared to jettison the doctrine altogether. The First Draft was a compromise in which the *ultra vires* principle was retained in a diluted form. A company was to be bound against third parties by the acts of its organs, unless these acts exceeded the limits laid down by the law (there was no controversy over that part) or unless they exceeded the charter purpose. A proviso was added, however, that even if the charter purpose was exceeded, the company was to be considered bound, if the third party had good reasons *(justes motifs)* to believe that the transaction was within the company's purpose.[161]

The argument in support of this compromise was that the third party—in view of the improved "publicity" requirement—will have ready access to the text of the charter, and will of course also be in a position to consult the appropriate law under which the company was organized and which "everyone is presumed to know," even though it may be foreign law.[162] The German experts were quite unhappy with this draft, and their acute dissatisfaction was heightened by the fact that, because of faulty drafting, the text could be interpreted—and was interpreted by some—as requiring the Federal Republic to re-introduce the *ultra vires* doctrine (or more accurately *"spécialité statutaire"*) into its own company law; this, however, apparently was not the intention of the Commission staff.[163] In any event, the Germans argued that if the compromise became a Community rule third parties would insist, prior to entering into any contract, even with a German company, upon obtaining the approval of the contract by the shareholders' meeting, or at least upon

161 *First Draft,* Art. 11, par. 1.

162 GOLDMAN, COURS at 219.

163 For German criticism *see, e.g.,* Gessler, in ENTWICKLUNGSTEN-DENZEN at 20; Fikentscher & Grossfeld, *The Proposed Directive* at 267.

the preparation of a legal opinion as to whether the contract fell within the charter purpose.[164] A warning came also from French quarters that the "good reasons to believe" formula would open the way to litigation.[165] On the other hand, the proposed formula was approved by the Economic and Social Committee[166] and defended by the responsible Commission official, also a German national, as a "decisive breach" into the "Romanic countries' *ultra vires* doctrine"; a frontal attack against this doctrine on an "all-or-nothing" basis—this official maintained—would have been futile, due to the intimate connection of the doctrine with the basic concept of the legal person in the five countries.[167]

In response to strong pleas from the German deputies, the European Parliament proposed a new compromise formula according to which, in the first place, a company would escape liability if the company organ exceeded its powers defined by the law; however, in addition the Member States would be left free to prescribe that the company could also escape liability if the charter purpose was exceeded (*ultra vires*), but only if the company could prove that the third party knew that the transaction exceeded the charter purpose.[168] Although still a compromise, this text at least would make it clear that the Federal Republic was not obliged to introduce the *ultra vires* concept into its law and, what was more important, in those States which retained the concept, it would be more difficult for a company to invoke it, because of the shift in the burden of proof in favor of the third party. In the plenary debate the Parliament rejected both a proposal by a French deputy to reinstate the text of the first

---

[164] Lamberth, *Der Richtlinienentwurf* at 70.

[165] GOLDMAN, COURS at 220; Dorat des Monts, *Vers un droit européen* at par. 16.

[166] AVIS at 3254. The Committee, however, in this connection raised a question of principle which will be referred to below.

[167] Bruns, in ENTWICKLUNGSTENDENZEN at 28.

[168] Resolution of the European Parliament, [1966] J.O. 1532. The text follows the proposed text of the Committee for the Internal Market, BERKHOUWER REPORT at 42.

draft and an amendment by an Italian law professor that would restore the *ultra vires* rule without restriction.[169]

The Commission was impressed by the views of the European Parliament and of "the diverse legal commentators"[170] including, no doubt, the International Federation of European Law (F.I.D.E.) representing lawyers in all Member States,[171] and accepted the substance of the new formula in its Second Draft; it was included ultimately with slight modifications (inserted at French insistence) in the final text.[172]

(d) Limitations written into the charter: a case of "real" coordination

Although the revised formula still did not satisfy the Germans completely the next provision in this section of the directive was hailed as a "true success" in German quarters.[173] This rule provides that a company will not be able to avoid liability against a third party by invoking a limitation upon the powers of its officials or organs *written into its charter or imposed by a decision of its organ,* even if the limitation was properly published. Consequently, a limita-

---

169 PARL. EUR., DÉBATS, [1966] No. 85, at 94.

170 *Second Draft,* EXPOSÉ DES MOTIFS at 6. The Commission referred also to the support of the Economic and Social Committee, even though there was nothing in the record of the Committee to this effect.

171 Comm. Working paper 7986/III/C/66-F, June 13, 1966, at 8. F.I.D.E. took the position that a limitation derived from the charter purpose can be invoked against a third party only if the company can prove that the third party was aware of the limitation. *See also* Houin, in 3ÈME COLLOQUE at 22.

172 *Final Text,* Art. 9, par. 1 (1) and (2), [1968] J.O. L 65 (March 14), at 11. The company's burden of proof was somewhat lightened at the request of France in that it is now sufficient if it proves that the third party must have known ("could not have been without knowledge") that the transaction exceeded the charter purpose, "taking into account the circumstances." But on the other hand the final text makes it clear that the burden of proof could not be met just by showing that the charter was published. For a critical view see Scholten, *Company Law in Europe* at 397.

173 Gessler, in ENTWICKLUNGSTENDENZEN at 20. *See also* Gessler, in 3ÈME COLLOQUE at 14-15.

tion of this type would be effective only in the internal relations within the company.[174] Stressing the security of transactions, in line with the arguments pressed by the German spokesmen, the Commission refused to accept an amendment, proposed by the European Parliament, that would have protected third parties only if they were "in good faith," and the Council of Ministers upheld the Commission.[175]

Agreement on this important provision was "very difficult to obtain from several states,"[176] in view of the difference between German law on the one hand and the law of the other States on the other. In the prevailing Belgian, Italian, Luxembourg, and Netherlands law, properly published limitations of this type in principle were considered operative against third parties who dealt with a company, and those parties therefore must consult the charter as well as the other published documents, such as the decisions of

---

[174] *Final Text,* Art. 9, par. 2. The most important addition to the *First Draft* was the clause on limitations imposed by a decision of a company organ. For an interesting analysis of the compatibility of the Swedish stock company law with the 1964 draft of the First Directive see Rodhe, *Svensk aktiebolagsrätt och harmoniseringen av EEC-Ländernas aktiebolagslagar,* in FESTSKRIFT TILL HÅKAN NIAL, STUDIER I CIVILRÄTT OCH INTERNATIONELL RÄTT 460 (Stockholm 1966). Prof. Rodhe believes that only in the *ultra vires* field would the rather modern Swedish Stock Company Act (of 1944) require material adjustment. According to that law, charter restrictions can be invoked against a third party, if he knew or should have known the restrictions.

[175] There was no agreement on this issue in the Committee of the Parliament but a majority tended toward the formula proposed by the Commission, subject, however, to the above amendment. BERKHOUWER REPORT at 34. In explaining the reasons why it did not follow the European Parliament's amendment the Commission said that the "good faith" qualification would introduce an ambiguity where security of transactions must prevail: "How, for example, would one determine the good faith of a third party which questioned a limitation that was duly published? The adopted solution, in moving away from the *ultra vires* principle, constitutes a marked progress in the direction of the German system, recognized as offering maximum security of transactions in this matter." *Second Draft,* EXPOSÉ DES MOTIFS at 7.

[176] Gessler, in ENTWICKLUNGSTENDENZEN at 20.

shareholders' meetings, in order to learn the extent of the powers granted to company organs and any limitations imposed upon them.[177] Thus, in contrast with German law, the shareholders are given protection at the expense of the third party who, therefore, carries the risk in the case of a transgression of a limitation by the company's negotiator even though, as was pointed out on the German side, the third party had nothing to do with his selection.[178]

Yet in this case also, the rigor of the "Latin" rule in national laws has been greatly tempered by a variety of devices such as "apparent authority," tacit ratification, unjust enrichment, various presumptions or by judicial interpretation in favor of third parties in good faith.[179] On the other hand, the rigor of the German rule[180] has also been mitigated by the courts as indicated earlier: Although the third party's mere knowledge of the limitations on the representative's power will not suffice to defeat his claim against the company, resulting from a contract made in excess of authority, the third party will not succeed in his claim if he was in a position to recognize that the company officer had abused his power, or, even worse, if he worked collusively with the representative.[181] In a declaration, adopted by the Council of Ministers, it was made clear that the provision in the directive will be interpreted similarly so as to exclude fraud.

(i) Converging national trends

It is evident that agreement on this rather significant rule would not have been possible without the distinct trend

---

[177] Van Ommeslaghe, Le régime No. 291; van der Heijden-van der Grinten, Handboek Nos. 234, 235 and 235.1 at 381-91; van Ryn & Heenen, 2 Principes de droit commercial No. 654 ff.; Encycl. Dalloz, Conseil d'administration No. 67 ff. (Paris 1967); Minervini, Gli amministratori di società per azioni No. 50 (Milan 1956).

[178] Gessler, in 3ème Colloque at 15.

[179] Van Ommeslaghe, Le régime No. 291.

[180] *E.g.*, Stock Company Law of 1965, § 82.

[181] *See* p. 288 *supra;* Schmidt, in Grosskommentar Aktiengesetz §§ 12, 74 (2d ed., Berlin 1961).

toward the German pattern in the other Member States. As in other instances, the situation in France was perhaps decisive. When the draft directive was first discussed, the rule excluding the effect of charter limitations on company officials' powers as against third parties applied in France to limited liability companies only;[182] however, the reform law proposal which was pending at the time, already envisaged extending this rule to stock and other companies.[183] In Belgium, the current draft of the reform embodies the same rule and, as I mentioned earlier, Luxembourg may be expected to follow Belgium. In the Netherlands and in Italy, however, the rule in the directive represents an innovation.[184] It was an Italian deputy who cast the only negative vote in the European Parliament against the directive because, he said, he could not conceive how the directive could provide in

---

[182] Art. 24, par. 2 of the Law of Mar. 7, 1925.

[183] GOLDMAN, COURS at 222-23. The new French Law No. 66-537 of July 25, 1966, as amended by Law No. 67-559 of July 12, 1967, applies this rule both to the powers of the "gérants" of the limited liability companies (Arts. 14 and 49) and to the conseil d'administration (administrative council), the president-director general, as well as to the optional, new "German type" directoire (executive board) of the stock company (Arts. 98, 113, 124).

[184] The Draft Law No. 10,400 "for the adaptation of the Netherlands legislation to the first directive of the Council of the European Communities of Mar. 9, 1968 relating to company law" which the Government submitted to the Parliament on Nov. 4, 1969, will, i.a., add a new Art. 47b to the Commercial Code which will modify the Netherlands law to conform to the above provision of the First Directive. This will be the most important modification of the Netherlands law in response to the First Directive. In Italy, Art. 5 of the Decree Implementing First Directive has modified Art. 2384 of the Codice civile to provide that "the 'amministratore' may perform all acts falling within the charter purpose, subject to any restrictions derived from the law or from the charter. Restrictions on the power to represent the company, derived from the charter, even if published, may not be invoked against third parties unless it is proved that the latter acted intentionally to the prejudice of the company." Art. 6 of the same Decree added a new Art. 2384 bis to the Codice civile, which provides that the company may not invoke, against a third party, the fact that an act performed by the "amministratore" was outside the charter purpose. Art. 17 of the Decree extends these provisions to limited liability companies.

one article that the company may rely on properly published information against third parties, and at the same time in another article exclude such reliance with respect to properly published limitations on the powers of company officials. He called the approved text "a beast with a Latin head and a German body and tail."[185] This may well be an isolated view, an amusing episode illustrating a case where unassailable logic makes little sense.

In any event, the Economic and Social Committee was justified in concluding that the solution reached was "inspired by the rather general tendency toward confining the effects of charter limitations upon the powers of company organs to internal affairs among the shareholders."[186]

(ii) A special problem of charter clauses on company representation

The last provision of this section of the directive deals with the effect of a charter clause providing that the company may be represented by a single person or by two or more persons. Again, differences in national law posed a problem. In the Federal Republic[187] a collegiate body, the executive board *(Vorstand)* of a stock company, is designated *by law* to represent the company in its dealings with third parties, but the same law makes it proper to provide in the charter that one or some members of this body may also be authorized to act for the company, and such provision is effective against third parties. In practice, such a clause is commonly included in the charter of at least the major German stock companies in the interest of speedier and more efficient decision-making.[188] This is not a "limitation" but, on the contrary, a broadening of the power of representation. In France, however, it is a single person, the

---

[185] Carboni, in [1966] PARL. EUR., DÉBATS No. 85, at 98, 99, 101.

[186] Avis at 3254, 2B.

[187] § 78, par. 2 of the Stock Company Law of 1965; § 35 of the Limited Liability Company Law.

[188] GODIN-WILHELMI, 1 AKTIENGESETZ § 78, note 7 (3rd ed., Berlin 1967).

president-general manager who by law has the sole power of representation with respect to third parties,[189] and any provision in the charter which would require him to seek concurrence of another member of the administrative council *(conseil d'administration)* would be a restriction on his power and thus a "limitation." In the Netherlands each member of the *bestuur* (administrative council or "managing committee") has the legal power to bind the company, but the general practice has been to require in the charter the signature of two or more members for certain transactions exceeding a specified amount.

The Commission's legal advisor, concerned with the problem, pointed out the difficulties of finding an acceptable coordinating rule in the light of this state of national law. He suggested wistfully that the best solution would be to enable a single person, be it the president-general manager or a member of the *Vorstand* or of the *conseil d'administration* or of the *bestuur,* acting alone, to bind the company as against a third party acting in good faith—a solution which was also adumbrated by the Economic and Social Committee;[190] but this, he noted with a sigh, unhappily would be hard to accept, at least in Belgium and Luxembourg.[191] Yet the Belgian reform proposal would embrace this solution. The final text of the directive—a compromise, adopted after the first faulty draft had been discarded—merely allows the company, *if this is permissible under its national law,* to rely *vis-à-vis* a third party on a charter clause granting the power

---

[189] Art. 113 of the Law of 1966, as amended by Art. 17 of Law No. 67-559 of July 12, 1967. For the text see note 194 *infra.*

[190] Avis at 3254-55.

[191] Leleux, in EUROPÄISCHE HANDELSGESELLSCHAFT at 51. The International Federation of European Law (F.I.D.E.) took the position that where the law prescribes joint representation, it should always be possible for the company to invoke it against third parties; but where such representation is required in the charter, the company should not be able to so invoke it unless the third party was aware of it— assuming that the requirement of joint or several representation was made public along with the names of persons authorized to act for the company.

to bind the company to one or several persons, providing, however—and this is significant—that the grant comprises the general power of representation.[192]

The scope of the coordination imposed by this provision is limited, and in this context the Economic and Social Committee observed that "in the absence of uniform legislation on the powers of company organs both as among the states and within the same state as far as different types of companies are concerned," the rule in the directive constitutes an "apparent" rather than a "real harmonization," and was apt to raise many questions, because of the differences in the distribution of powers among the different organs. In a similar vein, Professor Heenen also spoke of "half-measures," and the matter has come under discussion again in the Commission's working group in connection with a further coordination directive.[193] In the meantime, however, as we have noted, an important movement toward a "spontaneous" assimilation in the field of company structure has been taking place, with France having adopted the basic features of the German two-tier system as an optional form for stock companies, and Belgium, no doubt to be followed by Luxembourg, scheduled to embrace it as the exclusive form. In the Netherlands, despite important differences, in practice the more significant companies already operate under a system resembling in a sense the two-tier structure, and pending proposals envisage, as we have seen, a supervisory council with extensive powers defined in the law. France has moved a step closer to the German pattern in adopting the law of 1967 which defined further the powers of the company organs and in particular broadened the responsibility of the president of the *conseil d'administration*.[194]

---

[192] *Final Text,* Art. 9, par. 3.

[193] *See* p. 339 *infra.*

[194] Art. 98 of the Law of 1966 read originally: "Le conseil d'administration est investi des pouvoirs de gestion les plus étendus pour agir en toute circonstance au nom de la société. . . ." The words "de gestion" were eliminated by Art. 14 of Law No. 67-559 of July 12, 1967.

3.   When is a company invalid? Problems of "nullity"[195]

It would indeed constitute a threat not only to the company's creditors, but also to its shareholders and employees if, after years of operation, the company were to be declared "null and void" from the inception, because of some defect in its formation. In today's practice the question would hardly arise in these terms since national laws offer a variety of protective devices: the original defect may be cured in most instances, the action for invalidity may be barred by a statute of limitation, or a declaration of invalidity is given only a prospective and not a retroactive effect.[196] But even

---

The same law modified Art. 113 to read as follows (the italicized portion was added to the 1966 text):

"[1] The president of the administrative council shall assure, on his personal responsibility, the general direction of the company. He shall represent the company in its relations with third parties.

"[2] *The president shall be invested with the broadest powers to act in all circumstances in the name of the company,* subject to the authority that the law expressly assigns to the shareholders' meeting as well as the authority that it reserves in a special manner for the administrative council and within the limits of the charter purpose."

Arts. 98 and 113 were again modified (also Art. 124 concerning the new "directoire" and Art. 255 on the "gérant" of the limited liability company) by Arts. 3, 4, 5 and 6 of Ordinance No. 69-1176 of Dec. 20, 1969, modifying Law No. 66-537 of July 24, 1966, on commercial companies which was enacted in partial implementation of the First Directive.

In the general area of "validity of undertakings entered into on a company's behalf," the Netherlands Draft Law No. 10,400 "for the adaptation of the Netherlands legislation to the first directive of the Council of the European Communities of March 9, 1968 relating to the company law," proposes modifications of Art. 36g, insertion of Art. 36h, modifications of Arts. 40, 47a, 47b and omission of Art. 50a of the COMMERCIAL CODE.

195 The English term "invalidity" will be used in this section as a generic term to comprise "nullity" (nullité absolue, Nichtigkeit) and "voidability" (nullité relative, Anfechtbarkeit).

196 Even in the Member States which for all practical purposes have eliminated the problem, one encounters the retroactive effect as a still lingering consequence of the concept of the company as a contract. DE SOLÀ CAÑIZARES, LA CONSTITUTION DES SOCIÉTÉS PAR ACTIONS EN DROIT COMPARÉ 145, 147 (Paris 1959). In Belgian law, invalidity is

in the States where instances of invalidity have been reduced to a minimum the problem has remained, at least to
the extent that discontented shareholders have the possibility of harassing the company by actions for invalidity.[197] In
any case, since national laws on this subject differed substantially, it appeared useful to seek coordination for the benefit of those who deal with a company governed by foreign
law, which may not be readily ascertainable. In these circumstances, the Commission staff expected ready agreement that
the cases of invalidity should be reduced, and that coordination in this area should be in an "upward direction," to the
level of the national legislation which best protected the
security of transactions.[198] For that reason, the sharp conflict over this section of the directive that developed and was
resolved only at the eleventh hour, came as a "rather great
surprise" to the Commission staff.[199] In this area again, the
lingering devotion on the part of the "Latin" delegations
(Italy and France) to a basic doctrinal concept—the company
as a contract—seemed to have played a greater role than any
policy difference as to which of the competing interests
should prevail.

The principal purposes of this portion of the directive
were, *first,* to reduce the likelihood of invalidity by prescribing minimum "preventive" procedures or formalities to be
observed at the time when the company was organized;
second, to reduce the grounds on which invalidity could be
invoked and the categories of persons entitled to do so; and

---

given retroactive effect except where the action for a declaration of
invalidity is by a shareholder on the ground that the articles of incorporation were not given the proper legal form. VAN WYNENDAELE &
WAUTERS-DE NÉEFF, LE DROIT DES SOCIÉTÉS ANONYMES DANS LES PAYS DE LA
COMMUNAUTÉ ÉCONOMIQUE EUROPÉENNE at 117 (Bruxelles 1961). The
same is true in Luxembourg. Sinay, *La proposition de directive européenne* at 42, states that none of the Six has completely eliminated
cases of invalidity or provided for complete "purging" of the irregularities in the formation of companies.

[197] Jeantet, in 3ÈME COLLOQUE at 30.

[198] Sinay, *La proposition de directive européenne* at 41.

[199] Leleux, in EUROPÄISCHE HANDELSGESELLSCHAFT at 51.

third, to reduce the effect of a declaration of invalidity. The directive does not purport to deal with circumstances in which *acts of company organs* may be held invalid.[200]

(a)   Procedures to prevent faulty constitution of companies

(i)   Trends in national laws

There is logic in the proposition that an effort to reduce the grounds on which a company could be held invalid should be linked with a procedure that would assure that the law is observed when a company is constituted. In fact, the trend on the Continent has been toward judicial or administrative supervision of compliance, by the founders, with the rules governing the formation of companies, particularly of stock companies. It is another reflection of the pressures for increased public regulation of companies, and away from the "liberal" concept of a company as a freely negotiated contract. Nevertheless, important differences among the Member States remain. In Germany and Italy the "preventive" function is performed by the courts in conjunction with the company's registration,[201] in the Netherlands by the Minister of Justice.[202] Subsequent to the publication of the First Draft of the directive, the

---

[200] In the course of subsequent study the Commission staff and the special consultants (Conseillers spéciaux) suggested that the problem of "the régime of nullities of decisions" by company organs fell in the category of questions which, their practical importance notwithstanding, concerned above all internal effectiveness of company administration and—at least for the time being—did not need to be coordinated by a directive. Professor R. Houin, *Rapport sur l'administration et le contrôle des sociétés par actions,* COMM. DOC. 317/III/C/68-F, 2ème partie at 18, Jan. 18, 1968.

[201] Germany: § 38 of the Stock Company Law of 1965; Italy: Art. 2330 of the CODICE CIVILE; VAN OMMESLAGHE, LE RÉGIME at 142-44 (Germany), 203-07 (Italy); Banco di Roma, *Legal and Fiscal Provisions Regarding Companies in Italy,* in 2 FOREIGN PRIVATE ENTERPRISE IN ITALY 14 (2d ed., Rome 1959). In Italy, the public prosecutor is also consulted and this is unknown in Germany.

[202] Art. 36(e), WETBOEK VAN KOOPHANDEL; VAN OMMESLAGHE, LE RÉGIME at 231-34; Conard, *Organizing for Business* at 87.

French Government attempted to introduce a similar judicial procedure as part of the 1966 reform,[203] despite the vocal opposition of a portion of the French Bar,[204] but this effort was defeated in the Senate.[205] The Government refused to accept a counterproposal that, instead of the judicial supervision, the founders should be required to embody the charter of the company in a notarial act.[206] As finally enacted, the new law of 1966 required the founders only to submit to the clerk of the register a "declaration of conformity" in which they must relate all the prescribed steps that have been taken and in which they also must affirm that all the rules have been complied with.[207] However, the Government made it clear at the time that it viewed this as a provisional solution only, and that it intended to introduce the requirement of judicial supervision as soon as possible.[208] The principal practical obstacle emphasized in the Parliamentary debate was the prospect that the Paris court would be unable to cope with the thousands of applications for registration and thus would develop into a bottleneck of mammoth proportions.[209]

---

[203] *Rapport Le Douarec* at 3-5.

[204] Garcin, *Une initiative dangereuse pour la constitution des sociétés,* LA VIE FRANÇAISE, Nov. 13, 1964; Dalsace, *La réforme des sociétés commerciales,* 1964 BANQUE at 655 ff.; Burgard, *A propos du contrôle judiciaire de la constitution des sociétés et de certaines modifications statutaires,* 1964 JUR.-CL. PÉR. DOCTR. 1875; Dorat des Monts, *Vers un droit européen* at par. 17.

[205] See statement by M. Le Bellegou, DÉB. PARL., SÉNAT, Apr. 20, 1966, [1966] J.O. (France, Apr. 21), at 172.

[206] Thereafter no irregularity in the formation of the company could be raised but the notary might be held liable. The counterproposal coincided with Belgian and Luxembourg law.

[207] Arts. 6 and 7 of the Law No. 66-537 of July 24, 1966.

[208] LEFÈBVRE, LA RÉFORME DES SOCIÉTÉS COMMERCIALES at 18.

[209] In 1963, 5720 new companies were organized in the Département de Seine; if one includes modifications of the charter the court control would have extended to some 34,000 cases. M. Pleven in DÈB. PARL., ASS. NAT., June 1, 1965, [1965] J.O. (France, June 2), at 1667.

For the next step by the French Government see the following section.

(ii) Lowest common denominator

In view of the trend in four of the six national laws, the working group in Brussels explored the idea of prescribing some form of judicial procedure in the directive. It abandoned the effort, however, in the face of the strong objection by the Belgian and Luxembourg members who argued that national judges were not sufficiently familiar with business problems to be able to perform this type of role predictably and effectively. As a compromise, an article was included in the directive providing that in those Member States which did *not* have either a judicial or administrative "preventive" procedure, the charter will have to be drawn—under the penalty of invalidity ("nullity")—before a notary in the form of a notarial act.[210] A notary in civil law countries performs a different and much more significant function than in the United States and acts as a legal advisor in the preparation of documents.[211] Yet this article—which corresponds to the law of Belgium and Luxembourg and reflects the position pressed by the Belgian delegation—was criticized primarily in French quarters as a "useless complication," which not only will not add to the security of the parties in practice, but on the contrary will detract from it by creating a new ground for invalidity, in case the charter is not drawn up as a notarial act.[212] But some opponents of judicial supervision in France pointed to the absence of the requirement of such

---

[210] *Final Text*, Art. 10. The requirement applies to the articles of association and any amendments thereto.

[211] Conard, *Organizing for Business* at 69.

[212] Avis at 3255, 3A; Dorat des Monts, *Vers un droit européen* at par. 17; Sinay, *La proposition de directive européenne* at 38, and also *Le droit nouveau de la constitution des sociétés commerciales et de leurs modifications statutaires*, 1966 REV. DES SOCIÉTÉS 246, at 262-66. In response to this criticism it has been said that since the founders invariably require legal advice in any event, this requirement would hardly complicate matters. Moreover, the notary will see to it that the law is obeyed and if, despite this precaution, the constitution of the company should be held invalid, he could be held liable for damages.

supervision in the then proposed directive as an added argument to buttress their case.[213]

After the French Government had adopted the basic decrees of March 1967 implementing the new law, the Commission staff suggested that, with a minor modification, the new French procedure requiring a "declaration of conformity" would be the type of "preventive control" envisaged in the directive, since it would require the clerk of the register to bring to the attention of the judge any irregularity in the papers submitted by the founders, with a view to obtaining a judicial determination.[214] The French delegation found the suggestion quite acceptable. Actually, in the 1969 decree giving effect to the First Directive in French law, the French Government enacted the modification suggested by the Commission staff.[215]

The working group obviously decided not to deal with the questions to what extent compliance with the preventive procedure or notarial form should cure any irregularities in the formation of the company and thus preclude subsequent assertions of invalidity, and generally to what extent national laws should afford procedures for curing the grounds for invalidity.

(b) Grounds for invalidity of a company

(i) Only two grounds allowed?

The next, and the most important, article in this section of the directive prescribes a ceiling on invalidity—that is,

---

[213] M. Pleven in Déb. parl., Ass. Nat., June 1, 1965, [1965] J.O. (France, June 2), at 1667.

[214] The suggestion by the Commission staff (which was not to be viewed necessarily as the position of the Commission) was that Art. 16 of Decree No. 67-237 of March 27, 1967, concerning the commercial register which dealt with supervision of compliance with requirements *for admission to commercial activities* be extended specifically to cover also the requirements *for organizing commercial companies.* Judicial intervention is provided for in Art. 45 of the same decree.

[215] Art. 2 of Decree No. 69-1177 of Dec. 24, 1969, modifying Decree No. 67-236 of Mar. 23, 1967, on commercial companies, and Decree No. 67-237 of Mar. 23, 1967, on commercial register.

it directs the Members to remove from their respective laws all grounds on which invalidity of a company could be asserted, *except* those specifically enumerated; all or any one of these enumerated grounds *may* be retained or introduced in the national laws.[216]

The First Draft of the directive would have authorized only two such grounds, one relating to *form*, that is, the failure to prepare a charter or, depending upon the national law, to comply with the "preventive control" procedure or the notarial form,[217] and the other relating to *substance*, that is, a charter purpose that is illegal or in conflict with the *"ordre public."* However, any consensus on this formula, if there ever was one, disintegrated in subsequent proceedings, as its "radical" nature became better understood, and the contours of the differing national rules became more clearly apparent. A comparison revealed that the new French law which in other respects took the directive into account and sought to anticipate compliance, had failed to do so in this instance, and this upset the German delegation. The new French law provided that—in order "to assure all possible security particularly in European trade"—a company acquired its legal personality upon entry into the register, and this stressed the institutional nature of the company.[218] Nevertheless, the same law continued the rule that

---

216 This interpretation was confirmed in a Declaration by the Council of Ministers.

217 The question arose whether a failure to make public the charter should constitute an additional ground for invalidity. The directive indicates that this should be the case only in those States which consider "publicity" a prerequisite to the coming into existence of the company; in other States, failure to publish will have the same consequences as failure to comply with the general obligation to publish, that is, the unpublished documents or acts could not be invoked against third parties acting in good faith who, however, may nevertheless rely on them if they choose to do so. *See* Art. 9 of the *First Draft* which became Art. 8 of the *Second Draft,* but in the final text was covered in Art. 3, including Art. 3, par. 7, last clause.

218 Ass. Nat. [1963-64] No. 1003, Projet de loi sur les sociétés commerciales at 4; Art. 5 of the Law of 1966. *See similarly* § 41 of the

a company may be held invalid on any ground on which a contract might be challenged, and thus in this respect it retained the contractual concept of the company.[219] The most important of these grounds were the defect in the consent of the founder-shareholders[220] and their incapacity to enter into a contract,[221] neither of which was listed as authorized in the First Draft of the directive. The Italian law follows essentially the same rule as the French law. The Economic and Social Committee, again no doubt reflecting French attitudes, observed incredulously in its report on the First Draft that, in view of the "serious legal problems" which would arise from an excessively restrictive enumeration of the authorized grounds, the authors of the directive could not have possibly intended to exclude the contract-based grounds.[222]

(ii)　The Franco-German paradox

In striking contrast with the French pattern, the German law, having really abandoned the idea of the company as a contract, has done away with invalidity based on *contractual* grounds and, in lieu of an action for invalidity on these grounds, it offers other remedies[223] designed to protect

---

German Stock Company Law of 1965 and Art. 2331 of the Italian CODICE CIVILE.

[219] Art. 360 of the Law of 1966. In addition, invalidity may be based only on "an express provision of this law." However, the law has introduced a new procedure for *curing* invalidity. Art. 365. According to Art. 362 all types of invalidity may be cured except illegal or immoral charter purpose.

[220] Art. 1108 of the French CIVIL CODE.

[221] For a catalogue of the grounds for invalidity under the pre-1966 law see Escarra, ESCARRA & RAULT, 1 TRAITÉ THÉORIQUE ET PRATIQUE DE DROIT COMMERCIAL 245-62 (Paris 1950).

[222] Avis at 3255, 3A. In the same vein Dorat des Monts, *Vers un droit européen* at 18.

[223] Thus the Stock Company Law offers protection to the incapacitated person or the minor whose acts are considered void and who therefore cannot act as incorporator or be obligated to pay his contribution to the capital; but at the same time the participation of an incapacitated person has no effect on the acts of the other incorporators who have to assume his share. The company is *validly formed* among the remaining founders and no problem of invalidity

those interests that deserve protection, without impairing the existence of the company. This has also been the solution in Belgium and Luxembourg.[224] Paradoxically, however, the German (and Italian) law has retained action for invalidity on a number of grounds based on more or less *formal* defects, such as omission of certain required information from the charter;[225] yet no action is available on these grounds in French law.[226]

Apparently the French delegation became fully aware of this curious contradiction only at a later stage of the discussions. The showdown occurred during the final proceeding within the framework of the Council of Ministers, when the French and the Italians insisted that the defect-in-consent grounds be authorized, the Germans demanded the inclusion of the "formal" grounds of their own law, and the Italians finally produced—at the very last minute—a long list of grounds drawn from their own law, comprising such matters as the failure to observe rules governing subscription of stock. There is some evidence that the eleventh hour Italian demand was intended to serve also, if not primarily, for bargaining purposes, as a *quid pro quo* to induce the German delegation to mitigate its negative position on disclosure for limited liability companies.

At any rate, the final text, accepted after protracted and difficult negotiations, embodied the usual compromise.[227]

---

arises. Schmidt, in GROSSKOMMENTAR AKTIENGESETZ § 2 n.4 (2d ed., Berlin 1961).

[224] Art. 35 of the Belgian CODE DE COMMERCE holds the promoters liable for the obligations of the legally incapacitated persons; *see also* Art. 32 of the Luxembourg Law of 1915.

[225] §§ 23 and 275 of the Stock Company Law of 1965: the name of the firm, composition of the executive board (*Vorstand*), charter purpose, etc. Most of the formal defects may be cured and the company must be given opportunity to do so. § 275, par. 2. In Italian law action for invalidity for a formal defect is in principle available as long as the defect is not cured. Art. 2332, par. 3, CODICE CIVILE.

[226] Only an "action en régularisation" may be filed, aiming at curing the formal defect. Art. 6 of the Law of 1966. The responsible persons are subject to penal and civil liability.

[227] *Final Text*, Art. 11.

(iii)   At the end a compromise

In the final text, the original list containing the two authorized grounds of invalidity was substantially expanded to include four additions. In the first place, the French and the Italians, faced with a common front of the Benelux and German delegations and the Commission staff, abandoned their insistence on the contractual grounds,[228] but as a concession to them, one such ground, incapacity of *all* founder-shareholders, was added as an authorized ground.[229] Again, since the laws of the Six, with a single *prospective* exception of the Belgian reform, precluded incorporation by a single founder, a new ground was added, principally also in deference to Italian wishes, allowing invalidity where the number of *founder*-shareholders was less than two.[230] Of the two other added grounds, the first, absence of certain vital data in the charter (the name of the company, the contributions, the amount of the capital, charter purpose) was included to satisfy in part the Germans who in turn agreed to drop their other demands. The second new ground, failure to comply with national law requirements concerning minimum payment of the company capital, was added as still another concession to the Italians.[231]

---

[228] The argument by the majority was that to allow contractually based grounds for invalidity would create the danger of an excessively great opening for causes of invalidity (the possibility of having a company pronounced "null" by unanimous consent of the associates) and it would certainly lead to numerous litigations.

[229] Italian law tolerates a one-man company only after the company has been established with multiple incorporators. Art. 2362, Codice civile. Thus the Italian delegation was concerned lest in the case of incapacity of all founders *but one* the company became automatically a one-man company *from the outset*. The Commission staff argued that this would not be the case since the company would have functioned for a time before the invalidity was judicially declared. *See also* immediately *infra*.

[230] The new Belgian law would provide that a company may act as a single incorporator of its own subsidiary and, to accommodate this provision, a clause was added in Art. 11, par. f of the directive making it clear that this ground can be invoked only where national legislation requires more than one founder.

[231] A new last paragraph was also added principally to reflect Italian terminology ("*annullability*").

The end effect of the compromise was that each Member was required to modify its national law to a different degree, France and Italy the most, but even the Federal Republic to a minor extent. In fact, the Federal Law of Aug. 15, 1969, implementing the First Directive, eliminated from German law two grounds of invalidity which were not "authorized" by the directive.[232] In France, the rather significant adjustment was effected by an ordinance,[233] and in Italy by a Presidential decree.[233a]

---

[232] Pursuant to Art. 11, par. 2 of the First Directive, Art. 2, No. 19 and No. 20 of the Law Implementing First Directive has modified §§ 23, 275 and 276 of the Stock Company Law to reduce substantially the formal grounds for invalidity (see also Art. 3, No. 11, modifying § 75, par. 1 of the Law on Limited Liability Companies). However, as regards the more important grounds of invalidity due to defects in the charter which the directive did not authorize but which had existed in German law, Art. 5 of the Implementing Law introduces as a substitute for invalidity a special procedure before the court of the register; if the defect is not cured by the company a dissolution ensues. The Law did not introduce any new grounds authorized in Art. 11 of the directive which were not known in German law. The ground of invalidity provided in Art. 11, par. 2 (a) of the First Directive, based on the nonexistence of the entire charter is hardly imaginable but an omission of some of the essential data, specified in § 23, could occur although it is not likely to occur in Germany where a notary has the responsibility. Even if he "slips up" there are provisions for remedying the omission under § 276 and if this is of no avail the remedy is action for liquidation under § 277.

[233] Art. 7 of Ordinance No. 69-1176 of Dec. 20, 1969, modifying Law No. 66-537 of July 24, 1966, on commercial companies. Defect in the consent and incapacity may no longer be a ground for invalidity of stock companies or limited liability companies, unless it involves all founders; nor can invalidity result from the invalidity of clauses prohibited by Art. 1855 of the CODE CIVIL. In the Netherlands, Draft Law No. 10,400 "for the adaptation of the Netherlands legislation to the first directive of the Council of the European Communities of Mar. 9, 1968 relating to the company law," proposes modifications in the area of invalidity in Arts. 36, 36e, insertion of Art. 36i-l, modifications in Arts. 37b and 55 of the COMMERCIAL CODE. See Coebergh, De Nietigheid der Naamloze Vennootschap in het "Aanpassings ontwerp" 1969 N.V. 146.

[233a] Art. 3 of the Decree Implementing First Directive modified Art. 2332 of the CODICE CIVILE.

(c) Effects of invalidity: judicial declaration and no retroactivity

A company, the directive prescribes, cannot be considered invalid unless it is so declared in a judicial decision;[234] with respect to third parties the declaration will not have a retroactive effect and can be applied prospectively only. Prior undertakings by the company will not be impaired, and the shareholders will continue to be bound to pay in their part of the subscribed capital, to the extent that this will be necessary to satisfy the creditors in the ensuing liquidation proceeding. This "guarantee," which in several Member States reposes only on the doctrinal concept of *de facto* company, will thus become part of national written law as has been the case in France, Germany and Italy.[235] The judicial decision must be made public in accordance with the directive's general rules on "publicity," and its effect on third parties is governed by these same rules; where national law allows a third party to contest the decision, the action must be instituted within six months following the publication of the decision. This last provision is a compromise between those who favored an unrestricted effect "against all the world" *(erga omnes)* and those who would allow persons, not parties to the decision, as much as thirty years to file an objection against the judgment.[236] National law, however, continues to determine the effects of the declaration of invalidity upon relations among shareholders.[237]

---

234 *Final Text,* Art. 11, par. 1.

235 Germany: §§ 275-277 Stock Company Law of 1965. Italy: Art. 2332, CODICE CIVILE. France: Arts. 360-370, Law of July 24, 1966. *See also* LEHMANN, GESELLSCHAFTSRECHT at 37 (2d ed., Berlin 1959); Sinay, *La proposition de directive européenne* at 284 and 291.

236 Explanatory Memorandum of the Commission, 1964 Bull. E.E.C. Supp. No. 7, at 15, penultimate par. The six-month period of limitation was enacted in French law by Art. 1 of Decree No. 69-1177 of Dec. 24, 1969, modifying Decree No. 67-236 of Mar. 23, 1967, on commercial companies and Decree No. 67-237 of Mar. 23, 1967, on commercial register. This article introduced a new Art. 253-1 into Decree No. 67-237.

237 *Final Text,* Art. 12. The *First Draft* version of this article was modified in the *Second Draft* in response to the suggestions of the

4. Implementation of the First Directive in national laws

Of all the Member States, only the Federal Republic met the eighteen-month deadline for the implementation of the First Directive. The appropriate federal legislation was adopted in August 1969.[238] France and Italy acted before the end of 1969. In the Netherlands, the draft law has been pending before the Parliament,[239] but in Belgium delay occurred because two different Ministries had to reconcile their views on the modification of provisions concerning the commercial register. As a result, the draft law was still before the Belgian Conseil d'État early in 1970. A similar delay occurred in Luxembourg where the draft law was to be submitted to the Parliament and to the Conseil d'État in mid-1970.

In France and in Italy, in contrast with the other Member States, implementation was effected by executive action and no Parliamentary action was necessary. In France, the Government adopted a decree, based on its regular law-making powers attributed to it by the 1958 Constitution, and it also issued an ordinance, by virtue of a law of Parliament delegating to the Government the power to implement certain EEC directives.[240]

In Italy, the Presidential Decree[241] was based exclusively on legislation[242] which had delegated to the Government the power to implement EEC directives during the final stage of the "transitional period." The Parliamentary Committee, which was consulted on the decree before it was signed by the President, reacted with shocked disbelief when told that

Economic and Social Committee (Avis at 3255, B(a) and (b)), and in the final text.

[238] For full reference see Selected national legislation, *supra* p. xi.

[239] *See* p. 295 note 184 *supra*.

[240] For full references to the decree and the ordinance, see Selected national legislation, *supra* p. xii. The delegation of power was contained in Law No. 66-481 of July 6, 1966, based on Art. 38 of the Constitution. This law expired on Dec. 31, 1969, but the delegation was renewed by a new law of Dec. 26, 1969.

[241] For full reference see Selected national legislation *supra* p. xii

[242] Law No. 740 of Oct. 13, 1969.

the sacrosanct Civil Code will be modified by simple executive action. Yet the decree was clearly within the delegating legislation. This legislation, however, expired at the end of 1969, and there is some question whether the Parliament will be willing to renew it.

The fact that the First Directive concerned only some, and not all forms of commercial companies, has posed a technical problem in the countries with comprehensive codes on commercial companies.

Chapter 8

PROJECTS AND PROSPECTS

Since the mid-sixties, work has proceeded more or less simultaneously along three parallel lines: drafting of a series of directives for coordination of company laws to complete the process initiated in the First Directive, the elaboration of conventions bearing upon Community-wide recognition of companies, seat transfers and mergers ("fusions"), and a study of the ways and means for introducing a new European or "European-type" company form. In the opening chapter of this book I have described the legal bases for these activities and the *modus operandi* of the two principal working groups in which concrete proposals were "born." I have also mentioned that the "birth pangs" were reduced somewhat when all matters relating to company law, including tax problems, were brought within the competence of a single Directorate General. A notable, more recent development has been the growing awareness of the close nexus between company law on the one hand, and tax legislation and regulations governing capital markets on the other.[1]

---

[1] Tax Harmonization Programme, Commission Memorandum to the Council of Feb. 8, 1967, 1967 Bull. E.E.C. Supp. No. 8; Need and Methods for Action in the Sphere of Capital, Commission Memorandum to the Council, Europe, Documents No. 518, March 21, 1969, summarized in CCH COMM. MKT. REP. ¶ 9293, and in Comm. Spokesman's Group P-10/69, Mar. 1969; European Commission Guidelines on the Tax System Applicable to Shares and Interest on Debentures, Europe, Documents No. 519, Mar. 24, 1969; Vogelaar, "The Approximation of Tax Legislation in the European Common Market," Paper for International Fiscal Association Congress, Montevideo, Uruguay, Oct. 1968 (mimeo); Vogelaar, *Steuerharmonisierung in der Europäischen Gemeinschaft,* 1970 AWD 198.

1. Further coordination of company laws under Article 54, par. 3(g)

The emphasis has continued to be on capital companies and more specifically on stock companies. A series of co-ordinating proposals, limited to stock companies and dealing with the following subjects, has been under consideration:

(1) content of financial documents and accounting standards;

(2) formation and maintenance of capital (the subject of the "Second Directive");

(3) competence and structure of company organs, dissolution and liquidation, securities, "related companies";

(4) fusions of companies of the same nationality (the subject of the "Third Directive").

In addition, preparatory studies have been instituted in the following areas:

(1) limited liability companies (formation, capital, conduct of business, "quotas" (shares), financial documents, dissolution and liquidation, reorganization into another type of company, fusions of such companies of the same nationality);

(2) cooperatives;

(3) other companies formed in accordance with civil and commercial law;

(4) other legal persons of private and public law.[2]

(a) Working group "company law": atmosphere and orientation

The atmosphere in the working group on company law has undergone certain subtle modifications. In the first place, the continuing, close personal association of national experts and their growing knowledge and understanding of

[2] 1968 Bull. E.C. Supp. No. 5, at 13.

each other's legal system could not remain without influence on their attitude. Similarly, the Commission staff has become more effective as its knowledge of national laws became more sophisticated. The position of the Netherlands Government, reflecting, as we have seen, important differences between the Netherlands law and the laws of the other Members has continued to pose a problem. Nevertheless, the Netherlands governmental experts who initially opposed any coordination whatever, began to show an increasing inclination to cooperate, even though the hostility of the Netherlands legal profession at the bar, in the "private sector," and in the law faculties, continued unrelieved. In the Union of the Industries of the European Community (U.N.I.C.E.), as well as in the *Fédération bancaire* of the European Economic Community, the Dutch delegates were dissenters on important points.[3] When France blocked the United Kingdom's application for membership in the Communities for the second time late in 1967, the Netherlands Government threatened with a "boycott" of its own, forced a suspension of the important "Working Party Maréchal" on Scientific and Technical Research Policy in which France was interested,[4] and held up final approval of the Convention on Mutual Recognition of Companies for some two months as a gesture of protest. Yet at the time this episode did not seem to have "spilled-over" into the company law working group. Again, the posture of the German governmental experts has remained what could perhaps be best described as ambiguous, due to circumstances outlined earlier.

---

[3] Avis de l'U.N.I.C.E. au sujet du projet de deuxième directive tendant à coordonner, pour les rendre équivalentes, les garanties qui sont exigées, dans les État-membres, des sociétés au sens de l'article 58, alinéa 2 du Traité, pour protéger les intérêts tant des associés que des tiers, Bruxelles, Mar. 25, 1968, 22.6 A4 [hereinafter cited as *Avis de l'U.N.I.C.E.*]. Observations de la Fédération bancaire de la C.E.E. sur le projet de deuxième directive en matière de sociétés anonymes (doc. 7792/III/C/67 du 1er juin 1967 de la Commission de la C.E.E.), No. 95, Bruxelles, Jan. 22, 1968 [hereinafter cited as *Observations*].

[4] Commission of the Eur. Communities Spokesman's Group, Dec. 1968, P-64, Information Memo, 1968 IN RETROSPECT at 17.

After the working group had completed its labors on the first draft of the First Directive in 1964—and while the difficult negotiations proceeded in the Council of Ministers "on the other side of town"—the group turned its attention to the other areas of stock company law. Having drawn a lesson from past experience, the Commission staff eschewed the time-consuming and ineffective method of sending questionnaires to the governments for the purpose of obtaining information on their respective laws. Instead, a number of national company law experts, including some members of the group itself or the Commission's special consultants on company law, was commissioned to prepare comparative studies on selected aspects of national laws. These studies would contain more or less specific suggestions as to which rules could or should be coordinated and in what way.

(b)   The "Second Directive": more on stock companies

The first concrete proposal emerging from these studies was a draft of the so-called Second Directive, consisting of 36 articles on "guarantees" concerning acquisition and maintenance of stock company capital[5] which for all practical purposes was completed on June 1, 1967.[6] Initially, the

---

[5] Avant-Projet d'une deuxième directive de coordination des législations nationales en matière des sociétés anonymes, Doc. 6063/III/C/65-F, Bruxelles, Rév. 1, May 4, 1965; La riforma delle società, Progetti e documenti, 1966 RIVISTA DELLE SOCIETÀ 436; Projet de deuxième directive tendant à coordonner, pour les rendre équivalentes, les garanties qui sont exigées, dans les État-membres, des sociétés au sens de l'article 58, alinéa 2 du Traité, pour protéger les intérêts tant des associés que des tiers, Doc. 7792/III/C/67, Bruxelles, June 1, 1967. An undated modified text became available in Spring 1969. For the text approved by the Commission and proposed to the Council see [1970] J.O. C48 (Apr. 24) at 8-22.

See also M. le Prof. P. van Ommeslaghe, Rapport complémentaire sur certains problèmes examinés par le groupe de travail "Droit des sociétés" en 1964, Doc. 5706/III/C/65-F, Bruxelles, Apr. 28, 1965.

[6] Subsequent modifications were designed mainly to improve the drafting.

Commission withheld action on this proposal perhaps because of the aversion in some governmental, parliamentary and business quarters to "piece-meal" coordination; the implication was that the Commission would wait until the remaining proposals concerning stock companies were ready, whereupon it would submit them all at one time to the Council of Ministers. This plan was applauded by the Union of the Industries of the European Community (U.N.I.C.E.).[7] However, in February 1969, the Commission made it clear that it had chosen an alternative route and that it would propose a series of successive directives, each designed to coordinate one or more specific aspects of company law.[8] In fact, the Commission submitted a proposal for the "Second Directive" to the Council on March 9, 1970.[9]

(i)   The coverage: what of close companies and open-ended investment trusts?

The proposed text of the "Second Directive" contains no innovating or revolutionary ideas[10] but, because of the subject matter, it is of considerable practical interest. In the earlier drafting stages, the scope of the directive was in dispute; the disagreement centered again on the Netherlands "close stock company" *(besloten vennootschap)*.[11] When the Union of Industries of the European Community (U.N.I.C.E.) was consulted on the draft, it demanded "instant examination of the case" of these last mentioned companies and of "the open-ended investment funds," which in the Netherlands are organized as stock companies and in

---

[7] *Avis de l'U.N.I.C.E.* at 1; Houin, *Où en est le droit des sociétés* at 141.

[8] COMM. DOC. R 1325/69 of Feb. 27, 1969.

[9] For the text with an explanation see [1970] J.O. C48 (Apr. 24) at 8-22.

[10] Houin, *Où en est le droit des sociétés* at 141.

[11] Earlier, the group "reserved" its decision on possible exceptions or special provisions with regard to the Dutch close companies as well as companies listed on a stock exchange, banks, insurance companies, etc.

France (and under the Belgian reform law) as "companies with a variable capital."[12] In the current text of the proposal, however, Netherlands close companies are included along with all the other stock companies, even though certain exceptions are made for close companies. On the other hand, all investment companies with a variable capital which make public offering are specifically excluded,[13] except that they are required to identify themselves as such on all their business papers and in all forms of "publicity."[14] This provision, and other provisions in the introductory articles, are "throwbacks" to the First Directive; they set forth the minimum data that must be included in the charter[15] and thus complement Article 2 of the First Directive which prescribes the minimum information a company must make publicly available.

(ii)   Minimum required capital

One major purpose of the new text is the establishment of a uniform minimum capital amount for stock companies, since the differences in the required minimum levels could affect freedom of establishment, for instance, when a com-

---

12 *Avis de l'U.N.I.C.E.* at 2. In the Fédération bancaire, the Dutch delegation refused to agree to the proposed directive and argued that, in any case, Netherlands close companies must be excluded from its application the same way as limited liability companies. *Observations* at 8. On the "variable capital" company see *supra* p. 135.

13 That is, the Member States are free *not to apply* the directive to these companies.

14 The Fédération bancaire raised the question as to what will be the case in the event the requirement of "publicity" is disregarded by such a company: would the directive become applicable to the company "which would be inadmissible?" *Observations* at 2.

15 The prescribed data include the form and name of the company, its "seat," charter purpose, amount of capital with an indication whether this is subscribed or authorized capital, the securities, composition and powers of organs (except where determined by law), the duration of the company, the names of the incorporators, paid-in capital, number and value of shares issued for contributions other than cash payment, expenses of formation, special advantages and remuneration of the founders.

pany contemplates setting up a subsidiary in another Member State. I have mentioned earlier that only France, Germany and (theoretically) Italy now require a minimum stated capital, but the minimum levels vary between these countries, and the numbers of stock companies in proportion to limited liability companies are also different.[16] Yet apparently the experts found it difficult to decide whether they should set a minimum capital in the amount of 20,000 units of account ($20,000) or, in the alternative, leave the national legislators free to fix a minimum within the range of $20,000 to $50,000, with the possibility of requiring higher amounts for companies engaged in certain special activities or listed on a stock exchange. In the end, the proposal which was sent to the Council set a fixed minimum of $25,000, but it would allow a 10% upward or downward variation for the purpose of facilitating conversion into national currencies.[17] Moreover, two deviations are made possible. First, the minimum amount required for close companies (as defined in the First Directive) would be only $4,000, because they perform the functions of limited liability companies, and these latter companies are not subject to the directive. U.N.I.C.E. took the view that the minimum amount for stock companies should be set at $20,000 and that the Member States should *not* be allowed to require a higher minimum; moreover, the Netherlands close companies should be dealt with separately. The *Fédération bancaire,* on the other hand, took the position that the $4,000 minimum should apply to all close stock companies, not just those in the Netherlands, and pointed out that the Netherlands delegation viewed even this minimum as much too high.[18] According to the second deviation,

---

[16] *See* p. 200 *supra.* In the Federal Republic the minimum capital is 100,000 DM ($27,300), § 7 of the Stock Company Law of 1965; in France it is 500,000 Ffr ($100,000) for companies with public offering and 100,000 Ffr ($20,000) for others, Art. 71, Law of July 24, 1966; in Italy 1,000,000 Lire ($1,600), Art. 2327 CODICE CIVILE.

[17] The equivalent of $25,000 in Dutch and Italian currency cannot be expressed in round figures.

[18] *Avis de l'U.N.I.C.E.* at 4; *Observations* at 2-3.

a Member State could require a minimum amount in excess of $25,000 as a prerequisite for listing a company on a stock exchange or, pending further coordination, for companies engaged in activities requiring special treatment, such as banks and insurance enterprises.

If the proposed text is adopted, a substantial number of stock companies will no doubt be reorganized into other types of companies.

(iii) Acquisition of capital

Basic rules on acquisition and maintenance of capital are covered in considerable detail. Thus, stock subscribed for cash payments may be issued only if 25% of its nominal value is paid in.[19] The Netherlands delegation—in this instance supported by U.N.I.C.E.—urged that the minimum percentage payment be required only if the company capital did not exceed the minimum capital amount fixed by law (presumably $25,000); if the capital was higher, the required percentage should be reduced proportionately.[20] The *Fédération bancaire* on the other hand supported the rule as written, but expected exemptions for specially regulated industries such as insurance companies.

Contributions in kind, on the other hand, according to the proposal, must be made in full and a report thereon must be prepared by "one or more persons independent of the company, designated or approved by an administrative

---

[19] This is a compromise between the Belgium-Luxembourg law (20%) and the Italian law (30%). The French and German law already provide for 25%. Similarly, no-par value stock may be issued only if 25% of the value fixed for such shares is paid in. See explanation in [1970] J.O. C48 (Apr. 24) 8, at 10. No-par value shares may be issued in Belgium and Luxembourg, but the concept differs from no-par value shares in the United States. In the two European states, the value of a no-par value share is a fraction of an already fixed stated capital, while in the United States the stated capital represented by no-par value shares is the entire consideration received for such shares.

[20] The Netherlands U.N.I.C.E. delegation also insisted on the reduction of the percentage rate from 25% to 10%.

or judicial authority," and it must be published. Again, this
rule was opposed by the Netherlands private sector.[21] To
make sure that this rule is not circumvented, any acquisition
of property from a founder or shareholder within the first
two years of the company's existence is made subject to
the same audit (and must be approved by the shareholders'
meeting) if its value amounts to one-tenth or more of the
subscribed capital.[22] U.N.I.C.E. reported that this rule was

---

[21] Such audit of contributions in kind is required in existing
German (§§ 27, 34 of the Law of 1965), French (Art. 80 of the Law of
July 24, 1966), Belgian (Art. 29 of the CODE DE COMMERCE) and Italian
(Art. 2343 CODICE CIVILE) law. Luxembourg requires "publicity" only.
The Netherlands delegation in U.N.I.C.E. opposed this provision on
the ground that it would make mergers and transformations more diffi-
cult, and in the Fédération bancaire because it would constitute an
undue burden upon small close companies.

[22] This rule was inspired by § 52 of the German Stock Company
Law of 1965. Concerning the term "subscribed capital" see Conard,
Organizing for Business at 79-82. Conard states (at 79-80): "In five
of the six Common Market nations the amount of 'capital' stated in
the articles is quite a different thing from the 'authorized capital'
which is stated by the articles in most American states. 'Authorized
capital' means, in America, the amount which may be issued before
amending the charter; some of it may not be subscribed for some
time to come, and some may never be subscribed. Americans like to
have a 'cushion' of uncommitted stock to meet unforseen needs.

"In the Common Market (outside the Netherlands) the capital
contains no uncommitted cushion. The 'capital' means the *subscribed*
capital, and the corporation is not fully organized until the stated
amount is 100% subscribed. Some of the statutes say expressly that
the company is not perfected until it reaches this point; even when
the statutes are silent, the law is probably the same.

"In consequence, the stated capital should be set at an amount
for which present subscribers are readily available.

"If the incorporators foresee that future capital demands will exceed the amount for which present subscriptions are available, they
can sometimes make charter provisions for future increases by means
simpler than getting a shareholder's vote on a charter amendment.
Italy and Germany permit stock companies to adopt charter clauses
which authorize the managers to increase the capital. But the authorized increase must also be fully subscribed within a limited time—five
years in Germany, one in Italy. In this respect, it is quite unlike
American 'authorized capital.' France also has some statutory provisions permitting 'variable capital,' but they are somewhat inconvenient,
and are little used. Other kinds of companies can increase their initial

viewed as excessive by "delegations whose law does not know such a provision" (presumably the delegations from the Netherlands and Luxembourg). Again, the contributions to the capital must be "susceptible of being realized."[23]

In principle, no relief is allowed from the obligations to pay the subscribed portion of the capital, and dividends and interest may be paid only from net profits, lest the stated capital and required reserves be impaired. However, Member States may retain national provisions which authorize payment of interest in the absence of profits before the company becomes fully operative, subject to specified restrictions.[24] A company may not subscribe to its own stock directly or indirectly, and any intermediary and the administration are held liable in case of a violation.

(iv)   Acquisition by company of its own shares ("treasury shares")

The assumption here is that excessive acquisition by a company of its own shares may lead to a reduction of its capital and thus impair the position of *creditors*. Such acquisition may prejudice the position of the *shareholders* as well, if it enables the management to seize control over the company through this use of company funds; and it may reduce the value of the outstanding shares, if the purchase price paid by the company is excessive. Finally, the company's acquisition may artificially drive the price of the

---

capital only by charter amendment; this applies to limited liability companies in all five countries, and to stock companies in Belgium and Luxembourg." (Original footnotes omitted.)

23 This term was viewed by U.N.I.C.E. as lacking in clarity, and it was interpreted by the Fédération bancaire as embracing only assets on which execution may be levied. However, depending on the applicable national law, this definition would not exclude public concessions, goodwill, or the results of research and development in the form of "know-how."

24 A provision must be made for this in the charter, the rate must not exceed 4%, and the period must not exceed four years. See on this subject LUTTER, KAPITAL at 378.

shares up, to the prejudice of *potential investors*. Although the rules imposing limitations on such acquisition are thus relevant for the protection of both the creditors and the shareholders, the formulation of appropriate coordinating provisions proved perhaps the most difficult phase of the proceeding, because of the substantial differences among the legal systems of the Members. At the present, for instance, the Netherlands legislation imposes no maximum limit whatsoever on the acquisition of own shares, although in practice the Ministry of Justice insists on a 50% limit, apparently in order to prevent the management from obtaining control over the company.[25] At the other extreme, the 1966 French law originally forbade any acquisition of own stock, except for the purpose of capital reduction, but an amendment of 1967 has loosened the bar, subject to conditions similar to those in German law, and it has authorized acquisition also for the purpose of "workers' participation."[26]

The proposed directive would require those Member States which allow acquisition of own shares, to ensure that each such transaction is approved by the shareholders' meeting, with due regard to the principle of shareholder "equal-

---

[25] VAN DER HEIJDEN-VAN DER GRINTEN, HANDBOEK No. 315, at 499; Art. 41a, WETBOEK VAN KOOPHANDEL.

[26] Art. 217 of the French Law of July 24, 1966, as modified by Ordinances of Aug. 17 and Sept. 28, 1967, allows also acquisition of up to a 10% limit for the purpose of distribution to employees ("workers' participation") or for the support of the price of the shares, upon approval by the shareholders' meeting, but only if the current price on the stock exchange is at least 10% less than the real value of the share, calculated on the basis of the last balance sheet. The company must build a special reserve corresponding to the value of the purchased shares.

The German law was also modified somewhat in 1965. *See* § 71 of the Stock Company Law of 1965 and § 65 of the Law of 1937. German law gives the executive board a wider margin of discretion: to avoid serious harm, it may decide on an acquisition without approval by the shareholders' meeting up to the limit of 10%. There is no limitation on the source of the funds, even the capital may be drawn upon. The Belgian, Luxembourg and Italian laws authorize acquisition only from profits and free reserves and upon approval by the shareholders' meeting.

ity." No such acquisition is permitted, if it should bring
about a reduction of the net assets below the subscribed
capital and required reserves, and shares not fully paid are
excluded. Moreover, the company may not acquire own
shares beyond 25% of the subscribed capital, and previously
acquired own shares held in the company's portfolio ("treasury shares") must be counted. If, however, the acquisition
is "indispensable to avoid serious damage" (for instance when
a competitor purchases a block of shares), the approval by
the shareholders' meeting and the other conditions may be
disregarded,[27] but the acquisition must not have the effect of
reducing net assets below the amount of the capital; moreover, since the acquisition in this case is more "dangerous,"
the maximum limit is set at 10% (again including the treasury shares already held in the company's portfolio). Both
U.N.I.C.E. and the *Fédération bancaire* found the requirement of a special approval by the shareholders' meeting excessively burdensome.[28]

These rather severe limitations, however, would not apply at all if the company acquires its own shares for the
purpose of capital reduction, fusion or purchase of all of the
assets of another company which include the acquiring
company's shares; and the limitations would apply only in
part, if the purpose is to distribute the shares among the
company's employees. The last mentioned provision reflects the German and French policy of encouraging employee participation in the company's profits and growth.

The voting right based on treasury shares is suspended,
and if—as is permissible—the shares are carried as assets
on the balance sheet, a corresponding reserve must be
formed, in the image of the new French law.[29] In effect, that
part of the free reserve which corresponds to the price of the

---

[27] *See* § 71 German Law of 1965; BAUMBACH-HUECK, AKTIEN-
GESETZ § 71 n.6.

[28] *Avis de l'U.N.I.C.E.* at 8; *Observations* at 5.

[29] *Supra* note 26, p. 323.

acquired shares becomes required reserve and may no longer be distributed to the shareholders.[30]

Other provisions require the national legislator to impose limitations, for the protection of creditors, upon stock redemption in situations other than capital reduction.

(v) Capital increase

In principle, the proposal authorizes an increase of capital only when all outstanding shares are fully paid in, although the national legislator could allow and define exceptions to this rule. In U.N.I.C.E., the Netherlands delegation, joined in this instance by Italian interests, opposed this principle on the ground that it did not constitute any "guarantee" either for the creditors or shareholders; on the contrary, "any capital increase provides an added guarantee for third parties." The majority of U.N.I.C.E., however, was prepared to accept this part of the proposed directive, with the understanding that any exceptions to the principle should be defined in the directive and not left to the discretion of the Member States.[31] The *Fédération bancaire,* on the other hand, stated flatly that, because of the "diversity in the techniques of financing," the rule should be dropped and the matter should be left to national laws.[32] In reality, the *Fédération* did not view this matter as being important enough to be governed by a directive.

The shareholders' meeting must decide on a capital increase, and the rules governing the amendment procedure of the articles of incorporation (quorum, "publicity," voting) apply. Reflecting, however, in part the Netherlands law, the proposal provides that the "competent organ" of the company may be authorized, either in the charter or by the shareholders' meeting, to decide on an increase up to a fixed

---

[30] LUTTER, KAPITAL at 433, points out that this had been the practice in France even before the new law had made it a legal requirement.

[31] *Avis de l'U.N.I.C.E.* at 10.

[32] *Observations* at 6.

maximum within a period of not more than five years.[33]
This text would presumably cover the "authorized capital"
concept. Both the Italian and Netherlands delegations in
U.N.I.C.E., as well as in the *Fédération bancaire,* wanted the
time limitation removed, and the Netherlands representatives alone were opposed to other restrictions and prerequisites, such as the auditing of the contribution in kind,
brought in as a result of the capital increase.

In the event of a capital increase, the pre-emptive right
of the shareholders as regards the new shares is recognized,
with a view to maintaining their proportionate voting power
and participation in the assets. Only the shareholders' meeting may decide to exclude this right, but it may also delegate the decision on the exclusion to the administration. The
text does not impose any restrictions on this authority to
delegate the decision—and this omission was deplored by
U.N.I.C.E. Nor does the text define the legal consequences
in case the administration should have the authority to issue
additional shares (authorized capital) and to exclude the pre-
emptive right, if it should sell the stock to third parties at a
price which results in an impairment of the original shareholders' participation in the assets.[34] Presumably, in that
case members of the board could be held responsible for
damages to the original shareholders. The Netherlands representatives were the lone but vigorous dissenters in both the
U.N.I.C.E. and the *Fédération bancaire,* since the Netherlands law does not grant any such pre-emptive right to the
shareholders; a clause granting such right is included often in
the charter of the Dutch close companies, but very rarely in
the charter of listed companies. In practice, the Amsterdam
Stock Exchange Committee sees to it that new issues without
the right of pre-emption meet or closely approach the current

---

[33] This authorization would be renewable for subsequent five-year
periods. VAN DER HEIJDEN-VAN DER GRINTEN, HANDBOEK No. 164, at
210.

[34] On this problem in German law see Klette, *Der Emissionskurs
beim genehmigten Kapital,* 1968 BB 977; 21 BGHZ 354, 357 (1956);
33 BGHZ 175 (1960).

quoted price and—in the Dutch view—the imposition of the pre-emptive right would gravely impair the working of the Netherlands capital market.[35]

(vi) Capital reduction

The principal rule in this part of the proposal requires Member States to assure that the capital which becomes available as a result of a capital reduction, is not distributed to the shareholders, but remains available to the creditors.[36] Creditors whose claims had arisen prior to the publication of the required decision by the shareholders' meeting to reduce the capital, must be given appropriate security; however, national legislatures may dispense with this condition if the claims are otherwise secured, or if such security does not appear necessary in view of the available company assets. The provision on creditor security does not apply if the capital reduction is to cover losses. In any case, the capital must not be reduced below the minimum prescribed by law, or else the stock company must be transformed into another form.

(vii) "One-man" stock company

The doctrinal concept of the company as a contract which used to dominate the "Latin" legal systems, could not tolerate a "one-man" company in any form whatsoever. The proposed directive, however, recognizes the "one-man" company in a limited sense, only if all shares are acquired by a single person *after* the company's formation by more than a single founder. In that event, the company may no longer be held automatically dissolved, as is still the case in Belgium and Luxembourg; however, the Member States would remain free to require the liquidation of such a company.[37]

---

35 *Observations* at 7.

36 On this problem see LUTTER, KAPITAL at 384 ff., 531.

37 All of the national systems of the Member States require more than one "incorporator" for the founding of a stock company; LUTTER, KAPITAL at 59. However, the Belgian reform would allow a parent company to organize a wholly-owned subsidiary; *supra* p. 308. In the

If a judicial proceeding for dissolution is instituted, the court must allow the company a period of not less than six months "to regularize its situation." This proposed text appeared acceptable to both the industry and the bankers. However, a more "radical" Belgian proposal to allow a single person to organize a "one-man company" was not accepted in the working group, reportedly because it had "nothing to do with the protection of creditors or shareholders." The true reason may have been the lingering attachment to the doctrine of the company as a contract—and the fact that all Member States still require more than one stockholder for the formation of a stock company. It would be in the interest of creditors, at least, to coordinate national rules regarding the liability of the single shareholder. These rules are based in part on statute, in part on case law, and differ greatly from one Member State to the other.

(viii) Concluding observations

Several provisions in the proposed directive have already become law, or are in the process of becoming law, through the enactment of national reforms. Obviously, this fact makes

---

Federal Republic, acquisition of all shares *after* the incorporation has no particular legal consequences. WÜRDINGER, AKTIEN- UND KONZERNRECHT at 313; VAN DER HEIJDEN-VAN DER GRINTEN, HANDBOEK No. 94 at 104; Haardt, *La société d'une seule personne*, in RAPPORTS GÉNÉRAUX AU VIIe CONGRÈS INTERNATIONAL DE DROIT COMPARÉ, Uppsala, 6-13 août 1966, at 231-37 (Stockholm 1966). In German law, however, the provisions on related enterprises *(Konzernrecht)* must be observed. If the sole stockholder is the "enterprise" *(Unternehmen)* within the meaning of the law, he may not employ his power for the purpose of involving the company in an unfavorable deal, lest he be liable for damages. §§ 311-318 of the Stock Company Law of 1965. The concept of enterprise has not been clearly defined as yet. The case law concerning the piercing of the corporate veil must also be considered; 20 BGHZ 4, 14 (1956); 22 BGHZ 226, 231 (1956); WÜRDINGER, *id.* at 314. Present Belgian and Luxembourg law prescribe automatic dissolution. In the present French law, the company continues to exist but dissolution may be requested. Art. 9 of the Law of July 24, 1966. In Italy the company continues to exist but the single shareholder becomes liable personally. Arts. 2362, 2497, par. 2, CODICE CIVILE. This is the solution proposed also in the Belgian reform law.

the provisions more acceptable and less controversial. If one were to identify the delegation which exerted the strongest influence, it would no doubt be the Belgian group whose compromise proposals, designed to bridge the differences among national laws, received considerable support.

As in the case of the First Directive, some writers and the banking interests again raised the objection that most of the proposed rules were much too detailed and, if adopted, would compel the national parliaments in effect simply to transform these rules into national laws of the same wording. The Member States would thus be deprived of the margin of discretion, to which they were entitled in view of the Treaty concept of "coordination" and the Treaty definition of "directive." Moreover, the argument was advanced again that "coordination" under Treaty Article 54, par. 3(g), was limited to promoting freedom of establishment and no other purpose—a position that has not been accepted by the Commission.[38]

In contrast with this posture, the U.N.I.C.E. complained that in numerous instances the directive proposed to lay down minimum rules—a floor—to be observed by the national legislatures, but left them free to enact or maintain more severe rules on the subject. This approach, according to U.N.I.C.E., could not assure a coordination which called for "equivalent régimes" in *all* the Member States; yet in other instances such "equivalence" could be achieved, even though the Member States were allowed to choose different means and solutions.

On the whole, however, the legal debate on the scope of Article 54 and the power of the Community has tended to diminish; instead, the arguments have been framed more frequently in terms of good policy.

A continuing problem that has made coordination within a single subject area difficult, has been the organic in-

---

[38] Rodière, *L'harmonisation des législations* at 347; *Observations* at 1.

terrelationship between the various aspects of company law, and between company law and the laws and practices in other fields. On the other hand, this interrelationship has made it necessary to extend gradually the coordination studies from one aspect and area to another. Thus, it became obvious that, in the absence of common accounting standards, the amount of earnings available for distribution may differ from one Member State to the other. A prohibition of any distribution, in a situation in which net assets drop below the subscribed capital plus required reserves, becomes meaningful only if "net assets" are defined by uniform standards. Different methods of valuation of contributions in kind lead to different results, and the reliability of an audit becomes meaningful only if the professional qualifications of the auditors are comparable. Again, the rules in the proposal are incomplete as long as the level of required reserves is not determined. Finally, the rules on acquisition of own shares remain incomplete, as long as they do not regulate "indirect acquisition" through dependent subsidiaries. This problem was diagnosed by Professor van Ommeslaghe who suggested an appropriate formula in his preparatory report.[39] Yet his formula was eliminated from the text because the work on related enterprises had not progressed far enough at the time. These examples illustrate the reasons for the initial reluctance on the part of the Commission to submit its proposal for the "Second Directive" separately to the Council.

(c) Completing the coordination of stock company laws

(i) The reports by Special Consultants

The task of laying the groundwork for the completion of the coordination of national laws relating to stock companies was entrusted to the Commission's Special Consultants on Company Law, Professors Houin of Paris, Miccio of Rome, and Würdinger of Hamburg. In their individual

---

[39] Doc. 3714/III/C/65-F Rév. 1, at 44.

reports, Houin and Würdinger dealt with the internal organizational structure of the stock company, Würdinger
analyzed the problems of related and affiliated companies,
and Miccio considered the law on securities.[40] Although
portions of the Houin Report already reflect certain provisional attitudes taken by the national experts in the working
group on company law, the reports represent largely the
personal views of the learned authors and the proposed texts
of the additional directives are thus entirely tentative.[41]

(ii)   Company administration and shareholders' meeting: the Houin and Würdinger Reports

(1)   How much coordination?

Most of the subject matter of the First and Second Directives concerned unquestionably the protection of third
parties and shareholders within the meaning of Article 54,
par. 3(g). Moreover, in a general way, the trend in national
laws has been in the direction of reducing the differences
among the rules governing these subjects. Finally, most
issues—with some significant exceptions—raised technical
rather than policy questions.

---

[40] Houin, *Rapport sur l'administration de la société par actions,
Première partie,* Comm. Doc. 12.364/III/C/67-F, undated, and *2ème
partie,* Comm. Doc. 317/III/C/68-F, Jan. 18, 1968, cited below as
Houin Report I and *II; Les garanties des associés et des tiers qui se
rattachent aux valeurs mobilières de la société par actions,* Rapport
présenté par M. le professeur Renato Miccio, Comm. Doc. 16431/III/-
C/67-F, and *II, Les obligations émises par les sociétés,* Comm. Doc.
1060/III/C/68-F, cited as *Miccio Report I* and *II; Die Versammlung
der Aktionäre,* Arbeitsdokument vorgelegt von Professor Hans Würdinger, Hamburg, Comm. Doc. 14.653/III/C/67-D; *Note sur le
problème du droit des groupes de sociétés* par le Professeur Würdinger,
Comm. Doc. 5875/XIV/C/2/68-F, and *Sociétés liées,* Rapport présenté par le Professeur Hans Würdinger, Hamburg, Comm. Doc.
5928/XIV/C/2/68-F, cited as *Würdinger Report (Versammlung), Würdinger Report (groupes),* and *Würdinger Report (soc. liées).*

[41] According to Prof. Houin, the working group began examining
a draft of a directive on "administration, supervision and control"
in stock companies in February 1968. Houin, *Où en est le droit des
sociétés* at 144.

A somewhat different situation has prevailed in the area
covered by the Houin and Würdinger Reports, devoted to
the internal structure of stock companies. In the first place,
the relationship between the organization of a company and
the protection of shareholders and third parties is not always self-evident. Again, the problem of company organization evokes—it is said—"the continuing contest between
appearance and reality,"[42] a policy choice between "shareholder democracy" and modern effective management which
has faced the legislator in this field. While the corporation
laws in the United States and Great Britain had moved
toward a strong management at an early date, the lawmaker
on the Continent clung to the idea of a legally omnipotent
shareholders' meeting much longer, even though there, also,
the actual power had passed to the management a long time
ago. The German legislator was the first to seek an adjustment to reality by strengthening the legal position of the
company's management, to be followed—albeit in an attenuated form—by the French and Italian lawmakers.[43] The
current national reform trends point in the same general
direction, but the actual solutions often reflect a compromise.
Thus, the most recent German reform of 1965, as we have
seen, was a step in the opposite direction, because it curtailed
management's discretion somewhat, in the interest of more
effective protection of shareholders and investors. Finally,
since in some quarters, at any rate, the function of the company is no longer conceived exclusively in terms of profit-
maximization in the interest of shareholders, and as other
purposes come into view, the question is posed whether company organs should include representatives not only of the
shareholders but also of other groups, particularly the employees. While the problem of strengthening the management raises a policy question of some importance, it is on the
whole untainted by ideology. The issue of "extending the

---

[42] Franz Klein, quoted in Gessler, *Probleme und Wege von
Aktienrechtsreformen,* 1966 JURISTISCHE BLÄTTER 169.

[43] Gessler, *id.* at 170, 172.

corporate constituency" through workers' representation not
only involves socio-economic policies, but it also has deep
ideological connotations.[44]

Considering all these factors, it is not difficult to understand why the Houin Report in so many instances recommends against coordinating national rules on this or that
aspect of internal corporate organization. The reason given
for this restraint generally is that the relationship between
the rule in question and the protection of shareholders and
third parties is much too tenuous to justify Community
action under Article 54, par. 3(g). It is on this ground that
the Report for instance comes out against requiring the
Member States to adopt workers' codetermination or the
two-tier system with a supervisory council. Codetermination,
according to the Report, falls outside the scope of Article 54,
because it concerns more the internal relations between capital and labor than the protection of shareholders and creditors. A careful reading suggests that in reality, the learned
rapporteur's reasoning process combines legal analysis with
intuition. Having first examined and compared the national
rules on a specific aspect, he will advise against coordination
if he concludes that the differences among the national rules
are not such as to pose difficulties, particularly from the
viewpoint of creditor-shareholder protection. Similarly, he
will counsel against coordination if he feels that issues of
policy are involved which cannot be resolved at the present
time on a Community-wide basis, since integration of the
interested national groups on a transnational level has not
progressed far enough, and the existing lawmaking procedures in the Community do not provide for an effective parliamentary participation or for some other form of democratic legitimation. The general language of Article 54 offers
a convenient legal basis in support of these conclusions, even
though they are reached essentially by common sense and
realistic political judgment.

---

[44] Vagts, *Reforming the "Modern" Corporation* at 65 ff.

(2)   Company structure: a mandatory two-tier system?

In principle, the Houin and Würdinger Reports would leave each Member State broad discretion in determining the organizational scheme and the distribution of power within the stock company. The suggested text of a directive would not require the Members to define, in their laws, the division of functions between the administration and the shareholders' meeting,[45] but each Member would have to make sure that the shareholders' meeting possesses certain minimum powers, such as the power to decide on the appointment and recall of the board (or of the supervisory council in the two-tier system), the appointment of auditors, charter amendments, disposal of profits, waiver of claims against management, increase and reduction of capital.[46] Moreover, the authority of the shareholders' meeting could be extended by appropriate provisions in the charter.

In the same vein, the working group did not consider it possible to require the introduction of the supervisory council system as the *sole* organizational form, but it suggested that the Members should be obliged to introduce it "at least" as an *optional* alternative to the unitary single-tier system.[47] Yet as the negotiations unfolded, at least some expert observers became convinced that, with the sole exception of Italy, all Member States could be persuaded to introduce the two-tier system as the *exclusive* form.

No one can question that the problem of an effective supervision of management is related to the protection of shareholders. The German-type supervisory council, appointed by the shareholders, was conceived as one means for restoring shareholder control in a situation where proprietary interests had become separated from actual control, and such control devolved upon the management which in reality was responsible to no one.[48] Moreover, in the opinion of

---

45 *Würdinger Report (Versammlung)* at 27 ff.
46 *Id.* at 30.
47 *Houin Report I* at 4-5.
48 Vagts, *Reforming the "Modern" Corporation* at 48.

the working group, the supervisory council system, drawing a line as it does between the direction (management) of the enterprise and its supervision, has been "a legitimate success," and has responded to the practice of important companies.[49] We may recall in this context that, in German law and in the Belgian reform proposal, the supervisory council system represents the only form of the stock company; the Sanders draft statute for a European company[50] and the U.N.I.C.E. proposal for such a company would follow the same pattern. Nevertheless, the group did not wish to insist on its adoption as the only form, but was satisfied with an optional introduction "as a first step toward the ultimate, more complete coordination."[51] This, as we have seen, was the solution finally embodied in the French Law of 1966.

It is interesting to note that in Germany, where the supervisory council system in its present form has functioned since 1937 (although modified in 1965), the opinions on its effectiveness are by no means uniform. Some writers maintain the view—and the practice seems to confirm it—that the division between management and supervision is a difficult one to maintain. Effective supervision is possible only if the supervisory council becomes familiar with the details of the major operational decisions; but in that case, supervision ends in "co-management," which is bound to discourage the initiative of the executives. When the shareholding is closely concentrated, the big shareholders' representatives on the supervisory council tend to take over the active administration; and when it is widely scattered the management gains the upper hand, with the council rubber-stamping man-

---

[49] In practice, even the single-tier administrative council often confines itself to a supervisory role when it leaves almost all of the administering authority to the president-general manager.

[50] *See* p. 463 *infra.*

[51] The group noted that the Netherlands legislation was flexible enough to make it possible to provide *in the charter* for a system quite similar to the German pattern. *Houin Report I* at 4.

agement decisions.[52] One advantage of the supervisory council system—it is said—is that it precludes the election of the executive board members (*Vorstand*) by co-optation which, as the American experience has shown, may lead to abuse.[53] If vacancies on the executive board are filled by the supervisory council, an abuse could occur only as a result of collusion with the majority of the council, which is unlikely to materialize. Yet Vagts suggests that "[n]ew managers tend to be selected from within and, naturally, the present top managers know best who is ready for promotion. Eventually, the council comes to rely on the board even for suggestions as to filling vacancies on the council."[54]

In case of a potential conflict of interest, such as may arise from a contract with the company in which a member of the administration is directly or indirectly interested, the supervisory council performs a useful function as a forum for an impartial decision.[55] The alternative solutions in a unitary board system, that is, an approval by disinterested directors or by the shareholders' meeting, are not considered by some as equally effective, because the disinterested directors are exposed to the influence of their interested colleagues, and the shareholders' meeting is dominated by whoever assembles the proxies. Yet others feel, viewing the problem from the American perspective, that a disinterested quorum of outside directors can perform this and other functions as well as the supervisory council, "a cumbersome and expensive device," and even the advantages of an outside board

---

[52] Vagts, *Reforming the "Modern" Corporation* at 52, relying on WIETHÖLTER, INTERESSEN UND ORGANISATION DER AKTIENGESELLSCHAFT IM AMERIKANISCHEN UND DEUTSCHEN RECHT at 295-314 (Karlsruhe 1961). For a criticism see also MESTMÄCKER, VERWALTUNG at 83, 87-88.

[53] On the filling of the vacancies in the unitary board of directors see Sec. 38, MODEL BUS. CORP. ACT; *see also* Essex Universal Corp. v. Yates, 305 F.2d 572 (2d Cir. 1962).

[54] Vagts, *Reforming the "Modern" Corporation* at 52.

[55] On conflict of interest problems in American corporation law generally see LATTIN, JENNINGS & BUXBAUM, CORPORATIONS, CASES AND MATERIALS at 620 ff. (Chicago 1968).

are sharply contested by some American writers.[56] These widely divergent evaluations of the supervisory council are a telling illustration of the extreme difficulty encountered by those who seek to reach a realistic judgment on the effectiveness of a given corporate solution. Unless new methods of measurement and analysis are devised, the matter comes down to more or less subjective, if not visceral, reactions of corporate personnel.

Houin cautions that, on closer analysis, the French two-tier system differs from the corresponding German model, and such differences must be kept in mind when it comes to coordination. Thus, in contrast with German law, the shareholders' meeting in France retains its prerogatives, and the auditors *(commissaires aux comptes)* continue to function with all their powers and duties along with the supervisory council.[56a] Again, in contrast with the German practice of placing the company's executive employees on the executive board *(Vorstand)*, in France shareholders are often elected to the executive board *(directoire)*, and in that case the likelihood of conflict between the board and the supervisory council increases measurably. On the other hand, the theoretical differences between the old-line, single-tier, and the two-tier systems are often greatly reduced in practice. In the Federal Republic, as we have seen, the supervisory council at times assumes the direction of the company, so that the actual operation approaches the single-tier pattern. In France, on the other hand, the old-line, single-tier system often functions in reality as a two-tier system: the old-line administrative council, which according to the letter of the law is to direct the company, for all practical purposes acts as a supervisory council, with the president-general manager in effect exercising the powers comparable to those of the executive board in the two-tier system.

---

56 NEWCOMER, THE BIG BUSINESS EXECUTIVE; THE FACTORS THAT MADE HIM at 40 (New York 1955); Vagts, *Reforming the "Modern" Corporation* at 62.

56a *See* p. 119 *supra*.

(3) Company structure continued: division of jurisdiction

In line with the basic principle mentioned above, the jurisdictional delimitation between the administrative council and the president-general manager (or *administrateur délégué*) in the French-type "single-tier" system, and between the executive board and the supervisory council, is to be left to the discretion of the national lawmaker.[57] The reason given in support of this position is again that the matter relates essentially to internal organization and may remain within the national domain, without any serious inconvenience to the shareholders or third parties. This may have been considered a tenable position only because the First Directive has already decreed that, *against third parties,* the company may rely only on those restrictions upon the authority of the management which are defined in the law itself. More recently, however, the working group felt it necessary to propose an additional rule that would "complete" the First Directive on this point: The organ representing the company must be viewed as possessing all of the necessary powers to bind the company in transactions with a third party, subject only to the powers attributed by law to the shareholders' meeting; if the charter or even the law itself requires a prior decision or authorization of the transaction by the administrative or supervisory council, and if the company's representative acts in disregard of this requirement, the company is still considered bound as against a third party, acting in good faith. In the internal relationships within the company, of course, any additional restrictions upon the management would be given full effect, whether they are contained in the charter or in the law.

Logically, the First Directive should induce the national lawmaker to say in unmistakable terms which among the company's organs has the power to "represent" the company in its external relations *(e.g.,* the power to *conclude* a contract, even though the decision to enter into the contract may

[57] *Houin Report I* at 19-20.

be within the jurisdiction of another organ), and also to define clearly in the law itself the powers of the other organs (the shareholders' meeting, the supervisory council, etc.) which restrict the authority of the representative organ. The French and German delegations thought that it should be possible eventually to attempt drafting a coordinating rule which would specify the modalities for the designation of a company representative. The rapporteur did not undertake such an attempt, in view of the substantial differences among national legislations.[58]

The Houin Report suggests, with some hesitation since the matter is viewed again as one of internal structure, certain minimum arrangements for adoption by the national lawmaker in the "two-tier" States, designed to enable the supervisory council to exercise its supervisory function in an informed manner;[59] and a rule, proposed more recently, would require national legislations "in principle" to forbid the supervisory council to become involved in the direction or representation of the company.

The Houin Report also deals in some detail with the questions of conflict of interests and suggests that the di-

---

[58] As we have seen earlier in this book, the quality of a company "representative" is attributed to a collective body (Vorstand), or to individuals (president-general manager and general managers) in the French system employing the administrative council; to the president of the directoire and the general managers in the new French optional two-tier system; to the sole administrateur délégué or to several administrateurs délégués in Belgium, etc. In the rapporteur's view, the only text that could be possibly agreed upon at this time would read: "The laws of the Member States must identify with precision the person or persons who have the power to represent the company in relation to third parties." This text, however, was not considered to be of any use. Doc. 6752/XIV/C/68-F at 16-17.

[59] This includes receiving at least a quarterly report from the executive board, as well as the balance sheet and the statement of profit and loss, the authority of the supervisory council as a body (presumably not of individual members) to require special reports, and to inspect and verify the books and any documents at any time. *Houin Report II* at 20 ff. *See* § 90 of the German Law of 1965 and Art. 128 of the French Law of July 24, 1966.

rective should contain specified minimum protective provisions on that subject.[60]

(4)   Liability of company organs

The civil (tort) liability of the members of the management and supervisory organs would correspond to the
standards recognized in the Member States.[61] Of course, any
such liability is illusory if the law does not supply adequate
procedural remedies. Here we may note a significant difference between the laws of most Member States and the corporation laws in the United States. Although the laws in all of
the Six allow an action on behalf of the company if authorized by the competent company organ, the existing laws in
the Netherlands, Belgium and Luxembourg thus far do not
provide for any action upon demand by a minority of shareholders, not to speak of a derivative suit.[62] In the Federal
Republic and in Italy, a minority whose holding represents
at least ten percent of the capital may demand the institution
of an action for damages,[63] but since in practice this mini-

[60] Compensation of members of the administration or of the
supervisory council may not be fixed by their respective organs; contracts in which a member is personally interested must be approved
by the disinterested members of the administrative council or, in the
two-tier system, by the supervisory council (by the executive board
if a member of the supervisory council is involved). In addition, the
shareholders' meeting must be informed. *Houin Report II* at 6-18.

[61] Contravention of the law or of the charter, or failure to act as
an ordinarily prudent and conscientious person in the same position
would act. *Houin Report II* at 22. If authority is delegated, failure
to supervise entails liability. In order to ease the victim's burden
of proof, and also to encourage mutual control of the members of
an organ, the members of the collegiate organs would be held liable
jointly, but an individual member could escape liability if he is able
to show absence of any wrongdoing on his part (faute personnellement
imputable). *Id.* at 23-24.

[62] VAN RYN, 1 PRINCIPES DE DROIT COMMERCIAL at 396; *Houin Report II* at 25-26.

[63] § 147 of the German Law of 1965; Art. 2409 of the CODICE
CIVILE. But a derivative suit is allowed in German law in the case of
a dependent company. §§ 309, 310, 317, 318 of the Law of 1965. In
Italy, action may be instituted also by the public prosecutor.

mum prerequisite is difficult to meet and the minority bears all the legal expenses, the remedy is not very effective, at any rate in comparison with American law.[64] The French law alone provides a derivative suit by an individual shareholder or group of shareholders as a general remedy.[65]

The Report proposes to fill the gap in the shareholder protection by requiring the adoption not of the French, but of the German-Italian solution, leaving it to the discretion of each Member whether to introduce a derivative suit by one or several shareholders. Moreover, while the Houin Report would allow an action upon demand by a minority holding at least five percent, the Würdinger Report would raise this figure to ten percent.[66] Since this is a matter of a rather elementary protection, one might ask whether the proposed compromise solution represents sufficient progress. On the other hand, the text conforms to the principle that coordination should not be made at the level of the national rule providing for the *highest* degree of security.

The shareholders' meeting may decide not to pursue the claims for damages, but the directive would require minimum procedural safeguards and limitations in connection with such a decision. Again, the Member States would be required to make available an action for damages against company officers by creditors whose claims could not be satisfied from company funds; here the action appears to be in the nature of a derivative suit.[67]

---

[64] GROSSFELD, AKTIENGESELLSCHAFT at 211.

[65] Art. 245 of the Law of July 24, 1966.

[66] *Houin Report II* at 27; *Würdinger (Versammlung)* at 36. Subsequently, the working group suggested the ten percent figure, subject to certain qualifications. Doc. 6752/XIV/C/68-7, Art. 21.

[67] However, Member States would be free to allow a creditor an action in the amount of his individual claim, in which case the amount recovered would go directly to him. *Houin Report II* at 35. The "common law" of all Six allows individual action by a shareholder for "non-contractual" liability against company organs whose wrong ("faute") caused the plaintiff personal harm other than the harm suffered by the company. Although the modalities of this liability vary in the Member laws, it is not proposed to coordinate these provi-

(5) Shareholders' right to information and representation

In its first part, the Würdinger Report lists the minimum information that would have to be made available to the shareholders on a continuing basis, prior to the shareholders' meeting and in the course of that meeting.[68] The Member States would be free to fill in further details.

The practice concerning shareholder representation in shareholders' meetings differs widely from one Member State to the other: the banker's depositary vote in the Federal Republic; proxy-voting by the management in France, Belgium and Luxembourg; voting by banks or persons close to the management on the basis of blank powers in Italy; and voting by "trust companies" (*administratiekantoor*) in the Netherlands. The Report does not seek to "unify" the divergent patterns, but it limits itself to suggesting certain safeguards which the Member States would be required to enact. Thus, before he gives a proxy without voting instructions, the shareholder must be advised in what way the proxy-holder proposes to exercise the voting privilege. In addition, the authorization to vote must be limited in time and it must be revocable at any time, so as to avoid long-term separation of the shareholder from his voting right.[69] The Report follows the French and German law in prohibiting contracts re-

---

sions except for extending the joint liability rule to this situation and also to claims by creditors mentioned above. *Houin Report II* at 32-33. A subsequent draft indicates that no agreement has been reached thus far on the above subject.

[68] The "permanent" right to information would enable the shareholders at any time to receive data on the composition of the company's organs and the annual financial documents and business reports and the reports of the auditors for the last three years. Prior to the shareholders' meeting the shareholders must be given information and access to documents that would enable them to exercise their judgment. In the meeting the shareholders may pose questions relating to the items on the agenda. *Würdinger Report (Versammlung)* at 8 and 11. The shareholders would also have access to the lists of shareholders to check on the formal prerequisites for decision-making in the shareholders' meeting and to communicate with other shareholders. *Id.* at 13 ff.

[69] *Würdinger (Versammlung)* at 21.

garding the exercise of the voting right for the benefit of the management, as well as agreements to refrain from voting.[70] Voting trusts are not customary in the Member States, apart from the Netherlands *administratiekantoor*.

(6) Minority protection

The second principal topic of Würdinger's study deals with the protection of shareholder minorities. In addition to the right to demand an action for damages against the administration, which was mentioned earlier, a ten-percent shareholder minority would also be entitled to request court action. This latter action would be aimed at dismissing the auditors and appointing new or special auditors or, for a weighty reason, appointing a liquidator.[71] Würdinger would leave the Member States free to regulate minority protection in the voting process through quorum and majority requirements, except when it comes to charter amendments and basic changes such as fusion.[72]

The comprehensive fiduciary concept of the role of the majority in relation to a minority, as it was developed by English and American courts, is unknown in Continental company laws.[73] Instead, minority protection is grounded in "general clauses" or principles embodied in statutory or case law, such as the principles of equality of treatment and prohibition of misuse of the voting right for purposes alien to company interest. The minority is given the right to contest a decision which it considers harmful to its interests, on the ground that it was taken in violation of these principles. The Würdinger proposal would make these principles bind-

---

[70] *Cf.* § 136 of the German Law of 1965. For references to national laws see *Würdinger (Versammlung)* at 26, including reference to Art. 77 of the proposed Belgian reform law.

[71] *Würdinger Report (Versammlung)* at 37.

[72] *Id.* at 38.

[73] Lattin, *Equitable Limitations on Statutory or Charter Powers Given to Majority Stockholders*, 30 MICH. L. REV. 645 (1932).

ing in all Member States.[74] On the other hand, the proposal
would not accept the rule, observed in several Member
States, that *any* conflict between company and individual
interests necessarily entails a suspension of the voting right.[75]

(7) The auditors

Considering the importance of the subject, it is not surprising that an extensive portion of the Houin Report is
devoted to the position of auditors.[76] The functions of the
auditors are defined differently in the several legal systems,
depending upon the structure of the company, and this
divergence has made coordination in this area difficult.[77]
According to the law prevailing in the "single-tier" countries,
the auditors are not limited simply to a verification of annual
accounts; *in theory,* at any rate, they are to function on behalf
of the shareholders as an independent organ, charged with
the task of supervising all the accounting aspects of the administration, and in some instances even the legality of the
administration's conduct (in Belgium, Luxembourg, Italy
and in France).[78] In the two-tier system, there is no need for

---

[74] § 243 of the German Law of 1965; also the Belgian reform
proposal; CARTERON, *L'abus du droit et le détournement de pouvoir
dans les assemblées générales des sociétés anonymes,* 1964 REVUE DES
SOCIÉTÉS 161; WILLEBRANDT, DIE VERFASSUNG DER NAAMLOZE VENNOOT-
SCHAP IM NIEDERLÄNDISCHEN RECHT at 47-48 (Münster/Westf. 1965).

[75] Art. 2373 of the Italian CODICE CIVILE; *Würdinger (Versammlung)* at 22. According to the proposal, suspension from the voting
right would come into play only when the shareholders' meeting votes
on releasing the administration from the duty to institute action
against its members, or on a release from a claim for damages; in these
circumstances the shareholder concerned would have to refrain from
voting. However, more recently, the working group considering this
matter reportedly went further and agreed that a member of the administration should be required to refrain from voting on any question when there was conflict of interest between him and the company.
See also § 136, German Law of 1965; Art. 44c of the WETBOEK VAN
KOOPHANDEL; *Würdinger (Versammlung)* at 24.

[76] *Houin Report II* at 36-65.

[77] *Houin Report II* at 37 ff.

[78] I am advised by Prof. Heenen that in Belgium the auditors
have never really exercised their function of supervising the administra-

such extensive definition of the function of the auditors, in view of the existence of a separate supervisory organ. The supervisory council in the Federal Republic, in France (under the new law), in Belgium (under the proposed reform) and in the Netherlands (under the scheme proposed by the Social and Economic Council), is expected to perform the general role of surveillance of the administration—and so are the *"commissarissen"* under the present Netherlands law in those companies which adopt this institution. In that setting, one would expect the auditors to act merely as accounting technicians in support of the supervisory organ.[79] Another problem is posed by the fact that in certain Member States (Belgium, Italy and, in practice, the Netherlands) the auditors' position differs with respect to different categories of stock companies.[80]

The Report notes that the laws in five Member States already require the appointment of auditors; in the Netherlands the matter is dealt with in the charter or by the shareholders' meeting, and apparently all the "open" companies in fact do appoint an "accountant." The Report would require all Member States to prescribe that *all* stock companies must designate at least one auditor (*"commissaire aux comptes"*) with certain specified minimum attributes. The proposed specifications are intended to assure an independent and realistic verification.[81]

---

tion, and that the same situation may prevail in practice in the other Member States mentioned above, regardless of what the law provides.

[79] Houin advises that in the new optional two-tier system in France, the commissaires aux comptes have nevertheless retained their original broad function, and the resulting "duality of supervisory organs" may cause difficulties in practice.

[80] *Houin Report II* at 37-38. According to the Belgian reform law, auditors will perform the same function in *all* stock companies and will have to possess the same qualifications.

[81] The auditor's office is to be made incompatible with positions on the company's administrative and supervisory councils; certain minimum procedural rules are laid down for his appointment which would be for a term of not less than three years, with no possibility of recall without an important reason. In order to avoid conflicts of

The proposal in the Report does not attempt to set uniform standards for professional training, although this would be important from the viewpoint of assuring high quality of performance.[82] It relies for that purpose on national professional organizations. However, the proposal would require that at least one of the auditors be chosen from among the members of such organizations which set appropriate qualifications as a condition for membership. This is actually the state of the law in France, the Federal Republic, Belgium (for publicly held companies), Italy, and it is the practice in the Netherlands.[83] A more advanced draft, that has evolved from the Report, would extend the requirement of membership in a professional organization to *all* auditors.

Apparently it has never been suggested that the working group should write a uniform definition of the tasks of the auditors. If nothing else, the divergence of the functions adumbrated above would make it quite difficult. However, the proposed text would fix the *minimum* function of the auditors, which is to consist of verifying the regularity and honesty of the accounting for each business year, particularly in the balance sheet, the profit-and-loss statement and the annual report, and of certifying that the accounts correspond to the legal prescriptions and reflect truthfully the company's situation. In order to enable the auditors to fulfill their mission, the proposal would assure them of an extensive and continuing power of inquiry, extending to both parent and subsidiary companies. The auditors are to submit a report to the shareholders' meeting, and the annual accounts would be invalid if the rules concerning the audit were not observed.

---

interest an auditor would not be allowed to receive his compensation in the form of a participation in company profits, nor could he obtain a loan from company funds. *Houin Report II* at 38-47.

[82] *But see* EEC Art. 57.

[83] *Houin Report II* at 40-41. See on this von Caemmerer, in EuropÄische Handelsgesellschaft at 75. *See also* p. 362 *infra*.

(iii)   Würdinger Reports on dependent and related enterprises[84]

The Commission's effort to coordinate the provisions concerning the protection of shareholders and third parties might appear incomplete if it did not include the problem of dependent and otherwise related enterprises. At the core of the problem is the question whether a company, that holds a dominant power over another company, may use it to issue instructions to the latter, or even to subject it to unified economic direction. With the sole exception of the Federal Republic, which has a comprehensive system of statutory rules in this area, the laws of the Member States regulate only certain isolated aspects, such as the limitation on reciprocal participation, prohibition of the acquisition of the parent company's stock, and the requirement of consolidated financial documents. The German law, it will be recalled, allows the exercise of dominant power in the above sense pursuant only to an "agreement between enterprises." Such agreement must be approved by the shareholders' meeting of the dependent company and must provide for creditor and minority-shareholder protection through the right of withdrawal, guaranteed dividends, and obligation to assume any resulting loss.[85] Historically, the rules on "agreements between enterprises" derive from German tax legislation which has dealt with the enterprises tied together by such "integration agreements" *(Organschafts-* or *Gewinnabführungsvertrag)* as a unit, and has taxed the profits of the controlled companies only at the level of the controlling company, together with the latter's own profits.[86]

Because of insufficient practical experience, it has been impossible to evaluate the impact and utility of the rules enacted in the Federal Republic in 1965. It may be that the extremely detailed statutory regulation will prove much too

---

[84] *Würdinger Report (soc. liées); Würdinger Report (groupes).*

[85] §§ 291-310 of the German Stock Company Law of 1965, particularly §§ 302, 304, 305, 308. *See also* § 311. *See* p. 105 *supra.*

[86] *Würdinger,* Aktien- und Konzernrecht at 298.

rigid and confining, and that experience will counsel leaving a broader scope to the creative role of the courts. At any rate, Würdinger does not propose a wholesale adoption of this youthful legislation throughout the Community. Instead he uses it as an example and as a basis for his discussion of the general problem. As yet, the preparatory work in this field has not reached the stage when specific texts are drafted, and it is therefore quite uncertain what the ultimate tenor of the directive will be. However, the Commission's staff and consultants have been preparing a set of rules in this area to govern the proposed European Company.

(iv) Miccio Report on securities[87]

Professor Miccio's Report on the issue of securities of stock companies and limited partnerships with shares is the last document which remains to be mentioned in this sketch of activities in the working group on company law under Article 54, par. 3(g).

The Report deals with both shares and bonds, and it proposes, in accordance with the practice prevailing in five of the six Member States, that companies should be free to issue these securities either in bearer or in registered form.[88] Only Italy excludes bearer shares, and this divergence has already proved to be an obstacle in the elaboration of the plan for a European company.[89]

---

[87] *Miccio Report I* and *II, supra* note 40. Dott. Renato Miccio has been in the judicial branch since 1939, having reached the rank of Consigliere di cassazione. At the present time he is on detached service with the Ministry of Justice as vice-head of the legislative office. Throughout his judicial career he has maintained a close connection with the University of Rome, first as an assistant and since 1958 as "libero docente" (lecturer) in commercial law at the Law Faculty. He is the author of a two-volume commentary on the Civil Code and of several other books and some fifty articles in the field of civil and commercial law. Since 1966, he has been special consultant on company law to the EEC Commission.

[88] *Miccio Report I* at 26.

[89] *See* p. 462 *infra*.

(1) Issuance of shares

One question which the Report leaves unresolved is whether companies should be allowed to issue no-par value shares which exist in Belgium and Luxembourg, but are not authorized in French, German and Italian law. The rapporteur doubts that shares without a par value offer sufficient protection for creditors and shareholders, and he sees the danger of this American invention not so much in connection with the first issue, but rather at the occasion of subsequent issues of such shares. Leaving aside the differences between American and European concepts of no-par value shares, the fact is that American experience does not confirm these fears with regard to either the shareholders or the creditors.[90] Even though he admits that the European experience with this type of share is much too limited to permit a final judgment, the rapporteur would prefer to see them eliminated: the diversity of the systems would breach the uniformity of "the guarantees." Nevertheless, he suggests alternative texts from which the working group can choose.

In contrast with the corporation laws in the United States, full discretion would not be allowed in the setting of the par value; this is to avoid excessive fragmentation of stock which could lead to the control of the company by the manage-

---

[90] If the existing shareholders have the pre-emptive right to subscribe to the new shares they will not be hurt if the issue price is set below the real value; if the issue to outsiders or insiders is made on other than a pro rata basis the existing shareholders will have a claim for damages, if their participation is diluted as a result of an unduly low issue price of the new shares. BAKER-CARY, CORPORATIONS at 864 ff.; see also LUTTER, KAPITAL at 160, 400.

In case of a no-par value stock issue, the total of monetary and other contributions constitutes the guarantee amount, while in the case of a par value stock issue the guarantee amount is the total of the par values of the stock. There can be no payment of dividends if the guarantee amount were to be impaired.

In Belgium and Luxembourg, the issue of no-par value shares below the value expressed by the fraction of the stated capital is prohibited. In case of a subsequent issue based on an increase of capital, the protection of holders of no-par value shares is not inferior to the protection of those with par value shares.

ment.[91] Thus the Report would set the minimum par value at 100 units of account (dollars). One may wonder whether this amount is not much too high so as to impair trading in the shares and the possibility of broad acquisition by the public.

The draft contemplates various kinds of shares—preferred and common stock.[92] Preferred stock would give preference as regards dividend payments and liquidation. The voting right of the preferred shareholders may be limited in the charter to special shareholders' meetings, but the total of nonvoting preferred stock must not exceed one-half of the capital, in order to avoid power imbalance within the company. However, multiple voting shares would be prohibited in principle, except for a limited time period when an issue of such shares is necessary for the defense of the company's interests, for instance against a take-over bid by another company.

The rapporteur suggests that the founders should receive as compensation for their services not shares but special *certificats de jouissance* which would entitle them to participate in the company's profits but not in its capital.[93] The same form of compensation would be available to shareholders whose shares are called in as a result of a reduction of the capital or amortization.[94]

A logical consequence of the principle of capital maintenance is the prohibition of the issue of shares without consideration, except when capital is increased through transformation of free reserves into stated capital. In that case, new shares must be issued to all shareholders in proportion to their current holdings.[95] Although the rapporteur doubts the wisdom of including in the directive a provision on turn-

---

[91] *Miccio Report I* at 24, 27.

[92] *Id.* at 29 ff., 39 ff.

[93] *Miccio Report I* at 51 ff., 57.

[94] *Id.* at 72 ff., 77. *Cf.* actions de jouissance in Art. 210 of the French Law of July 24, 1966.

[95] *Id.* at 78-80.

ing company employees into shareholders, he nevertheless suggests what he thinks might be an appropriate text: when new stock is issued, one-fourth is to be reserved for the company's employees who could acquire it at nominal value, but could not sell it to outsiders; moreover, the company could distribute its shares gratuitously to the employees.[96]

Of some interest are the rapporteur's suggestions regarding the conditions for admission of stock companies to a stock exchange, although some might object that a directive on this subject would not fall within the scope of Article 54, par. 3(g).[97] Only companies with a minimum capital of one million units of account (dollars) and a record of profits during a "probation period" of three business years should be eligible. "The highest economic authority of the State" is to decide on the admission, after consultation with the local chamber of commerce. The reference to the "highest economic authority," presumably the Ministry of Economic Affairs, may raise questions in a federally structured state such as the Federal Republic of Germany. The admission to a stock exchange would entail a continuing obligation to report on the developments in the company so as to keep the market informed. This obligation, which goes beyond the filing of annual financial documents and also exceeds the "publicity" requirements of the First Directive, would apply also to other publicly held companies, not listed on a stock exchange.

(2) Issue of bonds

Bonds may be issued—according to the second part of the Report—upon approval by the shareholders' meeting, up to the amount of the paid-in capital only. This limitation is difficult to understand, since a company with a small paid-in capital may have substantial reserves, while another company with a large paid-in capital may be swamped with debts. This limitation would not apply to loans guaranteed by the

---

[96] *Id.* at 81-82.
[97] *Id.* at 88 ff.

state or secured by property; but in the latter case, no more than two-thirds of the company's real estate could be employed as security.[98]

An offer of a subscription must be accompanied by a prospectus indicating the amount of the issue, the par value of the individual paper, and the modalities of repayment and security. On the other hand, no data regarding the financial situation appear to be required in the prospectus, even though such information is essential for the investor.[99] I should mention in this context that a special working group has been preparing a uniform outline of a prospectus to be issued by companies which make public offerings of securities. Although in the Member States national rules on this subject are contained generally in special regulations concerning trading in securities, in the Italian reform law, at any rate, these rules would appear as a part of company law provisions. An argument could possibly be made that the subject does fall within the scope of coordination of company laws.

The Miccio Report would limit the possibility of a capital reduction during the lifetime of a bond issue, and in this instance also one may question the wisdom of this limitation. Fusion would be possible only if the resulting company is a stock company or a limited partnership with shares, because other companies are not permitted to issue bonds. Convertible bonds could be issued if authorized capital in the amount of the issue is available, or provision is made for a capital increase at the time of conversion. However, there appears to be no rule on the rate of conversion, which would protect other shareholders against the dilution of their participation in the absence of a pre-emptive right.[100]

The bondholders are to organize a collective organ whose task it is to protect the bondholders' rights as against the

---

[98] *Miccio Report II* at 8 ff.

[99] *Id.* at 32. The prospectus must be published in a journal for official notices.

[100] But issue of convertible bonds below the par value of the shares would be prohibited.

company.[101] Such an organ exists already in all of the Member States, but the scope of its authority varies. The meeting of bondholders may appoint a common representative to whom it would entrust the prosecution of its rights. The possibility of collective assertion does not exclude individual right of action, unless otherwise decided by the meeting.

(v) Summary and conclusions

The Reports discussed in this section constitute the final contribution to the preparatory work needed for the coordination of stock company legislation. Not all of these reports contain actual drafts of directives. They all reflect strongly the personal inclinations of the authors, and only in a limited part the tentative attitudes of the experts in the working group. This factor of personal predilection explains what one may consider a stronger propensity toward a more detailed regulation on the part of Miccio as compared with Houin and Würdinger. The major job of drafting and negotiation —and the rest of the complex process illustrated in connection with the First Directive—must be completed before the proposals mature into Community law. It would thus be entirely premature to seek to divine the eventual content of that law from these preliminary works. Although only the overall contours are visible, one thing appears certain: even if the coordination is completed according to the present plan, no uniform stock company law will emerge as a phoenix from the ashes. For reasons mentioned earlier, a directive does not seem to be the best instrument for unification, and, in the present state of the Community, the coordination process does not provide a sufficiently safe legal and political basis for shaping a uniform régime for a modern stock company. It may well be that uniformity is not essential and that coordination in the Treaty sense would suffice. But even coordination may require more broadly based processes than are presently available in the Community framework, when it comes to rules expressing the relationship between

---

[101] *Id.* at 51 ff., 68.

capital and labor within a company or the incidence of
public interest.

2. Proposed Directive on Annual Financial Documents of Stock Companies

(a) A "private" study group

We have observed earlier in this study that the impact of
the "publicity" rules in the First Directive and of a goodly
number of the proposed coordinating rules will depend
largely on assuring that the content of financial documents
of companies be meaningful and comparable. The Commission, relying again on Article 54, par. 3(g) of the Treaty, entrusted the elaboration of a preliminary draft of a directive
on this subject to "a study group," formed by national organizations of auditors and accountants under the chairmanship
of the President of the Institute of Auditors (*Institut der
Wirtschaftsprüfer in Deutschland e. V.*) in Düsseldorf, Dr.
Elmendorf.[102] The group submitted a preliminary proposal
(*Vorentwurf*) to the Commission in 1968,[103] and promised a
follow-up text on financial documents of related enterprises
(*Konzern*) at a later date. The legal status of the proposal is
ambiguous, since it was prepared by a group of private individuals rather than by the customary working group of government appointed experts. A working group organized by

---

[102] The group was composed of the members of the following
organizations, in addition to the *Institut der Wirtschaftsprüfer:* Bel-
gium, Collège National des Experts Comptables de Belgique; France,
Ordre des Experts Comptables et des Comptables Agréés, Institut Fran-
çais des Experts Comptables; Netherlands, Nederlands Instituut van
Registeraccountants; Italy, Ordine dei Ragionieri, Ordine dei Dottori
Commercialisti. An official of the Directorate for Establishment and
Services of the Commission also participated in the group.

[103] Kommission der Europäischen Gemeinschaften, Direktion
Niederlassungsrecht und Dienstleistungsverkehr, Rechtsangleichung,
Steuerfragen, Dok. 2800/IV/2/68-D, Brussels 1968, Gliederung des
Jahresabschlusses und Bewertung, Inhalt des Anhangs und des
Lageberichts, Prüfung des Jahresabschlusses durch den Abschluss-
prüfer sowie die Veröffentlichung des Jahresabschlusses.

the Commission has been considering the text with Dr. Elmendorf acting as a special advisor.

(b)   Scope of application of the directive

The planned directive is to apply in principle to stock companies only and not to limited liability companies. According to the First Directive, the financial disclosure obligation of limited liability companies was not to come into effect until after the coordination of the rules governing their financial documents. It appears that such coordination will not be undertaken until after the work in this field regarding the stock companies is completed. It is therefore likely that any financial disclosure obligation of limited liability companies will be delayed further, despite the peremptory two-year deadline prescribed in the First Directive.[104]

The proposal leaves it to the Commission to decide which categories of stock companies will be exempted from specified provisions of the directive. Family-owned and smaller-size enterprises are to benefit primarily from the exemption although the present, obviously tentative, broad formulation would also allow exemptions regardless of size. Presumably the Commission will see to it that the exemption clause is formulated in more precise terms. Enterprises such as banks and insurance companies, which require different methods for the preparation of financial documents, were not considered to fall within the scope of the study group. They will be dealt with separately.

(c)   The content of the directive

(i)   General observations

Reflecting the Commission's general philosophy on co-ordination under Article 54, par. 3(g), the study group did

---

[104] *See* p. 233 *supra*. The Commission is likely to delay final action on the proposal concerning financial documents of stock companies until a parallel proposal for the documents of limited liability companies is elaborated.

not feel that it should develop "fundamentally new, per-haps improved rules"; on the contrary, it viewed its task as being to determine to what extent the rules in the national laws and the legislative reform proposals and practices in the Member States could be "made uniform," with due regard to "internationally recognized standards." It is evident from the text of the proposal, that German and French law exerted considerable influence. The group made a studied effort to stay clear of questions of economic policy and general com-pany law.

In order to facilitate adjustment to new knowledge, con-ditions, and methods, deviations from the rules set forth in the directive are permitted, as long as the principles of proper and reliable accounting underlying the proposal are ob-served. Moreover, the directive is conceived as a minimum regulation and does not preclude inclusion of added content, either on a voluntary basis or in response to national laws.

(ii)   The extent of the obligation to report

The proposed text requires the preparation of a balance sheet, a profit-and-loss statement, and an explanatory report (an "annex" and a "situation report"). The purpose of the annex is to elucidate individual items in the documents, to indicate the valuation methods employed, including changes in such methods from those used in the preceding year, and generally to provide data that does not appear in the balance sheet or the profit-and-loss statement. The "situation report" should serve to deepen the insight into the financial situation of the company. For that purpose it must contain the ad-ministration's overall economic appraisal of the company's position (*Lagebericht*) and significant occurrences that took place after the closing date of the business year.

(iii)   The balance sheet and the profit-and-loss statement

The formal arrangement of the balance sheet relies heavily on the French balance sheet format which was first developed for balance sheets for tax purposes, but later was made compulsory also for balance sheets prepared for business purposes by large listed companies.[105]

In the interest of clarity, the proposal limits considerably the freedom to consolidate individual balance sheet positions. Insofar as such consolidation is allowed, separate explanatory information is to be included in the "Annex." Apparently this approach represents an attempt to accommodate those Member States which permit the practice of extensive consolidation of balance sheet positions, particularly the Benelux countries, and to a lesser extent Italy.

The form and order of the balance sheet are determined by the goal of providing the best possible insight into the financial structure and liquidity of an enterprise. The debit side must contain a detailed statement of the company's capital, reserves, and debts, while the credit side must show in detail intangible assets, fixed assets and investments as well as current assets (fixed and current assets have each a total of 15 separate items). The individual items are circumscribed by explanatory definitions so as to reduce the possibility of using them as repositories for hidden reserves.

In order to facilitate a check on the liquidity of an enterprise, accounts receivable and payable must be grouped according to their maturity date (up to one year, more than one year). This requirement is an improvement over the German

---

[105] On the Federal Republic see *supra* p. 245; on France *supra* p. 255. On accounting rules and profession generally see American Institute of Certified Public Accountants, Committee on International Relations, PROFESSIONAL ACCOUNTING IN 25 COUNTRIES (New York 1964); France, ch. 12; Germany, ch. 13; Italy, ch. 15; Netherlands, ch. 18. See further MUELLER, ACCOUNTING PRACTICES IN WEST GERMANY (Seattle 1964); MUELLER, INTERNATIONAL ACCOUNTING (New York, London 1967); Pavlock, A Comparison of Periodic Income Reporting Among the United States, West Germany, The Netherlands and Sweden (Ann Arbor, unpublished paper in the University of Michigan, School of Business Administration Library, 1965); Goodstein, *Comparative Accounting Concepts: A Tower of Babel*, 4 INT. LAWYER 295 (1970); Mueller, *Accounting Principles Generally Accepted in the United States Versus Those Generally Accepted Elsewhere*, 3 INT. J. OF ACCOUNTING 91 (No. 2, 1968).

law which differentiates long term from short term debts
on the basis of a maturity of four years. Insofar as debts are
covered by security they likewise must be shown separately.
In contrast with the usual practice in the United States, the
list of items does not begin with the most easily liquidated
forms of current assets (cash) but follows instead the order of
increasing liquidity so that the most easily liquidated assets
appear at the end.

In terms of economic policy, it is of some significance that
the proposal would require the disclosure of economic ties
with other enterprises and of the results of transactions with
them, although the disclosure obligation is not as far-reaching as that prescribed in American securities regulations.[106]
Separate information must be included regarding holdings
of securities and other investments in affiliated ("related")
enterprises, participation in "controlling" or "controlled"
companies, as well as claims by or against them. However,
the elaboration of a definition of the concept "related enterprises" is left to the working group on coordination of company laws. Similarly, the proposal fails to provide for a
consolidated balance sheet, presumably because a separate
exploration of accounting rules for groups of affiliated companies will be necessary before coordination of national rules
on this subject is attempted. Since the asset and earnings position of a subsidiary depends on the position of other subsidiaries and of the parent company, a reliable evaluation
can only be made on the basis of consolidated financial documents of the entire group.[107]

Inter-company comparisons would be improved if the
directive limited discretion in the manner of reporting depreciation taken on fixed assets. Currently, in most of the
Member States (France is an exception) the propriety of de-

---

[106] Regulation S-X, 17 CFR 210.3-19, par. b, and 210.5-02, paras.
9-12, 25.

[107] On consolidated financial statements see generally Swoboda,
*Comparison of Consolidated Financial Statements in the United States
and West Germany,* 1 INT. J. OF ACCOUNTING 9 (No. 2, 1966).

preciation cannot be readily judged on reading the balance sheet. For, in these countries, original costs are not shown, but only current book values less the depreciation taken during the accounting period. Where original costs of fixed asset items are indicated, it is customary to summarize the depreciation in one or two positions on the debit side (value adjustments). This method, however, does not make it possible to compute the remaining book values of the individual fixed asset items. The proposed directive does require separate disclosure of value adjustments for fixed and current assets, but the classification appears too rough to satisfy the requirement of the best possible insight into the asset and earnings position of the company. Moreover, the envisaged profit-and-loss statement does not require further classification of the depreciation according to individual items.

The rules governing the profit-and-loss statement proceed from the "gross" principle *(Bruttoprinzip)*, which requires disclosure of gross income and prohibits the consolidation of revenue and expenses. The principle prevails in France and in the Federal Republic. In Italy and the Benelux countries, on the other hand, the profit-and-loss statement is made on a "net" basis with numerous consolidations, mainly because of the fear that competitors might gain insight into the cost structure of the enterprise, if the "gross" principle were followed. Yet this fear appears unfounded, since even the French and German statements of the typical modern, multi-product enterprise have limited informative value for this purpose, unless they include a breakdown of sales and earnings by product groups.

The proposal offers an enterprise a choice between two different formats of profit-and-loss statements. The study group took the view that this range of discretion is justified in view of Article 54, par. 3(g), because the alternate procedures lead to the same end result and offer equivalent information with respect to important items. Nevertheless, some may question whether the coexistence of both forms is consistent with the goal of assuring the comparability of financial documents. The requirement for reporting depreciation in the profit-and-loss statement has been mentioned earlier.

(iv) Valuation rules

At this juncture, the differences in national valuation rules constitute a principal obstacle to meaningful international comparison of financial documents. The charge has been made primarily in American quarters that, as a rule, documents of European companies conceal hidden reserves,[108] and that the publicly reported profit has no relation to the true income position of the company. Such a broad charge can hardly be sustained against the Federal Republic and France after the adoption of the national reforms of 1965 and 1966.[109] It is, of course, a fact that hidden reserves continue to exist. They are produced by the depreciation of fixed assets far below their actual value, and by currency devaluation, if the assets are not appropriately revalued.[110] However, in the two countries mentioned, the creation of hidden reserves through deliberate undervaluation is now prohibited.[111] The objective of the proposed directive in this regard is to raise the valuation rules of all Member States to the level of French and German law. Thus the proposed valuation rules set not only maximum but also minimum values.

---

[108] Bookman, *An Accent on Foreign Stocks,* 66 FORTUNE 148, at 150 (July 1962).

[109] Robert Ball, *The Declining Art of Concealing the Figures,* 76 FORTUNE 136 (Sept. 15, 1967). *See also, generally,* Niehus, *Stock Corporation Law Reform in Germany and the Public Accountant,* 1 INT. J. OF ACCOUNTING 25 (No. 2, 1966).

[110] The purpose of a "revaluation" of assets is an adjustment for the loss of value of national currency through inflation. Revaluation in this sense is not permitted in the Federal Republic. In France revaluation was made obligatory in enterprises with a turnover exceeding 500 million old francs by Law No. 59-1472 of Oct. 28, 1959, as amended by Law No. 61-825 of July 29, 1961; for other companies it was made optional. *See* Garnier, *Théorie des bénéfices et des pertes,* JUR.-CL. SOCIÉTÉS, fasc. 18-3 (1967).

[111] *See* p. 246 *supra.*

As in the United States, the principle of consistency is assigned special importance in the proposal. Accordingly, the draft requires that accounting principles once employed should continue to be employed, and any change must be explained in the "Annex." Again, pursuant to the principle of prudent valuation, the proposed directive prescribes that unrealized losses must be shown, but it does not authorize taking into account unrealized profits.

In principle, fixed assets are to be valued according to their original or historic costs, current assets according to their original cost or fair market value, whichever is lower, while any of the customary methods[112] may be chosen for valuation of inventory. The Member States, however, would have the power to authorize deviating valuation rules, provided that such rules are compatible with basic principles of proper and reliable accounting; the differences resulting from the deviations must be explained in the "Annex." The requirement of compatibility with basic principles, which is to limit this power of the Member States, appears of little value, and the deviating rules will lead to different results, depending on whether the financial documents are to serve primarily the interests of creditors, shareholders, investors, or the public at large. Apparently the purpose of this power to issue deviating rules is again to take account of the divergent concepts prevailing in the Member States.

The draft directive leaves the method of depreciation up to the individual enterprise. It requires only that the chosen method follow a definitive and meaningful plan, so as to prevent an arbitrary determination of the depreciation rate. Although the depreciation method, employed in the elaboration of the balance sheet for business purposes, is independent of the method prescribed by tax law for the preparation of the tax balance sheet, the latter method often influences the choice of the former. Since at the present time,

---

[112] Fifo (first-in, first-out), lifo (last-in, first-out) and "average cost." *See* Döllerer, RECHNUNGSLEGUNG at 1412; and FINNEY & MILLER, PRINCIPLES OF ACCOUNTING 192-94 (New Jersey 1963).

at any rate, the rules governing the tax balance sheet are not included in the coordination effort, differences among these rules will continue to have a disfunctional impact on harmonization work relating to financial documents for business purposes.

(v) Verification through auditors

To be effective, an obligation to supply information requires assurance of some verification. Consequently, the proposal provides for an audit of the accounts by independent auditors to be elected by the shareholders' meeting, and it defines their most important duties. The auditors must meet the qualifications required by the Member State where the enterprise has its "seat";[113] but a coordination of the national rules governing these qualifications has not been attempted in this context, presumably because it will be undertaken in a separate directive on the basis of a different Treaty provision.[114] Nor did the group take a position on the question of *which* enterprises must submit to an obligatory audit, a question on which laws of the Member States differ, and which the group considered "predominantly a matter of economic policy." As we have seen, however, a directive on this subject is in the process of elaboration on the basis of the Houin Report. It will require all stock companies and limited partnerships with shares (except the Dutch close companies exempted from financial disclosure by the First Directive) to designate at least one "independent natural or legal person" as auditor.[115]

---

113 On the concept of "seat" see *supra* p. 28. On the European accounting profession generally see Treffers, *The Changing Nature of the European Accounting Profession,* 3 INT. J. OF ACCOUNTING 43 (No. 1, 1967).

114 EEC Art. 57, in the chapter on the right of establishment, provides for "directives regarding mutual recognition of diplomas, certificates, and other evidence of qualifications," and also for coordination by directives of legislative and administrative provisions "concerning access to and engagement in non-wage-earning activities."

115 Doc. 6752/XIV/C/68-F at 32. *See* p. 346 *supra.*

(d) Summary and concluding observations

There is little doubt that this proposal is a significant component of the coordination effort concerning companies. In fact, the success of a substantial portion of that effort depends on the realization of the objectives of the proposal. Yet the draft is limited in scope. In the first place, it applies only to stock companies. In its present form it does not extend to consolidated financial statements of corporate groupings although "without consolidated balance sheets, net figures are meaningless."[116] Again, the proposal deals with rules concerning financial documents prepared for business purposes only, and does not purport to treat rules governing documents compiled for tax purposes. Because of the important interaction between the two sets of rules, simultaneous coordination may have been worthy of consideration, although admittedly very difficult. Finally, there is an evident connection between the rules on financial documents and those governing the maintenance of capital and the allocation of competence among the company's organs with respect to disposition of earnings.[117] These latter rules, how-

---

[116] Claudio Segré quoted in Robert Ball, *The Declining Art of Concealing the Figures*, 76 FORTUNE 136, at 137 (Sept. 15, 1967).

[117] In the Member States, with the exception of the Federal Republic, it is in principle the shareholders' meeting that decides on the distribution of earnings. Thus the management will be inclined to employ valuation rules for the purpose of reducing the amount available for distribution by decision of the shareholders. This can be done, if the valuation rules permit deviations from the original or historic cost principle. Hence the desire to preserve the possibility of deviating rules which will continue to make comparability difficult.

The disposition of earnings is regulated by the following provisions: Federal Republic: according to § 58, par. 2 of the Stock Company Law of 1965, the executive board (Vorstand) has the authority to allocate up to 50% of the net annual earnings to reserves, the shareholders' meeting decides on the remaining earnings (§ 174) and under § 58, par. 3, it may form additional reserves; France: according to Art. 347 of the Law of July 24, 1966, the shareholders' meeting determines the reserves and dividends, but the charter may transfer the authority to build reserves to the administration. Dalsace, MANUEL DES SOCIÉTÉS ANONYMES No. 194, at 193 ff. (4th ed., Paris 1967). In Italy, Belgium and the Netherlands, the shareholders' meeting decides on the allocation of earnings (Art. 2433 Codice civile, Art. 80 of the

ever, have not been dealt with within the framework of this proposal, because the question of capital maintenance and the general problem of company organization fell within the terms of reference of another working group.[118]

If the proposed draft is adopted substantially in its present form it will be interesting to observe, considering the exceptions, dispensations and options among the various reporting systems, whether the directive will in fact achieve its purpose, that is, a meaningful comparability of financial documents of companies organized in different Member States. Much will depend also upon the attitude and activities of the accounting profession and its national organizations.[119]

3. Merger of companies[120]

(a) Concentration as an objective of economic policy: the "American challenge"

Assimilation of the laws on mergers raises problems of economic and social policy that are, if anything, more perva-

---

Belgian Code de commerce, Art. 42d Wetboek van Koophandel, respectively), but the creation of reserves may be provided in the charter. *See also* VAN OMMESLAGHE, LE RÉGIME at 132 (Belgium), 222 (Italy), and 245 (Netherlands).

In the United States, the board decides on the payment of dividends. *See, e.g.,* Sec. 170 of the Delaware General Corporation Law, DEL. CODE ANN. Title 8 (1968); Sec. 45 of the MODEL BUS. CORP. ACT. Sec. 70 of the MODEL BUS. CORP. ACT contemplates the possibility of open reserves, but they are not required unconditionally, since the board passes upon the payment of dividends.

[118] *See* p. 41 *supra.*

[119] *See generally* Niehus, *Generally Accepted Auditing Principles in Germany,* 4 INT. J. OF ACCOUNTING 113 (No. 2, 1969); Treffers, *The Changing Nature of the European Accounting Profession,* 3 INT. J. OF ACCOUNTING 43 (No. 1, 1967).

[120] The term "merger" is used here to connote any arrangement by which the businesses formerly conducted by two or more companies become the business of a single company. Prof. Conard points out that American lawyers more often use "reorganization" in this generic sense. For an enlightening analysis of this general area from an American viewpoint see Conard, *Corporate Fusion.* The article does not take into account fully the modifications of the French law in and after 1966.

sive than those involved in the regulation of financial disclosure. Since the mid-sixties, if not earlier, the policy in the Common Market on the national and transnational levels has been to encourage cooperation through agreements among enterprises (presumably within the limits of the laws against restrictive practices) and concentration through holdings and mergers (within the limits of the rules against the abuse of dominant power).[121] The assumption has been that concentration would advance specialization, mass production and higher productivity; provide capital for new investments and research; and generally help adapt the size of the enterprise to the new dimensions of the emerging Common Market and the expanding world market.[122] Added support for this policy was generated by

---

[121] The examples of the more spectacular "internal" mergers *within* a Member State in the mid-sixties are the Montecatini-Edison merger (the fourth and fifth largest Italian companies supplying about 80% of the Italian market for chemical products); the steel mergers between Thyssen and Phoenix Rheinrohr in the Federal Republic (some 25% of the German market) and the Arbed-Hadir merger combining virtually the entire steel production in Luxembourg. *See generally, Concentration and Competition in European Industry*, 1966 WORLD BUSINESS 7 (No. 2).

The Commission's policy on cooperation is reflected particularly in the following "Communications" (Notices):

Communication Concerning Agreements, Decisions and Concerted Practices in Cooperation Between Enterprises, [1968] J.O. C75 (July 29) at 3, CCH COMM. MKT. REP. ¶ 9248;

Communication of May 27, 1970, Relating to Agreements, Decisions, and Concerted Practices of Minor Importance Not Coming Within Article 85, Paragraph 1, of the Treaty Establishing the European Economic Community, [1970] J.O. C64 (June 2) at 1, CCH COMM. MKT. REP. ¶ 9367.

[122] Von der Groeben, *Competition Policy* at 5. Concentration of Enterprises in the Common Market, Memorandum of the Commission of the E.E.C. to the Governments of the Member States, submitted on Dec. 1, 1965, CCH COMM. MKT. REP. No. 26, Mar. 17, 1966. On concentration of enterprises and fusion see COOPÉRATIONS, CONCENTRATIONS, FUSIONS D'ENTREPRISES DANS LA C.E.E., Colloque Paris, Oct. 26-28, 1967, 1968 REV. MARCHÉ COMMUN (No. 109) (cited as *Coopérations):* reports by Lecourt at 6, Teitgen at 539; Conard, *Corporate Fusion* at 574; Sacco, *Industrial Concentration.*

the danger, real or imaginary, of American "satellisation" of European enterprises condemned—it has been argued—to a role of adjuncts of the powerful companies beyond the Atlantic. Unless the current trend of American penetration is halted, so goes the argument, American industry in Europe (rather than "European" industry) will become the third most powerful industrial complex in the world (after the United States and Soviet industry). In fact, American controlled companies, accustomed to operating in a continental and worldwide context, have perceived and seized the opportunities of the enlarged and affluent market well in advance of the European enterprises. Although the "American challenge" has often been exaggerated and used for extraneous political objectives, American acquisitions of substantial interests in entire industrial sectors have evoked concern not only in France, where "independence" has been the cornerstone of Gaullist policy, but in the Federal Republic as well. Those concerned emphasize the "research gap" and the "brain drain" that occur if research and development are concentrated in home laboratories of the American parent, as well as the disproportion in the dimensions, financial power, and research facilities of the enterprises on the two sides of the Atlantic.[123]

A statistical survey for the period of 1961-1969, based on incomplete data, indicates a significant increase in the number of agreements of cooperation as well as acquisitions and

---

[123] The most frequently cited examples of American "penetration" are the take-over of Machine Bull of France by General Electric, of Simca in France by Chrysler, of D.E.A. (Deutsche Erdöl Aktiengesellschaft) in the Federal Republic by Texaco. Sacco, *Industrial Concentration* at 59, reports 2290 transactions by American firms (new establishments, acquisitions, expansions) between 1958 and 1965. American interests control only 2% of the investments, but this figure is said not to tell the story since most of the specialized advanced industries are American controlled. See generally on this problem SERVAN-SCHREIBER, THE AMERICAN CHALLENGE (New York 1968); HELLMANN, AMERIKA AUF DEM EUROPAMARKT (Baden-Baden 1966); KINDLEBERGER, AMERICAN BUSINESS ABROAD at 74-98 (New Haven and London 1969); LAYTON, TRANS-ATLANTIC INVESTMENTS (Atlantic Institute, Paris 1966).

mergers, in the broad sense, within the Community.[124] However, the rate of growth of such transactions among companies of the same Member State has been substantially
higher than of those carried out across national frontiers by
companies of two or more different Member States.[125] The
Commission found "particularly disturbing" the fact that
acquisitions or absorptions of Member companies by third-
country companies have been almost four times as numerous
as those involving only companies of the Member States.[126]
Taking note of these trends, the Commission recognized that
the "restructuring" necessary to adapt the industry to the
new competitive conditions will often, but not always, call
for further concentration;[127] in fact some sectors have already

---

[124] The statistical study was carried out for the Commission by
"Opera Mundi Europe." It covers trends in expansion by means of
"unilateral" foreign subsidiaries, cooperation among enterprises, and
acquisition of controlling interests and mergers. The study is based
on some 15,000 operations in fifteen sectors of manufacturing industries. The data shows an increase in the total number of these transactions from 1507 in 1961 to 2096 in 1968; the estimated increase in
1969, calculated on the basis of the first six months, was 2716. The
first type of operation—"unilateral" formation of subsidiaries—was the
most commonly employed form (2300 as against 1001 cooperation
agreements and 257 "merger-acquisition" operations), but the trend
has been definitely toward the other two types (the growth rate has
been 26% for subsidiaries, 54% for cooperation agreements, 84% for
"merger-acquisitions"). Commission des Communautés Européennes,
COM (70)/final, Mar. 18, 1970, La Politique industrielle de la Communauté, Mémorandum de la Commission au Conseil, Première Partie:
La situation de l'industrie communautaire at I/45-I/51.

[125] In 1961 there were 100 cases of cooperation agreements within
a single Member State as against 104 cases of "across-frontier" cooperation agreements; in 1968 the relation was 231 to 160. Similarly in 1961,
there were 131 "merger-acquisitions" within a single Member to only
19 "Community" level cases; in 1968 the numbers were 272 as against
35. Id. at I/47.

[126] The specific figures were 820 to 257. There were 3546 subsidiaries formed by third-country companies and 2797 cooperation
agreements with third-country companies, as against 2300 and 1001
transactions of the same type by Member companies. Id. at I/49.

[127] Id. 2ème partie: Amélioration de l'environnement des Entreprises dans la Communauté at II/20. On the situation in French industry see Murcier, Le mouvement de concentration est-il allé trop
loin, Le Monde, Sélection hébd. Jan. 29-Feb. 4, 1970, p. 11.

reached a high degree of concentration and the number of these sectors must increase. Where, however, concentration turns into monopolization, "it must be treated as abusive exploitation of a dominant position."[128] The Commission sees a clear and urgent need of further concentration in advanced-technology industries (nuclear energy, space, aircraft, information retrieval and electronics industries) where national markets are still isolated, and the competitive position *vis-à-vis* the United States is particularly weak. Although the Commission is aware of the benefits deriving from foreign investment and does not wish in any way to recommend "a protectionist attitude,"[129] it nevertheless is concerned lest the combination of concentration at the national level and take-overs by third-country companies create a situation in which it would be impossible to evolve a common European policy in advanced-technology sectors. From the Commission's perspective, the gap between the competitive positions of the United States and Europe in products of advanced technology is still increasing, at a time when the United States seeks to limit European imports of products of "traditional" industries (steel, textiles, chemicals, shoes).[130] In these circumstances, the Commission has come out unequivocally in favor of a coordinated use of public loans, procurement contracts, and other means, with the view to stimulating formation of "transnational European enterprises." According to the Commission's definition, these enterprises "not only perform their activities in several countries, but their capital and management also belong to several countries [not exclusively to the Six] and their center of decision-making is situated in Europe." Such enterprises should be in a position "to face the competition of the giants from across the Atlantic, both in Europe and on world markets."[131] The

128 *Id.* at II/38.

129 *Id.* Introduction et orientations générales at 32.

130 *Id.,* Quatrième partie: La promotion des industries de technologie avancée at IV/15.

131 *Id.* Introduction at 21. The Commission "for the moment" does not advocate the formation of a Community-wide institution com-

Commission's definition, particularly the reference to the decision-making center in Europe, is reminiscent of the French insistence on confining the benefits of the EEC Treaty and Community law generally to "truly European" companies.

Vagts suggests that the "attractive idea" of matching American corporate giants by European countervailing companies needs further detailed analysis with a view to identifying both the potential benefits and possible dangers.[132] It would be the better part of wisdom for the United States Government and American companies, which on the whole have done extremely well in Europe, to consider seriously some of the matters raised by their European partners as possible issues for joint negotiation. These might include tax matters, such as elimination of tax-havens employed to avoid legitimate tax liabilities on both sides of the Atlantic, reciprocity in public procurement, better facilities for direct European investment in the United States, jurisdictional questions relating to extraterritorial application of national legislation (such as antitrust and trading-with-the-enemy laws) and to judicial jurisdiction over foreign companies, removal of non-tariff obstacles posed by old and new safety and health regulations, a modest coordination of basic economic policies, and last, but not least, technological cooperation in those areas where United States superiority is particularly pronounced at this juncture. Of course, the Community and the Member States would have to be prepared to give proper consideration to the legitimate interests of the United States in any such negotiations, both on the "bilateral" level and in multilateral forums such as GATT, the Hague Confer-

---

parable to the British Industrial Reorganization Corporation or the French Institut de Développement Industriel, but urges the use of the financial facilities of the European Investment Bank. *Id.* at 22. See also the position taken less explicitly on the proposed take-over by Westinghouse of the Belgian Ateliers de construction électrique and possibly of other French and Italian firms. Eur. Parliament, Written Question No. 156 by M. Glinne, [1969] J.O. C129 (Oct. 10) at 1.

132 Vagts, *The Multinational Enterprise* at 782.

ence, the Organization for Economic Cooperation and Development, and the various United Nations bodies.[133] Actually, the broader issue of reconciling the role of the multinational enterprise with that of the nation-state or a community of nation-states is involved here. At any rate, the evolution of the relationship between the United States and the Community will no doubt have an important impact not only upon the use of the emerging European economic power, but also upon the application of the Community's policies and laws—including the law on mergers, with which we are concerned in this section.

(b)   The concept of "fusion" in Community law[134]

The concept of "fusion" has acquired a specific meaning in the emerging Community law. Like the corresponding notions in American corporation codes,[135] "fusion" postulates a transfer by general assignment of all property *("universal succession")* from the submerged to the surviving company ("statutory merger"); or from the submerged company or companies to a newly organized company ("consolidation"). The submerged company or companies become extinguished *without liquidation* and their shareholders receive the shares of the surviving company in exchange for their original holdings.[136]

This concept of fusion does not comprise other related forms of concentration, such as the transfer of assets of

---

[133] *See generally* Vernon, *The Role of U.S. Enterprise Abroad*, DAEDALUS 113, at 124-32 (Winter 1969); Vernon, Statement Before the Joint Economic Committee of the U.S. Congress, Dec. 4, 1969 (mimeographed).

[134] Goldman, in COOPÉRATIONS at 299; Hauschild, *id.* at 8; Les fusions internes, Document de travail no. 6, Avant-projet de directive, Rapporteur: M.P. van Ommeslaghe, Doc. 11409/2/XIV/C/68-F.

[135] NEW YORK BUS. CORP. LAW § 901 (McKinney's Consol. Laws Ann., Book 6, Brooklyn, N.Y. 1963); see MODEL BUS. CORP. ACT §§ 71, 72.

[136] This notion of fusion would correspond to "type A reorganization" of the U.S. INTERNAL REVENUE CODE of 1954, § 368. *See* Conard, *Corporate Fusion* at 585.

one company in exchange for stock in another, whereby the former becomes a holding company, or an outright purchase by one company of assets of another for cash or bonds.[137] Not included are arrangements such as the "integration agreements" *(Organschaftsverträge)* in which a subsidiary gives up its rights to independent management and profit calculation, in consideration of certain guarantees of income from the parent. Such arrangements are permissible in Germany,[138] but exist in Belgium, for instance, only by extra-legal "gentlemen's agreements," not enforceable in law.

In contrast to fusion, a "scission" entails a "division" of a company into two new companies,[139] but the legal problems surrounding this and certain other related transactions appear quite similar. For this reason, rules governing fusion extend in principle, and as appropriate, to these transactions as well.

(c) "Domestic" and "international" fusion

The laws in five of the six Member States allow and favor, as we shall see, *"domestic"* fusions between companies of local nationality, but the national legal systems differ substantially. On the other hand, *"international"* fusions across national frontiers between companies of different nationalities have been unknown thus far in all of the Member States. Even in the absence of a specific prohibition, the requirements of national laws and procedures have made it practically impossible to undertake such transactions.[140] This situation has been due to the fear of the possible impairment of creditors and shareholders, a danger of the circumvention of important socio-political objectives such as

---

137 *Cf.* "type B," "type C," and "type D" reorganizations defined in the INTERNAL REVENUE CODE of 1954, § 368.

138 §§ 291-307 of the Stock Company Law of 1965. *See* pp. 106-07 *supra.*

139 *E.g.,* Art. 371 ff. of the French Law of 1966.

140 Loussouarn, in L'HARMONISATION at 28-29.

the workers' "codetermination," a possible loss of national tax revenue and, last, but not least, to economic nationalism. Consequently, the holding company has been the generally available device for international concentration.[141] The most celebrated illustration within the Common Market is the Agfa-Gevaert combination between the largest German and Belgian producers of photographic products.[142] The twin purposes of the arrangement were rationalization of production and improved position *vis-à-vis* the large American competitors, such as Kodak, Dupont, Minnesota Mining and Manufacturing, Polaroid and Xerox. Since, as indicated, a fusion was not possible, the two companies turned into holding companies, each acquiring 50% of two newly formed subsidiaries, one Belgian and the other German, which they established to operate the existing manufacturing and distribution facilities. The same persons sit in the administrative organs of both holding companies, and to that extent unity in the direction of the combined enterprises has been assured. That this arrangement has not proved entirely satisfactory will become apparent in the closing section of this chapter. Only a unitary company could assure truly unitary planning of the operations of the branches and plants. The new Convention, which is in the process of negotiation pursuant to Article 220 of the EEC Treaty, should make it possible to create such a company through international fusion. As Conard points out, however, it is not at all certain that a unitary company is always preferable to a holding company.[143]

One aspect of law-making in this field is of particular interest to American and other non-Member companies that have subsidiaries within the Community territory. In Community parlance, "international fusion" means fusion among companies of different Member States. The current Com-

---

[141] Goldman, in Coopérations at 297, 311.

[142] Bertrand Motte, President of the executive board of the Agfa-Gevaert Company, in Coopérations at 393.

[143] Conard, *Corporate Fusion* at 576 ff.

mission drafts are limited in this sense and do not purport to cover, for instance, a fusion of a Delaware company with a Member State company. On the other hand, a fusion between a French company, owned or controlled by an American parent, and a Member State company would be included. However, the French Government reportedly has suggested that foreign controlled subsidiaries be excluded from the Convention and from the proposed tax incentives to cross-frontier fusions, on the ground that only the Community-controlled companies needed incentives to merge "before they are all gobbled up by American companies." The Commission staff, supported by the Netherlands and Belgian Governments, has not been willing—it is said—to accept this view.[144]

(d)   Treaty bases: relation between Articles 220 and 54, par. 3(g)

A clear relationship exists between the introduction of international fusion, contemplated in Article 220, and coordination of national company laws in accordance with Article 54, par. 3(g). As national company laws—and the position of shareholders under these laws—become more similar through coordination or "spontaneous" assimilation, "the mistrust of foreign legal systems" is reduced and international fusion becomes more acceptable.[145] Consequently, the efforts of the working group on coordination of company laws under Article 54, par. 3(g), which I have described in some detail, are intimately related to the activities of the

---

[144] *Common Market Split on Mergers,* New York Times, Jan. 25, 1969, p. 1C, col. 2, and p. 38C, col. 1. The report that the Government of the Federal Republic supported the French has not been substantiated. The French attitude is consistent with that taken on aspects of the right of establishment and freedom of capital movement, *supra* p. 33. On tax-incentives for fusions see *infra* p. 384. *See generally* p. 387 *infra.*

[145] Goldman, in Coopérations at 303; Hauschild, in Europäische Handelsgesellschaft at 87; Beitzke, *Zur Anerkennung* at 95 ff. in the context of mutual recognition of companies.

working group established under Article 220, which was
also mentioned earlier.

(e)   A glimpse at differences in national laws on fusion

"Domestic" fusion without the requirement of a liquidation of the submerged company has been recognized in the
laws of all of the Member States with the exception of
the Netherlands; it is regulated by statute in France, the
Federal Republic and Italy,[146] and by case law in Belgium
and Luxembourg.[147] In the Netherlands, the law does not
provide for fusion in the above sense, entailing universal
succession to the assets of the submerged company and
extinction without liquidation of the submerged company.
Instead, the purpose of a fusion is achieved as a rule by an
exchange of stock or purchase of assets for stock.[148] The
Belgian reform proposal and the Netherlands new civil code
introduce statutory fusion and presage a statutory treatment
of the subject.[149]

The principal differences among the national laws on
fusion relate to the following issues:[150] the procedure, the
modalities of the protection of shareholders and creditors,
the fate of prior contracts with third parties, guarantees of
fairness and legality, and sanctions for violations of the
law.

---

[146] France: Art. 371, the Law of July 24, 1966; Federal Republic:
§§ 339 ff., the Stock Company Law of 1965; Italy: Art. 2501, CODICE
CIVILE. *See generally* Conard, *Corporate Fusion* at 584-92; FERNHOLZ, DIE
FUSION at 15 ff. FUSIONS DES SOCIÉTÉS, RAPPORTS AU COLLOQUE INTER-
NATIONAL DE DROIT EUROPÉEN organisé par l'Association belge pour le
droit européen, Bruxelles, 12-14 Octobre 1961 (Bruxelles 1962). However, the treatment of French law is out of date in view of the new
law of 1966.

[147] Renauld, *Les fusions des sociétés en droit belge,* 1962 REV. DROIT
INT. ET DROIT COMP. 217.

[148] Van Oven & van Leeuwe, *La fusion* at 108; VAN DER HEIJDEN-
VAN DER GRINTEN, HANDBOEK No. 378, at 580-81.

[149] Art. 2.1.12 NIEUW BURGERLIJK WETBOEK; on this subject see
Sanders, *La fusion.*

[150] Goldman, in COOPÉRATIONS at 306.

In France, the Federal Republic and Italy, the fusion agreement is concluded by the administrations of the companies concerned, with prior or subsequent approval by the shareholders' meeting.[151] The agreement must be embodied in Germany and Italy in a document prepared by a notary.[152] In France, the proposed agreement must be filed with the recording office of the commercial court and it must be published.[153] No formal fusion agreement is required in Belgium and Luxembourg, but appropriate resolutions must be adopted by the shareholders' meeting of the submerged company in accordance with the provisions governing charter amendment, and by the shareholders' meeting of the surviving company pursuant to the rules for charter amendment and increase of capital.[154] The rules governing the quorum and the voting majority required in the shareholders' meeting, as well as the provisions on the information that must be made available to the shareholders prior to the meeting, vary in part substantially.[155]

[151] Prior approval is required in Italy, Art. 2502, CODICE CIVILE. Subsequent approval in France, Art. 376, Law of July 24, 1966 and Art. 254 ff., Décret of Mar. 23, 1967; and also in the Federal Republic, § 340 of the Stock Company Law of 1965. The shareholders of the surviving company must in addition approve an increase of capital if there is no authorized capital which can be used for the issue of shares to be received by the shareholders of the submerged company. § 343 Stock Company Law of 1965.

[152] Art. 2504, Italian CODICE CIVILE.

[153] Art. 374, Law of July 24, 1966.

[154] FERNHOLZ, DIE FUSION at 70 ff.; Conard, *Corporate Fusion* at 587.

[155] *France:* Arts. 372, 373, 153 ff., Law of July 24, 1966: rules on charter amendment apply (with degressive quorum requirements), in the first meeting 50% of all shares entitled to vote must be represented, 2/3 majority must approve. The proposed fusion agreement has to be deposited in the recording office of the commercial court, Art. 374. *Federal Republic:* § 340, par. 2, Stock Company Law of 1965: no quorum required, but 3/4 majority. *Italy:* Arts. 2502, 2368, 2369, CODICE CIVILE: rules on charter amendment apply, more than one-half of the stated capital must approve. SIMONETTO, DELLE SOCIETÀ at 242 ff. (Bologna, Rome 1965). *Belgium:* Rules on charter amendment apply which require a quorum of 50% and approval by a majority of 3/4. If—as is the case invariably in large companies—the 50% quorum is

Only the Italian law may be interpreted as granting the shareholder who dissents from the fusion resolution the right to compel redemption of his shares at an appraised value, comparable to the "appraisal right" in American corporation codes.[156] However, Italian writers are not in unanimous agreement on this interpretation, since the relevant provision grants this right in so many words only in case of a change in the charter purpose, a change in the form of the company's organization or a transfer of the seat abroad, and does not mention fusion.[157] Decisions by corporate shareholders may be attacked if they are motivated by fraud.[158]

In those Member States where fusion is based on statutory provisions, it brings about an automatic transfer of the entire aggregation of assets and liabilities;[159] this is, of course, one of the principal characteristics and advantages of the fusion, as defined earlier. However, in Belgium and Luxembourg, where statutory regulation does not exist, some authorities nevertheless attribute to fusion the effect of a general assignment of *assets* (but not liabilities), while others would require separate conveyance of particular asset items. However, a general transfer of liabilities is not feasible, and assent by the creditors to the transfer of the debts is necessary.[160]

---

not obtained, a second meeting may be called which acts regardless of the number of shareholders present or represented. Thus in effect a majority of 3/4 of the shareholders present or represented is required. On the required information for the shareholders see Goldman, in COOPÉRATIONS at 587; FERNHOLZ, DIE FUSION at 164.

[156] MODEL BUS. CORP. ACT § 81.

[157] Franceschelli, in COOPÉRATIONS at 420 ff.; *contra* SIMONETTO, DELLE SOCIETÀ at 88.

[158] § 243 German Stock Company Law of 1965; abus de la majorité, which can cause the "nullity" of the vote, FERNHOLZ, DIE FUSION at 148; note 1968 TIJDSCHRIFT VOOR PRIVAATRECHT 92 ff.

[159] France: Arts. 381, 385, Law of July 24, 1966, and Art. 265, Décret No. 67-236; Federal Republic: § 346, par. 3, Stock Company Law of 1965; Italy: Art. 2504, par. 4, CODICE CIVILE. . .

[160] In support of a "general assignment" effect, Renauld, *Étude comparative de la réglementation des fusions de sociétés en droit belge et dans certaines législations étrangères,* 1955 REVUE PRATIQUE DES

Other differences concern the question when fusion takes effect,[161] and also the modalities of creditor protection. Although all three countries with statutory rules require either repayment of, or security for, creditors' claims, the procedures differ: mere notification by the creditor of his claim at the commercial register suffices in the Federal Republic and Italy, whereas in France "opposition" in the form of a complaint in court is necessary. In Italy, opposition by an unsatisfied creditor blocks the fusion, but the court may approve it if adequate security is offered.[162] In France, bondholders have the right to participate in the vote on the fusion unless they are repaid or secured, and in Luxembourg a provision granting this right in case of a change in the charter purpose or in the company form is construed as extending it to fusion as well.[163] Ordinary creditors in Belgium and in Luxembourg have no special rights defined by statute, such as they have in France, the Federal Republic and Italy, but they may rely on traditional remedies, such as contesting the validity of the transaction and pursuing the assets in the hands of the surviving company; if the submerged company has outstanding debts it is not extinguished automatically;

SOCIÉTÉS CIVILES ET COMMERCIALES 1, at 9; cf. del Marmol & Dabin, in JURA EUROPAE No. 20.70.6; Renauld, Les fusions at 220. For a Netherlands view see VAN LEEUWE, FISCALE PROBLEMEN at 27; and Sanders, La fusion at 2.

161 In France, Belgium and Luxembourg, fusion is effective "internally" upon the decision of the shareholders' meeting, and as against third parties upon publication only. It is not agreed whether in Italy the entry into the register has a declaratory or constitutive effect, but the prevailing opinion appears to support the declaratory effect. SANTAGATA, LA FUSIONE TRA SOCIETÀ at 378 (Napoli 1964). In German law (§ 346 paras. 3 and 4 of the Law of 1965) entry into the commercial register is constitutive.

162 Germany: § 347, Law of 1965; France: Houin & Goré, La réforme des sociétés at 172; Art. 381, par. 4, Law of July 24, 1966, and Art. 281, Décret No. 67-236; Italy: Art. 2503 of the CODICE CIVILE. See FERNHOLZ, DIE FUSION at 210 ff.

163 France: Arts. 380, 384 of the Law of July 24, 1966; Luxembourg: Art. 88, par. 7, Law of 1915; FERNHOLZ, DIE FUSION at 231 ff.; Conard, Corporate Fusion at 590.

and, although there is no liquidation proceeding, its shareholders may have to return the shares of the surviving company, if that is necessary to satisfy the creditors; the surviving company may also be held liable.[164]

As a further aspect of the shareholders' protection,
compliance with the prescribed rules is made the subject
of a report by auditors, in France pursuant to a statutory
provision,[165] and in Belgium on the basis of the provision
governing the issuance of shares in exchange for property;
the law in the Federal Republic and in Italy provides for
judicial control, while the future Netherlands law provides
for administrative control.[166]

(f) Proposed directive coordinating rules on "domestic" fusion

The proposed directive is based on the assumption that
"fusion" is "the most accomplished instrument of concentration"; since it exists in five of the six Member States,
it should be introduced in all six, so as "to create an
equivalence of the 'guarantees' offered to shareholders and
third parties in connection with this extremely important
transaction,"[167] and it is also to serve as a "bridge head"
for international fusion. The directive is again limited to
stock companies and embraces the concept of "fusion" as
described above. Thus the legislatures of all the Member
States would be required to provide in their legislative
arsenal for "fusion by absorption" of one stock company by

---

[164] Conard, *Corporate Fusion* at 592. Renauld, *Les fusions* at 58
ff. Luxembourg law contains a specific rule on transfer of assets for
stock. Art. 148 bis of the Law of 1915, as amended.

[165] Art. 377 of the Law of July 24, 1966.

[166] Germany: §§ 345-346, Law of 1965; Italy: Art. 2504, Codice
civile; Netherlands: Art. 2.1.12 Nieuw Burgerlijk Wetboek. Fernholz, Die Fusion at 148 ff.; Conard, *Corporate Fusion* at 590.

[167] Les fusions internes, Doc. de travail no. 6, Avant-projet de
directive, Commission des Communautés Européennes, Doc. 11409/
2/XIV/C/68-F, Rapporteur: M. P. van Ommeslaghe, Professeur à
l'Université de Bruxelles, Apr. 10, 1968, *Introduction* at 1. Somewhat
modified drafts of this "third" directive were prepared after the completion of this book: Doc. 3491/XIV/C/70-F and COM (70) final of
June 12, 1970.

another, and for fusion of two or more stock companies through the formation of a new company. Having thus defined the institution of fusion, the text sets forth the rules designed to coordinate the "guarantees" for the protection of shareholders, creditors and "other interested persons."

The shareholders of the submerged company or companies receive, in exchange for their stock, shares of the surviving (or newly created) company but, following the example of German law, an additional cash premium of up to 10% may also be paid.[168]

Fusion takes place through universal succession by the surviving (or newly formed) company to the assets and liabilities of the submerged company, in exchange for stock. It would be for the national legislator to determine the point of time at which the fusion takes effect, although the Commission staff hopes that a uniform rule on this rather important point could be agreed upon.[169] In any case, however, the provisions on "publicity" contained in the First Directive must be observed. Rights that cannot be assigned are excluded from the universal succession and, to the extent that given obligations could be performed by the submerged company only, the surviving company is liable for damages. If the performance of a contract proves incompatible with an obligation of the surviving company, or if it would impose an inequitable burden upon the surviving company, the national legislator may provide for special relief, such as adjustment of the obligation or outright release;[170] but this exceptional relief could not apply to employment contracts.

A fusion is executed by means of a contract among the "fusing" companies which must be approved by their share-

---

[168] § 344, par. 2, of the German Stock Company Law of 1965.

[169] The problem is to reconcile the Italian solution (shareholders' meeting decision, conclusion of an atto di fusione and its registration, at which time only the fusion takes effect) with French and German law (effect upon registration) and Belgian law (effect upon approval by shareholders' meeting).

[170] See § 349 of the German Stock Company Law of 1965.

holders' meetings. The fusion plan must contain specified
minimum information, and it must be communicated to the
shareholders a month in advance of the meeting, so as to
provide them with a factual basis for their decision. Moreover, each administration must make available to the shareholders its report, explaining the reasons for the fusion and
particularly the conditions of the exchange of stock which
must be verified by independent auditors. The balance
sheets and financial statements for the last three years must
also be made available.

According to the proposed directive, the quorum and the
voting majority required for the approval of the fusion in
the shareholders' meeting are governed by national rules
concerning charter amendment—an example of "renvoi" to
national rules—but the majority, necessary for the decision
to approve, must not be less than two-thirds of the capital
or of the voting shares represented in the meeting.[171] The
proposal does not assure the dissenting minority shareholder
of a right to compel the redemption of his shares at an
appraised value; but in case of negligent conduct, it does
require the national lawmakers to impose liability for
damages upon the members of the administration of the
submerged company and the auditors. The underlying assumption obviously is that a shareholder of the submerged
company will receive a fair consideration for his shares in
the form of the shares of the surviving or new company,
and that the prescribed auditing procedure reduces the possibility of undervaluation. Nevertheless, a gap remains in
the protection of the minority shareholder, if his potentially
substantial claim against the members of the administration
or the auditors cannot be satisfied because of their inability
to pay.

Protection is given only to the creditors of the submerged
company, although one can readily conceive of circum-

---

171 National legislators are entirely free to determine the quorum
and they also may require *more* than a majority of two-thirds for the
decision to approve.

stances in which the creditors of the surviving company are impaired. Several broad rules are to apply in this area, with details left to the discretion of the Members. In principle, the creditors whose claims have arisen prior to the public announcement of the calling of the shareholders' meeting should be given the right to obtain security for their claims, unless they are already otherwise secured; but this right may be eliminated by payment of the debt in advance of its maturity. As far as the bondholders are concerned, the Member States are given a choice, either to assure their protection in the same manner as that of ordinary creditors, or to require that their consent to the fusion be obtained either in a bondholders' meeting or individually. The surviving or the new company must give the holders of convertible bonds, dividend bonds and other types of debentures in the submerged company the same rights they enjoyed in that company; unless these rights are redeemed, they cannot be changed without the holders' consent.

Finally, the directive would provide that the rules governing fusion should apply by analogy to certain transactions "assimilated" to fusion, such as take-over of all assets of a wholly owned subsidiary, "scission,"[172] or the "short form merger" of German law,[173] and purchase of assets for stock of the purchasing corporation to be distributed directly to the shareholders of the selling company.

Article 54, par. 3(g), speaks, it will be recalled, of protecting the interests of both the shareholders and of "third parties." The original draft of the directive concerned itself with the interests of holders of securities, creditors and, to a limited extent, parties to contracts with the companies, including employment contracts. The "European" labor

---

[172] *Cf.* Art. 371 ff. of the French Law of July 24, 1966.

[173] *See* § 15 of Umwandlungsgesetz (Transformation Law) of Nov. 12, 1956, BGBl I 844, modified by the Introductory Law to the Law of 1965: where a parent company holds ninety percent of its subsidiary's stock it may take over the latter without the consent of the minority shareholders. Duden, *Umwandlung und Take-over* at 435.

groups which the Commission had consulted on the draft,
urged that the interests of workers employed by the fusing
companies should be taken fully into account in the draft,[174]
since these interests could be jeopardized as a result of a
fusion no less than those of the shareholders and creditors.
Since workers must be assured of their acquired rights and
accorded appropriate assistance in case of dismissal following a fusion, the administration should be required by the
directive to make available to workers' representatives the
report prepared for the shareholders and, in addition, in
ample time to allow consultation, a special report concerning job protection. More generally, the labor spokesmen
thought that fusions should be made subject to approval by
the governments; the approval ought to be granted only if
a showing is made of economic necessity. The broadening
of the scope of Article 54 is justified—it is said—by the fact
that over the last twenty years "the countries of the Community have required the inclusion in the constitution of
enterprises of provisions for the protection of workers which
have been integrated, if not *de jure* at least *de facto,* in
company law." An argument could be made that, although
the workers are a component part of an enterprise, they are
"third parties" in relation to the company with which they
have a contract, and since Article 54 speaks of "companies"
rather than enterprises, it supplies a broad enough basis for
consideration of workers' interests in the coordination of
company laws on the Community level. Actually, the most
recent draft of the directive goes some distance beyond the
original text toward recognizing the interests of the workers:
the management of each company planning fusion must submit to its employees a special report on the "more immediate" impact of the fusion on personnel. The report must

---

[174] Memorandum by the European Secretariat of the International
Confederation of Free Trade Unions (C.I.S.L.) and the European
Organization of the International Confederation of Christian Trade
Unions (C.I.S.C.) renamed to Confederation Mondiale des Travailleurs
(C.M.T.), summarized in 1969 LE DROIT ET LES AFFAIRES at 975, and
EUROPE No. 317 (new series), Apr. 18, 1969, at 8.

be made available one month in advance of the final decision and the employees must be given a hearing on the
report.[175]

(g) How to make "international" fusion possible

(i) Principal obstacles: national tax laws and proposals for their harmonization

In his unique study, Professor Conard has described the
obstacles to international fusion under the presently applicable national laws and the reasons underlying these obstacles.[176] In Germany, for instance, the statute providing a
procedure for fusion is limited by implication to fusions between companies of that country. Where there is no statutory fusion, general principles of company law and rules of
conflict of laws are manipulated to prevent a domestic company from voting itself into a foreign absorption over the
objection of any shareholder.[177]

---

[175] The Union Internationale des Avocats was also consulted on
this proposal, but the consultation with the Commission staff took
place in a meeting and no written opinion appears available.

[176] Conard, *Corporate Fusion* at 595 ff.

[177] Only the Italian company law expressly envisages a company
moving its seat to another country (and changing its "nationality"),
provided that dissenting shareholders are paid the value of their
interests. Art. 2437, CODICE CIVILE. This provision appears to apply to
absorption of an Italian company by a foreign company.

The Commission has described the present legal situation regarding international fusion in the following terms: "[I]n the Federal Republic, fusions are subject to judicial supervision. Since such supervision can not be lawfully exercised over a foreign national, fusion
between a German company and a company of a different nationality
is not possible.

"In the Netherlands, fusion does not exist in company law either
on the national or on the international level. 'Mergers' are accomplished by financial concentrations (acquisition of interest or of all
shares . . .).

"In Belgium, France, Italy and Luxembourg, international fusion
is legally possible when a foreign company is absorbed by a national
company. In other cases, company law in France, Belgium, and Luxembourg requires unanimous consent of all shareholders, a condition
which can not be met when capital is dispersed. In Italy such una-

This aversion toward international fusion has been due, Conard explains, not only to the differences among the national company laws, but also to the historic differences in political climate and economic policy, the past record of wartime seizure of shares in local companies held by "enemy aliens," and, last, but not least, to the interests of the national treasury.

Actually, even if all the other obstacles were removed there would remain the formidable problem of taxes, particularly taxes on capital gains and on transfer of property connected with a fusion, since most states which provide for tax exemptions limit them to fusions in which the surviving company is domestic.[178]

In the context of a general program for the harmonization of direct taxes, which the EEC Commission submitted to the Council on June 26, 1967,[179] a specific draft directive was elaborated in order to introduce "a common tax system" for fusions and assimilated transactions involving companies of different Member States, and this proposal was submitted to the Council on January 15, 1969.[180] It was

nimity is not required, and the shareholders who oppose the absorption have only the right to withdraw." Commission des Communautés Européennes, COM (70) 100/final, Mar. 18, 1970, La Politique industrielle de la Communauté, Mémorandum de la Commission au Conseil, 2ème partie at II/34.

[178] On the tax question relating to fusion see reports in COOPÉRATIONS: Hutchings at 467, Durang & Latscha at 475, Leboeuf at 487, Trebuth at 508, and Turq at 524. *See also* Albrecht & Schulze-Brachmann, *Die nationale und internationale Unternehmenskonzentration unter besonderer Berücksichtigung der europäischen Handelsgesellschaft,* 1968 AWD 81.

[179] Dok. R/959/67 (Eco. 104). This document was examined over a period of several months by a group of financial experts within the Council framework and was the subject of a report by the Committee of Permanent Representatives. Dok. R/319/68 (Eco. 26). In its meetings on March 4 and 5, 1968, the Council directed the Commission to submit appropriate proposals. Dok. R/411/68.

[180] Vorschlag einer Richtlinie über das gemeinsame Steuersystem für Fusionen, Spaltungen und die Einbringung von Unternehmensteilen, die Gesellschaften verschiedener Mitgliedstaaten betreffen. Dok. KOM (69)5 endg., Jan. 15, 1969. On this proposal see the opinion of the Social and Economic Committee, in [1970] J. O. C100 (Aug. 1) at 4.

accompanied by another proposal embodying a "common tax system for parent and subsidiary companies of different Member States"[181] which was intended to avoid double taxation of profits of foreign subsidiaries, and it contemplated eventually a consolidated "worldwide" profit system for companies with foreign affiliates. Both proposals are grounded on Article 100 of the EEC Treaty authorizing, as we have seen earlier, the issuance of directives for the "approximation" of national laws which "directly affect the establishment or functioning of the Common Market."

The first of these two proposed directives focuses directly on fusion situations and deals with the following subjects:

(1) Tax on capital gains of a submerged company resulting for instance from the abolition of hidden reserves at the time of a fusion. The directive would provide for a deferral of the tax until the capital gains are realized by the surviving (or new) company; but the State of the submerged company must be given an assurance that it will be able to levy the tax at that time. This means that appropriate entries must be maintained on the books of the surviving company as regards the continuing establishment in the submerged company's State, and that company's local assets (other than securities) must not be removed from that State's territory.

(2) Tax on capital gains of the submerged company's shareholders resulting from the exchange of stock. In principle, no tax would be imposed here, but the Member States would be free to deviate from this principle where shares of the submerged company were owned by a third company which, after the fusion, carried on its books the

---

[181] Vorschlag einer Richtlinie über das gemeinsame Steuersystem für Mutter- und Tochtergesellschaften verschiedener Mitgliedstaaten, Dok. KOM (60)6 endg., Jan. 15, 1969. *See generally* on both proposals CCH COMM. MKT. REP. ¶ 9281. On this proposal see the opinion of the Social and Economic Committee, in [1970] J.O. C100 (Aug. 1) at 7.

corresponding shares of the surviving company as a part of its assets, at a value higher than that of the exchanged shares.

(3) Tax on gains of the surviving company resulting from the cancellation of the shares it held in the submerged company, or from the cancellation of its own shares which it acquired from the submerged company as part of the fusion transaction. An exemption from such a tax is proposed in order to avoid double taxation, first at the time of the cancellation and then upon the realization of the capital gains.

(4) Taxation of establishments (defined in the broadest terms) of foreign companies. Here the purpose is to avoid double taxation and assure equal tax treatment of such establishments with domestic companies.

(5) Indirect taxes imposed upon transfer of property incident to fusion, which in some Member States are quite substantial, particularly where valuable real estate is involved.[182] In an earlier directive, approved by the Council on July 17, 1969, the Member States were required to set their "registration" tax on contributions to capital at a rate between one and two percent, but to reduce that rate by at least fifty percent in the case of a transfer of *entire assets* between Community companies.[183] Supplementing this text,

---

[182] Conard points out that the transfer tax problem is unlike any problem known to American corporation lawyers. Conceptually, these taxes may be compared to the former United States documentary stamp taxes on deeds or share issues, but they are much heavier. Conard, *Corporate Fusion* at 593.

[183] [1969] J.O. L249 (Oct. 3) at 65, unofficial English translation in CCH COMM. MKT. REP. ¶ 3032. The directive also ensures that the tax would be levied only once on any one operation (by the State in whose territory the actual administration office is located), and contemplates eventually a single uniform rate, to be proposed by the Commission before Jan. 1, 1971. Exemptions are provided. The directive also prohibits altogether any indirect tax on securities, including taxes on the creation, issuance or admission of securities to a stock exchange, but taxes on transfer of securities remain permitted. On the difficulties of obtaining agreement on the directive see EUROPE, No. 316 (new series) Apr. 17, 1969, at 5.

the present proposal would provide an exemption from taxes on transfers of property incident upon fusion.[184]

(ii)   Proposed Convention on international fusion

The preliminary draft of the Convention was prepared in 1967 by the working group established under Article 220, and it also is limited to fusions of stock companies.[185] This proposal, and a later 1969 version, left unresolved the question what "link" with a Member State a stock company must show in order to benefit from the provisions of the Convention.[186] One solution would be to apply the same criteria—with certain necessary adjustments—as are employed in the Convention on the Mutual Recognition of Companies for the purpose of deciding which companies are entitled to recognition of their legal personality.[187] However, the French experts urged, as I have adumbrated earlier, that companies belonging to an international group whose "center of decision-making" was outside the Community, should be excluded. The German delegation was concerned about another aspect of the problem: since in theory, fusion could be employed by companies as a device to escape the German requirement of workers' codetermination, the coverage of the Convention must be defined in such a way as to avoid this possibility.

(1)   Conflict-of-laws rules only?

From the *legal-technical* viewpoint, international fusion would become feasible if it were introduced uniformly by national legislation in all of the Member States. In that case, and if the *principal* differences among national rules per-

---

[184] KOM (69)5 endg., *supra* note 180, Begründung at 6.

[185] Comité des experts de l'article 220 alinéa 3 du Traité C.E.E., Droit des sociétés—Fusions internationales, Avant-projet de convention relatif à la fusion internationale de sociétés anonymes, Document de travail no. 4, 16.082/IV/67-F.

[186] Document de travail no. 7, 5873/XIV/69-F.

[187] *See* p. 409 *infra*.

taining to fusion (such as rules on the protection of shareholders and creditors, the acceptance of universal succession)
were removed by coordination, the only additional prerequisite for smoothing the path toward intra-Community fusion
would be an agreement on the applicable rules of conflict
of laws.[188] It was felt, however, that even if national company laws were substantially coordinated, some significant
differences among them would remain; moreover, under any
circumstances, special problems could arise in the case of
an international fusion. For instance, the pursuit of legal
remedies by creditors and shareholders is more difficult
abroad than at home, and this will be so presumably even
after the Convention on Judicial Jurisdiction and Execution
of Judgments in Civil and Commercial Matters becomes effective in the Member States.[189] Again, differences between
the laws of the States of the fusing companies in fields other
than company law, such as labor and social welfare laws,
would be likely to affect the legal position of employees of
the submerged company. Consequently, the proposed Convention is not limited to conflict-of-laws provisions, but includes a number of uniform "internal" rules to govern specifically international fusion. Thus, the question of which
national law is applicable would arise only in case the Convention does not supply such a uniform "internal" rule. In
that case, the controlling choice-of-law principle appears to
be that the law governing each company is to be applied
with respect to that company.[190] Thus, for instance, where

---

[188] Beitzke, *Internationalrechtliches zur Gesellschaftsfusion* at
14-36.

[189] For a reference to this Convention see *supra* note 55, p. 45, and
infra p. 405.

[190] Beitzke, *Internationalrechtliches zur Gesellschaftsfusion* at 20
ff.; *cf.* § 77 (a) of the MODEL BUS. CORP. ACT which reads: "Each
domestic corporation shall comply with the provisions of this Act with
respect to the merger or consolidation, as the case may be, of domestic
corporations and each foreign corporation shall comply with the applicable provisions of the laws of the state under which it is organized."
On the controlling choice-of-law principle in the field of company
law see *supra* p. 29.

the law governing one or more of the fusing companies requires judicial or administrative control over domestic fusion, these provisions must be observed with respect to each
such company. However, this choice-of-law rule is coupled
with a "minimum standard" "internal" rule that would
come into play only if the applicable law of a Member State
did not contain a comparable provision for public control
over domestic fusion; in that event, that Member would be
required by the Convention to modify its law to the effect
that the resolutions of the shareholders' meeting on fusion
must be embodied in a notarial act.

In evolving the "internal" rules, the authors of the Convention relied heavily on the proposed directive on domestic
fusions which I have discussed in the preceding section; but
they deviated from it in a number of more or less important
aspects, although the more recent versions have reduced
these deviations.

(2) Non-assignable contracts

In principle, as a result of the "universal succession,"
the surviving company assumes the contractual obligations
of the submerged company. The consequences of fusion
upon *non-assignable* contracts concluded by the submerged
or surviving company are to be determined by the law
governing such contracts in case of a domestic fusion. However, two variants have been under consideration as regards
contracts whose execution by either the submerged or the
surviving company becomes impossible or substantially
more difficult as a result of the fusion: first, a uniform
"internal" rule providing for damages, and possibly for recourse to a court by either party with a view to a readjustment of the contract and damages; second, a uniform choice-
of-law rule pointing to the law applicable to these contracts
in the event of a domestic fusion. Actions based on these
provisions may be brought before any court which has
jurisdiction in accordance with the new Convention on Judicial Jurisdiction and Execution of Judgments; but a party

to a contract with the submerged company retains his right
to sue before any court which would have been competent
in the absence of the fusion. The Convention on jurisdiction and execution should generally facilitate execution of
judgments on the surviving company's property located in
another Member State.

(3) A "ceiling" on procedural prerequisites; appraisal right; creditor protection

The national law applicable to each company in case of a
domestic fusion is to determine the modalities of the shareholders' meeting, called to decide on the international fusion, but the law of the submerged company may prescribe
special quorum or voting requirements for an international
fusion; in no case, however, may the requirements exceed
specified limits.[191] The suggested requirements differ from
those proposed in the directive on domestic fusion. The
purpose of a uniform rule in the Convention would be to
avoid as much as possible the development of "currents" of
international fusions which—it is said—could arise if rules
in some States were to remain more liberal than in others.
In contrast with the fusion directive, the Convention was to
give the dissenting minority shareholder an "appraisal right,"
presumably in recognition of the special need for shareholder protection in fusions across political frontiers. However, this provision, "inspired by Italian law," appeared to
pose so many difficulties, particularly as regards taxation,
that it is likely to be eliminated.

As far as ordinary creditors of the *submerged* company are
concerned, they would have the right to oppose the fusion
and demand security, unless a court finds that they already
are secured or that the company is sufficiently solvent, or

---

191 The maximum required voting majority is three-quarters of all
the votes cast, and the maximum quorum is one-half of the shares
entitled to vote in the first meeting and one-fourth of the shares in
the second meeting.

unless the court authorizes advance payment of the debt. A uniform jurisdictional rule identifies the court at the location of the submerged company's central administration as the competent tribunal. While some delegations favored outright extension of the same prerogatives to the creditors of the *surviving* company, others inclined toward a choice-of-law rule that would make the extension dependent upon the law applicable to domestic fusion. Bondholders of the submerged (and possibly also of the surviving) company would receive in principle the same protection as ordinary creditors, without prejudice to the rules of the national law applicable to the company concerned regarding the collective rights of the bondholders.

The Convention on international fusion would itself fix the point of time at which the fusion takes effect in internal relations and when it may be invoked against third parties.[192]

(4) Social aspects

No agreement has been reached thus far on the article of the Convention that would deal with a situation where the national law of a fusing company required representation of employees in the company administration. Because of the danger, real or imaginary, of circumvention of the German law on workers' codetermination, the German governmental experts have been extremely wary of the entire concept of international fusion. They reportedly took the position at one stage of the negotiations that international fusion would be acceptable only if the surviving company were organized in the form of a "European-type" company which would embody a workers' codetermination feature, but the Italian, Dutch and Belgian Governments apparently did not agree.

---

[192] Internally, upon completion, as appropriate, of the formalities of judicial or administrative control or execution of a notarial act; externally, national rules on "publicity" applicable to each company must be observed and the fusion cannot be invoked against a third party until the last formality of "publicity" is complied with.

The proposed Convention seeks to give assurance to employees of the submerged company that they will be protected in their acquired rights. An employment contract binds the surviving company in full measure and remains subject to the originally applicable law, even if the employee agrees to move with his job to another State.[193] If he refuses to move, the consequences are again determined by the contract and the same law, unless the employee elects instead to claim an indemnity amounting to a three-months' salary, with an increment depending on his seniority. Of course, national laws in this field differ—for instance as regards the right to strike—and thus problems with political implications may be involved. It would not come as a surprise if this provision were omitted from the final text.

After the effective date for an international fusion fixed in the Convention, the fusion may be contested as invalid ("null") only for violation of the rules on judicial or administrative or notarial control, but a court will not declare a fusion invalid if the ground for invalidity may be removed; the court may refuse to do so in any case if it is impossible to restore the state of affairs existing prior to the fusion.

(h)   Some closing observations

The negotiations both on the directive and the Convention have revealed an interesting aspect of the attitude of the Netherlands experts. Perhaps because the new Netherlands law will contain provisions on fusion, and also for reasons of economic policy favored by the Netherlands Government, the Dutch experts in Brussels have been extraordinarily cooperative. This attitude, as we have seen, is in sharp contrast to their generally negative posture toward coordination in other areas of company law. On the other hand, principally because of the politically "tainted" problem of codetermination, the German experts have proceeded

---

[193] *See* p. 381 *supra* on the proposed directive on domestic fusions.

with great circumspection, and the Italians have made things difficult by insisting that legal solutions of their own system be adopted in each instance.

Neither the proposed directive nor the proposed Convention offer original, innovating ideas, as compared with the solutions in the national laws. They will, however, have the practical effect, at least in some instances, of cumulating the national measures for the protection of shareholders and creditors, so that this protection will be stronger than it is today, even in those States with modern company laws. Examples of this effect are the provisions on information for the shareholders and verification of the exchange of stock by auditors. On the other hand, one may criticize the absence in the directive (and most likely also in the Convention) of the "appraisal right" of the dissenting minority shareholder. His position will be of course improved by the obligatory audit, but this is not an iron-clad safeguard, since valuation methods leave a wide margin for discretion. Moreover, the fairness of the exchange is not the only concern of the dissenting shareholder; he is also concerned with his position in the majority-dominated, surviving company, and here his voting right may not give him sufficient protection. The quorum and voting majority requirements in the proposed directive are based on the assumption that the fusing companies are independent and not linked together in the relationship of holding or otherwise affiliated companies. In the latter situation, the right to compel redemption of his shares at an appraised valuation is the only effective protective remedy. We should, however, recognize that a substantial body of opinion among the experts has questioned the value of the "appraisal right," and even in Italy, where it has been on the books, the experience is not considered uniformly as positive. In fact the practical value of this right is questioned in the United States as well.[194]

---

[194] Manning, *The Shareholder's Appraisal Remedy, An Essay for Frank Coker*, 72 YALE L.J. 223 (1962).

The principal obstacle to an agreement on the Convention appears to be political, the question of workers' codetermination.[195] In estimating the probable effect of the Convention, one must not lose sight of an important political fact of life. For the submerged company (or more accurately for its shareholders), fusion entails not only a change in the applicable law but also a transfer of political control from one government to another. Thus, for example, if a French company is submerged in a Belgian company, it is the Belgian Government that in principle would be able to impose "police-power" measures ranging from regulation to sequestration, to nationalization.[196] This effect of fusion cannot be removed by any assimilation or even unification of law. It could be mitigated by the introduction of a "European company," which I shall discuss later in this book, and fully neutralized only if national economic and political policies are closely coordinated in an effective institutional framework.[197]

4. Convention on recognition of companies[198]

The term "recognition" has many meanings. We speak of a "recognized child" in family law, recognition of a

---

[195] See also discussion of this problem *supra* p. 391, and in connection with the "European company" *infra* p. 464.

[196] On the problem of changing nationality see also *infra* p. 476.

[197] On the European Company see this chapter, section 5.

[198] Convention sur la reconnaissance mutuelle des sociétés et personnes morales, signed on Feb. 29, 1968; *Rapport concernant la Convention sur la reconnaissance mutuelle des sociétés et personnes morales,* présenté par M. Berthold Goldman, Professeur à la Faculté de droit et des sciences économiques de Paris (cited below as *Rapport Goldman),* reproduced with the Convention in 1968 REV. TRIM. DROIT EUR. 400; the text of the Convention in the four official languages and in an unofficial English translation is reproduced in the 1969 Bull. E.C. Supp. No. 2; *see also* an unofficial English translation of the Convention in CCH COMM. MKT. REP. ¶ 6083 and *infra* in Annex II p. 525.

Extensive literature deals with the problem of recognition of companies in the EEC and this Convention. CARUSO, LA SOCIETÀ NELLA

newly emerged state or newly installed government in public international law, recognition of foreign judgments or legal persons in private international law (conflict-of-laws). In both public and private international law it is the nation-state that grants or denies recognition. In public international law, the "recognizing" nation-state expresses "a value judgment acknowledging that a given fact situation is in accord with the exigencies of the international legal order."[199] In private international law, the "recognizing" nation-state agrees to extend to its own system certain legal

---

COMUNITÀ ECONOMICA EUROPEA 217 (Napoli 1969): RENAULD, DROIT EUROPÉEN DES SOCIÉTÉS at 6.02 (Bruxelles, Louvain 1969); van Hecke, *Erkenning, zetelverplaatsing en fusie*, in EUROPEES VENNOOTSCHAPSRECHT, LE RÉGIME JURIDIQUE DES SOCIÉTÉS DANS LA CEE, KATHOLIEKE UNIVERSITEIT LEUVEN at 149 (Antwerpen-Leuven 1968); Beitzke, *Zur Anerkennung von Handelsgesellschaften im EWG-Bereich*, 1968 AWD 91; Capotorti, *Il problema del reciproco riconoscimento delle società nella Comunità economica europea*, 1966 RIVISTA DELLE SOCIETÀ 969; Dieu, *La reconnaissance mutuelle des sociétés et personnes morales dans les Communautés européennes*, 1968 CAHIERS DE DROIT EUROPÉEN 532; Cerexhe, *La reconnaissance mutuelle des sociétés et personnes morales dans la Communauté économique européenne*, 1968 REV. MARCHÉ COMMUN 578; Drobnig, *Kritische Bemerkungen zum Vorentwurf eines EWG-Übereinkommens über die Anerkennung von Gesellschaften*, 1966 ZHR 93; Drobnig, *Conflict of Laws and the European Economic Community*, 15 AM. J. COMP. L. 204 (1966-67), particularly 207-10; Gessler, *Gegenseitige Anerkennung von Gesellschaften und juristischen Personen im EWG-Bereich*, 1967 DER BETRIEB 324; Goldman, *Le projet de convention entre les états membres de la Communauté économique européenne sur la reconnaissance mutuelle des sociétés et personnes morales*, 1967 RABELS ZEITSCHRIFT 201; Goldman, *La reconnaissance mutuelle des sociétés dans la Communauté économique européenne*, in ETUDES JURIDIQUES OFFERTES À LÉON JULLIOT DE LA MORANDIÈRE 175 (Paris 1964) ; Goldman, *The Convention Between the Member States of the E.E.C. on the Mutual Recognition of Companies and Legal Persons*, 6 C.M.L. REV. 104 (1968-69); van der Grinten, *Erkenning van vennootschappen en rechtspersonen in de Europese Economische Gemeenschap*, 1966 SOCIAAL-ECONOMISCHE WETGEVING 201; Grossfeld, *Die Anerkennung der Rechtsfähigkeit juristischer Personen* 1, at 16 ff., 46 ff.; Houin, *Où en est le droit des sociétés dans le Marché commun*, 1968 REV. TRIM. DROIT EUR. 131, particularly 145 ff.

[199] Rigaux, *Les personnes morales en droit international privé*, 1964 ANNALES DE DROIT ET DE SCIENCES POLITIQUES 241, at 245 (Bruxelles).

effects attributed to a fact situation in the legal system of
another nation-state.

In a pluralistic, horizontally organized community of nation-states, "recognition" has been a traditional instrumentality for cohesion, even though nation-states have exercised
wide discretion in appraising various fact situations and, particularly in public international law, have often employed
recognition in pursuit of national foreign policy, without
reference to the demands of the legal order. However, within
a more closely integrated federal or regional community of
states, public international law is displaced—to a greater or
lesser extent, depending on the degree of integration—by
"internal" public law; and the discretion of one member
state in granting or denying recognition to judgments or
legal persons, including companies, of another member state
is curtailed by normative constraints designed to protect common interests of the community.

*(a) Is there a need for uniform conflict-of-laws rules on recognition
of companies throughout the Community?*

If a company organized in one Member State is to do business in another Member State it must be "recognized" there
as a legal person.[200] Above all, "the freedom of establishment" (EEC Articles 52 to 58) and "the freedom to supply
services" (EEC Articles 59 to 66) across national frontiers
which the Treaty seeks to assure throughout the Community
territory for the benefit of Community companies, could not
become reality without the concomitant assurance of "recognition" of such companies. Although the obligation to
recognize in this context appears to be implicit in the Treaty,
the Member States undertook explicitly in EEC Article 220
to negotiate on securing "mutual recognition for companies
listed in Article 58."

Whether a foreign company will be recognized or denied
recognition has heretofore been determined in each Mem-

---

[200] *See* p. 43 *supra.* Beitzke, *Anerkennung* at 2; Grossfeld, *Die
Anerkennung* at 16-17.

ber State in principle by its own conflict-of-laws rules which have served to identify the applicable law. These conflict-of-laws rules vary. Thus, in the Netherlands, as we have seen, the applicable law is the law of the state of the company's incorporation, while in the other five Member States the law of the state of the company's "real seat" (central administration) applies. The "real seat" rule is reflected in national legislation, case law, and in some treaties, but there are variations in its application.[201] As long as recognition is governed by different national rules, freedom of establishment within the Community—it is said—could not be properly safeguarded;[202] moreover, the need for recognition may arise and recognition must be assured also outside of the estab-

---

[201] BATIFFOL, TRAITÉ at No. 193; VAN BOXSOM, RECHTSVERGELIJ-KENDE STUDIE OVER DE NATIONALITEIT DER VENNOOTSCHAPPEN at 56 (Brussels 1964); KEGEL, INTERNATIONALES PRIVATRECHT at 205 ff. (2d ed., München 1964); LOUSSOUARN, LES CONFLITS DE LOIS EN MATIÈRE DE SOCIÉTÉS at 126 ff. (Paris 1949); Beitzke, *Anerkennung* at 13 ff.; Goldman, *La reconnaissance* at 175-83; van Hecke, *Nationality of Companies Analysed*, 1961 NEDERLANDS TIJDSCHRIFT VOOR INTERNATIONAAL RECHT 223; Loussouarn, *Les sociétés étrangères en France*, 1958 JUR.-CL., DROIT INTERNATIONAL, fasc. 564 B No. 13. *See also* for detailed references to legislation and case law *supra* p. 29.

[202] Beitzke, *Zur Anerkennung* at 99; Dieu, *La reconnaissance mutuelle* at 534; Goldman, *La reconnaissance* at 176-85, where the differences in the statutes, case law and treaties are described in detail. These differences, and the additional reasons why a Convention was considered necessary, are briefly:

1. The Netherlands applies the "incorporation theory" *(see infra),* while the other Five in principle follow the "real seat" theory.

2. The "real seat" theory could result in a refusal of recognition when the real seat of the foreign company is in the state where recognition is sought (in the Federal Republic), or it could lead only to the application of local (forum) law to that company *(e.g.,* Art. 197 of the Belgian CODE DE COMMERCE, as interpreted by the Cour de cassation, *supra* p. 30).

3. Recognition in existing bilateral agreements does not comprise *all* companies and legal persons covered by EEC Art. 58, and the same applies to the Hague Convention on Recognition. *See* note 216 *infra.*

4. The traditional exception of public policy is much too broad for Community purposes.

lishment and supply-of-services context.²⁰³ For these reasons, uniform conflict-of-laws rules are necessary on this subject.²⁰⁴

When national company laws become more similar as a result of the coordination and "spontaneous assimilation" described earlier, the need for such uniform conflict-of-laws rules will be reduced, but it will by no means be eliminated, since company laws will continue to differ in many respects. Moreover, these laws will still be a part of the respective national systems and, in principle, will remain subject to change by the national lawmaker. In other words, in the foreseeable future, if ever, company law will not become "federal-type" Community law. It will, therefore, continue to be necessary to look to the appropriate conflict-of-laws rules in order to determine, first, whether a foreign company will be recognized as a legal person and, second, if the answer is in the affirmative, what law should govern its internal and external relationships.²⁰⁵ Although traditionally the problem has been posed in terms of these two distinct and separate questions, some believe that there is little sense in such separation.²⁰⁶ Indeed from a practical viewpoint, "any legal person is such only in relation to a specific legal issue, such

---

²⁰³ A company organized and operating in a Member State may want, for instance, to sue in another Member State on a contract with a local company of the latter State which is unrelated to any supply of services. Unless recognized as a legal person, it could be denied standing to sue.

²⁰⁴ Beitzke, *Zur Anerkennung* at 91.

²⁰⁵ Beitzke, *Anerkennung* at 10; Goldman, *Le projet* at 203; Grossfeld, *Die Anerkennung* at 3.

²⁰⁶ Drobnig, *Kritische Bemerkungen* at 113, 114, takes the view that recognition is a real issue only if linked with a conflict-of-laws rule determining the law that governs internal and external relationships of the foreign company.

The third and separate question in addition to the two stated in the text above would relate to the prerequisites for the "establishment" of the foreign company, or—in American terms—for its "qualification" to "do business" locally. In the absence of treaty obligations, these prerequisites are determined by the national law of the state of the establishment. Walker, *Foreign Corporation Laws: The Loss of Reason,* 47 N.C.L. REV. 1 (1968). *See* p. 52 *supra.*

as his capacity to sue . . ., to be sued . . ., or to hold property," and it is in a sense artificial to speak of a recognition
of a legal person in the abstract.[207]

(b)   Bases for recognition: the "real seat" or the "law of incorporation" rule?

(i)   The competing interests

The modern functional rationale for the Anglo-American
(and Dutch) rule of incorporation is said to be the need for
certainty and maximum uniformity in the choice of law.
There can be no doubt about the location of incorporation,
wherever the actual corporate administration and operations
may be. The Continental "real seat" rule, on the contrary,
favors the law of the central administration or principal
place of business because only that law secures proper regard
for the economic reality and prevents fraud on, or "abuse of,
the law."[208] This rule which is followed in all Member States
except the Netherlands, has been criticized on the ground
that the task of determining the location of the company's
real seat "might impose a burden upon the litigants and the
courts in close cases."[209]

In terms of the private and governmental interests involved, the problem may be posed in the form of a series of
questions: When private parties organize a company, should
they enjoy the same freedom or "autonomy" in choosing the
governing law for the company as they enjoy, particularly
on the Continent, and to a somewhat more limited extent in
the United States, in selecting the governing law for a contract?[210] Or is it necessary, in view of certain interests of a

---

[207] EHRENZWEIG, A TREATISE ON THE CONFLICT OF LAWS at 408.

[208] EHRENZWEIG, A TREATISE ON THE CONFLICT OF LAWS at 411;
BATIFFOL, TRAITÉ at No. 194.

[209] Reese & Kaufman, *The Law Governing Corporate Affairs* at
1127.

[210] KEGEL, INTERNATIONALES PRIVATRECHT 205 ff. On the autonomy
of the parties generally see Yntema, *"Autonomy" in Choice of Law,*
1 AM. J. COMP. L. 341 (1952).

higher order, for the company to be governed by the law of
the state of the "real seat" from which it is administered? At
times, the question is posed in a less detached formulation,
with a pointed reference to the Delaware and New Jersey
experience: Should a state be in a position to adopt—in pursuit of its own economic interests—an "exorbitantly" liberal
company law with a view to attracting an inordinate number
of companies which in fact would have little more than a
formal connection with its territory? And should that state
be entitled to expect other states—in the context of economic
intercourse—to "recognize" such companies as properly
constituted legal persons?[211]

A recent German study of policy considerations underlying the two competing principles[212] stresses the difference, in
terms of the socio-economic impact, between a simple contract and a commercial company which represents the common organizational form of the most significant enterprises
in modern national economy. Whereas contract law contemplates the widest autonomy of the parties, company law
in most Continental states contains a great number of mandatory rules which reflect national legal and economic policy.[213] As a result, the state seeks to have its law applied to
all those enterprises which center their activities on its territory; it wants to make sure that these enterprises do not
"escape" its control by claiming to be governed by the law
of another state with perhaps a more liberal or, in any
case, a different system. A variety of governmental interests,
real or imaginary, may be involved, including the protection

---

[211] On the movement in the United States opposing an excessively
broad application of the incorporation theory (the problem of the
"tramp" or "pseudo-foreign corporation") see Jennings, *The Role of
the States* at 194-96; Latty, *Pseudo-foreign Corporations,* 65 YALE L.J.
137, at 138-43 (1955-56) .

[212] Grossfeld, *Die Anerkennung* at 30.

[213] *Id.* at 22 ff., 29. See on this the conclusions of the Procureur
Général at the Belgian Cour de cassation in two ancient cases involving recognition of a French stock company, Pas. belge 1849. 1. 221;
1851. 1. 307; also French Cour de cassation, Recueil Dalloz 1847. 2. 171.

of local creditors and investors, and the competitive position of local companies. The assumption is, of course, that significant systemic differences exist between the legal orders concerned; as these differences give way to a measure of consensus on questions of economic, social and legal policy, the intensity of the governmental interest of the national lawmaker in the application of its own law decreases. Then, the freedom of parties to choose their own law may be given a broader scope, as is contemplated by the incorporation rule.

The theory of incorporation has been meeting with increasing favor from Continental lawyers in Germany, France, Switzerland, and Italy,[214] and it has been gaining ground in international forums such as the Institute of International Law,[215] and in the more recent international agreements, such as the 1956 Hague Convention Concerning Recognition of the Legal Personality of Foreign Companies, Associations, and Foundations, which has not come into force as yet.[216] Article 1 of the Hague Convention enunciates the incorporation theory in general terms, but Article 2 significantly limits the reach of that theory:

> If a company organized in one state establishes its real seat in another state it must be recognized in a third state only if the state of the real seat has accepted the incorporation theory.

---

[214] Beitzke, *Anerkennung* at 13; van Hecke, *Nationality of Companies Analysed* at 227.

[215] See the rules of the Institute of International Law, approved on Sept. 10, 1965, and recommended for adoption "to all States"; the rules are reproduced in 60 AM. J. INT'L L. 523 (1966) and discussed in Drucker, *Companies in Private International Law*, 17 INT'L & COMP. L.Q. 28 (1968).

[216] English text in 1 AM. J. COMP. L. 277-80 (1952). Five ratifications are required for the Convention to come into effect. Belgium, France, the Netherlands, Spain and Luxembourg have signed and all but Spain and Luxembourg have ratified. *Rapport Goldman* at par. 5. I am advised that, contrary to the statement in the *Rapport,* Luxembourg did not ratify.

If the opposition to the rule of incorporation has been receding somewhat, this trend may be due in some measure to the integrating effect of rapidly growing international trade, to the emergence of a multinational corporation which no longer operates in the confines of a single nation-state, and generally to the intensified transnational inter-course.

(ii)   The regional context

The important Article 58 of the EEC Treaty clearly mir-rors the changing currents within a regional context. Al-though it concerns only admission to business activities and not conflict-of-laws rules, Article 58 necessarily assumes rec-ognition since without it admission would be illusory. The article postulates Community-wide freedom of establish-ment and supply of services for companies and legal persons which are organized in accordance with the law of a Mem-ber State and *have their registered office, central administra-tion or principal place of business* within the Community. Thus, Article 58 does not require that the "real seat" (cen-tral administration) be in the State under whose law the company is organized or, for that matter, that it be any-where in the Community.[217] A literal interpretation would suggest that a mere registered office anywhere within the Community territory would suffice. However, this broad in-terpretation has not been entirely accepted because, pur-suant to Article 52, par. 1, individual nationals of the Mem-ber States may claim freedom of establishment in another State only if they are already "established" within the Com-munity, and companies are to enjoy the same, but not more extensive, benefits as natural persons. Accordingly, the Gen-eral Programs for the Removal of Restrictions on the Right of Establishment and on the Free Supply of Services,[218]

---

[217] *See* Goldman, *La reconnaissance* at 189 ff.; Beitzke, *Anerken-nung* at 13; Dieu, *La reconnaissance mutuelle* at 539 ff.; Grossfeld, *Die Anerkennung* at 17.

[218] [1962] J.O. 36, [1962] J.O. 32. *See* p. 25 *supra.*

adopted by the Council of Ministers, provide that when the companies "have only their registered office within the Community . . ., their business activity shall show a continuous and effective link with the economy of a Member State . . .," before they can claim the benefits of the Treaty.

The liberal posture embodied in Article 58 is obviously related to the coordination of national company laws on the basis of Article 54, par. 3(g). This coordination effort—and generally the assimilation of national laws and economic and social policies—is expected to advance freedom of establishment, and also to remove the obstacles to a more liberal recognition practice. As a short-range objective, however, the Member States agreed that the obligation to grant recognition should be strengthened; and they chose an international convention as the vehicle to achieve that objective.

(c)   Convention on the Mutual Recognition of Companies and Legal Persons[219]

(i)   The origin[220]

Earlier in this study, I discussed in some detail the considerations that had led to the establishment—at the initiative of the former Directorate General IV—of the working group of governmental experts which was to deal with the implementation of the clauses in Article 220 of the EEC Treaty concerning companies.[221] At that occasion I have also sought to identify the reasons why this group had arranged its priorities so as to take up first, on June 28, 1962, the problem of recognition of Community companies. Among the experts we encounter again the familiar names of Professors Gessler, van Ryn, and Houin, who were active also in the coordination work and in national reforms. With Professor Berthold Goldman of the Paris Law Faculty as an effective, albeit stern, chairman, the group labored for three years. Having at its

---

[219] For references to the text see *supra* note 198.

[220] *Rapport Goldman* at par. 1; Beitzke, *Zur Anerkennung* at 91.

[221] *Supra* p. 182.

disposal a report prepared by Professor Beitzke,[222] the group completed the first draft of the Convention on this subject on June 11, 1965. The Commission concurred in this draft on January 5, 1966, and the final text, containing certain modifications desired by the Governments, was ready in October 1967. The text was to be signed in December 1967, but this plan came to naught as a result of the Netherlands' reaction to General de Gaulle's attitude toward the admission of the United Kingdom.[223] The Convention was finally signed on behalf of the six Governments by the Ministers of Foreign Affairs on February 28, 1968.

A clause in the preamble affirms that the Ministers approved the Convention when *"meeting within the forum of the Council."* The Ministers had employed this somewhat controversial formula in the past, when they had reached an agreement on a matter not specifically authorized in the Treaty, but falling generally within its orbit. In the Commission's view, the recourse to this procedure endowed the Convention with a status different from an ordinary treaty: the agreement was, a Commission spokesman declared, "the first European Convention supplementing the Treaty of Rome."[224] Although this factor may be politically significant, in law the Convention is still an inter-state treaty governed in principle by international law; at any rate, it did not become a "Community act" in the technical sense and thus would presumably *not* fall within the jurisdiction of the Court of Justice.[225] However, in addition to the fact that it was drafted under the auspices of the EEC, the text itself bears out the close links between the Convention and the Community.[226] From the practical viewpoint, even more

---

222 Beitzke, *Anerkennung* at 1-47.

223 Beitzke, *Zur Anerkennung* at 91.

224 Comm. Spokesman's group (EEC), P14/68, Information Memo (undated).

225 *See* p. 420 *infra.*

226 See for instance the references to the EEC Treaty and specifically to Arts. 220 and 58 in the preamble of the Convention; Art. 10 of

indicative is the fact that the Convention was concluded among the Member States of the Community exclusively, and will come into effect only after all Members have ratified.[227]

The original draft of the experts contained an article similar to the corresponding provision in another "European Convention," the Convention on Judicial Jurisdiction and Execution of Judgments in Civil and Commercial Matters.[228] This article reflected the assumption that any state, which in the future will join the Community, will *have to* adhere also to the Convention on Recognition of Companies, perhaps with certain adjustments to be negotiated at the time. This

---

the Convention discussed *infra;* Art. 11, last clause, indicating the controlling role of the EEC Treaty; Arts. 12, 13, 15, 16, 19, assigning certain ministerial functions (in connection with the coming into effect of the Convention, etc.) to the Secretary General of the Council of the Communities; Art. 18 requiring the President of the Council of the Communities to call a conference for a revision of the Convention if requested by a Contracting Party; Art. 19 (four authentic texts), Art. 17 (unlimited duration) and Art. 14 (ratification by all Six is required) were obviously "inspired" by the corresponding articles in the EEC Treaty. It was also agreed to publish the Convention for information purposes in the Official Journal of the Communities. *Rapport Goldman* at par. 45.

The Convention refers throughout to "Contracting States" and "territories to which the present Convention applies"; but the preamble makes it clear that the States that concluded the Convention were "The High Contracting Parties to the Treaty establishing the European Economic Community."

[227] Art. 14. The Convention was approved by the French Parliament. Law No. 69-1134 of Dec. 20, 1969.

[228] Art. 63. The Convention was signed on Sept. 27, 1968. French text published by Conseil des Communautés européennes, undated. Unofficial English translation in 1969 Bull. E.C. Supp. No. 2; authentic texts of the French, German, Dutch, Italian versions in the same Supplement. *See* Hay, *The Common Market Preliminary Draft Convention on the Recognition and Enforcement of Judgments—Some Considerations of Policy and Interpretation,* 16 Am. J. Comp. L. 149 (1968); Nadelmann, *Jurisdictionally Improper Fora in Treaties on Recognition of Judgments: The Common Market Draft,* 67 Colum. L. Rev. 995 (1967); Nadelmann, *The Outer World and the Common Market Experts' Draft Convention on Recognition of Judgments,* 5 C.M.L. Rev. 409 (1968); Nadelmann, *The Common Market Judgments Convention and a Hague Conference Recommendation: What Steps Next?,* 82 Harv. L. Rev. 1282 (1969).

provision was dropped in the final text, and all that remains
is a Joint Declaration No. 2, included in a Protocol annexed
to the Convention, in which the parties declare their readiness to negotiate with any state "associated" (and by infer-
ence with any state that will become associated) with the
Community, with a view toward mutual recognition of companies along the lines of the basic principles of the Convention, and in the context of the agreement of association.[229] However, in the minutes of their meeting the
Ministers recorded their unanimous opinion that any state
which adheres to the Community must also adhere to the
Convention. This statement is of immediate interest in view
of the current negotiations with the United Kingdom, Denmark, Ireland, and Norway, concerning admission to membership in the Community.

(ii) The benefiting companies and legal persons

According to Article 1 of the Convention, all companies
formed under civil and commercial law, including cooperatives, must be recognized without more, if they were organized under the law of a State party to the Convention[230] and
if they have their registered seat (*siège statutaire, satzungsmässiger Sitz*) in the territories to which the Convention
applies. Article 8 makes it clear that any such company
may not be denied recognition even if it is not considered
a full-fledged legal person by the law under which it was
formed; it must be recognized so long as, under that law,
it has the capacity to sue or be sued in its own name, as
in the case of the German partnership (*offene Handelsgesellschaft*). In addition, Article 2 extends the benefit of rec-

---

[229] EEC Art. 238 provides that the Community may conclude
"with a third country, a union of States or an international organization, agreements creating an association embodying reciprocal rights
and obligations, joint actions and special procedures." A number of
such association agreements has been concluded, but the content varies
considerably.

[230] The term "State" will be used to indicate a State party to the
Convention.

ognition to all legal persons of public or private law, other
than companies, which meet the same conditions and which
are engaged in an "economic activity" performed normally
for remuneration.

A comparison of this definition of benefiting companies
and legal persons with that contained in EEC Article 58
reveals some interesting differences.[231] In the first place,
while Article 58 appears to exclude "non-profit companies,"[232] the Convention benefits companies of civil and
commercial law, whatever their purpose or nature of their
activity; their legal form is the determining factor. Thus
companies of civil law are also included, even though under
the laws of some Member States they may be organized for
a non-profit purpose.[233] Companies of commercial law are
conclusively presumed to exercise "commercial" activity and
thus to pursue a gainful purpose, even though in fact this
may not be so in a particular case.[234]

A second extension of the coverage, beyond the scope of
EEC Article 58, stems from Article 2 of the Convention
which includes all legal persons other than companies, pro-

---

[231] *See Rapport Goldman* at paras. 9-14; Beitzke, *Zur Anerkennung*
at 93; Cerexhe, *La reconnaissance* at 582 ff.; Dieu, *La reconnaissance
mutuelle* at 537; Goldman, *Le projet* at 214 ff.; van der Grinten, *Erkenning van vennootschappen* at 204 ff.

[232] Cerexhe suggests that Art. 58, "despite its rather paradoxical
language," in effect does not purport to require gainful purpose for
companies of civil or commercial law. Cerexhe, *La reconnaissance* at
584.

[233] In German law, § 705 of the CIVIL CODE, a company formed
pursuant to the Civil Code may pursue any purpose, including a
non-profit purpose. However, it is excluded from the coverage of the
Convention because it cannot sue or be sued in its own name. §§ 50,
736 of the ZIVILPROZESSORDNUNG of Jan. 30, 1877 (RGBl 83). Beitzke,
Zur Anerkennung at 93. On the other hand the società semplice of the
Italian law and the vennootschap onder firma of the Netherlands law
are included. *See* Joint Declaration No. 1, attached to the Convention.

[234] *E.g.*, a charitable institution run by a stock company. § 6 of
the German COMMERCIAL CODE. On the German partnership (offene
Handelsgesellschaft) under commercial law see § 105 of the COMMER-
CIAL CODE, which requires "commercial" and therefore gainful, purpose
(Handelsgewerbe).

viding they meet the prerequisite of "economic activity normally performed for remuneration."[235] This new concept[236] was substituted for the "gainful purpose" prerequisite of Article 58 because this article, if construed narrowly, might not include certain enterprises which, the national experts felt, should be covered by the Convention. The experts had in mind particularly nationalized enterprises, mixed private-public companies providing public services, and certain modern organizational forms of economic activity of entirely private nature, such as companies established by industrial enterprises to supply these enterprises with services in the fields of research, market surveys, or the protection of industrial property rights—fields in which the profit motive is not directly involved. Yet the experts were fully aware of the vagueness of the new concept.[237]

(iii) Prerequisites for recognition—Optional limitations

For recognition purposes, it is sufficient for the companies and legal persons comprised in Articles 1 and 2, to have their registered seat *anywhere* within the Community, even if they have their real seat outside the Community (for instance, a company organized under the Netherlands law with a real seat in the United States). Thus a registered seat—not a real seat—is the minimum contact required as a prerequisite to a claim to recognition—and this is in accord, as we have seen, with the *literal* reading of EEC Article 58 for the purpose of freedom of establishment and supply of services. The "real seat" is defined in Article 5 of the Convention as the place of the "central administration." This definition coincides with the Hague Convention and with the national

---

[235] More specifically, under this article are included those legal persons which either have "economic activity normally performed for remuneration" as their principal or subsidiary purpose, or which actually engage in such activity on a continuing basis without thereby infringing the law under which they were formed.

[236] *But see* EEC Art. 60 which speaks of "services normally supplied for remuneration."

[237] *Rapport Goldman* at paras. 10-12.

law in the Member States.[238] If this were the entire story, the victory of the incorporation theory would have been complete as regards recognition. However, following the Hague Convention pattern, the concession made in the first two articles by the "real seat" advocates is in part taken back in Articles 3 and 4.

In the first place, according to Article 3, each State is left free to declare that it will deny recognition to any company whose real seat is outside the territories to which the Convention applies, if the company does not maintain a *genuine link (lien sérieux, wirkliche Verbindung)* with the economy of one such territory. This limiting clause of an uncertain meaning differs somewhat from the corresponding (and equally vague) limitation grafted upon Article 58 by the General Programs,[239] and it may cause difficulties of interpretation. It is clearly designed to prevent a non-Community enterprise from claiming recognition within the Community on the basis of nothing more than a "post-office-box" address (a registered seat) in the Netherlands.

Second, Article 4 purports to deal with the position of a company which claims recognition in the State, party to the

---

[238] *Rapport Goldman* at par. 18. The draft of the Institute of International Law (Art. 5) defines "the actual seat of a company" as "the place at which it has its principal centre of control and management, even if the decisions which are taken at that place follow directives given by shareholders who reside elsewhere." Drucker, *Companies in Private International Law,* 17 Int'l & Comp. L.Q. 28, at 34 (1968). On the concept of "central administration" see Rabel, 2 Conflict of Laws at 40-41.

[239] "[A] continuous and effective link with the economy of a Member State." *See* note 32 *supra.* The Goldman Report acknowledges but does not explain the divergence. *Rapport Goldman* at par. 18. The International Court of Justice held that a State could not lay down rules governing the grant of its nationality and claim that these rules "are entitled to recognition by another State unless it has acted in conformity with the general aim of making the legal bond of nationality accord with the individual's *genuine connection* with the State which assumes the defense of its citizens by means of protection as against other States." (Emphasis added.) Nottebohm Case, Lichtenstein v. Guatemala, 1955 I.C.J. Rep. 4, at 24. *See also* the concept of "real connection" in the Hague Convention, *infra* note 241, p. 411.

Convention, where its real seat is located, although it was organized under the law of another such State, where it has its registered seat. In such a situation, under the prevailing national laws, if the real seat were located in the Federal Republic, recognition there could be denied, whereas if it were in Belgium, Italy, Luxembourg or (since the 1966 reform) in France, the law of the real seat would be applied *without* denial of recognition.[240] The formula for dealing with this situation was worked out in a special meeting of the Benelux Ministers of Justice. The Ministers considered the problem in the context of a company which had been incorporated in good faith in the Netherlands, and which, after it had operated for a time in and from the Netherlands, decided—for good business reasons—to transfer its central administration (real seat) to another State. According to the final solution embodied in Article 4 of the Convention, a State may declare that it will apply the mandatory provisions of its own law to a foreign company whose real seat is in its territory; however, it may apply its non-mandatory (optional) provisions to the company only if the company's charter does not contain a reference to its own law under which it was formed, or if the company is unable to show that it has in fact conducted its activity during a "reasonable time" in the State of its formation.

One problem with the formula is that it may be difficult to determine in some instances whether a provision is or is not of a mandatory nature in a given system. Again, the mandatory provisions of company law generally include rules on the formation of companies. Thus, the argument could be made that if, according to the mandatory rules of the State where the foreign company has its real seat, the company is not validly constituted, it may be denied recognition. The Netherlands experts strongly opposed such an in-

---

240 *Rapport Goldman* at paras. 3-4; Belgium: Art. 197 of the CODE DE COMMERCE; Italy: Art. 2505 of the CODICE CIVILE; Luxembourg: Art. 159 of the Law of Aug. 15, 1915; and France: Art. 3 of the Law of July 24, 1966.

terpretation as defeating the objective of recognition, and
they received substantial support from some other delegations. Without taking a position on this argument, the
German delegation posed a series of searching questions and
demanded that a uniform interpretation be agreed upon.
Evidently the German experts were again troubled by a
political nightmare: a foreign company, possibly organized
abroad by Germans with German capital, could maintain its
central administration on Federal territory and claim recognition there as a foreign company, even though the workers
would not be represented on its organs as required by the
Federal law on workers' "codetermination." Nevertheless, the
German demand was opposed by some who argued that the
experts should not be expected to interpret their own texts,
and by others who inclined in the same direction because
they considered the problem of limited practical importance.
It is reported that the experts have not reached an understanding on an interpretation. Thus any problems that may
arise will have to be resolved on a case by case basis, without
reference to an agreed interpretation. Nevertheless, the text
of Article 4 makes fairly clear the intention to prohibit a
refusal of recognition by the State of the real seat, and instead—as a compromise—to authorize that State to impose
its own law on the recognized company. The practical effects are uncertain and could vary from State to State. The
formula has all the disadvantages of complexity and ambiguity that characterize a laborious compromise. Although
this solution represents some progress over the Hague Convention,[241] the prospect of living under two different com-

---

[241] Art. 2 of the Hague Convention allows *refusal* of recognition
in this situation unless the real seat is transferred to a state which
follows the theory of incorporation. Similarly, Arts. 3 and 4 of the
International Law Institute Draft would permit refusing recognition
by the state of the real seat if the company charter does not accord
with its law, *unless* (and this is a deviation from the Hague solution)
the company carries on its principal business activity in the state of incorporation (Art. 3) or has a *"real connection"* with its territory (Art.
4). This "real connection must be established by facts other than the

pany-law systems is fraught with so many uncertainties (particularly if the requirements of the two systems should not be compatible) that the company is likely to feel compelled to transfer its real seat to the State where it was formed.[242]

The State's option in Article 4 to impose its own law upon a foreign company is limited to the situation where the company's real seat is in its territory. More specifically, a company organized in State A, with its real seat in State B, must be recognized in State C even if State B follows the real-seat principle. This is another small step forward and beyond the Hague Convention which demands recognition in this situation only if State B adheres to the principle of incorporation.[243] In this case the interest of the "third" State where recognition is claimed in having its own law applied is not as pervasive as it might be if the real seat were located in its territory. But the adopted solution could still lead to a situation where the same company is viewed in a third State as governed by the law of the State of its formation, while the State of the real seat is free to apply its own mandatory law to it. The fact that Article 4 allows for such an outcome indicates that the Convention on Recognition does not achieve the fullness of uniform treatment which is a major, if not the paramount, objective of private international law.[244]

---

mere indication of a registered office, and may in particular consist of a place of business in the territory, of the origin of the share or loan capital of the company, of the nationality or habitual residence of the shareholders or of those in control of the company" (Art. 4(2)).

[242] Beitzke, *Zur Anerkennung* at 94; van der Grinten, *Erkenning van vennootschappen* at 208. In order to reduce the threat to legal security posed by the options left open in Arts. 3 and 4, the States which desire to take advantage of the options must make the necessary declarations *at the latest at the time when they deposit their instrument of ratification* (Art. 15).

[243] Art. 2, par. 2 of the Hague Convention; *see also* Arts. 3 and 4 of the International Law Institute Draft.

[244] Grossfeld, *Die Anerkennung* at 47; *but see* Beitzke, *Anerkennung* at 20.

(iv) Effects of recognition

Reflecting the "traditional solution of private international law" which is followed also in the Hague Agreement, Article 6 provides that a company or legal person, which is entitled to recognition by virtue of the Convention, shall have the same capacity that was accorded to it by the law under which it was organized. But here again we encounter limitations designed to assure the forum State of a degree of freedom to apply its own law.[245]

The first such limitation derives from the reach of Article 4, which can come into play, as we have seen, when the real seat of the company is situated outside the State where it was organized and in the State where recognition is sought. Among the rules of its own law which the State of the real seat is free to apply to the foreign company might be a provision affecting the capacity of the company.[246]

In the second place, pursuant to Article 7, the State in which recognition is claimed may deny the foreign company specific rights which under its own law are also denied to its own companies of a "corresponding type," but any such limitation cannot have the effect of depriving the foreign company of its *basic* capacity to be the subject of rights and obligations, to enter into contracts and undertake other legal acts, and to sue and be sued.[247] However, the foreign company cannot itself invoke the limitations allowed by Article 7. Thus, the limitations are exclusively for the protection of local parties that contracted with the company.[248]

This complex of provisions is based on a rather esoteric distinction between two concepts: "the general capacity,"

---

[245] On analogies in American law see EHRENZWEIG, A TREATISE ON THE CONFLICT OF LAWS at 409, 413.

[246] *Rapport Goldman* at par. 23.

[247] *Cf.* also Art. 6 of the Hague Convention; further limitations are permitted in Art. 6 of the draft of the International Law Institute.

[248] This was considered by some to be an improper discrimination against foreign companies. Van der Grinten, *Erkenning van vennootschappen* at 209; *but see contra, Rapport Goldman* at par. 25.

consisting of the "abstract aptitude to take part in legal life" as "a distinct entity" which is determined exclusively by the law of the State where the company was organized; and the specific rights "which form the concrete content of the general capacity" and which, in the first instance, are also determined by the same law, but which the State where recognition is sought may deny by reference to its own law, within the limits described above.[249] This analysis lends support to those who consider it futile to attempt to draw a sharp distinction between "recognition" and the conflict-of-laws rules, which determine the law governing the foreign company's capacity and specific rights.

When we speculate on the application of these particular provisions, we should keep in mind that the Convention seeks to assure certain minimum rights derived from recognition, but does not deal with freedom of establishment or services, which involve rights *connected with specific activities*.[250] This means, on the one hand, that a German company need not be established in France, or supply services there, in order to claim the right to sue in a French court on its contract to purchase goods or to hire personnel in France. Its right to sue derives from the recognition in France of its general capacity and is specifically guaranteed in Article 7 of the Convention.[251] On the other hand, if under French law, a French limited liability company is excluded from banking business, a German limited liability company (of a "corresponding type") could also presumably be excluded from that business in France, in accordance with Article 7. Moreover, the German company could not rely on Articles 52 and 60 of the EEC Treaty concerning establishment and supply of services, since, under these provisions, France is

---

[249] *Rapport Goldman* at par. 24. *See* Art. 5 of the Hague Convention.

[250] See, in the same sense, Art. 7 of the Hague Convention.

[251] That right is also a necessary corollary of the right of establishment and supply of services, as applied to specific occupations and professions.

required only to accord the German company treatment equal to that accorded to its own companies. There is, finally, another group of restrictions relating to Article 7, which may be illustrated by the provision in German law confining membership on the executive board (*Vorstand*) of German stock companies to natural persons and making legal persons ineligible. It could hardly be argued that a foreign stock company, formed in a State which does not have such restrictions, could be denied recognition in the Federal Republic under Article 7, solely because its board includes another company among its members. Professor Goldman takes the optimistic view that in practice this type of question is not likely to arise very often. In his opinion, the differences among national laws governing the two types of companies which one is most likely to encounter in transnational business, that is the stock company and the limited liability company, are no longer very marked as far as the rules concerning capacity are concerned; and the differences that do exist will be further reduced in response to the coordination of national laws.[252] Not everyone may agree with this appraisal of the present law or with the estimate of the future development.

(v) Omissions

The Convention has been criticized for its omissions. In fact, in contrast with the draft of the Institute of International Law, it contains for instance no provision for the reverse of the situation contemplated in Article 7, that is, the situation in which the law of the State where recognition is claimed gives the company a broader capacity than the company's own law, to the possible prejudice of local creditors.[253]

---

[252] Goldman, *La reconnaissance* at 194-96.

[253] Beitzke, *Zur Anerkennung* at 95; Drobnig, *Kritische Bemerkungen* at 116. Art. 12 of the draft of the International Law Institute would make it impossible for a company to rely on a limitation on the power to act on its behalf imposed by its own law, if the contract was concluded outside the state of its incorporation and if the limita-

The differences between the national rules on *ultra vires* acts could lead to such a situation since, according to the basic principle underlying the Convention, the law of the State where the company was organized would apply unless Article 4 comes into play. As far as the law on *ultra vires* is concerned, the question will become moot for most practical purposes as between the Member States of the Community, when the First Directive on coordination of national company law is effectively implemented.

Similarly, it is said that the Convention should have provided appropriate conflict-of-laws rules to determine which law should govern the tort liability of the company for acts of its representatives (the "personal" law of the company or the law of the place of the wrong), the personal liability of members of "unincorporated" companies,[254] etc. The omission of such rules, it is said, will have disfunctional effects as long as substantial differences exist among the national laws of the Member States.

(vi)   The exception of public policy (ordre public)

In the field of conflict of laws, the exception of public policy *(ordre public)* traditionally enables the forum State to refuse the application of foreign law which would otherwise govern under its own choice-of-law rules. Thus, the Hague Convention stipulates that its provisions governing recognition may be disregarded by a State, party to the Convention, on the ground of *ordre public.*[255]

In the Community framework, a public-policy exception formulated in such general terms appeared inappropriate, and for that reason the draftsmen of the Convention on

---

tion does not exist under the law of the place where the contract was concluded, and if the other party had no reasonable notice thereof.

[254] Goldman, *Le projet* at 217, appears to suggest the law of the state of the company's formation, while Beitzke, *Zur Anerkennung* at 96, is concerned about the protection of local parties dealing with the foreign company.

[255] Art. 8 of the Hague Convention.

Recognition of Companies sought to restrict the scope of the exception.[256] In Article 9 they limited the application of the exception of public policy to situations where the company claiming recognition contravenes—through its charter *purpose,* through the *objective* which it seeks to achieve, or through the *activities* in which it is in fact engaged[257]—the principles which the *forum State* considers a matter of *public policy "in the private international law sense."*

It was suggested during the negotiations that the concept of public policy should be made a part of Community law, common to all States and applicable not only with reference to recognition of legal persons but also in other contexts, such as the Convention on Judicial Jurisdiction and Execution of Judgments. However, the Governments evidently were unwilling to go that far in the direction of unification. On its face, Article 9 seems to assume that, subject to the above mentioned restrictions of an uncertain reach, it is for each State to supply its own definition of public policy in applying the exception. Nevertheless, taking into account the consistent case law of the national courts, public policy "in the private international law sense" was clearly intended to comprise only the fundamental political, social and economic precepts of the forum State; in any case it was understood to be less comprehensive than the French "internal public policy" *(ordre public interne).*[258] Although the uncer-

---

[256] *See generally, Rapport Goldman* at paras. 27-32; Cerexhe, *La reconnaissance* at 588-90; Beitzke, *Zur Anerkennung* at 96; Dieu, *La reconnaissance mutuelle* at 545; van der Grinten, *Erkenning van vennootschappen* at 209.

[257] This formula, enumerating the "purpose," "objective," and actual activity, is an expanded version of the clause in the Franco-German Convention of Establishment and Navigation of 1956, which served as its "inspiration." It is designed to prohibit refusal of recognition on the basis of rules governing the *constitution* and *functioning* of the company. *Rapport Goldman* at paras. 28, 29-30.

[258] Art. 30 of the Introductory Law to the German Civil Code, which deals with the German equivalent of what the Convention de-

tainty of this changing concept of public policy has been reduced somewhat in the Convention, it probably still comprises not only certain fundamental rules of statutory national law, but the underlying principles and policies as well. The approach adopted in Article 9 resembles in a remote way the situation in the United States, where the exception of public policy in the choice-of-law setting remains operative as between the States of the Union and in principle its scope is defined by State law; its reach has been reduced by the courts and its application is subject only to a very loose control by the Federal Constitution. By way of contrast, courts have for all practical purposes eliminated "public policy" as a ground for refusal to "recognize" sister State judgments, relying on the Full Faith and Credit Clause of the Federal Constitution.[259]

---

scribes as the "ordre public in the private international law sense," provides that "the application of a foreign law is excluded if the application would be contrary to good morals or to the purpose of a German law." PALANDT, BÜRGERLICHES GESETZBUCH at 1766 (25th ed., München and Berlin 1966). Despite this broad language, the courts construe the exception narrowly, as contemplating refusal only if the application of foreign law should "attack directly the foundations of the German political or economic life" or if it should be "outright unbearable for the German legal order in terms of its legal concepts and in its measure of good morals." See KEGEL, INTERNATIONALES PRIVATRECHT at 184-87, citing cases at 184, 185. Similarly, Art. 31 of the Italian Codice civile provides in broad language that in no case may foreign laws, regulations, entities or contracts have effect in Italy "if they are contrary to the public order or good morals (costume)." Yet the courts have limited the exception to assuring "respect of the highest and most essential interests" of the Italian legal order. Corte di Cass., Oct. 21, 1955, No. 3399, and other cases cited in MARTINO, CODICE CIVILE, COMMENTO CON LA GIURISPRUDENZA at 33 (4th ed., Rome 1964). In France, distinction is made between "ordre public interne" (or more accurately "ordre public au sens du droit civil interne"), illustrated by Art. 6 of the Code civile providing that parties cannot derogate by contract from *mandatory rules* of the law, and "ordre public international" (or more precisely "ordre public au sens du droit international privé"). BATIFFOL, TRAITÉ at No. 367 ff. In France, still another notion of "ordre international public" concerns "les grands problèmes internationaux."

[259] *See generally* CURRIE, SELECTED ESSAYS ON THE CONFLICT OF LAWS at 196, 272-73, 625-26 (Durham 1963); Reese & Kaufmann, *The Law Governing Corporate Affairs* at 1137, 1143.

Article 9 of the Convention singles out one specific instance in which the exception of public policy may not be invoked. It provides that if the so-called "one-man" company may lawfully exist in its own State, it cannot be denied recognition in the other States on the ground of public policy. Although national company laws in the Community thus far do not allow a company to be initially organized by a single founder, the German and Netherlands laws do acknowledge the continuing existence of a company even if, after its constitution, all of its shares are acquired by the same person; and the French courts follow this view as regards *foreign* companies when the law governing those companies acknowledges such continuing existence. The Belgian courts, however, refuse to recognize the "one-man" companies on grounds of public policy.[260] From the viewpoint of the Belgian Government, this clause in Article 9 offers a convenient opportunity for getting rid of an outdated and obnoxious judge-made rule. The proposed reform of the Belgian company law, as we have seen, would go beyond any national law in the Community in the direction of admitting the "one-man" company.[261] Article 9 does not provide an express answer to the question whether the forum State could impose personal liability on the single shareholder, and there is no indication thus far that this thorny problem is being tackled in the context of coordination of company laws.[262]

The remaining provision in this section makes it clear that any "principles and rules" of national law that are contrary to the EEC Treaty may not be considered as national public policy for the purpose of denying recognition (Article 10). The experts apparently had in mind certain principles, such as discrimination on the ground of nationality in the field of establishment, which—although

---

[260] *Rapport Goldman* at paras. 28-29.

[261] The reform law would allow a stock company to act as a sole founder in forming a subsidiary. *See* p. 328 *supra*.

[262] *See* p. 328 *supra*.

eliminated as between the Members of the Community—
may remain applicable in the Member States to nationals of
third countries.[263] Yet one may think also of the non-self-
executing provisions of the EEC Treaty generally or of
directives which a Member has failed to implement in its
national law, although the experts obviously did not wish
to contemplate such noncompliance. One interesting "practical" effect of this provision may be that, in case of litigation before a national court, that court may be required,
in accordance with Article 177 of the EEC Treaty, to refer
to the Community Court of Justice the question of interpretation of that provision of the EEC Treaty which the
relevant national policy is alleged to contravene.[264]

(vii)   Toward a uniform interpretation?

The Court of Justice of the Communities would have
seemed the logical forum for ensuring an effective application, and above all a uniform interpretation of the Convention, since national courts are likely to diverge in their reading of some of the general and often ambiguous formulas.
Yet, as I have indicated above, the jurisdiction of the Court
does not extend to the Convention, although it could have
been so extended, had a clause to that effect been included in
the text. One possible legal basis for such a general clause is
Article 182 of the EEC Treaty, which enables the Court to
assume jurisdiction over Treaty-connected disputes between
Member States if these disputes are submitted to the Court
by virtue of a special agreement (*compromis, Schiedsver-
trag*). However, in that case the jurisdiction of the Court
could comprise only disputes *between Member States,* and
could not include controversies among private parties. Considering the nature of the Convention, this limitation would
gravely impair the utility of the Court's role. Moreover, the

---

[263] *Rapport Goldman* at par. 21 ff.
[264] Cerexhe, *La reconnaissance* at 590.

majority of the experts reportedly interpreted Article 182 to require a special agreement for each separate dispute; such a narrow interpretation would seem to preclude any practical arrangement on this basis.[265]

A more promising avenue is offered by Article 177 of the EEC Treaty according to which a national court, hearing a case between private parties, may, and if it is a court of last instance, must certify to the Community Court any question of "interpretation . . . of acts of the institutions of the Community," if a ruling on this question is necessary for the decision in the case. By inserting an appropriate clause in the Convention, it would have been possible to extend the authority of the Court under this article to cases before national courts involving questions of interpretation of the Convention. No amendment of the EEC Treaty would appear necessary to achieve this purpose.

At the time the Convention was drafted, however, the Member States apparently were not prepared to take this further step on the road toward legal integration. For one thing, it was argued that the Court of Justice was essentially equipped to deal only with questions of "public law"; it would have to form a separate chamber to deal with "private-law" cases of the sort that will arise under the Convention. A more weighty argument was based on the consideration that the question of the extension of the Court's role was of a more general scope, since it arose in connection with all the "European" Conventions which have been negotiated in accordance with Article 220. According to that argument, different arrangements might be required for different Conventions and an amendment of the EEC Treaty might be more appropriate. Thus, the working group confined itself to the Joint Declaration No. 3, which was attached to the Convention, and in which the parties affirmed their readiness to study the possibility of broadening the jurisdiction of the Court and negotiating an agree-

---

[265] See apparently contra 2 GROEBEN-BOECKH at 153.

ment to that effect. A special group has in fact been established for this purpose,[266] and it has reportedly reached an agreement on a draft of a Protocol that would extend the Court's jurisdiction so as to enable it to interpret the Convention on Recognition of Companies by reference from national courts in accordance with Article 177.

(viii)   Summary and Conclusion

As I have suggested elsewhere in this study, the decision to assign priority to the topic of recognition of companies was hardly justified by the realities of the emerging Common Market; it was based essentially on concerns for systemic symmetry which is endemic to Continental thought, and which also can be read into Article 220 of the EEC Treaty, if one is so inclined.

In the context of a regional, integrated market, law on recognition should serve to advance the security and growth of transnational intercourse and to free the corporate decision-maker from unnecessary legal restraints. The ultimate objective is, of course, a more rational use of human and material resources in the expanded economic arena. Perhaps because the negotiations for the Convention had begun at a relatively early date, when the Common Market was still more a mirage than a reality, the Convention in some respects falls short of meeting this purpose. It does advance a certain distance toward a stricter obligation to recognize, and toward greater uniformity, but, because of the options left open to the Member States, the Convention fails to assure true uniform treatment and legal certainty in the practice of recognition. The complexity of the solutions was due largely to the differences among the national laws, particularly to the divergence between the Netherlands law, which follows the incorporation theory, and the laws of the other five States, which still largely adhere to the "real seat"

---

[266] *Second General Report on the Activities of the Communities 1968,* at 88.

theory. The differences in the application of the real seat rule between the Federal Republic and the other four Members also posed a problem.

One may only speculate what sort of a document the experts could have produced if they had employed their considerable talents and expertise toward devising a truly new framework for recognition, based on a realistic analysis of the governmental and private interests in a modern economic union, rather than devoting so much attention to devising ingenious escape mechanisms, designed to pacify traditional national fears and to safeguard the sacrosanct preserves of national law.

In its basic approach and technique, the Convention differs little from the Hague Convention, which, of course, was not conceived in the context of an integrated, regional market. However, the EEC Convention has without question introduced improvements over the prevailing state of national law and over the Hague Convention. The EEC Convention has broadened the circle of the benefiting legal persons; it has increased the acceptance of the incorporation theory in situations where the registered and real seats of the company are separated; and it has also reduced somewhat the scope of the exception of public policy.

One may expect that the Convention on safeguarding the legal personality of a company in case of a transfer of its seat, which still remains to be negotiated in accordance with the EEC Article 220, will carry the progress toward greater "mobility" of companies further, particularly since mutual knowledge of national laws will be increased and the differences between them will be reduced by national reforms and presumably also by Community coordination.

In any event, one's judgment of the Convention must be tempered by the understanding of the political realities in Europe, including the fact that it was the first agreement reached in accordance with Article 220 to supplement the EEC Treaty, and thus was blessed with all the exaggerated care that lawyers everywhere tend to lavish upon a "precedent." To an American lawyer, hardened by the disconcerting process of interest analysis which characterizes the current uncertain state of the conflict-of-laws doctrine in the United States, the formulas of the Convention appear at the same time too rigid to meet the vagaries of actual life and too vague to be of real help. One must keep in mind, of course, that the Congress of the United States has never even entered the precincts of the choice-of-law area—although it has had ample and unquestioned constitutional power to do so under the Full Faith and Credit Clause and the Interstate and Foreign Commerce Clause—but rather has abandoned that area, for better or for worse, to the courts. The Full Faith and Credit Clause, as interpreted by the Federal Supreme Court, has proved to be a weak reed indeed in the choice-of-law field.

In the final analysis, the EEC Convention must be viewed in the broader perspective of the on-going effort described in this book. It demonstrates the difficulties incumbent in fashioning uniform conflict-of-laws rules among nations with divergent national laws, even when those nations are making a conscious effort to minimize the differences in their laws in the framework of an integrated, regional community.

5. The "European Company"[267]

(a) The why's and wherefore's

It is in the nature of things that a historian, even if he succeeds in tracing the origin of a new idea with some

---

[267] Despite the tentative nature of the plans for a "European Company" an astounding amount of literature has already been produced on this subject:

Belgium:

RENAULD, DROIT EUROPÉEN DES SOCIÉTÉS at 9.01 (Bruxelles, Louvain 1969); van Ryn, *La société européenne,* in L'HARMONISATION DANS LES COMMUNAUTÉS, INSTITUT D'ETUDES EUROPÉENNES, UNIVERSITÉ LIBRE DE BRUXELLES at 65 (Bruxelles 1968); Horsmans, *Quelques arguments pour une société de type européen,* 1964 REVUE DES SOCIÉTÉS 428; Leleux, *Faut-il créer la société commerciale européenne pour faciliter l'in-*

tégration économique dans la C.E.E., 1968 JOURNAL DES TRIBUNAUX 109; van Ommeslaghe, *La création d'une société commerciale de type européen*, 1960 JOURNAL DES TRIBUNAUX 457; van Ryn, *Faut-il instituer la société européenne?*, 1967 JOURNAL DES TRIBUNAUX 377.

France:

Houin, *La société européenne*, in L'HARMONISATION DANS LES COMMUNAUTÉS, INSTITUT D'ETUDES EUROPÉENNES, UNIVERSITÉ LIBRE DE BRUXELLES at 79 (Bruxelles 1968); Houin, *Les sociétés de type européen*, 1962-64 TRAVAUX DU COMITÉ FRANÇAIS DE DROIT INTERNATIONAL PRIVÉ (séance du 7 déc. 1962) 19; Thibièrge, *Le statut des sociétés étrangères*, in LE STATUT DE L'ÉTRANGER ET LE MARCHÉ COMMUN, 57ᵉ Congrès des notaires de France, Tours 1959, 240, at 270, 352, 360 (Paris 1959); Chartier, *Vers la société de type européen*, 1967 REV. MARCHÉ COMMUN 310; Chevallier, *Pour une société par actions de type européen*, 1960 BANQUE 495; Foyer, *La proposition française de création d'une société de type européen*, 1965 REV. MARCHÉ COMMUN 268; Goldman, *Le droit des sociétés internationales*, 1963 CLUNET 320; Houin, *Le régime juridique des sociétés dans la Communauté économique européenne*, 1965 REV. TRIM. DROIT EUR. 11; Houin, *Où en est le droit des sociétés dans le Marché Commun*, 1968 REV. TRIM. DROIT EUR. 131; Lepaulle, *Betrachtungen über die internationalen Gesellschaften*, 1960-61 AcP 126; Marty, *Les sociétés internationales*, 1962 RABELS ZEITSCHRIFT 73; Rault, *Pour la création d'une société commerciale de type européen*, 1960 REV. TRIM. DROIT EUR. 741; Vasseur, *Quelques arguments pour une société de type européen*, 1965 REV. DES SOCIÉTÉS 18; Vasseur, *Pour une société de type européen*, Mélanges offerts à René Savatier 903 (Paris 1965); Willemetz, *Faut-il envisager la création d'une société de type européen?*, 1960 REV. DES SOCIÉTÉS 364; Willemetz, *Une société de type européen*, 1960 REV. MARCHÉ COMMUN 38; Vers la société de type européen, Travaux et documents du Congrès international, Deauville, 13-15 avril 1967, 1967 Bulletin des Juristes Européens (No. 27-28).

Federal Republic of Germany:

Von Caemmerer, *Europäische Aktiengesellschaft*, in BIEDENKOPF, COING, MESTMÄCKER (eds.), FESTSCHRIFT FÜR KRONSTEIN 171 (KARLSRUHE 1967); Hauschild, Report in *Coopérations* at 317; Gessler, *Europäisches Gesellschaftsrecht am Scheideweg*, 1969 DER BETRIEB 1001; Bärmann, Book review of WANG, DIE EUROPÄISCHE AKTIENGESELLSCHAFT IN DER EWG (Freiburg/Switzerland 1964), 1966 AcP 545-46; Arnold, *Die Angleichung des Gesellschaftsrechts in der Europäischen Wirtschaftsgemeinschaft*, 1963 AWD 221; Bärmann, *Einheitliche Gesellschaftsform für die Europäische Wirtschaftsgemeinschaft*, 1961 AcP 97; Duden, *Internationale Aktiengesellschaften*, 1962 RABELS ZEITSCHRIFT 90; Duden, *Das Für und Wider einer europäischen GmbH*, 1962 GMBH-RUNDSCHAU 76; Eder, *Europäische Handelsgesellschaft*, 1965 GMBH-RUNDSCHAU 220; Gessler, *Grundfragen der europäischen Handelsgesellschaft*, 1967 BB 381; Lietzmann, *Stand der Diskussion über die europäische Aktiengesellschaft*,

degree of accuracy, is less able to identify the original motiva-
tions behind it. This observation certainly applies to the
schemes for a "European" or "European type" company, the

1961 AG 57; Lietzmann, *Die Vertretungsmacht gegenüber Dritten im
Schnittpunkt der geplanten europäischen Aktiengesellschaft,* 1961 AG
125; Lietzmann, *Zur europäischen Aktiengesellschaft,* 1961 AG 253;
Möhring, *Rechtsvereinheitlichung und Rechtsgarantien im EWG-Be-
reich,* 1965 NJW 2225; Seidl-Hohenveldern, *European Companies,* 1959
THE JOURNAL OF BUSINESS LAW 120 (London); Skaupy, *Europäisches
Gesellschaftsrecht,* 1966 AG 13; von der Groeben, *Auf dem Wege zu
europäischen Aktiengesellschaften,* 1967 AG 95.

Great Britain:
Thompson, *The Project for a Commercial Company of European
Type,* 10 INT'L & COMP. L.Q. 851 (1961).

Italy:
LA SOCIETÀ COMMERCIALE EUROPEA, ATTI DEL CONVEGNO DI VILLA
PIGNATELLI (Napoli 1968); Minervini, *Alcuni problemi connessi alla
creazione di una società di tipo europeo,* 1966 RIVISTA DELLE SOCIETÀ
984; Simonetto, *Problemi e perplessità intorno alla istituzione della
società per azioni europea,* 1963 RIVISTA DI DIRITTO CIVILE 313; A.T.B.,
*Alcune osservazioni su un progetto francese per la creazione di una
società commerciale di tipo europeo,* 1965 IL DIRITTO NEGLI SCAMBI
INTERNAZIONALI 79.

Netherlands:
Van der Grinten, *Het europees vennootschapstype,* in EUROPEES
VENNOOTSCHAPSRECHT at 37 (Leuven 1968); van der Grinten, *Contre
une société de type européen,* 1964 DE NAAMLOOZE VENNOOTSCHAP 8;
Sanders, *Vers une société anonyme européenne?,* 1959 RIVISTA DELLE
SOCIETÀ 1163; Sanders, *La société commerciale européenne,* 1968
RIVISTA DELLE SOCIETÀ 233; Scholten, *The European Company,* 4
C.M.L. REV. 9 (1967-68); Storm, *Statute of a Societas Europaea,* 5
C.M.L. REV. 265 (1967-68); *A European Company Law in the Making
—But Its Opportunity Is Questioned,* 7 COMM. MKT. 61 (1967). Feb-
ruary-March 1968 issue of *De naamlooze vennootschap* was devoted
to this topic.

Switzerland:
WANG, DIE EUROPÄISCHE AKTIENGESELLSCHAFT IN DER EWG (Freiburg/
Switzerland 1964); Patry, *La société anonyme de type européen,*
Mémoirs publiés par la Faculté de Droit de Genève, No. 18, at 29
(Geneva 1964).

United States:
Ault, *Harmonization of Company Law in the European Economic
Community,* 20 Hastings L.J. 77, at 113 (1968).

last and perhaps the most innovating proposal to be dealt with in this study.

(i)   No basis in the EEC Treaty

One would search the EEC Treaty in vain for any reference to a commercial "Community company" akin to the Dominion company of Canada, which is formed to carry on business in more than one Canadian province and which is incorporated as a federal rather than as a provincial company.[268] The "founding fathers" of the Community contemplated that enterprises in the Common Market will continue to be organized in accordance with the national law of one or the other Member State and in one of the existing legal forms available for commercial ventures. In this respect, the EEC pattern corresponds to the legal setting in the United States,[269] where company law (in the narrow sense) remains within the domain of the States and companies are organized under State law. In the United States, apart from the national banks which are incorporated under federal law, federal incorporation is possible only in isolated instances, for specific federal purposes and in accordance with special Congressional legislation. The varied and sundry proposals for a federal corporation law that would govern companies engaged in inter-state business, or for a federal licensing system that would preserve State laws, but superimpose certain federal rules in the public interest, have run against a successful resistance on the part of corporate executives and of State officials who have been opposed to such an extension of federal power.[270] Instead, the practice

---

[268] McDonald, *The Formation and Operation of Foreign Subsidiaries and Branches, Including the Extent to Which Foreign Subsidiaries Are Entitled to Special Treatment Under the Law of Their Incorporation or Under International Law: Canada,* 16 Bus. Law 416, at 427-28 (1961).

[269] *See* p. 56 *supra.*

[270] *See generally* Loss, 1 Securities Regulation at 107 ff. (2d ed., Boston and Toronto 1961). For an exchange of views concerning the relevance to the European situation of the Small Business Investment

has brought forth the mercurial and mobile "Delaware corporation" as the central instrumentality for a multi-state
enterprise. But this device has certainly not eliminated the
problems facing a company which operates in a multitude
of legal systems.

(ii) Economic grounds

It has been generally agreed on the Continent that the
enlarged market calls for a structural adjustment of enterprises which cannot be accomplished through natural growth
alone, and that a degree of concentration is necessary to
mobilize the necessary capital and other resources.[271] The
removal of internal barriers within the Community and the
reduction of the common external tariff resulting from the
Kennedy Round agreements have sharpened competition;
concentration among Community enterprises is a necessary
counterweight—it is said—to the competition and penetration by American enterprises, which enjoy more powerful
financial and technological resources than their European
counterparts. Until recently, the moves toward concentration
took place predominantly within the individual Member
States with the encouragement from the national governments.[272] Thus despite the emerging transnational Community, industrial concentration has been on a national level,
often with the participation of non-Community enterprises;
this trend has run counter to the objective of interpenetra-
tion across national frontiers within the Community, which
is considered essential for a "Common Market" and an
economic union.

I have dealt in some detail with the arsenal of legal
devices which the EEC Treaty makes available for over-

Act of 1958 and the idea of federally licensed corporations see Tiling &
Nissen, *Federal Corporations als Vorbild für die europäische Aktiengesellschaft? Ein Gegenvorschlag zu Sanders Entwurf*, 1968 AWD 330;
and Ficker, *Federal Corporations als Vorbild für die Europäische
Aktiengesellschaft*, 1969 *Id.* 182.

271 Hauschild, in Coopérations at 319; von der Groeben, *Auf
dem Wege* at 95; Leleux, *Faut-il créer* at 109.

272 Leleux, *Faut-il créer* at 109.

coming, in part at any rate, the obstacles caused by the continuing existence of separate and more or less different national legal systems: the freedom-of-establishment program, and coordination (but not unification) of company laws; the program for freedom of movement of capital; new treaties facilitating recognition of companies, transfer of company seat and transnational fusion; harmonization of tax law. However, there has been an undercurrent of feeling that the development of these instrumentalities has not kept pace with the new economic demands, and that the "European company" may offer a new avenue.

(b) "Psychological" and political grounds

It has been said that psychological factors, derived from the coexistence of diverse national legal systems, have posed a significant hindrance to the structural adjustment in the Community.[273] Only enterprises of substantial dimension, equipped with the necessary staff of legal and economic experts, can cope with the complexities of diverse legal systems and organize or acquire subsidiaries abroad; and even such major companies could reduce their administrative expenditures and improve management procedures significantly, if the parent and all affiliates were subject to identical law. Smaller companies are discouraged by the lack of knowledge of foreign law, practice and mentality. The lending policies of banks are also influenced by these considerations, and the flow of investment abroad and expansion of the capital markets are hampered. There has been some feeling that the "much worked psychological factor," based on the mistrust of foreign law, "disturbs only the lawyers and not the economic circles,"[274] but no reliable data seem to be available in the absence of a survey of attitudes.

The suggestion was made in the management circles which had negotiated the Agfa-Gevaert holding arrangement in

---

[273] Hauschild, in COOPÉRATIONS at 320; Leleux, *Faut-il créer* at 109.

[274] Rabels, *Bericht über die Diskussion,* in EUROPÄISCHE HANDELS-GESELLSCHAFT 100 at 103.

1964[275] that, even if a transnational fusion of the two companies had been legally possible at the time, it would have been inconceivable—for psychological and political reasons—for either the Belgian or the German component to have surrendered its national identification and to have agreed that the surviving company should assume the nationality of the partner; the situation would have been different if the emerging company could have taken on a truly "European identity" under "European law."[276] Again, the recent "joint venture" agreement between a French company (S. A. Citroën) and a German company (N.S.U.) for the joint development of a combustion engine with a revolving piston (Wankelmotor) led to the formation of a common subsidiary on "neutral" territory—in Switzerland. Although Switzerland may have offered certain tax advantages, I am advised that the solution would have been different if a "European company" had been available.

Finally, for the convinced "Europeans" the "European company" offered both a new symbol and a new potential incentive for the lagging integration movement. In France, some, but not all, of its protagonists saw in it an additional means for stemming the American "invasion."

Thus, the idea is rooted in a conglomerate of economic, legal, psychological and political considerations which do not always stand up to a critical analysis, particularly since no specific model was available before 1966 to serve as an authoritative basis for discussion, and consequently, until that time the concept of a "European company" meant different things to different participants.

(c) The history of the European Company: an unfinished symphony
(i) The first initiative

The suggestion for a commercial European company emerged in 1959 almost simultaneously in Tours at a meet-

---

275 See p. 372 supra.
276 See p. 372 supra, and p. 476 infra.

ing of French notaries, and in Rotterdam where Professor
Sanders, whom we had encountered as a member of the
national Verdam Commission,[277] delivered his well-known,
imaginative inaugural lecture. His thought was that the
new corporate form would exist along with the national
company forms, and that in principle it would be available to any enterprise wishing to engage in an activity on
the European level.[278] There followed a detailed discussion
at an international conference arranged by the Paris Bar
in 1960,[279] and although the EEC Commission displayed
some interest,[280] the reaction within the Member States was
largely skeptical, particularly in the Federal Republic and
in Belgium.[281] The only exception was France where study
and debate continued with considerable intensity, especially
in the French Committee on Private International Law
under the stimulus of Professor Houin, and in the "Comité
Hamel,"[282] which also elaborated the topics for the First
Directive on the coordination of company laws.[283]

Several reasons may have accounted for the negative response. The major enterprises that could have been expected to welcome the project feared that, when all is done,
the law which would govern the European company would
cumulate all the restrictive features of the various national
company laws, and for this reason they believed the new
entity would not be very attractive to the business community. Moreover, the proposal was confined to company

---

[277] *See* p. 148 *supra.*

[278] Von Caemmerer, in EUROPÄISCHE HANDELSGESELLSCHAFT at 56.

[279] For the documents of the Congress of Paris see 1960 REV.
MARCHÉ COMM. Supp. No. 27, 1-80. On the results see BÄRMANN,
Einheitliche Gesellschaftsform at 108-12; Sanders, *La fusion* at 2.

[280] Reply to question No. 47 of the member of the European
Parliament, Mr. Lichtenauer, dated Dec. 1, 1959, [1959] J.O. 1272.

[281] *See* BÄRMANN, *Einheitliche Gesellschaftsform* at 112 ff; Duden,
Internationale Aktiengesellschaften at 98; van Ryn, in L'HARMONISA-
TION at 65.

[282] Professor Vasseur made the principal contribution here.

[283] *See* p. 201 *supra.*

law, and thus the enterprises, desiring to cross national frontiers, would have to become acquainted in any case with
foreign tax, administrative, social security and labor laws.
In addition, they would continue to face the formidable
obstacles in the field of taxation. The medium size companies, including those in France, manifested little, if any,
interest. Again, some government officials feared that adding
another corporate form to the already numerous national
forms would only compound the confusion and, still worse,
would offer an escape from the burdensome, mandatory provisions of some national legislation. Finally, it was felt that
the negotiations for a uniform régime would take much too
long and would impair the prospects for the yet untried
coordination of national laws, which at the time appeared
to offer a more promising avenue.

(ii)   The French proposal and the Commission's response

By 1965 the situation changed. The EEC Commission
undertook a study of the means of advancing the growth
of medium size and smaller enterprises with an emphasis
on the concentration problem which, as we have seen earlier,
by that time had moved to the center of attention.[284]
The French Government, committed as it was to concentration as the major means for combating American "penetration," took the initiative. Drawing upon the preparatory
studies carried on in France, the Government early in 1965
submitted a note to the Commission in which it proposed
negotiations under EEC Article 220 for a "uniform law"
on a European-type company.[285] The move had the support
of the French Bar, allegedly in part because of the dissatisfaction with the then pending draft of the new French company law, which, some had hoped, might eventually atrophy,

---

[284] Denkschrift der Kommission, Das Problem der Unternehmens-
konzentration im Gemeinsamen Markt, Schriftenreihe Wettbewerb
Nr. 3 (Brüssel 1966); English text in 1966 Bull. E.E.C. Supp. No. 9/10,
3, at 6, 7, 15, 16, 17.

[285] Note of Mar. 15, 1965. French text in 1966 REV. TRIM DROIT
EUR. 409; English translation in CCH COMM. MKT. REP. ¶ 9025.

if the European company became reality. Moreover, those within the Government and in the legal profession, who had hoped for greater uniformity through coordination directives, realized by this time that this avenue did not offer any prospect for speedy results.

The Commission took up the French proposal with alacrity; yet more than a year was spent in an effort to reconcile the various views within that body, particularly since there was some insistence on the highest level that the Commission should come out for a "supranational" company as an alternative to the French-proposed national company of a uniform type. In its extensive memorandum of April 1966,[286] the Commission left this issue unresolved, but it concluded that the EEC Treaty provisions did not meet the requirements of the day from the economic and legal viewpoints in the same way as would the European company; only such company could assure full recognition, freedom of seat transfer, unobstructed formation of subsidiaries, transnational fusion and access to capital markets. Sensing correctly that a more concrete basis for discussion was needed, the Commission asked Professor Sanders, with a group of non-governmental expert advisors,[287] to prepare a concrete draft of a legal régime for a European company.

(iii)　The Sanders draft and beyond

The draft was in fact completed within a period of a few months. It represents a remarkable piece of work of more than two hundred articles, with an introduction exploring the legal bases and a detailed, illuminating commentary.[288]

---

[286] A European-Type Company, Memorandum of the Commission of the European Economic Community, 1966 Bull. E.E.C. Supp. to No. 9/10, CCH COMM. MKT. REP., Part I, No. 33, June 21, 1966.

[287] The group consisted of attorney Arendt, Luxembourg, and Professors von Caemmerer of Freiburg, the Federal Republic, Dabin of Liège, Belgium, Marty of Toulouse, France, and Minervini of Naples, Italy. *Sanders Report* at 7.

[288] *Projet d'un statut des sociétés anonymes européennes,* par M. le professeur Pieter Sanders, doyen de la faculté de droit de Rotterdam,

Although the advisory group was quite active, the text reflects a personal conception of the author rather than group consensus.[289]

The Commission transmitted the Report to the Council of Ministers and published it. In its resolution of May 11, 1966, on the "balanced" development of the Community, the Council included a statement to the effect that the "Council and the Member Governments shall consider, as soon as possible, the problems relating to the European patent law and to the creation of a European Company."[290] However, the Netherlands and Italian Governments still wanted to consider first whether a European company was really necessary; the large Netherlands enterprises apparently preferred the EEC Treaty avenue.[291] Moreover, France insisted that the negotiations take place entirely within the Council, and this led to a difficult procedural wrangle, raising again the question of the distribution of power between the Commission and the Council. In October 1966, the Council's Committee of Permanent Representatives organized a new expert working group, chaired again by Professor Sanders, which was to examine certain fundamental preliminary issues. In April 1967, the group presented a new report covering some ten basic questions and indicating the areas of agreement and disagreement. In September 1967, the Committee of Permanent Representatives asked the group to explore particularly what sort of enterprises could employ the proposed new company form, and under what circumstances (the "delicate problem" of "access"). In February 1968, the group resumed the examination of the question whether the European company should be free to issue bearer shares

---

COMMISSION DES COMMUNAUTÉS EUROPÉENNES, COLLECTION ETUDES, Série Concurrence No. 6 (Bruxelles 1967), cited as *Sanders Report*.

[289] The group met eight times during 1966 in meetings lasting several days. Von Caemmerer, in EUROPÄISCHE HANDELSGESELLSCHAFT at 59-60.

[290] EUROPE No. 2521, Oct. 4, 1966, at 6.

[291] *Id.*

—one of the more controversial items.[292] The Committee of Permanent Representatives—and the Council itself—wanted to be sure that no major obstacle would stand in the way of the European company before deciding definitely to go ahead with the project. The example of the treaty on the European patent was said to show that it was not very useful to start drafting a specific text before basic difficulties were resolved.[293] However, since no progress was reported by the Permanent Representatives, the Commission proposed on May 29, 1968, that a new Commission-based committee be established, with the chairman supplied by the Commission. In making this move, designed obviously both to give new impetus to the project and to assert control over it, the Commission relied on what it viewed as its Treaty mandate to submit proposals to the Council in the exercise of its own political responsibility: since the experts were understandably influenced by their own national laws the suggested new committee, the Commission claimed, was the only feasible forum for advancing the project. After a draft is worked out, it will then be for the Council to appoint its own *ad hoc* committee of competent Ministers to prepare the final decision on the draft.[294] However, no agreement was reached on this procedure, and the Commission's committee was never established.

Although the subject appeared from time to time on the agenda of the Permanent Representatives and of the Council itself, no progress was reported. The issue also became enmeshed with the politically charged efforts to have the United Kingdom participate, in one form or another, in the Community work. Finally, in January 1969, just short of four years after the French Government had made its initial proposal, the French delegation was reported to have announced to the Committee of Permanent Representatives that it

---

292 Houin, *Où en est le droit des sociétés* at 132.

293 Houin, *id.*

294 On the Commission's procedural proposal see *New Developments, European Company Statute*, CCH Comm. Mkt. Rep. ¶ 9261.

would refrain from requesting further discussion of the matter, because some Member States wished to use the European company project "for other ends, or to link it with other issues"; for this reason "it seems for the moment useless" to continue the negotiations. It was then decided to halt further work and to take "time for thought," so as "to allow those concerned to begin again later on a new basis."[295] One subsequent development of some interest was the report of the specialized section of the Economic and Social Committee. That report was prepared by M. de Précigout (who was also the rapporteur for the First Directive on coordination of company laws)[296] and it was received by the Committee for its information in March 1969. Although, in strict law, an opinion (avis) of this Committee was not required, the specialized section decided to deal with the matter and focused in its report on the four major issues on which agreement could not be reached. Suffice it to say here that the section wished to endorse the European company, particularly in view of the slow progress in the work on coordination of company laws, as a means to advance both the economic and political objectives of the Community.[297]

Since 1969, the Commission staff has been working with Professor Sanders on a new, comprehensive draft, which would resolve the major questions left open in his Report and which, hopefully, would serve as a basis for renewed negotiations. Although more recently the reaction in non-governmental circles has been more positive than in the earlier years, some adverse attitudes have persisted, particularly in Belgium and the Netherlands, based mostly on the conviction that the coordination and harmonization envis-

---

[295] *Community Work on European Company Again Halted,* EUROPE No. 264 (new series), Jan. 31, 1969, at 4.

[296] *Supra* p. 206.

[297] EUROPE No. 299 (new series), Mar. 21, 1969, at 7.

aged in the EEC Treaty were quite adequate.[298] The trend seems to be toward a widening consensus that a European company would be helpful, if it is assured access to national capital markets, where significant legal restrictions against foreign companies still prevail,[299] and if the agreement on its establishment is accompanied by a realistic harmonization of national tax laws.[300]

(d) The "international company"[301]

(i) Two abstract models

The concepts of an international non-governmental person in general, and an international company in particular, are the reflection of the endemic contradiction between social reality and legal form[302] which is due to the growing disfunctionality of the nation-state. As organized human activities overflow across national frontiers, traditional organizational forms, grounded in a single national legal system, no longer meet the requirements of the new reality.

One may think of an "international company" in terms of two *basic theoretical* models:

First, a legal person, that derives its personality from international law (a treaty or an act of an international organization) rather than from a given national system, and which

---

298 *E.g.,* van der Grinten, in EUROPEES VENNOOTSCHAPSRECHT at 37; van Ryn, *Faut-il instituer la "société européene,"* 1967 JOURNAL DES TRIBUNAUX 377.

299 *See* EUROPEAN ECONOMIC COMMUNITY: THE DEVELOPMENT OF A EUROPEAN CAPITAL MARKET, Report of a Group of experts appointed by the EEC Commission (Brussels 1966); EUROPE, Doc. No. 518, March 21, 1969, *Guidelines on the Progressive Creation of a European Capital Market.*

300 Leleux, *Faut-il créer* at 110.

301 On the subject of this section generally see WANG, DIE EUROPÄISCHE AKTIENGESELLSCHAFT IN DER EWG at 30 ff. (Freiburg/ Switzerland 1964); Duden, *Internationale Aktiengesellschaften,* 1962 RABELS ZEITSCHRIFT at 89; Geiler, *Die sog. Internationalen Juristischen Personen* at 177; Gutzwiller, *Die sog. Internationalen Juristischen Personen* at 116; *Corporations Formed Pursuant to Treaty,* 76 HARV. L. REV. 1431 (1963).

302 Gutzwiller, *Die sog. Internationalen Juristischen Personen* at 117.

is governed by international rather than a national law, and which is linked with international administrative and judicial institutions.

Second, a company, incorporated under a national "uniform" company law, which is set forth in, or annexed to, a treaty; the company derives its legal personality from the national law and is subject to national institutions only; but in the treaty, the parties assume specified obligations as to the treatment and privileges they will accord to a "foreign company" of the uniform type.

The first model is quite compatible with modern international law, and it would avoid the conflict-of-laws problems. However, it postulates a curtailment of national "sovereignty" in the classic sense, and it runs counter to the traditional concepts of national incorporation and "nationality" of a commercial company. Moreover, since international company law does not exist, it would be necessary to create a body of such law, presumably through a process of creative unification, and also to establish the required new international institutions.

The second model, however, which also postulates an agreement on a body of (uniform) company law, would not meet the principal requirements of a truly "international" company, if for no other reason, because of the identification of the company with a single nation-state.

If an international company in a legal sense becomes reality, it is likely to represent a "mix" of the two models. On that assumption, there are three basic issues: *First,* should the company be an international-law person or a "national of a nation-state?"; *second,* even if an agreement could be reached on a more or less detailed set of company law rules, recourse to "subsidiary law" will still be necessary, and how should this subsidiary source be identified?; *third,* should the company be subject to national administrative and judicial agencies, or to international institutions, or to a symbiotic combination of the two?

(ii) A precursor: "the treaty company"

Actually, the general idea of an international, non-governmental legal person was discussed as far back as 1910, in connection with non-profit associations organized on the international level. However, the concept of an international company was not given serious attention by professional circles until after the Second World War, in response to the pressing need for new forms of international cooperation.[303] The International Law Association, a private group, explored the legal issues in the late nineteen forties and fifties.[304] In this context, an attempt was made to draft a charter for companies engaged in activities requiring international regulation, such as civil aviation, but it offered only an incomplete set of rules. No comprehensive body of general law to govern international commercial enterprise has been worked out, and no treaty including such a law has been attempted. However, a number of bilateral and multilateral treaties has been concluded for the establishment of companies which were formed to perform a *specific* task or to conduct a continuing *specific* business, where the enterprise required drawing on capital, private and public, and on labor, from more than one country, or where the activities extended to several countries, or the function was of a vital interest to nationals of more than one country.[305]

The legal structures employed in these treaties draw upon elements from the two theoretical models, suggested above, in widely differing variants and combinations, responding to the specific needs of each situation. "At one end of the spectrum are the treaty companies incorporated under and largely subject to national law," such as the company established in a treaty between Belgium, France and Luxembourg

---

[303] See, however, the earlier forward-looking ideas of Karl Geiler, mentioned in Duden, *Internationale Aktiengesellschaften* at 89-90.

[304] International Law Ass'n, Report of the Forty-Third Conference 269 (Brussels 1948); Report of the Forty-Fifth Conference 43 (Luzern 1952); and Report of the Forty-Sixth Conference 406 (Edinburgh 1954).

[305] *Corporations Formed Pursuant to Treaty* at 1431 ff.

to operate Luxembourg railways. It was formed in Luxembourg, which was to supply the governing law; the Luxembourg Government was to hold the majority of the stock, with the Governments of the other two parties dividing the rest. Disputes concerning the execution of the treaty were to be submitted ultimately to the International Court of Justice.[306] In other instances, the treaty itself included the charter of the company setting forth a partial set of company law rules, but it referred also to a national company law as a supplementary source. This was the case of the convention for the "canalization" of the river Moselle which drew "subsidiarily" upon the German limited liability company law.[307] At the other end of the spectrum is the *Saar-Lothringische Kohlen-Union (Union Charbonnière Sarro-Lorraine)*, established by a Franco-German treaty as a "Franco-German stock company" for the selling of the coal from the two basins, with equal participation of the French and German interests, with two seats (head offices), one in France and the other in Germany, and with legal capacity in both states. The company charter is annexed to the treaty and in case of a conflict between the national stock company law and the charter, the latter is to prevail. If the charter law proves incomplete, it is to be supplemented not by reference to any one national law, but by "basic principles common to French and German law" and "the spirit of cooperation that has led to the transformation of the company into a Franco-German company." Arbitration is provided for the settlement of controversies, and the two Governments share the tax proceeds.[308]

---

[306] Convention Respecting Luxembourg Railways, Apr. 17, 1946, 27 U.N.T.S. 105.

[307] Vertrag zwischen der Bundesrepublik Deutschland, der Französischen Republik und dem Grossherzogtum Luxemburg über die Schiffbarmachung der Mosel, signed on 27 October 1956 at Luxembourg. Verträge der Bundesrepublik Deutschland, vol. 11, No. 116, at 34; 1956 BGBl II 1838. English translation in 1958 CLUNET 266.

[308] Traité sur le règlement de la question sarroise, Oct. 27, 1956, Statuts de Saarlor, Union Charbonnière Sarro-Lorraine, Société par

When the "European movement" brought about the establishment of the Council of Europe in Strasbourg, hope arose in some quarters that it will provide the necessary institutional framework for the development of a regional European company law. Nothing could have been further from reality. The draft convention which was recommended by the Consultative Assembly of the Council in 1952 would have made the "European status" available not, as originally contemplated, to all companies of more-than-national scope, but only to transnational companies holding a concession to operate a public service or to carry out a public work.[309] Even in this diluted form, however, the project proved unacceptable to the governments and interests concerned, and it was quietly dropped; instead, the Council turned toward the less controversial multilateral conventions on freedom of establishment.

The European Community treaties offered a substantially more integrated legal order than that of the Council of Europe. In the context of that order, the EURATOM Treaty introduced the institution of "joint enterprise," in some respects reminiscent of the abortive Council of Europe project. A "joint enterprise" is to carry out an undertaking of "outstanding importance to the development of nuclear energy in the Community."[310] The Commission transmits

---

Actions franco-allemande of Dec. 20, 1957 (Article 84 and annex 29 of the Treaty), J.O. (France) of Jan. 10, 1957, modified by the shareholders' meeting of Oct. 27, 1961, and approved by the two Governments. The company is entered in both the German and French commercial registers, its shares are expressed, and its accounts are kept, in both currencies; its tax is calculated as if one-half of its capital, assets and liabilities, including the reserves, as well as one-half of the turn-over, profits and dividends, were allocated to each of the two seats. The general principles for the coordination of the sales policies through the company must be approved by the two Governments. The charter contains 79 articles.

[309] Council of Europe Consultative Assembly: Documents: Doc. 71, *Draft convention in Recommendation 32,* Eur. Consult. Ass., 4th Sess., pt. 2, vol. 3, at 833 ff. (1952).

[310] Chapter V, Treaty Establishing the European Atomic Energy Community, 298 U.N.T.S. 167 (1958).

to the Council a plan for such an enterprise, including the proposed charter, and the Council approves by a "decision." The enterprise, so constituted, has a legal personality and the "most extensive capacity" accorded to legal persons by the Member State concerned, under its respective national law. The governing law is the Treaty itself, the approved charter and, as a subsidiary source, "the rules applying to industrial or commercial undertakings" (a curiously ambiguous clause), and the national law, if the charter refers to it.[311] In practice, the enterprise is formed under a national law of a Member State in a regular way, and thereafter the Council of Ministers grants it the status of a "joint enterprise," which entails privileges in the fields of taxation, customs, patent licenses, eminent domain and foreign exchange, as specified in the Treaty.[312] The system suggests a "federal"-type licensing of public interest enterprises.

---

[311] EURATOM Treaty Art. 49.

[312] Mathijsen, *Les entreprises communes,* in GANSHOF VAN DER MEERSCH (ed.), DROIT DES COMMUNAUTÉS EUROPÉENNES at 1119 (Bruxelles 1969); Décision du Conseil relative à la constitution de l'entreprise commune "S.E.N.A." ([1961] J.O. 1173); Décision du Conseil relative à l'approbation d'une modification des statuts de l'entreprise commune "Société d'énergie nucléaire franco-belge des Ardennes (S.E.N.A.)" ([1966] J.O. 2686); Décision du Conseil relative à la constitution de l'entreprise commune "Kernkraftwerk R.W.E.-Bayernwerk G.m.b.H." ([1963] J.O. 1745); Décision relative à l'approbation d'une modification des statuts de l'entreprise commune "Kernkraftwerk Rheinisch-Westfälisches Elektrizitätswerk Bayernwerk G.m.b.H." ([1964] J.O. 1557); Décision du Conseil relative à l'approbation d'une modification des statuts de l'entreprise commune "Kernkraftwerk Rheinisch-Westfälisches Elektrizitätswerk G.m.b.H." ([1965] J.O. 1896); Décision du Conseil relative à l'approbation d'une troisième modification des statuts de l'entreprise commune "Kernkraftwerk Rheinisch-Westfälisches Elektrizitätswerk-Bayernwerk G.m.b.H." ([1966] J.O. 1951) : Décision du Conseil relative à la constitution de l'entreprise commune "Kernkraftwerk Lingen G.m.b.H." ([1964] J.O. 3642); Décision du Conseil relative à l'approbation de deux modifications des statuts de l'entreprise commune "Kernkraftwerk Lingen G.m.b.H." ([1965] J.O. 3305); Décision du Conseil portant approbation d'une modification des statuts de l'entreprise commune "Kernkraftwerk Lingen G.m.b.H." ([1966] J.O. 4037); Décision du Conseil portant approbation d'une modification des statuts de l'entreprise commune "Kernkraftwerk Lingen G.m.b.H." ([1967] J.O. 7); Décision du Conseil relative à la constitution de l'entre-

In its 1970 blueprint for a new common "industrial policy," the Community Commission announced its intention to explore the idea of extending the "joint enterprise" status to certain non-nuclear industries, with a view to facilitating "industrial cooperation," particularly between public enterprises. This would be one of several arrangements designed to accelerate the creation of a "European industrial network"; the European company would be another.[312a]

(e) The European company: "Supranational" or "European-type" national company?

(i) Two prototypes

The discussion on the European company has taken place, as one would expect, against the background of the experience with the "treaty-companies" and the unification-of-law movement generally. It has polarized around two basic prototypes: a "supranational" company of "European law" and a national company of "European type."

In an extreme form, the first prototype would correspond to the first of the above-mentioned two models of an international company. It conjures a "supranational" legal person incorporated under Community law rather than under a national law, entered in a "European" commercial register and governed in principle by Community law, with a European Court assuring uniform application of that law. Since such a company would not be a "foreign company," no question of recognition in the conflict-of-laws sense would arise; and, since a transfer of the seat or a fusion among such

---

prise commune "Kernkraftwerk Obrigheim G.m.b.H." ([1966] J.O. 2681); Décision du Conseil portant approbation de trois modifications des statuts de l'entreprise commune "Kernkraftwerk Obrigheim G.m.b.H." ([1966] J.O. 4038); Décision du Conseil portant approbation d'une modification des statuts de l'entreprise commune "Kernkraftwerk Obrigheim G.m.b.H." ([1968] J.O. 16).

[312a] Commission des Communautés Européennes, COM(70) 100 final, Mar. 18, 1970, La Politique industrielle de la Communauté, Mémorandum de la Commission au Conseil, Introduction et Orientations générales at 18.

companies across political frontiers would take place within the same "supranational" legal order, the difficulties described above would be avoided. But the obstacles posed by tax legislation and restrictions on access to capital markets would remain, unless they were dealt with through parallel arrangements.

At the other pole is the solution reflecting the second model, and which is substantially akin to the plan advocated by the French Government in its note to the Commission of March 15, 1965, on the creation of a "European-type" commercial company.[313] The Member States would undertake to introduce into their national legal systems an identical "uniform law," adding a new corporate form to the existing national company forms. Thus the "European-type" company would be a "national" company formed under, and governed by, national law; its "European" character would be derived from the uniformity of its basic governing law in all Member States. Although the company would be subject to the jurisdiction of national courts, the French Government indicated that some arrangement would be necessary to assure uniform interpretation of the uniform national laws, but it did not give any clue as to the nature of such arrangement.

Considerable doubt has been expressed with regard to the value of the "European-type" company conceived in the French image.[314] The French Government argued that the uniform character of the law would reduce legal uncertainty and the mistrust of "foreign law" and thus facilitate intra-Community commerce. It would be easier to organize subsidiaries and joint ventures across national frontiers and to introduce unified management for establishments in various Member States, if the basic national company laws were identical; and a seat transfer would no longer require substantive changes in the charter. However, since the com-

---

313 See p. 432 supra.

314 See, e.g., most recently Gessler, *Europäisches Gesellschaftsrecht am Scheideweg* at 1004-05.

pany would preserve its "nationality" as any other nationally organized company, recognition abroad, seat transfer,
fusion or holding arrangements across political frontiers
would still involve two or more national systems, and the
existing basic difficulties stemming from the existence of the
separate national orders would persevere. Moreover, in case
of fusion, the fundamental political and psychological obstacle, inherent in a change of nationality and subjection to
another legal system, would also remain. Consequently, the
only saving grace of this solution, according to an authoritative German view, would lie in the hope that the European-
type company law form would gradually displace the existing, divergent national stock company forms, and thus bypass
the laborious effort of making the national laws more similar
through coordination.[315]

(ii) The legal bases for "enacting" the European company

Until recently, it has been generally assumed that the
Community institutions would not wish to claim the authority to pass a supranational "enabling act" for a European
company in the form of a directly applicable "regulation"
within the meaning of EEC Article 189.[316] However, if
there were the proverbial "political will," it would be quite
plausible for the Commission to propose that the Council
adopt such a regulation on the basis of Article 235.[316a] This
article makes available a specific procedure for "filling the
gap" in the Community lawmaking authority, where the
Treaty has failed to grant to the institutions the power of
action "necessary to achieve, within the framework of the

---

[315] Gessler, *id.* at 1005.

[316] Article 189 provides that "[r]egulations shall have general
application. They shall be binding in every respect and directly applicable in each Member State." However, as indicated *supra* p. 9,
a regulation may be adopted only when a provision in a "substantive"
Treaty article confers the authority to do so.

[316a] On Art. 235 and its application by the Council in 20 cases thus
far see Marenco, *Les conditions d'application de l'article 235 du Traité
C.E.E.*, 1970 REV. MARCHÉ COMMUN 147.

Common Market, one of the objectives of the Community."
Such assertion of Community power might be greeted with
raised eyebrows in some national capitals. Again, it has been
suggested—admittedly without much response—that a uniform law could be included in a Community "directive,"
possibly supplemented by a "recommendation," even though
unlike a "regulation," a "directive" is to bind the Member
States only with respect to "the result to be achieved," leaving
the form and means of enforcement to their discretion.[317]
The inextricable tie between substance and form in company law would justify, so goes the argument, reducing the
range of discretion of the national governments. If neither
a regulation nor a directive proves to be an acceptable form,
a new treaty would be the remaining alternative for establishing either a "supranational" European company or a
"European-type" company, based on a uniform national law.
In that case, if a uniform law becomes the chosen instrument, such law either could be included in a "self-executing" treaty, or it could be annexed to a treaty, in which
the Member States would stipulate to enact the implementing uniform legislation and to assure certain treatment for
the "European-type" company. The French Government
assumed that the uniform law would be introduced into
the national legal systems by means of a convention elaborated in the same way as the conventions based on Article
220, but it refrained from suggesting which of the two technical possibilities it would prefer. Article 220, it will be
recalled,[318] enumerates specific topics as subjects for possible
negotiations by the Member States (recognition of companies, seat transfer, fusion, etc.) but fails to mention a European company. However, it has been interpreted broadly
as supplying a basis for "European treaties" designed to supplement the EEC Treaty, as for instance the convention on

---

[317] Art. 189, par. 3. STRAUSS, FRAGEN DER RECHTSANGLEICHUNG at 17;
Zweigert, *Grundsatzfragen der europäischen Rechtsangleichung* at 413.
[318] *See* pp. 41, 183 *supra.*

the European patent.[319] Consequently, a European company, "supranational" or "European type," could presumably be realized through this type of convention.

(f) The Commission posture and the Sanders draft

(i) The Commission's 1966 Memorandum: benevolent neutrality

The Commission explored the implications of the two
prototypes at some length in the only comprehensive public
document on the subject, a Memorandum issued in April
1966 and marked by a studied posture of diplomatic detach-
ment. In this paper, the Commission praised the French
Government—as could be expected—for its initiative; the
Commission suggested that the "European-law" model would
fit the growing interest in creating "European firms," but
noted that, in practice, the impact of this "innovation" would
depend on a simultaneous solution of the difficulties in the
adjoining disciplines, principally tax law, regulations on the
issuance of foreign securities on national markets and access
to bank loans, and last, but not least, "social laws" such as
the patterns of workers' participation in the company's decision-making and in its profits. It is safe to assume that
the "European-law" (or supranational) alternative would be
more congenial to the Commission's interest in advancing
integration; but the Commission made it clear that it was
not prepared to face the dilemma and to make the choice
between the two models until further "careful studies" have
been made.[320]

---

[319] On the "Community features" of the "European treaties" see
supra p. 404.

[320] Memorandum by the Commission of the European Economic
Community on the Establishment of European Companies (submitted
by the Commission to the Council on 22 April 1966), 1966 Bull. E.E.C.
Supp. No. 9/10 at 20. On the options generally see *Sanders Report*
at 13; von Caemmerer, *Europäische Aktiengesellschaft* at 186; Leleux,
Le rapprochement at 129.

(ii) The Sanders draft: choice deferred

Professor Sanders, whom the Commission entrusted with such further studies, took his clue from the Commission's position of "neutrality on the legal form"; his primary purpose was to devise—in as concrete terms as was possible—a scheme of rules to govern a European company. As far as the legal basis was concerned, he proceeded on the assumption that a new treaty will be negotiated which would be linked closely to the Community institutions. However, he fashioned the draft in such a way that the new company law could come into effect either as a part of a "directly applicable" (self-executing) treaty, or in the form of national legislation enacted in pursuance of a non-self-executing treaty, to which the "uniform law" was annexed. The first of the two alternative methods would have the advantage of greater security, since in France, the Netherlands and Luxembourg, treaty law is superior to national legislation, and, in principle, it cannot be modified by a subsequent national statute; this is not the case in Italy, the Federal Republic and Belgium, although in the latter two countries the doctrine and certain case law appear to be moving toward attributing a higher normative value to Community law in relation to national law.[321] This advantage, however, should not be overrated since, in a common undertaking of this sort, it is difficult to conceive that a Member State would wish to abrogate or expressly modify a uniform law. Moreover, the danger of an application of a conflicting national law would be reduced, if the Community Court of Justice were given supervisory jurisdiction. The same arrangement would also reduce the risk of a divergent interpretation of the uniform law in national courts. In the past, differences in judicial

---

[321] *Sanders Report* at 12-14. For material illustrating the national constitutional practice see STEIN & HAY, LAW AND INSTITUTIONS IN THE ATLANTIC AREA—READINGS, CASES AND PROBLEMS at 26-63 (Indianapolis 1967). *See also* WAELBROECK, TRAITÉS INTERNATIONAUX ET JURIDICTIONS INTERNES DANS LES PAYS DU MARCHÉ COMMUN (Bruxelles-Paris 1969).

interpretation of uniform laws have been diluted, if not destroyed, uniformity, as illustrated by the fate of the Geneva
Convention on negotiable instruments of 1930 and 1931.
Yet if national courts are to look to uniform national legislation, rather than directly to the treaty text, the international or Community origin will be muted, and with it,
as von Caemmerer suggests, the integrating effect as well.[322]
It is not surprising that the trend of opinion in literature
has been in the direction of a "directly applicable" treaty,
which Sanders also appears to prefer.[323]

(iii)   Legal personality and capacity

As conceived by Sanders, the European company is a stock
company, reflecting the features of the existing national stock
company laws in the Member States. It is fashioned, however,
not as a compromise among these laws, but rather in a way
that would respond best to the particular objectives of a
Community-wide enterprise. The European company is to
be endowed with a legal personality in all Member States,
enjoying the same rights as are accorded to stock companies
formed under the existing national laws. In case the uniform-
law technique is employed, this provision would not form a
part of the uniform law itself but would be included as a
separate treaty obligation,[324] designed, among other objectives, to assure recognition of the company throughout the
Community.

Since "the European company is created to promote the
purposes of the Common Market," both its registered seat
(registered office) and its "real seat," that is, its central administration (home office), must be *within the Community*,
and they must be located in the same place specified in the
charter. If the decision is made to transfer the central ad-

---

[322] Von Caemmerer, *Europäische Aktiengesellschaft* at 192.

[323] Such a treaty would still require approval by national legislatures, but no separate legislation would be required beyond the "ratify-
ing law."

[324] *Sanders Report,* Art. I-1 and comment at 20.

ministration, the charter must be amended, presumably in order to make sure that the registered and real seat coincide again. The assumption is that the transfer is to another location within the Community. If the charter is not so amended the board members may be held personally liable to the company, and the company remains subject to the jurisdiction of the national courts of its registered seat. These would be the only consequences of a move without a charter amendment, since, as we shall see, the company's governing law is set forth in the treaty itself; hence, choice-of-law problems in this respect would not arise. Thus, it is said, "the registered seat is controlling" for judicial jurisdiction and tax and other purposes, and "legal security is reinforced."[325] Specific provisions sanction transnational fusion involving European companies.[326] Making such fusion possible is viewed, it will be recalled, as a major objective of the entire effort.

One may wonder whether the formulation of the initial prerequisite of geographic coincidence of the registered office and central administration is not too inflexible for a regional common market. Again, the condition that both the registered office and central administration be within the Community goes beyond the requirements of Article 58 of the Treaty, which makes it sufficient for a company, to be eligible for freedom-of-establishment and supply-of-services benefits, to have either the registered office or central administration on Community territory.[327]

It would not be surprising, if the Commission proposed abandoning entirely the "real seat" (central administration) theory and making the registered seat the only relevant contact for all purposes, except taxation. This registered seat would have to be within the Community territory. The Commission's idea is that a European company could have

---

[325] *Id.* at Art. I-4 and commentary thereunder.

[326] *Id.* Title XI. Fusion between European companies or between a European company and an ordinary stock company are covered, if they result in a European company. *Id.* at 124.

[327] *See* p .28 *supra.*

two or more registered seats in more than one Member
State. Since, however, the registered seat is the primary
basis of judicial jurisdiction over the company, a special
arrangement would have to be made to deal with the jurisdictional problem.

(iv) Governing law and judicial interpretation

A commercial company, we must keep in mind, functions in the context of a legal framework extending far
beyond company law proper. This applies necessarily also to
the projected European company, and the choice of the
source of the "subsidiary law," from which gaps are to be
filled, will greatly affect the character of the new organizational form. One obvious possibility would be to say that
whenever the new European law fails to provide a specific
rule, the appropriate national law would apply. Such a solution would reintroduce conflict-of-laws problems, jeopardize
uniformity, and reduce the European character of the company. For these reasons, Sanders pursued another avenue.
Instead, his draft contemplates[328] that, where a question
arises within the general area covered by the new company
law and that law provides no answer, the "general principles"
which "inspire" that law should supply a rule—a formula derived from Article 17 of the Hague Convention on the international sale of movable property;[329] if such principles fail to
offer a solution, reference is to be made to "common rules
or general principles preponderant in the legal orders" of
the Member States, a formula modeled after the Franco-
German "Saarlor" Treaty mentioned above,[330] and reminis-

---

[328] *Sanders Report,* Art. I-7.

[329] *See* von Caemmerer, *Rechtsvereinheitlichung und interna-
tionales Privatrecht,* in VON CAEMMERER, SCHLOCHAUER, STEINDORFF (eds.),
FESTSCHRIFT FÜR HALLSTEIN 63, at 79 (Frankfurt a. M. 1966); *1964 Hague
Convention Relating to a Uniform Law on the International Sale of
Goods,* 13 AM. J. COMP. L. 453, at 459 (1964).

[330] *Supra* p. 440.

cent also of Article 215 of the EEC Treaty.[331] Evidently, at this stage the judge is to employ the same comparative method that would have been used in the drafting of the European company law, and he is to extend his comparative inquiry, as appropriate, beyond the confines of national stock company legislation to the broader aspects of the national legal systems. In effect, the judge is to fashion a rule which the "European" lawmaker had failed to provide. In this way, the draft seeks to preclude or defer recourse to national law, evidently because such recourse would impair the European character of the company and the uniformity of its treatment. National law as such could be drawn upon as the ultimate "subsidiary" source, but only after the judge has determined, through a process of interpretation discussed below, that the matter was altogether outside the scope of the European company law, as for instance a contract of sale concluded by the European company, or questions of administrative law, industrial property, criminal law, labor law, general tort law, etc.[332] In that case, although the draft is silent on this point, the judge would very likely look to the law of the forum in order to decide which national law should supply the appropriate rule.[333] Finally, the judge is given a general guideline for the application and interpretation of the new law: he is to respect the basic purpose of creating "a territorial unit comprising the Contracting States

---

[331] Article 215 provides that ". . . [a]s regards non-contractual liability the Community shall, *in accordance with the general principles common to the laws of the Member States,* make reparations for any damages caused by its institutions or by its employees in the performance of their duties." (Emphasis added.) The principles of the EEC Treaty itself, such as prohibition of discrimination on the basis of nationality, free movement of persons, services and capital, would be included. *Sanders Report,* par. 3 of the comment on Art. I-7.

[332] For an analogous formula see Art. 89 of the *1964 Hague Convention Relating to a Uniform Law on the International Sale of Goods,* 13 Am. J. Comp. L. 453, at 470 (1964).

[333] In addition, there are scattered in the text of the proposal *express* references to national law (*e.g.,* Art. IV-1-2, par. 1); in other instances such references are *implied* (*e.g.,* Art. III-2-5, the definition of "delivery").

under a single law" ("*territoire de droit unique couvrant les États contractants*").[334]

This intriguing effort to lay the groundwork for judge-made European law through a frankly teleological interpretation, directed toward the common European purpose, invites a comparison with the evolution of the "federal courts law" in the United States after *Erie R. Co. v. Tompkins*.[335] In that case, the United States Supreme Court ruled that federal courts sitting in "diversity of jurisdiction" cases, must look to the law of the States of the Union, instead of applying federal common law to matters not governed by federal statutory law or by the Constitution. Nevertheless, federal courts, faced with statutory silence on a question which they have classified as "federal" because of a "radiation" from the federal Constitution or a Congressional act, have constructed the necessary rule on the basis of what they understood to be the federal policy underlying the Constitution or the act in question.[336] They have thus avoided applying State law. It is indicative, although not surprising, that the federal judiciary has employed this doctrine in order to extend federal power—including more recently the federal regulatory power over corporate securities[337]—at the expense of the States of the Union and beyond the specific confines set by the federal lawmaker.

---

[334] *Sanders Report,* Art. I-7 (1) and comment thereon. See on this also the *Wahl Report,* Council of Europe, Eur. Consult. Ass., Doc. 2005 (Jan. 4, 1966).

[335] Erie R. Co. v. Tompkins, 304 U.S. 64 (1938).

[336] *See, e.g.,* Clearfield Trust Co. v. United States, 318 U.S. 363 (1943); D'Oench, Duhme & Co. v. Federal Deposit Ins. Corp., 315 U.S. 447 (1942); *but contra,* Bank of America Nat'l Trust & Sav. Ass'n v. Parnell, 352 U.S. 29 (1956). *See also* the celebrated case of Banco Nacional de Cuba v. Sabbatino, 376 U.S. 398 (1964); Textile Workers Union v. Lincoln Mills, 353 U.S. 448 (1957).

[337] J.I. Case Co. v. Borak, 377 U.S. 426 (1964). *See* Friendly, *In Praise of Erie—and the New Federal Common Law,* 39 N.Y.U.L. Rev. 383 (1964). For a recent brief survey of the case law see Cramton & Currie, Conflict of Laws, Cases-Comments-Questions at 818-35 (St. Paul 1968).

In contrast with the federal system in the United States, which is endowed with a complete hierarchy of federal courts, judicial power in the Community remains in principle in the hands of national courts of the Member States. It is obvious that the elaborate formula on "subsidiary law" in the Sanders draft would have little meaning, if its application were left within the uncontrolled discretion of national judiciary, oriented naturally toward national law and national power. For that reason, Sanders proposes that the Court of Justice of the Communities should be given jurisdiction to rule, upon referral from national courts through a procedure analogous to that in EEC Article 177,[338] on questions of applicability and interpretation of the European law, on the subsidiary principles and common rules, and also on the interpretation of the individual charters of the European companies. It would thus be the Court of Justice that would perform the function of assuring the integrity and uniformity of the new law through its holdings on the "preliminary questions," to be referred to it by the parties in a case before a national court or by the national court itself.[339]

As I mentioned before, the French Government had recognized in its note the need for "a system for harmonizing national jurisprudence" but, we are told by Houin,[340] the group of national experts that had examined the Sanders text was unable to agree on the type of tribunal or judicial procedure which should be established for this purpose. Yet, this issue is not listed among those topics on which continuing disagreement has posed a serious obstacle to progress.

---

[338] *See* p. 421 *supra.*

[339] *Sanders Report,* Art. I-6 and comment thereon. The draft would substantially extend the jurisdiction of the Court of Justice as compared with Art. 177. In addition to giving the parties themselves a "certiorari-type" access to the Court of Justice, the Advocates General would also be given the authority to bring before the Court any final national judgment, with a view to determining whether it violated the new law, but this holding would not disturb the judgment itself. On the other hand, the national court would not be under an obligation to refer.

[340] Houin, *Où en est le droit des sociétés* at 136.

(v) How wide an "access" to the European company?

The first, if not the foremost, among the unresolved "hard core" issues is the question what type of an enterprise should be admitted to incorporation under the European law, and under what circumstances. To use the Common Market vernacular, the problem is one of "access."[341] For some authors, and perhaps also for some of the Governments concerned, the very *raison d'être* of the new institution may depend upon the way this hotly disputed issue is resolved.

It is generally assumed that the new organizational form would be optional and would "coexist" with the prevailing national company forms. But those who have been engaged in the negotiations have faced a dilemma: the wider and freer the access to the European company, the more the new form will "compete" with the coexisting national stock company forms, and the more difficult it will be to obtain agreement by those Governments which are attached to their national laws or strongly committed to a particular feature of that law; on the other hand, if the access is restricted so as to make the new form available to a few enterprises only, these Governments are more likely to accept it, even if it differed substantially from their own stock company form, but other Governments may no longer consider the whole enterprise worthwhile.

We may discern two opposing views: the first would make the new form widely available to any enterprise of a certain dimension; the other would make access dependent upon the existence of activities transcending the territory of a single Member State.

More specifically, the German delegation insisted that the access to the new form must be reserved only to those companies which were engaged in "international" or "European"

---

[341] *Sanders Report* at 9; von Caemmerer, *Europäische Aktiengesellschaft* at 182-85; Memorandum of the Commission, *supra* note 320, at 26; Leleux, *Le rappprochement* at 129; Storm, *Statute of a Societas Europaea* at 269 ff.

activities and which could not pursue their objectives as effectively in the form of "national" companies. According to this proposal, a European company form would be available only to a company with a branch in another State or with an interest in another State's company, or controlled by a foreign holding company, or whose stock was listed in different States, or which had set up a joint subsidiary or some other joint operation with companies organized in another State.[342] At the core of the German posture was again the fear that, unless access was restricted, the existing German companies would choose the European form in order to escape the provisions of German law, which are considered vital from the viewpoint of national economic and social policy, particularly the law on related enterprises (*Konzernrecht*),[343] but, more importantly, the stringent requirement of workers' codetermination.[344]

Sanders did not agree to condition access upon "European activities," but he sought to meet the German apprehension in part by proposing to make the new form available only to *existing* companies. More specifically, a European company could be established only by stock companies, which had been in actual operation over a period of three years; and it would be available only in case of a fusion, a holding arrangement or "transformation," or the creation of a subsidiary or a joint subsidiary.[345]

One may question the reality of a danger of a mass transformation of German companies into European companies. However, the German officials, conscious of the importance attributed to this matter by the German labor unions, did not feel free to go beyond the German proposal; their attitude encountered sympathetic understanding among the German-trained lawyers on the Commission staff.

---

[342] Houin, *Les sociétés de type européen* at 29.

[343] *See* p. 105 *supra*.

[344] *See* discussion by Leleux, v. Burchard, Ficker, Strauss, Mestmäcker, in EUROPÄISCHE HANDELSGESELLSCHAFT at 103-04.

[345] *Sanders Report*, Art. I-2, I-3.

Yet some other delegations, including apparently the French experts, were not at all averse to the idea of "competition" between the national and European company forms. They felt that if the national forms were to become obsolescent and progressively displaced by the European form, a significant step would be taken toward a complete unification of company law in the Community. These same experts opposed the criterion of "European activities" on a variety of grounds. In the first place, it raised questions of feasibility and legal security. The geographic scope of a company's activity could hardly be fixed as of the time of its formation since it might subsequently expand across national frontiers.[346] Again, the continuing involvement in the requisite "European activity" would have to be monitored on a permanent basis and the enforcement would be difficult. Finally, the German-favored criterion would work for the benefit of the existing groupings and cooperative arrangements, but would not stimulate concentration among smaller companies which heretofore had confined their operations to their respective national markets; and this—it was said—was incompatible with good "competition policy"; nor would the objective of an unhampered expansion of all enterprises within the Common Market be served.[347] The report of a specialized section of the Economic and Social Committee, prepared by M. de Précigout, reflected this general line of argumentation and supported the freest possible "access."[348]

The suggestion has been made that, at least as a provisional arrangement, access could be limited simply by requiring a minimum capital, although in the long run this criterion, based on "opulence," would satisfy "neither logic nor equity."[349] It is nevertheless generally agreed that the future

---

[346] Cf. Duden, *Internationale Aktiengesellschaften* at 100.

[347] Leleux, *Le rapprochement* at 111. In a sense, the Sanders proposal may also be said to favor large enterprises.

[348] Summary in Europe No. 299 (new series) of Mar. 21, 1969, at 7.

[349] Houin, in L'harmonisation at 82.

European company should have a certain minimum capital, and the Sanders draft includes this prerequisite.[350] Most national laws require a minimum capital for stock companies but the amounts vary and will—presumably—be harmonized in the "Second Directive."[351] Of course, if the minimum for a European company is set as high as $1 million across the board, as was suggested by the Italian delegation, the number of eligible companies would again be quite limited.

Be that as it may, the unwillingness of the experts to accept what the German delegation considered a good compromise on the "access" issue, and the disagreement on the related question of workers' participation, caused complete deadlock in the negotiations.

The wind in Brussels is blowing in the direction of narrowing the "access" so as to make the European company available only in three situations: fusion between companies of different Member States, formation of a holding company or formation of a joint subsidiary by companies of different Member States.

(vi) Should foreign-controlled and non-member companies be excluded from "access"?

One aspect of the access problem on which discord persists is of particular interest to the United States and other non-member states. It relates to the question whether non-Community companies should also be allowed to organize a European company. The question is analogous to the issue of access of "foreign" companies to the European patent under the proposed new patent convention.

The Sanders draft would allow a non-member company, whose *bona fides* is demonstrated by continuing active operation during a preceding minimum time period, to create

---

[350] One million dollars is the required minimum capital in case the European company is established by fusion or as a holding company, $500,000 in case of transformation, and $250,000 in case of the subsidiaries. *Sanders Report*, Art. I-3.

[351] *Supra* p. 319.

own or joint subsidiaries in the form of a European company. An effort to exclude legitimate third-country companies would make little sense since, as a Community official pointed out, a great many American concerns have subsidiaries organized as national companies in the Member States, and these presumably could not be denied access;[352] in any case, a third-country enterprise could always organize a national company within the Community and transform it, after a lapse of time, into a European company, if the transformation feature of the Sanders report is retained.

There is reason to believe, however, that the French Government in this instance, also, may pursue its objective of seeking to restrict Community benefits to "truly European" enterprises, as it has attempted in connection with access to the privileges of establishment, international fusion[353] and subsidies. Since, as shown above, the requirement of the company's "seat" (or nationality) in a Member State would not exclude companies organized within, but controlled from outside the Community, the French tentatively suggested that the location of the company's "center of decision-making" should be the determining factor. In other words, only those companies whose decision-making was centered within the Community territory would have access to the European company. It is interesting that here it is the French Government that advocates the narrowing of the access. Reportedly, the reaction to this suggestion on the part of the other delegations has been uniformly negative, if for no other reason, because the "center of decision-making" concept would be difficult to define. The risk of conflicting holdings by national courts would require an extension of the Community judicial power which the French Government apparently would not be prepared to accept.

Even under the liberal Sanders draft, however, companies formed in third countries would be excluded from organizing a European company by fusion, transformation, or

---

[352] Hauschild, in EUROPÄISCHE HANDELSGESELLSCHAFT at 103.
[353] See p. 373 supra.

as a holding company. One reason for the exclusion is
that fusion, which would lead to the extinction of the
third-country company and the transfer of its assets to a
European company, could not be made subject to the rules
of the new European law. It is conceivable that a third
country could adhere to the treaty on European company
law, without becoming a member of the Community. This,
however, would pose difficulties of a technical nature, considering the proposed links between the European company
and the institutions of the Community, particularly the Court
of Justice in which only Members participate.[354] Actually,
the possibility of adhesion of third states to the treaty was at
the center of the discussion in the Committee of Permanent Representatives. The Netherlands conditioned its consent to further negotiations on the acceptance of this possibility, while some other Governments took the position that,
since the institution of a European company presupposed a
complete customs union and an economic union in a fairly
advanced stage, participation in the treaty on a European
company by a non-member country was not acceptable.[355]

(vii)   The content of the European stock company law—
principal problems[356]

(1)   Company formation

The question who may act as founder of the European
company is intertwined with the problem of access. The
Sanders draft would allow only stock companies to become
founders, although the French and Italian experts would
admit individuals as well.[357] However, in contrast with

---

[354] The same consideration would apply to transformation and
formation of a holding. *Sanders Report,* comment on Art. I-3, at 21.
See also id. at 10.

[355] EUROPE No. 250 (new series), Jan. 13, 1969, at 3.

[356] For a detailed treatment see von Caemmerer, *Europäische
Aktiengesellschaft* at 196 ff.; Storm, *Statute of a Societas Europaea* at
276 ff.; *Sanders Report* at 15 ff.

[357] *A European Company Law in the Making—But Its Opportunity
Is Questioned,* 7 COMM. MKT. 61, at 64 (1967).

the present national laws, a stock company could act as the sole founder of its subsidiary, organized in the form of a European company;[358] only the Belgian reform proposal envisages this arrangement in the national arena.

In conformity with the legal and economic concepts prevailing in the Member States, no concession or license would be required for the formation of a European company; it would come into existence whenever the requirements of the law are met. In contrast with the choice left open by the First Directive,[359] the Sanders draft prescribes judicial supervision of the formation process by the Community Court of Justice. The purpose is to avoid irregularities which could be invoked as grounds for illegality ("nullity") of the company.[360] Houin points out that the Court of Justice could perform this supervisory function only if the number of European companies were quite limited. As an alternative, he suggests that the task of supervision might be entrusted in the first instance to national courts or administrative authorities, with a possibility of recourse, in one form or another, to the Community Court.[361]

The Sanders draft requires an entry of each European company into a European Commercial Register, which is to be constituted at the Court of Justice, and also a secondary entry in an "annex" of that Register, which is to be kept in the State where the new company has its seat.[362] The European company would come into existence upon appropriate publication in the Official Journal of the Communities, and thereafter it would no longer be possible to assert any faults in the formation.[363]

---

[358] On the problem of the "one-man company" generally see *supra* p. 327.

[359] *Supra* p. 303.

[360] *Sanders Report,* Art. II-1 ff.

[361] Houin, in L'HARMONISATION at 85.

[362] *Sanders Report,* Arts. I-8, II-1-6.

[363] *Id.* Art. II-1-7.

(2)   Shares: the problem of bearer shares

The Sanders scheme contemplates only par value shares, both registered and bearer. Although the law in five of the six Member States in principle permits the choice between registered and bearer shares, difficulties have arisen due to the fact that only registered shares are allowed in Italy.[364] The fear of tax evasion has been at the core of the Italian opposition to bearer shares, although it has been reinforced by the argument that registered shares permit a more effective surveillance of inter-company relationships. This argument, based on economic policy, is heard particularly in Italian socialist circles which have viewed the idea of the European company with a jaundiced eye, because in their opinion only large, predominantly foreign companies will take advantage of the new form. In business circles, on the other hand, one encounters the argument that an effective system of registered shares is necessary for monitoring the inflow of foreign capital to Italy. At any rate, the Italians fear that, if European companies could be organized in Italy with the authority to issue bearer shares, Italian national companies would seek the new form in order to escape disclosure of stock ownership, inherent in the Italian rule allowing registered shares only. It would avail nothing to provide that European companies with a seat in Italy would be subject to the present Italian rule prohibiting bearer shares, since in that case, so goes the argument, companies would set up their seat in another Member State. Houin opines that the only solution would be to prohibit bearer shares altogether in all six States, as is the case in the United States and the United Kingdom, but he doubts that this would be acceptable, particularly in France.[365] In fact, the prohibition of bearer shares was considered unacceptable

---

[364] *See* p. 348 *supra*. Exception is made in Italy for companies organized in Sicily and Sardinia.

[365] Houin, in L'HARMONISATION at 87.

in the report of a section of the Economic and Social Committee on the ground that it would impair the usefulness of the European company.[366] One may wonder, however, whether—when the chips are down—this question would pose an insuperable obstacle to an agreement. The experience has shown that to a large extent tax evasion could be controlled by requiring the company or the depositary bank to withhold the tax and by making stock exchanges report all transactions; and the disclosure of substantial stock ownership is achieved through a reporting obligation.[367] It is thus unlikely that the Commission will advocate a prohibition of bearer shares.

(3)　Structure of the European company

The internal organization of the European company did not seem to have caused particular difficulties, owing to the trend in the Member States toward the German-type, two-tier system. The Sanders draft falls in with this trend and adopts the German-type executive board and supervisory council.

The shareholders' meeting is competent to elect members of the supervisory council, to modify the charter and the capital, and also to decide on transformation or fusion. German law also served as a model for the self-financing provisions. The principle of transparency, or "glass pockets" applies to the formation of reserves. Valuation standards must be set forth and explained for each item of the balance sheet, as well as any changes in the valuation methods. The administration is given the authority to allocate up to two-thirds of annual profits to open reserves.[368]

---

[366] EUROPE No. 299 (new series), Mar. 21, 1969, at 7.

[367] *See, e.g.,* Art. 356 of the French Law of July 24, 1966; § 20 of the German Stock Company Law of 1965. *See* Storm, *Statute of a Societas Europaea* at 279-80.

[368] *Sanders Report,* Art. VI-6-1.

(4)   The problem of "codetermination" of workers[369]

We have seen earlier that the differences among national laws concerning the participation of employees in the direction and supervision of the companies has proved a formidable roadblock in the negotiations on the European company. In the German coal, iron and steel industry, representatives of employees constitute one-half of the supervisory council, and in addition a "labor relations director" (*Arbeitsdirektor*), elected by the workers, is a member of the executive board. In other stock companies, workers hold one-third of the seats on the supervisory council. The political trend in the Federal Republic is, as we have noted,[370] in the direction of widening this "right of codetermination." Consequently, the Federal Government has taken the position that it could not consent to any European company law that would omit this feature and thus offer an avenue for escaping its reach.

In France, two members of the plant committee (*comité d'entreprise*), organized on the enterprise level, sit on the company's administrative council (or supervisory council, where it exists) but in a nonvoting, advisory capacity only.[371] Except for France and the Federal Republic, the institution of workers' participation does not exist in the Member States at this time.

The group of government experts did not come anywhere close to finding a solution to the eminently political issue, whether or to what extent the European company law should contain this feature. Similar difficulties have arisen in the negotiations on transnational fusion.[372] The dilemma has been that the exclusion of the right of codetermination in the European company would clearly lead to a collapse of the entire undertaking, and, conversely, the German (or even

---

[369] For a survey of national legislation see *Sanders Report* at 76. *See also* pp. 94 ff. *supra.*

[370] *Supra* p. 96.

[371] *Supra* p. 119.

[372] *Supra* p. 391.

the French system) would hardly be acceptable to the other partners, except perhaps to Luxembourg and to the Netherlands.

As a possible way out of the political deadlock, Sanders has suggested a compromise solution based, in a sense, on the "territorial principle." If more than ninety percent of the company work force is employed in the Federal Republic or in France, the German or French law on codetermination or participation would apply; if less than one-fourth of the employees are employed in the establishments located in these two States, then there would be no workers' participation in the company's organs; if more than one-fourth are employed in France, the French version of participation would apply; but if more than one-fourth are employed in the Federal Republic, three alternatives are offered: either the Federal law would apply in full, or a separate "codetermination" organ could be created to function side-by-side with the supervisory organ and to have identical powers, or the matter would be regulated in the company's charter.[373]

Such a nuanced solution may be politically welcome, but it would sacrifice uniformity for flexibility. A European company, with most of its work force in the Federal Republic, would not have the same organs as other European companies.

Conscious of the need for further study, the Commission, in 1968, asked a group of experts to explore further the problem of workers' participation in the proposed European company. In the summer of 1969, the chairman of the group, Professor Gérard Lyon-Caen of the Paris Faculty of Law and Economic Sciences, submitted a report offering his own personal conclusions.[374] While Sanders conceives

---

[373] *Sanders Report,* Art. V-1-1 ff.

[374] Contribution à l'étude des modes de représentation des intérêts des travailleurs dans le cadre des sociétés anonymes européennes par le Professeur Gérard Lyon-Caen, Professeur à la Faculté de Droit et des Sciences économiques de Paris, Comm. Doc. 7. 974/XIV/69-F (undated).

of workers' participation exclusively in terms of the representation of workers on the company's organs, Lyon-Caen
seeks to broaden the spectrum of possible modalities by
employing a functional approach. Pursuant to a formula
evolved in the International Labor Organization,[375] Lyon-
Caen includes in the notion of participation all procedures
through which workers may take part in the preparation,
adoption and implementation of decisions, including such
methods as consultation, receiving information, negotiation,
as well as institutional representation. He concludes that
the European law which is to govern the proposed European company, should make the principle of workers' participation in the broad sense mandatory, leaving, however,
the management and the labor unions free to choose, by
negotiation, between several "equivalent" formulas:

(1) Membership of workers' representatives on the company's supervisory council, along with the representatives
of shareholders and possibly also of the general public
(consumers);

(2) institution of a "central economic committee or council" outside the company framework, similar to the existing
plant committees or councils;[376] the central council would
be composed of workers' representatives, and it would have
powers of inquiry, consultation, and perhaps also a veto
with regard to company decisions affecting personnel;

(3) institution of a new "special organ for codetermination," as suggested by Sanders, composed of workers' representatives, but functioning side-by-side with the supervisory
council, except that its powers would be confined to decisions concerning personnel, including pension plans, mergers, and plant transfers or conversions.

The negotiations, designed to obtain agreement on one
of these three formulas, would be conducted on the labor
side by a delegation from national labor unions, represent-

---

375 *Id.* at 5.

376 *See, e.g.,* in the Federal Republic p. 95 *supra.*

ing personnel employed in each of the several establishments of the European company concerned. The resulting contract could modify the chosen formula within certain limits, and it would have to be ratified also by the shareholders' meeting.

Lyon-Caen's principal innovation, however, is the idea that—as a further alternative—management and labor could agree on a contract to dispense with any institutional arrangement, and to stipulate instead, that specified types of decisions, which will have repercussions upon employment, must have prior consent by the signatory union. With an eye on American experience, and having in mind the attitude of labor unions in France and in Italy, Lyon-Caen sees no reason for being "more royalist than the king": why insist on institutional solutions, if the unions are content with a sort of "permanent negotiation on limited subjects"?[377] Even in the Federal Republic, he reports, where there is statutory, institutionalized co-determination, many personnel questions are actually negotiated in this manner, and the same is true of course in Italy, where no co-determination, or participation in the narrow sense, exists.[378]

The imaginative report, which goes beyond the normative aspects and suggests a framework for an inquiry into behavior and attitudes, necessarily leaves many questions unanswered.

Even though Lyon-Caen outlines a variety of safeguards, designed to preserve an "equivalence" of his optional formulas, the potential divergence, at least in theory, appears even greater in his plan than in the Sanders Report, and for this, if for no other reason, the Commission is not likely to embrace it in its totality. The Commission's staff is reported to be tending toward a compromise, that would prescribe a uniform minimum institutional arrangement, but it would give the parties an option to dispense with

---

[377] Contribution, *supra* note 374, at 218.
[378] *Id.* at 26.

certain forms of participation. More specifically, each European company with establishments in more than one Member State would be obligated to organize a "central" plant council, composed of workers' delegates from all of the establishments of a given European Company. This council's powers would exceed those of national plant committees or councils. The central plant council would have the authority to be kept fully informed by the management, to be consulted by it in advance of action taken, and to veto specified decisions. In addition, at least one third of the seats on the supervisory council would be filled by workers' representatives, but here—as suggested by Lyon-Caen—the parties would be free to "contract out" of the obligation to provide such institutional participation if two-thirds of all the employees agree. Finally, the management and the unions could, if they chose to do so, engage in collective bargaining with respect to working conditions generally, and any resulting agreement would apply to all workers employed by the European company anywhere within the Community.

(5) Law of related and affiliated companies (Konzernrecht)

In this field, the law of the Federal Republic alone offers a self-contained system of rules,[379] even the new French law is limited to a few provisions on subsidiaries and participations.[380] Yet, considering the significance of groupings of companies, Mestmäcker may be justified in remarking that the value of the European company law may depend in large measure upon its ability to realize, in legal terms, the economic unity of a group of related companies.[381]

No wonder then that the Sanders draft in this area also is guided by German law. In the few articles, containing basic

---

[379] *See* p. 105 *supra.*

[380] *Supra* p. 119.

[381] *See* discussion by Leleux, Burchard, et al., in EUROPÄISCHE HANDELSGESELLSCHAFT at 104.

provisions only, no distinction is made whether the controlling power of one company over other companies is based on contract or on factual control; in case of doubt, it would be for the Community Court of Justice to say whether the dependent relationship exists.

The minority-shareholder protection is ordered in such a way that they could demand the stock of the controlling company in exchange for their own stock,[382] or instead, if they so chose, an appropriate dividend, the level of which would be subject to review by the Court of Justice.[383] However, they could not claim fixed income in the form of a guaranteed dividend on the German law pattern.[384] The creditors would be protected through a simple, but rather brutal, device of across-the-board "piercing of the corporate veil:" the controlling company would be held jointly liable for all the existing and future debts of the dependent company.[385]

The "extraterritorial reach" of these rules would be of particular relevance for American enterprises. In principle, the rules concerning disclosure and liability toward minority shareholders and third parties would extend to companies controlled by the European company, but organized outside the EEC. Thus, these non-EEC companies would be included in the "publicity" requirement. Again, a European company would be required to file a consolidated balance sheet comprising its affiliates outside the EEC, which it controls; and a dependent European company would have the same obligation, if it in turn controls other companies in or outside the EEC. However, the liability for debts of companies, members of the "group," would be confined to the

---

[382] If the controlling company is a non-EEC company, they could claim cash indemnity. *Sanders Report,* Art. VIII-3-1 (2).

[383] *Sanders Report,* Art. VII-3-1 to VII-3-6.

[384] § 304, par. 2 of the German Stock Company Law of 1965.

[385] *Sanders Report,* Art. VIII-3-7. See generally on national laws, Cohn & Simitis, *"Lifting the Veil" in the Company Laws of the European Continent,* 12 INT'L & COMP. L.Q. 189 (1963).

debts of EEC companies, so that it would be possible to maintain affiliated subsidiaries outside the EEC, without the risk of potential liability for their debts.

(6) Taxation

In theory, a central problem is what authority, national or supranational, is to exercise "tax sovereignty" over the European company. The problem is posed of course only if one thinks in terms of a "supranational" rather than "European-type" company, and in that case the question arises whether the European Community rather than the Member State of the company's seat ought to be given the power to tax. The Community Commission already possesses a limited power to collect a levy on the production of coal and steel.[386] Such an extension of the "Community" taxing power would require the establishment of a Community tax administration which does not exist today. If the tax proceeds were to flow into Community coffers, they would provide the Community with an independent financial source, and in that sense constitute a significant increment in the power of the Community institutions in relation to the Member Governments.[387] Apart from the obvious political problems, this arrangement would entail a potentially significant loss of revenue for national treasuries, unless the proceeds of the tax were to be distributed by the Community to the Member Governments according to an agreed key.

Curiously enough, this problem has received little, if any, attention in public discussion, in part perhaps, because the idea of the Community as "tax collector" appears unreal in the current political context. In fact, the assumption has been that the taxing power with respect to European companies will remain in the hands of the Member States.

---

[386] Arts. 49 and 50 of the Treaty Establishing the European Coal and Steel Community, 261 U.N.T.S. 140 (1957).

[387] See in this context EEC Art. 201, envisaging independent Community resources particularly from duties collected under the common customs tariff. On the implementation of this provision see *supra* p. 21.

The Sanders draft contains only a few observations on the tax problem, but no specific solutions.[388] This is understandable, despite the intimate interaction between tax and company laws, which has now been generally recognized. The idea of a privileged tax treatment for the European company has been discarded, because it would inject an unacceptable discrimination against other companies. As long as Member States impose different taxes on the formation and income of national companies, it would be difficult to design a tax regime for the European company, which would avoid discrimination and at the same time assure a degree of uniform treatment. Thus, Sanders suggests, the problem should not be viewed in isolation from the general harmonization of national tax laws.

The tax questions arise, first, at the time of the formation of the European company, second, upon the transfer of its seat within the Community, and third, during its operations.

If a European company is formed as a new company (most frequently presumably as a subsidiary), it will be subject to the stamp-type tax on contributions to the company capital; the Council directive of 1969[389] assures partial harmonization by imposing a limit of one to two percent on the rate of this tax, with the ultimate possibility of a complete abolition of this tax. In case of the formation of a European company by transformation or fusion, or in the event of a seat transfer, the principal issue would be the treatment of previously untaxed reserves and capital gains, and here the proposed second directive, which I discussed in connection with fusion, would apply. The third directive, designed to prevent multiple taxation of the parent-subsidiary revenues, would provide relief in the course of operations.[390] It is difficult to estimate the chances of reaching an agreement

---

[388] *Sanders Report* at 128-29. On the tax problems see also Hauschild, in EUROPÄISCHE HANDELSGESELLSCHAFT at 96-99; Scholten, *The European Company* at 19; Storm, *Statute of a Societas Europaea* at 288.

[389] *Supra* p. 386.

[390] *Supra* pp. 384 ff.

on this complex of directives—yet without a measure of tax harmonization, a European company law would be of limited value indeed.

(viii) Summary and conclusions

The purpose of the European company law, whatever form it may take, is to remove or reduce the obstacles to transnational commerce and economic coalescence, which derive from the coexistence of separate and more or less divergent national legal systems within the legal order of the Community. The immediate impulse for serious negotiations came from two sources: *first,* the "sharpened competition," particularly from large American concerns, has brought about, it has been said, an urgent need for rapid concentration and expansion of European enterprises across national frontiers and, consequently, for new legal measures, beyond those contemplated in the EEC Treaty; and *second,* the difficulties and delays encountered in the negotiations for the coordination of national company laws have evoked a certain disenchantment and doubts about the effectiveness of that process. Yet the negotiations for the European company law have proved by no means easy. In addition to the controversial demand that non-member States be included in the discussions, the disputed issues concerned particularly the degree of freedom of "access" to the new European company form, the inclusion of the workers' codetermination and the admissibility of bearer shares.

The extent to which any European company law would achieve its avowed purpose may depend in large measure on the degree of its "European" character. The Sanders draft, the first concrete and detailed text of a European company law, is written in such a way that it could provide a basis either for a genuine supranational company or for a national company incorporated under a national uniform law, as was proposed by the French Government. However, Sanders attempted, with some success, to mitigate the differences

between the two alternatives and to reduce the identification
of the new company with any national system. He did so by
providing a close link with the Community institutions, in
partial replacement of national judicial and administrative
authorities, and by reducing to a minimum the recourse to
national law as a "subsidiary" source of the European law.

In his most recent writing, Gessler urged that only a
"truly supranational" company, not anchored in any national
law, with access to more than one national capital market,
could serve the desired purpose; and if—as may be the case,
particularly in view of the French opposition—this version
is not in the cards, the next best solution would be to provide for a company with a dual or multiple seat and nationality, anchored not in one, but in at least two, national
laws.[391] Such a company would, he believes, be viewed as an
indigenous component part of the economy in each State
where a seat is located, and this would overcome xenophobic
aversions and nationalist prejudices. The company would
have free access to the capital markets in all these States on
an equal basis with any other national company. The treaty
would contain a model charter, and the company would
comply with the formation requirements in all of the States
where it establishes a seat. So conceived, the new law would
not have to be as detailed as the Sanders draft (presumably
because the national law of each seat could be drawn upon
more freely), and consequently an agreement among Members may be less difficult to obtain. If unanimous consensus
proves impossible, the treaty could be signed by some, not
necessarily all, Member States. The model is the "bilingual"
Franco-German company "Saarlor,"[392] which could also supply a taxation formula. It took not more than 15 months to
negotiate the "Saarlor" company agreement which, according to Gessler, has worked so well that only one modification became necessary in the last ten years. The question
remains, however, whether an institutional design, tailor-

---

[391] Gessler, *Europäisches Gesellschaftsrecht am Scheideweg* at 1006.
[392] *Supra* pp. 440, 451.

made to fit a single significant enterprise, such as the politically important "Saarlor," could be readily transformed into
a general company law to serve a substantial number of
companies, including those of medium size. At first sight,
it would seem practicable for a limited number of large
enterprises only.

In this context, certain parallels in the American past
come to mind. Thus, the New York Central Railroad Company, created in 1914 by consolidation, was incorporated in
no less than six States of the Union. The multiple incorporation was undertaken because the laws of these States did
not then permit consolidation of the constituent corporations
into a corporation of a single State. The necessity to comply
with the laws of the six States, often conflicting and in some
cases antiquated, caused problems for the management until
the company was reincorporated as a Delaware corporation
almost half a century later.[393] Employing the theory of the

---

[393] The problem is explained in a proxy statement, dated April
22, 1960, prepared in connection with the reincorporation of the New
York Central Company as a Delaware corporation:

The Company has been, since its creation by consolidation
in 1914, a corporation incorporated in the States of New York,
Pennsylvania, Ohio, Indiana, Michigan and Illinois. This multistate status arose because the laws of these states did not then
permit consolidation of the constituent corporations into a corporation of a single state. Since then, the legal situation has changed,
through, among other things, the enactment of Section 5 of the
federal Interstate Commerce Act permitting the merger of rail-
roads upon approval of the Interstate Commerce Commission
regardless of restraints imposed by state law. Application will be
made to the Interstate Commerce Commission for approval of
the proposed merger, which will not be effected without such
approval.

The laws of the states in which the Company is presently incorporated conflict and are unclear in a number of significant
respects, which present increasing difficulty to the conduct of the
present and future activities of the Company. The Company
now derives income from profitable non-railroad operations and
intends to take advantage of opportunities, as they present themselves in the future, to operate other forms of transportation and
other forms of business. There is doubt under the provisions of
the railroad laws of some of the six states in which the Company
is now incorporated as to the extent to which such future opportun-

corporation prevailing at his time, Morawetz wrote: "[A]l-
though each charter of a company incorporated by different
States can operate as a grant of franchise only within the
jurisdiction of the State enacting it, yet the company itself
does not on that account cease to be one company, having
one undivided enterprise. A company thus constituted is in
reality but a single corporation, formed . . . for the purpose
of carrying on business in a corporate capacity in several
States. The several charters, taken together, form the constitution of the corporation. . . ."[394]

---

ities can be availed of. There is no doubt under the provisions of
the Delaware Corporation Law and of the charter of the Delaware
Corporation.

As a further instance, at present the statutes of several states
under whose laws the Company is incorporated purport to require
a majority of directors of a railroad incorporated in such state to
be residents of that state. Pennsylvania, Illinois, Michigan and
New York each purport to require that the annual meeting of a
railroad corporation incorporated within that state be held within
that state. Illinois restricts the duration of corporate existence
to 50 years (the Company was organized in 1914). Other conflicts
and ambiguities exist, which have cost the Company over the years
appreciable expenditures and have delayed or prevented actions
which appeared prudent and desirable from a business point of
view. Furthermore, in an Illinois case against the Company and
its directors the plaintiff, among other things, sought a declaratory
judgment from the Illinois Court that various important acts of
the directors were null and void for failure to comply with the
Illinois law. This case was finally settled by the Company and the
directors, after considerable expense, by a stipulation approved
by a decree of the Illinois Court in January, 1957, which provided
that the action might be reinstated at any time after five years
from the date of the decree upon a showing that the Company is
not "proceeding with reasonable diligence in connection with the
consolidation or organization of Central under the laws of a single
state."

I am indebted for this information to Mr. Ulrich Schweitzer, General
Corporate Counsel of the Penn Central. Other examples of multiple
incorporation were the Chicago and North Western Railway Company
(in Illinois, Wisconsin and Michigan), and the Minneapolis, St. Paul
and Sault Ste. Marie Railroad Company (in Minnesota, Michigan,
Wisconsin, North Dakota and South Dakota).

[394] MORAWETZ, 2 A TREATISE ON THE LAW OF PRIVATE CORPORA-
TIONS, Part II, CORPORATIONS CHARTERED BY SEVERAL STATES at § 995
(2d ed. Boston 1886). See also LEFLAR, AMERICAN CONFLICTS LAW at 597

Clearly, the analogy with the situation in the Community is not very compelling. For one thing, in the United States a corporation has no ties of loyalty toward the State of its incorporation or, for that matter, toward the State of its home office; in the Community on the other hand, nationalist feeling generally—and economic nationalism in particular—continues to be an important factor in business and governmental decisions. We have seen its manifestations quite recently in the negative attitude in France toward the attempt by Fiat of Italy to acquire a controlling interest in the Citroën of France; and the Government of the Federal Republic was similarly opposed to a take-over of a German petroleum concern by the Compagnie française des pétroles. Even the director of the Belgian component of Agfa-Gevaert, a Belgian-German holding combine, confessed to a continuing Belgian mistrust of the Germans.[395] It was this type of nationalist feeling that Gessler had no doubt in mind when he advanced his proposal for a company with dual or multiple nationality.

Another alternative to the European company scheme, supported in some German and Italian quarters "because of the known difficulties with the creation of a European commercial company," centers on a French model, the *groupement d'intérêt économique,* a special organizational form, introduced in 1967 in the context of governmental efforts to adjust the French economy to the new dimensions of the Common Market.[396] This greatly simplified, func-

---

ff. (1968) with references to cases; Foley, *Incorporation, Multiple Incorporation, and the Conflict of Laws,* 42 HARV. L. REV. 516 (1929).

[395] Farnsworth, *A Merger in Europe: Many Woes,* New York Times, July 20, 1969, at 8F, col. 3.

[396] Ordinance No. 67-821 of Sept. 23, 1967, on the "groupements d'intérêt économique", J.O. (France) of Sept. 28, 1967, at 9537. Bott & Rosener, *Das Groupement d'Intérêt Économique, Modell einer praktikablen Form grenzüberschreitender Unternehmens-Kooperation in Europa?,* 1970 NJW 364. *See also* Fenghi, *Ancora su "les groupements d'intérêt économique" (in Francia & Spagna),* 1969 RIVISTA DELLE SOCIETÀ 423; Langer, *Erfahrungen mit dem Groupement d'intérêt économique in Frankreich,* 1970 AWD 61.

tional new form of association is available to individuals and companies, wishing to join in cooperative arrangements for such purposes as selling or purchasing, research, exports, undertaking a public works project, or manufacturing a specific product. The "groupement" is formed by a simple contract, and it becomes a legal person with full legal capacity upon entry into the commercial register. It may issue only non-negotiable shares, but it may also be organized without any capital; the members, however, are liable personally. The organization consists of a members' meeting and one or more "administrators"; other organizational features may be defined in the contract. Substantial tax benefits accrue to a legal person organized in the new form, and this may be a principal reason why it has already proved rather popular in France. Moreover, in at least two instances, it was reportedly employed for transnational cooperation projects by German and French concerns. The suggestion was made that the Member States may find it easier to agree on a uniform law embodying this innovative, "concise and essentially practical" form, than to accept substantial harmonization of existing company laws.[397] The European Commission has shown interest in the French model.[398]

One may wonder whether some among those who display impatience and skepticism as to the prospects for both an early coordination of national company laws and an agreement on a European company, do not themselves bear a certain share of responsibility for the slowness of the pace, because of their passionate attachment to their own national law. In a more optimistic vein, von Caemmerer suggests that further serious work on a European company law,

---

[397] Bott & Rosener, preceding note at 367.

[398] Commission des Communautés Européennes, COM (70)/100 final, Mar. 18, 1970, La Politique industrielle de la Communauté, Mémorandum de la Commission au Conseil—Introduction et Orientations Générales at 18; 2ème partie: Amélioration de l'environnement des Entreprises dans la Communauté at II/28.

based presumably on the Sanders draft, may prove to be a
stimulant for accelerated work on the coordination of national laws; it may provide the *"Gesamtkonzeption,"* the
comprehensive concept, of a complete stock company law,
the absence of which has been deplored. Conversely, the
work on the coordination might advance the European company project, since any European company law would have
to respond to the minimum rules laid down in the directives
for national companies.[399]

---

[399] Von Caemmerer, in EUROPÄISCHE HANDELSGESELLSCHAFT at 55.

While this manuscript was in the process of publication, the Commission announced that it had approved its own draft of a European
stock-company law, and that it will propose to the Council the adoption
of the draft in the form of a regulation under EEC Art. 235. The complete text is contained in Doc. Com (70) 600 final, Partie I-III. The new
draft is likely to be modified in the course of negotiations. The following is an excerpt from the Commission's announcement, as set forth in
the Information Memo P-29/III, dated June 1970. Since the terminology
employed by the Commission's translators differs somewhat from my
own, I inserted my terms between brackets in a few instances.

"On 24 June 1970 the Commission of the European Communities
adopted the draft of a European law on joint-stock companies [stock
companies]. A proposal for the requisite Community regulation will be
forwarded to the Council in the next few days.

Access

"As a start it will be sufficient for this type of company to be available for very specific economic operations which must be made possible
and be given priority if conditions are to be created that are similar to
those of a domestic market. Three operations are concerned:

(a) Mergers between two companies which have their headquarters in
different Member States but wish to combine across the frontiers to
form a company under European law;

(b) Establishment of holding companies under European law by companies with their headquarters in different Member States;

(c) Establishment of joint subsidiaries under European law by companies with their headquarters in different Member States.

"To ensure that the rules are brief and simple, they will apply only
to joint-stock companies. Enterprises registered under other legal forms
can always reconstitute themselves as joint-stock companies under national law.

"Only joint-stock companies which opt for one of these three forms
of cross-frontier combination will be entitled to benefit from the Community's company law. The simple conversion of companies incorpo-

rated under national law into companies under European law is not envisaged. Even where such national companies have an international character (for instance with regard to their personnel, capital or type of operations, or because they have branches or subsidiaries in other Member States), their economic and legal relations are at least for the present sufficiently covered by the company law of the various Member States. Practical experience bears this out, and the EEC Treaty in fact confines itself to requiring that the national company laws be adjusted to the needs of the common market. The proposed law on European joint-stock companies will not therefore replace the national laws on joint-stock companies, but will operate side by side with them and so fill a gap which cannot be filled by approximation of national laws in this field. As the Treaty does not provide the powers needed to attain these Community objectives, and as it follows from what has been said that the Community must itself take the requisite action, the conditions are met for invoking EEC Treaty Article 235 as the legal basis of the regulation proposed by the Commission.

"Under this regulation, the minimum capital required of the European joint-stock company would be 500,000 units of account [i.e. $] in the case of mergers or the establishment of a holding company, and 250,000 units of account in the case of the establishment of a subsidiary. The minimum capital is fixed at a level which would enable even medium-sized enterprises to use the new company form.

"European joint-stock companies will be established under the judicial control of the Court of Justice of the European Communities and will be entered in a European register of companies to be kept with the Court of Justice. In each Member State there will be a branch office for this European register.

"A choice can be made between bearer shares and registered shares. To enable the shares of European joint-stock companies to be traded on the stock exchanges, the possibility of issuing bearer shares must be maintained.

"European joint-stock companies are free to set up their headquarters anywhere in the Community. They may have several headquarters. The location of headquarters is determined by the articles of association. For tax purposes, however, these companies are deemed to have their headquarters at the place from which they are actually managed.

"In line with progressive tendencies in all Member States, the European joint-stock company will have a board of management [executive board], which is the company's decision-making centre, a supervisory board [supervisory council], and a general meeting of shareholders.

Workers' participation

"The proposed regulation contains independent rules on the workers' right of participation, geared to the needs of the European joint-stock company. The arrangement proposed consists of three parts made to dovetail with each other; they cannot be taken separately but must be viewed as a whole. Under the proposal there would be a European works council [plant committee or council], workers would be given a say on the supervisory board and there would be arrangements for the possible conclusion of European collective wage agreements.

"First, a European works council will have to be set up in all European joint-stock companies having establishments in different Member States. Its competence is confined to matters that concern the whole of the company or several of its establishments. The national works councils in the establishments of a European joint-stock company are maintained, and will continue to fulfil their task to the extent that matters do not come under the competence of the European works council.

"The European works council consists of members from among the workers of the various establishments of the European joint-stock company elected under the rules applying in the individual countries. The European works council has the right to be informed and consulted and also the right to give or withhold its agreement. Its agreement is required for decisions by the board of management in the following matters: principles governing recruitment, careers, dismissal of workers and vocational training; measures relating to industrial health and safety; introduction and management of social facilities; establishment of pay principles and introduction of new pay methods; beginning and end of the working day; preparation of the leave schedule.

"Secondly, the workers have the right to have on the supervisory board one representative to every two representatives appointed by the general meeting. Over and above this statutory minimum of one worker's representative in every three members of the supervisory board, the articles of association of any European joint-stock company may provide for a larger number. The workers' representatives are elected from lists by the members of the national works councils. Proposals may be made by the national works councils, the European works council, the trade unions represented in the European joint-stock company, and the workers of the European joint-stock company. A trade union is represented in an establishment if it has members among the workers. If the workers have up to three representatives in the supervisory board, at least one of them must not be employed in an establishment of the European joint-stock company. If they have four or more representatives, at least two of them must not be employed in an establishment of the European joint-stock company.

"The workers will not be represented if at least two thirds of the workers of the European joint-stock company reject representation.

"No matter what the other arrangements, however, the regulation provides that when appointing the board of management the supervisory board must make one member responsible for personnel and labour relations.

"Thirdly, it will be possible for the working conditions of the staff of a European joint-stock company to be fixed by collective agreement between the company and the trade unions represented in its establishments if the two sides wish to conclude such an agreement. The European joint-stock company may therefore enter into collective agreements. The conditions of the work fixed by collective agreement apply directly and bindingly for all workers of the European joint-stock company who are members of one of the unions party to the collective agreement. For the other workers the employment contract may provide that the conditions of work fixed by collective agreement are to apply directly to the job.

"These proposals seek to make the fullest allowance possible for all differences in the actual, legal and psychological conditions found in the Member States. The Commission feels that the measures it has proposed are indispensable if the road is to be cleared for employers and workers in the European companies to co-operate as partners— and their co-operation is, in the Commission's view, essential.

Taxation

"From the tax angle, the European joint-stock company comes under the law of the State from which it is actually managed. There can be no tax preferences for the European joint-stock company, as it must be given the same treatment as joint-stock companies under the law of the individual States and as any preferences would be liable to distort competition.

"The principle will therefore be that European joint-stock companies are governed by the same rules as the Commission proposed at the beginning of 1969 in its draft directives on the common tax system that should apply to mergers between companies and to parent companies and subsidiaries from different Member States. Under these rules the profits of an establishment would continue to be taxed exclusively in the State where the establishment is located. Companies are, however, to be given the right to opt for the system of world profit. This would allow them to deduct in the country of tax domicile the losses suffered by establishments abroad. The regulation provides for rules to this effect.

Law on integrated groups [related or affiliated companies]

"Combination of enterprises under a single management (to form an integrated group) has everywhere assumed such great economic importance that the regulation cannot do without rules on integrated groups. Where a European joint-stock company is a controlling or controlled enterprise in a group, the regulation protects the independent shareholders outside the group and the creditors of controlled enterprises associated with the group. A European joint-stock company that becomes a member of a group is required to make the fact known immediately. Independent holders of shares in controlled enterprises may accept cash payment for their shares, demand that their shares be converted into shares of the controlling enterprise or in certain circumstances ask for an annual compensation to guarantee their dividend. If the controlling enterprise grants independent shareholders this guarantee, it has in principle the right to give instructions to the managing board of the controlled enterprise. The managing board of the controlled enterprise has to follow these instructions even if they run counter to its interests. The creditors of controlled enterprises are protected by the rule that the controlling enterprise has joint liability for the commitments of the controlled enterprise."

Chapter 9

AN OVERVIEW AND SOME CONCLUDING THOUGHTS ON THE PROCESS OF NATIONAL RE-FORM AND TRANSNATIONAL COORDINATION

We have been concerned in this volume with two separate but related legal processes. The *first* is the national law reform process, which aims at modernization and rationalization of company laws through national legislation. The *second* process—assimilation of national company laws on a regional level through prescriptive intervention of transnational institutions—is an aspect of a broader effort of constructing a regional legal framework for multinational "European" business. These two processes have interacted with an increasing intensity since 1961, but it is difficult to identify a cause-effect relationship on the basis of the presently available empirical data. For one thing, even before the establishment of the European Community, there was a detectable trend in national reforms toward "spontaneous assimilation"—that is, greater similarity among national laws, with German law often serving as the principal pole of attraction.

The state of fluidity in national legislation, created by the national reforms in progress, has been certainly helpful, and possibly indispensable, to the assimilation effort.

1. National reform

In the *Federal Republic of Germany,* the history of stock company law has been the history of its successive reforms. Today, that law is the most modern, most "regulatory" and

structured law among the Six—somewhat like the corporation and securities laws of California. The 1937 reform,
which greatly strengthened the hand of the management as
against the shareholders in the interest of efficiency, was followed by the important reform of 1965 which cut down
management discretion somewhat—particularly as regards
building hidden reserves. Moreover, in its *Konzernrecht*
provisions, the 1965 law sought to provide an organic legal
framework for the new reality of related and interlocking enterprises. The law as a whole was influenced by neo-liberalist thought and was designed primarily to protect shareholders and investors. The 1969 law on financial accounts
and disclosure by large enterprises was to serve in addition
the broader "corporate constituencies," including the public
at large. Although there has been ample communication between Bonn and Brussels, the 1965 reform shows no discernible impact of the transnational effort; but as the process
of reform continues in the Federal Republic, a new limited
liability company law has come under discussion and the
proposed provisions for partial financial disclosure reflect
the influence of the EEC assimilation process.

In *France,* a new comprehensive law dealing with *all* commercial companies was adopted in 1966. The reform was a
culmination of an effort extending over more than a quarter
of a century; it fit well into the Gaullist program of a general "renewal" of French institutions, even though in its
final form is represented only a modest modernization,
which conformed to general economic policy favoring private investment in private enterprise. The new law reflected
a conscious effort to assimilate to the German pattern, but
perhaps its principal value was that it put an end—for a
time at any rate—to what was described as *"obscurantisme
impénétrable,"* a labyrinth of laws, decrees and ordinances,
that had mushroomed since 1867. Yet by the end of 1969,
there were already a dozen amending and supplementing
laws and decrees. During its more advanced stage, the
French reform work exerted considerable influence on the

work of the EEC Commission, and it was in turn visibly influenced by the conclusions of the French reformers.

Belgium has been in the throes of a comprehensive reform of the 1935 version of its company law. The draft deals with all commercial companies, and, in 1970, it was undergoing a review in the Conseil d'État. The new text, not unlike the French reform, constitutes a modernization without revolutionary innovations, designed in many respects to sanction and codify existing case law and practice, and to increase only moderately the regulatory aspects. The draft was influenced profoundly by the business-oriented Belgian master-comparatists, and it reflects significantly the assimilation work in the Community, since these very same men have played a prominent part in that work as well.

A Belgian expert, Prof. van Ommeslaghe, and a national committee were entrusted with the task of drafting a reform for *Luxembourg,* and it is generally assumed that Luxembourg will adopt the new Belgian law as a model for its new law.

Italy has had a rather modern company law in its 1942 Civil Code, which consolidated civil and commercial law in a single codification. Because of this, and in view of the crying need for reforming other Italian institutions, such as the tax laws and public administration, a company law reform did not appear particularly pressing. Yet under the stimulus of the first center-left coalition program, in the early nineteen sixties, a draft reform law on commercial companies was worked out and went through the National Council of Economy and Labor as well as a high level Interministerial Committee. But like so many impressive reform schemes in Italy, it has been gathering dust in the Ministry since 1966, while the Government has moved from one crisis to another. The draft would strengthen the protection of the shareholder-investor, but it would also increase still further the already substantial governmental control over companies. The reform work in Rome did not take explicit note of the Brussels proceedings, but in several respects it points in the same direction.

The *Netherlands* has found itself in a peculiarly isolated position. It alone among the Member States has only a single corporate form, the stock company, since the limited liability company form does not exist there; it alone has adopted in full the Anglo-American "law-of-the-state-of-incorporation" rule as the controlling choice-of-law principle, in contrast with the "real seat" rule followed elsewhere; Dutch law alone requires Ministerial approval for incorporation; and, last, but not least, the Netherlands law resembles more the permissive Delaware "enabling-type" act than the laws of the other Five. In 1960, the Parliament approved a new, only slightly modified version of the stock company law as part of a general recodification, but the new law is not expected to enter into effect in the immediate future. However, two successive national commissions have been examining the "neuralgic areas" where political pressures are felt both at home and from the Community, which include the contents of corporate financial accounts, financial disclosure, introduction of a limited liability company, and even a form of workers' codetermination on the German pattern. As a result, several legislative measures are in various stages of readiness.

2. Transnational process superimposed

Superimposed on the national reform movements is the transnational mechanism for assimilation of company laws, built into the EEC Treaty. Two cardinal features of this mechanism must be kept in mind—one negative and one positive.

First, the Treaty does *not* give the Community institutions a *formal* power either to reform or to unify national company laws, but only to make them *more similar* to the extent *necessary* for the functioning of the regional Common Market. This functional orientation is in contrast with the objectives of the Nordic Council, for which unification is the purpose, although there also a gradual progression toward uniformity is envisaged in the company law field.

Second—and this constitutes the positive aspect—the task of wielding this power of assimilation is in the hands of Community institutions—lawmaking and judicial—which provide the necessary "organized impulse" and a measure of enforcement and uniform interpretation.

The objective, which the Community institutions are to pursue in exercising this power, is increased company mobility, in the broad sense of removing obstacles to multinational activities within the new regional market. In this volume, we have noted a four-pronged effort:

(a) Removing obstacles to entry into entrepreneurial activity, including setting up branches and subsidiaries across national frontiers. Over thirty directives have been adopted requiring each Member State to adjust its statutes, regulations and practices, so as to give "foreign companies" of the other Member States equal treatment with local companies regarding access to, and conduct of, specified businesses and occupations.

(b) Adjusting or "coordinating" national company law rules so as to make sure that shareholders and "third parties" dealing with a company will enjoy equal protection, regardless of the "nationality" of the company. The "First Directive," coordinating three areas of company law, has been adopted and four other directives are in more or less advance stages, with more to come.

(c) Introducing uniform conflict-of-laws rules, more appropriate for a regional market, and some "internal" norms required to overcome the territorial limitations inherent in a nation-state, through supplementing "European" conventions. The Convention on Recognition of Companies, which introduces in part the choice-of-law rule of incorporation and which makes more specific the obligation to recognize companies of the other Member States, is to be followed by conventions on transnational fusion, and on seat transfer. A new European stock company form is to be established either by a convention or by a regulation of the Council of Ministers.

(d) Eliminating differences among national laws which cause unequal competitive conditions in the Member States, and thereby affect "directly" the working of the regional market. This source of authority ("approximation") was drawn upon in the assimilation of certain tax laws and technical regulation, but has not yet been tapped with respect to company laws.

In principle, the articulation of company laws and of company law reform remains in the hands of the Member States, but national lawmaking must not contravene, and must take account of, the Treaty limitations and the new Community law. This means first, that national laws must be adjusted to give appropriate effect to Community directives or to the "European" treaties. Second, the Commission expects to be informed by the Governments of any new national legislation in the fields covered by the directives. However, the effectiveness of a preventive review of proposed national reform legislation will depend primarily upon the readiness on the part of the Member Governments to consult and to cooperate with the Commission.

3. National institutions in action

In all of the Member States, the initiative for, and the nerve center of, the law reform activity has been in the Ministry of Justice, an executive department headed by a member of the Government in power, but staffed from a body of law-trained civil servants, comprising judges, prosecutors, and administrators.

With one exception, the chosen instrument for preliminary exploration and drafting has been a special commission, appointed by the Minister of Justice. The composition has varied, but the most common mix has been one of

ministerial officials and university experts with a sprinkling
of practitioners. Only in the Federal Republic of Germany
has the drafting been done in the Ministry itself, without
any commission—in order, it is said, to keep "special interests" from unduly intruding at the formative stage.

The ideas for the reform have come in large measure from
a great variety of non-governmental "outside" sources, including learned writing, reports of professional organizations and (in France and Italy) drafts prepared by associations of stock companies.

The predominant influence has been in the hands of an
alliance among law-trained civil servants and law professors,
greatly concerned about theoretical concepts and doctrines
of company law. But those law professors in the working
groups, who are engaged also in law practice, and outside
lawyers, have reflected the prevailing climate and philosophy
of the business community. Even within the business circles, however, lawyers have represented the less "conservative" element, and they have been more likely to advocate
modernization and moderate reform than members of
management.

Paradoxically, in France, where "insiders" had kept tight
control, a vital phase of the 1966 law was placed in the
hands of a small committee, composed in large measure of
business-oriented outsiders, and presided by a leading political figure, a member of the Senate. This committee improvised an unusual, if not unprecedented, machinery for
extensive "hearings" of outside experts and interested
groups, but its comprehensive, albeit "conservative," draft
was greatly reduced in scope by the Minister of Justice,
who insisted on preserving the extensive lawmaking power
accorded by the 1958 Constitution to the executive at the
expense of the Parliament.

A studied effort has been made to keep company law
reform "non-political" and "technical," and thus to leave
such controversial issues as workers' codetermination or
participation to be dealt with by special legislation, as part of

the "law of the enterprise." In Italy, the reform became "tainted" for a time by "politics" as a result of its inclusion in a coalition program, and certain Netherlands reform legislation was initially proposed by a group of considerable political influence and awareness. In Italy, perhaps more clearly than elsewhere, one may note the two primary forces for reform, which at this juncture have fought each other to a stand-off: business lawyers pressing for modernization of the stock company in order to attract large entrepreneurial capital, and socialist oriented lawyers viewing the reform as a means for curbing corporate power through increased governmental control.

In France, Italy, the Netherlands, and Belgium, structured consultations with employers, labor and other interest groups take place in special councils established by law to advise the government on economic and social problems. No such body exists in the Federal Republic, and perhaps for this reason, the corresponding Economic and Social Committee, instituted at the Community level by the EEC Treaty, is viewed with some distrust in that country. In Italy, the Council tended in the direction of classic liberalism—toward less regulation and more freedom for companies. The impact of the Councils on the lawmaker is difficult to assess, but it does not appear to be overwhelming; it is noticeable in the Netherlands, where the Government appears to be taking a less negative posture toward workers' participation in response to an opinion rendered by the Council.

One phenomenon—somewhat unexpected in what is often viewed as a "technocratic" society—is the lively role played by national Parliaments, which exceeded the function of formal legitimation. Thus, in France, the innovative two-tier model of company structure was first introduced into the reform bill in the National Assembly by left-wing Gaullists, who viewed it as a first step toward workers' participation; in the Senate, on the other hand, a group of lawyer-parliamentarians of a more conservative business orientation asserted itself by obtaining a great number of modifications

—such as the elimination of judicial control over incorporation, which had been demanded by the Government, for the sake of assimilation to the German pattern, among other reasons. In Germany, the protracted examination of the Government draft of the new stock company law brought forth bitter complaints of the inadequacy of the parliamentary facilities for obtaining independent expert advice, as compared with those available to Congressional Committees in the United States.

In all of the Member States, legislative initiative is securely lodged in the hands of the executive, and this corresponds to the trend in lawmaking at the federal level in the United States. No uniform pattern is discernible in procedures employed by the States of the Union with respect to reforming company laws, but when a State legislature establishes a special commission, the State Executive as a rule plays a vital role in determining its membership.[1]

4. National attitudes in the transnational process

National attitudes and the character of the confrontations in the transnational process have been influenced greatly by the type of the norm under consideration. One may think of three categories of such norms in the field of company law:

(1)   Norms governing technical arrangements, such as the specific modalities of publication of the company charter and other data regarding its legal status.

(2)   Norms representing the lawmaker's compromise between the competing interests of the various corporate constituencies, particularly shareholders, creditors or other "third parties." The definition of "third parties" includes in

---

[1] The Michigan Law Revision Commission, however, which is now engaged in revising the State corporation act, was formed, and is controlled by, the State legislature, and thus appears to constitute an exception. Mich. Public Acts of 1965, No. 412, §§ 12-14; MICH. COMP. LAWS 1948, §§ 4.322-24 (MICH. COMP. LAWS ANN. §§ 4.322-24).

some States, but not in others, the employees, and to some extent the "public interest." Some of these norms are linked to traditional, albeit at times obsolescent, doctrines which States find difficult to discard (*ultra vires,* company as a contract in contrast with company as an institution).

(3) Norms which fall into the preceding category, but which, in addition, assume a distinct "political" coloring, because they evoke organized reaction of special interest groups or are linked to more general economic or social policies of governments. Examples are rules governing financial disclosure, codetermination or participation of workers in company organs, availability of bearer shares, and the extent of direct public intervention in the formation or life of companies. Moreover, two other types of norms are "political" in this sense. The first type comprises proposals to deny Community benefits to companies which are organized in Member States, but controlled from outside the Community. The second type comprises schemes for new institutional arrangements that would upgrade the powers of Community institutions at the expense of national institutions; such schemes are opposed by those who still conceive of the Community essentially as a customs union and a forum for cooperation of "sovereign" States.

Major problems in the Community process have arisen from differences among national norms and practices and from the absence of shared "common law," from substantial divergencies in the functions served by the same company form in different Member States, and to some extent from differences in the degree of industrial concentration.

Another difficulty, facing the national delegations, has been the lack of meaningful normative standards or empirically determined economic and social criteria for deciding whether coordination was necessary in a given area, what the priorities should be, and whether a uniform rule was required rather than a mere option among several national rules which have been appropriately adjusted to

assure "equivalence."[2] The traditional method employed—
a systematic comparison of national laws and practices, en-
riched by the experience of the experts—has proved adequate in dealing with predominantly legal-technical issues,
but it alone could not provide reliable indices when it came
to making value judgments on matters involving economic

---

[2] Drawing upon his vast experience, Professor van Ommeslaghe has
made a valiant effort to offer general criteria in the form of four
"stages" in the coordination work:

1. A complete and systematically ordered inventory must first be
   made of all company law provisions and related practices for each
   company form;
2. Each article, appearing in this inventory, must then be examined
   to determine whether and to what extent it concerns protection of
   shareholders or of third parties;
3. The articles which remain on the list after the examination in
   the second stage must then be further considered with a view to
   determining whether it is *necessary* to make them the subject of
   coordination, either because there exist disparities between the
   guarantees in the laws of the Member States, or because such
   disparities will develop as a result of the realization of complete
   freedom of establishment, or as a result of the entering into effect
   of the Convention on Mutual Recognition of Companies and
   Legal Persons. It is necessary for this purpose to examine each
   question concretely in each national law, taking into account the
   relevant practices, to compare legal institutions which lead to
   comparable results even if they appear to be quite different, and
   on that basis to exercise a value judgment as to the level of the
   guarantees and to the equivalence of the guarantees;
4. If the conclusion is to the effect that the guarantees are not
   equivalent, it is necessary "to intervene" through coordination.
   The form of the intervention would differ according to different
   circumstances. In some instances, it may be sufficient "to correct
   the existing systems so as to make them equivalent, leaving the
   Member States free to choose between the corrected systems. In
   other instances, it will not be possible to avoid laying down a
   more or less detailed uniform rule."

Thus, the drafting method, according to Professor van Ommeslaghe, consists of an intensive comparative analysis, which cannot be
limited to the "great principles," but must enter into the detailed
practices and concrete effects of the institutions. Taking this pragmatic
approach, it is necessary "to define the objectives in as concrete a
manner as possible, avoiding reference to legal concepts whose contents differ in the six countries." Van Ommeslaghe, *La première directive* at 519.

or social policy.[3] In the last analysis, decisions have been made on the basis of negotiated compromise, with the Commission staff, supported almost invariably by the French delegation, often advocating more, rather than less, coordination.

National delegations have insisted on the preservation of their respective national norms and solutions, partly because of inherent lawyers' conservatism and aversion to change, partly because of the nexus, real or imagined, between a national norm and a national economic interest. Fear of evasion of a national rule through new Community arrangements, and concern about the anticipated response of national parliaments, have reinforced the insistence on national solutions.

The Italian delegation, perhaps more than the others, has been unwilling to surrender its national rule. This may be due to the still highly conceptual nature of Italian legal education, dominated by inflexible positivist doctrines, to Italy's relative geographic isolation, and, last but not least, to the difficulty in sustaining continuity and quality of the preparatory work at the home base and effective coordination among the bureaus concerned. It has also been suggested that lack of governmental consensus on the text of a national reform law has caused the Italian delegation to be uncertain as to what changes in Italian law would be acceptable to its Government—and this factor is said to have contributed to its rigidity.

The delegation from the Federal Republic appeared at times equally inflexible, in part due to the dominant and authoritative personality of its leader. More important, however, has been the role of German legislation as the "target" law for the assimilation process, which has brought into play

---

[3] On the research method into extra-legal, economic and social bases of company law see Mestmäcker, *Das Verhältnis der Wirtschaftswissenschaft zur Rechtswissenschaft in Aktienrecht*, in DAS VERHÄLTNIS DER WIRTSCHAFTSWISSENSCHAFT ZUR RECHTSWISSENSCHAFT, SOZIOLOGIE UND STATISTIK 103, at 108 (Berlin 1964).

on the German side several contradictory considerations. On the one hand, the assimilation process has been viewed as a welcome device to reduce the real or apparent competitive disadvantage of German companies, which have been subject to stricter regulation and greater transparency than the companies of other Member States; on the other hand, there has been the concern, at the early stage at any rate, that co-ordination would require diluting German standards and, above all, that it would limit the freedom of the Federal Parliament in undertaking further reforms, and force it to accept Community-wide compromise solutions. Thus, it is generally recognized that German law has the most elaborate provisions for the preparation of annual financial documents by both stock companies and limited liability companies, but at present that law requires public disclosure for the former only, while in principle preserving privacy for the latter. Three of the Six, on the other hand, insist on a measure of public disclosure for limited liability companies as well, although their rules determining the content of the disclosed data are skimpy and the disclosure therefore somewhat illusory. The Belgian reform, however, would subject limited liability companies to almost as strict a disclosure as is required from stock companies. The Federal Government has been in the process of considering an extension of the disclosure requirement to limited liability companies; but in Brussels, the German delegation vigorously opposed a rule to this effect, unless and until the content of the disclosure was first prescribed and thus equalized throughout the Community. The Commission was, in effect, forced to accept this posture. The German delegation's concern about preserving its own unique model of workers' representation in company organs has posed perhaps the most serious issue, since thus far it has not proved acceptable elsewhere. In fact, negotiations on two major projects, the convention on transnational fusion and the scheme for a European company, have been deadlocked largely because of this issue. The division within the German Christian Democratic Party

regarding further extension of codetermination made the German delegation in Brussels particularly sensitive.

The French delegation has matched, if not surpassed, the German group in the quality of technical skill and ideas. However, the French attitude has been much more flexible because of the state of French law, and because of the ongoing national reform. Although generally cooperative, the French have shown strong opposition whenever a proposed norm implied increasing the powers of the European Commission or accepting new "supranational" arrangements, such as a European company governed by Community law. Again, they have sought to confine the advantages of Community arrangements to national companies whose center of decision-making is located within the Community. This has included certain benefits of free establishment and access to capital markets, recognition of companies under the new Convention, access to transnational fusion and the concomitant tax relief, and access to the new form of a European company. Thus far, this view has not been accepted by others.

The Belgian delegation has been the most flexible of all, and has often played the role of an *"amicable compositeur"* on the side of the Commission staff. This attitude may be explained in part by the fact that the Belgian reform, profoundly influenced by comparative studies of other systems, has been, and still is, in a relatively early stage; again, the Belgian draft, somewhat like the new French law, already anticipates the Community directives. Only when it came to extending governmental control beyond certain limits did the Belgians appear to take a strongly negative position. Thus they opposed—successfully—a Community rule that would have prescribed judicial or administrative supervision of company formation; they considered it an unnecessarily burdensome formality.

In the early phases of the proceeding, it was the Netherlands delegation that posed the most serious obstacle, because of its *a priori* opposition to any coordination whatsoever.

The Government, scholars, parliamentarians and industry, were united in this view, primarily for reasons inherent in the position of the Netherlands law as by far the most "liberal" in the Community, which presumably would have to be modified most in the process of coordination. As the negotiations progressed, and certain concessions were made to the Netherlands view, particularly for the benefit of Dutch close corporations, the Government delegation became more cooperative. But the sense of outrage in the Netherlands over the veto of the British membership application, and the desire to avoid, pending British adhesion, new commitments beyond those specified in the Treaty, have worked as new restraints. The powerful Anglo-Dutch concerns have continued to exert major influence.

5. Transnational institutions in action

(a) Interaction in lawmaking

At the transnational level, the Community Commission has the exclusive power of "legislative initiative" for coordination, and it has asserted its authority to initiate assimilation by convention as well. In fact, the Commission staff of Community civil servants performs functions comparable to those of a Ministry of Justice at the national level, while the role of a typical national reform "commission" is played by the two "working groups" (one for coordination, the other for new conventions). These groups, however, in contrast with a national commission, have mixed national and transnational membership, consisting of national "experts" (mostly officials of the Ministries of Justice and law professors) appointed by each Member Government, and Commission personnel. This small initial circle of lawyers has been gradually extended to include the special consultants to Commission bureaus and other outside scholars, who comment on the assimilation work in learned journals and professional meetings, often reflecting the particular perspective of the Commission bureau which they advise.

The draft of a directive that emerges from the working group is comparable to the German *Referentenentwurf* (official draft), in that it does not commit either the Commission or the Governments, even though the officials from the national Ministries exert an important, if not decisive, influence in the group. The circle broadens further at this stage when the Commission staff initiates informal consultations with special interest groups, organized on the Community level, including industry, banking, attorneys—and in the case of the directive on fusion—labor. For the purpose of fusion, at any rate, labor is viewed in a sense as a "third party," whose protection is involved in the coordination. In order to preclude conflict, however, the Commission personnel makes a studied effort to avoid direct communication with national special interest organizations which are the components of the transnational groupings.

This phase is concluded by what one may term the first "political" act, a decision of the EEC Commission approving the draft for submission to the Council of Ministers. In reality, the Commissioners rely largely on the recommendations by the staff and their "chiefs of cabinet." In the case of the First Directive, the phase of informal consultations was omitted and the Commission decided to give its approval despite the fact that the national delegations in the working group were unable to agree on the important issue of financial disclosure.

The approved proposal for a directive is reminiscent of the German *Regierungsentwurf* (Government draft); in forwarding it to the ultimate lawmaker, the Council of Ministers, the Commission performs the formal act of legislative initiative. Before the Council acts, it is required to seek the "opinions" of the Economic and Social Committee and of the European Parliament, the two Community bodies with essentially advisory functions, whose opinions, however, do not bind either the Commission or the Council. This phase of consultations brings in another group of actors, some of whom are also concerned with national reform work. Al-

though the experience relating specifically to company law
is still sparse, it may be said that the official national attitudes,
sketched in the preceding section, appear tempered, if not
submerged, in the two advisory bodies; the individual members tend to reflect the special interests of their respective
economic or political transnational group, and not necessarily the "national" interest articulated by official representatives. Thus the Netherlands and German labor spokesmen
in the Economic and Social Committee joined the transnational "workers' group" in opposing the German-Dutch employers' alliance on the issue of financial disclosure; and the
exchange between a German employer and a German labor
union spokesman resembled closely the debate in the Bonn
Parliament. In the European Parliament, the transnational
Christian Democrat group apparently was divided on the
issue of disclosure and this tempered the negative attitude of
its German spokesman, who as a rule has reflected the interests of German industry. The transnational "liberal" group,
however, strongly mirrored the French influence of its most
interested "conservative" members, who were also active in
the French Senate on the new company law. The socialists
inclined to reflect the transnational interest. Although not
obliged to do so, the Commission accepted some, but by no
means all, of the amendments to its draft of the First Directive, which were proposed by the two bodies, and it submitted a new, modified proposal to the Council.

The Council of Ministers, with the "opinions" of the two
advisory bodies before it, takes final action on the Commission's proposal. Up to this point, as the process unfolds, the
circle of actors widens somewhat at each successive stage.
However, in this final stage, when the proposal is prepared
for the Ministers' decision, the circle contracts to comprise
only some, but not all, of the members of the original working group, including the Commission personnel, and two
new components: a handful of national civil servants and
diplomats within the system of the so-called Committee of
Permanent Representatives, and the Secretariat of the Coun-

cil of Ministers. This arena represents a new, complex mix of national and transnational elements. The proceeding takes place in complete secrecy, through a progression of committees, and it amounts to intensive bargaining and "package deals," through which the still outstanding issues are finally resolved. It is at this stage that the Governments become committed to a text. Strong pressure to obtain consensus and dispose of the matter is exerted by the chairman of the busy group of senior national civil servants, who are responsible to the Ministers. Final agreement on the First Directive was reached at this level, so that the "political" act of approval by the Ministers, required by the Treaty, in fact was a mere formality.

When assimilation is effected through new conventions, the preparatory work is also done in a working group, organized at the initiative of the Commission, but in this case chaired by one of the government-appointed experts rather than by a member of Commission personnel. The Commission has no authority to intervene formally in what is essentially an intergovernmental undertaking, culminating in the approval of the convention by the Ministers, who sit in the Council but act as representatives of their own Governments—an improvised procedure, not envisaged in the Treaty. Finally, national parliaments must approve the convention in accordance with the normal treaty-making procedure.

In February 1970, responding to complaints of slow progress and in anticipation of increased membership of the EEC, Director General Vogelaar announced a modification in the preparatory phase of the coordination procedure.[4] The change was designed to eliminate the laborious and time-consuming collective drafting in the working group, by placing the responsibility for the drafting in the hands of the Commission staff and the permanent, special expert-consultants.[5] The function of the national delegations in

---

[4] Comm. Doc. 2926/XIV/C/70-F, Rev. 2, at 1-2.
[5] *See* p. 182 *supra.*

the working group would be, first, to discuss a general report prepared by one of the special consultants, and then to comment specifically on a "pre-draft" of a directive to be elaborated by the Commission's staff and consultants on the basis of the initial discussion. The staff would then study and evaluate the comments made by the national delegations, and it would prepare a "final" draft for approval by the Commission. The new procedure should make it possible to reduce the number of working group meetings, which escalated from three sessions in 1963 to fifteen in 1969.

It is much too early to estimate whether the innovation, which is also intended to strengthen the Commission's role of legislative initiative, will have the desired effect.

(b) Problems of parliamentary and judicial control

(i) Preserving the Commission's initiative; the principle of majority voting

Addressing the European Parliament in 1969, the Commissioner responsible for the assimilation work expressed his concern that the Commission's vital right of initiative was being thwarted, and its relative position of influence generally impaired, by the "administrative substructure of national 'delegations'" surrounding the Council of Ministers. He observed, "[F]ormal proposals of the Commission that in most cases have taken years to elaborate . . . are in practice often treated as mere working documents" when "the haggling among civil service experts starts anew from a different angle" at the final stage of the proceeding.[6]

To a certain extent, the experience with the First Directive confirms this complaint, since the Commission's text, elaborated over a period of more than four years, was

---

6 Approximation of Legislation: The Policy of the Commission of the European Communities, Address by Dr. Hans von der Groeben, Member of the Commission of the European Communities to the European Parliament, Strasbourg, Nov. 27, 1969, at 14, *Commission of the European Communities, Publ. Services* 8289/5/1/1970.

substantially redrafted at the final stage. This may have been due in part to the fact that the original drafting was less than perfect; moreover, the Commission personnel was able to participate actively in the "haggling," even though its bargaining position, by the nature of things, was not very strong. Yet there is little question that the development represents a certain deformity of the lawmaking process. Since national and transnational bureaucrats are encouraged to strike a bargain even on the more important "political" issues, the Commission itself is prevented from defending its position on such issues before the Ministers in the Council and from submitting an amended proposal, as is contemplated in the Treaty. At the very least, a sharper delineation of authority and responsibility in this secret phase would be desirable.

This issue is related to the problem of preserving the institution of majority voting in the Council, which some have viewed as an essential feature of the system and a hallmark of its supranationality. Since the end of the "first stage" of "the transitional period" on the last day of 1961, the Council has had the legal authority to approve a coordinating directive by a weighted majority vote. This possibility, and the Treaty rule to the effect that a Commission proposal may not be modified in the Council except by a unanimous vote, should have placed the Commission and its staff in a strong negotiating position during the final phase described above. Yet I was not able to find the slightest evidence in the records relating to the First Directive, that any of the actors, at any level, had contemplated the possibility of an action by majority vote.[7] This may or may not have been a consequence of the 1965 crisis in which the majority voting formula was a crucial point at issue. At that time, five Ministers refused to abandon the formula as demanded by France, but they did agree to waive its application to certain

---

[7] It is reported, however, that when the negotiations on the First Directive became deadlocked within the Committee of Permanent Representatives, a spokesman for the German delegation hinted at the possibility of a majority vote. A few days later the Italian delegation modified its position and unanimous agreement could be reached.

decisions on agricultural policy. The first coordinating directive may not have been the best occasion for considering other than unanimous approval, if one takes into account the ambiguity of Article 54, par. 3(g), the importance of company law in national economy, the sensitivity of national Parliaments and, last but not least, the absence of an effective Community procedure for political legitimation of Community law, as discussed in the next section. At any rate, there has been in this field no intimation of the "political will" that would be required to invoke the majority voting rule, if it should become necessary to do so. The same, strong consensual motivation appears to have prevailed generally in other fields as well, and in these circumstances the majority voting formula may have lost some, if not most, of its value as a "strategic deterrent" against exorbitant assertions of "national interest."

(ii)   Toward parliamentary control over the executive?

Another problem is posed by the fact that, for all practical purposes, assimilation through directives is within the exclusive control of executive power, national and transnational.

Although the communication with transnational interest groups may have improved somewhat, these Brussels-based professional and industrial organizations are still quite weak in relation to their national components; the role of the Economic and Social Committee has been episodic at best and does not seem to be growing. The new conventions do receive their legitimation through approval in national parliaments, but no comparable legitimation is available for directives. The European Parliament must render an "opinion" on a directive, but the opinion may be ignored by the Commission and by the Council. As a matter of law, the Parliament could force the Commission to resign, but it has no voice in the appointment of a new Commission and, in any case, it has no authority over the Council. The Commission has made an effort to make the consultation with the

Parliament in the field of legal assimilation more effective by programmatic statements and reports by the Commissioners in plenary sessions, by appearances of Commissioners in Committees, by submission of more or less informative memoranda and progress reports, and by answers to written questions. In response to some urging, the Commission also undertook to let the Parliament know on a regular basis what modifications have been made in a directive, *after* the Parliament had given its "opinion." However, there are obvious limits to the Commission's cooperation, since, according to the Treaty, it is the Council, not the Commission, that is required and authorized to consult the Parliament, and it is the Council that controls the final lawmaking phase. The Legal Committee of the Parliament recently suggested a more liberal Treaty interpretation which would at least allow the Commission to consult the Parliament directly, and to associate it thus more closely with the elaboration of the proposals.[8]

At the present time, it certainly cannot be said that the European Parliament exerts "political control" over executive lawmaking in the legal assimilation area. Nor is there any effective political control on the national level, since national legislatures are presented with a directive *after* it has become binding Community law; although they may choose "the form or means" of "enforcing" the directive in the national legal order, they have little, if any, discretion as to the substance, particularly when the directive is as detailed as some provisions of the First Directive. Yet a coordination directive may require, as we have seen, modifications of national codes and company law statutes, which would normally fall within the competence of national parliaments. In France and in Italy, the executive was able to implement the First Directive without recourse to the legislature;

---

8 The Legal Committee is reported to have adopted a "note" by M. Jozeau-Marigné (French Liberal) based on a new interpretation of EEC Art. 162, and suggesting negotiations for a modification of the present procedure. EUROPE, No. 515 (new series), Feb. 23, 1970, at 8.

in Belgium, the Federal Republic, Luxembourg, and in the Netherlands, however, an act of parliament is required, and there is no evidence thus far that the parliaments would be willing to delegate the necessary lawmaking power to the executive. On the contrary, in Italy, where the Government's delegated power had expired at the end of the transitional period, it now appears uncertain whether the Parliament will be willing to enact a new delegating law. In France, the Senate displayed some reluctance when it concurred in extending the delegated powers. A rule in a directive may well impose a readjustment, on a transnational level, in the balance of interests among corporate constituencies, which may disturb the compromise reached on the national level and written into a national norm. It may seem unwise and inappropriate for a national executive alone to undertake an irrevocable transnational commitment to this effect, without effective participation of the economic and political groups concerned. If legal assimilation is to become a significant feature of a Community-wide "industrial policy," a degree of political control will be unavoidable. The logical approach would be to strengthen the participation of the European Parliament in Community lawmaking beyond its present advisory role. It is noteworthy in this context that, as a result of persistent demands from parliamentary circles in the Federal Republic and in the Netherlands, in December 1969 the Member Governments agreed in principle to give the European Parliament very limited budgetary powers, effective in 1975. Moreover, they also agreed to study further the possibility of implementing the Treaty provision, which contemplates that deputies will be elected to the European Parliament by direct universal suffrage, rather than designated by national parliaments from among their membership, as is the present procedure.[9] An arrangement for a genuine participation by

---

9 EEC Art. 138(3). Unanimous approval by the Council and adoption in accordance with national constitutional procedures are necessary for introducing direct election.

the European Parliament in lawmaking including legal assimilation, accompanied perhaps by a scheme for direct election, could be accomplished in connection with the negotiations for admission of the United Kingdom and other new members, or—in the alternative—when the present three Communities, based on three separate treaties (the ECSC, EEC and EURATOM Treaties) are merged into a single Community, to be founded on a new, single treaty.

One measure, however, that could be adopted without complex negotiations, would noticeably improve the working of the European Parliament in the area of assimilation of laws. The experience with the first coordinating directive disclosed the difficulties faced by the Committees of the Parliament in obtaining expert information and advice. These Committees should be given means to order specialized studies, to employ consultants and to hold hearings, so as to be able to obtain a reliable basis for their report to the plenary Parliament. A modest beginning along these lines has already been made.

(iii) Judicial control of uniformity

The issue of institutional adequacy may be posed also in regard to the existing procedures for judicial enforcement and interpretation. There would be precious little assimilation, if the Members failed to give proper effect to the directives or conventions, or if wide interpretive divergencies were allowed to occur in national courts. According to the present Treaty, the Commission and any Member State have the right to complain before the Court of Justice of the Communities if a Member fails to adopt appropriate measures in compliance with a directive. In the context of this proceeding, the Court examines the national implementing law or regulation to see whether it conforms with the directive. The Court may not annul a defective national measure, but it may give an authoritative interpretation of the directive and declare that the measure does not conform to the directive and that the Member is in violation of Community law. The declaration is binding on the Member States and to that extent it may assure a degree of uniformity. However, past experience indicates that a Member State will not be prepared to press an action before the Court against a fellow Member in the absence of exceptional circumstances. The Commission, on the other hand, did start proceedings against Member States which it had considered clearly delinquent,[10] but it, too, may be inclined to tread gently, particularly where all of the Member Governments are in default, as was the case with the first "approximation" directive on pharmaceuticals.

Another means for fostering uniformity may evolve at the national level, in the context of another Treaty provision governing the sharing of judicial power between national and Community judiciaries. If a national measure implementing a directive becomes relevant in a judicial proceeding before a national court, that court would presumably wish to interpret such measure in the light of the directive; if it is necessary in this context to interpret the directive itself, the court may suspend the proceeding and obtain a "preliminary ruling" on the interpretation of the directive from the Court of Justice, in accordance with Article 177 of the Treaty. If it is a court of last instance, this reference is compulsory. However, this procedure has not yet been tested before the Court in this particular context, and some may question, whether a national court may look directly to a directive since, in contrast to the directly applicable "regulation," a directive is given effect in national law through measures chosen by the national Governments. It will thus depend upon the readiness of the Court to assert its jurisdiction in this manner, if and when a national court provides the opportunity.

As the law stands today, the new conventions concerning companies remain altogether outside the scope of the juris-

---

10 In 1969, for instance, eleven of the 77 new cases before the Court of Justice were complaints by the Commission against a Member State, brought in accordance with Art. 169. *Third General Report on the Activities of the Communities 1969,* at 472.

diction of the Court of Justice. Unless some new arrangement is made, one must expect that national courts and authorities, in applying the Convention on Mutual Recognition of Companies, for instance, will not necessarily adopt a uniform interpretation of what constitutes the required "genuine link" between a company and the economy of the Community. However, the need for an extension of Community judicial power appears to have been recognized, even though the modalities have not been definitely fixed as yet. These modalities may differ from one convention to another, depending upon the particular needs. One obvious method would be simply to broaden the reach of Article 177 by giving the Court of Justice the authority to interpret the new conventions upon reference from national courts. This appears to be the solution toward which the Governments have been moving in connection with the Convention on Mutual Recognition of Companies. Such an arrangement will constitute a modest, new step toward legal integration. According to the present text of Article 177, the reference of a question to the Court of Justice requires a decision by a national court. At this juncture, it is not probable that the Member States would be willing to extend access to the Court still further, by granting a party to a national proceeding an independent right to bring a question of interpretation of a new convention before the Court of Justice. However, serious consideration is being given to authorizing the Procureur Général ("Solicitor General") of the highest national court to ask the Court of Justice for an interpretation of the Convention on Judicial Jurisdiction and Execution of Judgments. The Governments are not likely to follow the suggestion that the Member States, and perhaps also the Commission and the European Parliament, could be given authority to request an interpretation of a convention, and for that matter also of an assimilation directive, from the Court of Justice in a non-contentious proceeding. The arrangement adopted for the Benelux Court could serve as a pattern. This might be the least controversial means, but Commission lawyers are concerned lest arrangements along these lines be employed to avoid access to the Court of Justice from national courts in accordance with Article 177. Such access is rightly considered important from both the legal and political viewpoints.

6. Some concluding observations

When the "transitional period" expired on the last day of 1969, the results of the assimilation work in the field of company law proper were limited indeed, if measured by the positive Community law. Yet any sensible appraisal must proceed on the assumption that the First Directive, with its modest but not insignificant reach, constitutes only the first step, to be followed by further measures of coordination in accordance with the plan outlined above. Similarly, it is reasonable to expect that the Convention on Recognition of Companies will be followed by further projected treaties.

The authors of the EEC Treaty must have thought of coordination as a relatively limited undertaking, linked more or less closely with the realization of the freedom of establishment; according to an early work program, it was to be completed rather speedily, and in any case not later than by the end of the transitional period. As we have seen, things have turned out differently on both accounts. The scope, as presently projected, is quite extensive, and the process has proved more lengthy and laborious than expected. Yet the end result, it is pointed out by some critics, will *not* be uniformity; differences among national laws will remain, and they may even increase in some respects. Moreover, it may be difficult to persuade national parliaments to engage in repeated modifications of national laws in response to successive directives, or to delegate the requisite power to the executive branches of the respective Governments. Disappointment with the pace of the progress has led some to suggest that the establishment of a uniform European company form should be pursued as an alternative to coordina-

tion. Yet the negotiations on the European company have proved no less toilsome and no more promising of rapid results; here again, a suggestion was made for an alternative, simpler scheme of multiple incorporation of national companies in as many Member States as business considerations demand.

It is, however, advisable to keep in mind that lawmaking and law reform are inherently a complex and slow process. In fact, as we have noted in the third chapter of this volume, there appears to be no record of a successful unification in the field of company law proper at the international level. The uninspiring experience in the United States illustrates how unification of state company laws has failed even in an integrated federal system, although the negative effect is of course greatly mitigated by federal securities legislation.

Again, whatever the theoretical objective of coordination may be, in reality it does impose uniformity at least in some instances, such as the provisions in the First Directive which read like specific statutory clauses, rather than rules allowing for a margin of discretion in the diverse national systems. Moreover, even where a directive envisages continuing divergencies among national laws within the framework of a coordinating rule, such rule, if well conceived, should bring about a measure of rationalization, which may be all that is necessary for the functioning of the regional market, taking account of local conditions and peculiarities.

Finally, in gauging the progress one ought to keep in mind that the latter sixties, following the 1965 crisis, were years of stagnation in the Community, with little progress on any front, except the building of the customs union, and with little evidence of a "political will" to advance toward an economic union. The "Hague spirit," if it continues, could infuse new life into the process and thus accelerate assimilation work as well. The "spill-over" mechanism, first identified by Ernst Haas, has functioned, albeit within rather narrow limits, in this as in other areas of Commission activities, because tampering with one component of company law has raised problems in other components of what is an organic body of law. Similarly, early formalistic and conceptual considerations of a problem (such as financial disclosure) have led inexorably to facing the real issues (the content and comparability of the disclosed data), and thus to a new subsector where coordination appeared necessary. Again, a scheme for an adjustment of conflict-of-laws rules and company law (such as the convention on transnational fusion) turns out to be an empty gesture when exposed to the stark light of business reality, unless it is followed by a modification in another field of the law (the tax system), and this leads to a new project in such a field. Finally, where Treaty instrumentalities appear inadequate to meet the needs of the day, new devices are conjured up (such as the European company, the European patent), which, not surprisingly, would have the incidental effect of upgrading Community power by creating new Community institutions (such as the European Patent Office) or increasing the authority of existing institutions.

In the long run, perhaps the most pervasive result of the process of assimilation of laws in this field will be the progressive socialization of the élite actors who, by the very nature of their profession, have traditionally operated in a "territorially intensive" network within a nation-state. The élite includes law-trained national and transnational officials, law professors, attorneys and business counsel, plus parliamentarians and spokesmen for economic and professional interest groups. The process started when a French civil servant on detached service with the EEC Commission brought to Brussels the ideas for the First Directive, evolved in a Paris study group. It has progressed not only in the formally constituted national and transnational arenas where law is made, but also in the variegated arenas where law is taught and discussed—in law faculties, research institutes, and in professional organizations, including such transnational bodies as the International Federation for European Law which has branches in all of the Member States. There is evidence of a distinct trend toward teaching and exploring national company law in the broader comparative context, at times even exceeding the confines of the Community.

This élite group is still quite small and it represents only a minute fraction of the lawyer population, even though it wields influence out of proportion to its size. Not infrequently, the same lawyer plays more than one of the many roles in the process: he drafts a national company reform law, he sits on a Commission working group preparing a directive, he drafts an opinion on the same directive as counsel for an economic interest group, he acts on the directive as a member of the national and European Parliaments, he introduces the directive into his course of company law at the university, he deals with the directive in a proceeding before a national court, he counsels still another government on its reform law project. One encounters lawyers wearing "a number of hats" particularly in the smaller Member States. As we have seen in the first chapter, assimilation work, far from being confined to the company law field, extends to a variety of other sectors where élites of varied professional background, including lawyers, interact in a similar way. Thus the process has been extending beyond the confines of the lawyers dealing with company law and beyond the legal profession.

One significant but little noticed effect of the Community system has been that it has encouraged the Governments to view isolated governmental measures in a broader context of national policies and to coordinate them at the national level. Such a coherent concept is obviously an indispensable prerequisite for a coordination of policies at the regional level, and for the formation of common Community policies. In its more recent declarations and "work programs," the Commission has sought to fit assimilation of company laws into the framework of what it hopes will become a common "industrial policy," consisting of two components.[11]

---

11 *See, e.g.,* The Communities' Work Programme (20th March 1969), 1969 Bull. E.C. Supp. No. 4, at 11 ff.

The first component is "the creation of a common legal framework as favorable as possible to the industrial development in the Community." The new framework should assure that the "diversity of national legal orders" will not "perpetuate" the existing obstacles to the mobility of factors of production and the dissimilar competitive conditions in industry. The program here would embrace assimilation of company laws in the broadest sense employed in this volume (including coordination of national laws, the European company form, and transnational fusions), as well as the creation of a European patent, trade-mark and design, with the necessary new European institutions and the concomitant harmonization of national legislation for the protection of industrial property. However, it would extend further into the field of "commercial law and procedure," through "harmonization of national legislation" on "industrial liability, bankruptcy and arbitration."

The second component envisages common action along the following lines: (a) "the strengthening of firms" through facilitating a regrouping of enterprises across national frontiers, adjustment of tax and credit systems to business needs, improved management methods and training of executives; (b) "structural adaptation" of sectors facing difficulties, through coordination of national policies on retraining, relocation and reemployment of labor (as illustrated by coordinated action already taken in the steel, textile, shipbuilding and paper industries); and (c) the development of new industries with emphasis on coordination of national programs for research and development, including public procurement and promotion of "multi-State industrial regroupings" for advanced industries, such as large-scale computer systems.

"Industrial policy" in turn is presented as one of no less than nine components of a still broader "common economic policy," which cuts across entire national economies and embraces important phases of national social policies as well.[12] It would seem that the Commission is not content with proceeding on the basis of what Nye describes as "the classic functionalist notion of solving a series of technical tasks and responding to specific needs until they add up to a web of relationships and institutions more important than the sovereign states."[13] Instead, in good neo-functionalist tradition, the Commission perceives the danger that work on "technical" topics, such as assimilation of company laws, may be condemned to triviality, with little impact on the important issues in the field, and with little, if any, effect on the integration process which the Commission wishes to advance. Thus it seeks to place the technical effort into the context of what it perceives as a vital common interest in industrial development, which in turn is presented as a plank in a still broader and more important platform, exceeding the specific confines of the Community Treaty-Constitution. Since "power and welfare cannot be kept radically separate . . . [t]he political game must be played, but played with a functionally oriented rather than legalistic or constitutional strategy." The constitutional strategy, which brings into the forefront demands for more formal institutional power and is characteristic of the federalists, was at times invoked when Professor Hallstein presided over the Commission, but now has clearly given way to the neo-functionalist approach.

----

[12] In addition to "industrial policy," the other components of "common economic policy" are: (1) General economic policy: (a) medium term policy, (b) anti-cyclical, financial and monetary policies; (2) commercial policy; (3) agricultural policy; (4) policy on research and technology; (5) energy policy; (6) transport policy; (7) regional policy; (8) social policy. The Communities' Work Programme, id. at 8-14.

[13] This and the subsequent quotations are drawn from a still unpublished chapter on "Regional Integration" by Professor Joseph S. Nye. See his earlier study entitled Comparative Regional Integration: Concept and Measurement, 22 INTERNATIONAL ORGANIZATION 855 (1968).

ANNEX I

First Council Directive
of March 9, 1968

designed to coordinate, in order to render them equivalent, the guarantees required in the Member States of companies defined in Article 58, par. 2 of the Treaty, for the protection of the interests of associates [shareholders] and third parties*

(68/151/CEE)

The Council of the European Communities,

Noting the Treaty establishing the European Economic Community, and particularly Article 54, par. 3(g) thereof,

Noting the General Program for the Removal of Restrictions on the Freedom of Establishment,[1] and particularly Title VI thereof,

Noting the proposal of the Commission,

Noting the opinion of the European Parliament,[2]

Noting the opinion of the Economic and Social Committee,[3]

Considering that the coordination provided for by Article 54, par. 3(g) and by the General Program for the Removal of Restrictions on the Freedom of Establishment is urgently needed, particularly with respect to stock companies and limited liability companies, since activities of such companies often extend beyond national territory;

Considering that the coordination of the provisions of national laws concerning publicity, the validity of undertakings of such companies, and invalidity ["nullity"] of such

---

* J.O. No. L65 of Mar. 14, 1968, at 8-12. This author's translation.
1 J.O. No. 2 of Jan. 15, 1962, at 36/62.
2 J.O. No. 96 of May 28, 1966, at 1519/66.
3 J.O. No. 194 of Nov. 27, 1964, at 3248/64.

companies is particularly important, notably with a view to ensuring the protection of the interests of third parties;

Considering that, in these areas, Community rules must be adopted for such companies simultaneously, since these companies offer only their assets as a guarantee to third parties;

Considering that publicity must make it possible for third parties to learn about the essential acts of a company and about certain data concerning it, particularly the identity of persons who are empowered to bind the company;

Considering that the protection of third parties must be assured by provisions limiting as much as possible the grounds on which undertakings incurred in behalf of the company may be declared invalid;

Considering that it is necessary, in order to assure legal security in the relationships between the company and third parties, as well as in the relationships between associates or shareholders, to limit the cases of invalidity ["nullity"], as well as the retroactive effect of the declaration of invalidity, and to prescribe a brief period in which third parties may contest such declaration,

Has adopted the following directive:

Article 1

The coordinating measures prescribed by this directive shall apply to the laws, regulations, and administrative provisions of the Member States, relating to companies organized in the following legal forms:

—in Germany:
Aktiengesellschaft [stock company], Kommanditgesellschaft auf Aktien [limited partnership with shares], Gesellschaft mit beschränkter Haftung [limited liability company];

—in Belgium:
naamloze vennootschap, société anonyme [stock company]; commanditaire vennootschap op aandelen, société en com-

mandite par actions [limited partnership with shares]; personenvennootschap met beperkte aansprakelijkheid, société de personnes a responsabilité limitée [limited liability company];

—in France:
société anonyme [stock company], société en commandite par actions [limited partnership with shares], société à responsabilité limitée [limited liability company];

—in Italy:
società per azioni [stock company], società in accomandita per azioni [limited partnership with shares], società a responsabilità limitata [limited liability company];

—in Luxembourg:
société anonyme [stock company], société en commandite par actions [limited partnership with shares], société à responsabilité limitée [limited liability company];

—in the Netherlands:
naamloze vennootschap [stock company], commanditaire vennootschap op aandelen [limited partnership with shares].

Section I. Publicity

Article 2

(1) The Member States shall take the necessary measures to ensure that mandatory publicity relating to companies covers at least the following acts and data:

(a) the act constituting the company and the charter, if it is the subject of a separate act;

(b) amendments to the acts referred to in (a), above, including any extension of the duration of the company;

(c) after each amendment of the act constituting the company or the charter, the full text of the amended act in the up-to-date version;

(d) the appointment, the termination of office, as well as the names of persons who, as an organ of the company prescribed by the law or as members of such organ

(i) have the power to bind the company in relation to third parties and to represent it in court,

(ii) take part in the administration, supervision, or control of the company.

The publicity measures must show clearly whether the persons who have the power to bind the company may do so alone or must do so jointly;

(e) at least once each year, the amount of the subscribed capital, where the act constituting the company or the charter refers to the authorized capital, unless an increase in the subscribed capital requires an amendment of the charter;

(f) the balance sheet and the profit-and-loss statement for each business year. The document embodying the balance sheet must give the names of the persons who are required by law to certify it. However, for limited liability companies in Belgian, French, German, Italian, or Luxembourg law, listed in Article 1, as well as for close stock companies [corporations] in Dutch law, the mandatory application of this provision shall be delayed until the effective date of a directive which will bring about the coordination of the content of balance sheets and profit-and-loss statements, and which will exempt from the publicity requirement all or a portion of these documents of such companies whose balance sheet total is below an amount to be determined by such directive. The Council shall issue such directive within two years after the adoption of the present directive;

(g) any transfer of the company seat [*siège social*];

(h) the dissolution of the company;

(i) the judicial decision declaring the company to be invalid ["null"];

(j) the appointment and names of the liquidators, as well as their respective powers, unless such powers derive expressly and exclusively from the law or the charter;

(k) the termination of the liquidation, and the cancellation of the company from the register in the Member States where such cancellation has legal effects.

(2) Companies that meet the following conditions shall be considered close stock companies [corporations] for the purpose of paragraph 1(f):

(a) they may not issue bearer shares;

(b) no person whatsoever may place in circulation a "bearer's certificate for registered shares" within the meaning of Article 42c of the Dutch Commercial Code;

(c) shares may not be listed on a stock exchange;

(d) the charter must contain a provision whereby any transfer of shares to third parties must have the approval of the company, except for devolution by death, and, if the charter so provides, except also for a transmission to a spouse, or to ascendants and descendants; the transfer must be executed either by an act under private seal signed by the transferor and the transferee, or by a notarized document, but not by a blank endorsement;

(e) the charter must state that it is a close stock company [corporation]; the company name must contain the words "Besloten Naamloze Vennootschap," or the initials "B.N.V."

Article 3

(1) In each Member State a file shall be opened, either at a central register, or at a commercial register, or at a register of companies, for each of the companies entered therein.

(2) All acts and all data that are made subject to publicity pursuant to Article 2 must either be deposited in such file or transcribed in the register; the subject matter of the transcription in the register must in any event be apparent from the file.

(3) Complete or partial copies of the acts or data referred to in Article 2 must be available upon written request. The charge for any such copy may not be in excess of the administrative cost.

The copies so transmitted shall be certified as true and correct unless the requesting party waives such certification.

(4) The acts and data referred to in paragraph 2 shall be published in an official bulletin designated by the Member State, either in full or as an extract, or in the form of a notation referring to the deposit of the acts in the file or their transcription in the register.

(5) The acts and data may not be invoked by the company against third parties until after the publication referred to in paragraph 4, unless the company proves that such third parties had knowledge thereof. However, the acts and data, relating to transactions that occurred prior to the sixteenth day after the day of the publication, may not be invoked against third parties who prove that it was impossible for them to have knowledge thereof.

(6) The Member States shall take whatever measures may be necessary to avoid any discrepancy between the substance of the text published in the press and that in the register or the file.

In the event of a discrepancy, however, the text published in the press may not be invoked against third parties; such third parties may, however, rely upon such text, unless the company proves that they had knowledge of the text deposited in the file or transcribed in the register.

(7) Third parties may, moreover, always rely upon the acts and data for which the formalities of publicity have not as yet been completed, unless the failure to publish them deprives them of legal effect.

Article 4

The Member States shall prescribe that letters and order forms shall carry the following information:

—the register at which the file referred to in Article 3 has been opened, as well as the company's registration number in such register;
—the legal form of the company, its seat [siège social], and the fact that it is in liquidation, if that is the case.

If the company capital is indicated on these papers, the amount of subscribed and paid-in capital must be given.

Article 5

Each Member State shall decide which persons must carry out the formalities of publicity.

Article 6

The Member States shall provide for appropriate sanctions in the event:

—the balance sheet and the profit-and-loss statement have not been published as prescribed in Article 2, paragraph 1(f);
—mandatory information required by Article 4 does not appear on business papers.

SECTION II. VALIDITY OF COMPANY UNDERTAKINGS

Article 7

If transactions are carried out in the name of a company which is in the process of formation, before it has acquired legal personality, and if the company does not assume the obligations resulting from such transactions, the persons who carried them out shall be liable jointly and severally and without limitation, unless there has been an agreement to the contrary.

Article 8

Once the formalities of publicity have been carried out with respect to persons who, as a company organ, have the power to bind the company, any defect in their appointment may not be invoked against third parties, unless the company proves that such third parties had knowledge thereof.

Article 9

(1) The company shall be bound as against third parties by acts of its organs, even if such acts are not related to the company purpose, unless such acts exceed the powers that have been given, or that may be given to such organs, by law.

However, the Member States may provide that the company shall not be bound where such acts exceeded the company purpose, if it proves that a third party had knowledge of the fact that the act exceeded the company purpose or, under the circumstances, could not have been unaware thereof; the fact that the charter has been published shall not in itself constitute such proof.

(2) Limitations upon the powers of the company organs imposed by the charter or by a decision of the competent organs may never be invoked against third parties, even if they have been published.

(3) Where national law provides that the power to represent the company may, notwithstanding any statutory rule on the subject, be delegated in the charter to a single person or to several persons acting jointly, such national law may provide that such provision in the charter may be invoked against third parties on condition that it concerns the general power of representation; the modalities for invoking such provision in the charter against third parties are set forth in Article 3.

SECTION III.   INVALIDITY ["NULLITY"] OF THE COMPANY

Article 10

In all Member States whose laws do not provide for a preventive administrative or judicial supervision over company formation, the act constituting the company and the company charter as well as any amendments thereto, must be embodied in a notarial act.

Article 11

The laws of the Member States may allow a company to be declared invalid ["null"] only under the following conditions:

(1) invalidity must be declared by judicial decision;
(2) invalidity may be decreed only in the following cases:

(a) where an act constituting the company is lacking, or where the formalities of preventive supervision or of the notarial act have not been complied with;

(b) where the purpose of the company is illegal or violates public policy;

(c) where the act constituting the company or its charter fails to show the name of the company, the contributions, the amount of subscribed capital, or the company purpose;

(d) where the provisions of national law relating to the minimum amount of paid-in capital have not been complied with;

(e) where all the founding associates or shareholders lacked legal capacity;

(f) where, in violation of the national law governing the company, the number of founding associates or shareholders was less than two.

Aside from these cases of invalidity, companies may not for any reason be held to be non-existent, or absolutely or relatively void or voidable.

Article 12

(1) Article 3 determines the modalities under which a judicial decision declaring the invalidity ["nullity"] of the company may be asserted against third parties. Where na-

tional law enables third parties to contest such decision, they must do so within a period of six months after publication of the judicial decision.

(2) Invalidity shall bring about the liquidation of the company in the same way as dissolution.

(3) Invalidity in itself shall not impair the validity of obligations incurred by or toward the company, without prejudice to the effects of a liquidation.

(4) The effects of invalidity on relationships among the associates [shareholders] may be determined by the law of each Member State.

(5) Holders of quotas or shares remain bound to pay the subscribed and not paid-in capital, to the extent required to satisfy obligations toward creditors.

SECTION IV. GENERAL PROVISIONS

Article 13

The Member States shall, within a period of eighteen months after being notified of this directive, effect whatever modifications may be necessary in their laws, regulations, and administrative provisions, to conform to the provisions of this directive, and they shall immediately inform the Commission of such modifications.

The publicity requirement prescribed in Article 2, paragraph 1(f) shall not take effect, for stock companies under Dutch law other than those subject to the present Article 42c of the Dutch Commercial Code, until thirty months after the notification of this directive.

The Member States may provide that the full text of the charter containing amendments adopted after the formation of the company need not be published for the first time until after the next amendment of the charter or, where no such amendment is made, not later than December 31, 1970.

The Member States shall see to it that the text of the essential provisions of internal law which they will adopt in the field governed by the present directive shall be communicated to the Commission.

Article 14

This directive is addressed to the Member States.

Done at Brussels, March 9, 1968.

ANNEX II

Convention on Mutual Recognition of Companies and Legal Persons*

PREAMBLE

The High Contracting Parties to the Treaty Establishing the European Economic Community,

Being desirous of implementing the provisions of Article 220 of the said Treaty concerning the mutual recognition of companies within the meaning of Article 58, paragraph 2,

Considering that it is necessary to ensure, as much as possible, the mutual recognition of companies within the meaning of Article 58, paragraph 2, without prejudice to the application to companies of the other provisions of the Treaty,

Have decided to conclude this Convention on the mutual recognition of companies and legal persons and have for this purpose appointed as their plenipotentiaries:

His Majesty the King of the Belgians:
M. Pierre Harmel, Minister of Foreign Affairs;

The President of the Federal Republic of Germany:
M. Willy Brandt, Vice-Chancellor and Minister of Foreign Affairs;

---

* 1969 Bull. E.C. Supp. No. 2. This author's translation

The President of the French Republic:
  M. Maurice Couve de Murville, Minister of Foreign
  Affairs;

The President of the Italian Republic:
  M. Amintore Fanfani, Minister of Foreign Affairs;

His Royal Highness, the Grand Duke of Luxembourg:
  M. Pierre Grégoire, Minister of Foreign Affairs;

Her Majesty the Queen of the Netherlands:
  M. J.M.A.H. Luns, Minister of Foreign Affairs;

Who, meeting within the forum of the Council, having
exchanged their full powers, found in good and due form,
  Have agreed as follows:

CHAPTER I

Scope of Application and Conditions for Recognition

Article 1

Companies under civil or commercial law, including cooperative associations, which were formed in accordance
with the law of a Contracting State which grants them the
capacity to have rights and obligations, and which have their
registered office [siège statutaire, satzungsmässiger Sitz] in
the territories to which this Convention applies, shall be
recognized as a matter of right.

Article 2

Recognition shall equally be granted as of right to legal
persons under public and private law, other than the companies referred to in Article 1, which meet the conditions
of Article 1, if their principal or subsidiary purpose is to
engage in an economic activity that is normally carried on
for remuneration, or if they in fact continuously engage in
such activity, without thereby violating the law under which
they were formed.

Article 3

Any Contracting State may, however, declare that it will not apply this Convention to any companies or legal persons referred to in Articles 1 and 2, whose real seat [siège réal, tatsächlicher Sitz] is located outside of the territories to which this Convention applies, if such companies or legal persons have no genuine link with the economy of one of these territories.

Article 4

Any Contracting State may further declare that it will apply such provisions of its own law as it considers mandatory to the companies or legal persons referred to in Articles 1 and 2, whose real seat is located in its territory, even though they were formed under the law of another Contracting State.

The non-mandatory provisions of the law of the State making such a declaration shall be applied in only one of the following two cases:

—if the charter does not provide otherwise, possibly also through an express, general reference to the law under which the company or legal person has been formed,

—if, in the absence of such a charter provision, the company or legal person fails to prove that it has actually exercised its activity for a reasonable time in the Contracting State under whose law it was formed.

Article 5

For the purpose of this Convention, the term "real seat" of a company or legal person shall mean the place where its central administration is located.

CHAPTER II

EFFECTS OF RECOGNITION

Article 6

Without prejudice to the application of Article 4, all companies or legal persons recognized by virtue of this Convention shall have the capacity accorded to them by the law under which they were formed.

Article 7

Any State in which recognition is sought may deny these companies or legal persons certain rights and powers which it does not accord to companies or legal persons of a corresponding type that are governed by its own law. However, this may not have the effect of denying to these companies or legal persons the capacity to have rights and obligations, to enter into contracts or to undertake other legal acts, and to sue and be sued.

The companies or legal persons referred to in Articles 1 and 2 may not invoke the limitations on their rights and powers dealt with in this Article.

Article 8

The capacity, rights, and powers of a company recognized by virtue of this Convention may not be denied or limited solely for the reason that it has no legal personality under the law under which it was formed.

CHAPTER III

PUBLIC POLICY

Article 9

A Contracting State shall be entitled not to apply this Convention only if the company or legal person that calls for its application violates—through its charter purpose, its objective, or the activity it actually exercises—principles or rules which that State considers to be a matter of public policy within the meaning of private international law.

If the law of the State under which a company was formed provides that such company can lawfully exist even if it has only a single shareholder, a Contracting State may not for that reason alone hold that such company violates its public policy within the meaning of private international law.

Article 10

Principles or rules which violate the Treaty Establishing the European Economic Community may not be deemed to be a part of public policy within the meaning of Article 9.

CHAPTER IV

FINAL PROVISIONS

Article 11

As between the Contracting States, this Convention shall apply notwithstanding any contrary provisions covering the recognition of companies or legal persons in other conventions to which the Contracting States are or will become parties.

However, this Convention shall not affect:

—rules of internal law,

—provisions of international conventions,
which are in force or shall enter into force and which require recognition in other cases or with broader effects, provided that this recognition or these effects are compatible with the Treaty Establishing the European Economic Community.

Article 12

This Convention shall apply to the European territories of the Contracting States, to the French overseas departments, and to the French overseas territories.

Any Contracting State may declare, by notifying the Secretary-General of the Council of the European Communities, that this Convention shall also apply to any country or territory designated in such declaration for whose international relations such State is responsible.

Article 13

This Convention shall be ratified by the Signatory States. The instruments of ratification shall be deposited with the Secretary-General of the Council of the European Communities.

Article 14

This Convention shall enter into force on the first day of the third month following the deposit of the instrument of ratification by the last Signatory State to perform this formality.

Article 15

The declarations provided for in Articles 3 and 4 must be made by any Signatory State no later than at the time when it deposits its instrument of ratification for this Convention. They shall become effective upon entry into force of the Convention. If the declaration provided for in Article 12, paragraph 2, is made before or at the time of the deposit of the sixth instrument of ratification for this Convention, it shall become effective upon entry into force of the Convention; if such declaration is made at a later date, it shall become effective on the first day of the third month following receipt of its notification.

Any Contracting State may, at any time, withdraw either or both of the declarations made under Articles 3 and 4. The withdrawal shall become effective on the first day of the third month following receipt of its notification by the Secretary-General of the Council of the European Communities. It shall be final.

Article 16

The Secretary-General of the Council of the European Communities shall notify the Signatory States of:

(a) the deposit of any instrument of ratification;

(b) the date on which this Convention enters into force;

(c) the declarations and notifications received in pursuance of Articles 3, 4, 12, paragraph 2, and 15, paragraph 2;

(d) the dates on which these declarations and notifications become effective.

Article 17

This Convention shall remain in force for an indefinite time.

Article 18

Any Contracting State may request that this Convention be revised. In such case, the President of the Council of the European Communities shall convene a conference on revision.

Article 19

This Convention, drawn up in one original in the Dutch, French, German, and Italian languages, all four texts being equally authentic, shall be deposited in the archives of the Secretariat of the Council of the European Communities. The Secretary-General shall transmit a certified copy to the Government of each Signatory State.

In Witness Whereof, the undersigned plenipotentiaries have affixed their signatures to this Convention.

Done at Brussels, February 29, 1968.

[Signatures omitted.]

PROTOCOL

Upon signing the Convention on the Mutual Recognition of Companies and Legal Persons, the plenipotentiaries of the High Contracting Parties to the Treaty Establishing the European Economic Community adopted the text of the following three declarations:

COMMON DECLARATION No. 1

The Governments of the Kingdom of Belgium, the Federal Republic of Germany, the French Republic, the Italian Republic, the Grand Duchy of Luxembourg, and the Kingdom of the Netherlands,

Declare that the "società semplice" under Italian law and the "vennootschap onder firma" under Dutch law fall under Article 1 of this Convention.

COMMON DECLARATION No. 2

The Governments of the Kingdom of Belgium, the Federal Republic of Germany, the French Republic, the Italian Republic, the Grand Duchy of Luxembourg, and the Kingdom of the Netherlands,

Declare their readiness to engage, as far as necessary and within the framework of association agreements, in negotiations with any State associated with the European Economic Community with a view to mutual recognition of companies and legal persons within the meaning of Articles 1 and 2 of the said Convention.

COMMON DECLARATION No. 3

The Governments of the Kingdom of Belgium, the Federal Republic of Germany, the French Republic, the Italian Republic, the Grand Duchy of Luxembourg, and the Kingdom of the Netherlands,

Being desirous of ensuring that the Convention is applied as effectively as possible,

Striving to avoid impairment of the unity of this Convention through diverging interpretations,

Declare their readiness to examine the means for accomplishing these objectives, particularly the possibility of granting certain jurisdiction to the Court of Justice of the European Communities, and if necessary to negotiate an agreement to this effect.

In Witness Whereof, the undersigned plenipotentiaries have affixed their signatures to this Protocol.

Done at Brussels, February 29, 1968.
[Signatures omitted.]

Index of Names

*Selected References to
Biographical Data*

Subject Index

Accounting rules. *See* Annual financial documents

Administrateurs gérants: in Belgian law, 133

Administratiekantoor (trust companies): in Netherlands law, 342-43

Agfa-Gevaert: as holding company effecting international concentration, 372, 429, 476

Amministratori ("administrators"): in Italian law, 143, 289 n.158. *See also* Codetermination, Houin Report, Würdinger Report, Lyon-Caen Report

Annual financial documents: under 1965 German reform law, 104; under 1966 French reform law, 118-19; need for comparability of, 254, 270; proposed directive on: content and purpose, 355-64; scope, 355; extent of reporting obligation, 356; balance sheet and profit-and-loss statement, 356-60; valuation rules, 360; auditors' verification, 362. *See also* Houin Report and First Coordination Directive

Anti-revolutionary Party: in the Netherlands, 148, 148 n.183 151 n.190

Anti-trust law. *See* Competition law; and Competition policy, EEC

Approximation: general Treaty basis (Art. 3 (h)), 9; specific Treaty authorizations for, 10 n.6; the concept of, 9-11; compared with harmonization and coordination, 11-13; the general "approximation of laws" clause (Art. 100), 49-50; D.G. IV and Art. 100, 176-77. *See also* Assimilation, Coordination, Harmonization, Transnational Coordination

Assimilation: definition of, 1; function of, in the EEC, 5-6; supplementing other patterns of lawmaking, 6-7; compared with approximation of law, 1, 12; achievements and prospects of, in general, 12-16, 19-21; and national reforms, 167-71; distribution of competence for, within the Commission, 173-74, 178; role of national élites in, 179-80, 189-94; of company laws under the EEC Treaty, *see* Establishment of companies, and Commercial company. *See also* Commission, EEC

manent Representatives, 227-29, 230-35; legislative initiative, 497, 501; new responsibility for drafting, as modification of coordination procedure, 500-01; legal action against Member States, 507

Committee of Permanent Representatives: generally, 227-29, 499; relationship to Commission and Council of Ministers, 227-29; Group on Economic Questions, 229; general composition of, 227; the First Directive before, 229-35

Communist Party: in the European Parliament, 213

Compagnie bancaire: French banking concern organized in new two-tier form, 125

Company law: as a subject for international unification, generally, 68-74; Scandinavian unification efforts, 70-72, 72 n.24, 73; developments in Central American Common Market, 70, 73 n.24

    in the United States: *see* Uniform Business Corporation Act, Model Business Corporation Act (MBCA), Securities Act of 1933, Securities Exchange Act of 1934, Securities Exchange Commission (SEC), Uniform Division of Income for Tax Purposes Act, 65-67; federal power compared with "Community power," 64-65; compared with emerging European system, 59-64

    in Europe: *see* Belgium; France; Germany; Italy; Luxembourg; Netherlands; Establishment of Companies; First Coordination Directive; Commission, EEC

    reform of, generally: role of corporation in society, 75-76; need for reform, 76-77; principal corporate forms, 78; schism between ownership and control as most significant issue—various schools of thought, 78-82; "the American challenge" as a reform impulse, 82-85

    national reforms: institutional aspects, 155-56, 298; compatibility with EEC Treaty, 162-67; *see also* Belgium, France, Germany, Italy, Luxembourg, Netherlands

Competition law: notification of restrictive agreements in EEC, 18; abuse of dominant position in EEC, 18; relation between German Law Against Restraints of Competition and *Konzernrecht,* 105. *See also* Competition policy, EEC, and Fusion

Establishment of companies: legal basis for, in EEC Treaty, 24-32; freedom to organize and manage, 26-32; diverging conflict-of-laws rules concerning benefiting companies, 29-32; limitation of right to "true" Community companies (Art. 58), 33-34; the French *carte de commerçant* as a compliance problem in field of, 35; protection of shareholders and "third parties" (Art. 54 (3)g), 36-37; German position on relationship between freedom of establishment and Art. 54 (3)g, 37-41; in the Common Market compared with a federal framework, 51-53; general significance of conflict-of-laws rules, 53-56. *See also* Commercial company, Conflict of laws, Company laws, European company, Recognition of companies, Convention on Mutual Recognition of Companies and Legal Persons

European company: generally, 50-51, 472, 488; no basis for, in EEC Treaty, 427; economic grounds for, 428-29; "psychological" and political grounds for, 429-30; history of, 430-37; as an "international company," models of, 437-38; the concept of a "treaty company," 439-43; supranational or European-type, 443-45; legal basis for "enacting" the European company, 445-47, 478-79 n.399; Commission position on, the 1966 Memo, 447

Sanders draft of: generally, 335, 433-37, 448-49, 472, 478 n.399; legal personality and capacity, 449-51; governing law and judicial interpretation, 451-54, 479 n.399; access to European company form, 455-58, 478 n.399; exclusion of foreign-controlled companies from access, 458-60; formation of company, 460-61; bearer shares problem, 462-63, 479 n.399; structure of European company, 463; workers' co-determination, 464-68, 479-81; law of related companies, 468, 481-82 n.399; taxation problems, 470-72, 481 n.399; draft regulation on, approved by EEC Commission, 478-82 n.399

European conventions (Art. 220): in general, 43-45, 53, 182-84, 404-05, 421, 432, 446-47, 487-88

European Economic Community: as an economic system, 5-6; history and policies, 12-22; institutions: *see* Commission, EEC; Council of Ministers; Court of Justice of the Communities; Economic and Social Committee; European Parliament. *See also* Company law

European Investment Bank, 21, 369 n.131

need for comparability of financial documents, 269; national reporting compared, 273; methods of publicity: failings of First Draft, 274-76; central file and bulletin, 276-80; required information on company stationery, 281; penalties, 281-82; action in Economic and Social Committee, 207-12; in European Parliament, 220-26; in Committee of Permanent Representatives, 232-35

on *"ultra vires":* generally, 282; doctrinal differences between Germany and the Five, 283-85; similarity of legal reality in the Six, 287-89; limitation by law and by charter purpose, 289-92; limitation in provision of charter, 292-94; special problem of charter clauses on company representation, 296-98; discussion in European Parliament, 221, 225

on "nullity": action in Committee of Permanent Representatives, 231, 233; generally, 299-301; national procedures to prevent faulty constitution of companies, 301-02; Franco-German divergence, 305-07; grounds for invalidity of a company, 308-09; effects of invalidity, 310

Foyer draft, 111, 114

France: *carte de commerçant (étranger),* 35; industry organizational pattern, 255; national disclosure rules, 255-56; Commission on Stock Exchange Transactions, *see Commission des opérations de bourse;* opposition to first draft of First directive, 258-59; valuation rules and "hidden" reserves, 360-62; *ultra vires* doctrine, 283; nullity doctrine, company viewed as a contract, 259, 259 n.58, 305-06; national law on fusion, 374-78

reform law: Law on Commercial Companies of 1966: reason for reform, 108; the reform process in France, 108-14; features of: generally, 116-19; "companies making a public offering," 116-17; extension of shareholder protection, 118; protection of third parties, 118-19; criminal penalties, 119; requirements for financial statements, 119, 255; two-tier administration, 119; impact on French practice, 124-26

Free Democratic Party (FDP): in Germany, 96, 102, 103, 158 n.202, 160, 161